THE PAPERS OF
Clarence Mitchell Jr.

THE PAPERS OF

Clarence Mitchell Jr.

Volume I, 1942–1943

Denton L. Watson, *editor*

Elizabeth M. Nuxoll, *associate editor*

OHIO UNIVERSITY PRESS

ATHENS

Ohio University Press, Athens, Ohio 45701
© 2005 Ohio University Press

Ohio University Press books are printed on acid-free paper ⊚ ™
The paper used in this publication meets the minimum requirements of the
American National Standard for Information Sciences—Permanence of Paper
for Printed Library Materials, ANSI Z39.48-1992.

13 12 11 10 09 08 07 06 05   5 4 3 2 1

Publication of *The Papers of Clarence Mitchell Jr.* has been made possible by a grant
from the National Historical Publications and Records Commission of the
National Archives and Records Administration and by the sponsorship of
the State University of New York College at Old Westbury.

This project was supported by the Harry Frank Guggenheim Foundation.

Dust jacket and frontispiece: Photo of Clarence Mitchell Jr. by Surlock Studio,
courtesy of Elmer Henderson Papers.

Library of Congress Cataloging-in-Publication Data
Mitchell, Clarence M. (Clarence Maurice), 1911–1984.
  [Papers. Selections]
  The papers of Clarence Mitchell, Jr. / Denton L. Watson, editor,
Elizabeth M. Nuxoll, associate editor.
    p. cm.
  Includes bibliographical references and index.
  ISBN 0-8214-1603-0 (cloth : v. 1 : alk. paper) — ISBN 0-8214-1604-9
(cloth : v. 2 : alk. paper)
    1. Mitchell, Clarence M. (Clarence Maurice), 1911–1984—Archives. 2. African Americans—Archives. 3.
Civil rights workers—United States—Archives. 4. African Americans—Civil rights—History—20th
century—Sources. 5. African Americans—Legal status, laws, etc.—History—20th century—Sources. 6.
Civil rights movements—United States—History—20th century—Sources. 7. United States—Race rela-
tions—History—20th century—Sources.   I. Watson, Denton L. II. Nuxoll, Elizabeth Miles, 1943– .
III. Title.
  E185.97.M63A25 2005
  323'.092—dc22
                                                                    2005022302

To Rose, Victor, and Dawn

The Papers of Clarence Mitchell Jr.

Volume I, 1942–1943
Volume II, 1944–1946
Volume III, 1946–1954
Volume IV, 1954–1960
Volume V, 1961–1978

CONTENTS

Volume I

DOCUMENTS

1942

Memoranda of Clarence M. Mitchell Jr. as Field Assistant and Assistant Chief under Robert C. Weaver, Chief of the Negro Employment and Training Division, Office of Production Management and War Production Board

Memoranda of Clarence M. Mitchell Jr. as Principal Fair Practice Examiner, Fair Employment Practice Committee (FEPC)

1943

Reports and Headquarters Memoranda of Clarence M. Mitchell Jr. as Associate Director of Field Operations, FEPC

Volume II

ILLUSTRATIONS

Volume II:

FIGURES

FOREWORD

The reports and memoranda of Clarence Mitchell Jr.—covering his years at the Fair Employment Practice Committee (FEPC), at the National Association for the Advancement of Colored People (NAACP) as labor secretary, and as director of that organization's Washington bureau—provide a window into a vast treasure trove of history that documents the beginnings of a seismic social movement that transformed the nation in the 1960s from one of racial exclusion to inclusion. The publication of Mitchell's papers is intended to strengthen Americans' knowledge of the constitutional processes of their government. As a lobbyist, Mitchell's mission was enlisting Congress to join the judicial and executive branches in upholding the Constitution by passing civil rights legislation and adopting constructive national policies to uphold the rights of minorities.

The publication of these documents begins with the present volumes covering World War II, when the FEPC sought to end employment discrimination in the defense and war industries based on race, creed, color, national origin, or alienage.

As Jervis Anderson in *A. Philip Randolph* noted, Executive Order 8802, which created the FEPC, "was the first major act by the national government to remedy distinct abuses suffered by black citizens."

Roy Wilkins, assistant executive secretary of the NAACP, affirmed that view: "Never in the history of the United States has a President issued an executive order which is at once a condemnation of racial discrimination as a policy and a powerful aid, economically, to the well being of Negro citizens."[1]

As did Lerone Bennett, the Johnson Publications historian and executive editor: "Up until then, the dominant issues in Negro life were poll tax legislation, anti-lynching legislation, 'separate-but-equal' school facilities and the white primary." From 1941 on, "Negro strategy would be based, implicitly and explicitly, on the necessity for decisive action by the federal government. It would be based, too, on the need for unrelenting pressure on the government."[2]

As did Denton L. Watson in *Lion in the Lobby: Clarence Mitchell, Jr.'s Struggle for the Passage of Civil Rights Laws:* "President Roosevelt's issuing of Executive Order 8802 on June 25, 1941, was the most celebrated act in the battle against discrimination in the war industries. That date marked the launching of the modern civil rights movement."[3]

The FEPC was an economic, political, and social movement. Implicit in the assessments of Wilkins, Bennett, and Anderson are the conclusions that the sociological and political currents that led to the creation of the agency, combined with the struggle in the federal courts by the NAACP for the reassertion of the true meaning of the Fourteenth Amendment, set a revolutionary new course for America on a promising path to achieving true racial equality.

The subsequent volumes will focus on Mitchell's role in implementing the NAACP's egalitarian philosophy, which was grounded in the Declaration of Independence and the Fourteenth Amendment.

These records reinforce the history of the parallel benefits of Mitchell's legislative advocacy; the nonviolent protests of the Rev. Martin Luther King Jr.; and the inspirational force of Malcolm X's black nationalism. As a constitutional humanist, Mitchell pushed Congress to join the judicial and executive branches of government in upholding the Constitution; as a moral humanist, King used nonviolent tactics to awaken the nation's conscience to the wrongs of racial injustices; and as a black nationalist, Malcolm X used his inspirational message to awaken African Americans to the strength of their racial heritage.

The State University of New York College at Old Westbury is proud of its sponsorship of *The Papers of Clarence Mitchell Jr.* Old Westbury was founded on a mission of strengthening and promoting the richness of social and cultural diversity through academic study. We are inspired by this body of work that reinforces our faith in American democracy.

Calvin O. Butts III
President, SUNY College at Old Westbury

NOTES

1. Anderson, *A. Philip Randolph,* 261.
2. Ibid.
3. Watson, *Lion in the Lobby,* 131.

PREFACE

On June 25, 1941, President Franklin Roosevelt issued Executive Order 8802 barring discrimination in the defense industry and creating the Fair Employment Practice Committee to administer the order. That action marked the beginning of the modern movement for full racial equality. At that time, African Americans were intensifying legal challenges to the denials of their constitutional rights of equality in professional education, in public schoolteachers' salaries, in interstate transportation, at the ballot box (through the system of all-white primaries), and through the use of restrictive housing covenants. In sum, blacks were awakening to their newfound political power and influence, at a time when liberalism was the guiding force in the national recovery following the Great Depression.[1]

Other pertinent aspects of this revolutionary period were the challenges of the radical communist left, which threatened to derail any forward movement of the most deprived sectors of society; development of a defense program well in advance of Pearl Harbor; use by African Americans of the national defense crisis as a wedge for opening up social and economic opportunities in wartime industries; and propaganda attacks by the Axis powers on America's racial Achilles' heel, using its Jim Crow practices as a powerful weapon to undermine support for its system of democracy abroad and at home itself.

Roosevelt's creation of the FEPC was the crystallization of the social and political unrest that had been building since the New Deal. The war was the catalyst. The potential benefits of the president's leadership in this struggle became immediately obvious to African Americans. Presidential leadership was what defined the historical importance of the FEPC and what would define the subsequent movement for a national nondiscrimination policy. From this point African Americans made the quest for presidential leadership central to their struggle for the federal government to establish such a policy to remedy not only the historical wrongs they were suffering in contradiction to the founding promise of equality but also the gross contradictions between their being denied the fundamentals of democracy at home while America was fighting abroad to protect those freedoms for white Europeans. African Americans thus saw the war as an opportunity to open a second front here at home while their nation was fighting Aryan fascism abroad and at the same time continuing to practice it at home.[2]

Clarence Mitchell Jr., a member of the FEPC staff, led in implementing the nondiscrimination policy. Subsequently, he led the struggle to persuade Presidents Harry Truman, Dwight Eisenhower, John Kennedy, and Lyndon Johnson to keep the FEPC idea alive by issuing executive orders barring discrimination in government employment and federal contracts until Congress passed national nondiscrimination laws. Next, he sought the leadership of not only President Johnson but Presidents Richard Nixon, Gerald Ford, and Jimmy Carter in enforcing and strengthening the laws. Mitchell also got the national government to establish constructive national policies to protect the rights of minorities.

Mitchell was born on March 8, 1911, in Baltimore, a vital port city and social entrepôt characterized by the daring of the legendary antislavery leader Frederick Douglass, who once lived and worked there. The city "grew up from the waterfront like a multilegged devil fish that decided to yawn and spread in all directions," Mitchell noted. In the 1940s shipping still played a significant part in the city's life. He was proud that, "unlike its sister, Charleston, South Carolina, Baltimore" had made "rapid strides forward in industry, commerce, and the mechanic arts." Steel mills, sugar refineries, and an automobile factory were among industries that provided jobs for workers. His papers—from 1942, when he began working for the FEPC, to 1978, when he retired as director of the Washington bureau of the National Association for the Advancement of Colored People and as legislative chairman of the Leadership Conference on Civil Rights—show how he marshaled the intricate political forces involved in ensuring the movement's success.[3]

Mitchell was conditioned for a life of civil rights activism in a milieu shaped by the clash of liberal ideas from the North and abroad with demonic racial ideologies from the South that made racial tension in border state Maryland palpable. He boasted about Baltimore's fame "for her home life and her beautiful residential districts" while complaining about the spread of residential segregation. Some white Baltimoreans, he said, "had the temerity to say that a white man has the same right to object to living next to a Negro as he has to object to being next to a horse stable." It required court fights, beginning in 1910 against the city's enactment of the nation's first residential segregation ordinance, and "actual physical battles" to halt opposition by whites in many instances to blacks' moving into white areas. There were still communities "where the blood of the hundred percenters boils at the thought of colored people in decent homes."[4]

After attending segregated schools in West Baltimore, Mitchell earned a bachelor's degree at Lincoln University, in neighboring Pennsylvania, and attended the Atlanta School of Social Work as an Urban League fellow from 1936 to 1937 and the School of Social Work at the University of Minnesota.

While still at Lincoln he was vice president of the City-Wide Young People's Forum, an activist, consciousness-raising organization in Baltimore that regularly had such speakers for its programs as Dr. W. E. B. Du Bois, editor of *The Crisis;* Walter White, executive secretary of the NAACP; Norman Thomas, the Socialist leader; and E. Franklin Frazier, the prominent Howard University sociologist, to fire up local blacks on social issues. Following his graduation, he became a reporter for the *Baltimore Afro-American* while serving as an activist in that city's branch of the NAACP.[5]

In 1933, Mitchell reported on the lynching of George Armwood, a black man, on Maryland's Eastern Shore. He covered the trial in 1935 of the lawsuit brought by Donald Gaines Murray, the Amherst University graduate, to gain admission to the lily-white University of Maryland Law School. All Maryland, he wrote, was "jubilant over the fact that through this case it is the first southern state to smash the color barrier in a state-supported educational institution." More than any other events, the sickening trauma of the lynching and the exhilaration of the Murray courtroom victory—under the direction of Charles Hamilton Houston and his young protégé Thurgood Marshall, attorney for the Baltimore NAACP branch—led Mitchell to devote his life to the civil rights struggle.[6] In 1937, Mary McLeod Bethune hired Mitchell as state director of the National Youth Administration in Maryland. He served in that position for six months.[7]

In 1937, Mitchell became executive director of the St. Paul Urban League in Minnesota. There he chipped away at racial discrimination by employers and labor unions. During his four years there, his crowning achievement was getting the Minnesota legislature to pass a law barring discrimination in the sale of liability insurance to blacks who used their cars and trucks for work. He regarded that problem as "one of the curious turns which race prejudice sometimes takes." It was a catch-22 for blacks. Some companies denied them coverage because they feared that juries were prejudiced and would always decide in favor of white litigants. Others discriminated by using such criteria as "moral characteristics" to determine insurability. St. Paul was a microcosm of Mitchell's subsequent national civil rights arena and his testing ground for marshaling disparate forces and allies to achieve social change.[8]

VOLUMES I AND II

First Phase, 1942–46: World War II, Foundation of the Movement

Mitchell's Place in the FEPC

In May 1941, Mitchell accepted the invitation of Robert C. Weaver, a Harvard University–trained economist and housing expert, to be his assistant in the newly created Negro Employment and Training Branch (NETB) of the National Defense Advisory Commission (NDAC). The companion Minority Groups Branch (MGB), which addressed discrimination problems relating to Mexican Americans and other minorities, was headed by Will Alexander. Subsequently Roosevelt abolished the NDAC and replaced it with the Office of Production Management (OPM). The NETB and the MGB were both transferred there. The following year, while still on Weaver's staff, Mitchell began working with the FEPC. Upon later joining its staff, he was successively principal fair practice examiner, associate director of field operations, and director of field operations, closing down the agency in 1946 after Southerners in Congress cut off its funding, thus killing it. Mitchell's FEPC collection, comprising volumes I and II, covers this period, 1942 to 1946.[9]

The FEPC was the first government agency in which black professionals were all line officers. Indeed, more than half the entire staff was black. Owing to Jim Crow in the South, whites served as directors of the FEPC's regional offices there, while blacks were regional directors in the North. The whites were needed in the South to give umbrella protection to their black associates. For blacks, the FEPC was a once-in-a-lifetime opportunity to attack employment discrimination.

Two of those blacks ran the FEPC: George M. Johnson and Clarence Mitchell Jr. As deputy chairman, Johnson directed the development of policy and led the legal division. It conducted hearings and did the legal work related to them, as well as for the division of field operations in preparation for hearings on discrimination cases. Mitchell led in implementing the policy set by the oversight group comprising the Committee (for an explanation of the policymaking functions see Jurisdictional Issues in the headnotes).[10]

The regional directors reported to Will Maslow, director of the division of field operations, but he turned over all their case referrals from the FEPC's fifteen regional and subregional offices to Mitchell for processing. That responsibility, which included referrals to the legal department, conducting field investigations, and helping to prepare for hearings, made Mitchell central to the FEPC's short-term mission. His papers document this short-term phase, as well as a part of the beginning of the long-term, political phase of the broader civil rights struggle, which was then being developed by the NAACP.[11]

Along with the division of field operations and the legal division, the FEPC's operating units were the division of review and analysis, the administrative division, and the information office. The FEPC's history incorporates two phases (see FEPC Chronology, below). The first, or old FEPC, lasted from 1941 to 1943. The beginning of the end of the old FEPC came when President Roosevelt created the War Manpower Commission on April 18, 1942, and, on July 30, 1942, abruptly transferred the FEPC and the War Production Board's two nondiscrimination units, the NETB and the MGB, to the labor division of the War Manpower Commission, headed by Paul V. McNutt. Bending to the public outcry over this change because McNutt was perceived as unsympathetic to the FEPC, Roosevelt on May 27, 1943, issued Executive Order 9346, creating the new, strengthened FEPC.

Before the FEPC's reorganization in July 1943, its staff was composed at most of only 13 officers and 21 clerical and stenographic employees. At the end of 1944, under EO 9346, the FEPC had 199 employees (56 professional, 63 clerical; for members, heads of divisions, and regional directors, see FEPC Staff).[12]

Responsible for overseeing staff functions was the group Roosevelt appointed as the governing or policymaking board, or the "Committee," as it generally was called. The bureaucratic structure was referred to generally as the "FEPC," although sometimes it was called the "committee" or the "agency." At the operating level, the agency's administration implemented policy.[13] The FEPC had an administrator and budget director, Theodore Jones, who reported to the chairman, but no executive director or chief executive officer. The administration hired staff and coordinated and controlled their functions. As chairman of the new FEPC, Malcolm Ross insisted that "the day-by-day direction of the staff and the appointment of members is the prerogative of the chairman under the Executive Order." Clearly, by staff he meant the division heads. The field and other staff reported to the division heads.[14]

The first Committee, created under EO 8802, was composed of a chairman and five other part-time, unpaid members who were appointed by Roosevelt on July 18, 1941. The first chairman, Mark Ethridge, was publisher of the *Louisville Courier-Journal*. Lawrence Cramer, former governor of the Virgin Islands, left his teaching post at Harvard to become its executive secretary. After Ethridge left, Roosevelt on March 25, 1942, appointed Malcolm MacLean, the white president of the all-black Hampton Institute, chairman of the Committee.[15]

Executive Order 9346 strengthened EO 8802 (see appendix 1). The new order placed the now organizationally independent FEPC within the Office of Emergency Management. The Committee was now composed of a paid, full-time chairman and six part-time, unpaid members. Three of the members were from labor (two from the AFL, one from the CIO) and the other three were from industry. Two members were African Americans. In 1943 one of the industry members headed a steamship company, another was a personnel expert, and the third a newspaper publisher.[16]

Roosevelt appointed the Reverend Francis J. Haas, dean of the School of Social Sciences at Catholic University and a well-known labor mediator, chairman of the new committee. Haas served until he was nominated bishop of Grand Rapids on October 7, 1943. On October 18, 1943, Roosevelt appointed Malcolm Ross, the Committee's deputy chairman, to succeed Haas. Ross was an author and former director of information of the National Labor Relations Board.[17]

Presidential Authority

The FEPC functioned in the name of the president, who delegated his authority under two prerogatives. The first was the constitutional power of the president as administrative head of the executive branch, which enabled him to direct the operation and administration of all federal agencies. Thus the president empowered the agency to investigate discrimination by the government, by government-sponsored training programs, and by private industries fulfilling government contracts. The second was his power as commander-in-chief to take all administrative actions necessary to assure adequate supplies for the armed forces of the United States. He delegated to the FEPC his authority to investigate discrimination in all essential war industries.[18] But the president gave the FEPC no enforcement powers. It could only investigate complaints, interpret the executive order, formulate policy, and adjust cases where possible. The FEPC developed procedures for consulting and assisting other government agencies, employers, and labor unions, and it provided information and conducted public relations.[19]

The FEPC was unique in that no other government agency had comparable knowledge about racial discrimination to implement the order. It relied on its prestige as an agency created by the president, as well as on the enforcement powers of other government departments and agencies, notably the War Manpower Commission, the army, the navy, the Maritime Commission, and the National War Labor Board, with all of whom it had working agreements. The FEPC imposed sanctions largely by relying on the actions of wartime contracting or regulatory agencies like the Civil Service Commission. For example, with the help of the WMC, the FEPC sought to have the United States Employment Services deny its manpower referral services to companies that refused to end discrimination. This process produced only spotty results, however, because it depended on the cooperation of the WMC's regional directors. The FEPC often invoked the persuasive powers inherent in the imperatives of war production that sought to obviate unnecessary delays caused by strikes and work stoppages. As it noted in a background document: "The nation cannot supply its fighting forces and those of its fighting allies on time in sufficient quantities without fully utilizing this 15% of its total manpower" that was at the time subjected to discrimination in employment (see Major Program Activities in the appendix). The FEPC depended on the negotiating skills of its staff and on embarrassing especially difficult employers through the public relations device of public hearings, which were also fact-finding affairs. When all else failed, it referred the case to the president.[20]

Complaints and Complainants

In January 1942, Roosevelt expanded the FEPC's jurisdiction over complaints to include alienage (or noncitizens, depending on their place of birth), in addition to race, creed, color, or national origin.[21] The FEPC's *First Report* explained that, between July 1, 1943, and June 30, 1944, the agency received complaints that resulted from twenty-two different types of alleged discriminatory practices. Refusal to hire accounted for almost 47 percent of the cases, and of these black male workers accounted for nearly 81 percent of the complaints. Other complaints alleged unwarranted dismissal, refusal to upgrade the worker to the level of his skill, and discriminatory working conditions. Mexican Americans and Japanese Americans complained mostly of discrimination based on their national origin. The FEPC *Final Report* noted that, generally, discrimination against the three million Mexican Americans paralleled that against African Americans. For example, a common complaint from African American and Mexican American workers in the Southwest was unequal pay for equal work done by whites in mining and oil industries. To a lesser degree, Jews, Italians, Germans, and Chinese also complained of discrimination based on national origin or alienage. Most creedal complaints came from Jews and Seventh-day Adventists, especially regarding the refusal of employers to recognize their Sabbath. Most of the discrimination complaints from Jehovah's Witnesses resulted from their refusal to buy war bonds or submit to the draft.[22]

Unions, training institutions, and employment agencies practiced indirect discrimination. Most complaints against labor unions involved their refusal to accept memberships from African Americans, issue them work permits, or handle their grievances, including disputes over seniority and upgrading. Another virulent form of discrimination was the segregation of blacks in local auxiliaries, in which they were denied the right to vote, bargain collectively, or participate equally in union negotiations. Separate training facilities, particularly those in the South, where *de jure* segregated schools existed, were another form of indirect discrimination. Other barriers to equal employment were segregated want ads in newspapers and employment agencies discriminating against African Americans, Jews, and aliens.

Complaints of discrimination were lodged by organizations such as the NAACP, National Urban League, Dallas Negro Chamber of Commerce, Anti-Defamation League, Japanese American Citizens League, Indian Confederation of America, the UAW and the CIO, and by private individuals. Because many individuals did not know how to lodge complaints, they often wrote to Roosevelt or, more frequently, his wife, Eleanor. These complaints were forwarded to the FEPC.

Mitchell's FEPC collection records the processing of those complaints and the struggles to resolve them. That was part of the back-and-forth process by which the agency developed the broad range of policies that subsequently guided Mitchell, the NAACP, other civil rights groups, and the federal government in developing nondiscrimination laws and constructive national policies.[23]

Processing Complaints

The FEPC required that complaints alleging discrimination be signed by the aggrieved person and be against a named employer, union, or government agency.[24] The staff could on their own act on complaints of discriminatory advertising, placement orders, or application forms. Additionally, a case could be based on evidence of violation of EO 9346 that was referred to the committee by another government agency.

The regional office in which the complaint originated first docketed the case. If the complaint was within the committee's jurisdiction, it investigated its validity. It could then seek further information from the complainant and conduct collateral investigations, after which a fair-practice examiner would contact the party charged. Upon being reminded of his nondiscrimination responsibilities, if the employer or union official eliminated the violations in accordance with the recommendations of the examiner and the regional director, the case was closed. Most cases were satisfactorily adjusted in that manner. When the regional director was unable to adjust a case, he referred it to the director of field operations in Washington.[25]

The committee frequently conducted negotiations with the WMC or with contracting agencies at both the local and national levels. When a case was especially difficult to resolve, the Washington office sent a senior fair-practice examiner to dispose of it. When attempts at settlement failed, the case was referred to the full Committee, which would order a public hearing. Only after this last resort failed did the Committee refer the case to the president. The Committee took that step in the epic struggle involving railways in the Southeastern Carriers Conference Agreement. In the Philadelphia Transportation Company strike in 1944, the president seized the company's equipment and operated it with army troops, thus forcing the workers to return to their jobs.[26]

The purpose of the hearings, as with those involving the railroads that were held in September 1943, was to determine the existence of discrimination, the duties of the employer, and the rights of employees under the executive orders. The hearings were informal, fact-finding proceedings. They were not limited by the legal rules of evidence and procedure. Sitting as an impartial body, the full Committee heard the case or authorized its chairman to appoint a hearing commissioner to conduct the proceedings. At times a panel of the Committee was delegated to conduct the hearings. Sometimes the FEPC investigated several concerns at once from the same industry or local area. In most of the public hearings the FEPC held, more than one company or union was involved.

To be fair, the Committee gave the party charged ample notice of the hearing and of the nature of the complaint. The accused either appeared in person or was represented by counsel, and witnesses were examined and cross-examined. The FEPC sometimes requested the accused to present material, but it had no power to subpoena witnesses or records. The full Committee reviewed the stenographic record of the hearings before it rendered its final decision and entered its findings. At that time it took corrective measures, which included recommendations and directives to the parties charged. It also made recommendations to federal agencies and to the president pertaining to steps they might take to eliminate whatever discrimination was revealed.

Eliminating Discrimination

A case was settled when the party charged complied with the FEPC's directive or request to take stipulated steps to correct discrimination or to guard against its recurrence. The FEPC implemented the agreement usually by including written instructions to personnel officers, placement agencies, training institutions, and labor unions that the accused employ persons solely on the basis of their qualifications.[27] The FEPC's directives usually advised the parties charged to issue formal instructions to their own personnel officers and employment agencies that the recruitment, training, and placement of workers must be done without discrimination.

Sometimes the FEPC directed companies to hire persons who had been discriminated against or to reinstate workers who were dismissed through discrimination. In December 1942, for example, following a hearing that involved charges brought by seven Jehovah's Witnesses, the Committee directed the accused company to immediately offer them reinstatement and reemployment with the full seniority rights they would have enjoyed had they not been discharged.[28]

The Committee consistently offered its views on methods for implementing the executive orders through directives. EO 8802 said that the Committee "shall take appropriate steps to redress grievances." The corresponding clause in EO 9346 implied the same power. It authorized the Committee to "take appropriate steps" to eliminate discrimination.

When directives were defied, the Committee's recourse was to refer the violation to the proper contracting agency, including the War Department, the Navy Department, or the Maritime Commission. Before the FEPC referred the case to the president, the contracting agencies could cancel or refuse to renew war contracts. The Committee could also refer cases to the chairman of the WMC. The formal agreement that the two agencies signed in August 1943 defined their respective responsi-

bilities in enforcing the government's nondiscrimination policies concerning train-
ing, placement, and use of manpower. In addition, the WMC, in implementing its
Employment Stabilization Program, could penalize violators of the policy. The
WMC could impose sanctions at both the local and national levels. Furthermore, the
WMC could deny workers who quit in protest over the employment of minority
workers certificates of availability for other employment.

The ultimate sanction could be imposed by the president using his powers as chief
executive and commander-in-chief. Roosevelt never did that, although in 1943 he
sent in troops to quell the violence in the Philadelphia Rapid Transit strike.[29]

Mitchell's Reports and Memoranda

Mitchell's FEPC headquarters reports and memoranda deal with multiple, substantive issues as well as topics based on individual complaints. Their coverage is
strongest for the West, Midwest, South, and Southwest, regions for which he was directly responsible. He also devoted interest to Philadelphia, particularly through his
direct involvement there in the transit strike, to Baltimore, his hometown, and to the
major shipbuilding areas in the Northeast.

Not published are Mitchell's letters and memoranda to the field staff. Many issues,
such as those related to endemic racial discrimination by private and government employers, to federal spending, and to labor unions' hiring practices continued throughout the life of the FEPC and into Mitchell's NAACP career up to the passage of Title
VII of the 1964 Civil Rights Act, which barred discrimination in federal spending.

The passage of Title VII was the fulfillment of Mitchell's FEPC grail. It similarly
barred discrimination in agencies like the Post Office Department, telephone and
other private companies, and throughout federal, state, and local governments. Subsequently, Mitchell worked for the enforcement of the laws as much as he had done
for a permanent nondiscrimination policy.

In effect, the FEPC, by establishing a national nondiscrimination program under
the president's leadership, defined the political core of the modern civil rights movement as much as the NAACP defined its judicial soul in its struggle to overturn the
1896 doctrine of separate but equal established in *Plessy v. Ferguson,* which it did in
its 1954 victory in the *Brown v. Board of Education* school desegregation case.[30]

Until the division of field operations was created on July 1, 1943, the agency's small
staff of examiners in Washington processed complaints largely through correspondence. Mitchell's reports became much more substantive and involved after Will
Maslow on December 17, 1943, made him fully responsible for the recording and processing of all the FEPC's cases.[31] The published texts—collected from the FEPC
repository at the National Archives (RG 228), Mitchell's personal collection in Baltimore, the NAACP Washington Bureau collection at the Library of Congress, and
the NAACP national headquarters—were supplemented by histories provided to
me by Mitchell, Robert Weaver, John A. Davis, William Maslow, Edward Rutledge,
and Elmer W. Henderson.

Regarding the FEPC collection, when Mitchell prepared the texts, he often attached letters and other documents to them. But as the documents were shunted

from office to office, many were separated or misplaced, especially in the FEPC's waning days, when the staff was rushing its *Final Report* to publication. That is one reason the microfilm collection, from which much of Volumes I and II were prepared, does not have Mitchell's, or any other staffer's, records all in one place. They are scattered throughout FEPC collections. Some texts, even ones identified by other scholars, are therefore missing from the edition because they were not found. Nevertheless, *The Papers of Clarence Mitchell Jr.* has prepared as comprehensive as possible a resource that should be instrumental in furthering scholarly research on this aspect of civil rights history.

In 1946, Walter Francis White hired Mitchell as labor secretary, working out of the NAACP Washington Bureau, to continue the FEPC's mission and to lead the struggle for such a permanent agency. Four years later, White relinquished his extended job as director of the NAACP Washington Bureau, naming Mitchell as his successor. Now the civil rights movement's lobbyist, Mitchell's extensive activities encompassed a broad spectrum of activities in all three branches of government.[32]

In addition to broadening and strengthening the FEPC's policies, Mitchell developed the strategies for getting them enacted into law. Subsequently, other social and political groups, including the powerful conservative countermovement, copied the political strategies he used through the NAACP and the Leadership Conference on Civil Rights for their own lobbying in Washington.

Mitchell's job was arduous and repetitive, and he achieved progress only incrementally. The key to his success was consolidating the pattern of leadership President Roosevelt established by enlisting the unequivocal support of subsequent chief executives. In carrying out his functions, Mitchell was restrained by the politics of governmental bureaucracy. The FEPC was a lightning rod in Congress for the South's venomous racism, which many Northern lawmakers supported. For the first decade of his career at the NAACP, Mitchell was the lone figure battling the Southerners. At least, though, he was now the legislative policymaker and the organization's leading strategist. How did he do it? He explained there were three basic areas in which groups like the NAACP contributed to legislative activities:

1. Mobilizing public opinion and support for broad national and international programs that benefited the country
2. Building a more informed electorate by providing information on important issues and where members of Congress stood on them
3. Assisting members of Congress in promoting good legislation, defeating bad ones, and strengthening others with amendments or clarifying the intent of Congress

A critically important development for the civil rights movement was Mitchell's broadening his FEPC goals to include implementation of the NAACP's constitutional victories in the courts through legislation. In addition to winning passage of laws barring discrimination in employment and federal spending, he secured passage of a broad range of laws that protected blacks and civil rights workers in the South from violence and segregation in public accommodations and that upheld the equal protection clause of the Fourteenth Amendment. He also gained passage of the 1965 Voting Rights Act and the 1968 Fair Housing Act. Poll taxes were abolished by the Twenty-fourth Amendment, by the Supreme Court in 1966, by decisions by federal courts, and by state laws, thus further consolidating the promise of full citizenship for African Americans.[33]

The following is an outline of the subsequent volumes in the edition.

VOLUME III

Second Phase, 1946–50: The Quest for Presidential Leadership

With the beginning in late 1943 of reconversion from wartime to peacetime, the FEPC and African American organizations had begun showing increasing concerns over the future economic progress of blacks. Because the wartime employment protection of EO 9346 ended with the war, African Americans faced the danger of losing the protection of the federal government in the crucial niche they were establishing in industrial America.

Mitchell attempted to devise a new program for the FEPC that would have enabled the federal government to continue fulfilling its constitutional obligation of protecting the rights of all its citizens without regard for race, creed, color, or national origin. Congress, however, blocked those transitional efforts by its abrupt termination of the wartime equal employment opportunity agency.[34]

Upon becoming NAACP labor secretary in 1946, Mitchell began his quest for a permanent FEPC. The FEPC set the foundation and direction for the continuing struggle. While phasing out its operations early in 1946, the FEPC made three basic recommendations to the president: that he "continue to urge upon Congress the passage of legislation which will guarantee equal job opportunity to all workers without discrimination because of race, color, religious belief, or national origin"; that the government "take steps not only to promulgate its policy more widely, but to enforce it as well," because the "mere existence of a Federal policy of nondiscrimination will not in itself result in fair employment practices"; and that appropriate government agencies report more widely statistics on "employment and unemployment by race and by sex within industries and occupations" in order to make the public more aware of the handicaps of minority workers.

Third Phase, 1951–54: Reasserting Citizenship Rights

Several developments helped shape the civil rights struggle.

Cold War

As the cold war intensified, America's need to counter Soviet propaganda throughout the Third World reinforced Mitchell's struggle for civil rights laws. While doing so, he had to combat the nefarious loyalty investigations into communist infiltration. Mitchell was particularly concerned about the false charges against NAACP leaders and other assertive blacks that they were fellow travelers. The intent was to destroy their professions and businesses as long as they fought for their civil rights.

Korean War

Contributing to Mitchell's success in 1957 in winning passage of the first civil rights law since Reconstruction was his use of the Korean War to intensify the struggle to end violence against black servicemen and segregation in the armed services. He thus ensured that gains obtained during World War II were not lost, but strengthened. In conjunction with White and Thurgood Marshall, NAACP special counsel, he joined the fight against racial segregation in the military, which Presidents Truman and Eisenhower ended.

Brown v. Board of Education

The second major milestone that shaped Mitchell's program was the Supreme Court's landmark ruling in 1954 that held that under the Fourteenth Amendment the "separate but equal" doctrine established in 1896 in *Plessy v. Ferguson* was inherently unequal. Previously at the FEPC, Mitchell had had to walk a fine line between segregation and discrimination to avoid worsening attacks on the agency from Southerners in Congress, who insisted that the two practices were distinct. Southerners maintained that by practicing segregation they were not discriminating because their Jim Crow system was within the separate-but-equal doctrine. Consequently, they insisted, there was no need for civil rights laws.

Now Mitchell used *Brown* to reinforce his struggle to get Congress to pass civil rights laws that were grounded in the Fourteenth Amendment in order to protect the rights of African Americans. The overriding challenge was defeating the Southerners' stranglehold on the Senate, where since the early 1920s they had used the filibuster to kill every civil rights bill. The Southerners' strength flowed from the one-party Democratic South. Furthermore, Southerners chaired the Senate's thirteen most important committees, especially Judiciary, which controlled the processing of civil rights bills. In the House, a Southerner was speaker, while another chaired the Rules Committee, through which all legislation had to pass onto the floor for debate. Southerners thus made Congress a civil rights graveyard.

Subsequent volumes of Mitchell's papers document how he achieved the legislative revolution.

VOLUME IV

Fourth Phase, 1955–57: Psychological Breakthrough

To win passage of the 1957 Civil Rights Act, Mitchell enlisted the support of Attorney General Herbert Brownell and created bipartisan committees in both houses of

Congress. Through self-study, he also matched the Southerners in their expertise on parliamentary procedures, created a political juggernaut through his combined use of the NAACP branch structure and the Leadership Conference on Civil Rights, and progressively strengthened presidential leadership for the struggle through his unrelenting agitation. It was only as a result of those efforts that he was able to defeat the Southern congressional phalanx and win passage of the 1957 Civil Rights Act, the first such law since Reconstruction.

Although the act was a weak voting rights measure, owing to the compromises Senate Majority Leader Lyndon Johnson had engineered, it vindicated Mitchell's conviction that Congress could be made to pass such measures. Despite its weakness, however, the act was major a psychological breakthrough. It also created the Civil Rights Division of the Justice Department and the U.S. Civil Rights Commission, both of which were needed for the passage of stronger laws and to enforce the 1957 act itself.

Fifth Phase, 1958–60: Political Interregnum

Until 1960, the NAACP was the civil rights movement. But the South's bitter opposition to any change in its Jim Crow system inspired an uprising by a younger generation of black activists who moved to the forefront of the struggle by physically confronting white resistance to integration through lunch-counter sit-ins and other nonviolent demonstrations. Though the NAACP shunned such confrontational tactics, the demonstrations reinforced the association's political strategy by creating a national emotional climate that demanded change.

VOLUME V

Sixth Phase, 1961–65: Holy Fire

Given the extreme difficulty in getting Congress to pass meaningful civil rights laws, many had abandoned the idea, preferring instead to get the president to issue an executive order to end discrimination—especially after John Kennedy's promise during the 1960 campaign to end discrimination in housing "with the stroke of a pen." Mitchell, however, was fiercely opposed to that alternative, knowing from experience that executive orders ended with a president's term. Furthermore, he knew that only a law passed by Congress that reflected the popular will could be effective. Consequently, early in the Kennedy administration those contesting views sparked fierce battles between Mitchell and the administration, which resisted his demands for civil rights laws because it was the more politically dangerous alternative.

By 1963 the civil rights drama pitted entrenched racism against the moral and constitutional rights of African Americans. National tension was heightened by the demonstrations in Birmingham; by President Kennedy's declaration that the struggle was a moral one; by his sending of a civil rights bill to Congress; by the assassination of Medgar Evers, the NAACP's field secretary in Mississippi, which pushed Kennedy to submit a stronger bill to Congress; by the NAACP's Legislative Strategy Conference in Washington, which brought branch leaders to the capital to lobby for the passage of the civil rights bill; by the unprecedented March on Washington, which drama-tized considerable popular support for civil rights; and by the assassination of the president. Mitchell's main battle with the Kennedy administration was over the scope of the civil rights bill, especially the inclusion of Title VI, barring discrimination in federally funded programs, and the line-in-the-sand Title VII, barring discrimina-tion in employment and creating an FEPC-type administrative agency.

In the White House, Lyndon Johnson, formerly Mitchell's wily opponent, became totally converted to the struggle and provided the type of committed presidential leadership Mitchell had long sought, leadership that prompted the lobbyist to char-acterize him later as "the greatest president on civil rights." Under Johnson's direc-tion, Congress passed the 1964 Omnibus Civil Rights Bill and a broad range of social legislation designed to uphold human dignity and fulfill America's promise as a land of equal opportunity for all. And with Johnson fully at the helm, Mitchell next led the successful struggle in Congress, for passage of the Voting Rights Act of 1965.

Seventh Phase, 1966–68: White Backlash

Passage of the 1968 Fair Housing Act was Mitchell's crowning achievement. It fur-ther vindicated his faith in the legislative process. Once more, Johnson's leadership was the defining moment. This struggle was especially complicated owing to the many swirling social currents caused, notably, by the raging urban riots; the racist presi-dential campaign of Governor George Wallace of Alabama that aroused the anti-civil rights passions of the so-called silent majority, which included white blue-collar workers; the birth of the black power movement among young, urban Northerners, who rejected the flagship NAACP's goal of integration and Martin Luther King Jr.'s tactics of nonviolence; the bitter protests against the Vietnam War and King's com-plication of the civil rights struggle by becoming involved in the antiwar movement; King's launching of his Poor People's Campaign in Washington instead of support-ing President Johnson's Great Society and other social programs; the birth of the stu-dent and the feminist movements; and the uncompromising demands by Southern blacks at the 1964 Democratic National Convention for full equality within their party, which tended to make the politically cautious Johnson look unsympathetic to their efforts to end their lockout in the South by their white counterparts. The ulti-mate elements of the national crisis were the assassinations of King and Attorney General Robert Kennedy, both in 1968.

The NAACP viewed the combined effects of those developments on the course of the civil rights movement as catastrophic. Mitchell was deeply frustrated by the lack of gratitude that King and many other blacks showed not only to President Johnson for his unprecedented contributions to the struggle, but also to Hubert Humphrey for his long, stalwart support for civil rights and his faithful leadership in the 1964 Senate battle for the civil rights act. Not only did the antiwar protests force Johnson not to seek reelection, but Humphrey lost to Richard Nixon by a tiny margin in the 1968 presidential campaign, thus implanting in the national government the forces of reaction.

Eighth Phase, 1969–78: Conservative Countermovement

The impact of the now fragmented civil rights movement on the legislative program was most obvious to Mitchell in a palpably conservative Congress and a hostile White House. In contrast to the previous presidents with whom he had worked and whose leadership he had invariably won, he now faced an angry Richard Nixon. As vice president, Nixon had supported civil rights. At a critical point in the maneuvering over the 1957 Civil Rights Act, when he was presiding as president of the Senate, he had made a ruling that allowed the bill to reach the floor for debate, thus enabling its passage. In 1968, when Mitchell was engaged in a do-or-die battle to win passage of the Fair Housing Act, Nixon, in a behind-the-scenes maneuver, agreed to Mitchell's request to speak with House Minority Leader Gerald R. Ford to get him to not take action that would have blocked passage of the 1968 Fair Housing Act.

Upon winning the presidency, Nixon helped Mitchell win renewal of the 1965 Voting Rights Act in 1970 and supported the expansion of affirmative action programs in the construction industry. But the president's Southern strategy continued to be an obvious appeal to the anti–civil rights forces in the North and South. Consequently, two of Mitchell's most notable battles with Nixon were over his nominations of federal judges Clement Haynsworth and G. Harrold Carswell to the Supreme Court. With the notable aid of the AFL-CIO, Mitchell, through the NAACP and the Leadership Conference, defeated the nominations. Nevertheless, Nixon continued his assault on the lower federal courts for their strong enforcement of *Brown* and their providing other constitutional protections for blacks. Those battles were the turning point for the conservative countermovement. Nixon ferociously used the highly controversial school busing issue to give the NAACP a whiplash and hand the civil rights movement its first significant defeat since the 1950s by getting Congress in 1972 to bar the use of federal funds to implement *Brown* in this manner.

As president, Ford continued Nixon's crusade against school busing as a court-mandated desegregation tool. Nevertheless, Mitchell won Ford's support, which was as forthright as Nixon's had been in 1970, for renewal in 1975 of the 1965 Voting Rights Act. Similarly, as with Nixon, he won Ford's support for affirmative action as a constitutional means for implementing Titles VI and VII of the 1964 Civil Rights Act.

In President Jimmy Carter, Mitchell found support that was as unequivocal as that which had cemented his bond with President Johnson. Carter felt the civil rights revolution was the greatest thing that had happened to the South. Because the revolution had ended when Carter was in office, however, his place in civil rights history was deprived of its due prominence. Civil rights had been the most potent national issue since World War II, but it was now receding as the country's driving social issue. There nevertheless could hardly have been a more satisfying moment for Mitchell than when Carter presented him in 1980 with the Presidential Medal of Freedom, saying, "It may well be that Hubert Humphrey and Lyndon Baines Johnson would not have been so notably acclaimed had it not been for the next gentleman who will be honored." The medal was inscribed:

> Clarence M. Mitchell, Jr., for decades waged in the halls of Congress a stubborn, resourceful and historic campaign for social justice. The integrity of this "101st Senator" earned him the respect of friends and adversaries alike. His brilliant advocacy helped translate into law the protests and aspirations of millions consigned too long to second-class citizenship. The hard-won fruits of his labors have made America a better and stronger nation.[35]

NOTES

1. Extensive collection of materials on the White House Conference on Negroes in Defense, 10–19–28–40, in NAACP, II A671, DLC; Watson, *Lion in the Lobby,* 120–51.

2. Klarman, *From Jim Crow to Civil Rights,* 171–86; Myrdal, *American Dilemma,* a summary of which is in HqR1, Office Memoranda. Bibliography, and Book Review; Watson, *Lion in the Lobby,* 83; Weaver, *Negro Labor,* 16–17; "War Crisis Forces Britain to Drop Army Color Bar," and "Whose Army Is It?" *Crisis,* 6/40, 179, 180; "The Negro in the United States Navy," *Crisis,* 7/40, 200–201, 210; "Brownsville, Tenn., U.S.A., 1940," *Crisis,* 8/40, 232; "Democracy in Brownsville, Tenn.," *Crisis,* 9/40, 289; "The Roosevelt Record," *Crisis,* 11/40, 343; "War on the Home Front," *Crisis,* 12/40, 375; "Now Is the Time Not to Be Silent," *Crisis,* 1/42, 7; "The Negro in the United States Army," *Crisis,* 2/42, 47; "Memorandum," "Yes, Negroes Know the Issues of War," and "Teachers' Salaries," *Crisis,* 3/42, 79, 100; "The Navy: Where Do You Stand? Pittsburgh (Pa.) *Courier,*" *Crisis,* 5/42, 160, 161, 165; Wilkins, "Negro Wants Full Equality," in Logan, *What the Negro Wants,* 113–32.

3. Watson, *Lion in the Lobby,* 83; Mitchell, "N.A.A.C.P.—Welcome to Baltimore!" *Crisis,* 7/36, 200–201.

4. Watson, *Lion in the Lobby,* 68–69.

5. Ibid., 87–96.

6. Houston created the NAACP's legal department and served as its first special counsel until 1938. Marshall succeeded him in 1939. Later, Houston became a policymaking member of the FEPC. Following Mitchell's death on March 18, 1984, Baltimore named the Baltimore City Courthouse, where the Murray case was tried, after him.

7. Mitchell, "N.A.A.C.P.–Welcome to Baltimore!" 200; Watson, *Lion in the Lobby,* 3–34, 94–96.

8. Watson, *Lion in the Lobby,* rev. ed., 108, 111.

9. Ibid., 122–26.

10. John A. Davis, interview by Watson, 1/19/84; Theodore Jones, interview by Watson, 11/19/82.

11. Part 1, "Wartime Experience: Value of National Policy against Discrimination in Industry," HqR2, Office Files of Malcolm Ross. Education Office of Vocational Training; *Final Report,* 1–7; Transcript of Proceedings, 2/12/44, 31, HqR64, Central Files.

12. As shown in the Committee on Fair Employment Practice (COFEP), "Its Beginning and Growth," the size of the staff varied; so did the number of regional offices, although there were usually twelve, paralleling the WMC's. In a news release on 7/8/43, the new Committee announced that at its first two-day meeting it had agreed to establish twelve regional offices and to proceed with several

cases, including the railroad hearings, pending on its docket. HqR85, Press Releases, 8/41–11/45. See also "Committee on Fair Employment Practice," Office of Labor Production, Chief Economic Adviser, JLM, July 13, 1943, in appendix 1.

13. Throughout the volume, I follow the FEPC's practice of using the term *Committee* for the policymaking body within the agency itself.

14. Transcript of Proceedings, 12/4/43, 57–59, HqR64, Central Files; Theodore Jones, interview by Watson, 11/19/82.

15. *First Report*, 9–17; COFEP, "Its Beginning and Growth," 3/44, an overview prepared by the division of review and analysis, HqR1, Office Files of Malcolm Ross. Extra Copies.

16. See FEPC Personnel, in appendix, as well as "Statement of Purpose," from which that list is prepared. HqR66, Regional Office, Releases.

17. *First Report*, 9–17; COFEP, "Its Beginning and Growth," 3/44; *Final Report*, viii; draft article by Malcolm Ross, FEPC chairman, for *NYT* on "Discrimination in War Industry," RG 228 (entry 8), Office Files of Malcolm Ross, box 64, DNA.

18. COFEP, "Its Beginning and Growth," 3/44.

19. For the FEPC's "Major Program Activities," see Minutes, 3/31/45, HqR1, Summary Minutes of Meetings. See also an overview of the FEPC, Office of Labor Production, Chief Economic Adviser, 7/13/43, and an "Analysis of Executive Order 9346," 7/43, both in appendix 1.

20. *First Report*, 3, 5, 46–48; "Major Program Activities," cited above. See references to War Labor Board throughout texts, such as 4/13, 5/17/44, 4/24/45. As an example of these agreements, see Johnson to Maslow, 3/6/44, "Agreement between NWLB and FEPC," which provides for:

1. NWLB will notify and arrange to have its Regional War Labor Boards notify FEPC upon request, whether the National or Regional War Labor Boards have on their dockets any cases involving a particular employer or labor organization.

2. NWLB will receive from FEPC its findings and determinations in any case pending before the National or Regional War Labor Boards and will give such consideration to these findings and determinations as the National or Regional Boards may deem appropriate.

HqR77, Central Files. Office Files of Ernest G. Trimble. Misc.

21. For a breakdown of the categories of group discrimination, see Operations Bulletin no. 1, FEPC folder, NAACP Washington Branch, DHU-MS.

22. *First Report*, 37, 42; *Final Report*, x.

23. In a memorandum of 12/17/43, Maslow, director of field operations, formally gave Mitchell his full assignment: "Until further notice, Mr. Mitchell will be responsible for the processing of all cases referred to the Director of Field Operations from the field, making and keeping records of assignments of these cases. Letters on such cases will be prepared for my signature under his supervision." In addition to Mitchell, Maslow sent the memorandum to Eugene Davidson, Emanuel Bloch, and Stanley Metzger. HqR6, Office Files of Emanuel H. Bloch. For a broader view of how the Committee developed its policy, see Transcripts of Proceedings, 8/41–4/46, HqR64, Central Files; HqR65, Central Files. U.S. Government; and HqR4, Office Files of George M. Johnson. Policy.

The Portland NAACP branch, for example, along with the Shipyard Negro Organization for Victory, in 1943 filed the employment discrimination complaint against the Kaiser Shipyard in Portland, Ore., with the NAACP. Noting that the Boilermakers Union at the shipyard barred blacks from membership, the complaint noted that their rights could not be protected in the Jim Crow Auxiliary Lodge A-32, which they were being forced to join. NAACP *Annual Report*, 7.

24. "A Study of Complaints of Discrimination against the Federal Government Because of Race, Creed, Color or National Origin Originating with the Civil Service Commission" provides considerably more details on how the system for resolving them was developed and how it worked. For example, the document notes that, immediately after the committee was organized, it "made vigorous attempts to strengthen the merit principle in Civil Service, especially with respect to the elimination of irrelevant consideration of race, creed, or national origin." HqR66, Central Files. U.S. Government, Civil Service Commission (Proposed Agreement), National.

25. See headnote on Jurisdictional Issues. For staff functions by job titles, see Operations Bulletin no. 1 in FEPC folder, NAACP Washington Branch, DHU-MS.

26. For a summary of the president's seizing the Philadelphia Transportation Co., see headnote on Street and Local Railways; *First Report*, 14–15. The Committee certified the case involving fourteen railroads that refused to cooperate with the agency and denied its jurisdiction to the president on 12/24/43. For the companies' letter of defiance, see Transcript of Proceedings, 12/17/43, 8–22, HqR64, Central Files. Railroads. For an internal overview, see "Railroads," in FEPC, RG 228 (entry 8), PI-147, Office Files of Malcolm Ross. Difficult Cases, box 67, DNA.

27. For a list of hearings held by the FEPC, see app. C, *First Report*, 108; for process involved, see Transcript of Proceedings, 9/30/44, 17–23, HqR65, Central Files.

28. Hearing on charges brought by seven Jehovah's Witnesses. See also the FEPC's referral to these complaints in FEPC's definition of "creed," Operating Bulletin no. 1, 8–9, FEPC folder, NAACP Washington Bureau, DHU-MS.

29. COFEP, "Its Beginning and Growth"; case flow chart in *First Report*, 18–19.

30. Watson, *Lion in the Lobby*, 594, 605, 609, 610, 618, 665, 670, 704; *Plessy v. Ferguson*, 163 U.S. 537 (1896); *Brown v. Board of Education*, 347 U.S. 483 (1954).

31. *First Report*, 11; Maslow, memorandum, 12/17/43.

32. Watson, *Lion in the Lobby*, 152–53, 183–86.

33. The Twenty-fourth Amendment banned the poll tax in federal elections, but it affected only five states: Alabama, Arkansas, Mississippi, Texas, and Virginia, which still had the tax on 1/23/64, when it was ratified. *Harman v. Forssenius*, 380 U.S. 528 (1964), covering federal elections, reaffirmed the Fifteenth Amendment, saying "no equivalent or milder substitute may be imposed." *Butts v. Harrison* and *Harper v. Virginia Board of Elections*, 383 U.S. 663 (1966), both decided as one. The 1965 Voting Rights Act also declared that it abridged the right to vote and directed the attorney general "forthwith" to challenge state poll taxes in lawsuits. For Mitchell's comments on *Forssenius*, see Watson, *Lion in the Lobby*, 652.

34. In addition to Mitchell's texts throughout the volume (8/17, 8/20, 8/25, 9/6, 9/14, 10/7, 10/9, 10/10, 10/29, 11/2/45), see appendix 1 for "Proposed Program for the Division of Field Operations." Other examples are the FEPC's report to the president on the "Impact of Reconversion on Minority Workers," HqR2, Office Files of Malcolm Ross. Education Office of Vocational Training for War Production Workers; and John A. Davis to Ross, memorandum, 12/16/44, with attached letters his division drafted to seven agencies on "FEPC and the War Mobilization and Reconversion Program"; W. C. Leland to Davis, memorandum, 10/31/44, on "Employment Impact of Cutbacks after V-E Day" on studies done by the WPB and the WMC, both in HqR3, Office Files of Malcolm Ross. John A. Davis. Numerous studies were done by such organizations as the National Urban League and the American Council on Race Relations, and articles were published on the subject in *The Crisis* and scholarly magazines.

35. Public Papers of the Presidents, Carter, 6/80, 1059.

ACKNOWLEDGMENTS

The work leading up to the editing and publishing of Mitchell's papers began some thirty years ago when Roy Wilkins, executive director of the National Association for the Advancement of Colored People, hired me as understudy to Henry Lee Moon, director of public relations. Unhappy with the exposure he was then getting from the public relations department, Mitchell began sending me materials for news releases on his work in Washington. The process of collecting the papers now being published was intensified and systematized during the five years before I began, in 1985, the full-time writing of my biography of Mitchell, *Lion in the Lobby* (Morrow, 1990; rev. ed., University Press of America, 2002), an essential supplement to Mitchell's papers.

A year after Mitchell's death in 1984, I asked Mary Giunta at the National Historical Publications and Records Commission about support for publishing the lobbyist's papers and received great encouragement. Sympathetically, however, she told me that ten years must pass between the death of the subject and support from the agency for editing his or her papers. Before I actually began the editing, therefore, many people helped me and I owe them an immeasurable debt of gratitude.

Roger A. Bruns, deputy executive director of the NHPRC, who enabled my dream to become reality by wholeheartedly endorsing the project in 2000 is at the top of the list. So is Hubert Keen, the newly appointed interim president of SUNY College at Old Westbury, who, upon first being informed about the proposed project, enthusiastically embraced it and agreed to Old Westbury's sponsoring it. Upon joining Keen's team as interim vice president for academic affairs, Jacqueline Ray was equally forceful in supporting it. It was her personal commitment to Roger that the project would have the full institutional support it merited that finally convinced him it was worth the NHPRC's support. Albert E. Smith, vice president for administration and finance was our "angel above" and was key to our launching the project. To all the others at SUNY College at Old Westbury who have been unstinting in their support and encouragement, I extend my deepest gratitude.

During this journey, which began in 1971 at the NAACP's national office, the staff endured my West Indian innocence of the organization's institutional and political artistry and of the civil rights movement in general. Perhaps it was because they did not feel threatened by me. The senior staff included, in addition to Moon, his able and dedicated assistant, Maybelle Ward. Both of them were big brother and big sister to me. Other veteran staffers were Gloster B. Current, director of branches and field administration, who was a cross between a big brother and a stern uncle who brooked no deviation from the old-guard NAACP book; Nathaniel R. Jones, general counsel, who was a friend and big brother too; and of course Clarence Mitchell Jr., whose support and nurturing won my undying admiration and respect.

With Roy's imprimatur, I traveled extensively throughout the country, especially the South, learning about the NAACP and its regional and local offices. To all the staff there, but especially to Ruby Hurley, director of Region V (the Southeast) during the most dangerous period of the struggle (as a reminder of the threats she constantly faced in the 1950s and 1960s, she kept in her Atlanta office a blonde doll, its neck slashed and splattered with red paint, that had been thrown on her porch one night), and to Virna Canson, director of Region II (the West Coast), I am indebted for their close tutoring, not only about the struggle but also about the NAACP's brutal internal politics.

I was further educated by a host of other NAACP activists, including Eugene Reed, president of the New York State Conference, who provided lessons about the uprising of young turks that began in the early 1960s within the organization owing to their dissatisfaction with Roy's leadership; Myrlie Evers, wife of Medgar, who was assassinated in 1963 in Jackson, Mississippi, for leading the local struggle as field secretary; Gilbert Mason, president of the Gulfport branch; Aaron Henry, president of the Mississippi State Conference; Kelly Alexander Sr., president of the North Carolina State Conference of NAACP Branches; and Delbert Woods, chairman of the labor and industrial committee of the South Carolina State Conference of NAACP Branches. I remain grateful for their lessons and insights into the nuances of the struggle and the importance of Mitchell's role in that struggle. Although most of them are not mentioned in volumes I and II, which cover the FEPC phase of Mitchell's career, they later play essential roles.

Shortly after joining the NAACP staff, I sought to write a biography of Roy Wilkins. His wife Minnie was most supportive and enthusiastic, to the point of granting me an interview. Roy, though, would have none of it, insisting that he should first write what in effect would have been his memoirs. Possibly because of that attitude, none of the other senior staff wrote their memoirs either. Wilkins did begin his (*Standing Fast*) following his retirement in 1976, but failing health robbed him of the opportunity to complete most of it, depriving history of his precious, unique insights and extensive knowledge of the movement dating back to 1931, when Walter White, executive secretary, hired him as assistant secretary. Because none of the other senior staff wrote memoirs to document not only their contributions but also those of the NAACP, Roy himself has been all but written out of modern civil rights history and the organization's role has been minimized. Yet, as head of the granddaddy NAACP, with its network of branches in every state and its Washington bureau, he was unquestionably the most influential of the Big Six civil rights leaders. (The other five: James Farmer, head of the Congress of Racial Equality; John Lewis, head of the Student Nonviolent Coordinating Committee; Whitney Young, head of the National Urban League; the Rev. Martin Luther King Jr., head of the Southern Christian Leadership Conference; and A. Philip Randolph, head of the Brotherhood of Sleeping Car Porters.) Roy's influence was buttressed by his chairmanship of the Leadership Conference on Civil

Rights—the powerful coalition of civil rights, civic, labor, religious, and fraternal organizations that he founded in Washington in 1950 that considerably expanded the NAACP's political clout. The Southern Christian Leadership Conference and the Student Nonviolent Coordinating Committee were LCCR members.

Because Roy refused to allow a biography of him to be written, I turned to Clarence, for whom respect throughout Washington had won him popular recognition as the "101st senator." Clarence earlier had begun exploring the possibility of writing his memoirs, but apparently he could find no trade publisher because he refused to cheapen his legacy by delving into personal and salacious gossip about lawmakers and government officials that would most certainly have made the work a best seller. Thanks to the persistent nudging of his wife, Juanita, Mitchell followed through on his commitment to me to cooperate in the writing of his biography after he had retired from the NAACP. The papers that are now being edited are the product of that long journey. I therefore hope that this project will adequately express my gratitude for his full cooperation and support and the undying inspiration of "Mrs. Mitchell." In addition to encouraging Clarence to cooperate with me, Mrs. Mitchell provided her eloquent and extensive knowledge and insights of the struggle during some of the many interviews I had with her husband.

Not only was she a griot, but her friendship enabled me to persevere in completing *Lion in the Lobby* and in the subsequent quest for a sponsor for the editing project until SUNY College at Old Westbury agreed to do so. Following her husband's death on March 18, 1984, in Baltimore, Juanita granted me total access to his private collection of papers, enabling me to not only chronicle her husband's contributions but also to begin planning the publishing of the edition. To the many other members of the family who cooperated so willingly—especially "Uncle" George Mitchell, Clarence's brother, who opened his private collection too, and Michael, his son—I am deeply indebted. That family support, too, encouraged Clarence to reach deep into his memory to provide the types of insights that no one else could have provided.

Following Clarence's death, I turned to Joseph L. Rauh Jr., his close lobbying partner from 1950 to 1978, the period of Mitchell's lobbying career, for guidance. (So close were Clarence and Joe that Senator Harry Flood Byrd Jr.—the "one who used to own the state of Virginia," recalled Joe—labeled them the Gold Dust Twins, after a popular scrubbing powder.) As the young lawyer who drafted Executive Order 8802 and was awed by the authoritarian bearing of A. Philip Randolph, who demanded a meaningful measure to bar discrimination in the defense industry, Joe's recollections too were priceless. ("Who the hell is this guy?" Joe wondered when Randolph, president of the Brotherhood of Sleeping Car Porters, held firm in his demand.) So were the insights of Robert C. (Bob) Weaver and John Aubrey Davis. Their insights were essential for the writing of the FEPC chapter in *Lion in the Lobby*. It was also Weaver's deathbed wish that I write a biography of him, but because I could find no financial support anywhere for that project, I turned my efforts to editing Mitchell's papers. Both Bob Weaver and John Aubrey remained friends for the rest of their lives and enabled a cross-checking of details about the FEPC and the modern civil rights struggle that, upon further cross-checks with each of them, inspired the outpourings of more details to me.

Others who shared their memories of the FEPC period were Will Maslow, another priceless source, especially on the genesis of affirmative action. Clarence, of course, explained the signal importance of the *Steele* and *Tunstall* decisions as demonstrating the need for affirmative action programs (see Railroad Unions), but it was Maslow who recalled that the FEPC itself was an affirmative action program. Overall, though, *The Papers of Clarence Mitchell Jr.* is rooted in the personal insights of Clarence himself and, of course, the texts themselves, which are overpowering in documenting the essential role he played.

The project's staff from its beginning has comprised two people: myself and my associate, Elizabeth M. Nuxoll, who leapfrogged from studying the career of Robert Morris (known as the financier of the American Revolution) into civil rights. To her, the project owes an immeasurable debt for her dedication to producing a work that will exemplify the principles of professional documentary editing. Also to be complimented for their work and support are the student assistants, whose typing and other skills enabled us to complete the massive transcription of the texts for all five volumes in near-record time. They were Natasha Cofresi, Georgianna Fitzgerald, Dulce Flores, Ankawa Jean-Louis, Eileen Maldonato, Shenella Mentor, Lori Ogiste, and Crystal Scott. Lincoln Van Sluytman, another assistant, was somewhat of an anomaly in that he was a professional returning to Old Westbury to obtain his degree. He demonstrated his maturity and professionalism by starting the biographical directory. Subsequent to Elizabeth's departure, Edward A. Bradley joined us as assistant editor.

Scholarly assistance was provided by Merl Reed, author of *Seedtime for the Modern Civil Rights Movement* and who, unknown to me in the early 1980s, was interviewing Mitchell for his work while I was doing the same for *Lion in the Lobby*. Reed shared with the project both the summary of his interviews and the identification of the FEPC staff in the group picture used in this volume.

In addition to the dedicated staff of SUNY Old Westbury's library, especially Norine Baskin and Stephen Kirkpatrick, we are indebted to Ronald Welton for helping us get established in our suite of offices; to P. J. Harlow, whose support from the college's sponsored programs office in preparing grant applications made her an invaluable asset; and to Marilyn Lombardi, grants manager in the SUNY Research Foundation.

Scholarly resources were also provided by the Freeport Memorial Library, thanks to Dave Opatow, executive director; Walter Hill and Dane Hartgrove, of the National Archives; and Ethel Earlene Henderson, widow of Elmer, who made her late husband's FEPC collection available. Interlibrary loans of FEPC microfilms were facilitated by Sally McMaster and Angela Valentine of the University of Rochester Library, Cindy Kristof of Kent State University Library, Ann Diseroad of Bloomsburg University Library, and Evelyn Silverman of Queens College (CUNY) Library.

Also providing us with their invaluable recollections, reminiscences, and evaluations of Mitchell's contributions at the Clarence Mitchell Jr. Symposium "His Struggle for Racial Equality" from January 30 to February 2, 2001, were John H. Bracey Jr., Afro-American Studies Department, University of Massachusetts, Amherst; Calvin O. Butts III, president, SUNY College at Old Westbury; Gwendolyn J. Cunningham, former secretary, NAACP Washington Bureau, and special assistant to the president, American Postal Workers Union, AFL-CIO; Onita Estes-Hicks, chair, English Language Studies, SUNY Old Westbury; Leonard Garment, White House civil rights liaison (Nixon administration); Evelyn Harvey, former secretary, NAACP Washington Bureau; Elaine R. Jones, president and director-counsel, NAACP Legal Defense and Educational Fund, Inc.; Nathaniel R. Jones, senior judge, U.S. Court of Appeals, Cincinnati; Gloria Browne Marshall, NAACP Legal Defense and Educational Fund; Harold McDougall, professor, Columbus School of Law, the Catholic University of America; Genna Rae McNeil, professor of history, University of North Carolina; Michael B. Mitchell and his daughters, Micah and Juanita; Matthew J. Perry Jr., senior judge, U.S. District Court, Columbia, South Carolina; Adelaide Sanford, New York State regent; Joseph R. L. Sterne, former editorial page editor, *Baltimore Sun;* Patricia Sullivan, W. E. B. Du Bois Institute for Afro-American Research, Harvard University; Michael H. Sussman, civil rights attorney; William L. Taylor, general counsel, LCCR; Timothy N. Thurber, assistant professor of history, SUNY Oswego; Charles Turner, dramatist; John Willertz, professor of history, Saginaw Valley State University; and Kenneth Young, former executive assistant to the president, AFL-CIO (George Meany and Lane Kirkland).

INTRODUCTION

The FEPC Years

My interest in the work of the Committee is over and above simply the problem of one minority in the country.
— *Clarence Mitchell Jr. to Will Maslow, March 3, 1944*

Before World War II the principle upon which the FEPC was founded, that equal job opportunity enabled Americans to establish a place in society based on their skills, was never reinforced by law. Or, as the FEPC said in its *Final Report,* "it was called upon to act in a field where Government never before had intervened." One reason was that Americans never felt the need for such protections because habits of assigning African Americans and Mexican Americans to the most menial, heaviest, or dirtiest work, at the lowest or unequal pay, were never challenged; the other was the belief that the only barrier to employment was inherent in the attitude of the individual. The FEPC was thus the first national step toward making equal job opportunity a protected right. National self-preservation demanded it. The FEPC's struggle for equal employment opportunity affirmed and sharpened the focus of the modern struggle for civil rights. Thus, there are two approaches to assessing Mitchell's contributions to the civil rights struggle through the FEPC. One is short-term, measuring his role in implementing the committee's nondiscrimination policy and program from 1941 to 1946 for opening up job opportunities to African Americans and others covered by the order; and the other is long-term, through the strategies he developed to preserve and strengthen the FEPC idea until Congress enacted a permanent agency and nondiscrimination program in 1964. *The Papers of Clarence Mitchell Jr.* is supplemented in its documentation of the historical significance of this phase of his work in the chapter "The FEPC Grail" in *Lion in the Lobby: Clarence Mitchell, Jr.'s Struggle for the Passage of Civil Rights Laws.*

Pearl Harbor shifted the nation from preparing for defense to preparing for war. The historical turning point, as Roosevelt stressed and African Americans realized, was that the nation had to use all available manpower to win the war. That dramatic change in national attitude came just before Pearl Harbor, building on the broad social, political, and international forces that began developing during the New Deal.

Six months before Roosevelt issued Executive Order 8802, *The Crisis,* the official organ of the NAACP, acknowledged his unprecedented, if reluctant, leadership during the New Deal: "Most important contribution of the Roosevelt Administration to the age-old color line problem in America has been its doctrine that Negroes are a part of the country as a whole. The inevitable discriminations, notwithstanding, this *thought* has been driven home in thousands of communities by a thousand specific acts. For the first time in their lives, government has taken on meaning and substance for the Negro masses."[1]

EO 8802 was more than a proclamation. It did more than reaffirm American ideals of democracy. It affirmed the duty of employers, labor organizations, the government, and citizens to uphold the president's national nondiscrimination policy in employment. Once African Americans obtained Roosevelt's leadership, they supported the FEPC in implementing the national nondiscrimination policy with the expansive principles of affirmative action that went beyond merely seeking to end inequalities against them, or their exclusion from the workplace, to correcting the historical legacies of such practices.[2]

During the new Committee's first meeting, in July 1943, Milton Webster asserted, "I think the effectiveness of the Committee is going to depend a good deal upon what happens to the complaints." Seeking to ensure that the FEPC fulfilled its promise despite its obvious shortcomings, Mitchell implemented its program by conducting investigations, such as those for the hearings involving the St. Louis, Missouri, war industries, and the Portland, Oregon, shipyards; ending race strikes, such as those involving the Alabama Dry Dock and Shipbuilding Company in Mobile, the Philadelphia Rapid Transit, and Bethlehem Steel in Baltimore; and handling a sizable number of cases himself, in addition to supervising the regional staff in resolving their cases.[3]

THE NATURE OF THE JOB

A proper understanding of Mitchell's job can be obtained only by reviewing developments leading up to the FEPC. He directed the field staff in working not only to persuade nervous or intransigent employers, but also labor unions and white workers, to remove obstacles to ending discrimination. Those obstacles included strikes and work stoppages to block the hiring or upgrading of blacks, most often men but sometimes women. Mitchell's job of implementing the nondiscrimination clause was the heart of the FEPC's mission. And "Clarence understood his job in its totality," explained John A. Davis.[4]

Upon joining Robert Weaver's staff in 1941 in the Office of Production Management, as one of a dozen or more highly trained professionals, Mitchell was regional director for New Jersey, Pennsylvania, and Delaware, where there was a concentration of industry. He also routinely worked on selected cases in Baltimore, no doubt at the insistence of Lillie Mae Jackson, his mother-in-law, who was president of the Baltimore NAACP branch.[5]

His October 26, 1941, report to Weaver, submitted as a letter on note pad paper he clearly typed, shows that their professional relationship began informally, but that they were equally committed to their work:

Dear Bob:

I have just finished talking with Mr. Saul M. Perdue, a member of the Baltimore school system who is in charge of employment at Glen Martin. Mr. Perdue informs me that there are 13 boys now at work in the Eastern Avenue Plant of the Martin Company. These persons are doing very well he states but the hiring og Negroes has been slwoed down because the company has been unable to get its requisitions for forty trainees filled. Mr. Perdue stated that the plan was to hire at least ten to fifteen Negroes a week.

So far as Albert Black is concerned, Mr. Perdue feels that the company will not hire him if it can get out of it because of the publicity which he has given the case. Off the record, he stated that he feels that the Martin Company would even be willing to pay damages assessed by a court rather than use Mr. Black.

One trainee from Philadelphia has been employed. His name is Richard Garrison. However, he got in by giving a Towson, Md., address. The company has adopted a policy of not hiring any Negroes except thos who give local addresses on their application blanks. Mr. Perdue, in response to a direct question from me, stated that if the trainees you have in West Virginia can come to Baltimore and give local addresses he feels that they will be hired. This of course would require some careful planning and I suggested that you would be glad to have him to lunch in Washington some time to discuss all angles. This brought up another point which is that Mr. Perdue feels that the Glen Martin Company is not satisfied with the equipment which is being used in the training courses in Baltimore. As an employee of the local department of education, Mr. Perdue cannot be quoted on this, but he feels that the school system's negligence is responsible for the lack of desirable equipment. He stated that he will perhaps be coming in to see you on this question.

Incidentally, Mr. Perdue says the people now employed are due for a raise next week. He also said that the Martin Company intends to transfer its Negro help to the Middle River Plant as soon as possible. You know, of course, that some of the colored people feel that the company intends to keep the Negroes in Canton permanently and never use them at Middle River. Mr. Perdue seems very honest and he denies this, you of course will know more about the whole thing later from the field man assigned to this territory or Ted. All of this [of] course is off the record so far as Mr. Perdue is concerned and I believe he will always be willing to co-operate with us if we respect his confidence.

Sincerely

Mitchell[6]

Subsequently, as his reports to Bob Weaver in 1942 show, their working relationship became more formal, further affirming Mitchell's deep respect for him.

Mitchell knew the FEPC's major shortcoming was its structure. The committee was established in the labor division of the OPM and was required to share Weaver's staff. The FEPC served as a board of appeal for Weaver's Negro Employment and Training Branch (NETB) and its companion Minority Groups Branch (MGB). "It seemed to me there was a potential for competition" in that arrangement, Mitchell explained. Before the FEPC's creation, Weaver was the principal person in government handling discrimination cases. Now the FEPC had that function and the NETB was demoted to facilitator. Weaver resented his unit's diminished status. But there was much to be done, and he and his team were committed to a common cause. Furthermore, they needed to survive, so they cooperated with the FEPC.[7]

"But there did come times when people would argue that the labor division had jurisdiction over a given matter, and therefore FEPC should stay out of it," Mitchell recalled. "I didn't really feel quite that way about it. The job was so big you could have had a hundred FEPCs and a hundred labor divisions, but still only scratch the surface." He thought it was possible that the FEPC suggested that it absorb OPM's labor division, but he did not want to get involved in unnecessary controversy. So he was never involved in those discussions or "maneuvering back and forth." When he felt he could be more useful at the FEPC, he "just walked over there."[8]

The FEPC's second problem was that it had no independent authority, so it could not enforce its orders. Its third was that its uncertain status reflected Roosevelt's ambivalence about the idea of equal employment opportunity for blacks. Outlining his job, Mitchell explained that he worked with employers and unions, respectively, to get their pledge to hire and to cooperate with the hiring of skilled African American workers. The unions' cooperation was necessary to accomplish the job "without friction and with the maximum good results," he said. He was especially grateful for the cooperation of the CIO unions in shipbuilding, aviation, the garment industry, and the automobile industry. Some circumstances demanded "courage and the belief in the fundamental principles of fair play," he said.[9]

The FEPC and the OPM's nondiscrimination units made progress in that very uncertain period while the defense program evolved in a makeshift manner. For example, on January 26, 1942, while Mitchell was in Philadelphia meeting with a contractor, the man held up a newspaper with the headline indicating that the OPM had been abolished and its functions transferred to the newly created and powerful War Production Board. During that short time Mitchell opened up skilled jobs for blacks in such firms as the Camp Shipbuilding Company, the Bendix Aviation Corporation, the Wright Aeronautical Company, Western Electric, RCA, and Westinghouse. Weaver therefore promoted him to assistant chief of the NETB of the WPB. On July 30, 1942, Roosevelt transferred the FEPC from the WPB to the War Manpower Commission, headed by Paul V. McNutt, where the NETB and the MGB were already functioning.[10]

Years later, Weaver would take credit for recommending Mitchell to the FEPC. Mitchell, however, recalled that it was Elmer Henderson, an FEPC staff member, who facilitated the arrangement. He remembered hearing of a conversation between Lawrence Cramer, FEPC executive secretary, and someone else in which Cramer said he did not know how Mitchell got on the FEPC staff. "He just looked up one day and I was there," Mitchell explained. Cramer assumed his assignment to the FEPC "had been cleared with everyone." Mitchell himself was surprised to learn that he was still on the WMC payroll.

On September 24, 1942, Mitchell and other staff of both the NETB and the MGB were immediately transferred to work for the FEPC, while Weaver was made chief of

xlvi

the Negro Manpower Service of the WMC. Weaver, nevertheless, and Will Alexander both had the official titles of assistant to the WMC's chairman.[11] In January 1943, Mitchell began working full time for the FEPC as senior fair practice examiner. He had begun submitting his reports to George Johnson, deputy chairman, in November, establishing a working bond whose cement was mutual respect, similar styles of proficiency, and commitment to a common cause. Despite his respect for Weaver, Mitchell was relieved that he was freed from divided loyalties. The FEPC provided him with leverage that no black government employee previously had ever had. Until the creation of the FEPC, blacks could only be race advisers to whites, as Weaver remained until he left the government in 1944.[12]

On Weaver's staff Mitchell had begun demonstrating an ability to handle employers who were hostile to his insistence that they stop discriminating and hire blacks. An official at the Sun Shipbuilding and Drydock Company in Chester, Pennsylvania, was typical. Mitchell recalled the official's response during their meeting: "Well, in all the years that I've been in the shipbuilding industry, I've never seen any Negro shipfitters." Mitchell was certain that there were black shipfitters, "but they weren't called that because it meant paying them a decent wage. We had some pretty rough going in some of those plants," he added. Sun also had a separate shipway for blacks, initiating a precedent for the Alabama Dry Dock and Shipbuilding Company in Mobile and elsewhere. On a later occasion, the vice president of the Goodyear Tire and Rubber Company in Akron concluded a long meeting about ending discrimination in defense plants by asking Mitchell, "Do you know where I could find a good cook?" At a similar meeting in Portland, Oregon, an official of the Boilermakers Union exploded, "God damn it, don't come in here waving the American flag." But rather than intimidating Mitchell, such encounters strengthened his resolve.[13]

Mitchell recalled that in 1941, Washington "was not morally ready to fight for democracy." The roots of segregation were deep, extending back to the administration of Woodrow Wilson. Battling the problem reached a new intensity in 1939, when the Daughters of the American Revolution barred renowned contralto Marian Anderson from singing at Constitution Hall. As the Anderson episode showed, however, the city's Jim Crow walls were cracking. She sang to a crowd of some seventy-five thousand at the Lincoln Memorial on April 9. The cadre of no-nonsense black bureaucrats like Mitchell, Weaver, and Henderson kept widening those cracks.[14]

The FEPC, too, suffered segregation. Mitchell recalled that when the agency moved into the Standard Oil building on Constitution Avenue at Third Street, which was shared by other government offices, there was a very unpleasant guard there who would not use courtesy titles in addressing blacks. So the FEPC got him transferred. The government-run cafeteria there was another problem. In addition to being located in a tiny room, with four or five tables, the "lady in charge" was most unpleasant, and the other tenants using the cafeteria often discriminated. Many years later, Mitchell would dismiss the problems as "little things" that arose constantly. But those problems were not regarded as little back then. So demeaning were they that Frank Hook, FEPC regional director, complained about them in a memorandum that Mitchell forwarded on January 21, 1944, to Theodore Jones, director of administration for the FEPC.

Jim Crow, of course, was not limited to Washington. Once when he visited the regional office in Dallas, which was headed by Carlos Castañeda, Mitchell learned that the FEPC staffers were not supposed to use the restroom on their floor. In addition to Castañeda, Virgil Williams (a young black man), a black secretary, and a German woman were in the office. Upon arriving there, however, someone simply handed Mitchell the key to the restroom. They had expected him to be white. With Mitchell setting a precedent, the practice was ended. Everyone got a key to the restroom. "In those days," explained Mitchell, a part of the problem was the "risk that Congressmen would retaliate" against the FEPC for promoting desegregation.[15]

COMMITTEE MEMBERS AND STAFF

Mitchell knew several members of the old Committee before they became members. He first met Malcolm MacLean, who succeeded Mark Ethridge as chairman, when he took social work courses at the University of Minnesota. MacLean then was head of its General College. Mitchell knew Frank Fenton well. He was director of organization at the AFL and alternate on the Committee for William Green, president of the AFL. Mitchell knew Ethridge through the NAACP. He knew Earl B. Dickerson, a black Mississippian, for a long time, probably as a result of his uncompromising stand on discrimination as an alderman in Chicago, where he had moved. He met David Sarnoff of the Radio Corporation of America at the WMC. Through mutual friends he knew Milton Webster, representing the Brotherhood of Sleeping Car Porters, casually in St. Paul. Boris Shishkin, also from the AFL, who was an "easy to know fellow and to work with," he had also known previously. Unlike Fenton, Shishkin was "more the intellectual." He met John Brophy when John Woods was organizing the CIO. Mitchell was there working for the *Baltimore Afro-American*. He first met Charles L. Horn in 1938 when Horn headed the Federal Cartridge Company in Anoka, Minnesota, and Mitchell led a concerned delegation to meet with him about hiring blacks at his plant. He supported Horn's nomination to the Committee. Subsequently, Horn hired Cecil Newman, publisher of the *St. Paul Advocate* and the *Minneapolis Spokesman* and a friend of Mitchell's, as personnel representative at the Twin City Ordnance plant operated by Federal Cartridge. Horn "hired a great number" of African Americans and thoroughly integrated them at the plant in many occupations. Mitchell added that Horn regularly made "very forthright statements" regarding the employment of African Americans in industry.[16]

Mitchell believed the members of the first FEPC were "a little at sea as to what they were supposed to do." Many of them "anticipated they would come in and start doing a lot of personal things," he said. "Cramer had the concept where he would be the focal point and wasn't quite prepared for the vigor," or demands of the job. By contrast, Milton Webster and Dickerson "would assert themselves." Cramer, though, was "a diplomatic person and tried to do a great number of things himself." Mitchell was not sure Cramer understood the "extent of the problem, and he might have assumed it was easier to handle it than it was."

Cramer had direct connections with the White House. Mitchell "got the impression he had talked with FDR a couple of times, but it was not clear there was a close, personal relationship." He heard a rumor that Cramer "was the son of a good friend of FDR and that was how he came into the picture." It was likely, Mitchell thought, that people wanted to cooperate with him. However, between the aggressiveness of some Committee members and the problems the agency had with politicians, "Cramer had a very difficult life." Mitchell therefore believed he was glad to go into the military, despite the difficulty he had using a hand as a result of a wound he suffered in World War I. Cramer got a waiver to enter the War Department.

Mitchell explained that other administrative challenges Cramer experienced resulted from the FEPC's inadequate staff and funding. Furthermore, in the FEPC's early days there were questions regarding its jurisdiction and scope and other policy issues. Under those circumstances, it "would have been difficult for anyone to show a clear pattern of administrative competence."

Mitchell felt that Malcolm (Mike) Ross, who succeeded Cramer, "had no knowledge in matters of racial problems." Instead of relying on people like George Johnson, deputy chairman, who knew discrimination firsthand, however, he turned to Will Maslow.[17] Maslow and Ross had been friends from their days at the National Labor Relations Board. Maslow had been a trial judge there when Ross was director of public relations. Maslow recalled that in May 1943, Ross, who had already joined the FEPC as deputy chairman, asked him to help draft a revision to EO 8802 to strengthen it. After Maslow did that, Ross submitted it to Ross's friend Attorney General Francis Biddle. That revision, Maslow said, became the new Executive Order 9346, which enlarged the FEPC's power and increased its budget. At Ross's invitation, Maslow left the NLRB and joined the FEPC staff as director of field operations. It was then that he met Mitchell, who was made his associate in the new FEPC. "What distinguished Clarence in my mind from everybody else on the staff was his integrity," said Maslow. "He had no other ambition but to serve the black people. He was absolutely unselfish, and did a very good and faithful job. I don't recall that we ever had any words of difference."

At that time, Maslow recalled, the FEPC's office was in a black neighborhood in Washington on R Street in "a ramshackle building" owned by the government. He estimated that two-thirds or three-quarters of the staff was black. "Because of my prior government experience I was given a lot of other tasks that would fit into the description of field operations. I would handle the meetings with the budget committee, the budget officer," Theodore Jones. "I was in charge of the liaison with people in the Congress, the legislative operations, and so on."

Maslow explained that it was he who hired the "regional directors after I had set up a plan, selected the cities that would have directors." He interviewed the candidates, and it impressed him that none had prior government experience. "There were very, very few blacks in government," on either the federal or state level. "I interviewed blacks and was dismayed to find how little contact they had with white people. In interviewing and selecting regional directors, I looked for people who had some experience, some contacts with blacks, because the regional directors had to meet, had to confer with white companies, to negotiate settlements, and things of that sort." Maslow said it was he who decided to hire white regional directors in the South, because "it was absolutely unworkable in those days to have a black regional director in a southern regional office. We tried to have a black deputy for each of the white regional officers."

Maslow recalled that he also induced A. Bruce Hunt to leave the NLRB and join the FEPC as regional director in its Atlanta office. "He was from Virginia. He was an idealistic fellow." He said Hunt wanted to hire a black secretary, but he could not find one. "Those women who were qualified went North. We finally induced the president of Atlanta University to give up his secretary so that Bruce Hunt could have a black secretary in his office."

In the headquarters building, said Maslow, "the problem rose about the toilets" because the FEPC had black female employees. "The white females from the other government offices would not allow the black girls to come in there. This problem went up to the White House. Eleanor Roosevelt worked with us in trying to solve the problem. She personally said we would make this black women's toilet so attractive, so much better, so much superior to the others that the white girls would come. And that worked out. After a few months, they [white women] forgot about it. They all began using the new and attractive toilets. But this was an idea of Eleanor Roosevelt." By contrast, it was Maslow's impression that the president "had no interest at all in the agency. He was no help at all."[18]

Maslow impressed Mitchell as "a brilliant fellow," a lawyer "steeped in NLRB problems." Maslow was "an excellent organizer, but he didn't really have a day-to-day background on the problems and personalities in the black community." Some blacks were "militantly aggressive, and, by any standard, that day or this, were very knowledgeable on where they wanted to go and how they would get there." Maslow did not understand that and neither did Ross.

Mitchell believed that "Mike may have felt he could not rely on George's loyalty to the same extent he could on Will's." But for Johnson to have been in the situation in which he was placed would have been "difficult for any black who knew the situation in the real world and knew Mike's lack of knowledge on it." So it was difficult for Johnson to have said, "I will be your confidant, I will show you how to do these things so you won't get into trouble." Mitchell's memoranda to Johnson, which sometimes revealed his own impatience with Maslow, helped cement the working relationship between him and the deputy chairman.

Furthermore, "Mike came into" the policy position "so suddenly and from an unknown point of origin" that there was "nothing in his background that any of us knew about that would" have indicated he was the right person for the job. Ross impressed Mitchell as a "gentle person" who "did not want unnecessary fights with anybody."

Mitchell wondered whether he would have taken the job if "he had known what was up the road for him." It was "difficult for him to crack down on anybody," so much so that Mitchell doubted that "Mike would have disciplined anybody for unauthorized press releases."

Mitchell recalled that once when a black politician was attempting to get G. James Fleming removed from the job as regional director in Philadelphia because he was a Republican, Ross joined in a meeting in an attempt to resolve the conflict. Mitchell became "disgusted" with Ross's indecisive manner in resolving the matter and started walking out. Ross surprised him by demanding in a raised voice that Mitchell "come back here." Ross then told him, "All I want to say is I am releasing you from any obligation in making a decision." Mitchell thought Ross would have reprimanded him more drastically. "But that was a drastic as he could get."

Owing to Ross's style, Mitchell suspected that St. Clair T. Bourne, information officer, gave the Negro press "a lot of stuff he shouldn't have." He suspected that Bourne, rather than protecting the agency, gave the press a lot of derogatory news about it.

In Mitchell's view, the Committee never kept too tight a rein on the staff, at least not on him, and, as he explained, he was in a significant position. He was "always grumbling to the legal staff about whether cases were moving fast enough, or being investigated properly," as some of his published texts show. He said he did not attempt to establish any special relations with Committee members, although he knew all of them. Totally immersed in his work, he never tried to find out what transpired at Committee meetings. But he knew that P. B. Young, Boris Shishkin, and Charles Horn were very hostile to Maslow. Mitchell respected Maslow as "very able," but he strongly disagreed with Maslow that the director of field operations was his boss.

That problem arose because when the FEPC was organized, some wanted Mitchell to be director of field operations, while others wanted Maslow to get the job. Maslow got it, but owing to the vague lines of authority, Mitchell could not tell whether or not he was Maslow's subordinate. Mitchell thus acted as Maslow's equal. He did not hesitate to reprimand Maslow, as he did in his memorandum of September 25, 1943, because of the manner in which he assigned Lethia Clore and Daniel R. Donovan from the national office to Region V under William T. McKnight. "In neither of these cases did the Regional Director have an opportunity to decide whether the individuals would fit the needs of his program," Mitchell wrote. "For this reason, I strongly recommend that, for the additional vacancy now in the Cleveland region, Mr. McKnight's judgment be the controlling factor in selection." He displayed a similar tone of authority in his May 31, 1945, memorandum to Maslow.

Mitchell believed Davidson wanted to be director of field operations, but "he went at it more vigorously" than Mitchell and "ended up as assistant director," because he evidently offended some people. Typically, Mitchell never wondered what his working relationship with Davidson was supposed to be. He simply fulfilled his duties by doing what he knew had to be done. Mitchell, furthermore, "avoided the various little political maneuvers" among the regional staff and tried to assist them in fulfilling their jobs. Never was he concerned about who was going to hold a given job. He nevertheless did openly oppose the transfer of Virgil Williams from the Dallas regional office to Chicago. He believed Williams wanted to remain in the South, even though it was a difficult place for a black person to work.[19]

Mitchell's assessment of selected staff, far from comprehensive, showed how he viewed people. He admired Dickerson because "he had deep convictions about things." Dickerson had served in World War I and seen how black troops were humiliated. The racial injustices blacks suffered in his hometown, Chicago, also bothered him. Mitchell believed anything Dickerson did to fight discrimination was done "because he conceived it to be the mission of the Committee." He had "a lot of brains and ability." To the extent that some might have found him abrasive, that would have been "his method of getting at the truth." He was not the type of person who kidded people. As a lawyer, he asked "questions that would get at the facts."

Mitchell saw the difference between the activist styles of Dickerson and Charles Hamilton Houston, another black lawyer on the Committee, as one between "a Harvard-trained person and a person trained in a less portly atmosphere." Houston "could get incisively at what he wanted, but in the most polished way, so that a person being probed would have a hard time taking offense." Dickerson exhibited a "more Midwestern frankness without trimmings," so one "would think he was trying to hurt feelings."

Mitchell regarded Hunt as a "great asset." He had an "unshakeable resentment against discrimination." A white lawyer with a Virginia accent who at one point also ran the Atlanta office, Hunt was acceptable in the South, until he voiced his position on discrimination. He "surprised those with whom he dealt"; they regarded him as a radical.

Hunt's successor, Witherspoon Dodge, director of the Atlanta regional office from 1944 to 1945, had a long activist history in church-sponsored work in the South. There, Mitchell explained, "church people would condemn what was wrong, but would never make any great waves" about racism. He was "cautious, very low key." On the other hand, "Bruce would come in as a lawyer and demolish the opposition." Dodge's lawyering included telling a few jokes and reciting poetry, "getting at the same thing in a different style, like what church people would use." Hunt's style would have been more acceptable "in today's world," Mitchell believed. As a child, Hunt's mother gave him a "horsewhipping" because "he did something offensive" to a black person. That "changed his perspective" on race, so that he "had an understanding of the problem." Mitchell believed Hunt was determined to help correct racial problems, but he was up against "impossible odds."

Don Ellinger "also had a lot of good will" and was "constructive." It was Maslow who recruited him to the headquarters, as well as Stanley D. Metzger, Emanuel H. Bloch, and Leonard M. Brin to the regional staff. Mitchell considered William T. McKnight, who "came in on his own steam" out of the Wage-Hours Administration, as similarly effective. Mitchell also regarded Elmer Henderson as "good and effective." By contrast, he found Roy A. Hoglund, a white regional director, to be a good man but not effective. Hoglund followed what Mitchell saw as a "political pattern of not wanting to antagonize any political person." Nevertheless, Mitchell respected him for his decent instincts. Hoglund got along with everyone—white, brown, and black. Joseph Evans, Mitchell explained, had served as "a career government person" for a long time before joining the FEPC's staff. But as director of Region IV, which included Washington, he was right under the "central Committee," so he was overshadowed.[20]

DEFINING DISCRIMINATION

Mitchell strengthened the policies that were established earlier in defining discrimination and continued to do so at the FEPC. Growing up in Baltimore, he did not pay much attention to discrimination, so it was no problem to him then. Blacks experienced discrimination as a normal part of their lives. Now, however, he followed a bureaucratic procedure for ending discrimination that built on earlier efforts that began in 1932, when he became vice president of the City-Wide Young People's Forum, an activist organization that his future wife, Juanita Jackson, began.[21]

Weaver had shown in the 1930s that the government previously had no criteria for determining discrimination. The federal government's efforts to end job discrimination began during the Roosevelt administration under Weaver's direction, when he was associate adviser in the Department of the Interior. He prepared a comprehensive study, "A Survey of White Collar and Skilled Workers," considered to be the most important to date on the economic status of blacks in the fall of 1934. The study provided the foundation for government programs against employment discrimination. Next, working in the housing division of the Public Works Administration, Weaver established criteria for defining discrimination and developed protections for the economic rights of blacks.

Weaver regarded public housing construction as the guinea pig for experiments in reducing discrimination against skilled black workers on publicly financed projects. Until 1929 black workers were almost totally excluded from the building industry. The situation began changing after 1930 as extreme competition developed for any type of construction work. In 1932, pressed by civil rights groups to end discrimination against black workers on public works projects, the United States Treasury issued a directive to construction engineers to end such practices. In 1933 the PWA followed the precedent and issued an order to state engineers that there should "be no discrimination exercised against any person because of color or religious affiliation." The orders, however, were not effective because they contained no definition of discrimination, and thus no criterion for proving that such practices existed or for dealing with contractors and labor unions that practiced them. Said Weaver, "It was humanly impossible to define discrimination (much less prove it) in a situation where a borrower, a contractor, and a labor union were involved." Weaver found that when discrimination was obvious because of the lack of black workers on a project, in order to satisfy the government's requirements, all the employer had to do to correct the problem was hire a few minority workers. But that action did not end discrimination against an entire class of people.

At Weaver's urging, the PWA's housing division adopted the policy that the failure to pay skilled blacks a minimum percentage of the total payroll for skilled workers was prima facie evidence of discrimination. The percentage was based on the most recent occupational census. That was the modern-day genesis of affirmative action programs. The policy was based on a principle of goals and timetables, and it was next adopted in 1938 by the newly created U.S. Housing Authority. But it was not adopted as a separate program or principle. The policy was inseparable from, or inherent in, the whole process of ending discrimination in employment to obtain meaningful, measurable results.[22]

The sweep of Hitler's panzer divisions through Europe at the close of the 1930s forced Washington to realize it had a major challenge in mobilizing American manpower for the defense of Western democracy. It had to integrate blacks into the war effort by using programs that not only addressed racial segregation by employers, but also were designed to correct a history of denying them training and job opportunities. So in July 1940 the government stepped up its efforts to prevent discrimination in essential industries.

The National Defense Advisory Commission created an office in its labor division to facilitate the training and use of African American workers. Later it reached an agreement with the AFL and the CIO in which each organization accepted responsibility for ending discrimination in their unions.

In October 1940, Congress included in its defense training appropriation a ban against discrimination in such state programs: "No trainee under the foregoing appropriations shall be discriminated against because of sex, race or color; and where separate schools are required by law for separate population groups, to the extent needed for trainees of each such group, equitable provision shall be made for facilities and training of like quality."[23] Implementing the law, the United States Office of Education announced it had established a nondiscrimination policy. The following month the commissioner of the Federal Security Agency of the Office of Education announced that his agency recently had held several conferences in Washington that dealt with problems of African Americans in the current emergency. He had "personally participated in a number" of them, some of which he had convened. From those conferences, one of which was with "State Agents for Negro Education representing" seventeen states with separate schools, he had prepared five suggestions, one of which was for state offices to implement the law's nondiscrimination policy by providing "for Negroes a sufficient number of courses and adequate equipment to give them training in a proportion, against all persons taken into training during the remainder of this fiscal year, equal to the ratio of Negroes on the rolls of the State Employment Service as of April 1940. This is a definite objective toward which to aim. Bear in mind that it deals with ratios on a State-wide basis."

Then, moving ahead of the inherent goals-and-timetable principle, the commissioner said,

> I fully realize that in providing training for Negroes on this basis it will appear that more Negroes are being trained than can immediately be employed. Some delay in employment is also occurring among white people who have been trained. I have the assurance of representatives of the Defense Commission that in view of the large percentage of Negroes *who have not had opportunity for training in the past* and the probable need for the employment of these Negroes in industries essential to national defense, it will not be expected that they will all be readily or immediately employed but it is certainly clear that if they are given essential training they will possess valuable assets which will facilitate their employment.

The FSA commissioner suggested, furthermore, that each state school officer call a staff conference of those who were "especially concerned with the defense training program, including the State Supervisor of Negro Education," to enable those leaders to present their views on implementing the policy. The commissioner noted that "one of the crucial problems" his department faced was the inadequate supply of competent black teachers prepared for the defense training programs. He suggested that the state supervisor of Negro schools prepare a list of teachers of mechanics and other activities to assist in organizing intensive training courses preliminary to launching the program.[24]

Another example of the Roosevelt administration's implementing of its nondiscrimination policy was the prohibition established by the administrator of the Federal Works Agency in January 1941 against job discrimination in the construction of defense housing projects. On April 11, 1941, Sidney Hillman, labor leader and codirector of the Office of Production Management, sent a letter to all defense contractors urging them to eliminate discrimination against African Americans in their hiring practices. But William S. Knudsen, formerly head of General Motors and the OPM's other codirector, did not sign it, angering African Americans. They were in no mood to settle for what the *New York Amsterdam News* called a "mere plea" from Hillman. "Nothing short of a major catastrophe" would shake America's policy of discrimination toward African Americans, it said. So the word to do so had to come straight from the White House. "Mr. Roosevelt must be prevailed upon to speak out."[25]

President Roosevelt, on June 15, 1941, did just that. He emphasized to Knudsen and Hillman the need for unity and placed "the full support of my office behind your statement to the effect that, 'All holders of defense contracts are urged to examine their employment and training policies at once to determine whether or not these policies make ample provision for the full utilization of available and competent Negro workers.'" Roosevelt stressed, "Every available source of labor capable of producing defense materials must be tapped in the present emergency." The reason, he explained, was that "No nation combating the increasing threat of totalitarianism can afford arbitrarily to exclude huge segments of its population from its defense industries. Even more important is it for us to strengthen our unity and morale by refuting at home the very theories which we are fighting abroad." But Roosevelt had issued a plea, not an order. So A. Philip Randolph announced his plans for the March on Washington, considerably heightening the climate of crisis. Roosevelt issued EO 8802 because blacks regarded the earlier steps as too weak.[26]

Mitchell's job included deciding when companies were in compliance with the nondiscrimination policy. On occasion he reprimanded a regional director for the inadequate manner in which he prematurely had declared a case closed. The challenge he faced in helping define the full range of discrimination was heightened by the common practice among war industries of ignoring pools of unemployed blacks in surrounding areas while they recruited white workers from distant places.[27]

Typical of the attitude the FEPC encountered was that of Edward S. Greenbaum of the War Department. He told Malcolm Ross in response to the Committee's efforts to end discrimination at the U.S. Cartridge Company in St. Louis, "Experience has shown, in dealing with racial matters, that orders and directives are not self executing. Very real consideration must be given to attitudes and customs that have been developing for years. Not to do this would result in work stoppages for which the War Department would be held responsible, and which, in the case of essential war supplies, would be inexcusable."[28]

In combating those attitudes, Mitchell helped the FEPC institutionalize and intensify its affirmative action process by systemically seeking to go beyond merely opening doors for blacks to enter the workplace to enforcing the national nondiscrimination policy as comprehensively as possible. That was the challenge Mitchell faced in December 1942 as he did his part in defining discrimination. He suggested to Johnson that the FEPC send a staff member to study "for a month or more" the employment practices of the Tennessee Valley Authority to be sure that it was not discriminating merely because it had followed the practice of other government agencies by citing the large number of blacks in its employ. Because the FEPC was created under a presidential executive order, its policy had the impact of law, although not nearly as strong as a policy created by the courts or Congress.[29]

Thus while the defense period accelerated the demand for economic security, Mitchell explored and used every means conceivable to implement the national nondiscrimination policy, including demanding equal opportunity in government-funded training programs as essential to remedying a history of racial exclusion in employment.

The Committee explained in its *First Report* that its hearings, held in accordance with paragraph 5 of the executive order that authorized it to conduct such proceedings, made "findings of fact," and took "appropriate steps to obtain the elimination of discrimination," and established "a body of interpretive principles." Those principles

> developed in the normal process of administrative adjudication as a necessary incident to the formulation of decisions in many controversies. By routine application of key provisions of the Executive order to specific fact situations, it has been possible to derive *a more elaborate statement of propositions than that contained in the order,* thus

implementing and clarifying in some degree, the basic tenets under which the Committee operates. Not all of the principles thus established have been included in its listing.

The Committee tailored the application of its principles to the facts of each case.[30]

The development of the definition of discrimination was the third principle defining the modern civil rights movement, after obtaining presidential leadership and adopting a national nondiscrimination policy. The process of defining discrimination by employers proceeded accordingly: through the hearings and internal policy debates, the Committee refined Weaver's opinion, helping it recognize that the absence, or the presence, of a few minority workers did not in itself justify a finding of discrimination. On the contrary, when an employer who hired no blacks contended that "certain skills were concentrated in certain nationalities," and plant guards refused at its gates to permit the entry of African Americans on the basis that they had the right to determine which applicants were entitled to be considered for employment, that was clear evidence of discrimination. The FEPC's case examples of this type of discrimination were *In re Bethlehem Shipbuilding Company, Vultee Aircraft Company, A. O. Smith Corporation, Nordberg Manufacturing Company,* and *Allis Chalmers Corporation.*

Discrimination by employers also could be determined when they required applicants to give their race or religion on application forms (see headnote). This was demonstrated in *In re Douglas Aircraft Corporation, Bethlehem Shipbuilding Company,* and *Gulf Shipbuilding Corporation.*

Facts themselves, such as those that showed it was the employer's policy to hire minority group members only as laborers or custodial workers, were another basis for determining discrimination. Case examples: *In re Lockheed Aircraft Corporation* and *Vega Airplane Company.*

So was an employer's selection of only white students from a technical school with available black and Jewish candidates. Case example: *In re Buick Aviation Engine Plant,* Melrose Park, Ill.

Newspaper advertising specifying a particular race was another indication of discrimination. Case examples: *In re Bearse Manufacturing Company, Simpson Construction Company,* and *Titeflex Metal Hose Company.*

Requests for workers specifying race was another indication, as *In re Carl Norden Incorporated* and *Titeflex Metal Hose Company.*

The discharge of employees who refused to salute the American flag or to stand during the playing of the National Anthem because of their religious convictions was another indication (see the headnote on Creedal Discrimination), as *In re Jehovah's Witnesses v. Pittsburgh Plate Glass Company.*

Another indication was an employer's expressed "preference" for workers of a particular race, as *In re St. Louis Shipbuilding Company.*

An employer's demand that workers obtain permission from a labor union that barred them from membership was also evidence of discrimination (see the headnote on the FEPC and Unions), as *In re Steamfitters Protective Association.*

An employer's quota system that restricted the presence of blacks on the workforce to a specified percentage was another form of discrimination, as *In re McQuay-Norris Manufacturing Company.*

Another example of the Committee's stand on quotas was its case involving the U.S. Cartridge Company of St. Louis, in which it held

> the racial quota system of employment to be contrary to the prescriptions of Executive Order 9346, since considerations of race or group rather than occupational qualifications provided the criterion and dominated the policy of the company in its determination as to whether an employee was to be employed or retained in employment.
>
> (This case is particularly instructive because it demonstrates "the difficulty, if not the impossibility, of affording equal job opportunities to all workers while confining one minority to jobs exclusively in one portion of a plant.")[31]

The *First Report* also listed several categories of discrimination by labor unions and government agencies.[32]

SEGREGATION VERSUS DISCRIMINATION

Mitchell's investigations across the country helped the FEPC document the extent to which racial discrimination and segregation were the same. Segregation was a manifestation of discrimination. From the shipyards of Portland, Oregon, to the war production plants of East Alton, Illinois, and the shipyards of Mobile, he showed that where one existed, so did the other. When he began working in 1942 on discrimination at the Portland shipyards, for example, he wanted to create "a great experiment—the importation of Negroes to work in the shipyards." Once he got the Kaiser Shipbuilding Company to agree to hire blacks, however, the Boilermakers Union insisted that they be segregated from white workers.[33]

But the FEPC's experience was that discrimination was not restricted to African Americans. Other groups, such as Mexican Americans, Japanese Americans, and Jews, also suffered discrimination based on their color, creed, or national origin or because they were aliens (see the headnotes on those groups; on National Origin, Alienage, and Loyalty; and on Race, Creed, Color, or National Origin on Employment Application Forms). As Mitchell declared in his March 30, 1944, memorandum to Maslow, he fought discrimination against all groups as fiercely as he did against African Americans. *Plessy v. Ferguson,* however, applied specifically to African Americans. So even though the FEPC was equally conscientious in attacking all forms of discrimination, its tortuous struggles to ensure equal employment opportunity for African Americans shaped its overall policy.[34]

The FEPC nevertheless had to follow the judicially contrived separate-but-equal distinction between *discrimination* and *segregation* to avoid legal and political traps. So it walked a nebulous, even invisible, line in fulfilling its mission for fear of bringing down on itself the wrath of its enemies, especially Southerners in Congress. Making its job, and existence, more politically tenuous was that the NAACP was then developing its strategy in the courts of making public school segregation so expensive to implement that the federal courts would force the South to abandon Jim Crow. For the FEPC, resolving the distinction was imperative if it was to function effectively, yet political wisdom forced it to proceed with caution after an initial period of optimism. Although the question of segregation had been before the Committee from its creation, it never took a position against it until July 6, 1943.

George Johnson noted at the Committee meeting on February 8, 1943, that the processing of several cases was being held up because it had "not definitely spelled out its policy" on segregation per se or in contrast to discrimination, regarding when the policy violated EO 8802. The Committee nevertheless had observed that in most, if not all, cases where attempts were made to segregate workers on the basis of race, discrimination resulted. Seeking to tackle the cases, Johnson noted, the Committee requested more information to determine whether discrimination was involved. Given how the FEPC functioned, it was highly likely that it was Mitchell who had referred most, if not all, cases to him. Johnson listed cases involving

- training programs in states where separate schools were required by law;
- segregation of war workers on bases operated by the Philips Coach Company of Lexington, Kentucky;
- segregation of government cafeterias, notably at the St. Louis post office;
- separate production lines at Kingsbury Ordnance Works, La Porte, Indiana;
- proposed separate departments for African American workers at Chrysler Corporation in Evansville, Indiana;
- failure to employ a black woman owing "to inability to obtain materials for separate toilet facilities";
- segregated ration boards at the Office of Price Administration;
- Jim Crow crews in the Seafarers International Union;
- Boilermakers Union Jim Crow auxiliaries on the West Coast;
- the Real Silk Hosiery Company in Indianapolis, which submitted a discriminatory job order to the United States Employment Service requesting two hundred white sewing machine operators; and
- a request from Cy Record of the WMC, working out of its Atlanta regional office, for a statement of the FEPC's policy on separate production lines, especially at Alabama Dry Dock in Mobile.[35]

The debate that followed demonstrated the hairsplitting in the determining process. Earl Dickerson agreed that the question had "bogged up with us ever since we started out." Dickerson cited the Sun Shipbuilding case as an example of the problem. When he was on Weaver's staff, Mitchell was very much involved in that case, especially as it related to providing the company's black workers with housing. But it was the Alabama Dry Dock case that, while portending trouble for Mitchell, defined the segregation issue.[36]

Dickerson noted that in *Missouri ex rel. Gaines v. Canada,* the Supreme Court had ruled in the case, which involved the University of Missouri Law School, that segregation was valid as long as the separate accommodations were equal. Because Missouri was unable to provide Lloyd Gaines, a black applicant, an equal law school within the state, the court ruled that it must admit him. Actually, the NAACP, which was representing Gaines, had not yet challenged the separate-but-equal doctrine in the lawsuit. But the association's parallel struggle, in seeking first to show that the separate-but-equal doctrine was unworkable, reinforced the historical significance of the FEPC's efforts to implement the national nondiscrimination policy beyond merely placing a token black on the job. Like the NAACP, the FEPC wanted to eliminate the doctrine because they knew that segregation violated the Fourteenth Amendment.[37]

But given the reality of the law, Dickerson wondered whether the Committee could not "look at these problems without taking a specific stand on whether" segregation violated the Constitution. He acknowledged that the Committee could not ignore segregation laws "without causing a lot of trouble and a lot of criticism which may hamper the further work of the committee." But in the North, in states like Illinois and Indiana, where there were no segregation laws, at least in "legal theory," he wondered whether the Committee could not take the position that segregation was contrary to the public policy "of the community" and insist, as in the Silk Hosiery case, that any work arrangement barring an employee from applying for a vacant position would violate the executive order.[38]

Through Socratic reasoning to determine how to guarantee jobs to blacks, whether they were segregated or not, Dickerson noted that in the Silk Hosiery case the company needed two hundred workers in the sewing machine department. It did not matter whether the company had such a separate department. If at the moment it needed the two hundred workers and fifteen African American women were immediately available for sewing machine jobs and they did not get any, that denial would be a violation of the executive order.

Applying that rule to the Alabama Dry Dock case, Dickerson reasoned that if a similar situation existed there, segregation had to yield to allow blacks into the workplace, otherwise the executive order would not have extended an equitable opportunity to them. "If they [the company] insist on segregation then they have to have departments of equal status from bottom to top, and the only reason they don't have to have them at the top is when there are no colored applicants qualified to be considered for the top positions." That was the only way blacks could be covered by the order, he insisted.

Supporting Dickerson, Cramer reasoned that where states had laws requiring separation of the races, the problem took "a different coloration" than in the North, where there were no such laws. "I think frankly that you have a practical consideration involved." The suggestion was that in the North the problem clearly would be one of discrimination. If Alabama Dry Dock agreed to set up equal working facilities and hired workers at their skill level, Cramer reasoned, the executive order would not be violated since the arrangement complied with the Supreme Court's separate-but-equal doctrine. But Shishkin maintained that industry did not tailor its operations to making facilities equal.[39]

John Brophy, furthermore, noted that sometimes there was no segregation at workplaces, such as coal mines, with which he was familiar. Once a worker was hired, he explained, "you had equality of opportunity" for everyone. There could be complaints, however, about the proportion of a racial group that was employed, or the unequal conditions under which a group of workers were employed. So, in view of the many variations of segregation that were possible, Brophy said simply he was "against segregation."[40] In other words, he, too, supported Dickerson.

The old Committee was unable to set a policy to guide Mitchell because in early 1943 its existence was uncertain. It primarily opposed the introduction of segregation where it did not previously exist or was not required by law. Consequently, the Alabama Dry Dock case caught him in a vortex of anger for helping to set a precedent. In June he accepted what he called a "temporary" fix, or an "interim agreement" for settling a violent racial conflict in which four separate shipways for bare-hull construction were set aside for black welders at the company's yard in Mobile. All other jobs on the remaining seven yards were set aside for whites. That was the approach Dickerson and Cramer had suggested. As a demonstration of the dilemma Mitchell faced, however, back in October 1942 he expressed his unhappiness with the acceptance by Anna Rosenberg, regional director of the WMC for New York, of the segregated plan the Boilermakers Union was insisting on for accepting blacks at the Kaiser shipyards in Portland, Oregon. Now Mitchell regarded the Alabama Dry Dock compromise as a practical means for getting whites to accept blacks working in skilled positions, though definitely not alongside them. Of the six thousand black workers there, five thousand were in unskilled positions. The rest were semiskilled workers who were capable of doing skilled jobs on the four shipways. So Mitchell agreed to the segregated setup.[41]

Defending the settlement in July before the new Committee against charges that he had done "a pretty dangerous thing," Mitchell said that it did "not preclude the upgrading of persons who were already employed at the yards." He said the Maritime Commission had very recently told him that Alabama Dry Dock had referred "approximately 426" blacks for courses in arc welding, acetylene welding, burning, and blueprint reading. That meant, he said, that those people were already employed and were being given supplementary training in hull construction.

Shishkin maintained, "Whether or not there was affirmative action by the old Committee on specific cases which it decided," the lack of action during the discussions that took place on segregation implied that it did not believe the practice violated EO 8802. That was not the Committee's intention, of course. A good reason for its not adopting an antisegregation policy most likely was that it had been transferred to the War Manpower Commission under Paul McNutt, who was no friend. After Roosevelt issued EO 9346, however, a stronger FEPC became more assertive, more inclined to take "affirmative action," or "positive action," in implementing the national policy.

Before the new Committee had met on July 6, 1943, Father Francis Haas, the new chairman, told his angry colleagues on that date that he had approved as "a practical settlement" the existing segregated work arrangement at Alabama Dry Dock. However, he explained, the Committee could not approve future restrictions regarding the upgrading of African Americans into the outfitting crafts, such as electrical work and pipefitting, because that would conflict with the executive order.

P. B. Young told the Committee that the compromise "was most unfortunate. I think a precedent was set which is going to give the Committee a great deal of trouble." He was right. The Committee was most concerned that the South would seek to spread or reinforce segregation throughout the North in places where it had not existed, such as at the Kaiser shipyards in Portland, Bethlehem Steel in Baltimore, and Timken Roller Bearing in Ohio.[42]

Mitchell, however, reminded the Committee that at its hearings in Birmingham in 1942 on the Brecon Bag Loading Company, Gulf Shipbuilding Company, and Alabama Dry Dock cases, it issued the directives against all of them. In the Brecon case, it approved an arrangement in which African American women were employed to operate power sewing machines "in a totally separate room from the other employees." Alabama Dry Dock officials cited that settlement, he told the Committee, in agreeing to the separate ways. Additionally, despite the Committee's directives to Gulf and another shipbuilding company in New Orleans, it had done not "a single thing" to enforce them, he said.

Young, a Southerner speaking as someone "with a realistic idea about the whole question of segregation," said he had "seen it improve in quantity and tone, and I have seen it degenerate, but we have seen in recent years in employment some improvement in economic status of the minority groups because of this Executive Order 8802." He was, however, pessimistic about getting "rid of segregation." He said "there will always be segregation unless this gets to be a much better world, but we don't want to aggravate and make it [race relations] worse."[43]

Mitchell, though, remained optimistic about ending segregation. He knew that Jim Crow was a racial caste system in which the dominant white group justified its oppression of blacks through an ideology of superiority. Mitchell knew that the process began in the mind as discrimination—a separateness, or intense hatred of the other. Thus, for example, the lynching of George Armwood in Princess Anne, Maryland, which he covered as a reporter for the *Baltimore Afro-American,* might not outwardly have been segregation, but inwardly, in the mind, in Jim Crow style the mob had segregated Armwood as a member of an inferior, hated caste. So it beat him mercilessly and, while he was still alive, poured gasoline on him, set him on fire, and left the charred remains in the town's square for all to see. Furthermore, the leaders of the mob, in Jim Crow style, were acquitted at the subsequent trial and treated as celebrities.[44]

The reality of economic exploitation that was endemic to Jim Crow characterized the FEPC's experience. Lawrence W. Cramer, executive secretary of the FEPC, for example, explained to the National Conference of Social Work in New York City that the government over the past twenty months had collected "ample evidence" that "available and needed workers" were barred from employment "solely because of their race, creed, color, national origin, or nationality." It was clear, he said, that the "morale of several racial and national groups made up of loyal and patriotic citizens" had "been adversely and seriously affected by the various forms of discrimination" they were experiencing. So, as a strategy of survival, Mitchell said he accepted the segregated ways because, first, it was the "practical" thing to do and, second, the Committee had not adopted a contrary policy. He further explained that under the settlement, blacks got equal pay and exactly the same work as whites. That was *Plessy* in practice.[45]

Mitchell's reasoned, lengthy explanation of why he thought the settlement was the best way to ease "a very explosive situation"—"this was no child's play going on down there"—showed not only his ability to work within the confines of administrative procedures, but also his persuasive ability. "Also in reaching this decision we were drawing on the background of previous experience which the Committee had had and which was facing us right in that area."[46]

Mitchell stressed, "I am against segregation. I think it is stupid, but I also know when I am facing a situation that you have one of two things facing you—either doing something about it or leaving it alone." He had to do something. He forcefully refuted the contention that the settlement set a precedent, emphasizing that neither did the Brecon Bag Loading arrangement, because it was the only way to end the impasse.[47]

Mitchell cited several reasons for the problems in Mobile. One was the influx of one hundred fifty thousand people from areas outside Alabama who "for the first time in their lives" were earning a living wage as welders and in industrial crafts. They regarded "any encroachment on those jobs" by blacks as a "threat to their survival." Additionally, there were rumors started by white men that all of them were being removed from the yard to be replaced by black men and white women. One step was bad enough, but together they were like putting a match to a powder keg. Another reason Mitchell mentioned in his report (see appendix 1) was the "totally inadequate guard force" present at Alabama Dry Dock. Mitchell expressed confidence that it was possible to avoid a recurrence of the problems there.

Mitchell's explanations turned a situation of criticism into one of compliments for himself and Haas and of appreciation for strengthening America's participation in the war effort. "I think that by acting promptly and accomplishing a settlement that has proved effective that the Chairman deserves a great deal of credit," said Shishkin. The Committee approved the settlement by an 8-to-1 vote (Milton Webster dissented), with the stated understanding that "The Committee accepts the accomplished fact of the settlement made in Mobile to end a crisis in war production, except that the Committee cannot give its approval to the complete segregation of Negroes on the four [ship]ways and does not consider this as a precedent."[48]

That was the same assurance Haas gave the NAACP, which, among other black institutions, protested the arrangement. The Committee's position was "that segregation *per se* on account of race is not within the jurisdiction of the Committee and that in any case where a complainant alleges that he had been discriminated against in connection with his employment because of segregation, efforts should be made at the local level to eliminate any discrimination found to exist, but that the case should be referred to the Committee for final disposition."[49]

But the Committee never completely resolved the distinction because it was politically impossible to do so, especially in the South, where as late as the end of 1945 not a single African American had been integrated into highly skilled positions in industry. Alabama Dry Dock, as well as Bell Aircraft Corporation in Atlanta, remained the best examples of that problem. At Bell there was a segregated department far removed from the main plant with 260 black workers, who were janitors and laborers. Both at Alabama Dry Dock and at Bell, blacks worked under white supervision. The Committee knew that segregation and discrimination were one, as Bell Aircraft's separate schools for whites and blacks also showed. Even though the white classes were not filled, black applicants were denied admission. But because it was the Supreme Court that had created the separate-but-equal doctrine, that court would have to reverse itself to remedy the problem.[50]

So when a "misunderstanding" arose in a regional office about a question of segregation, Maslow, in Field Instruction 47, unequivocally affirmed to the Division of Field Operations on April 14, 1945, the Committee's policy as given to the Senate Committee on Appropriations on June 5, 1944:

> The Committee has never taken the position that segregation per se is contrary to the provisions of Executive Orders 8802 and 9346. It recognizes, as it must, that its jurisdiction is limited to obtaining the elimination of discrimination in regard to hire, tenure, terms or conditions of employment, or union membership, and, in this case, where the issue of segregation is involved, as in all cases, the Committee's action will depend upon the existence or absence of evidence of prohibited discrimination.[51]

Mitchell's acumen in treading the Committee's segregation policy characterized his FEPC experience. No cases, however, had more personal significance for him than those from Baltimore: the Bethlehem Steel Shipbuilding Corporation at Sparrow's Point and the Western Electric works at Point Breeze. Although at the time the Chesapeake and Potomac Telephone Company technically was not a segregation case but one of refusal to hire black female operators, Mitchell considered it the same as the others. In seeking to resolve complaints in those cases, he refused to accept segregated training or work arrangements. Apart from his deep personal convictions, the Baltimore NAACP branch, under the leadership of Lillie Mae Jackson, never would have allowed him to do so. (For the details of Mitchell's handling of the Bethlehem Steel and Western Electric cases, see reports in appendix 1, related texts in the volume, and the headnote on Strikes and Work Stoppages.)

The problem began at Bethlehem Steel on July 6, 1943, when the company assigned a few blacks to its newly created riveting school. In protest, whites walked off the job, halting war work. For them maintaining segregation was more important than war production. When Bethlehem caved in and removed the blacks from the school, black workers staged their own walkout, halting all production.

The whites already working in the riveting department insisted that the workers already there be trained on the basis of seniority with a regular gang under actual conditions on the boat, where blacks had been excluded. They opposed the ground school, arguing that it did not afford the men already in the department a "fair opportunity." Blacks, though, demanded that blacks who successfully completed the program be eligible for top jobs. The Committee supported them by insisting that the riveting school be opened as originally planned to both white and black trainees, and it won.[52]

The Bethlehem Steel and Western Electric cases, like the Alabama Dry Dock case, considerably enhanced Mitchell's reputation for settling strikes. A significant reason was that he was able to win the trust of black workers and to reason with white management.[53] The Western Electric case was unique because since 1941 the company had voluntarily increased the number of African Americans on its staff to about eight hundred, or 10 percent of its workforce in 1943, and fully integrated them. Mitchell explained: "They use them in all types of jobs for which they were qualified. They use the same restaurant facilities; they use the same sanitary facilities, and in all respects are employees considered on an equal level with other persons working in the plant."

The problem arose in August 1943 when about twenty-five white women walked off the job to protest the use of the same toilet facilities by the one black woman in their work unit. When the Point Breeze Employees' Association, an independent union representing the workers, asked Mitchell to come to help resolve the problem, Mitchell responded, "I would decline to come to a meeting of that kind, and that, in my opinion, the company was doing a very excellent job and should not be interfered with." The company's position, he said, was that "if it attempted to segregate the workers, it would be in violation of the order."

Mitchell explained that ever since Western Electric integrated its plant, white women had been unhappy with the integrated toilets. "The protests have been coming in—you notice they came in since '42. You notice they go to a new department—and they always do when they get colored people qualified—there is always a little stir. Sometimes it is very indefinite; sometimes it isn't obvious. In this case the company took a good case and took a good stand," which was: "If you do not want to work under the conditions we have here, then you do not work at all." The white women elected to work. The walkout ended.

The problem reached the walkout point because the Point Breeze Employees' Association was being challenged by the International Association of Machinists as the workers' bargaining agent and was fighting for survival. So the employees' association sought to impress the workers by seeking to end integration at the plant. By contrast, Mitchell said, he got the impression that the Machinists "did not want to go along with this idea of having separate facilities."

Mitchell explained that, although the Western Electric problem was "reasonably well under control," the FEPC was "getting so many of these" cases. That day, another case involving the Brotherhood of Electrical Workers and the Anaconda Wire and Cable Company had come in "in which they raise the same question" of toilet facilities.

Welcoming the opportunity to oppose segregation unequivocally, Shishkin moved that the Committee notify the union that Western Electric's position was in accord with the executive order. A battle-shy Haas warned: "The chairman will follow the directions of the Committee, but the Committee should know that, in the judgment of the chairman, that action puts the Committee on record as opposing segregation. You may as well recognize it." To that alert, the no-nonsense Milton Webster asserted: "We do oppose it, don't we?"

John Brophy concluded that Western Electric's position was "a compliance with the spirit of the executive order. You can omit that spirit if you want to." But the reality stood. For two years Western Electric's practice of nonsegregation had been in compliance with the order.

The motion carried unanimously.[54]

Immediately, the Committee reinforced that position by again voting unanimously for the FEPC to seek an understanding on general procedure with the War Production Board to avoid butting into matters involving segregation the board was considering, such as the Western Electric case, in a manner that would violate the order.[55]

In a case involving the International Brotherhood of Electrical Workers, Mitchell next got the Committee to vote unanimously against "segregating or colonizing workers into particular plants solely because of their race."[56]

Leaving no doubt where it stood on the issue, as well as covering its previous stand against segregation, the Committee on November 16, 1943, agreed on the following statement: "[I]n circumstances of this case where there are frequent and temporary transfers of workers from department to department such installing of segregated duplicate facilities cannot but lead to discriminatory employment practices and would be in violation of Executive Order 9346."[57]

IMPLEMENTING THE ORDER

Two instruments the Committee used for guiding its implementation process were its hearings on what it called "difficult cases" and the nondiscrimination clause. Executive Order 9346 stated that it was the duty of all employers, including federal agencies and labor organizations, "to eliminate discrimination in regard to hire, tenure, terms or conditions of employment, or union membership because of race, creed, color, or national origin." The new order strengthened EO 8802 by requiring that "all contracting agencies of the government" include a nondiscrimination clause in contracts negotiated by them as well as to requiring such provisions in all subcontracts. The order furthermore empowered the Committee to "conduct hearings and make findings of fact," to promulgate "rules and regulations," and to "take appropriate steps to obtain elimination of such discrimination."

Because defining discrimination in employment and prescribing remedies were unprecedented steps in protecting citizenship rights that were not enforceable by law, obtaining compliance could be a tedious if not impossible process. In developing a bureaucratic procedure for determining discrimination, the Committee moved step by step, building on each case or group of cases as well as on hearings involving companies charged with discrimination.[58]

During its first two years the FEPC closed an average of two hundred and fifty cases each month. About one hundred of them each month were satisfactorily adjusted. But it was largely through the hearings that the Committee formally established its case when its jurisdiction or the veracity of the complaints was challenged. Functioning as a judicial body, the Committee heard evidence that might have been developed by its own staff serving as trial examiners, hearing officers, or trial attorneys.[59]

The hearings began in earnest in January 1942 with the Committee's second public one in Chicago, where eleven companies were cited for violating the order.[60] Although Mitchell helped to plan them, he said he did not "follow the hearings to a great extent"; he thought they were "nice window dressing." His conclusion that "they didn't in themselves accomplish a whole lot because of a lack of power to enforce decisions" had merit—that was, as far as immediately implementing the Committee's directives was concerned.

For Johnson, however, the hearings established a record of principles that enabled the Committee to develop its policy and function. That was their long-term benefit. In that regard, Mitchell did not dismiss the hearings entirely, even though there were not "a lot of instances where the body being charged accepted decisions." Some, nevertheless, like the shipbuilding hearings, he considered productive. Kaiser Shipbuilding, for one, wanted to be cooperative, but "it was lumped right in with the others" who would not cooperate.[61]

That intransigence led the Committee to create a category of "difficult cases," which covered aircraft, railroads, street railways, war industries in St. Louis and Cincinnati, West Coast shipyards, the Shell Oil Company, and the Boilermakers, Seafarers, and Teamsters unions.[62] Regarding Lockheed Aircraft, for example, witnesses testified at a hearing in 1941 that of the corporation's forty-eight thousand employees only thirty-nine African Americans were employed on mechanical operations. Because Lockheed's management expressed a willingness to obey EO 8802, by August 1944 there were thirty thousand African Americans in nearly one hundred occupations working there, and all of them had been integrated without difficulty. That success showed the potential benefits of embarrassing exposure where companies were unwilling to correct their socially disruptive behavior.

With the street railways (see the headnote on Street and Local Railways), cases ran the gamut of the FEPC's experiences, from compliance following negotiations to outright refusal to obey the executive order. The Philadelphia Transportation Company case was the third defining experience for the FEPC, after battles with Alabama Shipbuilding, which pushed the Committee to adopt a clear policy regarding segregated work arrangements, and the railway companies and railroad brotherhoods case, which exposed the extent of white determination to exclude blacks from economic benefits in the workplace. The Philadelphia Transportation case enabled Mitchell to demonstrate that the best way for the White House to lead in resolving industrial race strikes was to take a firm stand, even if it involved bringing in federal troops, as it did in that city.

That epic battle leading up to the railroad hearings began on March 30, 1942, when counsel for several railway labor organizations appeared before the Committee and charged that there was widespread employment discrimination by railways and their unions against African American firemen and other railroad workers. From June 18 to 20, 1942, the Committee heard evidence on those charges at its hearings in Birmingham. Owing to the nature of discrimination alleged and the lack of time at the hearings, the Committee decided to hold separate hearings on the railroad cases. The following month, the chairman appointed three members—Milton Webster, John Brophy, and Frank Fenton—as a subcommittee to supervise an investigation. In September the Committee scheduled the railroad hearings for December 7, 8, and 9. It engaged Henry Epstein, Charles Houston, and Harold A. Stevens as special counsel. On January 28, 1943, Mitchell informed Will Maslow he was leaving in accordance with his assignment to investigate complaints for the hearings. Subsequently, in order to complete the investigation, the Committee changed the dates to January 25, 26, and 27, 1943. But on January 9, 1943, Paul McNutt, the WMC's chairman, abruptly postponed the hearings indefinitely.[63]

Several hundred very complex complaints were lodged against thirty railroads and terminal companies and six labor unions. The complaints and the Committee's investigations showed that, except for a few railroads paying substandard wages, African Americans were no longer being hired as firemen, trainmen, or switchmen because of "custom." The railroads and unions institutionalized such discriminatory customs and practices by writing them into bargaining agreements. Blacks who were pushed out of those occupations were denied the right to exercise seniority along with whites. Subsequently, following postponement of the hearings, the Committee received several complaints from Mexicans and descendants of Mexicans who complained that they were treated similarly on the Union Pacific Lines.[64]

Because the outcry from several national organizations, including the NAACP, over cancellation of the hearings was fierce, the second FEPC rescheduled them for September 15 to 18, 1943. They ultimately were held against twenty Southern railway companies and thirteen unions of their employees, including those in the Southeastern Carriers Conference Agreement. These hearings produced some benefits, notably the upgrading of black workers by a few railways.[65]

Not only did the unions boycott the hearings, however, but on December 13, sixteen Southern railroads, in a joint letter to the president and FEPC, explained their defiance of the federal government by stating they would not obey the Committee because it was "wholly without constitutional and legal jurisdiction and power to issue the directives." For that reason, they said, the directives were "without legal effect." They insisted that the employment of black firemen would have "disastrous results" that "would antagonize the traveling and shipping public."[66]

The Committee referred the cases to the president, who in January appointed a committee headed by Walter P. Stacy, chief justice of the North Carolina Supreme

Court, to negotiate an understanding with the railroads and the unions on the charges. But, as Milton Webster said of the unions: "I can't see where the special Committee would have any more prestige than the President's Committee. They in substance ignored the President. The President issued an order and said, 'Stop discrimination; take such steps as you deem advisable.' They ignored the Committee." Committee members were dejected.[67] Said the FEPC, "The self-elected division of the carriers and unions into two groups—one which agreed to negotiate and the other which defied the Committee—provides a revealing contrast between the two attitudes and resulting outcome of the hearings." The limited benefits of the hearings only confirmed Mitchell's assessment about the FEPC's lack of power, even when the parties involved admitted their defiance of the order.

On December 30, 1943, the Committee announced its ruling that the Southeastern Carriers Conference Agreement (also known as the nonpromotable agreement) between the Brotherhood of Locomotive Firemen and Enginemen[68] and ten railroads[69] violated EO 9346 and must be set aside within thirty days. The purpose of the agreement, the Committee said, was to employ fewer blacks as firemen and to replace them with whites. That was being done by setting "definite percentages" for the two races through limiting firemen's jobs to "promotable" men and by excluding all African American workers from promotion.[70]

The Committee also cited as unfair the policy of some railroad unions that discriminated against African Americans "because of race, in regard to membership . . . thus rendering it impossible (for Negro workers) to have any adequate voice or representation with respect to grievances and the negotiation of agreements affecting working conditions, employment policy, practices and opportunities." In each of those instances, the Committee notified the union it must "cease and desist from . . . discriminatory practices affecting the employment of Negroes."[71]

Once more, as with the 1935 lawsuit that desegregated the University of Maryland, the U.S. Supreme Court buttressed Mitchell's faith in the nation's judicial process. The court's decisions of December 18, 1944, in the *Steele v. Louisville and Nashville Railroad Company, et. al.,* and *Tunstall v. Brotherhood of Locomotive Firemen and Enginemen* cases confirmed the Committee's findings of abysmal, endemic discrimination in the railroad industry. In those cases, the petitioners, independent of the FEPC, sought declaratory judgments and injunctive relief against the enforcement or recognition of the Southeastern Carriers Conference Agreement. The court also issued a declaratory judgment and injunctive relief against the brotherhood from acting as representative of all firemen under the Railway Labor Act as long as it refused to recognize African American minority nonmembers of the craft. Charles Houston, a member of the Committee, had argued those cases before the Supreme Court. The third companion case was *Wallace Corporation v. National Labor Relations Board,* which involved unfair labor practices under an NLRB contract. In sum, all three cases related to the employment problems of minorities under labor-management contracts.[72]

In the three cases the Supreme Court discussed the duty of labor organizations that had been recognized as "exclusive bargaining representatives" to represent all employees in the class or craft being represented. In *Steele*, the Supreme Court struck a sharp blow at the concept of the closed shop. It ruled that, in enacting the Railway Labor Act, Congress did not intend that a labor union, representing the majority of workers in a closed shop, could exclude the minority of workers from its protection. Thus, the court concluded, the union had a duty to "represent the interests of all its members." In his assessment of the importance of the Supreme Court's rulings that he circulated to the staff, Johnson explained that they all had an important bearing on the FEPC's operations because they covered matters with which the agency had been wrestling.[73]

One of the Committee's deep fears had been how it would get the railroads to comply with its directives since the practices of the brotherhoods were merely one aspect of what was being done to drive blacks out of the nation's industry. "The Negro is gradually being pressed down and down and down to the very bottom rail of our whole economic structure, being forced down to the position of substandard subsistence," said Young. "I think all of us know that as far as union labor is concerned, and I say that in the face of what has been developed in this Committee, what was brought out in these hearings, there is a determination that the Negro shall not have any skilled or semi-skilled employment if the unions can prevent it," Young said. So "we have got to get some affirmative action on this thing or else we have got to give up and say that as a laborer, as a wage earner, as a worker, we may consider the Negro no longer a factor in this country."[74]

Steele and *Tunstall* gave Mitchell and the Committee some hope for salvation. Justice Murphy said in *Steele*:

> The economic discrimination against Negroes practiced by the Brotherhood and the railroad under color of Congressional authority raises a grave constitutional issue that should be squarely faced.
>
> The utter disregard for the dignity and the well-being of colored citizens shown by this record is so pronounced as to demand the invocation of constitutional condemnation.

Murphy concluded:

> The Constitution voices its disapproval whenever economic discrimination is applied under authority of law against any race, creed or color. A sound democracy cannot allow such discrimination to go unchallenged. Racism is far too virulent today to permit the slightest refusal in the light of a Constitution that abhors it, to expose and condemn it wherever it appears in the course of a statutory interpretation.[75]

As happy as the Committee was with that resounding judgment, however, it could not escape the reality that

> [a]lthough the Court's opinions left no doubt as to the illegality of the discriminatory agreements, the agreements are so numerous and apply to so many railroads that to invalidate them by litigation would require a multiplicity of suits and the expenditure of much time and money. Moreover, the Steele and Tunstall cases touch

only on the rights of Negroes after they have been hired. They do not affect discrimination which bars Negroes from employment in the first place. Hence it is fair to conclude that, as a practical matter, only an administrative agency with the necessary authority can deal successfully with the problems presented by such discriminatory agreements.[76]

NONDISCRIMINATION CLAUSE

The Supreme Court's latest clarification of the constitutional foundations for challenging discrimination, as Shishkin urged, made the Committee's job of defining in "brief, clear" terms its "rules and regulations" for enforcing the nondiscrimination clause in EO 8802 imperative. The clause, he said, invited the Committee to *develop policies beyond the limitations of that instrument*" in the order. Reinforcing Shishkin's anxiety, Johnson told the Committee at its December 4, 1943, meeting that government agencies were repeatedly asking his department to interpret the requirement. He said, "you won't get any help from the executive order itself." The order stipulated that "all Government agencies shall include in all contracts negotiated or renegotiated by them" a nondiscrimination clause, whether they were wartime or peacetime. Consequently, the solicitor of the Department of the Interior sent the FEPC six or more types of contracts to determine whether the clause applied. The FEPC therefore held a conference with some fifteen or sixteen lawyers representing the departments of Interior and Agriculture, as well as the procurement division of Treasury.

As an example of the challenge, Johnson explained that the Department of Agriculture leased a portion of a building from the Louisville Stockyards for its inspectors' offices in Kentucky. "It is clear that the Louisville Stockyards must refrain from discrimination in the performance of the lease contract. That is to say, the maintenance of the office, the heating and janitorial service, etc., but does that non-discrimination clause extend to the whole stockyards business of the Louisville Stockyards?" That, Johnson said, was a "serious question."

The problem was that the order, in effect, specified a division between wartime and peacetime operations, when often such a division was impractical. So Maceo Hubbard confirmed Johnson's conclusion by explaining that the challenge was more complex than it seemed. The difficulty in stating that the clause applied only to the contract, Hubbard said, was that many times it was impossible to tell exactly where the owner of a building was performing under the contract with the related agency. "For instance, suppose we cite a company for discriminating, and we talk about a particular contractor, and his answer is, 'you haven't shown that the man who applied for the job made application to do the kind of work which I am doing under this contract.'" Furthermore, if a contractor was furnishing machines for the war effort, would that include his clerks and stenographers and other people in his office who might or might not have been performing functions related to the contract? Possibly they might write a letter related to the contract or perform some other related function, although the employee would spend the rest of the day doing other functions.

Shishkin responded that questions about that range of coverage were not new. He suggested that the legal department provide the Committee with a listing of tests and demarcations. And that it did.

As a first step, the Committee adopted the following statement for implementing Executive Order 9346:

a. The provision requires the inclusion of a nondiscrimination clause in Government contracts with non-war industries as well as war industries.
b. The provision requiring the inclusion of the non-discrimination clause refers to employment with respect to the performance of the contract containing the clause and does not extend to activities of the contractor unrelated to the contract.
c. The provision requires the inclusion of the non-discrimination clause in contracts between a Federal Government agency and a State or subdivision thereof.
d. The provision requires the inclusion of the non-discrimination clause in contracts required by law to be awarded to the lowest bidder.
e. The provision does not require the inclusion of a non-discrimination clause in contracts the performance of which does not require the employment of persons.[77]

At its December 27, 1943, meeting, the Committee more than doubled the coverage of the nondiscrimination clause, which it further increased on June 13, 1944.[78] The War Department's clause was typical:

a. The Contractor, in performing the work required by this contract, shall not discriminate against any employee or applicant for employment because of race, creed, color, or national origin.
b. The Contractor agrees that the provisions of paragraph (a) above will also be inserted in all of its subcontracts. For the purpose of this article, a subcontract is defined as any contract entered into by the contractor with any individual, partnership, association, corporation, estate, or trust, or other business enterprise or other legal entity, for a specific part of the work to be performed in connection with the supplies or services furnished under this contract; provided, however, that a contract for the furnishing of standard or commercial articles or raw material shall not be considered as a subcontract.[79]

Also typical was the clause the Treasury Department submitted to Johnson for approval:

The lessor, in performing the services required by this lease, shall not discriminate against any employee or applicant for employment because of race, creed, color or national origin. The lessor shall include in all sub-contracts a provision imposing a like obligation on subcontractors.[80]

But in attempting to enforce the clause, Treasury ran into the type of murky enforcement problem Hubbard had mentioned. What should it do, Treasury asked Johnson, when the "lessor" in Nashville, Tennessee, from whom it leased a considerable amount of office space, refused to execute a contract containing the nondiscrimination clause? Furthermore, Treasury said the problem would undoubtedly arise in connection with the renewal of its other leases. While it was apparently not possible for Johnson to provide Treasury with a reasonable response at the moment, he did direct Hubbard to inform the Congressional Appropriations Committee of the considerable amount of legal work required to enforce the nondiscrimination clause as justification for increased funding.[81]

Mitchell, too, had his hands full. A significant part of his duties was determining from the comptroller general which of the numerous contracts by the War and Navy Departments and the Maritime Commission contained a nondiscrimination clause. Additionally, he and the regional directors encountered difficulty in working through the hairsplitting process. An example was his response to Edward Lawson's inquiry in January 1944 concerning the army's announcement that it was hiring Japanese through the U.S. Employment Service, but that such hiring was subject to "satisfactory clearance." Mitchell said that, based on the information Lawson had provided, it did not appear that the army's action was discriminatory—that is, in violation of the nondiscrimination clause, within the meaning of the executive order.[82] However, he said, Lawson might

> wish to reread the attachment to R. D. No. 44 [regional directive], which states the War Department's policy on the employment of persons of Japanese ancestry. If, after you have done this, you still have some reservations, please submit a memorandum to us in order that we may obtain a ruling from the Deputy Chairman.
>
> I am attaching a copy of a memorandum concerning the conference with the General Accounting Office on the employment of Japanese.[83]

After grappling with the issue at its meeting on June 13, 1944, the Committee adopted the following positions:

> 1. The non-discrimination clause is not required in contracts renewed pursuant to an option to renew in accordance with the terms, conditions and provisions contained in the original contract.
> 2. The requirement that parties to contracts with the Government of the United States (or agencies of said Government) include a non-discrimination clause "in all sub-contracts" is not applicable to lessors of space in buildings except in cases where the Government of the United States (or an agency thereof) is the only tenant involved, or unless a sub-contract is entered into only for the purpose of performing an obligation (or obligations) imposed by the Government lease.[84]

Next, regarding the inclusion of the nondiscrimination clause in subcontracts, the Committee adopted the following policy:

> The requirements that parties to contracts with the Government of the United States (or agencies of said government) include a non-discrimination clause "in all

subcontracts" is applicable only in those cases in which the subcontract is entered into solely for the purpose of enabling the prime contractor to fulfill an obligation (or obligations) imposed by the government contract.[85]

Further help soon came. Vindicating the FEPC's policy as well as simplifying the process, the *Federal Register* on February 15, 1945, published a series of amendments to procurement regulations of the U.S. Army that Simon Stickgold, FEPC trial attorney, told Johnson appeared "to contain a concise formulation of the Committee's position with respect to the inclusion of non-discrimination clauses in government contracts" (see text of memorandum in appendix 1).[86]

TAKING AFFIRMATIVE ACTION

Mitchell used affirmative action, or positive action, as part of the normal process of implementing Committee policies. "I was personally involved," he emphasized. The terms were carryovers from the debates over the National Labor Relations Act (Wagner Act), which Congress adopted in 1935. Clearly owing to the benefits the act provided labor, Boris Shishkin used the term "affirmative action" as a normal part of the process in discussing how the executive order should be enforced. Will Maslow and other whites—such as Malcolm Ross, Emanuel Bloch, and Ernest Trimble, whom Maslow had brought over from the National Labor Relations Board—also introduced it to the FEPC.[87]

It was during that period beginning with the New Deal that Weaver established the prototype "goals and timetable" principle as a means for measuring progress in ending discrimination that was based on the proportion of skilled minority workers on a job in comparison to their representation in the surrounding community.[88] At every opportunity, Mitchell helped to expand the goals and timetable principle that Weaver and the Federal Security Agency had been seeking to ensure that, where possible, the proportion of African Americans employed in a given industry reflected their representation in the surrounding communities. "We were never just interested in lifting up just one person," Mitchell said. "We were interested in lifting up the whole group." He explained that

> [g]enerally speaking, in World War II, our big problem was the kind of arrangement under which the factories—if you were a helper, you could make more money than an apprentice. But you were frozen in the helper category. The only way you could get to be a skilled mechanic, that is, a master in the crafts, would be to start off as an apprentice and make less money for a time. Then you would move up to be a master and, of course, get more money. Unfortunately, because of that arrangement, blacks in most parts of industry, were frozen in the helper category.

Whether intentional or not, he said, the practice "kept blacks out of highly skilled jobs." Similar arrangements occurred in carpentry, where blacks were relegated to "so-called rough carpentry. That meant putting them in jobs where they would build scaffolding or put down heavy planks." But when the job involved hanging doors, installing window frames, or such other skilled work that was classified as finished carpentry, it was for whites only. The practice was not confined to "just one company. This was universal."[89]

Like the Committee, Mitchell was more determined than ever to break that historical pattern of confining African Americans and Mexican Americans to low-level, unskilled, and heavy-labor jobs and to ensure that they received equal training that enabled them to qualify and compete fairly for semiskilled and skilled jobs.[90]

The records are not explicit, but Mitchell also went well beyond opening up job opportunities in the usual war industries to include the top secret, huge new atomic bomb and atomic power plants in his quest. He fought discriminatory recruitment for the plutonium production plant at Hanford Engineering in Pasco, Washington, in 1943, where the lack of housing for black workers for a time led the company to seek to import only white workers. The FEPC negotiated with the War Department in 1945 for more inclusive employment opportunities at the Clinton Engineering facility and Eastman Tennessee operations related to atomic facilities at Oak Ridge. After the war, Mitchell and the NAACP would continue fighting for employment of blacks in the atomic industry.[91]

A compliance mechanism the FEPC used, as Mitchell reported on one occasion, was requesting the War Manpower Commission's Bureau of Placement to obtain statistical data from the Manning Tables and other sources to "show the extent of progress in terms of actual figures."[92]

Mitchell therefore was not surprised some forty years later when, as debate was raging over affirmative action, Maslow declared to an interviewer, "Do you know that the FEPC was an affirmative action program?" Mitchell explained that the FEPC "tried to get remedies" for the effects of past discrimination not just for one individual but for a whole class of people. "I was involved in those cases," he recalled. "We had certain forms [ES 270] to show just how many blacks they had employed, how they were employed, and how long they were employed." They were "major sources of information on trends in non-white employment in the country" and showed what was "happening to other minorities" as well.

Struggling, for example, to end discrimination in the Los Angeles transit system, Mitchell told the regional minorities representative of the WMC in August 1943 that the ES 270 reports he had obtained furnished "some of the necessary information" the FEPC needed but that they did "not indicate the breakdown of employees according to occupation." He therefore requested the information. "For example, how many non-whites are employed as brakemen, flagmen, conductors, janitors, repairmen, etc., and how do these figures compare with the total number of employees?" Mitchell said he needed the information for the Municipal Railway Company, Market Street Railway Company, and the California Street Railway Company. Another example of the benefits of this information was the report the U.S. Office of Education provided him in 1945 in response to his request for enrollment data on African American trainees in courses for war production workers at the Don Thompson Vocational

School in Tampa. The report said there were no African American trainees enrolled at the school in July 1943. But from then until December 1944 the report showed a cumulative enrollment of 816 African American trainees, of whom 609 had concluded training for such ship crafts as carpentry and woodworking, sheet metal, welding, and (heavy) electric work. Therein lay further evidence of the FEPC's role as the cornerstone of the modern civil rights movement. That experience taught Mitchell, as he showed then and subsequently, the extent to which discrimination was based on unfair practices against a group or class of people as opposed to an individual.

John A. Davis, too, confirmed the FEPC's affirmative action functions. The ES 270 report, which required a breakdown of race in employment, was central to the FEPC's work, Davis explained. "We had a big fight about referring workers by race," he said. The FEPC had to get employers "to take race off of all pre-employment forms" to end discrimination, but at the same time "there had to be some way to police compliance" with the executive order. For example, "there were no blacks in the New York Telephone Company when we came in" [in the operator's job]. So the FEPC required employers to record race on postemployment forms (see the headnotes on Race, Creed, Color, or National Origin on Employment Application Forms and on the Telephone Industry).[93]

CIVIL WAR PRECEDENT

A comparable national affirmative *movement,* similar to the FEPC, for ending grave historical wrongs was Reconstruction. Both sought to *remedy the legacy of wrongs* that had been inflicted on a group of citizens because of their race. Of the Emancipation Proclamation, the abolitionist William Lloyd Garrison said, "The first day of January, 1863, has now taken rank with the fourth of July, 1776, in the history of this country. The Proclamation, though leaving much to be done in the future, clears our course from all doubt and our process from all uncertainty."

Before the Civil War, President Lincoln said, "We feel[, therefore,] that all legal distinctions between individuals of the same community, founded in any such circumstances as color, origin, and the like, are hostile to the genius of our institutions, and incompatible with the true history [theory] of American liberty." Some months after signing the proclamation, Lincoln said, "Those who shall have tasted actual freedom I believe can never be slaves, or quasi slaves again." He therefore hoped that the states themselves would adopt some practical system "by which the two races could gradually live themselves out of their old relation to each other, and both come out better prepared for the new." Lincoln advocated education for the freedmen as well as the franchise so that they could become first-class citizens.

In effect, Lincoln hoped for much more from the Thirteenth Amendment than legal freedom for the slaves, and thus he laid the foundation for Reconstruction. He wanted real equality under the law and in the community. Following his assassination in April 1865, the Radical Republicans in Congress won enactment of civil rights acts, the Fourteenth Amendment, and other protections to make permanent the rights of blacks as citizens.

The enactment by Congress and the adoption by the states of the Fifteenth Amendment was further manifestation of the federal government's "positive action" to affirm the liberty of the new citizens of the republic. In seeking enfranchisement of African Americans in 1866, Senator Charles Sumner of Massachusetts said that Lincoln had promised in the Emancipation Proclamation to maintain freedom for blacks, "not for any limited period, but for all time. But this cannot be done so long as you deny him the shield of impartial laws. Let him be heard in court and let him vote. Let these rights be guarded sacredly."[94]

But even in the periods of national crisis in the 1860s and 1940s, there were those who begrudged the generous spirit of equality that enshrined the words of Lincoln and Roosevelt. Civil rights legislation during Reconstruction enunciated equality, but the laws had no teeth or heart. Executive Order 8802 called for an end to discrimination in employment, but it lacked the commitment of a soul, of a firm belief of faith in liberty for the racially oppressed and others who suffered discrimination. So from the beginning of the FEPC, freedom to earn a just living on the basis of equality had a hollow, temporary ring similar to Reconstruction.

The pulling of the political rug out from under Reconstruction in 1877 with the Hayes-Tilden compromise dashed the hopes implicit in the Declaration of Independence and Emancipation Proclamation in what historian John Hope Franklin called "one of the really tragic chapters in the history of the United States." Within two decades, in addition to being stripped of rights of citizenship, housing, employment, travel, and the franchise, which African Americans had enjoyed during Reconstruction, the race was subjected to the most degrading treatment inflicted on humanity in the New World under the theory that whites were the "master race." Education was the only gain that African Americans managed to cling to in any measurable form.[95]

The new status invited lynching, such as the parching George Armwood suffered in Maryland; race riots, such as the ones that wasted Detroit in 1943; and every practice designed to deprive blacks of any form of economic security and human dignity. Worse was that the federal government not only condoned the inhumane treatment but often was a party to it, notably during the Wilson administration. Then, one African American lamented, "We are given stone instead of a loaf of bread; we are given a hissing serpent rather than a fish." Later, in 1930, a member of the Black Man's Protective Organization of Macon, Georgia, wrote the attorney general: "It strikes us that the time is just about at hand when we must cast aside our Bible, stop offering so many solemn addresses to the Supreme Being and fight for our rights. . . . We shall defend ourselves by fighting like hell for once. . . . We would prefer death in lieu of remaining here on earth and have our manhood trampled upon." That was the type of militancy that Mitchell exemplified and that also ran throughout Milton Webster's participation in the Committee's intense debates on how best to confront the brotherhoods' callous disregard for the rights of blacks working on the railroads. One of his classic comments was, "The stupidity of the Boilermakers is so intense that they don't listen to any reason."[96]

A significant difference between Reconstruction and the FEPC was that it was the Congress that created Reconstruction over the objections of a hostile president, while it was the president who created the FEPC and was providing leadership in enforcing its national nondiscrimination clause over the objections of a hostile Congress. As with Lincoln's freeing of the slaves as a means of weakening the power of the Confederacy, Franklin Roosevelt had national strategic interests in mind when he created the FEPC in that he wanted to ensure that the republic was fully capable of defeating the Axis powers by avoiding crippling labor shortages and social disruptions at home. Mitchell, of course, did not care what Roosevelt's motives or purported strategies were; he simply joined other blacks in heralding the historic opportunities for social change that international pressures were forcing the president to make.[97]

THE FEPC'S HISTORICAL MEANING

For the Committee, affirmative action was not a concept based on a specific program, like those of the Kennedy administration or subsequent popular models, but a positive process of enforcing the nondiscrimination policy that went well beyond merely breaching the segregation wall to incorporate all possible efforts, such as training programs, to end a legacy of exclusion and provide job opportunities based on skill and potential achievement. The Committee reaffirmed that intention at its July 7, 1943, meeting by adopting the motion Sara Southall had offered to prohibit the acceptance by the staff of segregated work arrangements and to instruct the staff to prepare a pamphlet "with the aim of breaking down discrimination and furthering the employment of minority groups, using whatever material is available."[98]

But, prophetically, Shishkin warned that "if the strengthened nondiscrimination policy is a special treatment of the minority groups, I think it will aggravate the problem rather than help iron it out."[99] Nevertheless, Shishkin had no difficulty invoking the goals and timetable principle regarding the Committee's findings of discrimination against the railroads by saying that they and the related unions should be directed to

take the following affirmative action, and, in taking the affirmative action with respect to discrimination, it is not necessary to specify the timing [for ending such practices]. It is merely proper to say, as suggested here, that the discriminatory practice affecting employment be stopped immediately.

Regarding "the specific acts" the Committee was requiring the railroads and unions to take to end discrimination, he suggested that the force of the Committee's directive would be completely lost if the FEPC

did not specify the time limit within which the affirmative action should be taken. . . .
    Give them a certain length of time. There are a number of specific things. They [FEPC staff] direct that the company do so and so with respect to baggage men, etc.

If we specify and say within thirty or ninety days, or something, such action should be taken, that will give the Committee a basis to deal with the particular situation.[100]

On measuring progress, Elmer Henderson outlined a much more elaborate goals and timetable principle than that which Weaver had earlier established:

The test of the effectiveness of the President's Order and of the Committee's work does not lie in the number of complaints of discrimination successfully *adjusted* nor in the profusion of rules and regulations which may gain adoption. The basic criterion of success lies in the number of Negroes who have actually gained employment with the Government and the spread of occupations in which they are engaged. To determine this, the President's Committee requested all government agencies to submit progress reports on the employment of Negroes at periodic intervals. The statistics obtained in these reports furnish the basis for the present survey.[101]

Mitchell's responsibility for resolving complaints placed him at the center of the Committee's affirmative action activities. His struggles with discrimination by the Machinists and by the Boilermakers and other railroad unions, in particular, as well as the FEPC's extended, intense attention to the problems they posed made him aware of how disastrous past discrimination practices had been in eliminating blacks from many of the job categories the unions represented or in pushing them out of the better jobs altogether.

Mitchell cited *Steele* and *Tunstall* as examples of why affirmative action programs were necessary. He recalled how at the turn of the century whites drove blacks out of switchmen's jobs by waylaying and killing them as they performed their duties along railways. Similarly, whites took away the firemen's job from blacks following the introduction of the cleaner diesel-electric engines, which replaced steam engines, with their hot, unpleasant coal furnaces.[102]

That elimination was documented by the census, which counted 6,505 African American firemen in 1920. By the 1940 census, that number had dropped to 2,263. The 1920 Census recorded 8,275 African American brakemen, switchmen, flagmen, and yardmen; twenty years later, their number had dwindled to 2,739. The reason, Mitchell explained, was the big four brotherhoods (Brotherhood of Locomotive Engineers, Brotherhood of Locomotive Firemen and Enginemen, Brotherhood of Railroad Trainmen, and the Order of Railway Conductors), who provided a solid front against the hiring of African Americans. Diesel-electric engines made the new firemen's jobs cushiony and very lucrative, so whites craved them. Consequently, the goal of the big four operating brotherhoods since well before the turn of the century, Houston stressed to the Supreme Court, was the ruthless elimination of all blacks from the railroads through secret agreements and other chicanery. That history of exclusion and unfairness, Mitchell said, showed why affirmative action was needed.[103]

Mitchell's reports and memoranda help to show that the FEPC's battles with the railroads and the related unions, especially those covered by the Southeastern Carriers Conference Agreement, were far from unique. He was very familiar with the practices of the Boilermakers because, in addition to being a prominent member of the

Southeastern Carriers Conference Agreement, the union was the dominant bargaining unit in the shipbuilding industry. When the Committee was debating how best to serve the railroads and unions with its directives, he was in Portland, Oregon, conducting investigations for building its cases for the upcoming West Coast hearings, which included Los Angeles. The Committee complimented him for doing "some excellent investigation work in Portland." The railroad hearings reinforced for him the Committee's struggles to end discrimination by the Boilermakers in the manpower-hungry shipbuilding industry. The key issue was African Americans being deprived of their collective bargaining rights, once more under the closed-shop and master agreement.[104]

ASSESSING THE FEPC

By October 1944, as war industries continued laying off masses of workers, the FEPC, along with African Americans in general, became increasingly nervous over the implications of reconversion from a wartime to peacetime economy on its own future as well as the later prospects for employment of minorities. The Committee thus agreed to "recommend to the President that he instruct all agencies concerned with retraining and re-employment not to discriminate in carrying out their program and to advise such agencies that FEPC will handle problems of discrimination within its jurisdiction." Those letters, it said, were to be "broadly phrased so that agencies planning for the reconversion period consider special employment problems of minority groups." One of Mitchell's primary concerns was preparing lists of employers with postwar significance. At the same time, despite his desperate struggle to face the inevitable demise of the FEPC, Mitchell began preparing for continuing its legacy in the postwar period.[105]

On the eve of the committee's passing, *The Crisis* joined African Americans in beginning the mourning:

> The President's Committee on Fair Employment Practices is still breathing, but it is in its death throes, put there by no less a personage than Mr. Truman himself. When the President forbade the FEPC to issue a directive in the Capital Transit case, and refused the Committee an audience to discuss the issue, he cut the authority— and life—from FEPC.[106]
>
> With all but three of its offices closed for lack of funds and with those three manned by skeleton staffs, FEPC has been asked by Mr. Truman to do a fact-finding job on the operation of prejudice against minority group workers during the reconversion period. Thus we are back where we started; making surveys to find out what everyone already knows, namely, that there is brutal prejudice against Negroes, Jews, Spanish-Americans, so-called "foreigners," Japanese-Americans, Catholics, and others, and that this prejudice is denying them an equal opportunity at employment and promotion on the job.
>
> This fact-finding task will muddy the waters just long enough to make it most difficult, if not impossible, to pass legislation for a permanent FEPC. Mr. Truman

has made two fine statements for FEPC, but we must judge him and his party by what he did to it last month.[107]

Although Truman buckled to the same political pressure that had restrained Roosevelt, a totally new course in the civil rights struggle had been set. Mitchell was one of those African Americans who would not allow the president to shirk his responsibility to uphold the Constitution.[108]

Mitchell believed the FEPC "accomplished as much as it could have, but not as much as it should have." Because the agency's power stemmed from the president, a "great deal more could have been done, but it depended on the White House." The FEPC raised the standard of jobs blacks could get. For his part, Mitchell strengthened the nondiscrimination policy by always taking firm stands in implementing the executive orders.[109]

A typical problem he encountered was the "tendency to bring in as many blacks as possible" for such positions as janitors, charwomen, and automobile mechanics in an attempt to feign compliance. Another problem he cited was the Pennsylvania war plant that refused to hire blacks until the available supply of white workers in the area was exhausted. After the FEPC instructed the company to comply with the order it agreed to hire blacks. The FEPC, however, "helped raise sights on jobs" so that blacks were upgraded to skilled positions in such industries as steel, shipbuilding and aircraft. One notable achievement was that it changed the racial practices at Bell Aircraft. Overall, it changed the concept "of what constituted fair employment."[110]

Mitchell's reports and memoranda to the national staff do not by themselves provide a full measure of the difficulties the FEPC encountered in fighting discrimination. To obtain that information it is necessary first to refer to studies such as the WMC survey that, midway through the FEPC's life, explained that although there had been an increase in the total employment of African Americans in practically every branch of war production, there was a "serious time-lag both in" their wider use among the smaller individual firms and in their occupational upgrading in all firms. Their concentration "in relatively few large firms, has had the effect, together with slow occupational progress generally," of restricting their use, the survey said.

Thus the degree of African American employment varied widely among specific plants, areas, and industries. In the South, where there was a shortage of labor, African Americans were concentrated in heavy-labor, unskilled jobs. Furthermore, with few exceptions, no steps were taken to upgrade them to new occupations; nor were they hired to meet the demand for skilled workers.

In the North, where there were acute labor shortages, the employment of African Americans progressed much further, but they were concentrated in specific occupations, establishments, and industries. The WMC reported there was little indication of an increase in the diversification of their employment to meet manpower shortages. Furthermore, discriminatory job specifications remained a "formidable barrier in many plants and occupations."

So, concluded the WMC, the successful recruitment of African Americans for war work was fundamentally a problem of removing discriminatory barriers against their employment in many smaller companies and against their general use in all occupations for which they could qualify. There was a slow but promising trend that their use in war industries was increasing.[111]

Mitchell was among several staff members who provided their views on the committee's performance overall or on the obstacles it faced. They included George Johnson; John A. Davis, director of the division of review and analysis; Malcolm Ross; and Elmer Henderson, director of Region VI. Harry Kingman, director for Region XII, concluded that minority workers had "made some real gains since Pearl Harbor." He cited the shortage of manpower as the principal reason. But the federal intervention on behalf of fair employment practice contributed greatly. Many AFL unions did their part too, Kingman said, "but it would be unfactual to withhold the full credit to the CIO so far as union labor" was concerned. The CIO's national policy was "unequivocal and affiliates such as the Marine Cooks and Stewards" put "their announced principles into effect." Approaching the end of the war in 1945, he said, the FEPC was "hamstrung" because reconversion meant "the bitterest job rivalry" between majority and minority groups. It had "frequently been pointed out," he said, "that the severest test of a democracy" was "how to treat its minorities. Unfair treatment of Negroes, Jews, loyal persons of Japanese ancestry, and other minority people, could prove the entering wedge for the enemies of the American way of life."[112]

The FEPC's *First Report* and *Final Report* are other guides to understanding its effectiveness. Ultimately, though, Mitchell's contributions to that effectiveness must be judged against the history of the entire movement it initiated.

For Mitchell's part, one of his most measurable contributions to the FEPC's effectiveness and to the war effort was his ability to settle strikes by serving as both a conciliator and a no-nonsense leader in combating discrimination. But his reports on the Hazelwood By-Products Plant at Jones and Laughlin Steel Company in Aliquippa, Pennsylvania, in April 1944 provide further strong evidence of how he worked on those challenges. There, in conjunction with G. James Fleming, regional director, and Milo Manly, FEPC examiner, before allowing negotiations on ending the crippling strike by black workers to begin, the examiner "required the strikers to return to work in order that the production of vitally needed steel might suffer no further delay."

In that regard, another benefit of the FEPC's conciliation efforts was shown. Fleming welcomed the FEPC's successful efforts in getting Jones and Laughlin to adopt "a progression schedule to protect the promotional interests of the workers in the 14" mill." He complained, nevertheless, that the "[c]ompany reportedly has been applying this progression schedule only in the case of colored workers and has not extended to white workers its benefits. In keeping with FEPC principles when the progression schedule was suggested, we made clear that its virtue was in the direction of better management and personnel procedure as to all workers and not only for the advantage of some."[113]

Strengthening Mitchell's civil rights advocacy was his immersion in the broad social ramifications of World War II and the subsequent demobilization. The major factors that contributed to the progress he helped blacks make in industry during the war were a tight labor market in the principal war production centers, the president's leadership in establishing a national nondiscrimination policy and in enforcing it in order to break down racial barriers in employment, and the embarrassment America was suffering abroad and the cynicism it was arousing there owing to its racial practices at home. But jobs, especially ones higher than at the service level, were not the only opportunities blacks sought as a means of enjoying their full citizenship rights. They wanted decent housing, an equal right to vote, and all the other perquisites of full citizenship.

Thus, after the war, despite the loss of some of that progress, it was clear that the FEPC had accelerated the acceptance of blacks by labor unions and had demonstrated that people of various racial and ethnic backgrounds could work peacefully and productively together. Those were practical lessons employers understood. When confronted with charges of discrimination, many employers, such as Western Electric and Lockheed, sought to cooperate with the FEPC.

Executive Order 8802, therefore, had a much more profound and long-lasting impact than the ephemeral life span of the FEPC. It set the pattern for Mitchell's unrelenting struggle to get every president with whom he worked to promulgate a national nondiscrimination policy and to provide leadership in enforcing constitutional protections against all forms of discrimination until Congress passed civil rights laws.[114]

NOTES

1. *Crisis,* 11/40, 343; emphasis added.

2. George M. Johnson, "The Segregation of War Workers because of Race, Creed, Color or National Origin," HqR3, Office Files of George M. Johnson. Miscellaneous.

3. Transcript of Proceedings, 7/6/43, 19, HqR64, Central Files. See "Cases Currently Being Handled by Clarence M. Mitchell, 9/14/43," in appendix 1.

4. Part I of the "Wartime Experience" of black workers, "Value of the National Policy Against Discrimination in Industry," (no author provided) can be found in HqR2, Office Files of Malcolm Ross. West Coast Materials. Watson's interview with Davis, 9/22/85.

5. Watson, *Lion in the Lobby,* rev. ed., 122. See Mitchell's work on the Western Electric Point Breeze plant, the Chesapeake and Potomac Telephone, Bethlehem Steel and Baltimore Transit cases below.

6. Mitchell to Weaver, 10/26/41, MP.

7. Will Alexander complained that the FEPC's setup placed its enforcement "in the hands of a special commission." Weaver explained: "Faced with the pressure to produce immediate, dramatic results and constantly harassed by powerful economic and political forces opposed to its existence, the committee concentrated upon those activities which would corral support for it. This resulted in neglect of long-run planning and programming." Dykeman and Stokely, *Seeds of Southern Change,* 255–56.

8. Watson, *Lion in the Lobby,* 122–36; Merl Reed provides Mitchell's recollections in his "Notes on Interview" with Mitchell, 8/24/78.

9. Mitchell, speech to statewide conference of CIO, Bridgeport, Conn., 4/19/42.

10. Dykeman and Stokely, *Seeds of Southern Change,* 256–57.

11. Hardin, "Role of Presidential Advisors," 79–81.

12. Dykeman and Stokely, *Seeds of Southern Change,* 257–58.

13. Watson, *Lion in the Lobby,* 122–36, and the chapter "The FEPC Grail," 121–51, provide considerably more details of Mitchell's activities and related lessons. See also Reed, "Notes on Interview."

14. Lautier, "Jim Crow in the Nation's Capital," *Crisis,* 4/40, 107, 125; Watson, *Lion in the Lobby,* 224–25; Reed, "Notes on Interview"; White, *Man Called White,* 180–85. In 12/45 a three-judge federal court in Baltimore ruled that the regulations of the Southern Railway Company under which it failed to provide dining service to Henderson on 5/17/42 were inadequate, thus reversing a previous decision by the Interstate Commerce Commission, case 28895, *Elmer Henderson v. Southern Railway Company.* Henderson had applied to the ICC for injunctive relief by way of a cease-and-desist order to Southern Railway barring it from treating other African Americans in the manner it had treated him. That meant the company would have had to provide them with facilities equal to those for white passengers. A copy of the news release of 12/20/45 and other materials are in Henderson's private papers in Washington.

15. Reed, "Notes on Interview."

16. For the FEPC's evolving process, see Reed, *Seedtime,* 48–62; Reed, "Notes on Interview"; Transcript of Proceedings, 2/14/44, 4–8, HqR65, Central Files. On the attitudes of Randolph and Walter White on the selection of Committee members, see Hardin, "Role of Presidential Advisors," 46–54.

17. Reed, "Notes on Interview."

18. Watson, interview with Maslow, 11/23/83; for Maslow's study on the legislative struggles for a permanent FEPC, see Will Maslow, "FEPC—A Case History in Parliamentary Maneuver."

19. Reed, "Notes on Interview."

20. Ibid.

21. Watson, *Lion in the Lobby,* 87–91.

22. Ibid., 123–25; Weaver, *Negro Labor,* 10–13.

23. The FSA, in statement of 11/20/40, provided the excerpt from the appropriations act. HqR4, Office Files of George M. Johnson. Office of Education.

24. Ibid.; emphasis added.

25. Garfinkel, *When Negroes March,* 55; *Amsterdam News,* 4/19/41, 16.

26. Garfinkel, *When Negroes March,* 60, 61; Weaver, *Negro Labor,* 17–18; FEPC, "Its Beginning and Growth," 3/44. The text of Roosevelt's letter to Knudsen and Hillman is in HqR77, Office Files of Eugene Davidson. Speech Materials.

27. Transcript of Proceedings, 12/4/43, 131, HqR64, Central Files.

28. Greenbaum to Ross, 5/20/44, HqR1, Office Files of Malcolm Ross. Extra Copies.

29. See Mitchell to Johnson, memorandum, 12/23/42, and notes; Bloch, "Power of the President to Issue Executive Order 9346," in appendix 1.

30. *First Report,* 55; emphasis added.

31. Ibid., 55–59; HqR2, Office Files of Malcolm Ross. U.S. Cartridge Company (St. Louis Case), Compliance after Service of Complaint, Difficult Cases.

32. *First Report,* 55–59. See also the headnote on Jurisdictional Issues, which further explains how the Committee functioned.

33. See Mitchell to Weaver, report, 10/10/42, and other Mitchell texts on Portland, Ore. shipyards; Mitchell, love letter to Juanita Mitchell, n.d., MP.

As the 10/13/44 memorandum from John A. Davis to George Johnson showed, others independent of the FEPC and the NAACP were also documenting the inseparability of segregation and discrimination. Davis referred to studies by Leonard Ephraim Meece: *Negro Education in Kentucky* and *Survey Graphic.* He also said that two people who were "eminently qualified to testify on the effect of segregation in causing discrimination" were Dr. Charles H. Thompson, dean of the graduate school of Howard University and editor of the *Journal of Negro Education,* and Dr. Ina Corinne Brown of the Office of Education. Brown was a Lloyd Warner–trained cultural anthropologist and therefore was an expert on the broad scope of the effect of segregation and discrimination on African Americans. Davis's memorandum is in HqR38, Central Files. Memoranda, George Johnson, M—3, 12 /41–12 /43.

34. See John A. Davis to George Johnson, memorandum, 10/13/44, cited above.

35. Johnson's memorandum is at 2/8/43, in HqR1, Summaries of Actions Taken by the Committee at Its Meetings.

36. Johnson's memorandum of 2/8/43, which is discussed by the Committee, is in Transcript of Proceedings, 2/8/43, 11, HqR64, Central Files. See Mitchell's texts on the Sun Shipbuilding Company at 3/16/43, 4/3, 4/5, 4/17/44.

37. *Missouri ex rel. Gaines v. Canada*, 305 U.S. 337 (1938). The other NAACP case (originating in Texas and decided on 4/3/44) that reinforced the FEPC's struggle was *Smith v. Allwright*, 321 U.S. 649 (1944), in which the Supreme Court ruled that the right to vote was protected by the Constitution, clearing the way for blacks to vote in primary elections in the South.

38. Transcript of Proceedings, 2/8/43, 14–34, HqR64, Central Files.

39. Transcript of Proceedings, 7/6/43, 17–21, HqR64, Central Files.

40. Transcript of Proceedings, 2/8/43, 23, HqR64, Central Files.

41. See Mitchell to Cramer, memorandum, 6/1/43; Mitchell and Ernest Trimble, "Field Investigation Report," 6/8/43, in appendix 1, and related texts on this case throughout the volume; Transcript of Proceedings, 7/6/43, 20–37, HqR64, Central Files; Mitchell to Weaver, report, 10/10/42.

42. For a sample of texts on Kaiser shipyards in Portland, see 10/10/42; on Bethlehem Steel Shipbuilding, see report on the strike there at 8/1/43, in appendix 1; on the strike at Timken Roller Bearing, see 5/10, 7/31/43.

43. Transcript of Proceedings, 7/6/43, 20–37, HqR64, Central Files.

44. See Watson, *Lion in the Lobby*, 31–32.

45. Cramer speech, 3/11/43, HqR75, Central Files. Reference File. Releases. Further defending the settlement as limited, Ernest Trimble explained that it covered only workers with bare-hull skills. Transcript of Proceedings, 7/6/43, 39, HqR64, Central Files.

46. Transcript of Proceedings, 7/6/43, 35, HqR64, Central Files.

47. Transcript of Proceedings, 7/6/43, 36, HqR64, Central Files; for Brecon Bag Loading, see 4/23/42, 1/5, 3/39/43.

48. Transcript of Proceedings, 7/6/43, 44–45, 58, HqR64, Central Files; Davis, "Report on FEPC Action in Race Strikes," 5/25/44, in appendix 1; Minutes, 7/13/43 (of 7/6/43 meeting), HqR1, Summary Minutes of Meetings.

49. For selected policies on segregation, see selections at 2/5, 7/26, 8/7/43. For the NAACP's reaction, see NAACP, *Annual Report*, 1943, 28.

50. "Resume of Conference with Bell Aircraft Corporation," 1/18/45, in which Mitchell was one of the participants, FR80, Region VII. Administrative Files (A–Z), Bell Aircraft Corp.; Witherspoon Dodge to Maceo Hubbard, 12/3/45, FEPC FR 80, Region VII. Administrative Files (A–Z), Regional Director (contd.).

51. Maslow's field instruction is included in a batch Mitchell sent in Field Letter no. 77, 9/17/45, to the Division of Field Operations regarding "Attached Analysis of Immediate Problems Which Minority Group Workers Will Face" during reconversion. FEPC RG 228, Office Files of Clarence M. Mitchell: Approved Rough Drafts of R.D.'s, Field Letters, Field Instructions, box 457, DNA; Hearings, H.R. 4878, 158, 78th Cong., 2d sess.

52. Mitchell to Johnson, 11/1/43. See also Johnson's report of 7/31/43 to Haas on his conversation with Mitchell; Haas's memorandum of 8/1/43 on his participating in the case; Mitchell's 8/6/43 Field Investigation Report, all in appendix 1, and his related texts in the volume, especially his memorandum of 11/1/43 to Johnson.

53. See Davis, memorandum, 5/25/44, in appendix 1; headnote on Strikes and Work Stoppages.

54. Transcript of Proceedings, 8/28/43, 103–14, HqR64, Central Files.

55. Ibid.

56. Ibid., 114.

57. It approved the statement on 12/4/43. Minutes, 12/4/43 (of 11/16/43 meeting), HqR1, Summary Minutes of Meetings.

58. Transcript of Proceedings, 2/12/44, 29–31, HqR64, Central Files.

59. *Final Report,* 9; for an explanation of the hearings process, see *First Report,* 20–21; for Johnson's explanation of the hearings, see Transcript of Proceedings, 2/12/44, 29, HqR64, Central Files.

60. For hearings dates, see FEPC Chronology.

61. Reed, "Notes on Interview."

62. Mitchell, for example, helped plan the hearings in St. Louis. See Frank Reeves to Johnson, 7/22/44, HqR5, Office Files of George M. Johnson. Frank Reeves; *Final Report,* 11–23.

63. Maceo Hubbard provided this backgrounder, which varies in some details from others in the FEPC collection, to the Committee at its meeting on 7/6/43. See Transcript of Proceedings, 7/6/43, 171–72, HqR64, Central Files. See also another background document entitled, "Railroads," HqR2, Office Files of Malcolm Ross. Difficult Cases; Mitchell, 12/28/42; *Final Report,* 12. The NAACP *Annual Report,* 1943, 19, confirms 1/9/43 as the date on which McNutt cancelled the railroad hearings. It also noted that on 2/19/43 more than twenty leaders of organizations presented a solid front of protest against the treatment of FEPC. Speaker after speaker at the conference urged (1) restoring the FEPC to its independent status under the White House and removing it from the War Manpower Commission; (2) an immediate rescheduling of the cancelled railroad hearings and also the cancelled hearings on discrimination against Latin Americans in the Southwest; (3) giving the Committee sanctions in the form not only of public hearings but also of money penalties and liquidated damages; (4) giving the Committee an adequate staff and budget; and (5) keeping in service the members of the present Committee who had not resigned.

64. Transcript of Proceedings, 7/6/43, 172–73, HqR64, Central Files.

65. *First Report,* 13 (states 23 railroads and 14 unions); *Final Report,* 12–13, gives an updated and a fuller picture of the struggle. See Johnson's 12/4/44 memorandum, HqR38, Central Files. Memoranda 3, Legal Division; Summaries of Hearings in HqR3, Office Files of Malcolm Ross, where summaries of several hearings are located; HqR19, Records Relating to Hearings (throughout, for additional materials).

66. FEPC news release on letter from sixteen railroads defying the agency's 11/18/43 directive regarding the hiring and promoting of black railroad workers because doing so would seriously and irreparably prejudice the war effort, would be impracticable, and would violate the Railway Labor Act, in FEPC RG 228, Office Files of Ernest Trimble, box 469, DNA.

67. FEPC news release, 12/13/43, FEPC RG 228, IE-2–48–25–3, Office Files of Ernest Trimble, box 469, DNA; NAACP *Annual Report,* 1943, 21; Transcript of Proceedings, 1/15/45, 16–17, HqR65, Central Files.

68. The seven unions cited were the Brotherhood of Locomotive Firemen and Enginemen; Brotherhood of Railroad Trainmen; Order of Railway Conductors; Brotherhood of Railway Carmen of America; Brotherhood of Locomotive Engineers; International Association of Machinists; and International Brotherhood of Boilermakers, Iron Shipbuilders and Helpers of America.

69. The complaints involved twenty-three railroads. The ten cited as being involved in the Southeastern Conference agreement were Atlantic Coast Line Railway Co.; Atlanta Joint Terminals; Central of Georgia Railway Co.; Georgia Railroad; Jacksonville Terminal Co.; Louisville and Nashville Railroad Co.; Norfolk Southern Railroad Co.; St. Louis-San Francisco Railway Co.; Seaboard Air Line Railway; and Southern Railway Co. The other thirteen against whom complaints were also filed were: Baltimore and Ohio; Baltimore and Ohio Chicago Terminal; Chesapeake and Ohio; Chicago and Northwestern; Gulf, Mobile and Ohio; Illinois Central Railroad; Louisiana and Arkansas; Missouri-Kansas-Texas; New York Central; Southern Railroad; Pennsylvania Railroad; Union Pacific; Virginian Railway; and Union Pacific Railroad.

70. The Southeastern Carriers Conference Agreement was signed on 2/18/41 between the Brotherhood of Locomotive Firemen and Enginemen and several railroads. Northrup, *Organized Labor and the Negro,* 63–5, 75; *Final Report,* 12–13.

71. For the Committee's findings against the railroads, see FEPC advance news release, 12/1/43, OWI-2747, HqR64, Central Files. Railroads—Findings.

72. *Steele v. Louisville and Nashville Railroad Company, et al.,* 323 U.S. 192 (1944); *Tunstall v. Brotherhood of Locomotive Firemen and Enginemen, et al.,* 323 U.S. 210 (1944); *Wallace Corporation v. National Labor Relations Board,* 323 U.S. 248 (1944). See Johnson's assessment of the importance of the cases in HqR5, Office Files of George M. Johnson. Undesignated (blank) folder.

73. *Steele, Tunstall,* and *Wallace* cases; Office of War Information news release, Ross-WMC-2285, OWI-2439, in FEPC RG 228, Office Files of Ernest Trimble, box 469, DNA; advance release, 12/1/43,

Bourne-2285, OWI-2747, and OWI news release (Bourne-WMC-2285-N-618), in HqR64, Central Files. Railroads—Findings; FEPC RG 228, Office Files of Ernest Trimble, box 469, DNA; 12/13/43 letter from railroads responding to the Committee's directives of 11/18/43, in HqR1, Outgoing Correspondence. B; Transcript of Proceedings, 12/27/43, 24, HqR64, Central Files. Railroads—Findings; press release, 1/3/44, announcing appointment of Judge Walter P. Stacy to head a special committee with Mayor Lausche and Judge Holly as members, and Stacy statement, 5/18/44, noting that his committee had been meeting with the railroads and unions for the past two days, in HqR86, Press Releases; Houston, "Foul Employment Practice on the Rails," *Crisis,* 10/49, 269–71, 284–85.

74. Transcript of Proceedings, 10/18/43, 47–48, HqR64, Central Files.

75. *Steele v. Louisville and Nashville Railroad,* 234, 235.

76. *Final Report,* 13–14.

77. Transcript of Proceedings, 12/4/43, 134–43, HqR64, Central Files; Minutes, 12/4/43, HqR1, Summary Minutes of Meetings.

78. Statement, 12/27/43, with 6/13/44 addition, HqR38, "Statement Relating to Non-Discrimination Clause to be Included in Government Contracts, 12/27/43, with 6/13/44 addition," HqR38, Central Files.

79. FEPC's examples of "Typical Non-Discrimination Clauses," HqR5, Office Files of George M. Johnson. Non-Discrimination Clauses.

80. Administrative assistant to Secretary of the Treasury to George M. Johnson, 2/11/44, HqR5, Office Files of George M. Johnson. Non-Discrimination Clauses.

81. Johnson to Hubbard, memorandum, 3/2/44, HqR4, Office Files of George M. Johnson. Policy; *Hearings,* H.R. 4878, 158, 78th Cong. 2d sess.

82. Frank D. Reeves to Mitchell, memorandum, 7/12/44, requesting him to determine which of several contracts by the Maritime Commission and the War and Navy Departments in the St. Louis Area had nondiscrimination clauses, HqR66, Central Files. U.S. Government, Maritime Commission; Mitchell to Lawson, memorandum, 1/12/44, responding to the regional director's inquiry concerning Japanese, in HqR5, Office Files of George M. Johnson. Non-Discrimination Clauses.

83. Mitchell to Lawson, 1/12/44, cited above.

84. Minutes, 6/13/44, HqR1, Summary Minutes of Meetings.

85. Minutes, 9/30/44, HqR1, Summary Minutes of Meetings.

86. Stickgold memorandum to Johnson on Non-Discrimination Clause (*Federal Register,* 2/15/45), 2/19/45, HqR38, Central Files. Memoranda, Johnson, George M.—1944—.

87. The NLRB is an independent federal agency created under the National Labor Relations Act of 1935 (Wagner Act) that affirms labor's right to organize and bargain collectively through representatives of their own choosing or to refrain from such activities. For background on the NLRB, see *The Columbia Encyclopedia,* 6th ed., 2001. For the full text of the National Labor Relations Act, see 29 U.S.C. §§ 151–69; online, see http://www.union-organizing.com/nlra.html.

88. Mitchell, interview by Watson, 12/2/83; Watson, *Lion in the Lobby,* 123–25.

89. Mitchell, interview by Watson, 11/22/83. For similar problems, about which Mitchell also spoke in the interview, see also the headnotes on the Shipbuilding Industry and on the FEPC and Unions (esp. the Boilermakers).

90. Weaver, *Negro Labor,* is tantamount to a primary source on these problems.

91. On Hanford, see texts at 7/31/43, 3/6, 4/12, 5/1/44. On the Tennessee cases, see 1/27/44, 1/23, 2/6, 5/2, 6/5/45; Mitchell to Dodge, 5/25/45, and related texts, FR81, Region VII. Active Cases (A–Z), Tennessee Eastman. On later NAACP action, see Washington Bureau report, 12/4/50.

92. See Mitchell, 7/31/43.

93. Maslow, telephone interview by Watson, 11/21/83, in New York City; Mitchell, interviews by Watson, 11/21, 12/2/83; John Davis interview by Watson, 1/84, in New Rochelle, N.Y.; Mitchell to Robert C. Goodwin, director, USES, 10/22/45, HqR67, Central Files. U.S. Government, General, N–W; Mitchell to Clarence Johnson, regional minorities consultant, WMC, 8/25/43, HqR38, Central Files. Memoranda, Clarence Johnson; L. S. Hawkins, director, vocational training for War Production Workers, to Mitchell, 2/1/45, HqR3, Office Files of George M. Johnson. Mitchell, Clarence; Watson, *Lion in the Lobby,* 123–25, 140, 148.

94. Franklin, *Emancipation Proclamation; Crisis,* 3/63, 134.

95. Ibid., 135–36; Thompson, "Seventy-five Years of Negro Education," *Crisis,* 7/38, 202.

96. Franklin, *Emancipation Proclamation,* 136; for Webster's comment during discussion of the Boilermakers, see Transcript of Proceedings, 2/12/44, 75, HqR65, Central Files.

97. Du Bois, *Black Reconstruction,* 273–322.

98. For Southall's motion, see Transcript of Proceedings, 7/7/43, 96, HqR64, Central Files; Shishkin's affirmative action suggestions, in Transcript of Proceedings, 7/7/43, 10, HqR64, Central Files. For the interchangeable use of "affirmative action" and "positive action," see Transcript of Proceedings, 4/19/43, 24, 25, HqR64, Central Files. For an explanation of Kennedy's EO 10925, requiring positive action to further equal employment opportunities, see Morgan, *President and Civil Rights,* 47.

99. Transcript of Proceedings, 7/26/43, 9–10, HqR64, Central Files.

100. Transcript of Proceedings, 10/2/43, 12–13, HqR64, Central Files.

101. Elmer Henderson, "The Employment of Negroes in the Federal Government," [n.d.], HqR3, Office Files of George M. Johnson. Employment of Negroes in the Federal Government; emphasis added.

102. Mitchell, telephone interview by Watson, 12/2/83.

103. Mitchell, interview, 11/22/83; Houston, "Foul Employment," 269–71, 284–85.

104. Transcript of Proceedings, 10/18/43, 74–75, 82, 83; 12/4/43, 108, both in HqR64, Central Files.

105. See Mitchell's texts of 10/7, 10/9/44, 8/17, 8/20, 8/25, 9/6, 9/14, 10/29, 11/02/45. For an extended discussion by the Committee of staff proposals for action during the transition period and its results, see Transcript of Proceedings, 9/30/44, 29–74; 12/12/44, 90–92, both in HqR65, Central Files; Minutes, 9/30, 10/11/44, HqR1, Summary Minutes of Meetings.

106. See the headnote on Street and Local Railways.

107. "Truman Kills FEPC," editorial, *Crisis,* 1/46, 9. See also a lengthy collection of "Editorial Comments on the FEPC, 1944," HqR3, Office Files of Malcolm Ross. Editorials.

108. Simon Stickgold, "Statement of Principles," 2/20/45, HqR5, Office Files of George M. Johnson. Simon Stickgold; for their application, see "Stickgold's memorandum 'Statement of Principles,'" cited by Johnson to Hunt, 2/17/45, also in HqR5, Office Files of George M. Johnson. A. Bruce Hunt.

109. See the headnote on Street and Local Railways.

110. Reed, "Notes on Interview." See Mitchell, 7/24/43.

111. "Developments in the Employment of Negroes in War Industries," WMC, 10/18/43, HqR3, Office Files of George M. Johnson. Employment of Negroes in War Industries.

112. Kingman, speech, 7/25/45, at the National Convention of the CIO Marine Cooks and Stewards Union, HqR76, Office Files of Clarence Mitchell. Unarranged.

113. From Mitchell's unpublished strike data report of 5/44, used at 5/4/44, note 1, which is in HqR76, Office Files of Eugene Davidson. Strikes; selection from Fleming's weekly report for week ending 2/26/44, in series of weekly report excerpts from 9/18/43 to 3/4/44, HqR77, Office Files of Eugene Davidson. Strikes.

114. See Watson, *Lion in the Lobby,* 299–300, 307–10, 313–16.

EDITORIAL METHOD
AND ABBREVIATIONS

ORGANIZATION

This series will present Clarence Mitchell Jr.'s reports and selective memoranda, first as a staff member and director of the Division of Field Operations of the Fair Employment Practice Committee (1942–46), then as labor secretary of the NAACP (1946–50), and finally as director of the NAACP's Washington Bureau (1950–78). Texts are arranged in chronological sequence. Enclosures, attachments, and other related materials are printed at the discretion of the edition's editors. Identification of significant persons in the text is placed in the biographical directory at the end of the volumes. Less well known figures, such as complainants, local civil rights leaders, and lower-level officials with whom the FEPC and NAACP dealt, are also identified in the biographical directory when possible. To avoid repetitious annotation of related texts, headnotes coordinating the background for significant subject areas precede the documents in each volume. A timeline is provided as a guide for the FEPC's activities. Supplementary texts are placed in the appendices.

DATES

A dateline generally appears at the top of each manuscript. Where a dateline appears elsewhere in the manuscript, the editors have added one at the top in square brackets. Where the dateline was partly or wholly missing, the editors have assigned an approximate date based on internal evidence, adding question marks when in doubt. Such documents are placed according to the following rules.

- · If no day can be assigned, the document is placed after all others in that month.
- · If no month can be assigned, the document is placed at the end of the year.
- · If the year is missing but one can be inferred, it is inserted in square brackets and the document placed at the end of that year.
- · If no year can be assigned, inclusive dates are conjectured and the document is placed at the end of the first year.

PUNCTUATION

· In general, punctuation is rendered as it appears in the text.
· When a precise mark of punctuation cannot be determined, modern usage is followed.

SPELLING

The original spelling in the manuscript has been preserved, with the following exceptions:

· Proper names are always left unchanged in the document but are presented correctly in all editorial material.
· When the misspelling of a proper name is so unclear as to be misleading, the correct spelling is placed in square brackets immediately following it or in a footnote. When more than one person of the same last name appears in a volume and no title is given to identify the correct person, a first name is also added in square brackets.
· Missing letters are supplied in square brackets.
· Typographical errors are corrected at the discretion of the editors.

CAPITALIZATION

Manuscript capitalization is retained. In doubtful cases, modern usage is followed.

ABBREVIATIONS AND CONTRACTIONS

Abbreviations and contractions are retained as in the manuscript. A list of relevant abbreviations for this volume is provided below.

INDECIPHERABLE PASSAGES

In square brackets, the editors have supplied letters, words, and digits that are missing, illegible, or mutilated. When an addition is uncertain it is followed by a question mark. Passages that cannot be deduced are indicated by editorial insertions of an italicized explanation in brackets, such as [*illegible*] or [*torn*]. A blank left in the manuscript by the author is so depicted and the fact noted in a footnote.

REVISIONS IN MANUSCRIPTS

· Interlineations in the text and brief additions in the margin are incorporated silently in the text in the place indicated by the writer. Substantial marginal additions are also placed in the text at the appropriate point, either with the editorial insertion [in the margin] before and after the addition or with editorial comment suitable to the passage.

· Crossed-out passages are generally ignored. When excisions are significant or substantial, the deleted passages are either placed in the text in angle brackets </> before the words substituted or are presented in a footnote.

· When their importance warrants, variant readings derived from the collation of additional texts of a document with the basic or master text are entered in footnotes.

EDITORIAL APPARATUS

Classification of Manuscripts

When a document is represented by two or more manuscripts, the editors have selected the most authoritative for publication. The document type is listed in the source identification note following each document.

Manuscript Types and Descriptive Symbols

The nature of the original manuscripts, all of which are typed, is described accordingly:

Copy	copy [a carbon or mimeographed copy]
Draft	draft
D	document
DS	document signed
DI	document initialed
LH	letterhead (text, usually an original, placed on office letterhead)
MS	manuscript

Location Symbols

The original locations of documents in the edition are indicated by symbols. The guide used for our repositories was the *Symbols of American Libraries,* 11th ed.

(Washington, D.C.: Library of Congress, 1976). Each volume in the series will contain a table of symbols.

Repositories

DHU-MS   Moorland-Spingarn Research Center, Howard University
DNA   National Archives
DLC   Library of Congress
MP   Mitchell Papers, Baltimore

Abbreviations Related to FEPC Records

DFO   Division of Field Operations

EO   Executive Order

ES 270   Report prepared by the United States Employment Service that provided statistical and narrative information on projected labor requirements of specific plants, as well as information on current numbers of persons employed

ES 510   Report form used by the United States Employment Service to indicate that it had received a discriminatory order from an employer

FDR   Final Disposition Report

FR   (FEPC) Field Records. The citation format for Field Records is as follows: FR#, Region. + subcategory (where found), folder.

     FR1–2, Region I, Boston, July 1, 1943 (Connecticut, Maine, Massachusetts, New Hampshire, Rhode Island, Vermont)

     FR3–26, Region II, New York, July 1, 1943 (New York)

     FR27–41, Region III, Philadelphia, Aug. 30, 1943; Pittsburgh, Mar. 1, 1945 (Delaware, New Jersey, Pennsylvania)

     FR42–48, Region IV, Washington, D.C., Aug. 25, 1943 (District of Columbia, Maryland, North Carolina, Virginia, West Virginia)

     FR49–68, Region V, Cleveland, Sept. 27, 1943; Detroit, Aug. 1, 1943; Cincinnati, Feb. 1, 1945 (Kentucky, Michigan, Ohio)

     FR69–79, Region VI, Chicago, Sept. 15, 1943

     FR80–86, Region VII, Atlanta, Nov. 3, 1943 (Alabama, Florida, Georgia, Mississippi, South Carolina, Tennessee)

     FR87, Region VIII, Minneapolis, Sept. 15, 1943 (Illinois, Indiana, Iowa, Nebraska, North Dakota, South Dakota, Minnesota, Wisconsin)

     FR88–95, Region IX, Kansas City, Nov. 11, 1943; St. Louis, Nov. 1, 1944; Denver, Nov. 11, 1943 (Arkansas, Colorado, Idaho, Kansas, Missouri, Montana, Oklahoma, Wyoming, Utah)

     FR96–102, Regions X, XI, XIII, Dallas, Aug. 23, 1943; San Antonio, Mar. 1,

1945; New Orleans, Feb. 12, 1945 (Arizona, Louisiana, New Mexico, Texas)

FR103–17, Region XII, San Francisco, Sept. 1, 1943; Los Angeles, Sept. 16, 1943 (California, Washington, Oregon, Nevada)

HqR (FEPC) Headquarters Records. The citation format for Headquarters Records is as follows: HqR#, basic collection. + subcategory (where found), and folder. In the example "HqR48, Central Files. Reports, General Reports, N–Z," Central Files is the basic collection; Reports is the category; General Reports, N–Z is the folder. A folder also can be designated by a single letter, such as M. The collections most frequently used are:

HqR1, Documents File. Jan. 15, 1944–Aug. 1945

HqR1, Summary Minutes of Meetings. Jan. 18, 1942–Sept. 15, 1945

HqR1, Summaries of Actions Taken by the Committee at Its Meetings. Sept. 11, 1942–Mar. 15, 1943

HqR1–2, Office Files of Malcolm Ross. June 1940–June 1946

HqR3–4, Office Files of George M. Johnson, Deputy Chairman. Nov. 1941–Oct. 1945

HqR4–6, Office Files of George M. Johnson, Director. Dec. 1941–Nov. 1945

HqR6, Office Files of Emanuel H. Bloch, Hearing Examiner. July 1944–Jan. 1946

HqR7, Office Files of Maceo W. Hubbard. Jan. 1943–Jan. 1946

HqR7–8, Office Files of Frank D. Reeves, Trial Attorney. Dec. 1942–Aug. 1945

HqR8, Office Files of Evelyn N. Cooper, Trial Attorney. Sept. 1944–Dec. 1945

HqR9–22, Records Relating to Hearings. Dec. 1941–Mar. 1946

HqR37–67, Central Files of the FEPC. Aug. 1941–Apr. 1946

HqR73–75, Reference File. July 1941–Apr. 1946

HqR75, Tension File. July 1943–Oct. 1945

HqR76, Office Files of Will Maslow, Director. Sept. 1943–May 1945

HqR76, Office Files of Clarence M. Mitchell, Assistant Director. Oct. 1941–Apr. 1946

HqR76, Office Files of Ernest G. Trimble, Senior Field Representative. Nov. 1941–Nov. 1945

HqR83–85, Correspondence Relating to Cases. Dec. 1943–Oct. 1945

HqR86, Press Releases. Aug. 1941–Nov. 1945

PL Public Law

RD Formal memorandum from the Division of Field Operations to the regional directors transmitting the views of the director on timely subjects and current problems

RFA   Request for Further Action
RG   Record group in National Archives collections

Other Symbols and Abbreviations

ADA   Americans for Democratic Action
AFL   American Federation of Labor
BES   Bureau of Employment Security
CIO   Congress of Industrial Organizations
COFEP Committee on Fair Employment Practice
FEPC   Fair Employment Practice Committee
FSA   Federal Security Agency
GAO   General Accounting Office
GPO   Government Printing Office
HUAC House Un-American Activities Committee
IAM   International Association of Machinists
IBBISHA International Brotherhood of Boilermakers, Iron Shipbuilders and
       Helpers or America
IBEW   International Brotherhood of Electrical Workers
ILGWU International Ladies Garment Workers Union
IUMSWA Industrial Union of Marine and Shipbuilding Workers of America
IUERMW International Union of Electrical, Radio and Machine Workers
IWW   Industrial Workers of the World
LARY   Los Angeles Railway Corporation
LCCR   Leadership Conference on Civil Rights
LPB   Labor Production Board
MGB   Minority Groups Branch of the NDAC
NAPE   National Association of Postal Employees
NDAC   National Defense Advisory Commission
NETB   Negro Employment and Training Branch of the NDAC
NLRB   National Labor Relations Board
NWLB   National War Labor Board
NYA   National Youth Administration
NYT   *New York Times*
ODM   Office of Defense Mobilization
OEM   Office of Emergency Management
OEO   Office of Economic Opportunity
OMI   Oblate of Mary Immaculate (Catholic Religious Order)

OPA	Office of Price Administration
OPM	Office of Production Management
OWI	Office of War Information
OWIU	Oil Workers International Union
PCOFEP	President's Committee on Fair Employment Practice
PRT	Philadelphia Rapid Transit Employees Union
PTC	Philadelphia Transportation Company
PWA	Public Works Administration
SLU	Shipyard Laborer's Union
SNOV	Shipyard Negro Organization for Victory
TWU	Transport Workers Union of America
UAW	United Automobile Workers
UGCCWA	United Gas, Coke, and Chemical Workers of America
UREMWA	United Radio, Electric, and Machine Workers of America
USES	United States Employment Service
UTSEA	United Transportation Service Employees of America
WLB	War Labor Board
WMC	War Manpower Commission
WPA	Works Progress Administration
WPB	War Production Board
WSB	War Stabilization Board

FEPC CHRONOLOGY

April 1939

Elmer A. Carter, editor of *Opportunity* magazine, wonders: "The battlefield in modern wars extends into the factories and warehouses, the shipyards and dry-docks of the warring countries. . . . Knowing these things, and aware of the possibilities of war, it seems strange that the great industrialists of America should be so indifferent and prejudiced against the employment of Negroes. It has been established beyond a shadow of doubt that there is no skill which Negroes cannot acquire, no industrial process they cannot master if given the opportunity to learn. Negroes might well be inducted into America's industrial plants in every department now, so that in time of war there would be no question of the loyalty of the industrial personnel."

October 3, 1939

John T. Clark, executive secretary of The Urban League of St. Louis, Inc., expresses a growing concern among African Americans: "Today's world situation makes sharper than ever the wisdom of the suggestion made to industrial leaders by the Urban League last spring that America's national economy and national defense calls for a greater quantitative and qualitative inclusion of Negro workers in the nation's industries."

March 9, 1940

In a statement to the presidential nominees, delegates to the Washington Conference on Negro Needs—A. Philip Randolph, William H. Hastie, Robert C. Weaver, and Walter F. White—emphasize the plight of African Americans: "Any candidate satisfactory to Negroes must attest to his belief in democracy by unequivocal endorsement of the struggle of the Negro for full and free use of the ballot in all parts of the country. . . . He must support legislation for the eradication of lynching and the provision of civil rights for all citizens. He must stand for the full integration of the Negro into Government service through the selection of qualified colored citizens for policy-making positions in the Federal Government and the assurance of equity in employment in Civil Service positions." The statement also demands that the candidate "make plain his determination as Commander-in-Chief of the Army and Navy to integrate the Negro into all branches of our armed forces."

May 1940

President Roosevelt creates the National Defense Advisory Commission (NDAC) to oversee defense production and names Sidney Hillman chairman.

July 12, 1940

Hillman appoints Robert Weaver his administrative assistant in the NDAC's Labor Division and assigns him the responsibility for developing policies to integrate African Americans into training and job programs in the defense industry.

July 1940

The U.S. Office of Education, at the behest of the NDAC, announces that "in the expenditure of Federal funds for vocational training for defense, there should be no discrimination on account of race, creed, or color."

August 31, 1940

The NDAC announces a labor policy, stipulating that workers should not be discriminated against because of age, sex, race, or color.

September 15, 1940

In a message to Congress on the defense program, President Roosevelt cites the NDAC's nondiscrimination policy.

September 27, 1940

White House Conference on Negroes in Defense—Shortly after passage of the Selective Service Act, President Roosevelt meets with White, Randolph, and T. Arnold Hill, president of the National Urban League, to discuss their demand for the full use of blacks in the armed services. They also urge the abolition of discrimination in the armed forces as well as in employment at army arsenals, navy yards, and industrial plants with national defense contracts. This is the first delegation of blacks received by the Roosevelt administration during the defense period. Also present at the meeting are Col. Frank Knox, secretary of the navy, and Robert P. Patterson, assistant secretary of war.

October 7, 1940

At the behest of the NDAC, Congress includes the following provision in the legislation appropriating money for defense training: "No trainee under the foregoing appropriation shall be discriminated against because of sex, race, or color; and where separate schools are required by law for separate population groups, to the extent needed for trainees of such groups, equitable provision shall be made for facilities for training of like quality."

October 12, 1940

Hillman announces that the AFL and the CIO have reached an agreement with the NDAC to assume responsibility for removing barriers against African American workers in defense industries.

November 20, 1940

John W. Studebaker, U.S. commissioner of education, in a special letter to state and local boards of education, calls attention to the nondiscrimination clause in defense training legislation and urges all directors of defense programs to take special steps to facilitate the training of African Americans.

January 3, 1941

The Training-Within-Industry Branch of the OEM instructs all regional and field representatives to pay special attention to including African American workers in upgrading and apprentice programs in defense plants.

January 7, 1941

Roosevelt abolishes the NDAC and creates a stronger Office of Production Management (OPM) within the Office of Emergency Management, with Hillman as associate director general. Hillman's labor division is transferred to the OPM.

April 11, 1941

At the instruction of the OPM, Hillman sends a letter to all defense contractors urging them "to examine their employment and training policies at once to determine whether or not these policies make ample provision for the full utilization of available and competent Negro workers. Every available source of labor capable of producing defense material must be tapped in the present emergency."

April 11, 1941

Hillman creates within the labor division of the OPM the Negro Employment and Training Branch and the Minority Groups Branch and names as chiefs Weaver and Will Alexander, respectively. The NETB is responsible for problems experienced by African Americans, the MGB for Mexicans and ethnic Americans.

June 12, 1941

Roosevelt, in a memorandum to Hillman and William S. Knudsen, co-director of the OPM, places the full support of his office behind Hillman's letter to defense contractors: "Our Government cannot countenance continued discrimination against American citizens in defense production. Industry must take the initiative in opening the doors of employment to all loyal and qualified workers regardless of race, creed, color, or national origin. American workers, both organized and unorganized, must be prepared to welcome the general and much-needed employment of fellow-workers of all racial and nationality origins in defense industries."

June 13, 1941

New York mayor Fiorello La Guardia arranges a meeting between Randolph and White and representatives of President Roosevelt (La Guardia himself, Eleanor Roosevelt, and Aubrey Williams, head of the National Youth Administration) in which they urge the two black leaders to call off the threatened march; but they decline to do so.

Frank Knox, secretary of the navy, wires Randolph, urging him to come to Washington "for a conference on your project."

June 18, 1941

Randolph and White meet with Roosevelt to press their demands for an end to discrimination in war production industries and segregation in the armed services.

Roosevelt appoints a committee headed by La Guardia to prepare a plan to end discrimination.

June 24, 1941

La Guardia meets with Randolph and White and informs them that the president is prepared to issue an executive order barring discrimination in the defense industry.

JUNE 1941 TO APRIL 1944

June 25, 1941

Roosevelt issues Executive Order 8802: "[T]here shall be no discrimination in the employment of workers in defense industries or government because of race, creed, color, or national origin."

The order creates a Committee of Fair Employment Practice as an administering agency within the OPM that is to "receive and investigate complaints of discrimination in violation of the provisions of this order" and to "take appropriate steps to redress grievances which it finds to be valid."

July 1, 1941

Hillman emphasizes the drive for nondiscrimination in defense employment by appointing Weaver and Alexander among the twelve officials from government agencies who compose the Federal Labor Supply Committee. Members of the Negro Employment and Training Branch and the Minority Groups Branch of the OPM are assigned to Regional Labor Supply Committees.

July 18, 1941

Roosevelt issues EO 8823, expanding the Committee from four to five members, exclusive of the chairman.

Roosevelt appoints Mark Ethridge, publisher of the *Louisville Courier-Journal,* chairman of the Committee and Lawrence Cramer, former governor of the Virgin Islands, executive secretary. Other Committee members are Earl B. Dickerson, alderman, City Council of Chicago; William Green, president of the AFL; Philip Murray, president of the CIO; David Sarnoff, president of the Radio Corporation of America; and Milton P. Webster, international vice president of the Brotherhood of Sleeping Car Porters. Frank Fenton, director of organization for the AFL, and John Brophy, chairman of the CIO Industrial Union Councils, are later appointed alternates for Green and Murray.

September 3, 1941

A letter from Roosevelt to the heads of all departments and independent establishments of the government states, "[I]t is my desire that all departments and independent establishments in the Federal Government make a thorough examination of their personnel policies and practices to the end that they may be able to assure me that in the Federal Service the doors of employment are open to all loyal and qualified workers, regardless of creed, race, or national origin."

October 20–21, 1941

Public hearings are held in Los Angeles before the full Committee on charges against ten firms and three unions.

January 3, 1942

A letter from Roosevelt to the Committee places complaints of discrimination because of alienage within the Committee's jurisdiction.

January 12–20, 1942

Public hearings are held in Chicago before the full Committee on charges against eleven firms.

January 26, 1942

The FEPC is transferred to the War Production Board upon the dissolution of the OPM.

February 16–17, 1942

Public hearings are held in New York City before the full Committee on charges against eleven firms.

March 25, 1942

EO 9111 increases the number of Committee members to seven (including the chairman)

Malcolm MacLean, president of Hampton Institute, is appointed chairman to succeed Ethridge, who continues to serve as a Committee member.

March 28, 1942

In a letter to the Committee Roosevelt reaffirms his message of September 3, 1941, with regard to fair employment by federal departments and suggests that the Committee "ascertain, by direct reports from them, the degree of progress which has been achieved by the respective departments and agencies."

April 4, 1942

A public hearing is held in Chicago before a subcommittee on charges against two unions.

June 18–20, 1942

Public hearings before the full Committee are held in Birmingham on charges against five firms, two unions, and one defense training program.

July 21, 1942

A rehearing is held in Washington, D.C., before the full Committee on charges against two companies that appeared at the New York hearings in February.

July 30, 1942

The FEPC is transferred as an "organizational entity" to the War Manpower Commission (WMC).

August 17, 1942

Roosevelt tells the Committee that the transfer is to "strengthen, not to submerge" it.

August 22, 1942

The undersecretaries of war and the navy issue a joint statement on the employment of aliens and of citizens without birth certificates.

December 1, 1942

The FEPC directs Capital Transit Company to bring employment policies into compliance with EO 8802.

January 9, 1943

Paul McNutt indefinitely postpones planned hearings on the railroad industry, as instructed by Attorney General Biddle.

Railroad special counsels Charles Houston, Harold Stevens, and Henry Epstein resign.

January 18, 1943

Houston writes Roosevelt sharply protesting the postponement of the railroad hearings.

January 1943

MacLean resigns to become a race relations adviser in the Navy Department.

February 3, 1943

Roosevelt announces a special conference of minority group leaders to reconsider the status, scope, and powers of the FEPC.

February 4, 1943

The FEPC is informed it will be reorganized.

February 19, 1943

The minority group conference recommends that the FEPC be removed from the WMC and restored to independent status with adequate budget and personnel.

March 1, 1943

The FEPC complains to Roosevelt that the WMC is not carrying out the WMC-FEPC agreement and requests independent status.

March 1943

Civil rights organizations request immediate and satisfactory action on the FEPC.

April 19, 1943

At the FEPC's meeting the Committee votes to go forward with hearings and permits its members to make their own announcements. An official press release on the decisions is suppressed by the WMC.

April 19, 1943

Dickerson, acting chairman, holds a press conference and announces scheduling of Detroit hearings and Capital Transit hearings and plans for railroad hearings and hearings in St. Louis, Cleveland, Philadelphia, and Baltimore.

May 5, 1943

The FEPC meets with presidential aide Marvin McIntyre.

May 17, 1943

Capital Transit hearings are postponed until June 2 at White House request until after new chairman takes over.

May 27, 1943

Roosevelt issues EO 9346 enlarging upon EO 8802 and establishing a new Committee on Fair Employment Practice, to function as an independent organization within the OEM. Monsignor (later Bishop) Francis J. Haas, dean of the School of Social Sciences at Catholic University, is appointed as the Committee's first paid chairman. Other members are Brophy and Webster from the old Committee; Boris Shishkin, AFL economist (who replaced Fenton as the alternate for Green on the old Committee); Sara Southall, supervisor of employment and service, International Harvester Company; P. B. Young, publisher and editor of the *Norfolk Journal and Guide;* and Samuel Zemurray, president of the United Fruit Company.

July 1, 1943

The FEPC's first regional office opens in New York City.

August 2, 1943

An operating agreement is executed between the FEPC and the WMC.

September 15–18, 1943

Railroad hearings held in Washington, D.C., before the full Committee on charges against twenty-two railroads and thirteen unions.

September 28, 1943

A public hearing is held in Midland, Michigan, before a Committee-appointed hearing commissioner on charges against the Dow Chemical Company.

October 1, 1943

A public hearing is held in Clearfield, Pennsylvania, before a Committee-appointed hearing commissioner on charges against the Northwest Mining and Exchange Company.

October 7, 1943

A ruling by Comptroller-General Lindsay Warren interprets EO 9346 to the effect that the inclusion of a nondiscrimination clause in defense contracts is a directive rather than a mandatory requirement.

October 18, 1943

Malcolm Ross, deputy FEPC chairman and former director of public relations for the National Labor Relations Board, is appointed to succeed Monsignor Haas as chairman.

November 3, 1943

The opening of the FEPC's office in Atlanta completes the organization of the Committee's field division, with nine regional offices and two suboffices.

November 5, 1943

A letter from Roosevelt to Attorney General Biddle makes clear the mandatory nature of the nondiscrimination clause under EO 9346.

November 15–16, 1943

Boilermakers hearings held in Portland, Oregon, before the full Committee on charges against two companies and four unions.

November 19–20, 1943

Boilermakers hearings are held in Los Angeles before the full Committee on charges against three companies and three unions.

December 8, 1943

A public hearing is held in Philadelphia by a subcommittee on charges against the Philadelphia Transportation Company and the Philadelphia Rapid Transit Employees Union.

December 13, 1943

Fourteen railroads issue a joint reply to the Committee's directives.

December 27, 1943

The cases of the fourteen railroads are referred to Roosevelt, as are the cases of the seven unions to whom directives were issued.

January 3, 1944

Roosevelt appoints the Stacy Committee to investigate further the railroad cases.

January 11, 1944

The first of the hearings on the FEPC are held before the Select Committee to Investigate Executive Agencies (Rep. Howard W. Smith, chairman).

March 6, 1944

The White House announces new Committee members to replace Young and Zemurray: Charles L. Horn, president of the Federal Cartridge Corporation, and Charles H. Houston, Washington, D.C., attorney.

March 14, 1944

Ross files a statement on the railroad cases with the House Select Committee.

March 23–25, 1944

The Subcommittee on Deficiencies of the House Committee on Appropriations holds a hearing on the FEPC budget.

APRIL 1944 TO JUNE 1946

February 10–12, 1944

FEPC regional directors meet in Washington, D.C.

May 25–26, 1944

The House of Representatives debates appropriations for the FEPC. Debates continue in June until appropriations bill passes on June 20, allocating the FEPC $500,000 for one year.

August 1–4, 1944

White operators of the Philadelphia Transportation Company strike in response to a requirement from the WMC that the company hire black operators without discrimination. Roosevelt issues orders to seize the company's properties and for the army to operate the lines. Mitchell travels to Philadelphia to investigate the situation (August 1–3) and reports on August 4. White House aide Jonathan Daniels pledges the government will not back down. He relays a request from the mayor of Los Angeles to postpone FEPC hearings on the Los Angeles Street Railway. The FEPC opposes a postponement.

August 1–2, 1944

Hearings are held on eight companies in St. Louis, Missouri.

August 7–8, 1944

Hearings on the Los Angeles Railway Company and rehearings on other major cases are held in Los Angeles.

September 4, 1944

Mitchell submits a report on FEPC complaints against the Machinists Union (IAM). The FEPC agrees to have a subcommittee meet with union president Harvey W. Brown.

September 7, 1944

Mitchell submits a report on complaints against the Post Office Department. The FEPC agrees to ask for a meeting with the postmaster general.

October 7–10, 1944

Mitchell and Eugene Davidson submit reports on FEPC cases involving industries with postwar significance.

October 10, 1944

A subcommittee hearing is held in New York City against the Seafarers International Union.

October 18, 1944

Full Committee hearings are held in Portland, Oregon.

November 25, 1944

Mitchell meets with Postmaster General Frank C. Walker and obtains acknowledgement that the Post Office Department is within FEPC jurisdiction. They reach an understanding that postal employees who accept war service appointments are entitled to their old jobs at the cessation of hostilities if they cannot be retained in the positions to which they have been promoted.

December 18, 1944

The Supreme Court decides three cases concerned with the employment problems of minorities under labor-management contracts: *Steele, Tunstall,* and *Wallace.*

December 18, 1944

Mitchell meets with Maritime Commission officials regarding Gulf region shipbuilding companies. The Delta Shipbuilding case is subsequently resolved.

December 28–30, 1944

An examiner's hearing is held in Houston against the Shell Oil Company and Oilworkers International Union, Local 367.

January 8, 1945

Mitchell issues a further report on Machinist Union cases; the report is submitted to union president Brown for study.

January 12, 1945

An examiner's hearing is held in Zanesville, Ohio, on the Line Material Company.

January 15, 1945

Full Committee hearings are held in Washington, D.C., on the Capital Transit case.

January 31, 1945

Hearings are held in East Alton, Illinois, on the Western Cartridge Company; they continue February 23 and 24.

February 9, 1945

A conference is held with the WMC on the failure by its regional offices to comply with the FEPC-WMC operating agreement.

February 27, 1945

A further meeting is held with the WMC on regional problems regarding FEPC access to employment data.

March 9, 1945

An examiner's hearing is held in St. Louis on the General Cable Company.

March 15–17, 1945

Hearings are held in Cincinnati on eight war industries.

March 19–23, 1945

An examiner's hearing is held in Oakland on Key System and Division 192, Amalgamated Association of Steel, Electric, and Motor Coach Employees of America; the hearing continues June 1 in San Francisco.

March 21, 1945

Roosevelt requests the House to pass a war agencies appropriation bill that includes $599,000 for the FEPC. The House appropriations committee refuses to comply. Consequently, the appropriation bill for 1946 includes no FEPC appropriation; efforts on the House floor to restore the FEPC appropriations fail. A subsequent amendment from Sen. Dennis Chavez for an appropriation of $446,000 for the FEPC is attached to the Senate appropriations bill, but it too fails.

April 12, 1945

Roosevelt dies; Harry S. Truman becomes president.

April 27–July 13, 1945

Hearings and debates are held on FEPC appropriations.

April 1945

FEPC regional directors meet in Washington, D.C.

May 4, 1945

Hearings are held in Houston on the Texas and New Orleans Railroad and the Brotherhood of Railway Trainmen.

May 14, 1945

Hearings are held in Akron on the Goodyear Aircraft Corporation.

May 23, 1945

A conference is held with the Navy Department on the employment of citizens of Japanese ancestry in West Coast establishments.

June 1945

The FEPC's *First Report* is published.

June 2, 1945

An FEPC hearing is held in Detroit.

June 27–29, 1945

A filibuster is staged in the Senate against FEPC appropriations

June 1945

Will Maslow resigns as director of field operations; Mitchell takes over, first as acting director, then as director in July, serving until May 1946. Mitchell continues to send memoranda and reports to Malcolm Ross and other remaining FEPC officials.

July 13, 1945

Congress passes the National War Agencies Appropriation Act of 1946, providing $250,000 for the FEPC to be used for "completely terminating the functions and duties of the Committee," with the stipulation that "in no case shall this fund be available for expenditure beyond June 30, 1946."

August–December 1945

The FEPC reduces its staff from 128 to 31 and closes all its field offices except those in Chicago, Detroit, and St. Louis.

September 6, 1945

President Truman informs Congress that the FEPC will continue during the reconversion period and urges the establishment of a permanent agency.

September 18, 1945

The FEPC notifies Truman of eight categories of pending cases for which decisions and directives are being prepared, including the Capital Transit and Cincinnati cases.

November 23, 1945

The White House orders the postponement of the directive to the Capital Transit Company. In protest, Charles H. Houston submits his resignation from the Committee to Truman.

December 20, 1945

Truman issues EO 9664, continuing the Committee's work for the period, subject to the conditions stated in its appropriation legislation, which limits the FEPC to investigative functions, with no enforcement powers.

April 8, 1946

Mitchell reports to Ross on statements of compliance with the nondiscrimination executive orders solicited from unions.

May 3, 1946

All remaining employees are put on leave without pay. Except for volunteer efforts, all staff operations cease.

June 28, 1946

Along with the resignation of all its members, the Committee submits its *Final Report* to the president. Truman accepts the resignations.

NOTES

The prehistory section was prepared by the editors from HqR6, Proposed Hearings; "Washington Conference on Negro Needs," and "White House Conference on Negroes and Defense," September 27, 1940, NAACP, II A671, DLC; United States, Committee on Fair Employment Practice, *Minorities in Defense*, RG 179, WPB 015.737, PCOFEP, DNA; Reed, *Seedtime*, 13, 175, 176; Garfinkel, *When Negroes March*, 34, 60, 61; Watson, *Lion in the Lobby*, 122; Hardin, *Role of Presidential Advisors*, 79–80; *Facts on File, 1941*, 76; Kryder, *Divided Arsenal*, 247.

The history to April 1944 was prepared by the Division of Research and Analysis, April 1944. The editors have modified the format for style and incorporated additional dates from *Minorities in Defense*. For more timeline details in this period, such as the appointment on May 25, 1942, of McLean as chairman of the FEPC to replace Mark Etheridge, and information on the location of these records, see Zaid, *Preliminary Inventory*.

The history from 1944 to 1946 was compiled by the editors from FEPC Records, RG 228, DNA; and Reed, *Seedtime*, 331.

All entries after August 22, 1942 (except for May 27, 1943) were added by the editors from FEPC records.

FEPC PERSONNEL LIST

MEMBERS OF THE FAIR EMPLOYMENT PRACTICE COMMITTEE

John Brophy (1941–45)
Earl Dickerson (1941–43)
Mark Ethridge (1941–43)
Frank Fenton (alternate, 1941–42)
William Green (1941–43)
Charles L. Horn (1944–46)
Charles Hamilton Houston (1944–45)
Philip Murray (1941–43)
David Sarnoff (1941–43)
Sara E. Southall (1943–46)
Boris Shishkin (alternate 1942–43; member 1943–46)
Milton Webster (1941–46)
P. B. Young (1943–44)
Samuel Zemurray (1943–44)

MAJOR STAFF MEMBERS OF THE FAIR EMPLOYMENT PRACTICE COMMITTEE

Headquarters Staff

Executive Secretary	Lawrence Cramer (1941–43)
Assistant Executive Secretary	George M. Johnson (1943–46)
Chairman	Mark Ethridge (1941–42)
	Malcolm MacClean (1942–43)
	Francis J. Haas (1943)
	Malcolm Ross (1943–45)
Deputy Chairman	George M. Johnson (1943–45)
Assistant to the Chairman for Latin American Affairs	Carlos E. Castañeda (1944–45)

Administration

Director of Budget and Administrative Management	Theodore A. Jones (1943–45)
Administrative Manager	Sinclair V. Jeter (1943–45)

Legal Division

Director	George M. Johnson (acting, 1943–45)
	Maceo W. Hubbard (1945–46)
Hearing Examiners	George W. Crockett (1943–44)
	Maceo W. Hubbard (1943–45)
	Emanuel H. Bloch (1944–45)
	Evelyn Nesbitt Cooper (1944–45)
Trial Attorneys	Simon Stickgold (1945?)
	Frank D. Reeves (1944–45)
Counsel, Western Division	A. Bruce Hunt (1944–45)
Special Counsels	Bartley C. Crum (1943)
	Benjamin Dreyfus (1943)
	Marvin C. Harrison (1943)
	Charles Hamilton Houston (1943)
	Joseph Sharfsin (1944)
	Harold Stevens (1943)

Division of Research and Analysis

Director	John A. Davis (1943–45)
	Marjorie M. Lawson (1945–46)
Assistant Director	Marjorie M. Lawson (1942–45)
Compliance Analysts	Joy A. Davis (1943–45)
	Cornelius L. Golightly (1943–45)

Information Office

Information Officer	St. Clair T. Bourne (1943–45)

Division of Field Operations

Director of Field Operations	Will Maslow (1943–45)
	Clarence Mitchell Jr. (1945–46)

Associate Director	Clarence Mitchell Jr. (1943–45)
	Eugene W. Davidson (1945–46)
Assistant Director	Eugene W. Davidson (1943–45)
Field Representatives and Investigators	John Beecher (1941–42)
	Eugene W. Davidson (1941–43)
	Daniel R. Donovan (1941–43)
	Maceo W. Hubbard (1942)
	A. Bruce Hunt (1943)
	Ruth S. Landes (1941–45)
	Clarence Mitchell Jr. (1943)
	Ernest G. Trimble (1941–43)
Examiners	Ernest G. Trimble (1943–44)
	Emanuel H. Bloch (1943–44)
	Stanley D. Metzger (1944)
	W. Hayes Beall (1944–45)
	Richard J. Roche (1944)
	Muriel Ferris (1945?)

Regional Office Staff

Region I (New England) (see Region II)

Director	Edward Lawson (acting)

Region II (New York Office)

Examiner in Charge	John Beecher (1942–43)
Director	Edward Lawson (1943–45)
Examiners	Madison S. Jones (1943–45
	Daniel R. Donovan (1944–45)
	Robert G. Jones (1942–43), (1944–45)
	Samuel R. Risk (1943–44?)
	Lethia W. Clore (1943)
	St. Clair T. Bourne (1942–43)
	Mildred R. Greenblat (1943)

Region III (Philadelphia Office)

Director	G. James Fleming (1943–45)
Examiners	Milo Manly (1943–44)
	Mildred R. Greenblat (1944–45)
	Samuel R. Risk (1944–45?)
Examiner in Charge, Pittsburgh	Milo Manly (1944–45)

Region IV (Washington, D.C., Office)

Director	Frank Hook (1943–44)
	Joseph H. B. Evans (acting, 1943; 1944–45)
Examiners	Alice R. Kahn (1944)
	W. Hayes Beall (1944–45)
	Richard J. Roche (1944–45)

Region V (Cleveland Office)

Director	William T. McKnight (1943–45)
Examiner in Charge, Cincinnati	Harold James (1945)
	Lethia W. Clore (1945)
Examiners	Lethia W. Clore (1944–45)
	Daniel R. Donovan (1943)
	Olcott R. Abbott (1944–45)

Region VI (Chicago Office)

Director	Eugene W. Henderson (1943–46)
Examiners	Harry H. C. Gibson (1943–45)
	Joy Schulz (1944–45)
	L. Virgil Williams (1944–45)
Examiner, Detroit	G. James Fleming (1943)
Examiner in Charge, Detroit	Edward Swan (1943–45)

Region VII (Atlanta Office)

Director	A. Bruce Hunt (1943–44)
	David Witherspoon Dodge (1944–45)
Examiners	John Hope II (1943–45)
	James H. Tipton Jr. (1944–45?)

Region VIII (see Region VI)

Region IX (Kansas City and St. Louis Offices)

Director	Roy A. Hoglund (1943–46)
Examiner in Charge, St. Louis	Theodore E. Brown (1943–45)

Region X (Dallas Office)

Director	Carlos E. Castañeda (acting, 1943; 1945)
	Leonard M. Brin (1944)
	W. Don Ellinger (acting, 1944–45)
Examiners	Clay Cochran (1943)
	L. Virgil Williams (1943–44)

Region XI (Kansas City and San Antonio Offices)

Director	Roy A. Hoglund (1943–45)
	Carlos E. Castañeda (1945)

Region XII (West Coast Office)

Director	Harry L. Kingman (1943–45)
	Edward Rutledge (1945)
	Bernard Ross (1945)
Examiner in Charge, San Francisco	Edward Rutledge (1943–45)
Examiner in Charge, Los Angeles	Robert E. Brown (1943–45)
Examiners	Frank Pestana (1943–45)
	Jack Burke (1944–45)
	Harold James (1944)
	Bernard Ross (1944–45)

Region XIII (New Orleans Office)

Director	W. Don Ellinger (1945)

A copy of the FEPC's entire schedule of personnel with base pay, as of 12/27/43, is in the HqR18, Records Relating to Hearings. Smith Committee Correspondence.

HEADNOTES

JURISDICTIONAL ISSUES

Because the Fair Employment Practice Committee was created by executive order, not by legislation, it faced constant, open challenges in Congress and elsewhere to its authority to enforce the unprecedented national nondiscrimination policy established by the president. It was nevertheless pushed by the complaints it received to extend its jurisdiction into areas not conceived by its creators. Its stated purpose was not to achieve social change, nor to enter the legal and political segregation thickets, but to strengthen the nation's ability to win the war by ensuring that no individual was denied an opportunity to contribute because of discrimination based on race, creed, color, or national origin. The challenges to the FEPC's authority were particularly intense, not only because of the political nature of Executive Order 8802 but also because the authority granted the Committee applied only to employment discrimination, lasted only for the duration of the war, and was limited to:

> Federal government agencies, including administrative agencies under Congress.
> Plants owned and operated by the federal government.
> Plants owned by the federal government but privately operated.
> Privately owned and operated companies with federal government contractors or with subcontractors.
> Other essential industries, including railroads; steamship lines; radio, telephone, and telegraph companies; vital street railway systems.
> Industries listed as "essential" by the WMC.
> Labor unions whose practices related to or affected employment in war industries or in the service of the federal government.
> Private educational institutions receiving federal funds for war training programs.

Agencies that definitely were not within the FEPC's jurisdiction were:

> Privately owned and operated plants not holding government contracts or subcontracts and not engaged in essential war production.
> Retail stores or professional enterprises, such as specialty shops, beauty parlors, and law offices that held no government contracts or subcontracts and were not engaged in essential war services.
> The armed forces.
> Enterprises that were listed by the WMC as "nonessential."

Agencies that, depending on the circumstances, could fall under the FEPC's jurisdiction were:

State agencies or their political subdivisions.
Enterprises in Hawaii.
Private employment agencies without government contracts.
Quasi-governmental agencies, such as the American Red Cross.
Private educational institutions not receiving federal funds but which were
    training war workers.[1]

Executive Order 9346 had a stronger nondiscrimination clause than EO 8802 and more explicitly forbade discrimination by unions.[2] Even though gender discrimination was not a civil rights issue then, the FEPC devoted considerable attention to opening up employment for African American women. A unique challenge the FEPC faced in those instances was the demand from white women that industry provide them separate toilet facilities. That sometimes meant that African American women had to walk considerable distances from their work stations to the toilet. In the telephone industry, white women opposed the hiring of black women as operators because the job not only required workers to sit side by side but also to cross over each other to connect telephone calls.[3]

The FEPC was defined by the extent to which it was able to establish its jurisdiction. Mitchell's texts are important not for their comprehensive presentation of how the committee achieved that goal, but for demonstrating the manner in which the agency worked to do so and the political, legal and constitutional nuances involved in the process. When the division of field operations was stumped in determining whether it had jurisdiction over a case or employer, it referred the matter to the legal department, which, if it was unable to render a final decision, requested the Committee to do so.[4]

Central to the process of establishing jurisdiction was the first paragraph of EO 9346:

All contracting agencies of the Government of the United States shall include in all contracts hereafter negotiated or renegotiated by them a provision obligating the contractor not to discriminate against any employee or applicant for employment because of race, creed, color, or national origin and requiring him to include a similar provision in all subcontracts.

The mandatory inclusion of the nondiscrimination clause in government contracts gained its major significance as an obligation on war contractors, and it was enforced through government contracting agencies. Despite repeated challenges, the FEPC insisted there was no question regarding the obligation of the government contractor to obey the executive order by including and obeying the nondiscrimination clause. The Committee's jurisdiction was called into question, however, in cases where there were no contracts, especially in the nonproduction war industries.

The FEPC also encountered other problems in establishing its jurisdiction. Owing to the FEPC's case-by-case mode of operating, every challenge to its jurisdiction had to be considered individually. The legal division documented this onerous task in its report covering the period from December 11, 1943, to March 8, 1944, showing it received fourteen cases for opinions on either the interpretation and application of the executive order or of the FEPC's jurisdiction regarding a case. In that same period generally, the legal division handled another eleven cases that were referred to it for a recommendation on whether a hearing should be held.[5]

In the early stages of the FEPC's functioning, President Roosevelt was most helpful in clarifying his intentions regarding the scope of his order. When in 1941 he learned that employers were "discharging workers who happen to be aliens or even foreign-born citizens," he declared on January 2, 1942, that that policy was "as stupid as it is unjust." The following day, at the FEPC's request, he reaffirmed its jurisdiction over aliens:

> I have given careful consideration to the problem raised by you as to the jurisdiction of the Committee on Fair Employment Practice over cases involving alleged discrimination in defense industries based on national origin of noncitizens.
>
> It was the original intent of Executive Order 8802 of June 25, 1941, to include noncitizens in the scope of the Committee's responsibilities. I, therefore, feel it appropriate that your Committee investigate cases in which noncitizens allege that they have been discriminated against because of their national origin in a manner more restrictive than required by the law governing their employment in defense industries.[6]

Confusion, nevertheless, over the extent to which the FEPC could act regarding aliens from countries with which the United States was at war led the agency to suspend action on such cases in 1944. In general the FEPC deferred to the War Department on loyalty issues, but it could challenge the government when it seemed to violate the nondiscrimination policy in barring employment.[7]

In cases involving creed, where the most common conflict was more one of balancing religious worship requirements of workers against the exigencies of war production than of settling jurisdictional challenges, the FEPC resorted to guidance from the War Department policy in addition to shaping its own policy based on its own experiences and authority. The other creedal challenge the FEPC encountered occurred when Jehovah's Witnesses were fired from their jobs because they refused to salute the flag or purchase war bonds. The Committee resolved that religious conflict accordingly:

> Creed was interpreted by the first Committee [on Fair Employment Practice] as embracing adherence to a formalized religious faith, membership in a particular religious denomination or sect, or identification with a particular group which is presumed to be devoted to a code of principles and practices of a religious character. Personal "conscience unrelated to the religious code of an organized sect was not considered creed as a basis of discrimination within the meaning of Executive Order 8802."[8]

On October 7, 1943, Roosevelt was confronted with a more profound challenge when the comptroller general ruled that the first paragraph of EO 9346 "was intended only as a directive," not as a mandate to the contracting government agencies, "so that failure to include such a provision will not render void an otherwise proper contract or render objectionable otherwise proper payments thereunder." The president was unequivocal. At the Committee's request, he wrote Attorney General Francis Biddle on November 6 "to make it perfectly clear that these provisions are mandatory and should be incorporated in all Government contracts. The order should be so construed by all Government contracting agencies."[9]

Challenges by government agencies, such as the Post Office Department, to the Committee's jurisdiction made the FEPC clarify its jurisdiction in this area. The Government Printing Office and the District of Columbia also unsuccessfully challenged the agency's jurisdiction over them.[10]

By 1943 the FEPC was also exploring the interpretation that all agencies receiving federal funds were covered by the nondiscrimination policy, but apparently it could not get around the Lanham Act, which, as George Johnson indicated in his October 24, 1944, memorandum (published herein), prohibited it from intervening.[11]

The War Manpower Commission had by 1942 developed a list of essential war industries based on its own jurisdiction. The Committee accepted as a general guide the WMC's list, but it reserved the right to determine in each case whether the party charged was a war industry based on the FEPC's own unique mission. At the same time, it sought rulings from the general counsel of particular agencies regarding its jurisdiction over various industries. That year, for instance, the Office of the General Counsel of the WMC affirmed that radio broadcasting companies and stations, telephone and telegraph companies, and local and street railways and bus lines were "defense industries." The office reverted to a federal law adopted in 1918 that defined "war utilities" to include, among other things, telephone and telegraph plants, as well as the poles, wires, and fixtures of wireless stations and the buildings connected with their maintenance and operations, which were used to supply communication facilities to any premises related to the war effort, military or naval forces, or any associate nation.

The Office of General Counsel explained that EO 8802 reaffirmed "the policy of the United States that there shall be no discrimination in the employment of workers in *defense industries*" based on race, creed, color, or national origin. The Office of General Counsel concluded that the president's intent regarding the scope of the term "defense industries" could be best appreciated by the order's entire context, which supported a broad interpretation of the term. The first "Whereas" clause declared it to be "the policy of the United States to encourage *full participation in the national defense program* by all citizens of the United States." The policy was reaffirmed "as a prerequisite to the successful conduct of our *national defense production effort*" (emphasis in original). Those words, he said, were broad enough to include any industry and firm whose activities furthered the defense program. Nevertheless, the policy was constantly challenged by companies, unions, and members of Congress, but for the most part it was upheld.[12]

Progressively, especially after the hearings in 1944 by the Select Committee to Investigate Executive Agencies, which was headed by Rep. Howard Smith of Virginia, a battle-shy FEPC became more careful yet more resolute than ever in determining its jurisdiction.

In the wake of the Smith Committee hearings, it stated:

> The power of this Committee, according to the Order, extends to all "war industries." There are numerous industries whose successful functioning and the expeditious satisfaction of whose manpower needs directly and intimately affect the successful prosecution of the war, notwithstanding they have no formal contractual arrangements with any Government agency. The Committee has consistently asserted its jurisdiction in such instances in accordance with its opinion that its power "to investigate" and to "take appropriate steps to obtain elimination of such discrimination" as violates the Order, extends to all industries classified by the War Manpower Commission as "essential" to the effective prosecution of the war. *A fortiori*, its power extends to all employees' unions in those industries.[13]

Nevertheless, in its ruling of March 18, 1944, on the Screen Actors Guild case, for example, the Committee said it had jurisdiction over the motion picture industry in that it would consider any industry a "war industry" if it was classified "essential" by the WMC, "unless there are facts present which warrant a different conclusion." However, it declined jurisdiction over that particular case because the relationship of the work in question to the war effort was "too remote." Thus, despite its assertion following the Smith Committee hearing, the FEPC did not assume jurisdiction over every industry the WMC labeled essential.[14]

In April, Johnson recommended against using the qualifying phrase "unless there are facts present which warrant a different conclusion" in determining jurisdiction. He said that stance afforded "an opportunity to exclude from the Committee's jurisdiction industries which for some reason the Committee does not wish to regard as subject to its jurisdiction." He suggested, instead, basing a general rule of exclusion on a formulation originally developed by George Crockett for hospital cases. Crockett had noted that the WMC listed all hospitals as "essential activities." He acknowledged, "Such a designation by the Commission is entitled to careful consideration," but it should not be regarded as controlling the FEPC's determination of what were and what were not "war industries" or "industries engaged in war production."

The WMC had a broader mandate than the FEPC, Crockett noted, and its authority was not strictly confined to war production activities. He asserted that in the absence of evidence that the institution served primarily war workers, neither state nor private hospitals should be considered war industries or subject to FEPC jurisdiction. Johnson supported Crockett's argument that the FEPC should deal with only those aspects of "essential" industries closely related to war production.[15]

At its April 20 meeting, the Committee concurred with Johnson's and Crockett's reasoning. It agreed that to assert "jurisdiction over all industries classified as 'essential' by the War Manpower Commission was too broad" for its purposes. On May 27 it reiterated its flexibility in a ruling regarding newspapers: "The Committee has concluded that the term 'war industry' is limited to enterprises engaged in (1) the production of war materials, and (2) activities necessary for the maintenance of the production of war materials." The Committee also decided that the tentative definitions it established on coverage of war industries should be submitted to the attorney general and that he be asked to assist in coordinating those definitions with the actions of other agencies for the purposes of enforcing the policies established by EO 9346.[16]

In guidelines the FEPC adopted on September 9, 1944, it reiterated that only two categories of industrial activities were within its jurisdiction: (1) production of war materials and (2) activities essential to the maintenance of war production activities.[17]

Each defense of its jurisdiction, nevertheless, only seemed to invite more challenges. Rep. Lindley Beckworth requested the FEPC's reaction to a statement from another congressman regarding its authority to require the inclusion of the nondiscrimination clause in government leases being renewed. Malcolm Ross, the Committee's chairman, responded that in such instances his agency was only operating under EO 9346:

> It will be observed that the command to include non-discrimination clauses in Government contracts emanates not from FEPC but from the President. It is to be noted further that his command is not to FEPC but to the "contracting agencies of the Government." Hence, it is not accurate to say or imply that non-discrimination clauses are placed in contracts because of "mandatory instructions" from the Committee. The truth is that the Committee is bound by the Executive Order just as other Government agencies are. It has no more authority than they to disregard the Order's provisions.[18]

Ross, of course, was understating the Committee's determination to enforce the order, a resolve not necessarily shared by other agencies. On September 30, 1944, as the nation prepared for reconversion, the Committee declared:

> FEPC's jurisdiction continues even though a portion of the industry is converted to non-war activity so long as the war and non-war activities are commingled or interdependent.
>
> FEPC has jurisdiction over industries not engaged directly in war production so long as their facilities and services are used for the maintenance and services of war industries.
>
> FEPC's jurisdiction over Federal Government employment continues so long as Executive Order 9346 is in effect.

The FEPC clarified its jurisdiction over labor unions by stating that it

> extends to all practices and policies which effect hire, tenure, terms or conditions of war employment including practices and policies in regard to union membership. (Any union discrimination which excludes workers from having an equal voice in the selection of agents handling collective bargaining and grievance procedures, results in discrimination in regard to terms and conditions of employment because of such exclusion).[19]

Johnson's November 1, 1944, memorandum to the legal division, a revision of one he prepared October 27, 1944, explained:

> You will note that this revision attempts to distinguish between those opinions with respect to jurisdiction over the party charged and those opinions with respect to jurisdiction over activities. Moreover, the revision attempts to leave the way open for further consideration of the Committee's jurisdiction under paragraph numbered 4 of the Executive Order as distinguished from its jurisdiction under paragraph numbered 5:

A. Opinions involving the status of the party charged.

1. *Retail Credit Company.* A company making character and loyalty investigations of workers or applicants for work is not a "war industry" subject to the jurisdiction of the Committee. (Whether the character and loyalty investigation of war workers affects employment so as to bring these activities within the jurisdiction of the Committee is not decided).

2. *Banks.* A bank is not a "war industry" subject to the jurisdiction of the Committee.

3. *Animal and Poultry Food Company.* A company engaged in the manufacture of animal and poultry food and extracting "fats" and selling fats to soap makers who in turn extract glyceria may or may not be subject to the jurisdiction of the Committee depending on such factors as whether the raw materials from which glyceria is extracted or used solely for such purpose and the proportion of the business devoted to production of such raw material.

4. *Montgomery Ward and Company (Chicago Plant).* The retail, mail order and warehousing activities of the company at Chicago are not "war industries" within the [intentions?] of Executive Order 9346, nor in the case submitted was there evidence that these activities involve employment related to the performance of the company's contracts with the government.

5. *Stockyards.* Stockyards upon which large packing companies must depend in the execution of government contracts are "war industries" subject to the jurisdiction of the Committee.

6. *Newspapers.* Newspapers of general circulation are not "war industries" subject to the jurisdiction of the Committee.

7. *War housing construction companies.* Companies engaged in the construction of houses for war workers are "war industries" subject to the jurisdiction of the Committee.

8. *Nursery and child care centers.* Nursery and child care schools operated for the benefit of the children of war workers, supported by federal funds pursuant to provisions of a Congressional Act (Lanham Act) are immune from FEPC interference.

9. *Hospitals.* Hospitals which are not devoted primarily to serving war workers are not "war industries" subject to the jurisdiction of the Committee. (Whether rendering medical service to war workers is an activity affecting employment which is subject to the jurisdiction of the committee is not decided).

10. *Private employment agencies.* Private employment agencies engaged in the solicitation, recruitment and placement of war workers are not "war industries" subject to the jurisdiction of the Committee. (Whether solicitation, recruitment and placement of war workers are activities affecting employment is not decided. It is reasonably apparent, however, that these activities are subject to the jurisdiction of the Committee).

B. Opinions involving the nature of activities.

1. *Vocational training.* Vocational training for other than war work is not subject to the jurisdiction of the Committee.

2. *Services of radio broadcasting systems.* Radio communication services are activities subject to the jurisdiction of the Committee. However, the mere dissemination and entertainment services of radio systems are not activities subject to the jurisdiction of the Committee.

3. *The rendition of opinions by the National Railroad Adjustment Board.* A decision of said board holding that the duties of brakemen are to be performed only by regular brakemen and may not be performed by train porters, does not in itself violate the provisions of Executive Order 9346, where the decision does not touch the question of whether Negroes may or may not be employed as regular brakemen.

4. *Refusal of employer to supply employment statistics.* The refusal of an employer to furnish statistics showing the breakdown of his employees by race is not a violation of the provisions of Executive Order 9346.

5 *Discharge of Jehovah's Witness for refusal to buy war bonds.* Discharge from employment for refusal to buy war bonds does not violate the prohibition against discrimination in employment because of creed in the absence of a showing that the purchase of war bonds is contrary to an established precept of the creed. (Committee action)

6. *Refusal of employer to repeal an unsatisfactory decision of a local draft board.* The refusal to make such an appeal on behalf of a Jehovah's Witness does not in itself constitute discrimination in employment because of creed. (Committee action)

7. *Discriminatory advertisements.* Committee statement of policy is as follows:

> "The Committee deems that for an employer within its jurisdiction to publish advertisements for employment which specify that only workers of a particular race or color or creed or national origin are desired, or in anyway specifies a particular race, color or creed or national origin, is discriminatory with respect to hire and employment, and as such violates Executive Order 9346. Such publication is no less a violation because the employer involved employs members of the particular race that the discriminatory advertisement seeks to bar."

8. *Refusal to admit to union membership.* The refusal to admit to union membership because of race does not constitute discrimination in violation of the provisions of Executive Order 9346 in the absence of a showing that such refusal resulted in discrimination in hire, tenure or terms or conditions of employment. (Whether discriminatory exclusion from participation in the

collective bargaining process constitutes discrimination in terms or conditions of employment is not decided.)[20]

Thus in fields only marginally connected to defense, if at all, the FEPC declined jurisdiction or limited jurisdiction only to those establishments or activities that primarily served the war effort. In addition to those exclusions Johnson listed, others were laundries, prisons, and baseball. The *First Report* also listed bakeshops, theaters, hotels, restaurants, wholesale druggists, pottery manufacturers, and educational institutions not conducting war-training programs supported by federal funds as enterprises over which it had declined jurisdiction.[21]

The legal division also considered requests in early 1945 for a ruling on whether the committee had jurisdiction over agricultural workers. In a detailed analysis, attorney Evelyn Cooper told Johnson that the explicit jurisdiction of the WMC and the War Food Administration over agriculture militated against the FEPC's having such authority in that area. For example, she explained, that among other things the WMC was empowered to "estimate the requirements of manpower for industry; receive all other estimates of needs for military, agricultural and civilian manpower;" to "establish policies and prescribe regulations governing all Federal programs relating to the recruitment, vocational training, and placement of workers to meet the needs of industry and agriculture." Thus the WMC's authority over agriculture was not only explicit but also distinct from its authority over industry.[22]

Given the strong distinction between agriculture and industry under the WMC order, Cooper did not believe the FEPC order could be interpreted as covering agricultural employers. However, because 50 percent of processed foods went to the armed forces, it was conceivable to conclude that food processing was a "war industry and hence that growers engaged interdependently and to a substantial extent in processing" were engaged in war industry that came under the FEPC's jurisdiction. In other words, whether or not the FEPC had authority over discrimination cases involving agricultural workers depended on the particular circumstances and the type of documentation the field offices provided.[23]

Although it battled workplace segregation, the FEPC had no explicit mandate to deal with that problem unless it could show that segregation directly caused discrimination in employment.[24]

Because executive orders expired with the end of a president's term, the death of President Roosevelt and the accession of Harry Truman reopened the jurisdiction question. Rather than issuing a new executive order, President Truman merely issued a statement to Congress on September 6, 1945, that the Committee would "continue during the reconversion period" and requested Congress to create a permanent agency. The FEPC feared its jurisdiction over war industries, and particularly over reconverting industries, was at an end and asked Truman to clarify its status, but he did not respond. So business continued as usual. Mitchell reported on September 27, 1945, that regional offices were taking action on various cases and that "so far, the question of FEPC jurisdiction over these companies has not arisen." Mitchell therefore suggested that the FEPC carry on "an aggressive program with the hope that we can make the most of what voluntary cooperation we can obtain." In December, Truman issued EO 9664, authorizing the FEPC to investigate, to make findings and recommendations, but not to issue directives, and to report discrimination in industries contributing to military production or to the effective transition to a peacetime economy.[25]

In addition to continuing challenges to its authority, the FEPC faced doubts over its right to issue directives and the extent to which parties had to comply. Its lack of enforcement powers meant that certain industries were able to defy its directives with impunity, while others were able to stall until it went out of existence. The Smith Committee challenges helped sharpen the FEPC's awareness of its limitations. Truman added salt to the FEPC's wounds by blocking its issuance of a directive in the contentious Capital Transit Company case. Finally, Congress terminated the FEPC's authority, first by denying it appropriations and then by refusing to authorize a permanent agency after the war.[26]

NOTES

1. These details are taken from Maslow's Field Instruction no. 7, 9/11/43, to all regional directors regarding the jurisdiction of FEPC as to parties charged, which is in HqR78, Field Instructions. Aug. 1943–May 1945 (entry 46) Field Instructions, 1–19. See also the text of Executive Order 8802 in appendix 1; *First Report*, 5–7; George Johnson memorandum to Legal Division, "Jurisdictional Problems Handled by the Legal Division," 10/27/44, and, "Statement of the President's Committee of Fair Employment Practice Adopted September 9, 1944, Relating to Its Jurisdiction over 'War Industries' as That Term is Used in Executive Order 9346," both in HqR5, Office Files of George M. Johnson. Maceo Hubbard.

2. See the text of EO 9346 in appendix 1.

3. For cases involving discrimination against minority women, see, for example, Mitchell's memoranda of 3/16, 7/16/43, 12/6/44, 2/19/45 (–2); and the headnote on the Telephone Industry.

At the 8/28/43 Committee meeting, Mitchell held up the exemplary progress the Western Electric Company in Baltimore had made in achieving "complete integration" of its workforce. In 1941, he noted, the company had approximately eleven African American workers there. The Baltimore plant at Point Breeze decided to follow the company's national policy and as a result increased the number of African Americans there to eight hundred, or roughly 10 percent of the total workforce. Faced with efforts to introduce segregated toilet facilities at Western Electric Point Breeze plant, nevertheless, the Committee at its 12/4/43 meeting approved the following statement of action it had adopted at its 11/16 meeting: "Following has Committee approval for use in Western Electric Case—the Committee takes the position that in the circumstances of this case where there are frequent and temporary transfers of workers from department to department such installing of segregated duplicate facilities cannot but lead to discriminatory employment practices and would be in violation of Executive Order 9346." Transcript of Proceedings, 8/28/43, 102–3, HqR64, Central Files; Minutes, 12/4/43, HqR1, Summary Minutes of Meetings.

4. For a detailed exposition on the FEPC's jurisdiction, see *First Report*, ch. 6, "Interpretation of the Executive Order," 46–64.

5. See the Committee's interpretation that EO 9346 required the inclusion of the nondiscrimination clause in all governments contracts in Minutes, 12/4/43, and its approval of a nine-point statement of policy on the subject, Minutes, 12/27/43, both in HqR1, Summary Minutes of Meetings; the joint letter from Henry L. Stimson, secretary of war, Frank Knox, secretary of the navy, and E. S. Land, chairman of the U.S. Maritime Commission, 7/2/42, stipulating the responsibilities of their agencies

for enforcing the nondiscrimination principles regarding (a) government establishments, such as navy yards and army arsenals, (b) government-owned, privately operated plants, and (c) privately owned, privately operated plants having government contracts, in HqR67, Central Files. Reports, U.S. Government, War Department; and *First Report,* 46–47.

The FEPC defined discrimination accordingly:

(1) the submission of any hiring specification which excludes from employment occupationally qualified workers of a certain race, color, creed, national origin, or citizenship; (2) the refusal to hire because of race, creed, color, national origin or citizenship of an occupationally qualified worker referred by the USES or the repeated refusal to hire for vacancies for which they are referred, available occupationally qualified workers of a certain race, creed, color, national origin, or citizenship, except that the refusal to hire available occupationally qualified workers because of citizenship, in instances where an employer is engaged in production under "classified" or aeronautical government contracts and the government contracting agency has refused approval for the employment of such workers, shall not be considered discrimination; (3) the failure to request consent for the employment of an alien or to employ him upon securing such consent, if except for his alien status he would have been hired.

Discrimination by an employee of the United States Employment Service is defined as the failure to properly register and classify occupationally qualified applicants because of their race, color, creed, national origin, or citizenship; or the failure to refer such applicants when qualified. (Operations Bulletin No. 1, President's Committee on Fair Employment Practice, War Manpower Commission [Confidential], in NAACP Washington Branch, FEPC, DHU-MS)

6. *First Report,* 49–50. For press release, 1/2/42, in which Roosevelt called the discharge of aliens "stupid," see HqR86, Press Releases; for text of Roosevelt's letter, and the joint statement on the "Application of Antidiscrimination Clause," by the secretary of war, attorney general, secretary of the navy, and chairman of the Maritime Commission, see *First Report,* app. 1, 146–47.

7. See *First Report,* 49–51, and the discussion on alienage cases.

8. *First Report,* 54n16. Also see the headnote on Creedal Discrimination.

9. For full text of Roosevelt's letter, see *First Report,* 47; app., 145.

10. The Post Office Department becomes the United States Postal Service in 1971; on jurisdiction over post offices, see Mitchell's memorandum of 5/3, and notes, 9/7/44, 11/25/44, and his weekly reports of 5/8, 5/17, 11/27/44, and the headnote on Relationships with Federal Agencies. On GPO, see Office of the General Counsel, WMC, to George Johnson, 9/25/42, HqR5, Office Files of George M. Johnson. Opinions. In 11/43, regarding a case involving the District of Columbia Boxing Commission, Johnson concluded that the government of the district was covered by the presidential executive orders and hence was under FEPC jurisdiction. See Johnson to Maslow, 11/4/43, HqR63, Central Files. Will Maslow; FR45, D.C. Boxing Commission, Washington, D.C., 4-GR-171, Dr. G. Herbert Marshall. That this formulation was adopted is shown by the inclusion of the District of Columbia under the heading of government in the in-house statement regarding jurisdiction cited in note 12, below. For the opinion of the Office of the General Counsel on the Application of Executive Order no. 8802 to Government Printing Office, 9/25/42, see Operations Bulletin no. 1, note 14, in FEPC Files, Papers of the Washington, D.C., NAACP Branch, DHU-MS, app.

11. The Lanham Act, or National Defense Housing Act of 1940, authorized the War and Navy Departments and the Housing Authority to cooperate in providing public housing for servicemen and defense workers in areas of acute need. Apparently included in the act was a provision that barred the FEPC from applying the nondiscrimination clause to certain areas of federal funding. *Congress and the Nation,* 473, 1196. See also Mitchell's memorandum of 4/28/43.

12. On the development and application of the concept of "essential" industries, see *First Report,* 47; Office of General Counsel memorandum, 9/28/42, in HqR6, Office Files of George M. Johnson. Miscellaneous; Mitchell's memoranda of 1/8/44, and notes, 2/21/44, 5/17/44; rulings of the General Counsel of the Office of Production Management in Operations Bulletin no. 1, app., nn15–17, FEPC files, Papers of the Washington, D.C., NAACP Branch, MSCHU. "Statement of the President's Committee on Fair Employment Practice," HqR5, Office Files of George M. Johnson. Undesignated (blank) folder.

The Office of the General Counsel of the Office of Emergency Management had declared railroads to be defense industries early in 1942. See Minutes, 1/18/42, HqR1, Summary Minutes of Meetings. For rulings regarding steamship lines, see Office of the General Counsel, WMC, to George Johnson, memorandum, 4/29/42, HqR5, Office Files of George M. Johnson. Opinions.

13. Draft statement, n.d., "The Jurisdiction of FEPC over Complaints Alleging Discrimination Employment Practices in Essential War Industries," in HqR5, Office Files of George M. Johnson. Legal Division.

14. See Minutes, 3/18/44, HqR1, Summary Minutes of Meetings; Johnson to Committee Members, 4/5/44, in HqR5, Office Files of George M. Johnson. Shishkin.

For the Committee's discussion of the Screen Actors Guild case and the motion picture industry, which the WMC listed as essential, see Transcript of Proceedings, 4/20/44, 2–8, HqR64, Central Files; Mitchell's weekly reports of 2/28, 3/6, 4/3/44, and notes. On the Smith Committee hearings, see the headnote on Street and Local Railways; for the FEPC's battles with the railways and railroad unions, see the introduction.

15. See Johnson to Committee members, memorandum, 4/5/44, HqR5, Office Files of George M. Johnson. Legal Division; Crockett to Johnson, memorandum on Bridgeport Hospital case, 3/13/44, HqR4, Office Files of George M. Johnson. Frank Reeves.

16. Crockett to Johnson, memorandum, 5/4/44, on Application of Executive Order 9346 to Baking Companies and Dairies, in HqR3, Office Files of George M. Johnson. George W. Crockett; "Proposed Committee Statement of Policy in re Jurisdiction over Newspapers," 5/26/44, HqR5, Office Files of George M. Johnson. Sara Southall; Transcript of Proceedings, 4/20/44, 2–8, and, for its discussion of jurisdiction over hospitals, 5/27/44, 51–64, both in HqR65, Central Files.

17. Johnson to Mitchell, 10/6/44, on hospital cases, FR2, Region I. Closed Cases G–Z, Peter Bent Brigham Hospital, 1-BU-69; and "Statement Adopted September 29, 1944," HqR5, Office Files of George M. Johnson. Undesignated (blank) folder.

18. Ross to Beckworth, 11/3/44, responding to his letter of 9/21/44, in HqR4, Office Files of George M. Johnson. Committee Matters.

19. Minutes, 9/30/44, HqR1, Summary Minutes of Meetings.

20. HqR5, Office Files of George M. Johnson. Maceo Hubbard. For the Committee's extended discussion of jurisdiction over all aspects of union activity, see Transcript of Proceedings, 9/30/44, 33–56, HqR65, Central Files.

21. *First Report*, 47–48; and Mitchell's weekly report, 5/1/7/44; related texts in HqR8, Office Files of Evelyn N. Cooper. (entry 18) Opinions on Jurisdiction; and HqR63, Central Files. Reports, Rulings, General.

On hospitals, see Mitchell's reports of 5/8, 5/17, 5/24, 10/16/44 and memoranda of 2/22, 5/5, 5/20/44, and notes; and Johnson to Mitchell, 10/6/44, and related texts, FR2, Region I. Closed Cases G–Z, Peter Bent Brigham Hospital, 1-BU-69. On baseball, see Mitchell's memorandum, 8/3/45. On radio, see Mitchell's memorandum of 7/7/44 and notes. On newspapers, see Minutes, 5/27, 6/13/44, HqR1, Summary Minutes of Meetings. On movie theaters, see Mitchell's second memorandum of 1/8/44, and notes, and his report of 1/14/44. On employment agencies and employee investigation agencies, see Mitchell's memoranda of 8/7 (3), 8/14/44, and notes; and the discussion of the Retail Credit Corporation cases in the headnote on National Origin, Alienage, and Loyalty. On prisons, see Mitchell's memoranda, 4/28/43, 8/24/45. On department stores, see Mitchell's memorandum of 8/8/44. On the food industry, especially the baking and dairy industries, see Mitchell's report of 5/17/44, and notes. On the laundry industry, defined as locally essential by WMC, see the weekly report of 4/17/44.

22. Johnson to Evelyn Cooper, 2/10/45, request for an analysis of the problem, and her detailed response of 3/3/45, both in HqR4, Office Files of George M. Johnson. Evelyn Cooper; and EO 9139, creating the WMC.

23. Cooper to Johnson, 3/3/45, HqR4.

24. On the segregation issue, see Mitchell's memoranda of 7/24/43, 1/10/44, 8/8/45, his weekly report of 5/8/44, and his field investigation report of 6/8/43, and notes, in appendix 1; and the headnote on Strikes and Work Stoppages. See also Field Instruction no. 47, 4/14/45, which quotes Ross's testimony before the Senate Committee on Appropriations 6/5/44: "The Committee has never taken the position that segregation *per se* is contrary to the provisions of Executive Orders 8802 and 9346. It rec-

ognizes, as it must, that its jurisdiction is limited to obtaining the elimination of discrimination in regard to hire, tenure, terms or conditions of employment, or union membership, and, in this case, where the issue of segregation is involved, as in all cases, the Committee's action will depend upon the existence or absence of evidence of prohibited discrimination." HqR78, Field Instructions, 8/43–5/45, 40–59.

25. Minutes, 9/4, 9/15/45, HqR1, Summary Minutes of Meetings; Reed, *Seedtime*, 329–32, 337.

26. For Johnson's response to denial that FEPC directives had the force of law, see his memorandum to the legal division, 1/28/44, on "Legal Questions Presented by the Positions Taken by the Parties Charged in the Railroad Hearings, the West Coast Hearings and the Philadelphia Transportation Company Hearings," HqR5, Office Files of George Johnson. Legal Division. Newspapers and magazines widely covered the Capital Transit debacle. See also the headnote on Street and Local Railways; Reed, *Seedtime*, 332–43; Watson, *Lion in the Lobby*, 149–51.

RELATIONSHIPS WITH FEDERAL AGENCIES

The FEPC had informal working relationships with many government agencies and formal operating agreements with eight.[1] In several cases, the FEPC's regional directors negotiated local agreements with their counterparts at other agencies, which generally led to the signing of national agreements.

The War Manpower Commission was primarily responsible for mobilizing the nation's manpower, while the War Shipping Administration assigned seamen to vessels. In addition to hiring, the WSA was responsible for promoting and training without regard for race, creed, color, or national origin. The War Department, the Navy Department, and the United States Maritime Commission were the contracting agencies. They were "obliged to insert a nondiscrimination clause in every war contract, and in theory, at least, a violation of this clause put the whole contract in jeopardy," the *Final Report* explained. "Such obligations to assure equality in war-work opportunities, although legally air tight, in practice had many leaks," it said. Hard-pressed government agencies often saw policing implementation of the nondiscrimination clause as an unwelcome extra chore. Furthermore, some officials were not sympathetic to the FEPC's goals, while others feared work stoppages by white workers if they employed or promoted minorities. The FEPC was an administrative agency. It administered statutory requirements related to stated forms of discrimination. It became involved in a discriminatory situation only upon the request of a complainant, and then it sought to address the problem along established procedures. It saw its role as a dual one: "to cooperate with all other agencies in their independent handling of discrimination problems and to process charges which these other agencies could not themselves solve." In many cases, it simultaneously was involved with several other agencies on both the local and national levels in efforts to resolve complaints.[2]

The FEPC did not have the sanction power to back up its regulations. Consequently, it relied on the cooperation of other government agencies with power to take such actions as lowering the priority ratings of businesses, making it harder for them to secure workers and material; refusing to refer workers to discriminating firms; or, in extreme cases, denying or revoking their contracts. Additionally, cooperating agencies could revoke draft deferments of striking or otherwise recalcitrant workers and deny clearances for them to work in other defense industries. In cases of plant shutdowns by strikes or violence, the military could, and sometimes did, take over "essential" businesses and operate them until order was restored.

Working agreements, which were intended to establish predictable courses of action, set timetables for responses and signaled to other departments that their staffs were expected to cooperate with the FEPC in implementing the national nondiscrimination policy. In general, agreements specified that the government agency would exhaust its remedies in eliminating discrimination and inform the FEPC of the results. The FEPC entered a case only when a department or agency could not, or would not, resolve it. When they had been fully established, the FEPC's regional offices assumed more responsibility for handling agreements.[3]

Negotiating agreements could be time consuming and delicate, and some staff of the other agencies refused to abide by them, particularly in the South, and their superiors were unwilling to risk local upheavals or damaging political consequences to enforce nondiscrimination measures. Good examples of such problems can be found in the reports on the FEPC's dealings with the WMC and the United States Employment Service.[4]

The WMC and USES

The War Manpower Commission's comprehensive programs in training, placing, and using workers in a nondiscriminatory manner were especially valuable for the FEPC. When the old FEPC was under the WMC's jurisdiction, between mid-1942 and mid-1943, the agency conducted investigations with WMC personnel. The problem then was that although that administrative arrangement was ostensibly designed to improve cooperation between the two agencies, many interpreted Roosevelt's shifting it to a place where it was under the control of Paul McNutt, the unfriendly chairman of the WMC, as an effort to muzzle the FEPC. Those fears were confirmed by the WMC's abrupt cancellation of the crucial railroad hearings the FEPC had scheduled for early 1943 and its general go-slow policy toward discrimination.

Bending to criticism, Roosevelt reversed himself in July 1943 and made the FEPC an independent agency in the President's Office of Emergency Management. Nevertheless, several jurisdictional questions continued to hamper a smooth working relationship between them even though both agencies had a well-established history of cooperation. There was also a deep reservoir of suspicion within the FEPC about the motivation and willingness of WMC leaders to act on discrimination complaints. Under a new operating agreement they signed on August 2, 1943, the WMC was responsible for handling complaints and evidence of discrimination. Procedures were adopted for dealing with various types of cases, and each WMC regional office was required to appoint a staff member to coordinate its nondiscrimination activities with the FEPC.[5]

Under the agreement, the United States Employment Service was not to clear discriminatory hiring or training requests. The WMC was to persuade the offending employer or agency to remove such discriminatory specifications; if the company did not comply within ten days, the USES was to submit a "510 report" on the discriminatory work order to the regional FEPC director. If after further negotiations no settlement was reached, the FEPC was to process the case in cooperation with the WMC. In training programs, similar steps were to be followed to end discrimination. If, under state law, training programs were segregated, the WMC was obligated to see that there was no other discrimination involved. Complaints involving firms not already in contact with the WMC fell under the FEPC's immediate jurisdiction and were handled by its regional director. The regional director could request the WMC to act on a complaint; if it did not act on time, the FEPC would take over the case.[6]

The most common complaints were against Regions IV (Maryland, the District of Columbia, Virginia, West Virginia, and North Carolina), VII (the Southeast), and X (the Southwest), where WMC regional directors were especially unwilling to comply with the operating agreement. The FEPC charged that the WMC in those areas also failed to ensure equal access to training programs.[7] In the South, USES offices were segregated. They often accepted and complied with discriminatory work orders from companies and refused to file an ES 510 report regarding the order; and they failed to provide the FEPC with information from ES 270 reports indicating the extent of minority employment. There FEPC regional and national officials, with only limited success, spent much time seeking to obtain cooperation from the WMC and USES staffs.[8]

Although Mitchell and other FEPC staff complained about many WMC officials, they singled out some for praise, particularly Anna Rosenberg, director of Region II (New York). Initially, Rosenberg accepted a segregated arrangement for minority workers recruited in New York by Kaiser shipyards for work in Portland, Oregon, and Vancouver, Washington. Following intense criticism, her office defined segregation as a form of discrimination and developed instructions for the region that went well beyond those in the manual of operations of the WMC. Region II's guidelines explained in detail the practices that constituted discrimination and set forth steps to eliminate it. Rosenberg appointed a regional staff committee on discrimination and assigned it to assist and advise the regional director on policy and procedure. Consequently, the WMC's Region II automatically denied referral services to employers and training agencies that submitted discriminatory orders. Agencies in Region II, such as the War Shipping Administration and Civil Service Commission, to which WMC functions had been delegated also were required to observe the nondiscriminatory policy. Although no other region established equally desirable guidelines, some WMC regional offices worked well with the FEPC, especially those on the West Coast and in the Midwest.[9]

At war's end, as the FEPC faced its own demise, it negotiated with the WMC to ensure appropriate consideration for minorities in its peacetime reconversion plans and sought to include FEPC staff in planning meetings. It expressed concern over the return of the USES to the states, where segregation and discrimination were likely to go unchallenged. However, it did not succeed in blocking the return of those services, leaving Mitchell and the NAACP to continue that battle after the war.[10]

The War Department

Loyalty Investigations

Executive Order 8972 authorized the secretaries of war and navy to protect defense material and facilities from sabotage. This policy, though, invited conflicts with EO 8802, which barred discrimination based on race, creed, color, national origin, or alienage (see the headnote on National Origin, Alienage, and Loyalty). Under EO 8972, the War Department issued instructions for determining the loyalty of persons with access to defense material, premises, and utilities. The instructions often included asking questions about race, creed, and national origin that conflicted with the nondiscrimination policy.

To avoid jurisdictional conflicts with the War Department while still checking for potential abuses, the FEPC negotiated an agreement with the provost marshal's office. Under the agreement, signed March 10, 1943, the FEPC agreed, contrary to its general policy, to permit government agencies to inquire about race, creed, and national origin in security investigations after a worker had been hired. It also agreed not to object to such questions in investigations of members of the armed services and the Women's Army Auxiliary Corps or in investigations conducted at the request of the War Relocation Authority, which had authority over Japanese aliens and Japanese Americans. The provost marshal general, though, agreed to ban the release of that data to outside parties. The agreement also permitted employers or government representatives concerned about an employee's loyalty to refer the case to the provost marshal general or his representatives for a loyalty investigation. The final determination of the person's employability then rested with the provost marshal general, acting for the War Department. In such cases, it was also agreed that race, creed, color, and national origin could be considered in making the necessary loyalty determination.[11]

Although it generally had to defer to the War Department when loyalty issues arose, the FEPC did question some government policies that it thought exceeded security requirements. It challenged a General Accounting Office ban on the hiring of Japanese Americans. It got the Coast Guard to end its restriction on the hiring of Japanese American merchant seamen, but it was unable to get the Navy Department to end its ban on the employment of Japanese Americans in naval installations on the West Coast.[12] For a time, the FEPC also handled individual cases of discrimination based on alienage or national origin. However, because of controversy over cases involving enemy aliens, it suspended action on alienage cases in 1944, pending a requested clarification of its authority from the White House, which never came.[13]

Adhering to the Nondiscrimination Policy

The War Department owned or operated innumerable defense plants and signed thousands of military contracts. As the largest government employer of civilian workers in the nation, the department therefore drew a large number of FEPC complaints that often made their relationship prickly. Mitchell frequently charged that responses from the War Department were dilatory, evasive, or an apparent attempt at "covering up rather than cooperation." Finally, on November 20, 1944, he complained:

> Our experiences in recent weeks with the War Department show that our present relationship is of no real value. In an effort to facilitate the handling of cases, I have made trips to the War Department for the purpose of reviewing files. After reviewing such files, I have attempted to rely on informal agreements, in addition to written requests for the accomplishment of results. It now appears that nothing has been gained by such visits, and shortly I shall present a recommendation on this problem.

On November 24, after long negotiations, the FEPC and the War Department revised their operating agreement. It authorized FEPC local examiners investigating complaints to request conferences with a plant's commanding officer or other representatives. Only if no compliance was obtained through negotiation at the local level was the case to be referred to the FEPC for negotiations. Should that process fail, the case was to be referred to the full Committee.[14]

Many cases were resolved at the local level. Unresolved ones that reached the FEPC were in fact negotiated by Mitchell and Truman K. Gibson, the War Department's civilian aide. Because one of the War Department's primary concerns was avoiding conflicts that would disrupt war production, it was vulnerable to threats of strikes in attempts to enforce the nondiscrimination policy. It often acted with less speed and resolve on complaints than the FEPC wanted. Consequently, Mitchell often criticized Gibson and other War Department staff for being insufficiently cooperative or even obstructionist.[15]

Mitchell, as well as Malcolm Ross, cited the War Department's attempt to obstruct the General Cable Company's implementation of the nondiscrimination policy as an example of their frustration. While the FEPC was attempting to get General Cable to hire African American women alongside white women at its St. Louis plant, the department sent two generals to the agency to urge it to end its efforts there. But Dwight Palmer, the company's president, began integrating the women without incident. Both Mitchell and Ross lauded Palmer's courage. Facetiously, Ross commented that "a two-general call meant a first-class crisis." The *Final Report* more tactfully explained that there were "powerful reasons" behind the department's policy of "production first," and praised the army for its contribution to eliminating discrimination. "FEPC through experience knew that most strike threats were bluff," the report said, and the Committee therefore "differed with Army personnel on occasion." Nevertheless, these "exceptions aside," it clearly appreciated the army's cooperation in implementing the president's executive order.

The *Final Report* also sought to pave the way for future nondiscrimination efforts by the army. It noted the War Department's admonition to commanding generals to retain the nondiscrimination policy during reconversion, and published Secretary of War Patterson's letter of March 16, 1946, which promised that the department would be "unrelaxing in its efforts to further the purposes and objectives of the FEPC."[16]

The Navy Department, War Shipping Administration, and Maritime Commission

Because of the extensive wartime shipbuilding and shipping programs, the FEPC's relations with the Navy Department, War Shipping Administration, and Maritime Commission were also crucial. As early as July 2, 1942, the Maritime Commission issued a joint statement with the War and Navy departments indicating its working relationship with the first FEPC. The second FEPC signed operating agreements with the Maritime Commission on November 5, 1943; with the War Shipping Administration on June 16, 1944; and with the Navy Department on December 9, 1944.

The Maritime Commission required a nondiscrimination clause in all its contracts, and it worked with the FEPC to develop orderly procedures for handling complaints arising in its shipyards or those filed originally with the first FEPC. The procedures were sorely tested at Southern shipyards, especially at two major locations, Alabama Dry Dock in Mobile and Delta's shipyards at New Orleans. Both yards expanded tremendously during the war, importing many laborers from throughout the region. They desperately needed skilled workers, especially welders, but the white workers opposed the hiring or training of blacks for that job. After its hearings in Birmingham in 1942, the FEPC directed Alabama Dry Dock to end hiring discrimination. When the company sought to comply by placing black welders on a night shift, a group of whites the next day attacked them and drove them from the yard. To end the strike, the FEPC and the Maritime Commission agreed to a controversial settlement that accepted black welders on segregated shipways.

The FEPC also directed Delta Shipbuilding to end its discrimination following the Birmingham hearings in 1942. In 1944 the Maritime Commission ordered the firm to use the black welders available, despite warnings of violence from the company. Black welders were thus employed without incident. Nonetheless, despite considerable progress in the employment of skilled blacks in Northern and West Coast yards, the FEPC and Maritime Commission were able to make only limited progress in using them as anything but unskilled laborers in Southern shipyards (see the headnote on the Shipbuilding Industry and the Boilermakers Union).

With its requirement of a nondiscrimination clause in all its contracts, the Navy Department became a major employer of minority wartime workers at government-owned and -operated yards. It hired more minority workers and provided them with more opportunities for skilled work than did privately owned and operated naval facilities. That admirable record notwithstanding, the FEPC received many discrimination complaints that were usually related to assignments, working conditions, promotion, upgrading, and discipline. The placement by navy yards of racial identification on employee badges was another strong source of complaints, and thus they were removed (see the headnote on Race, Creed, Color, or National Origin on Employment Application Forms). The FEPC also fought bans on the employment of Japanese Americans on merchant vessels and at West Coast shore facilities. Through its negotiations with Ralph Bard, undersecretary of the navy, the FEPC resolved most of its cases. In 1946 the FEPC secured a navy pledge to continue the nondiscriminatory policy after the war, but segregation and discrimination still remained serious problems, especially in the South.[17]

The FEPC's operating agreement with the Maritime Commission also included a requirement for the inclusion of the nondiscrimination clause in all its shipbuilding contracts, enabling it to play an active role in settling discrimination complaints at shipyards. The commission's commitment was tested early during the Alabama Dry Dock strike as a result of its participation in the agreement that established the segregated shipways.[18]

The FEPC was also involved in implementing some provisions for upgrading blacks at Delta's shipyards. The *Final Report* explained that the commission helped ensure considerable use of minorities on the East and West coasts, but it made little progress in securing the upgrading of blacks in Southeastern and Gulf Coast shipyards. There African Americans remained limited largely to unskilled positions.

The War Shipping Administration, through its Recruitment and Manning Organization, recruited huge numbers of merchant seamen. But the Smith Committee during its hearings strongly attacked the RMO for its opposition to discrimination. The RMO conducted training that respected equal opportunity and practiced no segregation in eating or sleeping arrangements. In cooperation with the FEPC, the RMO persuaded some shippers to hire without discrimination. Primary hiring authority on merchant vessels lay with the relevant unions. The RMO became involved only if unions could not provide full crews. It applied a rotary dispatching system whereby the first available man on the department list was referred to a job, irrespective of race or color. Under an agreement with the FEPC, the RMO first attempted to end discrimination. Only after its efforts failed did it refer the case to the FEPC. By that time, though, the ship probably had sailed without the seamen who had filed the complaint, because the RMO was unwilling to interfere with the prompt sailing of a vessel. Nevertheless, RMO officials publicly denounced discrimination as both unlawful and inefficient. The RMO further contributed to the nondiscrimination struggle by presenting evidence of peaceful shipboard relations on integrated ships, a situation confirmed by the FEPC's investigations in New York. Some unions, however, remained opposed to implementing the nondiscrimination policy. One was the Seafarers International Union, which complained to Congress because the RMO was unwilling to sanction segregated crews. Owing to those complaints, the Smith Committee charged that the RMO's top New York officials were radicals or Communist sympathizers because they were promoting "social equality" aboard ship. Since the

Seafarers Union disregarded the FEPC's directive against discrimination at war's end, and the War Shipping Administration was dissolved, the problem of seaboard discrimination remained "to be solved by the peacetime American Merchant Marine service," the *Final Report* explained.[19]

The U.S. Civil Service Commission

The CSC, with which the FEPC signed an operating agreement in November 1943, had jurisdiction over employment discrimination by federal agencies. The CSC pledged to forward copies of discrimination complaints to the FEPC and to send it reports on actions it had taken. Under the agreement, if the FEPC's regional directors did not consider the reports satisfactory they could docket and process cases.[20]

The CSC conducted loyalty investigations of government employees, and it developed policies on the employment of Japanese Americans. Its practices in both areas aroused charges of discrimination that the FEPC considered. Although African Americans made greater progress proportionately in public employment during the war than in any other area, the FEPC and civil rights groups remained generally unsatisfied with the CSC's record.[21] Mitchell complained that the CSC rarely found discrimination, no matter how much evidence the FEPC provided it. He classified the government (see his July 1946 article in volume II) as a major discriminator and cited the State Department, the Justice Department, and the General Accounting Office as having poor records on employing blacks and other minorities.[22]

The NWLB, WPB, and U.S. Conciliation Service

In addition to the military services and the WMC, several federal agencies were involved in resolving labor issues that might interfere with wartime production. Among them were the War Production Board (WPB) and its Office of Labor Production, the National War Labor Board, and the U.S. Conciliation Service of the Department of Labor. Established in 1942, the WPB superceded the Office of Production Management and various other agencies, and remained in existence until November 1945. It exercised general direction over federal war procurement and production programs. For a time, both the Negro Employment and Training Branch, where Mitchell worked in 1942, and later the WMC were under its jurisdiction. The NWLB, also established in January 1942, made final determinations on all outstanding industrial disputes that might hinder wartime production. The tripartite board included representatives from the public, industry, and labor sectors. Its scope expanded in October 1942 after it was assigned much of the task of administering salary and wage regulation under the war stabilization program. Enacted on October 2, 1942, the stabilization program froze prices, wages, and salaries to their September 15, 1942, levels, but it permitted adjustments to inequities in wages and working conditions. The NWLB then became part of a more comprehensive program of economic stabilization, controlling civilian purchasing power, including prices, rents, wages, salaries, profits, rationing, and subsidies. The NWLB's stated goals were prevention of avoidable increases in the cost of living, minimization of migration of labor from one industry to another, and the facilitation of wartime production.

As a result of this increased workload, twelve regional boards were established, with the same tripartite structure as the national board. The regional boards made final decisions in labor disputes and rulings on wage and salary adjustments if collective bargaining and the efforts of the U.S. Conciliation Service had failed. The board adopted and sought to enforce a policy of equal pay for equal work and it supported equal opportunity for promotions, often challenging discrimination based on race, creed, or national origin.[23] After the FEPC's regional offices were established in 1943, the FEPC often interacted with the board on both the national and regional levels.[24]

The FEPC signed agreements with the NWLB on March 11, 1944, and with the Office of Labor Production of the WPB on May 30, 1944.[25] In addition to providing for sharing of information and forwarding of complaints, the agreements permitted the FEPC to request the boards to withhold material and labor allocation priorities and other privileges from employers who discriminated on the basis of race or creed. Mitchell received amicable cooperation from these agencies, but there were occasional conflicts. The Non-Ferrous Metals Commission, a subagency of the WPB, cooperated with the FEPC in investigating mining cases in the Southwest, and the WPB upheld on appeal the Non-Ferrous Metals Commission's ruling requiring equal pay for equal work (see the headnotes on Mexican Americans and on the Mining Industry). The WPB invited the FEPC to assist in the labor disputes at Jones and Laughlin Steel near Pittsburgh, and the local WLB sought its assistance in settling complaints at General Box Company in Kansas City, Missouri, enabling those cases to be resolved.[26]

The WLB and FEPC shared information on firms, and the WLB reported complaints as required to the FEPC. WLB officials and mediators worked with the FEPC and other agencies on some cases, including the Philadelphia transit strike and the Wright Aeronautical and the Bethlehem Steel strikes. When a case reached an impasse it was certified to the NWLB, paving the way for further intervention by other federal agencies. For example, Mitchell complained in 1942 that the WPB had told the Western Electric Company in Baltimore, which was in a dispute with its employees' association over demands that it provide separate toilet facilities for African American workers, that under EO 8802 the facilities could be provided if they were equal. The suggestion threatened to undermine the FEPC's efforts to block the introduction or expansion of segregation in the workplace. When the case was referred to the NWLB in December 1943, however, the board ruled that the company did not have to provide separate facilities, and the government enforced the decision when white workers went on strike over the issue.[27]

Similarly, the FEPC's relations with other agencies could be difficult, depending on the individual with whom it was working, rather than on official policy. Mitchell complained about the role of George Streator, an African American WPB staff member who, during negotiations of the Monsanto case in St. Louis, agreed with those who dismissed black workers' complaints as radical or communist influenced or inspired by union rivalries; Streator thus sabotaged settlement of the case.[28] But Mitchell obtained access to WPB postwar planning meetings in 1945 and forwarded information acquired there to the FEPC's field staff.[29] Looking back in 1946, however, he criticized the WPB for not supporting the FEPC, while he cited the collapse of the NWLB as harmful to the successful settlement of certain important cases.[30]

The Post Office Department

Beginning with Reconstruction, the United States Post Office was probably the first federal agency to employ blacks in other than menial jobs in the South. During the Woodrow Wilson administration, when Jim Crow was officially introduced to Washington, however, segregation and related discrimination were extended even to the cemeteries. African Americans were then often pushed out of higher-level postal positions throughout the nation. Nevertheless, when World War II began, blacks in Norfolk, for example, still held jobs as special delivery messengers, clerks, letter carriers, transportation workers, and custodians.[31]

In 1942, with the federal government undermining Jim Crow through President Roosevelt's nondiscrimination policy, complaints against post offices poured in from individuals, from the National Alliance of Postal Employees, and from civil rights organizations. Major cases arose in Los Angeles; Seattle; Houston; Dallas; San Antonio; New Orleans; Durham, North Carolina; Fredericksburg and Newport News, Virginia; St. Louis; Cleveland; and Philadelphia. Charges ranged from outright refusal to hire blacks for any positions in some communities to the restriction of black workers to certain positions, branches, or shifts, and to failure to upgrade or promote blacks and other minorities regardless of qualifications. Post office administrators manipulated civil service regulations to avoid hiring blacks for higher positions. In some areas, blacks were even barred from carrier or clerical jobs. Rarely were they made supervisors. It was only the severe shortage of labor that led the New Orleans post office and others to open clerical positions to blacks, Mitchell reported, and those hired were given only war-service appointments, making their jobs vulnerable to elimination after the war.[32]

Although most post office cases were handled through negotiations in Washington, the FEPC considered one of the earliest, that of Rone Sidney of Newport News, at a hearing in December 1943. The case was based on a complaint that Sidney filed on March 22, 1942, alleging that the postmaster had denied him employment as a postal clerk because of his race. He said he had passed the civil service examination twice, that his name had been submitted to the postmaster, that he had been certified a number of times, but that he still had not been appointed. Following an FEPC directive issued in February 1944, the post office initiated some reforms at Newport News. However, Sidney himself never got the job he wanted.[33]

Through the negotiations, the FEPC reached "understandings" on complaints with the department. But, unlike other agencies, it never entered into an agreement with the FEPC. Furthermore, unlike other agencies, the department did not permit its local post office officials to negotiate with the FEPC's regional staff. All complaints had to be referred to the Post Office Department in Washington, where the FEPC conducted the negotiations. The long struggle over the department's racial policies was most often very bumpy. In April 1944, for example, Joseph F. Gallagher, post-master of the Philadelphia post office, challenged the FEPC's jurisdiction over it. The FEPC defeated the challenge by providing evidence of its authority, and in November 1944 the department confirmed that it did indeed have that jurisdiction over local post offices.[34]

Just before achieving that major victory, however, George Johnson, the FEPC's deputy chairman, expressed a general frustration by telling the Committee that the FEPC was "confronted with something in the nature of defiance by other government agencies." Among the several post office cases the FEPC had received, he said, was one in Chicago the agency was able to adjust without going to a hearing. But he said the FEPC's efforts to negotiate settlements or to adjust cases at the field level ran into the department's "stern position" that all complaints had to be considered in Washington. Explaining Gallagher's challenge, Johnson said he had been told that "top officials in Washington" had "advised postmasters not to do business with the committee at the regional level." Meantime, he said, the FEPC was asked to hold a hearing on the Los Angeles post office case, which, not surprisingly, it had been unsuccessful in settling at the local level.

Mitchell told the Committee that because Gallagher's hostility apparently had been dictated from Washington, he concluded that the only thing that could be done was to have a conference with the postmaster general in which the FEPC would ask that the department correct specific complaints and change its racial policy so that there would be "a minimum of such complaints occurring in the future." Furthermore, the FEPC would ask the Post Office Department in Washington to instruct local postmasters to cooperate with the FEPC at the local level and also to work out some kind of machinery in Washington in which matters that were not adjusted at the local level would be referred to the FEPC for adjustment.

Mitchell cited the frustrations of blacks in Detroit cases as a demonstration of the need for forceful action from the FEPC. There, he said, when the FEPC did not follow through with a promised hearing on their complaints, "the complainants became discouraged and finally adjusted most of them themselves"—no doubt unsatisfactorily from the Committee's perspective.[35]

Mitchell's memorandum of August 24, 1945, on his latest conference with the Post Office Department provided a comprehensive update on his struggles:

> As stated in my memorandum of August 22, we are still giving attention to complaints filed against the Post Office Department. I had planned to have a joint conference with the Postal Alliance and the Post Office Department on these matters. However, Mr. Joseph F. Gartland, Chief of the Operations Board of the Post Office

Department, declined to participate in this kind of meeting and it was necessary for me to talk with him on Thursday alone. The Alliance is having its meeting with him today.

Mr. Gartland argued in his conversation with me that the Post Office Department considered itself a "family group" and preferred to discuss its problems in the absence of other government agencies. He stated that he recognized FEPC's authority to act on behalf of employees, but felt that this responsibility should not be exercised unless the Post Office Department itself could not resolve the problem.

We then reviewed many changes made by the Post Office Department since FEPC's conferences with the Postmaster General on November 27, 1944. It does appear that some progress has been made. For example, the Philadelphia Post Office, which formerly denied FEPC jurisdiction has been instructed to recognize it. 2. Also in Philadelphia Negroes have been appointed as Civil Service monitors in certain additional window jobs, and some persons who charged they were denied clerical assignments now have them. Philadelphia postal employees, of course, still feel that opportunities for upgrading must be expanded. 3. In Los Angeles the colored employees complained of concentration in the hand stamping section, flat alley work, and rating table. The Los Angeles Branch of the National Postal Alliance now states that this type of discrimination has been corrected. On the other hand, it also feels that there is additional need for opportunities to be upgraded. 4. In Houston the Postal Alliance indicates that four Negroes have been employed as special delivery messengers. This is the first time that this has happened. This was one of the complaints filed with FEPC. 5. The Post Office Department has issued a statement of procedures on posting of vacancies in preferred assignments which the Alliance representatives regard as a step forward.

I showed Mr. Gartland the original of a letter I had received from Mr. Aldrich, the former First Assistant Postmaster General. This letter charged that the Postal Alliance members who had submitted letters of complaints to FEPC were radicals and had been voted out of office by the local branch of the Alliance. I also had with me a copy of the regular Alliance publication in Los Angeles which reaffirmed the branch's desire to correct discriminatory policies. I then stated that many of the postal employees seem to feel that charges of radicalism brought against them when they complain are unjust attempts to use pressure to prevent progress. Mr. Gartland agreed that such charges of radicalism were improper in most instances and stated that he was personally impressed with the men who represent the Alliance.

I said that I would make a new effort to settle the remaining grievances which the Alliance's representatives complained about. I stated that if the Alliance obtained satisfactory adjustment of the complaints in the meeting with him on Friday, it would be very desirable. On the other hand, if such adjustment was not obtained, FEPC would continue the processing of its cases. He agreed that it would be well to have reasonably frequent meetings with Mr. Donaldson, the First Assistant Postmaster General, to discuss the matters in the hands of FEPC.

On the whole, I believe that we will ultimately make additional progress in the Post Office Department although until our status is clarified, it will be rather slow. It is interesting to note that Mr. Gartland closed the conference by saying that although he does not agree with all of FEPC's procedures, he was in favor of the agency and felt that it should be continued.[36]

Mitchell continued to welcome any report on progress in the Post Office Department. Responding to Robert E. Brown's memorandum on the Los Angeles Post Office cases, Mitchell stated:

> Mr. James Robinson, who was present in Washington during our conferences on post office problems, informed me that some of the complaints have been resolved. He stated that Negroes are no longer concentrated at the Rating Table, in the Flat Alley, and in the Hand Stamp Section. I will appreciate it if you will verify this statement.
>
> It is difficult to know how much, if any, improvement is due to FEPC's action, but since it does appear that there were some discriminatory policies in the Los Angeles post office and we have done work on those, I believe you are entitled to satisfactory adjustments on the portions of the ones which have been adjusted. This will also enable us to narrow the issues to the unresolved questions.[37]

In 1947, recalling the Los Angeles case, Mitchell said that the department had denied any discrimination there. Reform was only possible, he said, when the department ceased its policies of "fleeing into the protection of a virtual jungle of rules and technicalities" and of "intimidating those who complain[ed]" and gave protection not only to those entrusted with administrative authority but also to the "humblest employee or the most obscure job applicant." The absence of "protection for the little people was the evil of the Los Angeles case," he said. He added that that absence was also the real source of trouble in Alabama, Louisiana, Tennessee, Texas, and many other states.[38]

Despite the difficulties, the FEPC, as Mitchell noted, did make progress, and it praised examples of cooperation whenever possible. For example, on October 22, 1945, Mitchell provided Gartland with a "refreshing illustration of cooperation" between a FEPC regional staff member and a local postmaster. He told him of the successful outcome of Bernard Ross's negotiations on behalf of a nisei war veteran previously denied employment at the San Francisco post office because of his national origin.[39]

Of major concern at war's end was the fate of black postal workers hired or promoted to temporary positions during wartime who would be displaced by returning veterans reclaiming their former positions. The FEPC negotiated a pledge that those who were upgraded would at least be able to return to their previous positions. The FEPC also hoped that returning black veterans, along with white veterans, would benefit from hiring preferences. Mitchell later reported that in many post offices such preferences were disregarded.[40]

On March 23, 1946, Robert E. Hannegan, postmaster general and Democratic Party leader, responded to a query from Malcolm Ross for a summation and evaluation of his department's nondiscrimination policies. Hannegan affirmed the department's adherence to nondiscrimination and said that local postmasters had been informed of this policy. Although he said that discrimination complaints were "comparatively few," and that "in each case steps have been taken to eliminate the cause," the FEPC's experience showed that the department still had serious racial problems.[41]

A reason for the FEPC's frustrations, Mitchell noted, was that the department showed "great zeal in 'proving' that there was no discrimination, but little interest in getting at the facts." He said that Hannegan and a few "fixers" tried to play up insignificant appointments. However, "a glance at the Congressional Directory and the Government Manual will show that the various bureaus are like Mr. Hannegan's Post Office Department. That is, they have numerous assistants, dozens of deputies, scores of administrative assistants and other functionaries but all of these are white."[42]

NOTES

1. The eight, including the dates on which the agreements were signed: War Manpower Commission, 8/2/43; Maritime Commission, 9/27/43; Civil Service Commission, 11/5/43; National War Labor Board, 3/11/44; Office of Labor Production, War Production Board, 5/30/44; War Shipping Administration, 6/16/44; War Department, 11/24/44; and Navy Department, 11/24/44.

2. President Roosevelt sent a letter to all federal agencies on 9/16/41, requiring them to examine policies to ensure that positions were open to all loyal and qualified workers, regardless of race, creed, or national origin. See Wynn, *Afro-American and the Second World War,* 56–57.

Analysis on FEPC's relationship with other federal agencies is derived primarily from *First Report,* 23–28. Copies of the most important related texts are located in HqR66, Central Files. Reports, U.S. Government Agencies, Specific Agencies; and in HqR67, Central Files. Reports, U.S. Government Agencies, Specific Agencies. See also the undated digest of agreements with other agencies HqR68, Office Files of John A. Davis. Agreements with Other Agencies. Other sources are indicated below, where applicable. See also Boris Shishkin's explanation of the Committee's function in Transcript of Proceedings, 4/20/44, 13, HqR65, Central Files. For additional details on the FEPC's relationship with other agencies, see Zaid, *Preliminary Inventory,* 1–5.

3. See Charles Hamilton Houston's explanation during the Committee's extended discussion of their limited authority involving discriminatory advertising in Transcript of Proceedings, 4/20/44, 14, HqR65, Central Files; local handling was resisted by the Post Office Department during the often tense negotiations held with FEPC officials, and no formal Post Office-FEPC working agreement was adopted. See Mitchell's memorandum of 11/25/44 and his weekly report of 11/27/44.

For examples of implementation of sanctions, particularly the denial of referral services and lowering of priority ratings, see the discussion of the Western Cartridge case in the headnote on Major Cases in St. Louis; Mitchell's report of 4/17/44 and his memoranda of 7/14/44, 2/8, 3/28, 5/17, 7/28/45.

As another form of sanctions, Major General Hayes—the head of the army who was called in to curb violence and run the Philadelphia transit system in 1944—threatened strikers not only with permanent job loss but also with immediate cancellation of their draft deferments and reclassification as 1-A unless they immediately returned to work. See Wynn, *Afro-American and the Second World War,* 53. Cancellation of draft deferments apparently also was used as a sanction against shipyard workers in Portland who refused to work with blacks in 1942 (Reed, *Seedtime,* 270–71).

4. In his report of 5/17/44, Mitchell indicated that he would have primary responsibility for handling contacts with the War Department, the Maritime Commission, the War Manpower Commission, and the General Accounting Office, while his colleagues Emanuel Bloch and Stanley Metzger would cover the other agencies; however, since both Bloch and Metzger left the Division of Field Operations shortly afterward, Mitchell later had to deal with many other agencies as well.

5. See *First Report,* 23–25. For the FEPC-WMC operating agreement of 8/12/43 and related texts, see HqR4, Office Files of George M. Johnson. Agreements-WMC. On its implementation, see especially Mitchell's memoranda of 2/10, 2/26, 4/12, 11/1/44, 2/9/45 (and notes), 2/28, 9/26/45; and the discussion of the Western Cartridge and other cases in the headnote on Major Cases in St. Louis.

6. For examples of 510 reports, see HqR48, Central Files. Reports: Reports of Discriminatory Hiring Practices [USES Form 510].

7. For efforts to ensure greater access to training programs, see Mitchell's memoranda of 2/2, 11/28, 12/17/42, 1/11, 1/18, 2/5, 3/16, 3/29, 7/24, 8/7, 12/9/43, 4/28, 7/10, 12/4, 12/18, 12/20, 12/29/44 (and notes), 1/4, 2/5, 3/5/45; Reed, *Seedtime*, 175–204; King, *Separate and Unequal*, 96–103. On rising access to training programs, see Wynn, *Afro-American and the Second World War*, 77.

8. The USES was the government agency most cited in FEPC cases. On complaints against the USES, especially in WMC regions IV, VII, and X, see Mitchell's weekly reports dated 1/22, 1/29, 2/5, 2/17, 2/28, 3/6, 3/18, 3/27, 4/17, 9/25/44, 1/23, 2/9 (and notes), 3/28, 4/12/45, and his memoranda of 2/10, 4/12, 11/1/44, 1/25, 2/6/45; Reed, *Seedtime*, 63–65; Merl Reed, "FEPC and Federal Agencies in the South," 47–54; Dodge and Cooke, *Southern Rebel in Reverse*, 150–51; King, *Separate and Unequal*, 172–89; Kryder, *Divided Arsenal*, 111–33.

9. On Rosenberg's acceptance of segregation for workers recruited by Kaiser and the Machinists Union, see the section regarding labor unions above, and Mitchell's memorandum of 10/10/42. For Mitchell's praise of Rosenberg's efforts, see his memorandum of 2/10/44; *First Report*, 24; Mitchell, epilogue; Mitchell, interview by Merl Reed, 8/24/78; digest of FEPC-WMC regional relationship in Mitchell's memorandum of 2/10/44. On Midwest offices, see also Mitchell's memorandum of 10/18/43; report of 3/27/44; and Ruchames, *Race, Jobs, and Politics*, 45, 109–10.

10. On reconversion planning and minority groups, see Mitchell, memoranda, 2/9, 8/8, 8/17, 8/25, 8/28, 9/6, 9/14/45; Davis to Ross, 4/3/45, FR80, Region VII. Administrative Files (A–Z), Regional Director (cont'd.). On the turning over of the employment service branches to the states and subsequent discrimination, see NAACP, Washington Bureau report, 9/30/45, NAACP Papers, DLC; Mitchell, epilogue; Mitchell, reports as NAACP labor secretary, 11/30, 12/30/46, 5/2, 12/2/47, 4/30/48, 4/3/50; Mitchell, testimony before a subcommittee of the Senate Appropriations Committee, 4/17/47, and before the House Appropriations Committee, 4/17/48, U.S. Congress, House, *Supplemental Federal Security Appropriations for 1949*; King, *Separate and Unequal*, 63–64, 172–89.

11. See Mitchell's memorandum of 5/6/43, and notes; and the copy of the agreement of 3/10/43, included with Field Instruction 19 of 10/4/43, in appendix 1.

12. See Mitchell's memorandum of 11/17/43; on the exclusion of Japanese Americans from certain facilities by the Coast Guard and the Navy Department, see Mitchell's reports of 2/17, 4/24/44, 5/21, 5/26, 6/5, 8/9/45; and the memorandum on Important Cases Being Handled at Regional Level, 4/22–5/22/44, in appendix 1; Reed, *Seedtime*, 238–51; HqR66, Central Files. U.S. Government, Aliens in Defense, Specific Groups, Japanese; and Field Instruction no. 20-A, 4/24/44, HqR78, Field Instructions, 20–39.

13. See Mitchell's memoranda of 5/6/43, 1/27, 2/26, 11/21/44, and his report of 2/17/44.

14. See Field Instructions no. 19, 10/4/43, and no. 19B, 11/24/44; Robert P. Patterson to Ross, 11/23/44, in appendix 1.

15. For Mitchell's dealings with civilian aide Truman Gibson, see his memoranda and reports of 7/12, 11/9/43, 5/17 (and notes), 11/22, 11/27, 12/4, 12/14, 12/28/44, 2/19/45; Mitchell, epilogue. On army reluctance to deal with the General Cable case, see Mitchell's report of 5/17/44.

16. See *Final Report*, 24–24; Mitchell, epilogue; Ross, *All Manner of Men*, 72–79; and Kryder, *Divided Arsenal*, 33–38, 74–78, 144–46, 150–54, 163, 171, 181, 238–41. For Mitchell reports praising the role of army officers, see, for example, his memoranda of 6/6, 6/9/44, on the Wright Aeronautical strike. For other interaction with the War Department, see his reports of 3/27, 4/17, 5/1, 5/8, 10/9, 11/20, 12/14, 12/18/44, 1/9, 1/30, 2/6, 2/20, 3/20/45, and his memoranda of 7/[31]/43, 1/25, 3/13, 3/22, 6/5/45; discussions of Western Cartridge and other cases in the headnote on Major Cases in St. Louis; and, more generally, HqR67, Central Files. U.S. Government, War Department, A–L, M–Z; and the Mitchell-Gibson correspondence in Records of the Office of the Civilian Aide to the Secretary of War, Records of the Office of the Secretary of War, 1791–1947, RG 107, boxes 190, 191, DNA. On the role of the civilian aides and their assistants, see also Osur, *Blacks in the Army Air Forces during World War II*, 63–67, 70–71, 73–76.

See also the acrimonious correspondence over War Department handling of investigations requested by the FEPC contained in Joy P. Davis's analysis of the subject, 11/26/43, Louis Lautier's caustic comments on it of 12/10/43, Gibson's memo of 12/23/43 enclosing them, and Davis's reply of

4/20/44, found in HqR68, Office Files of John A. Davis. Miscellaneous; HqR85, Correspondence Relating to Cases. War Department; Records of the Office of the Civilian Aide to the Secretary of War, Records of the Office of the Secretary of War, 1791–1947, RG 107, box 190, COFEP, DNA.

17. See *Final Report,* 25–26; Kryder, *Divided Arsenal,* 122–26; Mitchell's memoranda and reports of 3/16, 7/24/43, 3/27, 4/3 (and notes), 5/1/44, 2/14, 3/13, 3/20, 3/22/45; FEPC files relating to the Brooklyn Navy Yard, HqR67, Central Files. U.S. Government, Navy Department, and in HqR83, Correspondence Relating to Cases. (A–K); the numerous texts included in HR84, Correspondence Relating to Cases. (L–Se), Navy, Identification Badges; and the files relating to discrimination in the navy, 1941–44, Records of the Office of the Assistant Secretary of the Navy (Ralph Bard), Records of the Secretary of the Navy, General Records of the Department of the Navy, 1798–1947, RG 80, DNA. On the exclusion of Japanese Americans from certain facilities by the Coast Guard and the Navy Department, see Mitchell's reports of 2/17, 4/24/44, 5/21, 5/26, 6/5, 8/9/45; and memorandum on Important Cases Being Handled at Regional Level, 4/22/44–5/22/44, in appendix 1. On Delta Shipbuilding, see Mitchell's reports of 1/29, 2/28, 3/27, 5/1, 5/8, 5/17/44, 1/9, 1/15/45; and his memoranda of 3/16/43, 5/5/44, 8/14 (2), 11/1/44 (3), 1/8, 1/12/45; and the memorandum on "Important Cases Being Handled at Regional Level," 4/22–5/22/44, in appendix 1.

18. On the Alabama Dry Dock case, see Mitchell's memorandum of 6/1/43, and Mitchell and Trimble's field investigation report of 6/8/43 (and notes), in appendix 1; Watson, *Lion in the Lobby,* 141–43.

19. *Final Report,* 28–29; Malcolm Ross, *All Manner of Men,* 103–17; Hill, *Black Labor and the American Legal System,* 218–34; texts in HqR67, Central Files. U.S. Government, War Shipping Administration; Field Letter no. 42-E, 9/17/45, enclosing Committee's Decision on SITU, 9/6/45, HqR4, Office Files of George M. Johnson. FEPC Miscellaneous. See other Delta citations in note 17, above.

20. See King, *Separate and Unequal,* 65; HqR68, Office Files of John A Davis. Agreements with Other Agencies; "The Wartime Enforcement of the Non Discrimination Policy in the Federal Government: Techniques and Accomplishments," n.d., RG 228, box 358, Civil Service—Negro, DNA.

21. See Wynn, *Afro-Americans and the Second World War,* 56–57; King, *Separate and Unequal,* 75, 81–88, 277n12.

22. On FEPC-Civil Service Commission negotiations and agreements, national and local, see the texts in HqR66, Central Files. U.S. Government, Civil Service Commission. For FEPC cases involving the civil service commission itself, see 9/14/43, 3/6, 5/8/44. On the FEPC relationship with the Commission, see Mitchell's reports and memoranda of 10/8/43, 1/27, 4/17, 5/17/44, 1/25, 7/31/45, and Mitchell, epilogue. For an analysis of the procedures by which Civil Service guidelines were manipulated to permit continued discrimination, see King, *Separate and Unequal,* 49–71, 88–96; Reed, "FEPC and the Federal Agencies." On civil service policies affecting Japanese Americans, see Mitchell's reports of 4/17/43, 3/27/44, 5/21, 5/26, 8/9/45.

23. See Cramer memorandum on wage increases, 11/25/42, and other materials in HqR4, Office Files of George M. Johnson. Wage Increases; note 1 to Mitchell's memorandum of 3/13/43; "National War Labor Board Cases Involving Racial Discrimination," n.d., HqR2, Office Files of Malcolm Ross. West Coast Materials; and *First Report,* 26.

24. See the finding aid to the Records of the U.S. National War Labor Board, Labor Archives and Research Center, San Francisco State University; and the aid to the War Production Board Records, DNA.

25. See HqR68, Office Files of John A. Davis. Agreements with Other Agencies; "Agreement between FEPC and the Labor Production Office of WPB," HqR3, Office Files of Malcolm Ross.

26. On the Jones and Laughlin case, see Mitchell's memoranda of 9/4, 9/9/43. On the General Box Company case, see Mitchell's report of 4/13/44. For FEPC involvement with both boards regarding the strike at the National Lead Company in St. Louis, see Eleanor Rogers's memorandum to Mitchell of 7/27/44. For another instance of interagency cooperation, in this case securing training and employment for African Americans in Macon, Ga., see Mitchell's report of 3/5/45. For criticism of the willingness of the local WPB staff to bargain with the Philadelphia transit strikers, see Mitchell's field report of 8/4/44; Weaver, *Negro Labor,* 190. Apart from the WPB action, Robert Weaver praised the Philadelphia case as one in which the relevant federal agencies successfully took a strong and united stand (ibid., 189–90).

27. On the Western Electric case, see Mitchell's memoranda of 8/26, 11/11/43, and notes.

28. For the FEPC complaints against George Streator's actions regarding the Monsanto case, see Mitchell's reports of 4/3, 4/17/44, and their notes; Harry Gibson's report to Elmer Henderson of 4/10/44, and Stanley Metzger's memorandum of 4/15/44 on the incident in HqR84, Correspondence Relating to Cases. (L–Se), Monsanto Chemical Co., Region VI. For more details on reports on Streator's activities, see also 4/3/44, note 2.

29. See Mitchell's memoranda of 9/14/43, 4/3, 5/8/44, 6/19/45 and report of 4/17/44.

30. See Mitchell, epilogue.

31. Reed, "FEPC and the Federal Agencies in the South," 44–45; King, *Separate and Unequal*, 3–4, 29–30, 53–54.

32. For background on Post Office Department discrimination before and during World War II, see Mitchell's memorandum of 12/14/44, and notes; Transcript of Proceedings, 9/7/44, 44–51, HqR65, Central Files; and King, *Separate and Unequal*, 29–30, 44, 53–54, 69, 85–86, 262n167, 271nn72–73. On the role of NAPE in bringing complaints before the FEPC, see memoranda of 12/9/44, 5/31, 6/5, 11/8/45. For NAACP negotiations with the Post Office Department during the war, see the Washington Bureau report of 9/23/43, NAACP Papers, DLC. For cases in which blacks were barred from carrier positions, see 3/20/45 report. For obstacles to clerical positions, see memoranda of 9/7, 9/23/44, 9/12/45. For discrimination in promotions and in supervisory positions, see Mitchell's memoranda of 9/12, 12/9/44. For the correspondence regarding discrimination at the Durham, N.C., post office, see FR48, Region IV. U.S. Post Office, Durham, N.C. For the continued discrimination in New Orleans, and other southern cities, see Mitchell's testimony of 12/9/47, 7–13; Mitchell's testimony of 12/9/47, Hearing Before the Committee on Civil Service, U.S. Senate, 80th Cong., 1st sess., on the Confirmation of Jesse M. Donaldson to be Postmaster General and Paul Aiken to be Second Assistant Postmaster General (Washington, D.C.: GPO, 1947), 12–13; Arthur Marsalis et al., NAPE, New Orleans branch, to Ralph Handlin, Acting Postmaster, New Orleans, 4/28/45, HqR76, Office Files of Will Maslow. Post Office.

33. For the Rone Sidney case, see Mitchell's memorandum of 12/14/42 and notes to 5/3/44; "Rone Sidney vs. Post-Master of Newport News, Virginia, Facts of the Case," HqR4, Office Files of George M. Johnson. Ernest Trimble; Transcript of Proceedings, 3/4/44, 74–76; 4/1/44, 15–27; 4/20/44, 27–32, all in HqR65, Central Files.

34. On FEPC jurisdiction over post offices, see Mitchell's memoranda of 5/3 (and notes), 5/8, 9/7, 11/25, 11/27/44. For negotiations with post office officials, see 5/1, 9/7, 11/13, 11/25, 11/27, 12/12/44, 3/20, 5/21, 9/21/45; and George Crockett's detailed memorandum to Johnson on "Application of Executive Order No. 9346 to the Philadelphia Post Offices," HqR3, Office Files of George M. Johnson. George W. Crockett.

35. Transcript of Proceedings, 9/7/44, 44–48, HqR65, Central Files.

36. Mitchell to Brown, Castañeda, Fleming, and Hoglund, 8/24/45, HqR84, Correspondence Relating to Cases. (L–S), Post Office Department (General). Mitchell's list has no item 1.

37. HqR84, Correspondence Relating to Cases. (L–S), Los Angeles Post Office. Brown's memorandum of 8/29/45 is also in the file.

38. See Mitchell's testimony of 12/9/47, cited in note 32, above. For the Los Angeles cases, see 5/1, 9/7, 9/23, 11/21, 11/25, 12/9/44, 3/13/45. On Houston, see 9/7, 11/21, 12/11, 12/18/44, 2/4, 3/5, 3/13, 9/12/45. On Philadelphia, see 12/14/42, 5/3, 5/8, 9/7, 11/21, 11/25, 12/11, 12/18/44, 2/14, 4/12/45. For an example of the nature of the communist smear, see Curtis W. Garrott, member of Special Committee to Investigate Promotional Discrimination, letter, 5/23/45, HqR84, Correspondence Relating to Cases. (L–S), Los Angeles Post Office. See also HqR84, Correspondence Relating to Cases. U.S. Post Office, Houston Post Office, and Philadelphia Post Office; Transcript of Proceedings, 9/4/45, 79–80, HqR65, Central Files.

39. See Mitchell to Gartland, 10/22/45, enclosing an excerpt from the monthly report from Region XII for the period ending 10/15/45, HqR76, Office Files of Clarence Mitchell. Unarranged.

40. On the postwar status of black postal employees, see 11/25, 11/27, 12/12/44, 3/20, 9/12/45.

41. *Final Report,* 127–28.

42. Mitchell's report of 3/13/45; Mitchell, epilogue.

CREEDAL DISCRIMINATION

In seeking to redress complaints involving creed, most frequently from Jews, Seventh-day Adventists, and Jehovah's Witnesses, the FEPC was guided by national policy against racial and religious discrimination that was rooted in the Constitution and several federal statutes.[1] Although just 8 percent of its docketed cases involved religious discrimination, the Committee devoted a representative amount of time to resolving those problems. Complaints from Jews represented 70 percent of the cases and were concentrated in geographic areas where substantial numbers of Jews resided, such as New York, California, and Chicago. Jewish groups were among the FEPC's earliest supporters, and a number of FEPC staff members were Jews. Jewish organizations forwarded complaints to the FEPC and were among the prime initiators of FEPC efforts to remove religious questions from employment applications and personnel and security investigations of applicants.[2] The most frequent complaint was the refusal of employers to hire them. Other charges included discriminatory advertising and failure to promote or upgrade. Jews also sought further accommodation of work schedules to their Sabbath and to religious holidays. At the time of its disbandment, the FEPC sought data from Jewish organizations for use in its *Final Report* and referred several unresolved religious discrimination cases to Jewish organizations to follow up on their own (see the Committee's definition of creed in the headnote on Jurisdictional Issues).[3]

In its *Final Report* the Committee contended that it had largely handled valid cases of anti-Semitism through negotiation. It stated it had "much success" in removing from newspapers discriminatory advertisements for "Gentiles only" that were submitted by companies under FEPC jurisdiction. "Persuasion only was used; no directorates issued," the agency proclaimed, and "private organizations were primarily instrumental in barring such advertisements." Many employers had contended subordinates acted without authority. The Committee cited one case in which a major employer, reminded of his duty under the executive order, posted this notice: "Let us not in this shipyard help the enemy by provoking incidents based on religious or racial prejudice."[4]

Even though the Committee in its *Final Report* seemed equally pleased with its success in resolving complaints from Seventh-day Adventists and other Sabbatarians, the prominence its *First Report* gave to these cases indicated that initially it did encounter serious resistance in doing so. The problem that was common to both Jews and Seventh-day Adventists was their refusal to work on Saturdays. For Orthodox Jews the issue was thornier because their Sabbath began at sundown on Fridays. Complying with their needs would require readjusting work schedules during wartime. Defense plants, many of which operated around the clock, seven days a week, sometimes resisted accommodating them, especially at times of acute labor shortage.

The FEPC patterned its policy on religious holidays on one the War Department announced in September 1942:

The policy of the War Department is to permit absence from work to those
whose conscience leads them to spend certain holy days in religious devotion.

If possible those employees should seek some method by which they can make
up the production time so lost. Wherever the situations permit, work schedules should be rearranged so as to provide substituted work time.

Where work schedules cannot be rearranged, the absence shall be charged
against annual leave accredited to the employee.

Whenever the employee has no annual leave to his credit, his absence shall be
recorded as leave without pay with no prejudice to the employee's standing.

The Committee reasoned that since freedom of religion was one of the objectives
of the war, it was "desirable that the Government adopt a liberal position regarding
the arrangements for the observance of religious holidays." Consequently, the Committee recommended to the Civil Service Commission that "such policy be established throughout the Government, preferably patterned along the lines of the policy
adopted by the War Department."[5]

The War Department's position regarding employers holding government contracts was that refusal to accommodate the religious holidays of a particular group
was not discriminatory if no provisions were made for the holidays of other groups.
However, the department's guideline stated:

Although the refusal to employ workers whose religious convictions require them to
be absent from work on Saturday, or to follow other practices which interfere with normal work schedules, is not considered to be a violation of the anti-discrimination
clause in war contracts, employers should be encouraged to find means of adjusting
work schedules to make use, whenever possible, of employees whose particular religious convictions conflict with customary schedules.[6]

Responding to complaints from employees of navy yards and other defense establishments that did not find it feasible to accommodate them, and that had in some
cases fired or failed to promote those who were absent on their Sabbath days or religious holidays, the FEPC negotiated cases with the War and Navy Departments and
with individual employers. In July 1943 the Navy Department sent new instructions
to its shore establishments strongly urging them to accommodate religious beliefs
whenever possible. In September 1943 the second FEPC promulgated a stronger statement of policy:

In cases in which it is alleged that a person has been discriminated against in connection with employment in war industries or Government service, because of
creed, and it appears upon investigation that such person has been denied employment or dismissed from employment because he or she on account of his or her
creed conscientiously cannot perform secular work on certain days, the committee
takes the position that if it is possible, even at considerable inconvenience, for the
party charged to arrange work schedules so as to permit such person to absent himself or herself from work on days on which he or she because of creed conscientiously cannot perform secular work, failure to arrange such work schedules will be
regarded as a violation of the provisions of Executive Order 9346.[7]

The FEPC succeeded in getting many employers to adapt. Nevertheless, it could not easily challenge those instances where defense plants contended that accommodations to religious belief would substantially damage their contributions to the war effort.

More difficult to resolve than the Sabbatarian cases were those involving religious groups with pacifist or antiwar tenets that came into conflict with wartime patriotism, particularly the Jehovah's Witnesses. Such cases "were relatively few in number" but required "a considerable amount of time in negotiations." For example, a case involving complaints from Jehovah's Witnesses fired by the Pittsburgh Plate Glass Company plant at Clarksburg, West Virginia, was especially contentious because the complainants had "inflamed" their coworkers by refusing to stand during the singing of the national anthem and absenting themselves from a flag-raising ceremony. After a hearing on this case, the Committee ruled that in these instances, in violation of Executive Order 8802, Pittsburgh Plate Glass had unjustly dismissed the men because of their creed.[8]

Other cases involved Jehovah's Witnesses' refusal to buy war bonds, their demands for deferral from the draft, and their employers' refusal to request an appeal to an unsatisfactory decision by a local draft board. However, in March 1944, upon ascertaining that the Jehovah's Witnesses had "no formalized body of religious principles" on the issue and left actions like the purchase of war bonds up to "individual determination," the FEPC refused to act on such complaints. The first FEPC, it noted, had decided that "personal 'conscience' unrelated to the religious conduct of an organized sect was not considered creed as a basis of discrimination within the meaning of EO 8802." The FEPC therefore declined jurisdiction over cases of discrimination on religious grounds "unless it is shown that the action taken by the complainant was related to some established precept of a creed." Thus, it declared that "the mere fact of discharge for such refusal [to buy war bonds] is not evidence of discrimination because of creed. Nor does the Committee consider a complaint by a Jehovah's Witness alleging that an employer refuses to request draft deferment or refuses to appeal from an unsatisfactory decision by a local draft board, to involve discrimination because of creed."[9] Mitchell was among the FEPC staff members who questioned the Committee's decision to define religious discrimination cases narrowly in dealing with the Jehovah's Witnesses cases. He contended that important religious principles were involved in the cases and complained that he did not have an adequate opportunity to express his views before the Committee acted.[10]

NOTES

1. For the Committee's interpretation of creed, see the FEPC report of 2/8/44, in appendix 1 and the headnote on Jurisdictional Issues. For an overview of the FEPC's actions on religious discrimination, see Reed, *Seedtime,* 251–66.

2. See Mitchell's memorandum of 8/14/44, and notes, and the headnote on Race, Creed, Color, and National Origin on Employment Applications.

3. On complaints by Jews and the activities of Jewish organizations, see Reed, *Seedtime,* 251–60; Hayes Beall to Maslow on Complaints of Discrimination against Jews, 1944, 5/28/45, HqR2, Office Files of Malcolm Ross. Difficult Cases, Sects, Tensions. Among other things, discriminatory experiences led Jews to intense introspection in an attempt to inspire understanding of the historical roots of anti-Semitism. See Philip Bernstein, "Some Facts about Jews," *Harper's,* 4/39, 501–6; Stanley High, "Jews, Anti-Semites, and Tyrants," *Harper's,* 6/42, 22–29. For an example of the data collected at war's end, see "Survey of Employment Discrimination against Jews since V-J Day" [ca. 3/46], HqR1, Office Files of Malcolm Ross. West Coast Materials.

4. *Final Report,* 39; Beall to Maslow on "Complaints of Discrimination against Jews, 1944," 5/25/45, HqR2, Office Files of Malcolm Ross. Difficult Cases, Sects, Tensions, on which the section of the report on Jewish cases is largely based.

5. *First Report,* 52–53; Rough draft, "Operations Bulletin Re: Sabbath Observers and Absences for Religious Purposes," HqR4, Office Files of George M. Johnson. Records of the Legal Divisions, Application for Employment; Harry B. Mitchell to Mark Ethridge, 2/12/43, HqR1, Office Files of Malcolm Ross. Extra Copies.

6. *First Report,* 53.

7. Ibid., 53–54. For other FEPC action on War Department policy, see Maslow to Edward Lawson, 5/1/44, "Request for Interpretation of Ruling Regarding Seventh Day Adventists," HqR67, Central Files. Reports, U.S. Government, Seventh Day Adventists-Sabbatarians.

For naval efforts to establish flexible policies on religious holidays, see Bard to Cramer, 12/4, 12/10/42, enclosing "Memorandum to All Shore Establishments on Absence from Work and Holidays" (issued 12/17/42); Cramer to Bard, 12/12/42, all in HqR67, Central Files. U.S. Government, Navy Department; Bard to All Shore Establishments, 7/7/43, HqR67, Central Files. Seventh Day Adventists, Sabbatarians, and Religious Discrimination. For instances when naval establishments declared it not feasible to permit such flexibility, see Mitchell's memorandum of 8/23/43, and notes; Reed, *Seedtime,* 261–62; Cramer to Harry B. Mitchell, 4/24/43, and Harry B. Mitchell to Cramer, 4/20, 5/10/43, HqR67, Central Files. Reports, U.S. Government, Religious Discrimination.

8. See Mitchell's memorandum of 4/5/43; *First Report,* 56; HqR1, FEPC Summary of Hearings with Findings and Directions, 12/21/41 (this document is dated 12/21/43, which apparently is an error), in the case of "Jehovah's Witnesses versus the Pittsburgh Plate Glass Company"; and McLean's letter of 11/23/42 to Pittsburgh Plate Glass Company, both in HqR1, Office Files of Malcolm Ross. Committee Members; hearings transcript on Pittsburgh Plate Glass Company case, 12/21/42, HqR18.

9. See Mitchell's weekly reports of 2/5, 3/18/44, memoranda of 4/5/43, 3/30/44, and notes; *First Report,* 54; Minutes, 3/4/44, HqR1, Summary Minutes of Meetings; Reed, *Seedtime,* 262–65. Despite the 3/44 decision, the Committee continued to handle some Jehovah's Witnesses cases. See Mitchell's memorandum of 1/23/45.

10. See Mitchell's memorandum of 3/30/44; Maslow to the Committee, n.d., HqR66, Office Files of George M. Johnson. Records of the Legal Division, Miscellaneous.

NATIONAL ORIGIN, ALIENAGE, AND LOYALTY

Ending discrimination based on national origin and alienage, or noncitizenship, was especially challenging for the Committee because questions of loyalty and national security were oftentimes intertwined in those issues, and the distinction between them could be fuzzy. Furthermore, many employers did not distinguish between noncitizens and citizens of foreign origin, so the issues of national origin and alienage often merged or overlapped. Practically all complaints of discrimination based on national origin the Committee received, for example, were from Mexicans, whether or not they were American citizens. Their complaints were similar to those from African Americans. National origin complaints from Japanese and Jews, and sometimes from Germans and Italians, however, were essentially alienage cases, often resulting from national security concerns.[1] (See the headnotes on Mexican Americans, on Japanese Americans, on the Mining Industry, on the Oil Industry, and on Race, Creed, Color, and National Origin on Employment Application Forms.)

Because it felt that discrimination against any ethnic group undermined its efforts to obtain fair treatment for African Americans, the FEPC made no distinction in its aggressive treatment of complaints based on race, creed, national origin, or alienage. Similarly, it fought to ensure that temporary, foreign agricultural workers, notably Mexicans, Jamaicans, and Bahamians, were covered by its nondiscrimination policies.[2]

National Origin, Alienage, and Loyalty

Disclosures in Europe over fifth-column activities in countries that had been conquered by the German war machine made Americans especially worried about their national security. Here at home, an article in the *Saturday Evening Post* reinforced the growing alarm: "No one, not even the agents of the Federal Bureau of Investigation, knows how many alien propagandists, professional culture carriers, spies, and *agents provocateurs* the war has unloosed in the United States. Few of them turn up to have their noses counted." The article explained that in September 1939, when the president put the nation in a state of "limited emergency," he assigned the problem to the FBI, but it was already too big for the agency. So, by the time the FEPC was created, aliens, as in past periods of war, were already regarded as a people apart. One section of Public Law 671, passed June 28, 1940, "to expedite national defense, and for other purposes," provided that

> no aliens employed by a contractor in the performance of secret, confidential, or restricted Government contracts shall be permitted to have access to the plans or specifications, or the work under such contracts, or to participate in the contract trials, unless the written consent of the head of the Government department concerned has first been obtained.

Its precursor, the Air Corps Act of 1926, stated that

> no aliens employed by a contractor for furnishing or constructing aircraft, or aircraft parts, or aeronautical accessories for the United States shall be permitted to have access to the plans or specifications or the work under construction or to participate in the contract trials without the written consent beforehand of the Secretary of the Department concerned.[3]

Another law, the Alien Registration Act of 1940, which the president signed on June 29, 1940, required the Department of Justice to fingerprint all aliens as part of the process. In signing the law, Roosevelt said it "should be interpreted and administered as a program designed not only for the protection of the country but also for the protection of the loyal aliens who are its guests." He cautioned, "It would be unfortunate if, in the course of this regulative program, any loyal aliens were subjected to harassment." In enacting the law, he said, Congress intended "to provide a uniform method of handling this difficult problem of alien registration." The main objective of this law was to destroy the American Communist Party and other left-wing political groups in the country as well as fascist and Nazi organizations (William Green, president of the AFL, also named the German American Bund as another organization that engaged in "traitorous activities"), but the law's scope covered all aliens, whether loyal or disloyal. Under this law, nearly five million aliens were registered. Section 1 of the act, which subsequently assumed a notoriety of its own as the Smith Act of 1940 (named after Congressman Howard W. Smith of Virginia, who sponsored it), prohibited certain subversive activities and made it a crime to advocate violent overthrow of the government.[4]

Owing to those laws and the general suspicion of aliens, some employers had a rule of not hiring them. Many labor unions, too, made citizenship a requirement for membership, in effect presenting aliens with a closed shop because without membership they could not be employed in related areas. Furthermore, many states, including New York (noted for its large immigrant population), federal agencies, and the civil service for years prohibited the employment of aliens on public works.[5]

Consequently, before the issuance of EO 8802 an employer had discretion to apply for a permit to employ an alien and to base his decision solely on the person's citizenship status or national origin. With the issuance of the order, the employer was still responsible for vouching for the employee's loyalty. Nevertheless, at least he was prohibited by a national nondiscrimination policy from excluding a person solely on the basis of national origin, so he had to find other reasons for doing so.

That procedural looseness made the FEPC's challenge considerable. The dangers of sabotage were widely publicized, and the belief that aliens were the most likely to engage in such actions worsened their plight. The problem was compounded by employers' misdirected patriotism. A study by the Bureau of Employment Security (BES) of the Federal Security Agency revealed that of about forty thousand persons hired over a short period by the aircraft industry, 99.99 percent were required by their employers to be citizens; out of sixty-six hundred shipbuilding employees hired, 94.1 percent had to be citizens; in the automobile industry, 93.5 percent of nine thousand hired had to be citizens. The study showed that the tendency was aggravated by federal statutes that restricted the employment of aliens on certain types of contracts, which provisions were widely misinterpreted to completely prohibit the employment of aliens. In some areas of the country, discrimination was extended to people of foreign-born parents and with foreign-sounding names. Those attitudes of defense employers were often copied in nondefense industries.[6]

Consequently, twelve days after EO 8802 was issued, the BES began efforts to establish standard procedures by issuing an Operating Policy and Procedure regarding statutes and their interpretation relating to the employment of noncitizens in defense industries. The bureau felt it was essential that local employment offices have information on procedures and laws concerning the employment of those persons in defense industries by private employers on government contracts.[7]

A draft government statement on the employment of aliens and persons of foreign origin in national defense industries similarly noted that the negative attitude toward foreign-born and alien workmen did not contribute to the national welfare, and neither was it in the best interest of the defense effort. The practice, it said, held many dangers for the entire country. Shortages of labor, it said, were developing in many industries vital to the national well-being, so it was "imperative that the skills and services of all able-bodied and loyal persons—citizens and aliens alike—be utilized. Unnecessary dislocations of labor and turnover of employees must be avoided." The statement explained that federal laws contained "no absolute prohibitions against the employment of aliens in national defense industries." It reiterated that in certain special instances involving government contracts an employer must secure permission under Public Law 671 to employ them from the head of the government department concerned.[8]

The Japanese attack on Pearl Harbor brought the issue to a new peak. On December 7 and 8, Roosevelt issued proclamations prescribing regulations "for the conduct and control of alien enemies." Attorney General Francis Biddle promptly announced that the FBI had been directed to take a selected group of Japanese aliens into custody for questioning and temporary detention. Throughout the country, he said, "a comparatively small number" of Japanese were "being rounded up in view of the situation." On December 12, 1941, Roosevelt issued EO 8972, which specifically suspended the employment of Japanese Americans pending a careful investigation of their loyalty by the War Department. Previously, Japanese, as well as Chinese, long had been barred from naturalization. With exceptions made in a few special cases, furthermore, they had not been allowed for many years to settle in the United States. Therefore only those born in the United States were citizens.[9]

Alarmed, however, about the harmful impact of the hysteria over aliens on the war effort, Biddle tried to moderate anti-Japanese passions. He had a tough job doing so given the security concerns and often blatant racial prejudices of the War Department and the FBI. He appealed to state and local law enforcement agencies and to the general public to "help guard at home the freedoms our country is now fighting to defend by protecting the civil liberties of our loyal non-citizen population." He said the response to the appeal to keep the hysteria and antagonism toward noncitizens at a minimum was heartening. Nevertheless, he said, there remained "a serious problem in adjusting our sights to our one great objective; it is the problem of discrimination against aliens in private employment."

He reminded employers who were "discharging workers because of some vague 'suspicion' that they may be disloyal aliens," or because they had "foreign-sounding names" that of America's total noncitizen population of about five million, fewer than three thousand—six out of ten thousand—had been regarded as dangerous. Federal authorities, he repeated, had taken those persons into custody. He also reminded those employers that many of the "foreigners" they had discharged had sons serving in the U.S. Army and Navy. "Among those who died fighting off the treacherous attacks on Manila and Pearl Harbor were men named Wagner and Petersen and Monzo and Rossini and Mueller and Rasmussen." War, Biddle said, threatened all civil rights,

> and although we have fought wars before, and our personal freedoms have survived, there have been periods of gross abuse, when hysteria and hate and fear ran high, and when minorities were unlawfully and cruelly abused. Every man who cares about freedom, about a government by law—and all freedom is based on fair administration of the law—must fight for it for the other man with whom he disagrees, for the right of the minority, for the chance for the underprivileged with the same passion of insistence as he claims for his own rights. If we care about democracy, we must care about it as a reality for others as well as for ourselves; yes, for aliens, for Germans, for Italians, for Japanese, for those who are with us as well as those who are against us: For the Bill of Rights protects not only American citizens but all human beings who live on our American soil, under our American flag. The rights of Anglo-Saxons, of Jews, of Catholics, of negroes, of Slavs, Indians—all are alike before the law. And this we must remember and sustain—that is if we really love justice, and really hate the bayonet and the gun, and the whole Gestapo method of a way of handling human beings.[10]

President Roosevelt, too, sought to ease the hysteria: "It is one thing to safeguard American industry, and particularly defense industry, against sabotage; it is very much another to throw out of work honest and loyal people who, except for the accident of birth, are sincerely patriotic." He said such a policy was as "stupid" as it was "unjust." Responding to the FEPC's request for clarification of his now contradictory policy on aliens, Roosevelt wrote the Committee on January 3, 1942, that it was his intention to include "non-citizens in the scope of the Committee's responsibilities. I, therefore, feel it appropriate that your Committee investigate cases in which non-citizens allege that they have been discriminated against because of their national origin in a manner more restrictive than required by the law governing their employment in defense industries."

The BES study and the draft statement showed that the problem was not isolated to the Japanese, Germans, or Italians. The *First Report* confirmed that reality. On January 23, 1942, Eugene Davidson, FEPC field representative, wrote Lawrence Cramer, "The situation in regards to employment of aliens in New York City is exceedingly serious." He inquired "whether or not our Committee had jurisdiction over aliens in law as well as in fact" and asked whether he should continue handling such cases. One question he had was whether volunteers working at the Office of Civilian Defense came within the FEPC's jurisdiction. Another question resulted from the practice by the "great majority of private defense contractors" in the New York area who were "refusing employment to aliens even to the extent of advertising in newspapers that American citizenship was essential." Davidson cited the case of Arnold Burger, whom a company refused to hire because "they did not employ aliens." Cramer told Richard F. Prichard Jr. of the War Production Board, "This obviously is something that should not be left to private individuals to do, but should be a function of the Government itself."[11]

Thus the government was hard pressed to improve on its earlier efforts to moderate its policies, especially since some job applicants could not produce birth certificates to prove their American citizenship. In a July 3, 1942, operations bulletin to all USES personnel, John J. Corson, USES director, noted that, on June 4, 1942, the War and Navy departments had issued a joint statement to prospective army and navy contractors and subcontractors that previous instructions on the hiring of persons without birth certificates given in a memorandum of July 16, 1941, had been suspended. The July 16 memorandum had sought to enforce restrictions that existing laws placed on the employments of aliens for "specified contracts" and had recommended a procedure for facilitating the employment of people who were unable to produce birth certificates. "That [July 16] memorandum was concerned primarily with establishing proof of birth in the United States in case of prospective employees who [were] unable to produce birth certificates," the joint June 4 memorandum said. However, the June 4 memorandum explained, recent experience had shown that obtaining a birth certificate had caused "considerable delay during which the services of the individual were not available in connection with the contracts in question." Consequently, the War and Navy departments recommended the following revision, which was intended to speed the hiring of persons who lacked birth certificates:

[T]hat contractors and subcontractors require applicants for employment in the performance of any secret, confidential or restricted contract, or any contract for furnishing aircraft, aircraft parts, or aeronautical accessories, to sign a statement in the presence of an Army or Navy District Procurement, Factory or Plant Protection representative, to the effect that he is a citizen of the United States and that he has read and understands the pertinent provision of the act of June 28, 1940 (Public Law 671, 76th Cong.), as indicated by the inclosed form entitled "Declaration of Citizenship."

The foregoing recommended procedure does not relieve the employer from the duty of seeking further investigation when there is any reason to doubt the truth of applicant's declaration that he is a citizen.

Corson thus instructed local USES offices to refer applicants without birth certificates "to the contractor with the suggestion that they request the employer to accept their 'Declaration of Citizenship' as a basis for employment."[12]

Nevertheless, the mass evacuations of the Japanese from the West Coast under Executive Order 9066 heightened concern over enemy aliens. The Council for Democracy noted that the slightly more than one million aliens of German, Italian, and Japanese origin listed by the Alien Registration Act could be "swelled" by the inclusion of Hungarians, Bulgarians, and Rumanians. Unquestionably, the council said, the overwhelming majority of these aliens were loyal. Many had been in the United States for decades. Many others were essential workers in war industries. Approximately two hundred thousand of them were refugees whose citizenship in a majority of cases had been revoked by the Axis powers. Their bitter experience with fascism abroad gave them more reason to fight against the system than most Americans. Nevertheless, the council said, "news of the Japanese evacuation, plus inept announcements from the military authorities," had created increasing "uneasiness among all aliens of enemy nationality, and only to a slightly lesser degree among naturalized citizens." The council explained that grave psychological harm had been wreaked, a problem worsened by the widespread use of the invidious term *enemy alien*, it said.[13]

On July 11, 1942, Roosevelt clarified the nondiscrimination policy, which also covered the Japanese (see his statement in appendix, which apparently elaborated on the October 20, 1941, FEPC draft).[14] On January 28, 1943, the secretary of war, further attempting to moderate his department's harsh policy toward Japanese Americans, announced its "confidence in loyal Japanese Americans" and that he was extending to them the right to serve as soldiers in the army:

> It is the inherent right of every faithful citizen, regardless of ancestry, to bear arms in the Nation's battle. When obstacles to the free expression of that right are imposed by emergency considerations, those barriers should be removed as soon as humanly possible. Loyalty to country is a voice that must be heard, and I am glad that I am now able to give active proof that this basic American belief is not a casualty of war.

The War Department also informed the FEPC that it was collaborating with the War Relocation Authority in examining the loyalty qualifications of all Japanese Americans released from the War Relocation Centers for work in essential war industries. The U.S. Civil Service Commission in a letter to its regional and division chiefs, also once more sought futilely to provide a coherent policy and procedure for the use of American citizens of Japanese origin who had been in the centers.[15]

The *First Report* further documented the struggles within the government with the issue. It provided an excerpt of a joint statement by the secretary of war, the attorney general, the secretary of navy, and the chairman of the Maritime Commission on the employment of aliens:

> [The nondiscrimination clause] has been included in all War and Navy Department and Maritime Commission contracts entered into since June 25, 1941. This clause requires the granting of full employment opportunities to all loyal and qualified workers regardless of race, creed, color, or national origin. This clause is intended to apply equally to citizens and noncitizens. For contractors or subcontractors of the War or Navy Department, or of the Maritime Commission to require American citizenship as an essential condition for employment is considered a breach of the clause in the contract and is contrary to the national policy as expressed in the Executive order.
>
> Even on aeronautical and classified contracts, if a qualified applicant whose services the contractor needs is an alien whose loyalty to the United States the contractor has no reason to doubt, the contractor is obligated to cooperate with the applicant in applying for consent to his employment. Failure to request consent for the employment of, or to employ such an alien upon securing consent, if except for his alien status he would have been employed, constitutes a breach of the antidiscriminatory

clause of the contract and is contrary to national policy as expressed in the Executive order. If a contractor refuses employment to a qualified and authorized alien worker, he should be prepared to present specific and sufficient reasons to avoid a charge of discrimination.[16]

Nevertheless, with policy and practice conflicting, Congressman Vito Marcantonio had told Roosevelt that the procedures of the War and Navy departments were creating many serious problems. Marcantonio's experience was that many employers were willing to cooperate in enforcing the federal policies that Roosevelt himself had established, but they were being discouraged from using noncitizens by the manner in which the War and Navy departments were administering the law. He noted that one of the problems deterring employers from hiring or continuing to employ an alien, was that they had to apply to the one of the two departments for permission to do so. After applying for such permission, however, employers had to wait several months before receiving a decision. The employer could not be expected to hold the position open indefinitely, Marcantonio explained, so many stopped giving consideration to noncitizens.

Marcantonio said the situation was further aggravated by the insistence of the departments that an employer receive renewed permission for the employment of an alien for each job that person performed. "Thus a sub-contractor, working on a series of jobs, each of two weeks duration, must obtain permission again and again to employ the same alien." Probably the greatest demoralizing factor, he said, was the refusal of the two departments to give reasons for their denying permission to employ an alien. The practice caused "widespread confusion and hopelessness among great numbers of non-citizens and their families," he said. Another consequence of the practices of the War and Navy departments was that a noncitizen who had worked for a firm for many years and was fired when that firm was converted to classified work had great difficulty in finding other employment in a nonclassified firm because he could not give a reason for his dismissal, because those departments gave him none.[17]

Roosevelt's assertions notwithstanding, the government required contracting agencies to obtain certain information to aid them in their investigations of workers they hired. The enforcement of PL 671 required plants executing confidential—or more explicitly, secret, restricted, or aeronautical—contracts to submit an application to the contracting agency involved for consent before hiring an alien. Consequently, the employer had to have the information about the nationality or citizenship status of applicants. In order to facilitate an investigation, additional information, such as the applicant's national origin, was considered helpful.

The Committee therefore held that in those cases it could not take exception to the inclusion of such inquiry on employment application forms regarding national origin. The Committee maintained:

> Where, however, it cannot be shown that the information on nationality or national origin has a direct relationship to national security, these inquiries should be eliminated.

Inquiries on application for employment forms pertaining to "Descent," in which the applicant is asked to disclose whether he is "Aryan," "Semitic," "Asiatic," "Non-Caucasian," etc., rather than specific information pertaining to nationality, are not acceptable and should be eliminated, since such information concerns *racial origin*.[18]

In January 1944, however, the FEPC still had no policy regarding aliens, and that gap was making it difficult for its field staff to resolve related issues. George Johnson therefore suggested to the Committee that the position of members in the "field operation" should be that the policy on aliens is similar to that with respect to other minority groups. He said "the staff was concerned with what variations, if any, should be made." The AFL's Boris Shishkin, too, stressed that there was "no clear delegation to this Committee to deal with aliens. If we have that jurisdiction we ought to have it defined so there is no question. If we want to assume jurisdiction we ought to have it defined, so there is no question."[19]

Shishkin saw the loyalty issue in a much broader context that involved groups other than Japanese aliens, namely Jews. Discussing the case of a Mr. Miyakawa, who charged he was denied employment because of his Japanese ancestry even though he was born in California, Shishkin reiterated that

> a tremendous amount of abuse in cases of this kind has occurred to American citizens who are eligible to jobs because of the inadequacy of the procedure and the incompetence of the staff of the Civil Service Commission. One flagrant example was a case where a supervisor of the Civil Service Commission who was investigating a girl who had been in my employ came to my office. He asked about her locality, patriotism, etc. This was not a direct investigation. He said, "she had been with the International Labor Organization, a 'commie' outfit from the name of it, and I wonder what you know about that organization, what its purpose is and what its objectives are."

Miyakawa, Shishkin noted, was denied a job that did not involve war production but that handled work in civilian requirements in the area of nonferrous metals.[20]

With the Committee's approval, Johnson suggested a policy that the Committee adopted at its March 4, 1944, meeting:

> Executive Order 9346, issued May 27, 1943, refers to "the policy of the United States to encourage full participation in the war effort by *all* persons in the United States" and specifically states that the new Committee "shall assume jurisdiction over all complaints and matters pending before the old Committee." The intention to vest the new Committee with such jurisdiction over alien complaints as was given to the old Committee, is clear.
>
> The Committee, therefore, recognizes its jurisdiction over problems of discrimination in employment in war industries because of non-citizenship and exercises the powers vested in it by Executive Order 9346 to obtain the elimination of such discrimination in this field as it finds to exist.[21]

Emphasizing his approval of the policy, Charles Hamilton Houston said it seemed to him that the president expressly extended the Committee's jurisdiction "to include all workers, whether they are citizens or aliens." Shishkin, however, who had been absent from the March 4 meeting, strongly dissented from the statement at the Committee's meeting on March 18. He said he objected to "government by press release" and to basing FEPC authority on informal statements of the president. Neither EO 8802 nor EO 9346, he said, explicitly referred to discrimination because of noncitizenship. The Committee's assumption of jurisdiction in such cases placed on it "the responsibility for action involving legal rights and equities of persons." Yet it was "doubtful that such action by the Committee, if subjected to a judicial test, would be sustained by the courts in the absence of a clear and valid grant of authority." Noncitizens, he noted, were "denied employment by the federal government itself and by the majority of state governments. This fact must be faced and its implications met." FEPC policy would have to be accommodated to civil service law. He therefore urged the Committee to seek clear and explicit grants of power regarding the employment of aliens.

In response, the Committee on March 18, 1944, modified its decision and agreed to "request the President to issue an Executive Order giving the Committee jurisdiction over alien complaints, spelling out the authority extended to other specified agencies of the government in cases of alien employment involving questions of national security, and an explicit enumeration of wartime employment policy of the federal government with regard to aliens." The Committee further agreed that regional offices should continue processing such complaints but if they got to the Committee level they would be held pending action on the Committee's recommendation to the president. Roosevelt took no action on the request.[22]

On March 23, 1944, Congress also took up the jurisdiction issue when members of the House Sub-Committee on Appropriations considered the FEPC's budget request for fiscal year 1944–45. Johnson reported that the congressmen questioned the FEPC's representatives regarding its "authority to process complaints involving 'enemy aliens.'" He said the FEPC's representatives responded that the agency did so according to its "jurisdiction over complaints of this type." Although it had "processed only a small number of complaints involving 'enemy aliens' there appeared to be no basis for distinguishing between complaints from 'enemy aliens' and those received from other aliens." Nevertheless, the FEPC's representatives agreed "that pending a clarification of its jurisdiction over all alien complaints, the Committee would suspend processing complaints of this type." Subsequently, Malcolm Ross said that by unanimous action of its seven members on March 27, 1944, "the agency had voted to stop processing all complaints involving aliens, and its regional directors have been so instructed." Processing alien cases was still suspended in January 1945, when the Committee agreed to further discussions with Congressman Ellis D. Patterson, chairman of the House subcommittee, who had recommended that the FEPC handle "resident alien complaints."[23]

With the end of the war, the overriding focus of loyalty concerns shifted to communists, real or imagined. The FEPC suffered many of those attacks during the Smith Committee hearings, when it was suggested that the FEPC was "communist" for promoting "social equality," and subsequently from racist demagogues like James O. Eastland and Theodore G. Bilbo, both senators from Mississippi, during debate on budget appropriations in 1945. Several FEPC staff members were also labeled subversive. But those attacks were a political stretch of fears concerning national security.[24]

NOTES

1. See draft report, "FEPC and Discrimination against Mexicans" (n.d.), used in note at 12/4/43; U.S. Civil Service Commission Circular Letter no. 3982, 3/27/43, used in note at 4/17/43.

2. See Mitchell's memoranda of 5/6, 6/28/43, 1/27, 2/26, 11/21/44, and his report of 2/17/44; *Final Report*, 40.

3. Milner and Dempsey, "Alien Myth," 374–78; High, "Alien Poison," 9–11, 75; the texts of the two statutes, provided in a Bureau of Employment Security advisory, 7/7/41, to all Statement Security Agencies informing them of operating policy and procedures under them, are in HqR65, Central Files. Aliens in Defense, D–H. Section 11 (a) of the Act "To expedite national defense, and for other purposes" (Public Law 671), 6/28/40, 76th Cong., 3d sess. For complete text of the act, see: *United States Statutes at Large*, 76th Cong., 2d, 3d sess., 1939–41, vol. 54, part 1, Public Laws and Reorganization Plans (Washington, D.C.: Government Printing Office, 1941), 676–83. (Section 11 is on pp. 680–81.)

4. The Alien Registration Act, HR 5138, also of 6/28/40, Public Law 670, required the Department of Justice to register all aliens over fourteen years old. For the text of the act, see *United States Statutes at Large*, 76th Cong., 2d, 3d sess., 670–75; *Survey Monthly*, 9/40, 264. "The Alien Registration Act," http://www.spartacus.schoolnet.co.uk/USAalien.htm; "The Alien Registration Act," http://tucnak .fsv.cuni.cz/~calda/Documents/1940s/Alien%20Registration%20Act%20of%201940.html; *NYT*, 6/30/40, 5; *Congress and the Nation, 1945–1964*, 1647–48; http://www.bc.edu/bc_org/avp/cas/comm/free_speech/ smithactof1940.html.

5. "Number of Alien Registration Schedules Received Cumulative Through and During the Week Ending November 1, 1940," HqR65, Central Files. Aliens in Defense, D–H. See Boris Shishkin, cited in note 18, below. The texts of the 1926 and 1940 acts, provided by Bureau of Employment Security, 7/7/41, also can be found in HqR65, Central Files. Aliens in Defense, A. See also "Discrimination against Aliens in Defense Industries," 8/23/41, HqR66, Central Files. U.S. Government, Department of Justice; and news bulletin of Public Administration Clearing House, 9/22/41, "Few Laws to Restrict Aliens' Occupations Enacted in 1941," HqR66, Central Files. U.S. Government, Aliens in Defense, Specific Groups, Japanese.

6. Cramer to Edward F. Prichard Jr., of the WPB, memorandum, 3/9/42, HqR66, Central Files. U.S. Government, Aliens in Defense, Specific Groups, O–S.

7. Martin F. Carpenter, chief, USES Division, to all state employment security agencies, advisory with interpretation attached, 7/7/41, HqR65, Central Files. Aliens in Defense, A.

8. Draft of general statement of 10/20/41, HqR65, Central Files. Aliens in Defense, D–H; Bureau of Employment Security advisory to all State Employment Security Agencies, 7/7/41, HqR65, Central Files. Aliens in Defense, D–H.

9. In EO 9066, issued 2/19/42, "Authorizing the Secretary of War to Prescribe Military Areas," Roosevelt said it did not modify or limit "in any way the authority heretofore granted under Executive Order 8972," issued on 12/12/41, "Executive Order No. 9066," http://www.library.arizona.edu/images/ jpamer/execordr.html; *NYT*, 12/8/41, 6. For the extent of discrimination they suffered, see the headnote on Japanese Americans; "Memorandum of Understanding between the FEPC, War Department, and Provost Marshal General," 3/10/43, HqR4, Office Files of George M. Johnson; Cole, *Enemy Aliens*, 88–100. For a contemporary bibliography, see, in addition to *Enemy Aliens*, "Further Reading—US Government Violation of Japanese American Civil Liberties," http://humanrights.uchicago.edu/ enemyaliens/furtherreading.html; "The Enemy Alien Files: Hidden Stories of World War II," http://humanrights.uchicago.edu/enemyaliens/; "Name Administration, Inc.," http://www.enemyaliens .com/facts.html; "World War II—The Internment of German American Civilians," http://www .foitimes.com/internment/; "WWII Violations of German American Civil Liberties by the U.S. Government," http://www.foitimes.com/internment/gasummary.htm; "Internment of Japanese Americans," http://academic.udayton.edu/race/02rights/intern01.htm; "Confinement and Ethnicity," http://www.cr .nps.gov/history/online_books/anthropology74/ce3d.htm.

10. Cole, *Enemy Aliens,* 88–100; Daniels, *Prisoners without Trial,* 22–48; Department of Justice press release, 12/28/41, HqR75, Tension File. Statement by Attorney General Biddle—employment of aliens in private industry.

11. Press release on statement by the president, 1/2/42, HqR86, Press Releases; Davidson's letter and Cramer's response, as well as Robert Glen's circular letter, are in HqR65, Central Files. Aliens in Defense, D–H; "Discrimination against Aliens in Defense Industries," 8/23/41, HqR66, Central Files. Department of Justice; Roy L. Glen, labor representative, OPM, circular letter, 1/9/42, attached to text of Roosevelt's 1/2/42 statement regarding employment of aliens and foreign-born citizens, HqR65, Central Files. Aliens in Defense, D–H; *First Report,* 146–47.

12. Joint statement, 6/4/42, by the undersecretaries of war and navy, in HqR66, Central Files. U.S. Government, Employment of Aliens, T to XYZ; Bureau of Employment Security, USES Operations Bulletin No. C-29, Supplement No. 2, 7/3/42, in HqR66, Central Files. U.S. Government, Application Forms.

13. For reference to the text of EO 9066, issued 3/18/42, see "The Alien Registration Act," http://www.library.arizona.edu/images/jpamer/wraintro.html; "Plan for Reclassification of Aliens of Enemy Nationality," 6/26/42, Council for Democracy, HqR65, Central Files. Aliens in Defense, A.

14. Excerpt is in Operations Bulletin no. 1, a copy of which is in the collection of the NAACP Washington Branch, FEPC, DHU-MS. See also U.S. Civil Service policy, "Positions Excepted from the Citizenship Restrictions of Appropriation Acts," note 11, app. of Operations Bulletin no. 1; Davidson to Cramer, 1/23, 1/28/42, Cramer to Davidson, 1/29, 1/31/42, and related texts, HqR77, Office Files of Eugene Davidson. Laws on Employment of Aliens; memorandum on "Discrimination against Aliens in Defense Industries," 8/23/41, HqR66, Central Files. U.S. Government, Department of Justice; Department of Justice press release, 12/28/41, HqR75, Reference File. Statement of Attorney General Biddle, Employment of Aliens.

15. John J. McCloy, assistant secretary of war, to Cramer, 4/23/43. Circular Letter no. 3982, 3/27/43, which amended Circular Letter no. 3615, 3/7/42, HqR66, Central Files. Japanese.

16. Employment of Aliens (para. 6 and 7, 6/7/43), in app. 1, *First Report,* 147.

17. Marcantonio's letter, 9/4/42, along with "A Report on Utilization of Non-Citizens in War Industries," and other materials are in HqR65, Central Files. Aliens in Defense, A.

18. Rough draft, "Operations Bulletin Re: Application for Employment Forms," ca. 3/14/44 (estimate based on letter of 1/4/44 by Roy A. Hoglund), HqR4, Office Files of George M. Johnson. Application for Employment; emphasis in original.

19. Transcript of Proceedings, 1/15/44, 63, HqR66, Central Files.

20. Transcript of Proceedings, 2/12/44, 62–66, HqR66, Central Files.

21. Transcript of Proceedings, 3/4/44, 10–13; 3/18/44, 73–78, HqR66, Central Files; emphasis in original; Minutes, 3/4/44, 3/18/44, HqR1, Summary Minutes of Meetings. See also *First Report,* 49–50; press release, statement by the president, 1/2/42, HqR86, Press Releases; Johnson to Maslow, 3/7/44, HqR38, Central Files. Meetings; FEPC Chronology in front of volume.

22. Minutes, 3/4/44, HqR1, Summary Minutes of Meetings. See also "A Report on Utilization of Non-Citizens," cited above; Houston's comment is at Transcript of Proceedings, 3/4/44, 15, HqR65, Central Files; Shishkin's is at Transcript of Proceedings, 4/18/44, 78, HqR65, Central Files; HqR1, Summary Minutes of Meetings, Jan. 18–Sept. 15, 1945, item 5; Shishkin memorandum, 3/14/44, to the Committee, on "Policy on Aliens," in which he strongly complained about the Committee's action at its 3/4/44 meeting, in HqR4, Office Files of George M. Johnson. Committee Meetings.

23. "Exhibit A," regarding FEPC action on 3/27/44, HqR4, Office Files of George M. Johnson. Policy; Johnson to Congressman Ellis D. Patterson, 1/26/45, HqR4, Office Files of George M. Johnson. Records of the Legal Division, Correspondence from Congressmen; *First Report,* 97–98. For references to individual alienage cases, suspension of action on them, and continued handling of them, see Mitchell's memoranda of 1/14, 1/27, 2/26, 10/12, 11/21/44, 1/23/45.

24. For attacks on the FEPC, see, for example, Ross, *All Manner of Men,* 113; "Legislation in the 79th Congress," *Crisis,* 1/45, 29–30; "Negroes! Jews! Catholics!" *Crisis,* 8/45, 217–19, 237–38; Charles L. Horn to Malcolm Ross, 4/19/45; Ross to Horn response, 5/2/45, noting the FEPC staffers, including himself, who had been labeled "subversive," HqR38, Central Files. Memoranda, Charles L. Horn.

RACE, CREED, COLOR OR NATIONAL ORIGIN
ON EMPLOYMENT APPLICATION FORMS

When the FEPC was created, a common practice by employers was to require designations of race, creed, or color on application forms, and since 1914 the Civil Service Commission had been requesting photographs from job applicants for its written examinations. Some employers placed these designations on employees' badges. Because the required information was unnecessary for measuring job performance and could encourage racial and religious discrimination, the Committee opposed the requirements. It was stymied, in part, in developing a clear-cut policy, however, because the requirement of noting race, creed, and color was often intertwined with national origin, alienage, and loyalty.[1]

The FEPC implemented its national nondiscrimination policy, under which it attacked those requirements, according to the following criteria:

Race: Distinguishing physical characteristics of a people, inherited from a common ancestry. The committee distinguished race from nationality, which connoted geographical differentiations of a political nature. Its basic distinctions, of course, were black (or Negro) and white.

Creed: Adherence to a formalized religious faith, membership in a particular religious denomination or sect, or identification with a particular group that is presumed to be devoted to a code of principles and practices of a religious character. Groups fitting that interpretation were Catholics, Jews, Quakers, Mormons, Moslems, Jehovah's Witnesses, Seventh-day Adventists and various Protestant denominations and sects. It did not consider personal "conscience" unrelated to the religious code of an organized sect (such as the refusal to salute the flag or say the Pledge of Allegiance) as aspects of creed that was covered by Executive Order 8802.

Color: A distinguishing personal or group feature based on skin pigmentation rather than national or racial origin. Most often color discrimination was practiced against African Americans, Filipinos, dark-skinned Mexicans, Latin Americans, American Indians, and Portuguese.

National Origin: The birth of a naturalized American citizen in a foreign country (such as Mexicans or Japanese). That form of discrimination was not based on noncitizenship, as was alienage (see the headnote on National Origin, Alienage, and Loyalty).[2]

President Roosevelt agreed with the FEPC's efforts to end the designation requirements. On September 3, 1941, he wrote Mark Ethridge, chairman of the FEPC, that designations of race, religion, and national origin on the employment forms of government agencies and private employers under its purview should be removed. Ethridge promptly implemented the instruction by recommending to those employers that they revise their application forms, and "if they now require the applicant to specify his race or color, to eliminate this requirement."[3]

The principal war-contracting agencies and most government agencies agreed to the proposal to end the requirement. As George Johnson told J. B. King of the Federal

Communications Commission, the proposal was further extended to all employers in government-owned but privately operated industrial plants of the War and Navy Departments and the Maritime Commission. In a joint letter to the Committee on July 2, 1942, the heads of those departments reported they had removed the requirement and said they would instruct contractors to do the same. Johnson said the Committee subsequently requested war contractors in privately owned and operated plants to do the same.[4]

The Committee also opposed the use of photographs "for the same reason." L. A. Moyer, executive director and chief examiner of the U.S. Civil Service Commission, in a departmental circular of November 10, 1943, explained that since 1941 it had discontinued the reference to race and the use of photographs on any of its forms. Previously, he said, the commission had required photographs "with applications as a method of identification to prevent impersonation." Instead, departments and agencies were authorized to accept the CSC's application form 57 "for original appointment or transfer." Clearly in response to the FEPC's insistence, Moyer reminded departments and agencies of the policy.[5]

Agreeing with the proposal, the CSC established uniform application forms that did not include requiring a photograph. Although the Committee's priorities did not include political attacks, even though it was suffering some, it was relevant that section 2, rule 1, of the commission's regulations barred such inquiries except where required by law for wartime security purposes.[6]

Because of those wartime security concerns, the Committee found it much more difficult to end national origin identification and requirements for citizenship on employment application forms, which particularly concerned Jews. The Committee initially was ambivalent about it. Responding to a complaint from Eli Cohen, executive director of the Coordinating Committee of Jewish Organizations Dealing with Employment Discrimination in War Industries, Lawrence Cramer said that Colonel Schmidt of the John J. Doe Company of Baltimore was not familiar with the War Department's policy on the employment of aliens and its deletion of inquiries into race, creed, or color on job application forms. Cohen said Schmidt's position was that "religion was requested as a means for checking an applicant's character and reputation through a priest, rabbi or minister." The Minnesota Jewish Council, which had raised the issue with Schmidt, informed Cramer that a War Department memorandum of August 17, 1942, outlined a sample letter to contractors asking them, among other things, to delete references to race or religion on their employment application forms. Protesting the references, Cramer sent the company a copy of the president's July 11, 1942, statement clarifying the government's policy on the employment of aliens in war industries. But that did not resolve the matter, and it remained a thorn for Jewish groups.[7]

Johnson subsequently explained to the Committee that a person of German ancestry who was born in New York might have to provide the information on national origin where the form required him to do so. That requirement was a must on FBI forms in war plants. The discussion showed a significant difference in the attitudes of blacks and Jews over the requirement. Charles Houston said he saw no objection to the question, "Where were you born?" But he could see one to the question, "Where was your mother or father born?" because, at a certain level, "it depends on what you are shooting at." Boris Shishkin said that the FBI some years earlier had approved a question on the census inquiring about a mother's maiden name. Such a question did exist on the CSC's form 57, Johnson noted. It was also in all Security Division forms. Item 41(a) asked:

> Were any of the following members of your family born outside Continental U.S.A.? Wife, Husband, Father, Mother.
> If so, indicate which by marking the appropriate space and show under Item 45 for each (1) full name, including maiden name of wife or mother; (2) birthplace; (3) native citizenship; and (4) if U.S. naturalized, date of naturalization.

Item 41(b) asked:

> Have you any relatives, by blood or by marriage (excluding persons in the U.S. armed forces) now living in a foreign country?

Johnson informed the Committee that Abel E. Berland of the Chicago office of the Anti-Defamation League was "making a strong plea" for the FEPC to strongly oppose the requirement. He reminded members that while they had adopted a policy opposing inquiries about race or religion on the forms, they did not adopt a similar one on national origin. Berland complained that the question had "nothing to do with the man's ability to do a job." He said it would be better to ask for his citizenship status, adding:

> There can be no valid objection to an employer seeking to determine whether he is hiring a citizen or a non-citizen. That would appear to be relevant and fair.
> There frequently is a misconception as to what the questions of nationality and descent really mean. Many people, when asked what their nationality is, even though they be American citizens mistakenly reply that they are Scotch, Irish, Jewish, etc. Add to this lack of understanding on the part of many as to what information these questions are intended to elicit, the fact that the inclusion of these questions provides personnel officials with the opportunity to interpret them in such a manner so as to obtain frequently the kind of data which may be used in violation of the President's Executive Order. It is difficult to understand how one can justify the elimination of the questions of race and religion from application forms and at the same time permit the use of nationality and descent, providing the same loophole for the development of discrimination in employment procedures. Either the reasoning which supports the contention that an employer does not require information concerning the race, creed or national origin of the applicant is sound in toto or it should be abandoned. It cannot be justified in one instance and then defeated in part in another.

Berland said that, given the FEPC's procedure of dealing with discrimination only when there was an indication that such bias arose "out of the inquiries relating to nationality and descent," it was needless for him "to point out the difficulty of securing a clear-cut case under" the circumstances. "Even if it were possible to do so," he said, "it would appear to be more desirable to prevent, in the first instance, the development of the discrimination just as in the case of the deletion in the questions of race and religion."

He stressed that government agencies concerned with internal security had to admit that individuals determined to conduct disloyal activities would conceal the information concerning their origin if that was a factor involved in their being employed and kept under surveillance. "United States citizenship presumes that a man's background and record have been investigated if he is naturalized, or requires no special investigation if he is a citizen by birth," he said. That should satisfy the requirements of the FBI and other agencies, he said.

Shishkin stressed that if a person was naturalized or a citizen by birth, the investigation was thorough, so Berland's point was well taken. He explained that some of those questions were introduced because until quite recently a certificate of naturalization was not required of older persons who became naturalized through their parents or under a blanket provision for those arriving before 1930—or whatever the actual legal cutoff year was. He recalled that until 1911 there had been mass migration to the United States. "Naturalization for parents was committed to any youngsters whose parents secured naturalization prior to their becoming of age. They did not have any evidence, there were no naturalization papers and that kind of evidence. It was the only means of establishing their claim to citizenship. It was the correct one."

Subsequently, the naturalization process changed. Shishkin said certificates of naturalization were then granted to certify citizenship. Like Berland, he thought such evidence should be sufficient proof of citizenship. But Sara E. Southall responded that if the process was to be challenged, it should be done through the FBI and the Civil Service Commission because they were the ones imposing those requirements on government and private employers, "and we are in a quite hopeless position to tell employers that they have got to take it out when the FBI and intelligence services are telling them they have to put it in."

Even though the members agreed to discuss the matter with the other agencies, Houston said he saw another problem, in addition to Berland's letter being faulty. The question, he said, was one of "divided loyalties," and there was no "particular divided loyalty on the ground of just race as race. White and black are in this thing all together, and there is no divided loyalty as to creed. Protestant, Catholic and Jew are all in this together, but when it comes down to origin, you have serious questions of divided loyalties." In Chicago, Houston said,

> [Y]ou have all your spite trials where you have these second generations arguing. If in a family, even though a citizen just might have been naturalized, the whole leaning of the family has been against naturalization and keeping active ties with the old country, you have at this particular stage danger.
>
> Viewing it against the background of the existing war, you have an entirely different reason for asking as to the origin of the family than you would have, it seems to me, asking for either race or creed.

So, Houston said, he would be opposed to the inclusion of questions of national origin on application forms in peacetime, "or I would be opposed to any inquiry which did not reflect the existing situation, but it strikes me if the younger brother is naturalized and the old folks aren't and they have been back in Germany repeatedly and they have had swastikas hanging in the house."

"That is not a question. I don't agree with you," Shishkin said, cutting off Houston. "I don't think that is a question of national origin. That is a question of subversive attitude. That is entirely in a separate category."

Persisting, Houston said, "I carry it to the point where unquestionably you pick me up, but at the same time it does seem to me an issue where you have a question like this that the foundation information is an inquiry as to the origin of the family."

Concurring, Southall said, "You have no idea how many times they run into some member of a family that is tied up with a subversive gang, and the only way they ever locate him is back through those things. The FBI is always looking through those things."

But Shishkin insisted that his concern was with wartime. He therefore demanded "a factual, comprehensive report on the views of" concerned agencies, which the Committee agreed to have the staff provide. The rapidly approaching end of the war, however, soon made the issue irrelevant.[8] (For related loyalty issues see the headnote in National Origin, Alienage, and Loyalty.)

Badges

Responding to complaints to the New York regional office, the Committee similarly protested the Navy Department's placing of racial designations—W for white, N for Negro—on employees' badges at the Brooklyn Navy Yard. Ralph A. Bard, assistant secretary of the navy, in his response, revealed the department's increasing sensitivity to racial issues. He explained that the navy's circular letter of November 18, 1942, prohibited intimidation or reprisal against an employee who complained about discrimination or registered a grievance. On that date, he said, the department established a "uniform procedure with the approval of the Civil Service Commission to handle cases of complaints and grievances." The department's August 20, 1943, letter provided for the giving of "full consideration" to requests for absences on holy days, and its letter of April 1, 1944, established a "uniform policy" barring racial designations on badges beginning on that day.[9]

Personnel Forms

However, the Committee said that the recording of race and religion on personnel forms after a person had been employed did not lead to discrimination. It therefore required such record keeping because reports based on that information were necessary for measuring progress in implementing the executive order and for submission to the president.[10]

Refusing to comply with the request, Harry B. Mitchell, president of the Civil Service Commission, told Lawrence Cramer that his agency was able to obtain from its division chiefs and regional directors "complete tallies on the distribution of colored employees by organization units." The tallies, he said, "could be consolidated into the type of report" the FEPC used. Therefore, he said, unless there was "indication that more information than heretofore requested by you will be needed in the future, the entry of race data on post-employment forms" seemed unnecessary to him. Of course, that system was not as efficient as the one the FEPC sought to implement, he said.[11]

Nevertheless, Johnson told Clarence Mitchell that Robert Weaver had received several reports indicating that the refusal to submit the nonwhite employment information was "rather widespread" and that employers were attributing their defiance to the FEPC's prohibition of placing race and religion information on preemployment forms. Mitchell therefore suggested to Weaver that he draft a statement, which he did. The Civil Service Commission was one of those that never budged from its refusal to gather the information.[12]

In a letter of October 6, 1942, to heads of all federal departments and independent establishments under its jurisdiction, the FEPC affirmed its policy. Its statement, it said, "in no way qualifies the Committee's firm position that designations of race, creed, or color be removed from application-for-employment forms wherever they may still be present."[13]

On January 11, 1944, the FEPC got significant support from the War Manpower Commission in its draft bulletin to state manpower directors and regional division chiefs in clarifying the agency's position. The bulletin noted that the FEPC was experiencing difficulty in collecting postemployment race data owing to the impression among government and private employers that the Committee had ruled that such action violated the executive order. The WMC was particularly concerned that the information was being omitted from many ES 270 reports, which kept track of minority hiring. It stressed that "race must be deleted from preemployment forms *only*. Such records that are kept of race, after addition to the payroll, *are not* in violation of Executive Order 9346."[14] Many employers voluntarily complied with the FEPC's request. A good example of the benefits of collecting the data was a WMC report of March 1944, "Utilization of Reserve Workers: Recently Reported Placements of Negroes in Skilled Occupations."[15]

General Motors, though, adamantly refused to cooperate. On January 4, 1944, M. W. Howe, Chevrolet–St. Louis plant manager, explained to Roy A. Hoglund, FEPC regional director, that, in keeping with the FEPC's directive, GM had, beginning on March 10, 1942, repeatedly ordered its plants to eliminate all racial records. Howe said, "General Motors' position on this matter is that maintaining *any* records on race in the employment or other operating office of the plant *after* the person's employment is just as open to misinterpretation and criticism as such an inquiry prior to employment." Consequently, he said, GM would continue its "policy of maintaining no racial records." Many other war contractors in recent months also had cited the FEPC's policy of barring racial or religious designations on employment forms for refusing to do so on personnel records.[16] The resistance caused Vernon McGee, deputy executive director of the WMC, which still supported the FEPC, on March 28, 1944, to write Clarence Mitchell that the commission had "no authority for requiring the maintaining of such records."[17]

On September 19, 1944, Johnson acknowledged to Maceo Hubbard, FEPC counsel, "Whether or not the company's stated reasons for refusing to supply these statistics are bona fide, they do raise a rather embarrassing question." Hubbard subsequently told Johnson that Mitchell had concluded, based on information he had received, that the WMC had "no power to compel an employer to furnish the sort of statistical information requested" in this case. "Such information" was voluntarily furnished. Unless the FEPC found proper authority in Executive Order 9346, it was "without right to demand or attempt to require the company to furnish the information requested." Mitchell therefore said that the requirement was "beyond the Committee's power and jurisdiction."[18]

Boris Shishkin agreed. He suggested to Johnson that it seemed "desirable, however, for the FEPC to explore the feasibility of recommending to the War Manpower Commission and to the Bureau of the Census a procedure whereby such information be required of the Company by those agencies." There the issue remained unsettled for the FEPC.[19]

NOTES

1. Policy outlined in the statement "Reference to Race and/or Religion on Company or Agency Forms," with the suggestion that the new committee decide on its position on this matter, HqR2, Office Files of Malcolm Ross. Materials from July 26 Meeting.

2. Operating Bulletin no. 1, NAACP Washington Branch collection, FEPC, DHU-MS.

3. Lawrence Cramer referred to Roosevelt's letter of 9/3/41 in his letter of 10/7/43 to Harry B. Mitchell, commissioner, U.S. Civil Service Commission; Brig. Gen. Lewis B. Hershey, director, Selective Service System; James Lawrence Fly, chairman, Federal Communications Commission; and R. Adm. Emory S. Land, chairman, U.S. Maritime Commission, copies of which are also in HqR66, Central Files. U.S. Government, Application Forms.

4. See Johnson to J. B. King, 5/21/43, and Lawrence Cramer to P. Minor, 7/27/42, HqR66, Central Files. U.S. Government, Aliens in Defense, General, Application Forms. An example of a company that complied was Transcontinental & Western Air, Inc., which in a letter of 1/14/43 to Johnson provided the racial breakdown based on skilled and unskilled positions held by blacks and whites. Other related materials can be found in HqR1, Summary Minutes of Meetings. Committee Meetings, 1/11/44. The letter is also mentioned in rough draft, "Operations Bulletin, Re: Application for Employment Forms" [ca. 3/10/42—date is based on M. W. Howe to Roy A. Hoglund, 1/4/44], Operations Bulletin.

5. Moyer, Departmental Circular no. 449, 11/10/43, HqR66, Central Files. U.S. Government, Civil Service Commission. For examples of complaints regarding such problems, see Barron B. Beshoar to Cramer, 12/22/42, 1/20/43, and Cramer to Beshoar, 1/11/43, same location. On the Civil Service Commission's requirement for photographs, see King, *Separate and Unequal*, 48.

For the Committee's position on photographs, see Lawrence Cramer to John J. Doe Company, Baltimore, 3/31/43 (sparked by a complaint from Eli Cohen, 3/31/43), HqR2, Office Files of Malcolm Ross. Holiday; rough draft, "Operations Bulletin Re: Application for Employment Forms," n.d.— however, M. W. Howe's letter of 1/4/44 to Hoglund regarding General Motors' refusal to keep postemployment records places the date at around 3/14/42. HqR4, Office Files of George M. Johnson. Application for Employment.

6. Copy of Civil Service Commission, section 2, rule 1, which was attached to rough draft, "Operations Bulletin Re: Application Forms" [ca. 3/14/42] is in HqR1, Summary Minutes of Meetings. Committee Meetings. The draft's source was Operations Bulletin no. 1, n. 7, a copy of which can be found in FEPC, NAACP Washington Branch, DHU-MS. See the nondiscrimination policy section of the introduction for the broader scope of section 2, rule 1 of the regulations as it reinforced the Committee's work.

According to a 9/29/44 memorandum from Maceo Hubbard to Johnson, the Committee reaffirmed the policy on 8/9/43. HqR5, Office Files of George M. Johnson. Maceo Hubbard.

7. A copy of the Coordinating Committee's letter of 3/26/43, as well as Cramer's letters to Cohen and to the John Doe Company, both of 3/31/43, are in HqR2, Office Files of Malcolm Ross. Holiday. See also USES Operating Bulletin no. C-29, supplement no. 2, "Operating Policy and Procedure," regarding "Discrimination in Employment on the Basis of Citizenship Requirements; Local Provisions Governing Employment under Certain Types of Navy and War Department Contracts," 7/3/42, regarding the USES revising its procedure for facilitating employment of persons who were unable to produce birth certificates, HqR66, Central Files. U.S. Government, Application Forms. Citizenship issues, as they related to issues of birth, are covered in the headnote on National Origin, Alienage, and Loyalty.

8. Transcript of Proceedings, 3/4/44, 24–33, HqR65, Central Files. See also Minutes, 3/4/44, HqR1, Summary Minutes of Meetings. Berland's letter is also in HqR4, Office Files of George M. Johnson. Committee Matters. In response to the Committee's request for the legal division to draft a policy statement, Johnson provided them on 5/16/44 with one dated 5/11/44, prepared by Ernest Trimble. Johnson explained that the memorandum was presented to the Committee at its 5/13 meeting in Chicago and, according to his understanding, it was approved. The position the Committee then took was "that inquiry as to nationality or place of birth and citizenship on application for employment forms is not inconsistent with the provision of Executive Order 9346." Malcolm Ross scribbled on the memorandum, "This is my understanding of the Committee's position." HqR4, Office Files of George M. Johnson. Committee Matters.

9. Bard to Malcolm Ross, HqR67, Central Files. U.S. Government, Navy Department. Related materials are also in HqR84, Correspondence Relating to Cases. (L–S). Materials on racial designations on identification badges are in Brooklyn Navy Yard materials in HqR84, Correspondence Relating to Cases. Navy Department; and in HqR83, Correspondence Relating to Cases. (L–Se), Navy Identification Badges.

10. Committee statement, "Reference to Race and/or Religion on Company or Agency Forms," n.d., HqR2, Office Files of Malcolm Ross. Materials from July 26 Meeting. See also draft statement by Weaver on maintaining postemployment race records, attached to his memorandum to Johnson, 7/28/43, HqR38, Central Files. Memoranda, George Johnson, M—3, 12/41–12/43.

11. Cramer to Harry Mitchell, 9/20/41, Harry Mitchell to Cramer, 10/21/42, HqR66, Central Files. U.S. Government, Application Forms.

On private employment firms, see the references to the Retail Credit Company cases in Clarence Mitchell's weekly reports of 2/17, 3/18, 5/24, 9/18/44, and his memorandum of 8/14/44; Cramer to L. A. Moyer, 12/18/42, executive director and chief examiner, U.S. Civil Service Commission, transmitting a letter of that date from Retail Credit Company to Moyer; Walter C. Hill, president, Retail Credit Company, to Cramer, 1/6/43, explaining his company's reasons for seeking the information; Cramer to Col. Alton C. Miller, director, personnel security division of the Office of Provost Marshal, War Department, 5/18/43, on Retail Credit Company; Cramer to Col. M. S. Battle, chief, personnel security section of the internal security division of the War Department, 3/3/43, on the Hooper-Holmes Bureau, another private employment company. All correspondence is in HqR66, Central Files. U.S. Government, Application Forms.

12. Johnson, memorandum of 7/29/43, to Mitchell, and Weaver's memorandum of 7/28/43, with a draft statement, to Johnson, all in HqR38, Central Files. Memoranda, George Johnson, M—3, 12/41–12/43. See also Harry Mitchell's exchange of letters with John A. Davis, 9/11, 9/12/45, HqR66, Central Files. U.S. Government, Application Forms; Clarence Mitchell, memorandum, 4/16/43, regarding the difficulty in measuring progress in training programs for problems caused by the failure of the U.S. Office of Education to keep race statistics; Clarence Mitchell, memorandum, 11/5/43, on problems caused by a group of firms in Region IX that also resisted keeping the records.

13. The 10/6/42 quotation is in Henderson to Johnson, memorandum, 3/1/43, HqR66, Central Files. U.S. Government, Application Forms.

14. The WMC draft bulletin, 1/1/44, is in HqR4, Office Files of George M. Johnson. War Manpower Commission; HqR66, Central Files. U.S. Government, Application Forms, emphasis in original. See also WMC Draft Bulletin no. RO-111-92, HqR4, Central Files. U.S. Government, Application Forms.

15. See, for example, Otis F. Bryan, general manager, Transcontinental & Western Air, to George Johnson, 1/14/43, HqR6, Office Files of George M. Johnson and Emanuel Bloch. The WMC's 3/44 report is in HqR4, Office Files of George M. Johnson. War Manpower Commission.

16. Howe's letter and Hoglund's response are in HqR1, Office Files of Malcolm Ross. Outgoing Correspondence, 8/41–5/46, Committee Meetings; emphasis in original. See also materials in HqR2, Office Files of Malcolm Ross. Reference to Race and/or Religion, and Materials from July 26 Meeting.

17. McGee to Mitchell, HqR83, Correspondence Relating to Cases. (A–L), General Motors, Region V. See also Mitchell to Maslow, 4/12/44.

18. Both Johnson's 9/19/44 memorandum and Hubbard's 9/29/44 response are in HqR1, Office Files of Malcolm Ross. Outgoing Correspondence, 8/41–5/46, Committee Meetings. Also see HqR5, Office Files of George M. Johnson. Maceo Hubbard.

19. HqR5, Office Files of George M. Johnson. Shishkin.

JAPANESE AMERICANS

Before Pearl Harbor, Japanese Americans, otherwise called nisei, were experiencing difficulty in getting defense industry jobs because of strong cultural differences. Their plight became critical after President Roosevelt, on December 12, 1941, issued Executive Order 8972 suspending their employment pending a careful investigation of their loyalty by the War Department. The order authorized and directed the secretary of war and the secretary of the navy to take whatever action they deemed necessary to protect from injury or destruction national-defense material, premises, and utilities, as broadly defined in the Sabotage Act. In keeping with the order, the government issued instructions and took action to ensure that everyone who had access to important national defense material, premises, and utilities was loyal to the country.[1]

The policy, however, conflicted with Executive Order 8802. Consequently, the FEPC in September 1942 sought the opinion of the general counsel of the War Manpower Commission. He responded that "there is no question that the Committee has jurisdiction to receive and investigate complaints made by persons of Japanese ancestry suspended as a result of the War Department's present policy, and . . . to make recommendations to the War Department and to the President." The counsel's opinion boosted the FEPC's prestige when he explained that ordinarily the FEPC would have had no "authority to inquire into the appropriateness of measures taken by the Secretary of War in the exercise of his discretion under EO 8972." However, "[w]here the measures taken are based primarily on considerations of race or national origin . . . and where they allege to be in violation of Executive Order 8802, the President's Committee may inquire into their appropriateness."[2]

The FEPC's concern about the treatment of the Japanese was especially pertinent because, as Baron B. Beshoar, WMC special groups consultant in Colorado, noted, their predicament was "not only injurious to the war effort and the morale of the

Japanese-Americans themselves, but" it had "an indirectly adverse effect on the employment of members of other minority groups, such as Spanish-Americans and Negroes." Discrimination against Japanese Americans, Beshoar added, was "open and widespread."

> It will be said that we must treat the Japanese-Americans as a distinct group, because we are at war with their ancestral country, but in response to this I call your attention to the fact that we do not treat citizens of German or Italian ancestry in the same manner. In fact, German and Italian nationals are permitted much freedom in areas where Japanese-Americans are banned through [sic] we are just as much at war with Germany and Italy as with Japan.[3]

The FEPC noted that, in contrast to the pervasive discrimination against Japanese Americans, complaints filed by Italians, Germans, Chinese, and aliens were insignificant in number and primarily reflected local prejudice.[4]

The FEPC thus vigorously defended the rights of Japanese Americans whose loyalty was established, and particularly those who had served in the military. The FEPC stated that its policy toward Japanese Americans was consistent with that toward other groups, which was that all Americans were entitled to equal protection under EO 9346. It therefore challenged a General Accounting Office ban on the hiring of Japanese Americans.[5]

The FEPC had good support from President Roosevelt, who on September 14, 1943, in a message to the Senate, said: "Americans of Japanese ancestry, like those of many other ancestries, have shown that they can, and want to, accept our institutions and work loyally with the rest of us . . . it is important to us to maintain a high standard of fair, considerate, and equal treatment for the people of this minority as of all other minorities." The following month he issued a field instruction clarifying the policy. Despite that protection, government-instituted discrimination toward Japanese Americans was relentless and systematic. They were confined in large numbers to relocation centers and forced to leave their homes on the West Coast and subsequently scattered throughout states like Colorado, Wyoming, Montana, Idaho, and Utah, the FEPC's Region XI.[6]

The FEPC, however, never gave up. As an example, Stanley Metzger in October 1943 told Maslow he was seeking a relaxation of a Civil Service Commission policy that provided for lengthy investigations of Japanese Americans. A January 10, 1945, policy statement from Harry Kingman regarding "Workers of Japanese Ancestry on the West Coast" that Maslow amended and approved, said,

> [R]egarding complaints from a worker of Japanese ancestry alleging denial of equal employment opportunity by employers or unions in war industry or in government, the FEPC "will investigate to determine whether the complaint is valid. If discrimination is found to exist, the Committee will do its best to obtain elimination of the unfair employment practices. The same attempt will be made in this case to carry out the provisions of the national Non-Discrimination Order that is made in behalf of any other minority worker over which the FEPC has jurisdiction."[7]

The FEPC got the coast guard to end its restriction on the hiring of Japanese American merchant seamen. As the war drew to a close, many Japanese Americans returned to the West Coast, where some sought employment in defense-related industries. But the FEPC could not get the Navy Department to end its ban on employment of Japanese Americans in naval installations on the West Coast.[8]

Kingman confirmed this to Mitchell, who apparently was preparing to meet with CSC representatives in Washington. The navy's "most flagrant discrimination against all persons of Japanese ancestry" persisted, he said. The commission had instructed its West Coast representatives that it was navy policy not to certify or recruit them for naval establishments in California, Oregon, Washington, or Hawaii. "This policy is particularly flagrant in that it applies to veterans as well as non-veterans," Kingman said. "It appears that it is the Navy and not the Civil Service Commission which is responsible." Outside the West Coast, he said, the appointments of Japanese American citizens were subjected to investigations by the commission that were not made of German Americans. Kingman suggested to Mitchell that he ask commission representatives why was it necessary for the agency, before certifying a Japanese American citizen to a West Coast governmental agency, to stipulate that the job was not closely related to the war effort nor was it of a confidential nature. "If this is not stipulated, an investigation is required which takes considerable time and naturally increases the difficulty of securing the position," he said. Again, Japanese Americans whom the army had permitted to return to the West Coast were singled out for special treatment. "Someday," said Kingman, "the United States is likely to look back with shame upon its treatment of a racial minority many of whose members have proven their loyalty the hard way."[9]

There were promises of positive changes, though, as the FEPC's *Final Report* noted:

> All sources agree that the return of the Japanese-Americans has been far more successful than many people believed possible. The "success" is admittedly the result of their own initiative, rather than the interest of the community. As a matter of fact, the return of the Japanese has not occasioned as much tension, especially of an overt nature as may have been anticipated by some, but the stereotypes of employment have been reestablished. The Japanese relief case load is now well over a thousand and at least 4,000 returnees are stranded as to housing. The chief source of racial tension in Los Angeles is not employment, but housing. The main difficulties are chargeable to restrictive covenants which cause overcrowding.[10]

NOTES

1. EO 8972 is paraphrased in "Memorandum of Understanding" of 3/10/43, between the FEPC, War Department, and the Provost Marshal General, War Department, HqR4, Office Files of George M. Johnson. Agreements, War Department. For historical overviews, see Hosokawa, *Nisei: The Quiet Americans;* "Historical Overview of the Japanese American Internment," at www.momomedia .com/CLBEF/history.html.

2. Earl Dickerson, acting chairman of FEPC, to Robert P. Patterson, undersecretary of war, 3/1/43, and related exchanges, HqR66, Central Files. U.S. Government, Aliens in Defense, Specific Groups, Japanese; other texts are in HqR1, Office Files of Malcom Ross. Outgoing Correspondence, 8/41–5/46, Extra Copies.

3. Beshoar's detailed overview to Lawrence Cramer, 3/31/43, HqR66, Central Files. U.S. Government, Aliens in Defense, Specific Groups, Japanese. In a 4/15/43 telegram to Cramer, Beshoar also expressed grave concerns over the impact on recruiting workers by companies in the mountain states of a statement by General Dewitt before a congressional committee in San Francisco: "A Jap's a Jap, and it makes no difference whether he is an American citizen or not. . . . You can't change . . . a Japanese by giving him a piece of paper. . . . They are a dangerous element whether loyal or not." Ibid.

4. *First Report,* 51, 98; *Final Report,* 39, 40.

5. See Mitchell's memorandum of 11/17/43 and his report on his conference with the comptroller general's office given at the FEPC meeting of 1/15/44, in Transcript of Proceedings 1/15/44, 45–48, HqR65, Central Files; also his concerns expressed to Ross, 2/4/44, over the GAO's field instructions, chap. 16, "Procedures Applicable to Limited Groups," HqR1, Office Files of Malcolm Ross. M.

6. FEPC draft, "Statement for January 10th Conference," Central Files. U.S. Government, Aliens in Defense, Specific Groups, Japanese. Also in this location is a copy of the War Relocation Authority's independent leave policy circular, published in the *Federal Register,* 9/28/42. An example of the FEPC's efforts on behalf of three persons of Japanese and German backgrounds and a Jew are provided in Maslow's letter of complaint, 11/8/43, to Major Sidney Suffrin, Labor Branch, Industrial Personnel Division, Army Service Force, War Department, HqR66, Central Files. U.S. Government, Aliens in Defense, Specific Groups, Japanese. For a current background of Japanese internment, see Roger Daniels, "Incarcerating Japanese Americans."

7. Metzger to Maslow, 10/23/43, in which he sends the CSC's relaxation of circular 405, is in HqR66, Central Files. U.S. Government, Aliens in Defense, Specific Groups, Japanese. Lawrence Cramer, too, remained deeply involved. See his 3/10/43 letter from L. A. Moyer, executive director and chief examiner of the commission, regarding the FEPC's concerns over another circular that also resulted in lengthy investigations, ibid.

On 12/20/44 Kingman asked Maslow for the latest interpretation of the FEPC's Field Instruction 20 of 10/8/43. Maslow's 1/10/45 approval of Kingman's draft apparently represented the FEPC's most recent policy on the question. Those documents are in FEPC FR103, Region XII. Administrative Files (A–Z), Policy, American-Japanese.

8. On the exclusion of Japanese Americans from certain facilities by the Coast Guard and the Navy Department, see Mitchell's reports of 2/17, 4/24/44, 5/21, 5/26, 6/5, 8/9/45; and his memorandum on "Important Cases Being Handled at Regional Level," 4/22–5/22/44, in appendix 1; Reed, *Seedtime,* 238–51; HqR66, Central Files. U.S. Government, Aliens in Defense, Specific Groups, Japanese; headnotes on Jurisdictional Issues and on Relationships with Federal Agencies.

9. Kingman, memorandum, 5/1/45, FR103, Region XII. Administrative Files (A–Z), Policy, American-Japanese. See Mitchell's memorandum of 5/26/45 on his 5/23/45 conference with the Navy Department on its policy, and his 8/9/45 memorandum to Ross on his continuing struggle with the Civil Service Commission's regulations on this issue.

10. *Final Report,* 83.

MEXICAN AMERICANS

The FEPC's concern about the treatment of workers of Mexican origin or descent throughout the Southwest, both citizens and noncitizens, was aroused in May 1942, when it began receiving complaints from them alleging discrimination in war industries because of their race or color.[1] In addition to Region X (Louisiana, Texas, New Mexico, and Arizona), cases involving discrimination against Mexican Americans were concentrated to a lesser extent in Regions IX (Missouri, Kansas, Oklahoma, Arkansas, Colorado, Utah, Wyoming, Idaho, Montana) and XII (Nevada, California, Washington, and Oregon). A few cases originated in the Chicago area. Although, as aliens, Mexican nationals sometimes experienced additional difficulties getting clearance for work in defense plants, in general no distinction in discrimination was made in favor of those who were American citizens. Many industries discriminated equally against Mexican nationals and Mexican Americans (or Spanish Americans, as they were sometimes called), African Americans, and, in some places, Indians. Mining, a principal industry in New Mexico and Arizona, nevertheless gave slightly more opportunities to Mexicans and relied primarily on their labor.

Mexican American leaders feared that because they had no strong tradition of labor organization or protest and had played no role in establishing the FEPC, their grievances would be overlooked. That fear was confirmed by the scant attention given to discrimination against them at the FEPC hearings in Los Angeles in 1941, even though they were the largest minority in the area. However, even though the three million Spanish Americans in the Southwest were an important labor source, and prevailing practices both prevented their full use and undermined Roosevelt's Good Neighbor policy with Latin America, the FEPC was not as involved in combating discrimination against them as it was against African Americans and other groups.[2]

Regarding agricultural workers imported from Mexico and the West Indies, the FEPC established that the nondiscrimination policy also applied to them, but it did not become directly involved in those cases because those foreigners were primarily under the jurisdiction of the Departments of State and Agriculture. Large numbers of Mexicans also worked on the railroads throughout the country, and in the mining and oil industries. Consequently, their cases were the most significant ones involving Spanish Americans that the FEPC handled. Their complaints involved dual wage structures, improper job classifications, and their relegation to the dirtiest, most arduous, and lowest-paying jobs, with little or no possibility of advancement or training.[3]

Catholic Church leaders, particularly Bishop Robert E. Lucey of San Antonio; Adolfo G. Domínguez, the Mexican consul in Texas; other Mexican officials; and key union leaders increasingly pressed for action to end discrimination against Spanish Americans. Additionally, the Mexican government refused to permit its citizens to migrate to the United States for work unless discrimination against them was ended. Furthermore, the International Union of Mine, Mill, and Smelter Workers, CIO, fearful of an influx of workers at substandard wages, for a time objected to their importation unless the related agreement included a ban on discrimination. The War Manpower Commission also hoped that its joint efforts with the FEPC and the War Production Board could eliminate discrimination so that additional Mexican workers could be obtained. However, with the mines unwilling to modify their practices, the Roosevelt administration did not approve a new labor agreement with Mexico for mineworkers.[4]

In August 1943, the FEPC hired Carlos Castañeda, a librarian and historian at the University of Texas, as an examiner. He served as acting regional director in Region X in 1943 and 1945, and as special assistant to the chairman of the FEPC on Latin American problems in 1944 and 1945.[5] His job was to focus on discrimination against Mexican Americans, while other FEPC staff dealt with problems relating to African Americans and other minorities. However, given the small staff and the fact that many firms discriminated equally against both African Americans and Spanish Americans, the division did not always work. Despite a substantial Mexican population in Region XII, the FEPC received few complaints from them and devoted comparatively little time and resources to them.[6]

In conducting the FEPC investigations throughout the Southwest in November 1943, Castañeda and another examiner, Clay L. Cochran, traveled to Corpus Christi, Texas, to discuss mining industry complaints with representatives of the American Smelting and Refining Company and locals of the Zinc Workers Federal Labor Union, AFL, and of the Alkali Workers of America. They uncovered discriminatory "gentlemen's agreements" between management and unions and a two-tiered salary structure that consigned Mexican Americans to minimum-wage positions.[7] In December, Castañeda's investigations of three oil firms, Humble, Sinclair, and Shell, also revealed wage discrimination and an upgrading policy that permitted Hispanics to rise no higher than janitor and gardener.[8]

Although the International Oil Workers Union sought to cooperate with the FEPC in ending oil industry discrimination against both Mexican Americans and African Americans, several of its locals signed contracts that placed ceilings on the positions to which either group could be promoted. Leaders feared the union would lose white members if it acted on its own against discrimination, so they sought FEPC hearings and directives to justify any action it took. Furthermore, members of its Texas locals insisted on retaining bans on minority upgrading, and deposed any of its leaders who supported a nondiscriminatory policy. Occasionally too they resorted to unauthorized wildcat strikes when Spanish-speaking and African American workers were upgraded.[9] Consequently, while the FEPC reached agreements with some firms and settled some individual complaints, there was little change in the occupational structure (see the headnote on the Oil Industry).

In his testimony before a subcommittee of the Senate Education and Labor Committee in September 1944 and in March 1945 headed by Dennis Chávez (D-NM), Castañeda stressed the pervasive systematic discrimination against Mexican Americans, particularly in the mining and oil industries. He reported better progress in the aviation, shipbuilding, and other defense industries but lamented that they were not likely to provide significant employment after the war. While he acknowledged that some reduction in discrimination against Mexican Americans had been achieved through persuasion, Castañeda said, "the roots of prejudice are so deep-seated in the Southwest that it is going to take something more than persuasion to bring about a change of conditions." Consequently he and other Mexican Americans supported legislation for a permanent FEPC: "We in Texas are convinced that the solution to the problem is legislation . . . that can be effectively enforced so as to restrain that small minority, but very aggressive minority, that, because of ignorance, perhaps, practice[s] discrimination that brings shame upon our American democracy."[10]

NOTES

1. Malcolm Ross to Jonathan Daniels, 11/4/43, HqR66, Central Files. U.S. Government, Aliens in Defense, Specific Groups, Mexicans (Miscellaneous).

2. Daniel, *Chicano Workers*, 5–8. For overall analysis of Hispanic cases, see *Chicano Workers*, 28–44, 53–105, 119–33, 144–89; Reed, *Seedtime*, 231–38.

3. See Mitchell, memoranda, 6/28, ca. 7/24/43, 4/12/44; *Final Report*, 38. For additional information on wartime workers imported under agreements with Mexico, see "Agreement of 8/4/42, for the Temporary Migration of Mexican Agricultural Workers to the United States as Revised on 7/26/43"; Marjorie Lawson to Edward Lawson, 11/19/43; J. H. Bond to Ross, 3/8/44, HqR66, Central Files. U.S. Government, Aliens in Defense, Specific Groups, Mexicans (Miscellaneous).

On State Department pressures, see Sumner Welles to Lawrence Cramer, 11/13, 12/3/42; Cramer to Welles, 11/21/42; Ross to secretary of state, 2/17/44; related texts, all in HqR66, Central Files. U.S. Government, State Department; Transcript of Proceedings, 2/12/44, 104–6; 3/4/44, 114–16, HqR65, Central Files; Almaráz, *Knight without Armor*, 245–6; Reed, *Seedtime*, 232–33, 236–37; Daniel, *Chicano Workers*, 153–58; Zamora, "Failed Promise of Wartime Opportunities for Mexicans," 329n14; Hardin, "Role of Presidential Advisers," 83–93. State Department officials did, however, press some of the firms to reduce their discrimination.

4. See Mitchell, memorandum, 3/1/44; Castañeda to Mitchell, 3/13/44; to Maslow, 1/1/45; to Ross, 1/5/45; to Johnson, 1/25/45, all in HqR38, Central Files. Memoranda, Carlos Castañeda, 7/44; "Memorandum on Discrimination in the Mining and Oil Industries in the Southwest," n.d., HqR2, Office Files of Malcolm Ross. Meetings, Material from the 7/6 and 7/7/43 Meetings; Daniel, *Chicano Workers*, 77–79; Reed, *Seedtime*, 237.

5. Almaráz, *Knight without Armor*, 217–66.

6. Daniel, *Chicano Workers*, 172–73.

7. Almaráz, *Knight without Armor*, 226. For Mitchell's visit to the office to consult on its organization and procedures, see his memoranda of 10/11, 10/12/43.

8. Almaráz, *Knight without Armor*, 232.

9. See Zamora, "Failed Promise," 327–29, 334, 336–37, 347–48.

10. The text of Castañeda's statement before Senator Chávez's Subcommittee of the Senate Education and Labor Committee, Hearing on S. 2408, 9/8/44, is in HqR4, Press Releases; similar materials are in HqR6, Office Files of George M. Johnson. Permanent FEPC. See also statement by Alonso A. Perales, "The Mexican-American's Argument for a Permanent FEPC," 3/19/46, HqR2, Office Files of Malcolm Ross. Tension Areas; Almaráz, *Knight without Armor*, 257–60; and Daniel, *Chicano Workers*, 173. For the full hearings records, see U.S. Congress, *Fair Employment Practices Act*; U.S. Congress, *Fair Employment Practices Act, S. 2048*.

THE MINING INDUSTRY

The FEPC's concern about the treatment of workers of Mexican origin or descent throughout the Southwest who were either citizens or noncitizens was aroused in May 1942, when it began receiving complaints from them alleging discrimination in war industries because of their race or color. The Committee therefore opened a temporary office in El Paso in July and assigned Ernest G. Trimble, Daniel R. Donovan, and G. James Fleming from its staff, and Barron Beshoar, on loan from the WMC's Denver office, to work there as examiners. They began investigating copper-mining cases in the Southwest (see the headnote on Mexican Americans). For six weeks they investigated complaints in Texas, New Mexico, and Arizona against the larger copper companies, including Phelps-Dodge Corporation, Kennecott Copper Corporation, Miami Copper Company, and Inspiration Consolidated Copper Corporation.[1]

The FEPC found that the patterns of discrimination were similar in the mining and oil industries in two respects (see the headnote on the Oil Industry). First, there was a wage differential between two classes of common laborers, one of which was composed primarily of Mexicans and a few African Americans; the other was composed entirely, or almost entirely, of Anglos, who were paid a higher wage. Next, there was a "general failure to upgrade Mexicans" among the common laborers into skilled and semiskilled jobs.

The Committee therefore scheduled a public hearing in El Paso for August 14 and 15, 1942, in order to fully disclose those practices. The State Department, however, early in August got the White House to have the FEPC cancel the hearings in order to avoid further complicating U.S. relations with Mexico. The reason was that while the copper companies depended on the importation of Mexican laborers, the Mexican government was reluctant to permit its citizens to emigrate for that purpose as long as they suffered such discrimination. The field investigation that Trimble led was in lieu of the hearings. (His full report, "Discrimination in the Mining Industry," is in appendix 1. See also the headnote on Mexican Americans.)[2]

Between May and September the Committee collected more than one hundred fifty notarized complaints. While it continued the investigations, it attempted to negotiate agreements with the companies in an effort to adjust the cases. After it closed the El Paso office, which was open for about ten weeks, it maintained its correspondence with the complainants and interested labor organizations and other persons. In some instances, the Committee managed to obtain "formal paper compliance with requests to companies for implementation of their obligations under Executive Order 8802." It achieved some token upgrading of Mexican workers and minor adjustments of low wage scales. In other cases, however, its requests and directives met open defiance. Because the hearings were cancelled, companies no longer feared public exposure and embarrassment.

Further complicating the Committee's efforts were the jurisdictional conflicts between the International Union of Mine, Mill, and Smelter Workers, CIO, which was unionizing Mexican workers, and the Metal Trades Council and its affiliated AFL organizations, which represented Anglo-Americans in skilled jobs through its craft unions. The upgrading of Mexican workers usually involved transferring them from the CIO to the AFL, which did not welcome them. Companies frequently used the potential conflicts as an excuse for barring promotion of Spanish-speaking Americans even though, in some instances, union contracts contained antidiscrimination clauses. Furthermore, some disputes could be handled through the grievance procedures provided in contracts. Consequently, the National Labor Relations Board frequently was required to settle disputes between the two organizations.[3]

By November 1943 the FEPC therefore found that the Spanish-speaking workers in the Southwest were greatly discouraged, owing to the cancellation of the hearings, the withdrawal of the Committee's representatives from the region, and the refusal of companies to comply with the executive orders. In many cases, the minimum gains of the summer of 1942 were lost. Consequently, the complainants, the labor unions that supported them, representatives of the Mexican government, and the liberal leadership of the Southwest were all convinced that only broad-based government action could eliminate the discrimination.

The FEPC found that resident Mexicans and Spanish-speaking citizens served as a link between the United States and the Mexican government, which was well aware of the economic and social status of its people in the Southwest. Malcolm Ross, chairman of the FEPC, told Jonathan Daniels, administrative assistant to the president, that the Good Neighbor policy could "flourish only as we implement our pronouncements of democracy with democratic action." He said that, aside from the urgent problems of national unity and morale, "the demands of war production" could not be met if America continued "a policy of underutilization of an important group of experienced workers." Ross said the Committee considered it "expedient to reopen the Mexican cases," which had "been quiescent since December, 1942," and added, "It would be futile, however, to raise these issues again without prior consideration of the ultimate steps which may be required for the adjustment of these grievances. The eventual necessity of a public hearing appears to be inevitable. The history of Committee action in the Mexican cases has deprived it of prestige and the confidence of the workers, who will be reluctant to cooperate without assurance that the Committee, this time, will prosecute the investigation to its logical conclusion."[4]

In February 1944 and again in the summer of 1944, Carlos Castañeda examined conditions in mining communities in Colorado, New Mexico, and the El Paso area, where Hispanics represented as much as 80 percent of the mining workforce.[5] That was the second field investigation on which Stanley Metzger reported, a copy of which Mitchell attached to his memorandum to Johnson of July 17, 1944.[6]

Castañeda documented pervasive patterns of segregation and social discrimination, as well as discrimination in wages, job classifications, and promotions against Spanish-speaking residents. The revelations set the stage for all subsequent negotiations in the area. Certain units of the Phelps-Dodge Company were identified as flagrantly abusive to Indians as well as Chicanos, and as particularly uncooperative during the investigations. Reforming Phelps-Dodge, the country's largest copper-mining corporation, was thus seen as the most likely way to change the industry as a whole by setting a pattern.[7]

The FEPC's investigations were confirmed by others conducted by the WMC, the Non-Ferrous Metals Commission, and the War Production Board.[8] Furthermore, Catholic Church officials, Latin American community leaders, and the Mexican consul joined in demanding action.[9]

Because the FEPC found it difficult to obtain well-documented cases of discrimination, the staff debated whether to hold a hearing based on individual cases or to present evidence to indicate discrimination by industry policy against an entire group (illustrated by individual cases). This policy would be documented by patterns of job assignments or treatment of the group. Mitchell won Johnson's approval for, as the deputy chairman said, "varying our procedure and building a hearing around expert testimony." The only question, Johnson said, was who would be the expert. Frank Reeves explained that that approach was recommended

> on the theory that since technical aspects of the problem are so broad, little good would be accomplished by presenting only the individual cases and restricting re-medial steps within such confined limits.
>
> While I appreciate the arguments advanced in favor of proceeding on a broad policy basis, consideration must be given the question of whether the Committee has, or can obtain, the expert testimony and detailed technical information neces-sary to support findings on this basis. For instance, where, as alleged in certain of the complaints, Spanish-Americans are precluded from opportunities for upgrading into certain job classifications, it would seem necessary that we be able to present evidence based upon exhaustive job and qualification analysis, indicating that Ang-los working in those classifications were advanced thereto, or hired therein, in pref-erence to Spanish-Americans having equal or better qualifications. Although circumstantial evidence of this might exist in the case where we can show that a par-ticular Spanish-American complainant was discriminated against, it is questionable whether such circumstances, coupled with the absence of other Spanish-Americans in the job classification, would be sufficient to justify a finding of discrimination on a policy basis. It is my opinion, therefore, that careful analysis of the evidence at hand should be made before a final decision is reached.[10]

For the reasons Reeves outlined, the Committee repeatedly postponed a hearing until it ran out of time and resources owing to its impending demise, making it aban-don such plans. The postponements led Castañeda to invoke in January 1945 the complaint of a representative of the International Union of Mine, Mill, and Smelter Workers in the El Paso area, that "mine workers in northwestern Texas and southern New Mexico are completely disillusioned with the Committee; that the members at large in recent meetings have questioned the Committee's efficiency to help them in any way to eliminate the deep-rooted discrimination which they have suffered for years." The Non-Ferrous Metals Commission in Denver, Castañeda reported, had taken a more positive stand against discrimination than was exhibited by any of the various FEPC representatives who visited mining areas to investigate complaints.[11]

The FEPC had in fact cooperated with the Non-Ferrous Metals Commission in its investigations into dual wage structures. Aware, however, that the commission's ju-risdiction over the industry was better established than its own, and that it had au-thority to order payment of back wages, the FEPC agreed to have it make the ruling against dual wage scales. The commission's directive of February 5, 1944, was ap-pealed to the War Labor Board, which sustained it on August 26.[12] As Castañeda noted, Mexicans perceived the ruling as the most important action ever taken on their behalf during the war. Despite their perception of the FEPC's ineffectiveness, Mexicans did support legislation for a permanent agency at the end of the war.[13]

The exodus of white miners to more lucrative defense jobs on the West Coast opened more mining jobs to Mexicans. Furthermore, over the course of the war, labor shortages and pressure from various federal agencies besides the FEPC induced some promotions. By the end of 1944, the *First Report* noted, fourteen thousand Mexican Americans were working in the mining industry in Arizona and New Mexico, 60 percent of whom were common laborers, 35 percent were in semiskilled jobs, and 5 percent were semiskilled craftsmen. The FEPC's negotiations resolved some 40 percent of individual cases. The ruling of the Non-Ferrous Metal Commission and the War Labor Board against dual wage scales as well as cooperation from key unions helped the FEPC make progress in ending the wage discrimination. Although cutbacks at war's end deeply affected Mexican Americans, some progress remained. Later passage of a state FEPC act in New Mexico in 1948 also helped preserve those gains.[14]

NOTES

1. Malcolm Ross to Jonathan Daniels, 11/4/43, HqR66, Central Files. U.S. Government, Aliens in Defense, Specific Groups, Mexicans (Miscellaneous) (also in HqR2, as in note 2); Trimble to Cramer, [ca. 12/42], memorandum on the temporary Southwest office, HqR19, Records Relating to Hearings. Mining; another copy of that text, and Trimble to Cramer 8/15/42, and Donovan and Beshoar, "Report on Phelps Dodge Corp. Operations at Bisbee, Ariz., and Douglas, Ariz.," n.d. [1942], in HqR77, Office Files of Ernest G. Trimble. Unarranged; and Daniel, *Chicano Workers*, 52–76.

2. Ross to Daniels, 11/4/43, and backgrounder, "Discrimination in the Mining Industries of the Southwest," both in HqR2, Office Files of Malcolm Ross. Materials from 7/6, 7/7 Meetings.

3. Ross to Daniels, 11/4/43; Frank D. Reeves memorandum to Bruce Hunt, Western counsel, 10/13/44, HqR19, Records Relating to Hearings. Southwest Hearings.

4. Ross to Daniels, 11/4/43; other materials related to the second Area-Wide Mining Industry Investigation in the Southwest are in HqR19, Records Relating to Hearings. Mining. See also report on "Discrimination in the Mining and Oil Industries of the Southwest," HqR2, Office Files of Malcolm Ross. Materials from 7/6, 7/7 Meetings; and the headnote on the Oil Industry.

5. Almaráz, *Knight without Armor*, 234–37.

6. See Mitchell, memoranda, 10/11, 10/12, 12/6/43. For accounts and interpretations of the reasons for the FEPC's abandoning the hearings that sometimes do not jibe with those of the editor of *The Papers of Clarence Mitchell Jr.*, see Daniel, *Chicano Workers*, 28, 37, 40, 52–55, 62, 63, 124, 146, 158, 175, 178–84; Almaráz, *Knight without Armor*, 212–52; Johnson's memorandum of 7/22/44 replying to Mitchell, in which he said he could see no objection to varying the procedure for the hearings Castañeda proposed, and related texts in HqR19, Records Relating to Hearings. Southwest Hearings and Mining.

7. On Castañeda's findings, see Mitchell memorandum, 7/17/44, to Johnson. On Phelps-Dodge, see esp. Almaráz, *Knight without Armor*, 243–45, 247; Daniel, *Chicano Workers*, 81–83, 88–105.

8. For those other confirmations, see "Discrimination in the Mining and Oil Industries of the Southwest," HqR2, Office Files of Malcolm Ross. Materials from 7/6, 7/7 Meetings; Johnson to Mitchell, 7/22/44, HqR19, Records Relating to Hearings. Southwest Hearings and Mining. Other related documents, such as "Recommendations on the Manpower Problem in the Copper Industry in Arizona," are also in HqR19.

9. See *Final Report*, 38–39; Castañeda to Maslow, 3/25/44, HqR66, Central Files. U.S. Government, Aliens in Defense, Specific Groups, Mexicans (Miscellaneous); Castañeda to Maslow, 7/4, 8/26, 9/1, 9/29/44, and to Ross, 1/5/45, HqR38, Central Files. Memoranda, Carlos Castañeda, 7/44.

10. Johnson to Mitchell, 7/22/44, and Reeves to Hunt, 10/13/44, HqR19, Records Relating to Hearings. Southwest Hearings.

11. Castañeda to Johnson, 1/25/45, HqR38, Central Files. Memoranda, Carlos Castañeda, 7/44. On the action of the Non-Ferrous Metal Commission against dual wage rates, see Metzger to Ross, 11/13/43, and to Maslow, 12/16/43, HqR66, Central Files. U.S. Government, Aliens in Defense, Specific Groups, Mexicans (Miscellaneous).

12. See Maslow to Johnson, 11/8/43, HqR3, Office Files of George M. Johnson. Will Maslow; Castañeda to Maslow, 9/1/44, HqR38, Central Files. Memoranda, Carlos Castañeda, 7/44; Transcript of Proceedings, 3/4/44, 116–23; 3/18/44, 79–82, HqR65, Central Files.

13. See, for example, Alonso S. Perales, "The Mexican-Americans' Argument for a Permanent FEPC," 3/19/46, HqR2, Office Files of Malcolm Ross. Tension Areas.

14. See Mitchell, report, 8/25/45; *Final Report*, 38–39; Reed, *Seedtime*, 238; Daniel, *Chicano Workers*, 185–89.

THE OIL INDUSTRY

The FEPC began investigating complaints against the oil industry in 1943 and continued to do so throughout its existence because oil was one of the industries expected to have continued significance in the postwar period. Initial complaints against the Gulf, Humble, Republic, Shell, Sinclair, and Texas oil companies charged wage discrimination and refusal to upgrade Mexican and African American workers beyond laborers. Texas Oil's desire to utilize segregated black deck crews on some of its tankers also came before the FEPC for a ruling on whether such work arrangements were discriminatory. The FEPC saw settlement of the oil cases as a way of overcoming local minority workers' fears that nothing would be done about their cases and that they would face retaliation for complaining. The Committee also hoped success with these firms would create precedents for compliance by other oil companies.[1]

The FEPC's initial negotiations by FEPC Region X officials Carlos Castañeda and Clay Cochran, and subsequently by Leonard Brin and Don Ellinger, bore little fruit. At first Mitchell believed all the cases would have to be brought before the FEPC for a hearing.[2] However, the cases against Sinclair and Humble were settled locally with pledges to void discriminatory clauses in union contracts and to abolish discriminatory job classifications and wage rates.[3]

Shell, which had a contract with its Oil Workers International Union (OWIU), Local 367, barring the upgrading of African Americans and Mexican Americans above laborers, janitors, and gardeners, stated its hiring policies were typical for the region and refused to change them unless other firms in the area also did. The OWIU, though supportive at the national level, was unwilling to take action locally without an FEPC hearing and directive to strengthen its hand. The union had only recently succeeded in being chosen to represent the workers at the company, defeating the previous company union, and feared it would be forced out by the workers if it insisted on a nondiscriminatory policy.

Prominent Catholic clergymen as well as the Mexican embassy and Mexican consul in Texas demanded action. Mitchell recommended, and the Committee voted at its

March 18, 1944, meeting, to hold a hearing on the Shell Oil case. Because of its connection to such key issues, the FEPC saw its battle with Shell as an attack on "a whole area of discrimination." Nonetheless, the hearing continued to be postponed pending a decision on whether to hold it about Shell alone or about the oil industry generally. By the fall Castañeda warned of a loss of faith in the FEPC by Mexican workers in the area.[4]

The FEPC finally held a hearing in Houston in December 1944, with A. Bruce Hunt serving as hearing commissioner and Emanuel Bloch as the FEPC attorney. But the Committee recessed the hearing to permit continuance of negotiations that were then making progress. The FEPC reached an agreement with Shell and the union local on an upgrading plan. It directed them to eliminate from their existing bargaining agreements the provisions limiting promotional opportunities for African Americans and Mexican Americans at the company's Deer Park refinery in Houston and to apply a nondiscriminatory policy in the hiring of new workers. The FEPC gave Shell Oil and the union ninety days to comply.[5]

Two Mexican Americans who had filed complaints were upgraded without incident, but when several African Americans were upgraded to worker's helper, whites threatened a walkout unless they were removed. After Shell's management complied, the workers insisted that the upgraded Mexican workers also be removed. Regional director Ellinger obtained assistance from army and navy officials, from the Petroleum Administration for War, and from leaders of the OWIU. George Weaver of the CIO Committee against Discrimination also intervened in the negotiation.[6]

Shell refused to upgrade minority workers unless it was assured there would be no strike. It proposed to upgrade the forty black and Mexican workers eligible on the basis of seniority, then to pledge to the white workers there would be no further upgrading for six months, since in any case no other minority workers would be eligible under seniority rules during that period. The FEPC said it could not officially be a part of such an arrangement but it would not oppose it if it did not jeopardize the rights of the upgraded workers.

After many more meetings, the FEPC and the relevant federal agencies insisted that Shell comply with the nondiscrimination clause, and the white workers again threatened a wildcat strike. On April 27, 1945, they walked out, but they returned to work upon agreement to hold an official strike vote. On June 7 the workers formally voted to strike if the upgrading took place.[7] White workers next agreed to upgrade on a two-tier segregated basis and with discriminatory wage levels—higher wages for themselves and lower ones for Mexican and African Americans. Mexican American workers rejected the segregation proposal, and the African Americans did so in addition to objecting to the wages offered.[8]

With war's end and the closing down of the FEPC and other federal agencies, the nondiscrimination efforts largely ended. Failure at Shell discouraged compliance by other firms and unions. In his final appraisal of the OWIU in April 1946, Mitchell noted that the union's leadership was more supportive than the membership and that while individual cases had been resolved, there had been little change in the overall practices in the oil industry.[9]

NOTES

1. See Mitchell, memoranda, 10/12/43, 1/12/44; weekly reports 2/28, 3/6/44; Ernest Trimble memorandum, 7/9/43, to Haas, HqR38, Central Files. Memoranda, Francis J. Haas. For oil's inclusion on the list of industries with postwar significance, see Mitchell, memoranda, 10/7, 10/10, and 11/1/44. For overall background, see Obadele-Starks, "Road to Jericho," 71–97; Zamora, "Failed Promise," 323–50.

2. See Mitchell, weekly report, 1/22/44.

3. See Mitchell, weekly report, 2/5/44; press release prepared by Castañeda at request of regional director, Region X, [5/44], and related texts, HqR38, Central Files. Memoranda, Carlos Castañeda.

4. See Mitchell, memoranda, 1/25, 3/1/44; report, 3/27/44; Castañeda to Mitchell, 3/13/44, HqR38, Central Files. Memoranda, Carlos Castañeda; Johnson to Maslow, 5/1/44, HqR3, Office Files of George M. Johnson. Will Maslow; Cooper to Mitchell, 10/19/44, HqR4, Office Files of George M. Johnson. Evelyn N. Cooper.

5. Castañeda to Maslow, 10/28/44, 1/1/45, HqR38, Central Files. Memoranda, Carlos Castañeda; FEPC press release, 1/31/45, HqR86, Press Releases. Shell Oil Company; copy of FEPC directive to Shell, 1/45, in Obadele-Starks, "Road to Jericho," 228–31, from manuscripts in RG 228 (entry 70), Shell file, DNA. See also backgrounder, "Discrimination in the Mining and Oil Industries of the Southwest," n.d., HqR2, Office Files of Malcolm Ross. Intergovernmental.

6. On Weaver's intercession, see Mitchell, memorandum, 3/26; reports, 6/5 and 6/19/45.

7. See Mitchell, weekly reports, 4/24, and 5/21/44; notes, 6/5 and 6/19/45; memoranda, 3/26 and 4/12/45. For the voluminous documentation on this case, see HqR21, Records Relating to Hearings. Shell Oil Company; HqR85, Correspondence Relating to Cases. (Sh–Z), Shell Oil Company.

8. *Final Report,* 23; Obadele-Starks, "Road to Jericho," 92–97.

9. See Mitchell, memorandum, 4/8/46, on the Oil Workers Union; *Final Report,* 23.

THE AIRCRAFT INDUSTRY

The aircraft industry grew rapidly during the early war years, jumping from about one hundred thousand workers in 1940 to over two million by the end of 1943. It encountered labor shortages by mid-1942 that opened new opportunities for black workers, who before the war represented a minuscule 0.2 percent of the workforce. In his 1943 survey of racial tension areas, sociologist Charles S. Johnson showed how "the almost universal prejudice of the aircraft industry against Negroes" was making the position of African American workers an "extremely marginal one." After mid-1942 aircraft plants hired large numbers of black workers in many areas, but they often had to accept segregated work arrangements and discrimination in upgrading and promotion.[1] The FEPC's first task was to secure African Americans' access to industrial training, especially in segregated areas. Later, it tackled the issues of discrimination in hiring and promotion.[2]

The International Association of Machinists and the United Automobile Workers, CIO, dominated the industry. Where the Machinists, with its ritual ban on black membership, prevailed, it presented its typical obstacles to the employment of blacks that were similar to those in the shipyards. The Boeing plant in Seattle, one of the few in which the Machinists held a closed-shop contract, was a noted example.[3]

According to Robert C. Weaver, however, where management made a firm decision to hire black workers, the union generally went along. As with the shipyards, the union then granted work permits or special work clearances, or it organized black auxiliaries. In the case of the Lockheed plant in California, the local actually admitted some blacks as members, although it was later stopped from doing so by the international union.

The UAW-CIO, by contrast, adopted and generally implemented a nondiscrimination policy. As a result, even within the same firm, policies could vary at local plants depending on the location and which union predominated. For example, at the Consolidated Vultee Aircraft plant in California, where the UAW held the contract, African Americans were employed; but at its Nashville plant, where the Boilermakers held a closed-shop contract, blacks had difficulty obtaining even low-level jobs.[4]

Based in San Diego, Consolidated Vultee in 1941 informed the National Negro Congress that its policy was not to employ "people other than of the Caucasian race." The FEPC issued a directive against its Nashville plant as early as November 17, 1942. Key issues there and at the company's Fort Worth plant were lack of access to training and upgrading and the refusal to hire black women. After drawn-out negotiations by the FEPC national staff and regional directors A. Bruce Hunt and W. Don Ellinger accomplished little, the agency sought assistance from the War Department.[5]

Eventually, the War Department recommended appeals to the San Diego headquarters, but Mitchell considered their responses dilatory and evasive. He strongly favored a hearing on the case.[6] In February 1945, Vultee proposed a program for training and upgrading blacks at the Fort Worth plant. Mitchell did not consider the plan very significant and worried that because it included segregated work arrangements it would cause trouble "up the road," but he eventually admitted in March 1945 that it showed some progress. By August 1945 he had to recommend that a hearing was then useless because the company was already undergoing major reconversion cutbacks.[7]

In the South, discrimination presented a solid front not only at the Consolidated Vultee plants in Nashville and Fort Worth, but also at Bell Aircraft in Marietta, Georgia, and North American Aviation in Dallas. Complaints about plants in segregated border cities like St. Louis and Cincinnati, particularly those of Curtiss-Wright Corporation and Wright Aeronautical Corporation, also required extensive FEPC negotiations. In most of these cases, FEPC settlements met with long delays in implementation that caused progress to come too late in the war to benefit materially African American workers.[8]

Mitchell cited Eastern Aircraft Corporation in Baltimore as an integrated plant, similar to Western Electric there.[9] Extensive negotiations with Curtiss-Wright and Wright Aeronautical secured black access to more positions in St. Louis, but they were limited by retention of segregated workplace patterns. Wright's Cincinnati plant employed more African Americans than any other aircraft plant, but efforts to integrate work arrangements there triggered a brief strike by white workers. Gradually, with UAW support, more jobs and departments were opened to black workers, including black women, but the company retained its segregated work arrangements.

While the firm asserted it would continue to employ blacks in the postwar era, it refused to promise to tackle segregation within its plants.[10]

Similarly, at Bell Aircraft's plant in Marietta, which produced B-29 bombers, African Americans were admitted to training programs, but regional FEPC efforts to learn if the trainees were being hired were initially blocked. In defiance of the WMC-FEPC operating agreement, the local USES offices took no action against discriminatory work orders from the company. Ultimately, the FEPC instructed its New York regional director to appeal to officials at the company's headquarters in Buffalo, where with UAW support Bell had initiated a nondiscrimination policy in 1942. Bell's management pledged cooperation. Nevertheless, complaints continued regarding the failure to hire skilled African American workers, and segregated workplace arrangements limited the number of jobs available to blacks. In March 1945, Bell submitted a segregated plan for training and upgrading black workers similar to that of Consolidated Vultee, but since drastic reconversion cutbacks were already underway, little was accomplished.[11]

Despite the difficulties, however, some progress was made. Lockheed Aircraft Corporation and Vega Airplane Company, the manufacturer's subsidiary, whose discriminatory policies were investigated during the 1941 FEPC hearings in Los Angeles, subsequently became the aircraft producer in California with the largest number of African American employees. Its progress came despite its contract with the Machinists Union. Although there were some complaints about the firm's plant in Texas, the FEPC cited the merged Lockheed-Vega Corporation as one of its particularly successful cases. Douglas Aircraft Company, after initially employing few blacks, also eventually hired many blacks in California, including for higher-level positions.[12]

Discrimination complaints involving North American Aviation, based in California, which had major operations in Texas and plants elsewhere, were particularly varied. The FEPC successfully resolved most of the cases, in some instances by appeals to the company's headquarters. Responding to pressure from the FEPC and the local African American community, North American's Kansas City plant hired blacks in almost all departments and skill levels. That compliance, however, was not equally true of their plants in Texas and Louisiana.[13] Complaints of hostile acts against black workers by foremen led to the dismissal of the foremen at a time when the company's policies were reported to be creating racial tensions. Another group of complaints alleged that the UAW was not properly representing blacks at the Texas plant. After receiving complaints of long delays in hiring Mexican aliens at the Dallas plant, the FEPC succeeded in speeding up the loyalty review process to permit employment of these workers. Religious discrimination complaints were levied against the firm over its dismissals of Seventh-day Adventists. Since the firm began major cutbacks by late 1944 and its layoffs were not disproportionately directed against minority workers, the firm subsequently attracted little FEPC notice.[14]

According to its *First Report*, the FEPC helped in raising black employment in the industry from 0.2 percent of the workforce in 1940 to 2.9 percent in July 1942, and 6.4 percent in November 1944. However, it anticipated that in the postwar period, no more than ten to twelve thousand African Americans would find employment in peacetime aircraft manufacture. Extensive cutbacks and the lower seniority of black workers were the expected causes of the lack of continued opportunity in the field.[15]

NOTES

1. See Northrup, *Organized Labor and the Negro,* 205–9; Weaver, *Negro Labor,* 128–29; Johnson, *To Stem This Tide,* 20–21. Johnson's comments on the prevailing prejudice in the industry apparently derived in part from his article "Half a Million Workers," *Forbes,* 3/41, 98, 163. The information was also quoted in Weaver, "Negro Employment in the Aircraft Industry," 599n3; and in Northrup, *Organized Labor,* 206; *First Report,* 90–91.

2. For the FEPC's efforts to secure training, see Mitchell, memoranda, 2/2, 11/28/42, 1/11/43.

3. For housing and union membership problems at Boeing later in the war, see Mitchell, report, 11/27/44; memorandum, 1/8/45; Weaver, *Negro Labor,* 116–17.

4. Northrup, *Organized Labor,* 207; Weaver, *Negro Labor,* 111–12.

5. See Office of War Information, WMC, news release, 1/4/43; Mitchell, weekly reports, 1/29, 9/18/44, 2/6/45; memoranda, 1/25, 10/12/44; Weaver, *Negro Labor,* 109; Northrup, *Organized Labor,* 206.

6. See Mitchell, reports, 11/27, 12/4, 12/18/44, 1/9, 2/6, 2/14, 3/13/45; memoranda, 12/14/44, 1/4/45.

7. On Consolidated Vultee, see Mitchell, memoranda, 2/12, 4/12, 4/23, 8/17/45; weekly reports, 2/14, 2/20, 3/5, 3/29/45, and notes; Weaver, *Negro Labor,* 115–16.

8. See "Important Cases Being Handled at Regional Level," 4/22–5/22/44, in appendix 1; HqR83, Correspondence Relating to Cases. (A–K), Bell Aircraft, Consolidated Vultee Aircraft, and Curtiss-Wright Corporation.

9. See Mitchell, memoranda, 11/11/43, 4/8/46.

10. On Curtiss-Wright, see Mitchell, reports, 3/14/44, 4/24/45; memorandum, 5/18/45; HqR83, Correspondence Relating to Cases. (A–K), Curtiss-Wright Corporation; Weaver, *Negro Labor,* 120, 125–27.

11. On Bell Aircraft, see Mitchell, memoranda, 1/11, 2/5, 3/29/43, 8/19/44, 1/23, 5/18/45; weekly reports, 2/28, 3/6, 5/1/44, 1/23/45; "Summaries of Important Cases," 4/22–5/22/44, in appendix 1; Mitchell, epilogue; texts in FR80, Region VII. Administrative Files (A–Z), Bell Aircraft Corporation; Weaver, *Negro Labor,* 111–12, 125. On the rapid cutbacks as the war ended, see Matthews, *Cobra! Bell Aircraft Corporation, 1934–1946,* 378; Pelletier, *Bell Aircraft since 1935,* 13.

12. On Lockheed-Vega, see *Final Report,* 11–12 (Weaver sometimes refers to the companies separately, sometimes as one corporation. Furthermore, see 9/14/43 text in appendix 1.); Weaver, *Negro Labor,* 196–99; Mitchell, memoranda, 9/14 (in appendix 1), 10/12/43, 8/25/45. On Douglas Aircraft, see Weaver, *Negro Labor,* 199–200; Northrup, *Organized Labor,* 208.

13. Northrup, *Organized Labor,* 208; Weaver, *Negro Labor,* 118–20.

14. On North American Aviation, see Mitchell, memoranda, 10/12, 12/9/43, 1/27, 11/01/44, 8/25/45; reports, 2/28, 3/6, 5/1, 5/8/44; "Important Cases Being Handled at Regional Level," 4/22–5/22/44, in appendix 1; Transcript of Proceedings, 3/18/44, 24–27; 4/1/44, 38–47; and 5/13/44, 19–34, HqR65, Central Files; HqR84, Correspondence Relating to Cases. (L–Se), North American Aviation.

Responding to a question from Charles Horn about the propriety of "forcing" black workers into communities that had never hired any before, Milton Webster argued in 4/44 that had the FEPC not done so, there would not be any black workers in the aviation industry on the West Coast. "Two years ago they weren't going to hire Negroes, Chinese, or dark-skinned Mexicans. North American made a public statement in the *Kansas City Star* that they were sympathetic to the Negroes, but were not going to hire any. We would have suffered; the war effort would have suffered. They just didn't intend to do it." See Transcript of Proceedings, 4/20/44, 74, HqR65, Central Files.

15. *First Report,* 90–91, 141; *Final Report,* 90; Mitchell, memoranda, 5/18, 8/25, 9/27, 10/9/45. See also Weaver, *Negro Labor,* 268; and Northrup's updated comments in the reprint edition of *Organized Labor,* xe.

THE SHIPBUILDING INDUSTRY AND THE BOILERMAKERS UNION

Of all the wartime industries, shipbuilding experienced the most dramatic increase in nonwhite employment, considerably outstripping the rapid workforce growth as a whole. Consequently, the FEPC devoted a considerable amount of its meager resources to fighting discrimination there, notably by the dominant Boilermakers Union. The *Final Report* explained that the problems on the West Coast that defined its struggles in the industry "ranked with the FEPC railroad cases in complexity and difficulty."[1]

African Americans had long been working in ship construction, mostly in unskilled and helper capacities. A sizable number of them had been carpenters, caulkers, fasteners, and helpers in the older shipyards, as in Baltimore, where Frederick Douglass, the abolitionist leader, had worked, and in the South. After gaining recognition in World War I as outstanding shipbuilders, however, their numbers sharply declined with job cutbacks in the industry. The replacement of wood with steel in construction further reduced demand for their labor, owing to the switch to welding as a primary trade, and contributed to the barring of blacks from the new training programs. Blacks were also excluded from electrical work, which also was now a major industry skill.[2]

Promptly after its founding in 1941, the FEPC began receiving complaints from blacks about discrimination in the industry. The basic problem was that African American shipyard workers were being denied certain types of work or applicants were being denied employment altogether. There was a significant increase in their use, nonetheless, at such large shipyards as the Newport News Shipbuilding and Drydock Company in Virginia. There, more than five thousand African Americans were employed toward the end of 1941, but primarily as laborers.

The U.S. Navy yards were the first to open appreciable opportunities to African Americans, while private yards slowly followed that lead. The Sun Shipbuilding and Drydock Company in Chester, Pennsylvania, for example, created a training program that enabled it to employ thousands of African Americans in 1942. But they were confined to a separate shipway, which imitated the prevalent practice in the South. Mitchell vigorously opposed such workplace segregation. Other yards on the East Coast that employed blacks in large numbers were New Jersey's Federal Shipbuilding Company, the New York Shipbuilding Company, the Bethlehem Steel and Shipbuilding Company in Baltimore, and Newport News Shipbuilding and Dry Dock Company.

In the newer shipyards on the Gulf Coast, only slight progress was made in employing African Americans by the end of 1941. At the West Coast shipyards, hundreds of blacks were hired, but there the racial policies of the AFL-dominated craft unions, notably the Boilermakers, limited the kinds of jobs they could hold, and that policy in turn put a cap on the number of blacks who could be hired. Through a "master agreement" between the yards and the AFL's Metal Trades Department,[3] the Boilermakers Union got exclusive bargaining rights for about 65 percent of workers in most of the shipyards. The agreement gave the Boilermakers a closed shop, which provided that the "employer agrees to hire all workmen it may require hereunder . . . through and from the unions and to continue in its employ . . . only workmen who are members in good standing of the respective unions signatory hereto."

Under a ritual it adopted in 1937, the Boilermakers barred African Americans from becoming members and limited their employment to the job category of laborers. In response to protests from African Americans and government agencies, the union created auxiliary locals exclusively for blacks. A large number of African Americans, nevertheless, refused to join and maintain membership in the auxiliaries because, although they paid the same dues as whites, these units were totally subordinate to the white local and had no rights.[4]

In 1942, Mitchell became involved in the discrimination problems on the West Coast when he helped to plan the recruitment of black workers for Kaiser Shipbuilding Company shipyards in Portland, Oregon, and Vancouver, Washington, and for the Oregon Shipbuilding Corporation, also owned by Kaiser, at Portland. Out of a total of eighty to one hundred thousand workers in the Portland-Vancouver area, approximately six thousand were blacks, a ratio that underscored the need to recruit them as workers from outside the region to help Kaiser meet its production goals. Kaiser, nevertheless, had a closed-shop agreement with the Boilermakers Union, which barred blacks as members. Consequently, although the two hundred African Americans who were recruited in New York were told they would be upgraded, on the train to Portland, Kaiser's representatives upgraded the white workers but left the blacks as laborers. Upon arriving in Portland, the blacks protested against the discrimination. Consequently, Kaiser sent eighteen of them to school as welder trainees.[5]

Thomas Ray, business agent for Boilermakers Local 72, unhappy with Kaiser's attempt to mollify the blacks, brought charges against the company, apparently of violating the closed-shop agreement in the union contract. Meantime, the black workers protested the union's requirement that they join the Boilermakers' Jim Crow auxiliary 32-A as a condition for employment. Auxiliary 32-A was created by the Boilermakers as a temporary means of responding to pressure for blacks to be allowed to work. About this time, in December 1942, blacks rejected the auxiliary and created the Shipyard Negro Organization for Victory (SNOV) with the intention of chartering it as their own bargaining agent. Ray, however, refused to recognize it by meeting with a committee it apparently had chosen for that purpose.[6]

Before the war, Boilermakers Local 72, based in Portland, also had covered Vancouver. In December 1942, while limiting Local 72's coverage to Portland, the Boilermakers created Local 401 for whites at Vancouver and ordered all blacks to go to it so that they could be placed in auxiliary 32-A, which would have jurisdiction over them in the Portland-Vancouver area. By mid-July, because three hundred fifty blacks, including experienced welders, refused to pay dues to the auxiliary, they were dismissed. Another two hundred fifty who had joined the auxiliary were kept on the job. The FEPC therefore concluded that Kaiser, at the request of the union, had discriminated against the workers who were discharged; that Locals 72 and 401 had discriminated against the workers "with respect to security and tenure on the job and promotions"; that, regarding "eligibility for membership," there had been discrimination since white workers up to age seventy could join the union, while black workers could pay union dues to the auxiliary up to the age of sixty; and that , under the union's bylaws, the union's international president had the power to suspend members of the auxiliary, while, under the constitution, the lodge had the power to suspend members of the white locals, and that authority was "hedged about by many safeguards to the member."[7] Kaiser willingly supported the union's practices by not hiring blacks who did not join the auxiliaries, or by discharging workers at the union's request who protested by refusing to pay dues solely on the basis of race.[8]

Mitchell's appraisal of the industry in his memorandum of March 16, 1943, showed a solid appreciation for the challenges the FEPC faced. His experience was boosted that year by his investigation of especially difficult race-related strikes at two major shipyards, Alabama Dry Dock and Shipbuilding in Mobile, and the Bethlehem Steel Shipbuilding Company (see especially his field investigation report in appendix 1 and other details in related texts and in the headnote on Strikes and Work Stoppages). Unlike the West Coast yards, where racial problems were caused primarily by the Boilermakers, both of these cases resulted from the fierce opposition of white workers to the hiring of blacks in skilled positions as well as the creation of integrated workforces based on full equality. The conflicts were resolved after considerable interagency cooperation that permitted greater participation of blacks in skilled jobs. By contrast, during the war neither the FEPC nor the courts were able to end discrimination by the Boilermakers and other unions.[9]

Another appraisal in 1943 by Daniel R. Donovan for George Johnson on racial discrimination in the industry on the West Coast stressed the importance of the USES 510 reports as the chief source of complaints for documenting discrimination in the industry. In addition to the details the *First Report* provided, Donovan said that in almost every instance the complaints were directed against labor unions with exclusive contracts with the shipbuilding company. In view of the collective bargaining agreement between the West Coast shipbuilders and the Metal Trades Department of the AFL, he once more confirmed, the matter of hiring control was completely in the hands of the local unions of the respective craft unions. Clearance for hiring was provided under the master agreement. That year, based on the recommendation of the chairmen of the FEPC and the Maritime Commission, the FEPC held a conference on August 20 with representatives of four of the major companies in the region: Kaiser Company, Consolidated Steel Corporation, California Shipbuilding Corporation (Calship), and Western Pipe and Steel Company and agents of the Boilermakers Union in an attempt to end discrimination in the industry. But the union remained uncooperative, and Kaiser accused the FEPC of ordering management to abrogate its contract with the unions. So the FEPC proceeded with its plans for hearings.[10]

Mitchell conducted an extensive investigation in Portland for the Committee's planned hearing and subsequent hearings in Los Angeles. When Mitchell arrived in Los Angeles on October 22, he met with WMC and USES officials, sympathetic white members of Boilermakers Local 92, and black auxiliary union officials. He interviewed many FEPC complainants, evaluating their cases and their potential effectiveness as witnesses. Like most observers, he identified the union as the primary culprit in discrimination and reported that the union's business agent, E. V. Blackwell, had stated that if admitted as regular members, blacks would remain in the union during peacetime, but auxiliaries could and would be eliminated at war's end. When he finished his investigations, Mitchell strongly recommended proceeding with a hearing.[11]

On November 15 and 16, 1943, the Committee held hearings in Portland on the problems at the Kaiser and Oregon shipbuilding yards and right afterward, on November 19 and 20, in Los Angeles on problems at Calship, Consolidated, and Western Pipe and Steel. Kaiser contended it was willing to hire without discrimination but that it was prevented by its master agreement with the union and that federal law banned their interference with the internal affairs of unions. Edgar F. Kaiser, general manager of the Portland yards, also testified that a big part of the labor problem was caused by the lack of housing for blacks. Local 72 officials blamed the international union. They contended they were willing to admit blacks but were precluded from doing so by the international and the requirement that their members be white. Black workers, many of them witnesses Mitchell recommended, testified that they were assigned to the more marginal shipyards and the more undesirable shifts. That treatment, they said, indicated that it was likely their jobs would be eliminated as the war ended.[12]

The Shipyard Workers Committee for Equal Participation in Unions, in Los Angeles, and the Bay Area Council against Discrimination, in San Francisco-Oakland, similarly challenged the auxiliary system and the requirement that blacks pay union dues as a condition for employment. They initiated no-dues-paying pledge campaigns among workers. Many black workers at several shipyards complied and were consequently fired for not paying the dues. The organizations interpreted the dismissals as evidence of collusion between management and union. The resulting increase in militancy among blacks led to picketing and threats against those who joined auxiliaries. Walter Williams, president of the Shipyard Workers Committee, warned that race riots could result from the tensions; local political leaders voiced similar fears.[13]

On December 9, 1943, the Committee found that the companies and Boilermakers were parties to a closed-shop agreement obligating them to hire and retain in their employ only persons who were acceptable to and in good standing with the unions— in other words, those who paid their dues. The union did not admit African Americans but relegated them to auxiliary lodges in which they were denied rights and privileges accorded members of the regular lodges of the union. The Committee further found that the policies and practices of the companies and the union violated the nondiscrimination provisions of Executive Order 9346. Consequently, the Committee directed the union to take the necessary steps to eliminate the discrimination. It directed the companies, pending the compliance of the union with its directive, to desist from discharging blacks who refused to join the auxiliary.[14]

Both management and unions immediately challenged the directive. The companies complained that they were told evidence was being given regarding union discrimination only and that therefore they had not been adequately prepared in presenting their case. They insisted that the FEPC was interfering with legal labor agreements and that they were barred by the Wagner Act from interference in the internal affairs of unions. Charles MacGowan, the Boilermakers' president, demanded that the companies adhere to their master agreement regardless of the FEPC's opinion, which he contended was a mere guideline and lacked the force of law. He warned that compliance with the FEPC's instructions would "alienate the goodwill of organized labor and its support of the war effort because of this arrogant attempt to destroy collective bargaining agreements." Most firms agreed to comply with the union's demand that they adhere to the master agreement and discharge non-dues-paying members. Boilermakers' locals promptly presented lists of workers to be dismissed by the shipyards.[15] The union also complained in a letter to the Smith Committee, prompting it to investigate the FEPC's handling of the case.[16]

Despite its defiance, the Boilermakers had agreed to bring the subject before its executive council and requested time to take it up at the next union convention, in February 1944. Joseph Keenan of the War Production Board negotiated with the union. Ross met with MacGowan and other union officials for several hours before the convention. Boris Shishkin, a member of the FEPC, attended it and attempted to exert some influence. The Boilermakers agreed to some concessions regarding the auxiliaries, including admission of their representatives to international conventions and equal insurance coverage for black members, but it left the auxiliaries subordinate to the white locals and with little ability to elect their own officers or handle their own grievances. It still denied the right of universal transfer of membership that whites had. Shishkin initially contended that the concessions were a "tremendous step forward," but Milton Webster, a black Committee member, strongly challenged that interpretation. After considerable debate, the FEPC informed the union it was still not in full compliance with EO 9346. Meanwhile, the FEPC continued to receive complaints, especially on the West Coast and in Florida, but it could not adjust them until it had resolved the overall issue of the Boilermakers' policies. The cases were generally referred to the FEPC's legal division for inclusion as part of the overall settlement with the union.[17]

Concerned that the unrest in the industry was adversely affecting production in the FEPC's Region XII, the House Subcommittee on Production in Shipbuilding Plants invited the FEPC to brief it at its meeting on January 19, 1944. The subcommittee's chairman said he wanted to see how Congress could help. One obvious measure of the problem, George Johnson testified, was that, as of November 1943, 348,466 persons were engaged in the industry on the West Coast, and only 29,069 were nonwhite (the great bulk of those were black). Attempting to enlist the committee's help, Johnson added:

> When you consider that approximately 65 percent of all shipyard workers are employed in skills under the jurisdiction of the Boilermakers union, you get some idea of the number of persons involved.

> Unless this problem is settled, you are faced with this possibility: Either the Negro shipyard workers will submit to the discriminatory membership, or they will seek work elsewhere.

"Thereby draining from the manpower which is necessary for the upkeep of the shipyards on the West Coast," the subcommittee's chairman concluded.

Furthermore, Johnson testified, the problems of the auxiliary were compounded by the intransigence of the international union. As an example, he explained that when Local 308 attempted to "get rid of this discrimination policy," the international officers from Kansas City blocked their effort. He said the local "even went as far as to elect a Negro as one of its delegates to the convention." But the international officers declared the election invalid, he explained. The international seized the ballots. The local then went into court and got an injunction, and the judge, ruling that the auxiliary union setup was invalid, enjoined the international officers from taking those ballots out of the state, Johnson explained.

Citing another example, Johnson said Local 308 even permitted blacks to attend a membership meeting. But the international officers there objected, saying: "no meeting could be held so long as those Negroes were present. The Negroes quietly retired, and the vote was taken as to whether a Negro auxiliary should be established in Providence, R.I. All the white members voted. They voted 363 to 59 against the establishment of an auxiliary, and yet the international tells them that they cannot take Negroes in." So, Johnson continued, in order to be able to work in the closed-shop setting, the blacks paid their dues, and the international told the local to send the payments to Kansas City, "and we will carry them in the international organization in Kansas City, but you cannot carry them in your membership."[18]

Mitchell testified on two areas, the union's acceptance of Chinese, Japanese, and Mexicans as full members in the union and thus for work in the industry, and its denial of the same opportunity to African Americans. The union, he said, accepted into full membership African Americans "whose parents had registered them as persons of various nationalities such as Portuguese and that sort of thing when they were born." But if the true racial identity of the African American who had been admitted under that subterfuge was discovered, he would be terminated.

Mitchell explained that there were differences in intensity between discrimination at the West Coast yards, where the Boilermakers were dominant, and at the East Coast yards, where other unions were involved. In between, at the Delta Shipbuilding Company in New Orleans, he explained, discrimination by the Boilermakers was as bad as that on the West Coast. A similar problem could also develop at the Gulf Shipbuilding Company and at the yards in Mobile, where the Boilermakers also had closed-shop agreements, he said. "In both yards," he said, there was "a very hard line of demarcation" that prevented African Americans from "being upgraded beyond the skilled level to other jobs for which they" might have been qualified or were qualified.

Mitchell noted the East Coast companies that employed "a great many" African Americans. Nevertheless, he said, there were situations that arose from time to time when there was a need for workers, but because of "certain customs and regulations," it was impossible to upgrade African Americans. That was because, he said, some yards had union problems similar to those on the West Coast that limited the effective use of blacks at higher skills.[19]

In his later reports on the segregated Sun Shipbuilding yards, Mitchell noted that another factor contributing to racial problems in the industry was a shortage of housing that helped spark a brief strike by black workers who were dissatisfied with the company's upgrading and hiring policies. The shortage of housing had also contributed in 1943 to the violence at the Alabama Dry Dock Company. In May 1944, he said that Sun Shipbuilding was among the shipyards that had to modify their segregation policies in the interest of workplace flexibility.[20]

That month, Frank Reeves, the attorney heading the FEPC's legal action against the industry and its unions on the West Coast, informed Johnson that the San Francisco office (Region XII) had twenty-one discrimination cases based on seventy-four individual and organizational complaints pending against the seven shipbuilding companies and eight Boilermakers locals in northern California, Oregon, and Washington. Reeves divided those cases roughly into three categories. The first originated before and were considered at the Committee's November 1943 hearing against the Boilermakers. The second originated before but were not considered at the November hearings (principally cases in the San Francisco Bay area). The third arose subsequently.

The first category was based on complaints against the Kaiser Company, Oregon Shipbuilding Corporation, and Boilermakers Locals 72 and 401 in the Portland-Vancouver area. After the hearings, the companies petitioned the FEPC for a rehearing. Reeves gave more importance to the position of the Boilermakers Union, nevertheless, which declared that the Committee's directive that laid out steps for it to end its discrimination was "inoperative as affecting the obligation of the companies to comply with the provisions of their closed shop contract with the Union, specifically that provision obligating the companies to hire and retain in their employ only persons who are members in good standing with the union." That meant those who had paid their dues.

Those cases that originated before the November hearings but that were then not considered arose principally in the Bay area, Reeves said. The controlling interests in those cases were identical to those in the Portland-Vancouver area, Los Angeles, and elsewhere on the West Coast. The companies in both areas were represented by the same counsel and were all signatories to the same master agreement involved in the other cases.

The problem in the Bay area, he said, was complicated by court action against the Marinship Corporation (in Sausalito) and Boilermakers Local 6 that was instituted independently of the FEPC by organized groups of black shipyard workers who were seeking to enjoin the companies and union from continuing their discrimination and practices that the Committee had found to be in violation of EO 8802. Further action against the companies and the union, he said, was effectively suspended pending a decision in the case by the Supreme Court of California.

Of the fourteen cases based on complaints that were filed with the FEPC's San Francisco office since the Los Angeles–Portland hearings, Reeves added, it was significant that seven were against companies and unions that previously were not charged in the current Boilermakers' dispute. Another disturbing development, he said, was a plan by the union to take advantage of the Committee's suspension of its actions against it pending final resolution of the court case. The union, he said, was seeking to "pick off" the African American leadership who were opposing the auxiliary union.[21]

Further betraying his desperation, Johnson later in the year provided the Committee with a concise history of its action regarding the policies and practices of the West Coast shipyards and the Boilermakers Union. He said the FEPC's "failure to bring about a satisfactory adjustment of numerous complaints received from Negro shipyard workers alleging violations of Executive Order 8802 and 9346 by west coast shipyards and Boilermakers is exposing the Committee to severe criticism, and the operation of the Committee's regional office in San Francisco now are being seriously hampered." He characterized the FEPC's actions as a most revealing series of frustrating exercises.[22]

A report by W. Hayes Beall, fair practice examiner, of March 9, 1945, on negotiations he and Mitchell had conducted with the Maritime Commission regarding Southern shipyards, confirmed that the FEPC had managed to change very little in the industry:

> The most common complaint [of discrimination against the larger shipyards] is refusal to hire at highest skill because of race. Such cases are pending against the Charleston Navy Yard, Boston, Mass; Federal Shipbuilding and Drydock Company, Kearny, N.J.; St. Johns River Shipbuilding Company, Jacksonville, Florida; Brown Shipbuilding Company, Houston, Texas; and several others. Some yards that have good records for the employment of Negro men, refuse to hire Negro women. Bethlehem-Fairchild, Baltimore, Maryland, discontinued all hiring of women after being charged with refusal to hire Negro women. Allegations of refusal to upgrade and of discriminatory classification in lower wage brackets are frequent. Negro men state that they are refused advancement beyond the classification of a laborer or a helper. In the Todd Houston Shipbuilding Company of Houston, Texas, more than twenty trained Negro welders are working as laborers after being refused upgrading upon completion of courses in welding that were offered in a government school. An estimated 1,500 trained Negro welders have left the Houston area. Such shipyards as St. Johns River, Jacksonville, Fla., refuse to train Negroes for welding. In numerous instances, employers contend that unions prevent the hiring and upgrading of Negroes to perform semi-skilled and skilled jobs. The Boilermakers and the International Association of Machinists, as well as others are allegedly (in some cases, admittedly) guilty of those types of discrimination. Members of religious groups and persons belonging to other minorities also appear frequently among the complainants in the shipbuilding industry.[23]

On January 2, 1945, the Supreme Court of California handed down its decision in the pathbreaking case of *James v. Marinship et al.*, which outlawed the auxiliary system and laid the foundation for breaking it up. In *James*, which resulted from the frustrations of blacks with the FEPC's failures, the court declared that segregated and discriminatory unions were illegal in California. Where closed shops existed, it said, unions were not mere private clubs entitled to choose their own members but quasi-public organizations holding a monopoly over labor. Thus they were not free to discriminate. The ruling, though limited in geography, strengthened the FEPC, winning from the companies some compliance with its directives. The victory still did not lessen the Boilermakers' determination to continue racial discrimination. The case was instituted by an injunction proceeding brought by an African American employee of the Marinship Corporation when he was threatened with dismissal for refusing to join the local Boilermakers' auxiliary.[24]

Johnson explained in a memorandum to the field staff of February 15, 1945, that the case was based on the appeal of an order by the lower court that enjoined the company from discharging or refusing to hire African Americans because of their refusal to join the Boilermakers' auxiliary. The order enjoined the union from continuing its discrimination against and segregation of African Americans. The lower court, he said, "declared the union's auxiliary system to be contrary to public polity and the closed shop contract between the company and the union to be invalid." The order was affirmed on appeal. Consequently, he said, the union was

> restrained specifically from (1) compelling blacks to join or pay initiation fees, dues or other moneys to the local auxiliary, (2) compelling, inducing or requesting the company to discharge or refuse to employ blacks because of their refusal to become or remain members or pay dues, (3) preventing the employment of blacks because of their non-membership or refusal to pay dues, (4) refusing to admit blacks into membership in the white local on the same terms and conditions as white persons, or refusing to accept tendered initiation fees and dues to the white local from the plaintiff and other Negroes similarly situated, (5) refusing to give work clearances to blacks who fail to join or pay dues, and (6) attempting to enforce the by-laws governing auxiliary lodges of the International.

Moreover, Johnson said, the company was restrained from discharging or refusing to employ blacks because they did not have work clearances from or were not members of the white local or the auxiliary, provided that if the blacks were accepted into full membership on the same terms and on an equal basis with white persons, they should then be required to obtain and present work clearances from the white local.

Johnson explained further that the court observed that the question to be resolved was whether "a closed union coupled with a closed shop was a legitimate objective of organized labor." It responded:

> In our opinion, an arbitrarily closed or partially closed union is incompatible with a closed shop. Where a union has, as in this case, attained a monopoly of the supply of labor by means of closed shop agreements and other forms of collective labor action, such a union occupies a quasi-public position similar to that of a public service business and it has certain corresponding obligations. It may no longer claim the

same freedom from legal restraint enjoyed by golf clubs or fraternal associations. Its asserted right to choose its own members does not merely relate to social relations; it affects the fundamental right to work for a living.

Johnson said the court examined the Boilermakers' auxiliary system and affirmed the basic complaints of blacks. Johnson explained that the court rejected several contentions of the union and the company, most of which had been made to the Committee in the West Coast shipyards cases. Some of those contentions, he noted, also had been made in other FEPC cases. They could reappear from time to time. Thus, he said, the court rejected the argument that the company should not have been joined as a party to the case because it was bound by the NLRB to enforce the closed-shop agreement and therefore could not go behind notice from the union that a particular employee was not a member in good standing. The court rejected the argument that a state court lacked jurisdiction over a labor controversy involving an industry under the jurisdiction of the NLRB because the board's jurisdiction was exclusive. It also rejected the contention that action by a state court would improperly invade the jurisdiction of the WLB, as well as the contention that the plaintiff had failed to exhaust his administrative remedies through the FEPC.

Johnson explained that the principles established by the decision were:

> 1. A closed shop contract would be void as to African American employees or job applicants who were barred from equal membership rights in the contracting union. That meant that they had to be employed without clearance from the union so long as discrimination in union membership continued.
> 2. Employment could not be conditioned upon joining a subsidiary union affording unequal union membership rights.
> 3. An employer entering into a closed shop contract with a union known to discriminate against African Americans or, with knowledge, acquiescing in a union's discriminatory policy under an existing closed shop contract was also responsible for the discrimination.

Johnson said that the effect of the decision, from the union's standpoint, was that it would lose the membership of the auxiliary; it would lose the support, including dues payments, of blacks within its jurisdiction; and it would lose its complete control over the hiring of employees.

The decision was binding, Johnson stressed, only within California, but, together with the U.S. Supreme Court's recent decisions in the *Tunstall, Steele,* and *Wallace* cases, it "should be useful in all of our compliance negotiations with unions having discriminatory policies, inasmuch as these decisions point to the likely self-destruction of unions which continue such policies."[25]

That year, Mitchell continued to work with the FEPC's Regions VII, X, and XIII, on shipyard cases in the South. (Region XII was carved out of Regions VII and XII, covering Louisiana and parts of Texas.) The most important was the Delta Drydock and Shipbuilding case. In addition to Alabama Dry Dock, the FEPC had investigated discrimination at Delta's shipyards in New Orleans during the Birmingham hearings of

1942, and it issued an FEPC directive on October 8, 1942, to the firm to open skilled jobs to African Americans. Tensions in the yard led to violence against black workers in which the state-assigned security guards took part and that in 1944 led to a walkout of large numbers of unskilled black workers. After Delta refused to revise its promotion policies, the FEPC began negotiations with the Maritime Commission to enforce the nondiscrimination clauses in its contracts with the firm and to do so without sanctioning segregated work arrangements. Initially afraid to take a strong stand for fear of disrupting production, the commission ultimately stood firm on a requirement that the company hire black welders. Fifteen were finally placed on the job without incident in January 1945 and the company pledged to raise the number to seventy-five (see Maritime Commission in the headnote on Relationships with Federal Agencies).

Elsewhere, as many shipyards began cutbacks, negotiations were not as successful. At St. Johns River shipyard in Florida, workers threatened violence if black welders and burners were hired. At Todd-Johnson Dry Docks in New Orleans, white workers went on strike in July 1945 when an African American was promoted to boilermaker's helper, while black workers threatened to walk out in response to conditions at the yard. The FEPC rejected the Maritime Commission's request for it to abandon its demands that the USES refuse to assign workers to the plant because of its failure to employ blacks. The FEPC continued its negotiations with national company officials and union leaders to resolve the case.[26]

In its analysis of postwar prospects in the industry, the FEPC noted that, just as in World War I, African Americans had in World War II experienced their highest wartime use of skills in shipbuilding. However, it warned, all the gains from World War I had vanished by 1930. It predicted that only ten to twelve thousand blacks could expect to be employed when the industry returned to normal, and that "some 182,000 Negroes must eventually seek work elsewhere."[27]

Shipbuilding was not one of the industries the FEPC considered to be potentially significant for employment for African Americans after the war. Follow-up appraisals by Herbert R. Northrup, noted economist and labor expert, confirmed that while blacks retained or even increased their share of jobs, shipbuilding declined so much after the war that it provided few future opportunities for African Americans. But shipbuilding did play a major role during the war in defining the extent and depth of labor union discrimination, and this problem continued well into the future to help define the struggle in Washington against racial discrimination that Mitchell would subsequently lead.[28]

NOTES

1. The *First Report* noted that nonwhite employment in the industry rose "from 10,099 in the whole industry in 1940 to 157,874 in 96 shipyards in 3/44. While total employment increased 888.9 percent, nonwhite employment during the period of wartime growth rose 1,463.2 percent." *First Report,* 91. See also *Final Report,* 19; Weaver, *Negro Labor,* 7; Harris, "Federal Intervention in Union Discrimination," 325–48.

See the section on the Boilermakers in the headnote on the FEPC and Unions; for a contemporary, chapter-length report that traces the history of racial problems in the industry, see Northrup, *Organized Labor;* for a chapter-length study that highlights the struggles of A. Philip Randolph, president of the Brotherhood of Sleeping Car Porters, and other blacks in the AFL against the racial policies of its Metal Trades Department and of the FEPC's against discrimination in the industry, see Hill, *Black Labor.*

2. Weaver, *Negro Labor,* 34–37, 97–99.

3. A master agreement is a collective bargaining agreement that generally applies to different sectors of an industry or in different geographic areas within the union's jurisdiction. The AFL chartered its Metal Trades Department (MTD) in 1908 to coordinate the negotiating, organizing, and legislative efforts of its twenty international affiliated craft and trade unions. They include the Machinists, Boilermakers, Electrical Workers, and the Plumbers and Steamfitters. The MTD operates under its own constitution and by-laws within the laws of the AFL-CIO.

4. Northrup, *Organized Labor,* 211; Weaver, *Negro Labor,* 34–37; "Progress Report, War Manpower Commission, March 1943," in Spero and Harris, *Black Worker,* 231–32; Harris, "Federal Intervention," 326; Hill, *Black Labor,* 185–208; testimony by Johnson and Mitchell, Hearings, House Resolution 52, Subcommittee on Production in Shipbuilding Plants of the House Committee on Merchant Marine and Fisheries, 78th Cong., 2nd sess., 1173–84; *Final Report,* 19–20.

5. Watson, *Lion in the Lobby,* 130–31; Mitchell memorandum, 10/10/42, to Weaver; Zaid, *Preliminary Inventory,* 20; WPB memorandum from Dorothea de Schweints to Phillips L. Garman, logged at FEPC on June 18, 1943, on "The Shootings at Sun Shipbuilding and Dry Dock Company on June 16," in RG 179, Records of the War Production Board, WPB 323.42, Shipyards–Labor–Strikes and Disputes, DNA; Malcolm Ross memorandum, 7/29/43, to Father Haas, on "Facts on Boilermakers Situation," HqR1, Office Files of Malcolm Ross. R.

6. Ross to Haas, 7/29/43, "Facts on Boilermakers Situation," HqR1, Office Files of Malcolm Ross. R. See Mitchell's memoranda to Johnson, 10/18/43–1, 10/18/43–2, 10/18/43–3, for a detailed background of the creation of SNOV and other aspects of his investigation. Report by Leslie Perry, 8/11/43, in MP. Perry, administrative assistant in the NAACP Washington Bureau, reported:

> On July 21st a representative of the Bureau [Perry] participated with Rev. James Clow, President of the Portland, Oregon [NAACP] Branch; Julius Rodriguez, President, Shipyard Negro Organization for Victory, Portland; M. Moran Weston, Field Secretary, Negro Labor Victory Committee, New York; and Rev. W. H. Jernigin, Fraternal Council of Negro Churches, Washington, D.C., in a conference with Father Haas, Malcolm Ross and George Johnson of the Fair Employment Practice Committee. At this conference an informal complaint was lodged against the Kaiser Company Inc., Oregon, Vancouver and Swan Island Shipyards and Subordinate Lodge No. 72 of the International Brotherhood of Boilermakers, Iron Shipbuilders and Helpers of America, for alleged discriminatory practices in violation of Executive Order 9346. The essence of the complaint is that Negro workers in these shipyards were being discharged for non-union membership as a result of their refusal to join a jim-crow auxiliary set-up to obviate the failure and refusal of the subordinate lodge to admit them as members. A formal complaint was to be prepared and submitted immediately.

7. Ross to Haas, 7/29/43, "Facts on Boilermakers Situation," HqR1, Office Files of Malcolm Ross. R.

For Mitchell, a major problem was Thomas Ray, leader and business agent of Local 72. Mitchell considered Ray "a browbeating kind of fellow," the big stumbling block to getting blacks into the skilled trades in the shipbuilding industry. He described the Kaiser Company as "actually enthusiastic" about employing blacks. He depicted Anna Rosenberg, a small, "very perceptive" and "tough New Yorker," as more than a match for Ray and credited her with knocking out his power. Merl Reed interview with Mitchell, 8/24/78.

8. Merl Reed interview, 8/24/78.

9. See Mitchell, reports, 6/8, 8/6/43, in appendix 1; memorandum, 6/1/43, and notes; "Important Cases Being Handled at Regional Level," 4/22–5/22/44, in appendix 1.

10. Donovan memorandum, 7/5/43, to Johnson, HqR1, Office Memoranda, D; Johnson to Haas, memorandum, 8/24/43, providing a detailed report on the conference, HqR1, Office Memoranda, J.

11. Mitchell's four memoranda, all of 10/18/43 and 11/6/43, to Johnson.

12. Hearings materials are in HqR83, Correspondence Relating to Cases. Kaiser Company, Inc., and Kaiser Shipbuilding Co.

13. Mitchell, memoranda, 11/1/43–3, 11/13/43–2.

14. "The Boilermakers Case," a summary of the Committee's findings and directives, HqR5, Office Files of George M. Johnson. Undesignated (blank) folder. See also Summary, Findings, and Directives, 12/9/43, Portland Hearing, Exhibit File, HqR14, Records Relating to Hearings; Reed, *Seedtime,* 284–85; Harris, "Federal Intervention," 339.

15. On the responses to the decision of 12/9/43, see the Transcript of Proceedings,12/27/43, HqR64 Central Files; Transcript of Proceedings, 3/4/44, 92–114, 123–49, HqR65, Central Files; testimony of George Johnson at the hearings of the Subcommittee on Production in Shipyards of the House Committee on the Merchant Marine and Fisheries, 1/19/44, Hearings, House Resolution 52, 78th Cong., 2nd sess., 1175–76; Ross, *All Manner of Men,* 145–49; Reed, *Seedtime,* 285–86; Harris, "Federal Intervention," 339–41. At least in the case of the Richmond shipyard in California, union president MacGowan pledged in 3/44 to Joseph Keenan of the WPB that no black workers would be discharged for nonpayment of dues until the Boilermakers case was settled (see Mitchell, weekly report, 3/14/44). On the continuing complaints against the union and the referral of most to the legal division, see Mitchell, memoranda, 6/26, 7/21, 7/25, 10/12, 11/21/44. On the Boilermakers Union issues at Florida shipyards, see Mitchell, memoranda, 1/2, 1/23/45; weekly report, 2/6/45.

16. For the Smith Committee investigation on the FEPC's handling of the Boilermakers cases, see the union's complaint of 12/21/43 and the lists of materials regarding the Boilermakers hearings that the FEPC provided the committee in 1/44, HqR18, Records Relating to Hearings. Smith Committee Hearings; Transcript of Proceedings, 12/27/43, HqR64, Central Files; Reed, *Seedtime,* 142.

17. See Transcript of Proceedings, 2/11/44, 50–58; 2/12/44, 67–89; 4/1/44, 13–15, 48–72; 4/20/44, 125–36; 5/13/44, 90–104; 5/27/44, 2–3, 71–102; 6/13/44, 27–89; 9/9/44, 22–45, all in HqR65, Central Files; Harris, "Federal Intervention," 340–46.

18. Hearings, House Resolution 52, 78th Cong., 2nd sess., 1173–84; Reeves to Johnson, 5/9/44, "Current Status of the Boilermakers Auxiliary Union Issue as It Affects Region XII," HqR6, Office Files of George M. Johnson. Summaries.

19. Hearings, House Resolution 52, 78th Congress, 2nd sess., 1173–84.

20. For tension caused by shortage of housing, see Mitchell, memorandum, 4/17/44. On the Camden, Philadelphia, and Wilmington shipyards, see Mitchell, memoranda, 3/16/43, 5/5/44; reports 4/3, 4/17/44.

21. Reeves to Johnson, memorandum, 5/9/44, "Current Status of the Boilermakers Auxiliary Union Issue," HqR6, Office Files of George M. Johnson. Summaries; memorandum, 5/27/44, "Compliance Analysis in re the Committee's Directive of December 9, 1943, to the International Brotherhood of Boilermakers, Iron Ship Builders and Helpers of America," HqR1, Office Files of Malcolm Ross. Committee Meeting, 6/13/44. See also Reeves memorandum, 3/7/44, to Johnson, "Recent Court Decisions Involving Negro Membership in the I.B. of B.M., I.S.B. & H. of A."; memorandum, 10/6/44, "Cases Involving Discrimination in the West Coast Shipbuilding Industry—Analysis and Recommendations, pt. 1 (Los Angeles and Portland-Vancouver)," both in HqR5, Office Files of George M. Johnson. Reeves; Reeves to Mitchell, "Boilermaker Cases Referred to the DFO (Miss Rogers' memorandum September 29, 1944)," providing a list of Kaiser Company cases (Portland-Vancouver) that were filed prior to and were involved in the hearings, HqR38, Central Files. Stanley Metzger; Reeves, 12/27/44 memorandum to Johnson, "Chronology re Kaiser Company, Inc., and Oregon Shipbuilding Corporation Request and Inquiry Concerning FEPC-Maritime Commission Operating Agreement and Procedures," relating to new issues raised at the rehearing held in Los Angeles on 8/7/44, HqR5, Office Files of George M. Johnson. Reeves (for other materials relating to the Kaiser Company rehearing, see HqR1, Committee Meetings); OWI, advance news release, 12/14/43, on FEPC findings and directives resulting from hearings held on 11/15–16/43 in Portland on Kaiser Company and the Oregon Shipbuilding Corporation and on 11/19–20/43 in Los Angeles; FEPC, "Summary Findings and Directives Relating to the Hearings Held on 11/19–20/43 on California Shipbuilding Corporation, Western Pipe and Steel Company, Consolidated Steel Corporation (Shipbuilding Division), International Brotherhood of Boiler Makers, Iron Ship Builders, Welders and Helpers of America, A.F. of L., Subordinate Lodge no. 92, Auxiliary Lodge no. A-35," issued 12/9/43, HqR6, Office Files of George M. Johnson. Summaries.

22. Johnson to Committee members, 11/22/44, HqR38, Central Files. Memoranda, All Committee Members, 1944–1945.

23. At the end of 1944, Mitchell, accompanied by Beall, conducted extensive negotiations with the Maritime Commission regarding the Southern shipyards (see Mitchell's memorandum, 12/19/44). Beall documented the dramatic changes in employment by regions. Report, 3/9/45, HqR38, Central Files. (entry 25) Will Maslow, 1945.

24. *James v. Marinship Corp.*, 25 Cal. 2d 721 (1944). In defending the FEPC at Smith Committee's investigation into the agency's actions against the Boilermakers Union, Leslie Perry, administrative assistant in the NAACP Washington Bureau, noted that as early as 1935 in the case of *Cameron v. Alliance of Theatrical, Stage Employees and Moving Picture Operators of the United States and Canada, Local Union No. 384 of Hudson County*, 118 N.J. Eq. 11 (1935), the court, in ruling on a comparable situation, held that auxiliaries violated sound public policy. It said:

> Their status is not even that of nominal members. They are under the absolute control of this body, but are in no sense a part of it. Thus liberty of contract is unreasonably restrained; the design is not to advance the public welfare, but the individual members of the senior members solely. It is a perversion, an embezzlement of power.

Perry's draft letter, 1/6/44, from Roy Wilkins, NAACP executive secretary, and William H. Hastie, chairman, NAACP national legal committee, to members of the Special Committee to Investigate Executive Agencies (Smith Committee), with copies to Congressmen Sam Rayburn, speaker of the House, John W. McCormack, majority leaders, and Joseph W. Martin Jr., minority leader, in NAACP II A269, DLC.

25. Johnson, memorandum, 2/15/45, HqR6, Office Files of George M. Johnson. Miscellaneous. For more detail on the *Tunstall, Steele,* and *Wallace* cases, see the headnote on the FEPC and Unions.

26. On the Southern shipyard cases generally, see Mitchell, memoranda, 12/19/44, 1/2, 7/24, 7/28/45; weekly reports, 2/14, 2/20, 2/26, 4/3/45. For background, see Reed, "FEPC, the Black Worker and the Southern Shipyards." On Delta, see esp. Mitchell, weekly reports, 2/19, 2/28, 3/6, 3/27, 5/1, 5/8, 5/17/44, 1/9, 1/15/45; memoranda, 3/16/43, 5/5, 8/14/44, 1/8, 1/12/45, and notes; "Important Cases Being Handled at Regional Level," 4/22–5/22/44, in appendix 1; related texts in HqR83, Correspondence Relating to Cases. (A–K), Delta Shipbuilding, and in FR96, Region X. Active Cases (A–Z), Delta Shipbuilding.

27. *Final Report,* 90.

28. Northrup, *Organized Labor,* xe–xf.

THE STEEL INDUSTRY

World War II provided a significant increase in opportunities for jobs and upgrading for African Americans in the steel industry, which had a long tradition of employing them.[1] According to Sterling Spero and Abram Harris,

> The Negro became an important factor in steel during the war-time [WWI] labor shortage. "If it hadn't been for the Negro at that time," said a former official of the Carnegie Steel Company in Pittsburgh, "we could hardly have carried on our operations." When the migration failed to bring colored labor to the mills in sufficient numbers, the companies sent their agents to the South and brought thousands of black workers back with them. "The nigger saved the day for us," declared a company official who had personally supervised the importation of thousands of colored men into the Pittsburgh district.

By World War II, however, African Americans were no longer content with doing the most menial jobs without prospects of moving up to better jobs.[2]

Although the FEPC dealt with many cases involving the steel industry, particularly over the questions of upgrading and the hiring of African American women, in general they were handled through negotiations and did not require hearings. The United Steelworkers Union officially supported a nondiscrimination policy and signed a working agreement with the FEPC for handling discrimination charges related to the union. Locals, however, were not always supportive and white workers occasionally went on strike to protest upgrading of African Americans into skilled positions (see, for example, the strike at the American Steel Foundry plant, East Chicago, Indiana). Black workers also periodically staged walkouts to protest discriminatory working conditions at steel mills. The most prominent of those cases were the Carnegie-Illinois Steel Corporation plant at Clairton and the Jones and Laughlin Steel plant at Hazelwood, both in Pennsylvania, which were successfully brought under control by the FEPC's Region III staff.[3]

Unlike most other industries, at war's end the FEPC saw steel as continuing to offer good prospects for black workers. "The industry's future is good, its manpower needs are acute, and the Negroes' position is generally backed by union policy," the Committee noted.[4] Reviewing the postwar situation in 1971, Herbert Northrup noted that the industry remained "something of a paradox." It employed large numbers of African Americans, including many in skilled positions, but it excluded them from some jobs. The Steelworkers Union admitted blacks, officially on a nondiscriminatory basis. In practice, however, it sometimes tolerated discriminatory seniority systems or declined to challenge discriminating locals. Moreover, stagnation of the industry and the shift away from blast furnaces reduced the employment opportunities the industry could provide African Americans in the future.[5]

NOTES

1. *Final Report*, 89.

2. Spero and Harris, *Black Worker*, 25. In a study of the economic status and industrial position of African Americans in industry and labor unions, Horace R. Cayton and George S. Mitchell provide extensive coverage of their struggle for equality in the iron and steel industry. Cayton and Mitchell, *Black Workers and the New Unions*, 3–103. In *Negro Labor*, Weaver also discusses the problems of African Americans in the iron and steel industry.

3. See Mitchell, first memorandum, 4/8/46, and notes. On the racial unrest and strikes at American Steel Foundry plants, see memoranda, 7/16, 9/14/43, 7/31/44. On the Carnegie-Steel cases, see memoranda, 9/14/43, 3/6, 3/27, 4/13, 10/7/44. On Jones and Laughlin, see memoranda, 9/4, 9/9, 9/14, 9/29/43; report, 5/1/44. For overall background, see the headnote on Strikes and Work Stoppages. On the general steel industry situation along the Gulf Coast, see Obadele-Starks, "Road to Jericho," 154–79; and for the Midwest, see Kersten, *Race, Jobs, and the War*, 62–63. See also Reed, "Black Workers, Defense Industries, and Federal Agencies in Pennsylvania, 1941–1945."

4. *Final Report*, 89.

5. Northrup, *Organized Labor*, xe.

STREET AND LOCAL RAILWAYS

Before World War II a large number of African Americans worked on most local transit systems as maintenance workers and often in skilled positions that did not necessitate contact with the public. An incomplete report from the Office of Defense Transportation indicated that as of March 1943 nonwhites constituted 44 percent of the total number of local transit employees throughout the country. Barred to them in most cities, nevertheless, were jobs as operators—motormen and conductors, popularly known as platform jobs—on street, elevated, and subway rail systems. The exceptions were New York City, Buffalo, Cleveland, Detroit, Tulsa, Winston-Salem, and Tacoma, where African Americans worked as operators. As labor shortages began to emerge in World War II, civil rights organizations that had long been campaigning unsuccessfully to open platform jobs to blacks stepped up their efforts, especially when companies began hiring white women for those jobs.[1]

The FEPC began receiving complaints about such discrimination in 1942, when manpower shortages were leaving equipment idle because those transportation systems refused to hire or train African Americans for the coveted positions. One such system was the Capital Transit Company in Washington, D.C. At the Committee's meeting on November 23, 1942, representatives of management and labor said they believed the employment of African Americans as operators would precipitate violence and interrupt transportation service—a common claim throughout most wartime industries. The president of Capital Transit admitted that his company had submitted discriminatory orders to the USES and said it would "continue to refuse to employ Negroes as bus and car operators."

The Committee agreed to send a directive to the Capital Transit Company and that it should be "cleared through regular channels for publication." Pending clearance, it agreed, Milton Webster, a black Committee member, would get in touch with the international officers of the Amalgamated Association of Street, Electric Railway, and Motor Coach Employees of America, AFL, to see whether they wanted to take action. "It was agreed that unless the International officers acted the directive should issue as of November 28." At its subsequent meeting on December 7, 1942, the Committee voted to deny Capital Transit's request for an extension of the deadline.[2]

On December 23, 1942, the Committee announced that Capital Transit, which had "been declared a war industry" and thus fell under the FEPC's jurisdiction, agreed to "abide by directions issued to it to bring the employment policy of the bus and trolley system into line with Executive Order 8802." The FEPC said that W. D. Mahon, the international president of Amalgamated, in effect had tried to win the local's support. Mahon said he had urged J. G. Bigelow, president of Division 689 of the union, which had the contract with Capital Transit, to "take into consideration the fact that we are now engaged in a war in which the colored man is called upon to do the same line of duty that the white man is called upon to do." He reminded Bigelow that African Americans had been full-fledged members of the union for years and suggested that it was time for them to hold platform jobs.[3]

For the next three months, despite Capital Transit's commitments to the FEPC to place blacks in platform jobs, it took no action. In fact, rather than improving, the problem worsened as the company's ratio of African Americans declined, Lawrence Cramer told the Committee on April 19, 1943. He added that the Los Angeles Railway Corporation (LARY) case, which was similar to Capital Transit, had been struggling on for four months. The Committee therefore scheduled hearings on Capital Transit for May 18 in Washington. It also agreed that it should schedule hearings on LARY, the Chicago transportation system, and the Baltimore Transit Company.[4]

Capital Transit made one attempt to employ an African American as a conductor early in February 1943. But even though there were over four hundred blacks working with Capital Transit in other capacities, skilled and unskilled, whites refused to work with him. They said they would stop working if blacks were hired as operators. Consequently, the company did not implement its December 23 assurances. At its May 17, 1943, meeting, the Committee postponed the May 18 hearing to June 2. Webster reported that "MacIntyre called up for the president and asked the Committee to postpone it in view of the fact that the new chairman had been appointed and would be in Washington within 48 hours." That was in the wake of the "indefinite postponement" of the railroad hearings on January 9 by Paul McNutt, WMC chairman, which aroused widespread fears over Roosevelt's intentions for the future of the FEPC. On May 31 the Committee agreed to a request from the new chairman, Francis Haas, for a further postponement, evidently because he wanted to try negotiations.[5]

On June 1, 1943, Haas met with the president of the company and its attorney. Three days later Haas spoke by telephone with the union's international officers, and Ernest Trimble continued negotiations, but the company never relented in its insistence that it could not end whites' opposition to blacks working as operators despite its purported educational program that was supposed to help end racial antagonisms.[6]

Webster noted in July 1943 that Capital Transit had had no difficulty training the one black conductor with eleven whites, revealing the sociological dynamics of racial discrimination. A large part of the resistance by whites involved their determination to show their racial superiority. For upon attempting to put the black conductor on a streetcar for his first run with an older white conductor, "progressively 18 conductors refused to take him out." So, "not a train moved in that barn for 20 minutes." A big problem, Webster concluded, was "collusion between the union and management. They become bolder as time goes on."

Boris Shishkin added, too, that a major problem was that Capital Transit was expanding its operations and consequently "drawing very large proportions of the men from the farm areas in Virginia and in North Carolina and in West Virginia." They "were farm people coming in to take these jobs who were not even trained union men—I mean, not experienced union men. There was very little union discipline." The "main reasons for the difficulties, why they can't apply the [nondiscrimination] policy very effectively, is that the jobs in Washington are not frozen, and if you try to force this issue these men know it is very easy for them to try to find jobs elsewhere and leave."[7]

At its December 4, 1943, meeting, the Committee agreed that an "Agreed Upon Statement of Facts" should be presented to the Capital Transit management and union and that subsequently they should be given an opportunity for a public hearing on unresolved issues. The Committee also agreed that its findings and directives should be ready for issuance at its next meeting.

Meantime, workers at the Philadelphia Transportation Company and LARY, which both employed large numbers of Mexican Americans and African Americans, continued to complain about racial discrimination at those companies. (See the headnotes on the FEPC and Unions and Strikes and Work Stoppages.) The complaints began in August 1941 when African American employees at the PTC sought promotion to platform and clerical jobs. The company blamed the Philadelphia Rapid Transit Employees Union for blocking consideration of their request because a clause in the collective bargaining agreement provided that "customs bearing on employer-employee relationship shall continue in full force and effect." The PRT Employees' Union confirmed its opposition by refusing to consider the demand to change.[8]

Early in 1943, the WMC and the USES had attempted to place blacks in those jobs, but the company balked, saying that only a directive from the government could make it do that. The WMC therefore referred the matter to the FEPC, which then received several complaints about the discrimination.

Following the establishment of the new FEPC regional office in Philadelphia in August 1943, the agency had held several conferences with the company and the union. The company agreed that its operations in providing transportation to war workers placed it under the FEPC's jurisdiction. It stipulated that it had never hired African Americans in platform jobs and it expressed its willingness to comply with a FEPC directive to end the discrimination. But it said that the "customs" clause in its contract with the PRT Employees' Union provided that there should be no change in employment arrangements without the union's agreement, and it had not agreed.

On December 8, 1943, the FEPC held a public hearing in Philadelphia, and on December 27 it directed the PTC and the PRT Employees' Union to cease interpreting their contract in a manner that prevented compliance with the national nondiscrimination policy. The union promptly told the FEPC that it would not comply with the directive because the agency did not have jurisdiction over it. (The PTC was not a government contractor, and, ostensibly, that was the reason for the union's refusal to comply. See the headnote on Jurisdictional Issues.) Under cover of the union's challenge that the FEPC had issued its directive without legal authority, the company on January 14, 1944, informed the Committee that it would not comply with the order "until the validity of the Committee's Directives, now challenged, shall be finally established." The reference was to the union's complaint to the House Select Committee to Investigate Executive Agencies (the Smith Committee). Judge Howard Smith of Virginia, a leading Southern opponent of the FEPC, created his committee to investigate complaints that various federal agencies were exceeding their lawful jurisdiction. The PTC's response was an in-your-face reversal of its earlier willingness to comply with the FEPC directive. Furthermore, the issue of the FEPC's authority had not been raised at the hearing. The company insisted the issue had to be settled before it would comply.[9]

On January 11, 1944, the Smith Committee held a hearing on the employees' union's challenge to the FEPC's jurisdiction over the PTC. At the conclusion, Smith asked Ross to provide his committee with a statement on the legal issues involved in the hearings, namely the FEPC's jurisdiction over war industries in the absence of government contracts, and its authority to issue directives.[10]

On January 15, 1944, reporting to his Committee on the brief he had filed that day with the Smith Committee in response to Judge Smith's request, Ross said that there were three jurisdictional questions involved: the power of the president to set up the FEPC and give it the authority it had; whether or not that authority extended to war industries that did not have contracts with the federal government; and whether or not, under the executive order, the FEPC was authorized to issue directives.[11]

Ross said that the Department of Justice shared the Committee's view that the first question, about the president's authority, was one it "should not take on itself. It might be embarrassing later on if we omitted to mention some little power over here that had been overlooked. So it was the conclusion we don't argue that point in our brief."[12] Among the points the FEPC limited itself to in its brief, therefore, were its jurisdiction over war industries that did not have contracts and its power to issue directives.

Regarding the Committee's jurisdiction over industries without contracts, he said, the brief noted that in the final analysis Executive Order 9346 had two goals. First, it sought to promote the fullest use of available manpower, which meant manpower in all industries that were engaged in war production, whether or not they had contracts. Second, it sought to eliminate discrimination against employees in the federal services and in other operations that were subject to federal control.

Ross cited another question that was subject to federal control:

> the whole business of entering into a contract with any industry. So that the President, pursuant to his powers as President and not as Commander-in-Chief, made that direction that executive agencies do not enter into any contract without putting in this provision. In that respect he is acting as Chief Executive and not as Commander-in-Chief. We made that clear so that we could draw the conclusion from that that the mere fact of his actions in this instance as President is no indication he intended to limit this Committee when this Committee was acting by virtue of authority given him as Commander-in-Chief.
>
> The second point necessarily carried with it the authority to take all administrative action necessary to promote the waging of a total war, which included bringing in all available manpower. What I tried as much as possible to do was to get away from the idea that the purpose of this Order was to end racial discrimination and so on. The fundamental purpose of the Order was to get available all the country's manpower.

So, he stressed, falling back on the language of the executive order, "the Commander-in-Chief has specifically authorized his Committee to ' . . . receive and investigate complaints of discrimination forbidden by this Order.'" And when the president instructs the Committee to take appropriate action, he is telling it "to indicate what we think should be done in order to come into compliance with the Order." So by implementing his instructions "in the form of a directive, we are, in effect, stating our conclusions based upon the findings of fact we made as to what should be done."

Ross then read into the record the FEPC's interpretation of a directive:

It is the informed conclusion of the expert impartial agency mandated by the President to "take appropriate steps to obtain elimination" of discrimination and bring employment patterns in line with national policy. It is a direction to take or refrain from taking certain action. It is not self-enforcing, but it does enable the President to evaluate the practical steps which the FEPC believes will eliminate discrimination and dispose of a public controversy.

Ross explained further that the staff had been bothered by the question of "whether or not we are in the habit of issuing directives without fact-finding hearings," because in the PTC case the Committee had issued what it called "proposed directives before there had been any hearing." That action, he said, "was permissible, since the proposed directive was not final and provided in so many words that the party could obtain the public hearing prior to the time any final directive would be issued." In any event, he said, such a hearing was subsequently held.

Ross said he explained to the select committee that the FEPC did not issue directives

as a matter of course in every case before it; and never without full opportunity to all affected parties to be heard. It is only in those rare cases when every conceivable means of amicable adjustment has failed that the FEPC, after hearings and findings of fact, issues directives. To argue that the language, "take appropriate steps," does not envisage the issuance of directives under these circumstances informing the parties of the proper corrective measures which, in the Committee's judgment, are necessary to effectuate the purposes of the Order is, we submit, to rob those vital words of the Order of their commonly understood meaning, and make the Committee's fact-finding functions a nullity.[13]

At the March 4, 1944, Committee meeting, in response to a question about "what could the Smith Committee do at its worst," Ross responded: "Recommend to Congress that we are either usurping powers or denying constitutional rights to people, and they can give us a lot of bad language, which they will, but that is the only effect of it. It is a sounding board for all our enemies." What Ross could not have realized, of course, was that the Smith Committee hearing on the PTC was Congress's first nail in the FEPC's coffin. Smith held three other hearings on complaints against the FEPC, one of which was from the Boilermakers Union on March 13, 1944. And other lawmakers were lining up to take their shots.[14]

Events leading up to a strike on August 1, 1944, were further complicated by intense rivalry among unions contesting to represent the PTC workers even after the Transport Workers Union of America, CIO, had won the representation battle in March 1944, replacing the PRT Employees' Union. The TWU favored ending the discrimination.

On July 1 the PTC informed its employees that it must henceforth comply with the WMC's new employment stabilization plan for the Philadelphia area that required it, in part, to hire workers through the USES without regard to race. Toward the end of the month, the company attempted to use eight blacks it was training as operators. A group of white workers then staged a work stoppage that led Roosevelt to seize the company's properties and call in the army to operate them and implement the WMC's employment stabilization plan with the use of black operators.

Meanwhile, as Cornelius Golightly reported, there was horrendous pressure on all sides, especially on Washington, to settle the strike quickly:

> The output of vital war material from scores of Philadelphia plants and installa-tions fell off, the War Department said, when one third of the city's war workers were kept from their jobs by the walkout of trolley, bus, subway, elevated and electric train operators.
>
> The War Department pointed out that the tie-up of heavy artillery and ammuni-tion, heavy trucks and radar equipment was particularly serious because of the ur-gent need for these items at the fighting front. Production of all these items have been behind requirements, the department said.[15]

During the war the PTC strike was the most publicized. Its causes were intensely de-bated. Many like Mitchell, who led in settling it, attributed the strike to "flying squads," or provocateurs. Mitchell and others insisted that a majority of the workers did not support the strike. After the strike, when several of its participants were charged with violating the Smith-Connolly Act, their lawyers were reported to have said that the strike was not a rank-and-file movement. Instead, they said a claque had instigated it and company and union officials had injected the race issue in an effort to "smash the bridgehead that organized labor" had gained in winning the labor election.

Mitchell and others considered it significant that after the strike black and white operators worked together without further problems, and the public accepted the blacks, one of whom was promoted to supervisor. Members of the TWU also elected a black as vice president and four others as members of the union's executive committee.[16]

Mitchell's experience with the PTC considerably strengthened his handling of the Los Angeles Railway case, which had developed along similar lines. His memoran-dum to the files of August 4, 1944, illustrated his intense involvement in the disputes in both Philadelphia and Los Angeles. In both cases the FEPC gained compliance, but only after Roosevelt had called in the army to operate the PTC system in order to force the workers to end their strike and after overcoming substantial political pres-sure to cave in on the Los Angeles case.[17]

Successes in the PTC and LARY cases made them the best examples of govern-ment action inspired by the FEPC. To win both battles, the FEPC had to convince a queasy White House that with strong leadership from the president the strikers would promptly return to work.[18] The government's success in Philadelphia imme-diately opened up jobs for blacks as streetcar conductors and operators and bus drivers throughout the city's transit system. It also strengthened the government in ending satisfactorily the Los Angeles Railway case. Settlement also was helped by LARY's severe manpower shortage, which reduced service and caused overcrowding. Although the railway association supported discrimination in other places, it did not do so officially in Los Angeles. Instead, representatives from the Chicago local went to Los Angeles to support an end to discrimination in hiring there.

The WMC assisted by lowering LARY's priority rating in March 1944 because the corporation refused to employ all available manpower. Mayor Fletcher Bowron, though anxious to avoid a hearing, took an active role in seeking a solution through appointment of a six-member committee. Nevertheless, after long negotiations, the case reached an impasse; union and management relations became increasingly strained and each sought to blame the other for the impasse over upgrading blacks. The FEPC's decision to proceed with hearings in August 1944 and to issue a cease and desist order immediately, and the strong actions taken in Philadelphia two days before the hearings paved the way for peaceful settlement.

An earlier success, in 1943, in Chicago was facilitated by a long effort there by civil rights organizations to open up platform jobs and by the effective action of the newly opened FEPC regional office. Both management and labor supported working out a solution. Even though resistance among white workers was relatively slight, the union leadership personally sought to reduce it and took a strong stand on the right to work regardless of color. The hiring of African Americans was therefore introduced without trouble. The contrast between the strong and effective union action taken in Chicago and the suspicion of union leadership by workers and union rivalries in Philadelphia and Los Angeles helped to explain why a settlement proceeded much more rapidly in Chicago than in those two cities.[19]

Robert Weaver too emphasized that the three cases indicated that contrary to widespread fears of upheaval, the public showed little resistance to employment of blacks in platform jobs. Nevertheless, in Baltimore, as in Washington, officials remained afraid of protests and walkouts; support from labor, management, and government was weak, and action was delayed until war's end, when the FEPC was too weak politically to achieve its goals.[20]

The Capital Transit case, unlike the PTC, LARY, and Chicago cases, showed neither political leadership nor union cooperation. Unable to gain compliance in 1943 with what the company called "suggestions" for ending the discrimination in the platform service positions, the FEPC suggested to Capital Transit that it create a Joint Labor-Management Committee to help resolve the impasse, and this it did. The labor-management committee hired Paul S. Lunt to study the attitudes of employees toward the hiring of blacks.

Completed on January 10, 1944, the Lunt study rehashed the common knowledge that 80 percent of the company's platform employees were born and raised in the South. By contrast, only 20 percent of PTC employees were from Dixie. The study therefore concluded that 80 percent of Capital's white workers would walk out if African Americans were employed as platform workers—even though African Americans were full members of Local 689 of the railway union. Even the intervention of a top official each from the Office of Defense Transportation and the WMC, the chairman of the board of directors of Capital Transit, and the union's lawyers could not change the company's position.[21]

In a January 2, 1945, press release, the FEPC announced that by still refusing to hire qualified black workers, Capital Transit had failed to use available manpower on its trolley and bus lines in violation of Executive Order 9346. It thus announced that it would hold a hearing on January 15 and 16 on complaints by fourteen black men and women who charged that they had been refused employment. The release said that in reviewing the hiring policies of Capital Transit over the past two years, the Committee had found that the company had revised its original order to the USES for "white only" workers and expressed a willingness to accept referrals without regard to race. One hundred and five blacks consequently applied for jobs as bus operators, motormen, conductors, and checkers. When the company did not hire them, the FEPC said that "the company's refusal to utilize available manpower" had "resulted in inadequate transportation service to Government and District war workers."[22]

At the hearings, Capital Transit reiterated its earlier position that it was willing to comply with the FEPC's demands. However, it dodged behind Lunt's prediction by saying there was "a distinct possibility of a complete stoppage of transportation if" it hired blacks in platform jobs. So it did not do so.

Praising the agency for rejecting continuing calls, including those from some blacks, to postpone the hearings, the *Washington Post* said, "For the committee to have yielded to this counsel of expediency would have been, we think, to destroy its own prestige and effectiveness." Regarding the prospects of violence, the *Post* said it did not "think that the Government ought to yield in this or any other situation to the threats of a bigoted and truculent minority. It was clear in Philadelphia that the whole resistance to the hiring of Negroes was inspired by a handful of hoodlums. The same, we are convinced, will be found to be the case here."[23]

The FEPC's struggle with Capital Transit came to a head on November 23, 1945. As the Committee was about to issue its directive to the company to comply with EO 9346, a politically vulnerable Harry Truman, who was seeking a law from Congress to curb industrial strikes during the reconversion period, ordered the FEPC not to issue the directive because it would further complicate his efforts to win support for the measure. Extremely incensed that Truman had pulled the rug out from under the FEPC, Charles Hamilton Houston told the president:

> It is my position that the order to hold up the Capital Transit decision involves grave public responsibility which must be properly established. In view of the urgency and gravity of this matter, and in accord with the position of certain committee members taken when the committee decided to issue the directive, that the committee should withhold the same only upon direct orders from you to be followed by an immediate conference with you, I herewith on behalf of the committee request such a committee conference with you. We sincerely trust that the conference can be held within the next twenty-four hours.[24]

Receiving no response from the White House to the letter, which was delivered on November 26, Houston resigned from the Committee on December 3, 1945. He told Truman that "the effect of your intervention in the Capital Transit case" was "not to eliminate discrimination but to condone it" and that "you not only repudiate the committee, but more important you nullify the Executive Orders themselves." Accepting Houston's resignation, Truman rejected his allegations that he had blocked the agency's operations and abandoned its principles. The FEPC's doomsday mood was severely aggravated by the impending battle in Congress over S.101, the bill to make the agency permanent.[25]

Because no action was taken, the NAACP and other organizations had to continue the struggle well into the 1950s before African Americans could be hired for platform jobs in the nation's capital. By war's end, many other transit companies had integrated their line operations, including those in Albany, Syracuse, Flushing, Pittsburgh, Cleveland, Phoenix, Sacramento, San Diego, San Francisco, and Seattle. But the Baltimore, Kansas City, and Gary, Indiana, transit systems were among those the FEPC failed to change.[26]

Thus, while the PTC and LARY cases showed the benefits of strong political leadership in resolving racial conflicts, the Capital Transit debacle showed the exact opposite. For Mitchell, the Capital Transit case illustrated "how a few misguided planners and high strategists muffed the ball." They thought they could get Congress to establish a permanent FEPC only if they did not insist that Capital Transit hire blacks as platform workers. But in neither the White House nor Congress, he said, was there any commitment to establishing a strong agency.[27]

NOTES

1. Weaver, *Negro Labor,* 153–55; Hill, *Black Labor,* 309–10; "Equal Employment Opportunity for Negroes in Local Transportation Systems," speech by George Johnson to Louisville Pan-Hellenic Council, 5/23/43, in HqR76, Office Files of Will Maslow. Transportation Systems; copy of Johnson's speech also in FEPC RG 228, entry 40, PI-147, Office Files of Clarence M. Mitchell, Transportation Systems, Local Negro Employment, box 459; *Final Report,* 14.

2. On the claim by management and union regarding violence, see Minutes, 11/23/42, HqR1, Summary Minutes of Meetings. Regarding ostensible fears of riots, in discussing the Chesapeake and Potomac case, Milton Webster said, "Everybody comes before this Committee and predicts a riot." His comments are in Transcript of Proceedings, 7/6/43, 118, HqR64, Central Files; Hill, *Black Labor,* 322–24; headnote on the FEPC and Unions.

3. OWI press release, 12/23/43, HqR86, Press Releases. Capital Transit. For early background of the problems with Capital Transit, see Paul S. Lunt, report, HqR4, Office Files of George M. Johnson. Capital Transit. For discussion on presenting Capital Transit with "an agreed-upon statement of facts" with all the "pertinent facts in the situation" for them to sign, see Transcript of Proceedings, 12/4/43, 31, HqR64, Central Files.

4. Transcript of Proceedings, 4/19/43, 18–21, HqR64, Central Files.

5. Transcript of Proceedings, 4/19/43, 18; 7/6/43, 131–33, 148, HqR64, Central Files.

6. Minutes of 12/4/43, HqR1, Summary Minutes of Meetings.

7. For Webster's and Shishkin's quotes, see Transcript of Proceedings, 7/6/43, 136, 148, HqR64, Central Files; *Final Report,* 15–16. For a broader look at developments, see Reed, *Seedtime,* 89–91, 333–37; Kersten, *Race, Jobs, and the War,* 49–50.

8. For the FEPC's "Chronological Summary of Philadelphia Transportation Company Case Non-Governmental Action," Exhibit no. 462 for the Smith Committee, see HqR18, Records Relating to Hearings. Smith Committee Hearings.

9. In the matter of Philadelphia Rapid Transit Employees Union, Case no. 55, "Summary of Evidence with Opinion and Order," of hearings before Malcolm Ross, chairman, and Committee member Milton P. Webster, held in Philadelphia 12/8/43, in FEPC RG 228, entry 8, PI-147, Office Files of Malcolm Ross, Philadelphia Rapid Transit, box 71, DNA; summary, "Philadelphia Transportation Company Case," HqR5, Office Files of George M. Johnson. Undesignated (blank) folder; Hunt to Ross, memorandum, "Compliance Obtained—Philadelphia Transportation Co.," 4/11/46, HqR2, Office Files of Malcolm Ross. Difficult Cases; FEPC press release cleared through OWI, n.d., with Ross announcement that, following the 12/8/43 directive to the PRT Employees Union, it informed the Committee that it did not propose to comply with the directive to end discrimination, HqR86, Press Releases. Appointment of Sharfsin, Philadelphia RTEU—Statement.

At its meeting on 12/27/43, the Committee discussed the proposed "summary of the evidence with opinion and order" in the PTC case that was previously issued and voted to make it permanent. The Committee also voted to direct both the PTC and the PRT Employees Union that in the event there was any opposition to the company's implementing the directive, it should report the names of the persons or company responsible for such opposition. Transcript of Proceedings, 12/4/43, 24–38, HqR64, Central Files; Minutes, 12/27/43, HqR1, Summary Minutes of Meetings.

10. Reference to the PRT Employees Union's letter of 12/29/43 to the Smith Committee is made in Crockett, memorandum, 1/15/43 (i.e., 1944) on "Legal Issues in PRT Employees Union Case," HqR3, Office Files of George M. Johnson. George W. Crockett, Jr.; and Hunt to Ross, 4/11/46, "Compliance Obtained—Philadelphia Transportation Co.," HqR2, Office Files of Malcolm Ross. Difficult Cases.

11. Transcript of Proceedings, 1/15/44, 24–29, HqR65, Central Files; HqR66, Central Files. U.S. Government, Aliens in Defense, General, A–N; Ross, statement on jurisdiction before the Select Committee to Investigate Executive Agencies (HR 102), 1/15/44, HqR3, Office Files of Malcolm Ross. Maslow, Will.

12. See "Power of the President to Issue Executive Order No. 9346" (ca. 5/44), in appendix 1.

13. Transcript of Proceedings, 1/15/4, 24–29, HqR65, Central Files.

14. For Ross's downplaying of the danger of Smith's attacks, see Transcript of Proceedings, 3/4/44, 62, HqR65, Central Files. See also Ross's statement to the Smith Committee on the Railroad Cases, 3/13/44, HqR6, Office Files of George M. Johnson. Railroad Cases.

Ross presided at the 12/27/43 Committee meeting at which, immediately preceding discussion of the PTC case, three representatives of the Smith Committee—Aaron L. Ford, gen. counsel; Harold F. Hanes, asst. counsel; and Joseph H. Stratton, asst. counsel—appeared before the Committee to ask permission to go through the FEPC's "files to see how you are operating; to determine whether or not you are exceeding your congressional authority." Ford said his delegation "would like to have a roster of the organization, the names, and the whole setup, particularly the Washington office." He said he had a complaint from the Association of Railroads—the Southeastern Carriers Conference—in reference to its recent directive to the members, and he wanted to go into the files on that matter. When Ross balked, Ford asked him, "Do you want to be technical, Mr. Ross? We have a subpoena here. We can take all your files. They [the railroads] have seen the Chairman personally." The Committee then authorized George Johnson to show the representatives the records of the Boilermakers case and the railroad cases, and Theodore Jones to show them the personnel records. Transcript of Proceedings, 12/27/43, 23–31, HqR64, Central Files.

For the FEPC's schedule of personnel, 12/27/43, and the "Contents of Exhibits Submitted to the Smith Committee on January 11, 1944," by Alice Kahn, 1/13/44 for Maslow, see HqR18, Records Relating to Hearings. Smith Committee, Correspondence.

In a newsletter of 4/19/44, from the National Federation for Constitutional Liberties, the organization noted the increasing pressure on the FEPC. It reported that for many months the FEPC had been threatened and attacked from several different sources, notably the Southern railroads, the poll taxers in Congress, the "white supremacy" campaigners of the South, and the Smith Committee, including Rep. Clare Hoffman (R-Mich.), because of its nondiscrimination policy. The federation reported that early in the congressional session, Rep. Vito Marcantonio introduced a bill, HR 1732, to create a permanent FEPC with punitive powers. Other congressmen, including William A. Dawson (D-Ill.) and Thomas Scanlon (D-Pa.), had introduced similar bills.

But the FEPC's enemies had found that their most effective weapon was oblique attacks on the agency's operating funds. Sen. Richard B. Russell (D-Ga.) attached an amendment to the Independent

Offices bill to make it impossible for the president to appropriate funds to any agency in operation for more than one year, but that had not been given statutory powers by Congress. Russell publicly announced that the amendment was intended to eliminate the FEPC, which had been financed by such a presidential allotment. Despite widespread protests from the FEPC's supporters, the amendment was passed. That left the FEPC no alternative. Then pending before the House Appropriations Committee was a request for $585,000. Three groups on the committee held power: the poll tax Democrats, the liberal Democrats, and the Republicans. The federation explained that only a combination of the last two groups could pass the appropriation. Although the FEPC's request was a very small part of the total wartime budget, the agency was carrying the major burden of the crucial fight, not only to realize in practice the basic tenets of the U.S. Constitution and Bill of Rights, but also to achieve the barest practical necessity in this worldwide war—the full use of all the manpower in this country.

The passage of the Russell Amendment, the continued attacks of the Smith Committee, and the extremely precarious position of the pending FEPC budget request before the House Appropriations Committee indicated the genuine crisis of the whole pivotal antidiscrimination policy.

Another National Federation for Constitutional Liberties newsletter, prepared by the NAACP's Washington Bureau (5/44), noted that, in addition to the hearings on the FEPC and the Boilermakers Union, the Smith Committee held one on complaints filed by the Seafarers International Union against the Recruitment and Manning Organization of the War Shipping Administration (see the headnote on the FEPC and Unions):

> The Smith Committee has not published its report on FEPC, but if it does publish one, it may do so while FEPC's appropriation is being debated. An unfavorable report by the Smith Committee should be carefully analyzed and voters should contact their Congressmen about it with a view to preventing them from opposing FEPC's appropriation because of anything reported by the Smith Committee. All of the complaints filed with the Smith Committee against FEPC opposed the efforts to eliminate discrimination against Negro workers in activities essential to the war effort.

The newsletter noted that several congressmen had gone on record about the FEPC and that most of their positions were reported in the *Congressional Record*. The newsletter listed accordingly: 12/3/43, John E. Rankin (D-Miss.), attacking FEPC for seeking to end employment discrimination in the South, *CR* 90, no. 3, 133; 1/12/44, Clare Hoffman (R-Miss.), attacking FEPC for "stirring up trouble," *CR* 90, no. 3, 133; 3/21/44, George E. Outland (D-Calif.), favoring FEPC, *CR* 90, no. 53, app., 1510; 3/22/44, Hugh D. Scott (R-Pa.), favoring FEPC, *CR* 90, no. 53, app., 1549; 4/14/44, John S. Gibson (D-Ga.), attacking the FEPC for the large number of blacks on its staff, *CR* 90, no. 65, app., 1918. Both newsletters are in FR 3, Region II.

15. For additional background on developments in the PTC strike, see Hoover to attorney general, memoranda, 8/17/43, n.d.; FEPC RG 228, Office Files of Clarence M. Mitchell, entry 40, PI-147, Transportation Systems—Local Negro Employment, box 459, DNA; Golightly's brief summary of "Industrial Side of the Philadelphia Transportation Company Strike," FEPC RG 228, entry 29, PI-147, Office Files of Cornelius Golightly, Preview and Analysis Philadelphia Strike and Mitchell Report, box 398, DNA; Hill, *Black Labor*, 275–308; Watson, *Lion in the Lobby*, 143–47.

16. Watson, *Lion in the Lobby*, 143–47; Hunt to Ross, memorandum, 4/11/46, "Compliance Obtained," HqR2, Office Files of Malcolm Ross. Difficult Cases; Mitchell to Maslow, report, 8/10/44, "Investigation of Transit Company Strike"; N. Jeanne Clifton to Mitchell, notes of his telephone conversation on the Philadelphia Transportation Company Case, 8/7/44. See also John Davis to Mitchell, "PTC Strike," 8/6/44, reinforcing the conclusions that several other issues were involved in the strike, HqR38, Central Files. (entry 25) Memoranda, Clarence Mitchell.

The Smith-Connolly Act, formally the War Labor Disputes Act, was enacted by Congress 6/25/43, over President Roosevelt's veto. Limited to the war period, it gave the president power to block national emergency strikes. *Congress and the Nation*, 627–28.

For a tiny sample of the press coverage, see "Race Trouble in Philadelphia Brings Test of Wartime Powers," *Newsweek*, 8/14/44, 36; "Trouble in Philadelphia: Transportation Strike," *Time*, 8/14/44, 22–23; *NYT*, 7/9/44, 38, 8/2/44, 1, 8/3/44, 1, editorial, 8/3/44, 18; "Philadelphia's Hate Strike," *Crisis*, 9/44, 281–83, 301; "Philadelphia—Postwar Preview?," *Crisis*, 9/44, editorial, 280.

17. Mitchell, memo, "Conference with Jonathan Daniels re: Philadelphia Transit and Los Angeles Street Railway," 8/4/44. For a concise FEPC background on LARY, see Bloch to Maslow, 12/31/43, HqR21, Records Relating to Hearings. Los Angeles Railway Corporation (LARY Case), Exhibits. In addition to Mitchell's several other texts on the LARY, see esp. his memorandum to the files, 8/4/44; Mitchell to Maslow, memorandum, 8/10/44; N. Jeanne Clifton to Mitchell, memorandum, 8/7/44, on his telephone conversation. For the FEPC update, see Paul Tillett to Ross, 9/13/44, HqR21, Records Relating to Hearings. Exhibits. In response to Maslow's memorandum to Johnson, 11/6/44, "Final Dispositions Philadelphia Transportation Company, Inc.," Johnson on 11/14/44 informed him that the matter was presented to the Committee at its meeting on 11/11/44, and it determined that the cases "should be considered adjusted." Both memoranda are in HqR38, Central Files. Memoranda, George M. Johnson—3 and Office Files of George M. Johnson. Also see Hill, *Black Labor,* 309–16; Watson, *Lion in the Lobby,* 145–46.

18. Watson, *Lion in the Lobby,* 143–46.

19. For analyses of the factors in successful settlement, see Weaver, *Negro Labor,* 186–91; Ross, *All Manner of Men,* 153–56, 163–69; Mitchell, epilogue. For Mitchell's praise of the quick action of the Committee on the LARY directive, see Transcript of Proceedings, 9/9/44, 65, HqR65, Central Files.

John Davis prepared a report of 10/20/43 that is in the field records for Region XII, LARY case files, FR103. Reports on the handling of the PTC strike, copies of which are in that file, had also been forwarded immediately to Los Angeles for use in the hearings there. See also Alice Kahn, report, 9/13/43, "Employment of Negroes in Local Transit Industry," HqR48, Central Files, General Reports, N–Z.

20. Weaver, *Negro Labor,* 186–91. Hill, *Black Labor,* 325–33; *Final Report,* 15–17.

21. Edmund L. Jones, Capital Transit counsel, opening statement before the FEPC, "Stipulation of Facts," by the company and the FEPC, n.d. [1945], and other documents, HqR4, Office Files of George M. Johnson. Capital Transit. For background, see also HqR1, Documents File. H and T; HqR2, Office Files of Malcolm Ross. Materials from July 6 and 7 [1943] Meeting and Materials from July 26 [1943] Meeting.

22. FEPC, press release, 1/2/45, announcing the hearing; press release, n.d. [1/16/45?], quoting Jones at the hearing, HqR86, Press Releases. Capital Transit.

23. Editorial, "Test of the FEPC," *Washington Post,* 1/18/45, a copy of which is in FEPC RG 228, Office Files of Malcolm Ross, box 64, DNA.

24. Houston to Truman, 11/25/45, cited in McNeal, *Groundwork,* 173.

25. McNeal, *Groundwork,* 173; *NYT,* 12/8/45, 11. See also editorial, "Truman Kills FECP," *Crisis,* 1/46, 9; editorial, "FEPC Filibuster Shows the Way," *Crisis,* 2/46, 40; Watson, *Lion in the Lobby,* 156–57.

26. For the FEPC's progressive steps in Capital Transit, see Mitchell, memoranda, reports, 2/9, 5/7, 5/9, 5/17, 5/21, 8/8/45; FEPC, press release, 1/2/45; "Manuscript #35," 1/12/45, both in HqR86, Press Releases. Capital Transit; *Final Report,* 15–17.

For progress on the several transit systems, see Mitchell's epilogue. On Sacramento, see Mitchell, report, 3/27/44. On Gary and Kansas City cases, see "Important Cases Being Handled at Regional Level," 4/22–5/22/44 (in appendix 1).

See also Kersten, *Race, Jobs, and the War,* 126, 132–34; Hill, *Black Labor,* 311–12, 328–30; Gardner, *Truman and Civil Rights,* 24–39; Eagles, *Jonathan Daniels and Race Relations,* 145–48; Kesselman, *Social Politics of FEPC,* 201–14; Reed, *Seedtime,* 332–37; and Watson, *Lion in the Lobby,* 149–51. On later efforts to secure platform jobs for African Americans at Capital Transit, see, for example, Mitchell's NAACP reports, 7/31/46, 2/2, 3/5, 8/31, 12/28/51; Watson, *Lion in the Lobby,* 231–32.

27. Mitchell, epilogue. For other reasons advanced by Ross, see Ross, *All Manner of Men,* 153–56, 160, 163–69. On the transit employment situation by the 1970s, see Hill, *Black Labor,* 331–33.

THE TELEPHONE INDUSTRY

In *Negro Labor,* Robert Weaver portrays a scene in 1942 in a small Connecticut city where seven hundred African Americans had assembled to hear a speaker discuss war jobs. Most of the men in the audience had jobs. However, the majority of the audience, who were female, were confined to domestic work because black women were barred from manufacturing jobs. The manager of the local U.S. Employment Services confirmed this deliberate exclusion. He said he feared that encouraging black women to apply for manufacturing jobs would arouse the wrath of the wives of the city's influential employers because doing so would deprive them of the services of black domestics.[1]

As widespread as that form of discrimination was, no industry more typified the discrimination African American women experienced than the telephone companies. The problem there was the intimate working relationship among telephone operators, who not only sat close to each other but also had to cross over each other to plug and unplug telephone calls. So, while several companies hired black women in clerical and other positions, they refused to hire them as operators. That pattern persisted among telephone companies even as African American women nearly doubled their presence in nondomestic jobs between 1940 and 1944 (from 4.7 to 8.3 percent).[2]

The FEPC regarded the telephone industry as especially important because it would continue to be an important source of employment after the war. Most of the settlements of the telephone cases were achieved through negotiations. Region II achieved a significant breakthrough in opening up the New York Telephone Company to employment of African American operators in 1944, which served as a precedent for other companies elsewhere. Nevertheless, early in 1945 the Committee was considering hearings on several companies, notably Ohio Bell, Chesapeake and Potomac, Southern Bell, and New Jersey Bell.[3]

The debate among the FEPC's national staff in March 1945, with Mitchell insisting on hearings and Cooper favoring the softer approach of returning the cases to FEPC field staff for further negotiations, was another demonstration of the FEPC's lack of real enforcement power. No hearings were held because the FEPC ran out of time. It nevertheless continued efforts to resolve cases through negotiations. The one against New Jersey Bell's operations in Atlantic City was settled in 1945 when the company agreed to hire some black operators. However, the Chesapeake and Potomac Telephone Company case in Baltimore, in which Mitchell was directly involved in negotiations, was still unresolved when the FEPC dissolved.[4]

In its *Final Report*, the FEPC stated that African Americans entered both the telephone and telegraph industry and the manufacturing of communications instruments in significant numbers for the first time during World War II. Their overall prospects continued to be "improved" in the postwar era, according to the FEPC, because "both the managements and unions are generally attempting to be fair."[5]

NOTES

1. Weaver, *Negro Labor*, 17–18, 21, 38–39, 81, 270.

2. For in-depth reports on the FEPC's progress in tackling telephone company discrimination as well as on remaining problems, see Mitchell, weekly report, 11/27/44; Evelyn Cooper, weekly report, 3/7/45 (in appendix 1).

3. In addition to Cooper's 3/7/45 memorandum in appendix 1, for overviews of the telephone cases, see Mitchell, texts, 10/7, 10/10, 12/2, 12/11/44, 3/8, 3/13, 5/21, 9/27/45. For the background on the New York cases, see Lawson to Maslow, memorandum, 10/17/44, HqR3, Office Files of George M. Johnson. Will Maslow. On the importance of the breakthrough in New York, see Mitchell, memorandum, 12/11/44, and epilogue.

4. Johnson also expressed his desire to join Mitchell, Maslow, and Davis in another meeting with Cooper. See HqR3, Office Files of George M. Johnson. Will Maslow.

See Davis to Johnson, memorandum, 3/13/45, HqR38, Central Files. Memoranda, George Johnson, M—3, 1944. On the FEPC meeting of 2/12/45, see Minutes, 2/12/45, HqR1, Summary Minutes of Meetings. On the Chesapeake and Potomac and New Jersey Bell cases, see texts, 7/5, 9/14/43, 2/5, 12/2/44, 2/14, 2/20, 3/8, 3/13, 3/15, 5/21/45.

Mitchell noted Cooper's meeting with Leo Craig, vice president of the American Telephone and Telegraph Company, concerning complaints of discrimination the FEPC had received. "Recently," he said, indicating that this was a fruit of the meeting, New Jersey Bell agreed to employ black operators. As of that date, the pledge had not been honored, but "it is our hope that some will be on the job within thirty days." Mitchell to Joseph Evans, Region IV director, memorandum, 5/15/45, HqR5, Office Files of George M. Johnson. Telephone Company. For the ultimate success of the New Jersey Bell case, see memorandum, 5/21/45, in the same folder.

5. *Final Report*, 89.

MAJOR CASES IN ST. LOUIS

Defense-related industries in the St. Louis area provided the FEPC with one of its biggest workloads, and cases there culminated in some of the FEPC's greatest successes and failures. Despite being in the North, St. Louis was rigidly segregated and its dominant unions were lily white. Owing to a major growth in defense industries there, the Negro Employment and Training Branch of the Office of Production Management conducted an investigation of racial practices among them. To forestall further investigation by the FEPC in late 1941, many of the defense contractors initiated a 10 percent quota system, based on the proportion of African Americans in the population. The FEPC objected to the quota system, arguing that it placed a ceiling on the employment of blacks even when workers were badly needed. Quotas, it insisted, would substitute "considerations of race rather than qualifications and availability as the criterion for hiring or retraining" employees, thereby subverting the rationale of the president's executive order. The FEPC, however, could do little to prevent its implementation, and the quota system did open more job opportunities to blacks during the war than generally existed elsewhere.[1]

In 1942 the FEPC began investigating those problems, but it took the less confrontational course of attempting to resolve them through negotiations. The Curtiss-Wright Corporation and United States Cartridge Company further expanded job opportunities by opening huge new plants in the area that hired hundreds of black workers, skilled and unskilled. Like the earlier firms, they adopted quotas and segregated workers. Other contractors, though, still refused to hire blacks, while some hired large numbers as needed, but only for low-level positions. Such inequalities sparked complaints to the FEPC. Those problems, along with inequalities in training, upgrading and promotions, and the hiring of black women, remained unresolved in many plants.[2]

Olin Industries, another major St. Louis firm, presented special problems. It was the biggest small-arms manufacturer in the world, producing every third bullet fired by the U.S. armed forces during the war. Some of its component companies in other areas were models of nondiscrimination, notably the Winchester Repeating Arms Company in New Haven, Connecticut. However, Western Cartridge, which was Olin's parent company and its largest unit, was located at East Alton, about twenty-five miles from St. Louis. East Alton was a small "sundown town" that since the 1890s had banned blacks from living or working there. Olin's location within that geographical and racist environment shaped its policy, leading to one of the most socially revealing of the FEPC hearings and one of its noteworthy defeats. Although its contracts included the mandatory nondiscrimination clauses, Olin contended that because of local customs it could not hire any African Americans in East Alton without triggering a plant shutdown that would hamper the war effort.[3]

So in 1943, Western Cartridge, despite severe labor shortages, rejected the WMC's nondiscriminatory referrals through the USES and hired only whites. The WMC then told the company it had to end such discrimination. Western Cartridge still refused, prompting the WMC to impose sanctions by withdrawing its referral services from the firm and refusing to permit it to recruit employees outside the area while black workers were available in nearby towns. Months of subsequent negotiations failed. The regional WMC, caught between nondiscrimination regulations and pressures from the War Department not to let anything interfere with production, referred the case in November 1943 to the FEPC, with which it had an operating agreement. On December 2, after further negotiations with Local 825 of the United Electrical, Radio, and Machine Workers of America, CIO; the WMC; the FEPC; and military officials, Western Cartridge reached an agreement that seemed to promise the hiring of African Americans if federal and state officials and civic organizations undertook a range of conciliating and educational actions and induced other local firms to employ black workers.

The slowing of demand in 1944 for munitions as the nation began preparing for reconversion, however, led Western Cartridge to start cutting its workforce. So it ended its concessions. Moreover, it contended, other parties to the agreement had not accomplished everything they had pledged. Western Cartridge thus announced that it would be unable to hire African Americans. The WMC and local military officials then declared the agreement at an end and reported its collapse to the FEPC in May 1944. A field visit by Charles L. Horn, a Committee member, failed to elicit any changes, so the agency held a public hearing at East Alton in February 1945.[4]

Similarly, after making little progress with United States Cartridge, McQuay-Norris, Wagner Electric, Carter Carburetor, Amertorp Corporation, Bussman Manufacturing, St. Louis Shipbuilding and Steel, and McDonnell Aircraft, the FEPC held hearings against them in August 1944. Those major firms also cited community sentiment, fear of walkouts by whites, or lack of separate toilet facilities as reasons for their racist practices, particularly regarding the hiring or upgrading of black women. Following the hearings, the FEPC issued directives to most of the companies in December 1944 and January 1945. They were ordered to cease and desist discriminatory policies and to take "affirmative action" accordingly: hire black workers who had filed complaints, educate white workers about nondiscrimination regulations, develop and publicize a nondiscriminatory employment and promotion policy, and submit reports to the FEPC. The firms made, at most, only token concessions. A positive development, nevertheless, was that the War Department began cooperating more closely with the FEPC, enabling the agency to make additional progress during 1945.[5]

United States Cartridge was another huge Olin company. It employed large numbers of African Americans, although it kept them segregated in one of its eight buildings. In 1942 layoffs of black workers had prompted protests by the St. Louis March on Washington Movement that succeeded in getting the workers reinstated. The protest also mobilized local civil rights groups to demand more opportunities, including the hiring of black women and increased training and upgrading. When the company, facing labor shortages, attempted to use blacks in one of the seven "white" buildings, workers there went on strike, despite the opposition of union leaders, who consequently resigned.

Surrendering, Gen. Edward S. Greenbaum of the War Department warned the FEPC in May 1944, "Experience has shown, in dealing with racial matters, that orders and directives are not self executing. Very real consideration must be given to attitudes and customs that have been developing for years. Not to do this would result in work stoppages for which the War Department would be held responsible, and which, in the case of essential war supplies, would be inexcusable." Greenbaum said, "I cannot agree that segregation in the United States Cartridge Company case was discriminatory or in violation of Executive Order." Stanley Metzger noted that the statement amounted to a War Department refusal to take any action on the grounds that "community custom" excused the practices of discrimination caused by segregation in company operations.[6]

Theodore Brown, the FEPC's regional examiner in charge, contended, however, that since both management and union leaders favored employing blacks, the FEPC could strengthen their hands by immediately issuing a directive to cease discrimination. Eventually, with union assistance, the firm's management did introduce black workers into new nonsegregated work settings, and the case was resolved without further upheaval.

The United States Cartridge success, however, did not encourage Olin to take a stronger stand at its Western Cartridge plant at East Alton. There the company's lawyer contended that the FEPC had no authority to compel nondiscrimination if it might hamper the war effort, and he marshaled witnesses from the town to document community sentiment. Despite the presence of a group of hostile "brass mill workers," according to Malcolm Ross in *All Manner of Men,* the FEPC hearings proceeded peacefully but brought no concessions. The FEPC regarded the Western Cartridge case as a complete failure. In contrast to the United States Cartridge case, where there was a comparatively strong management and union and government support for change persisted, at Western Cartridge the community was unusually hostile and management and union support were weak. As Ross explained, at East Alton, the FEPC met opposition as stiff as any it encountered in its five years of existence. The town staged a "successful rebellion against a war agency of the United States Government." There, not only the company's lawyers, but the mayor, the ministers, the workers, and the superintendent of schools in effect "told FEPC to go fly a kite." Although the WMC and the FEPC took strong stands, the army, Ross noted, got "cold feet." Thus, even within one area and one company's affairs, two drastically different outcomes occurred.[7]

The most successful of the FEPC's St. Louis cases was General Cable Company. Its eight plants, which were producing much-needed communications cable for the army, were all in the North including the one at St. Louis. There the issues were the hiring of skilled black workers to work with whites on production lines and the employment of black women in any capacity. Local managers needed workers, but they feared that if they placed blacks and whites together, the whites would walk out. The company succeeded in mixing white and black male workers without incident, but had faced a strike when it attempted to place black and white women together. The company backed off and initiated an educational program to promote acceptance of an integrated workforce. Little change occurred in the attitudes of white "farm girls from the Ozarks" working at the plant. Although the union agreed to the hiring of black women, the army liaison officer at the plant informed the FEPC's regional staff that his superiors had directed that he observe a "hands-off" policy to avoid risking a walkout. Learning that the company's president, St. Louis–born Dwight Palmer, intended to go forward with hiring the black women workers needed, despite "white girl opposition," the War Department sent prominent officials to the FEPC to urge it to stop him. Palmer, however, had already gone to the plant, given a rousing patriotic pep talk to the workers, and succeeded in winning them over to acceptance of the new employees. Staff integration moved forward without incident. Ross, Mitchell, and other FEPC staff members lauded Palmer's patriotism and courage at the same time they broadcast the military's failure of nerve.[8]

The St. Louis cases reinforced the FEPC's conviction that even in segregated areas with "Southern" racial attitudes, discrimination could be reduced when the government took a strong public stand, and when company and union leaders showed initiative and courage and appealed to the patriotism and "decency" of most Americans. They regarded threats of violence and walkouts as mostly bluffs that would recede in the face of strong government action and criticized the military and other federal officials for often getting cold feet. Other government officials, though, continued to believe they acted properly by compromising or avoiding action if war production or the administration's political survival seemed threatened. Overall, the efforts of the FEPC and its allies in St. Louis succeeded in winning blacks a somewhat higher share of wartime employment in defense industries than elsewhere, but they had little impact on long-term employment patterns or segregation in the area.

NOTES

1. *Final Report*, 17; Kersten, *Race, Jobs, and the War*, 112–16; Summary of the Evidence with Opinion and Order on Hearings Held in St. Louis, Missouri [on the McQuay-Norris case], 8/2/44, 5–6, HqR3, Office Files of George M. Johnson, Records for the Committee Meeting of 9/3/44; Emanuel Bloch, "U.S. Cartridge Company (St. Louis Case): Compliance after Service of Complaint," n.d., HqR2, Office Files of Malcolm Ross. Difficult Cases.

2. For complaints related to Curtiss-Wright, which, unlike those about the other companies listed, were largely settled without a hearing, see Mitchell, memorandum, 5/18/45; reports, 4/24, 5/7, 5/21/45. On the National Lead Company, another St. Louis firm whose issues did not go before a hearing, see Mitchell, memoranda, 5/29, 7/27, 8/2, 8/8/44; 2/19/45–2, and notes; report, 5/7/45. Also see Mitchell, reports, 4/3, 4/17, 5/17, 12/18/44, 3/20, 4/12, 5/7/45; memoranda, 7/7, 12/18/44, 2/19, 3/13, 5/18/45. For overall background, see Kersten, *Race, Jobs, and the War*, 112–25.

3. On employment in the armaments industry in St. Louis, see Kryder, *Divided Arsenal*, 115–16n87. For overviews of Olin Industries and of the situation in East Alton, see Ross, *All Manner of Men*, 48–68; *Final Report*, 17–19. For full documentation, see the transcript and related files of the hearing held in East Alton, 2/45, HqR20, Records Relating to Hearings. HqR85, Correspondence Relating to Cases. (Sh–Z), Western Cartridge.

4. On the Western Cartridge case, see Mitchell, memorandum, 5/11/44; agreement of 12/2/43, and related texts, HqR85, Correspondence Relating to Cases. (Sh–Z), Western Cartridge; W. H. Spencer, A. H. Brawner, and Elmer Henderson to Western Cartridge, 5/20, canceling the agreement; company's reply, 5/26/44, HqR20, Records Relating to Hearings. Western Cartridge.

5. See Bloch, report, "St. Louis Cases, No Compliance after Service of Complaint," n.d.; report "U.S. Cartridge Company (St. Louis Case): Compliance after Service of Complaint," n.d., both in HqR2, Office Files of Malcolm Ross. Difficult Cases; reports cited in note 2, above. See also St. Louis hearings transcripts and related records, HqR19, Records Relating to Hearings. Bussman Manufacturing Company, Carter Carburetor Company [etc.], and throughout HqR20, Records Relating to Hearings; and Kersten, *Race, Jobs, and the War*, 122–24.

6. Bloch, report, "U.S. Cartridge Company (St. Louis Case): Compliance after Service of Complaint," HqR2, Office Files of Malcolm Ross. Difficult Cases; E. S. Greenbaum to Ross, 5/20/44, HqR1, Office Files of Malcolm Ross. Extra Copies; Metzger to Maslow, memorandum, 5/24/44, HqR5, Office Files of George M. Johnson. Shishkin; "Memorandum on Employment and Training Problems in St. Louis Resulting from Segregation," n.d., HqR2, Office Files of Malcolm Ross. Materials from July 26 Meeting.

7. See Mitchell, memorandum, 2/19/45; Davidson to Maslow, 12/19/44, HqR76, Office Files of Clarence Mitchell. U.S. Cartridge Company; Ross, *All Manner of Men*, 49–66, 166–67.

8. On General Cable, see Ross, *All Manner of Men*, 67–79; Mitchell, reports, 4/3, 4/17, 5/17/44, 3/29, 4/12/45; memoranda, 2/19, 3/13/45; Mitchell, epilogue; and *Final Report*, 18.

THE FEPC AND UNIONS

By leading the struggle for Executive Order 8802, A. Philip Randolph, president of the Brotherhood of Sleeping Car Porters, served as a social and political catalyst during the war period. Milton Webster, vice president of the union and one of two African American members on the Committee throughout its existence, was unflappable, sometimes caustic, in explaining how discrimination worked against his people. Other black unions, such as the National Alliance of Postal Employees, played important roles in fighting employment discrimination by filing complaints with the FEPC. Further extending hope to black workers were the UAW, which was the only union to sign an operating agreement with the FEPC, and the CIO, which supported the national nondiscrimination policy. The AFL's representative, Boris Shishkin, another member on the Committee, served as organized labor's social conscience despite the craft unions' abysmal racial policies. With the help of its union representatives, the Committee attacked endemic discrimination in labor unions. Its combat with some of the nation's most powerful unions to end those practices helped to shape the character of the agency and further demonstrated its own catalytic role in social change.[1]

The New Deal strengthened the economic position of labor unions. The desire to avoid labor unrest and the need to achieve social progress during wartime induced the government to sanction closed shops and other agreements beneficial to the unions. In exchange, the government got no-strike pledges and the acceptance of labor stabilization agreements for war industries. In fields with the greatest wartime employment expansion, such as shipbuilding, steel production, munitions production, and aircraft building, AFL unions in the metal trades generally controlled access to jobs. Several such unions had barriers against blacks as members in their rituals or constitutions. Many others simply discriminated. Civil rights organizations protested those practices.[2]

The CIO, though, offered hope. Growing in membership, it adopted a nondiscriminatory policy, authorized in 1941 the formation of antidiscrimination committees, and usually cooperated with the FEPC. Consequently, as Herbert R. Northrup explained in 1944, "in so far as this writer has been able to determine, no national CIO union excludes Negro workers from membership nor segregates its colored members into Jim Crow local unions." By contrast its rival, the AFL, fiercely resisted change and defied FEPC directives. One of the more sinister forms of discrimination was the requirement that blacks join segregated, subordinate, and unequal auxiliaries in order to get jobs in companies where unions had closed-shop agreements with management that constituted monopoly over employment. In other instances, unions granted temporary wartime work permits to blacks without admitting them as members. Thus, after the war blacks lost their jobs and union segregation once more became the norm.[3]

The railroad brotherhoods (for the FEPC's battle with the railroad unions, see the introduction), notably the International Brotherhood of Boilermakers, Iron Ship Builders, and Helpers of America, were the worse offenders. Among the other unions commanding the FEPC's attention were the International Association of Machinists; the International Brotherhood of Teamsters, Chauffeurs, Warehousemen, and Helpers of America; and the Seafarers International Union. In addition to the UAW, the FEPC had much better relationships with the United Packinghouse Workers of America, the United Steelworkers of America, and the International Brotherhood of Electrical Workers.

With the transfer of the WMC's nondiscriminatory functions to the new FEPC in mid-1943 and the subsequent expansion of the FEPC's staff, the agency became more assertive in investigating union discrimination. Unlike Executive Order 8802, EO 9346 explicitly extended the FEPC's jurisdiction over unions, thus enabling it to challenge more aggressively discrimination in labor organizations.

Railroad Unions

One of the earliest, longest, and most troublesome investigations for the FEPC involved the railroad industry, in which unions colluded with management to restrict the access of African Americans to most jobs. The agency's case against twenty-three railroads and fourteen labor unions was its first after it was reorganized in 1943 under EO 9346. In his testimony at the FEPC's railroad hearings in 1943, Northrup said that the

> Negro railroad worker is in an anomalous position. He is denied a voice in the affairs of nearly all railroad labor organizations; yet, collective bargaining on the railroads has received wider acceptance than in almost any other American industry. He is, for the most part, ineligible to promotion although promotion in the industry is based almost exclusively upon seniority. He frequently receives lower pay than white men when doing the same work, a fact which is often disguised by separate occupational classifications for white and colored workers who perform identical tasks.
>
> The result is that the Negro has become a pawn in industrial relations: Employers have used him to fight unions and to depress wages; unions have retaliated by attempting either to limit the employment of Negroes or by driving those already employed from the railroads.[4]

The *Final Report* declared that the FEPC's struggle against discrimination in the railroad industry "must be counted among the Committee's outstanding failures." The truth, though, was that its struggle, in conjunction with the Supreme Court's decisions in *Steele v. Louisville and Nashville Railroad Company et al., Tunstall v. Brotherhood of Locomotive Firemen and Enginemen,* and *Wallace Corporation v. National Labor Relations Board,* were a landmark in the African American quest for equal employment opportunity. All three cases related to the duty of labor organizations that had been designated "exclusive bargaining agents" to represent all employees in the class or craft that was being represented.

In the *Steele* and *Tunstall* cases the court held that, when acting as bargaining agent under the Railroad Act for an entire craft or class of railroad workers, the union could not use its bargaining right to negotiate an agreement that was preferential to union members and discriminated against other employees on the basis of race. The decisions substantially nullified the Southeastern Carriers Conference Agreement, which was found to be a master pact designed to restrict and eliminate African American firemen and trainmen. The agreement set the pattern for the industry. The decisions meant that the bargaining representative had to represent all members of the craft, class, or unit without hostile discrimination.

In *Wallace* the court ruled against the closed-shop contract when it was knowingly used to achieve the discharge of a group of workers: "We do not construe the provisions authorizing a closed shop contract as indicating an intention on the part of Congress to authorize a majority of workers and a company, as in the instant case, to penalize minority groups of workers by depriving them of that full freedom of association and self-organization which it was the prime purpose of the Act to protect for all workers." George Johnson explained that the *Wallace* decision was not clear-cut, but, nevertheless, he considered it a resounding victory.[5]

In *Steele* and *Tunstall,* the Supreme Court agreed with the Committee's findings and directives that refuted the carriers' position that their actions were legal. Charles Hamilton Houston, who led the battle before the Supreme Court, proudly noted that both cases were the culmination of a five-year struggle. They were initiated, financed, and fought by the Association of Colored Railway Trainmen and Locomotive Firemen, Inc., and the International Association of Railway Employees. The *Final Report* explained that although the *Steele* and *Tunstall* cases rendered the Southeastern Carriers Conference Agreement illegal, such pacts throughout the industry were so numerous that to invalidate them by litigation would have required multiple lawsuits and the expenditure of great amounts of time and money. Moreover, the Supreme Court's decision in those cases applied only to the rights of African Americans after they had been hired and did not affect those who were barred altogether from employment. Both Houston and the *Final Report* concluded that only a permanent FEPC with sufficient authority could deal effectively with all the discriminatory union agreements, but Congress refused to create one.[6]

Union collusion with management to restrict the hiring of blacks was also involved in FEPC cases involving street railways, particularly the Philadelphia Transportation Company case (see the headnotes on Street and Local Railways and on Strikes and Work Stoppages), in which the FEPC met with mixed success in ending discrimination.[7]

The Boilermakers

The FEPC's struggle against the International Brotherhood of Boilermakers, Iron Ship Builders, and Helpers centered on its Jim Crow practices in the shipbuilding industry, particularly on the Pacific Coast (see the headnote on the Shipbuilding Industry). Although there were many unions involved in ship construction, the Boilermakers' control of 65 percent of jobs in the industry set another historic, hard-line pattern of discrimination.[8]

Among the complaints from blacks that resulted from the Boilermakers' policies were that the companies had hired them, but the union refused them access to the jobs because they refused to join the union's auxiliaries. Some worked in the shipyards pending union membership because they would not participate in the auxiliary. Others complained that to hold their jobs they had to pay dues to the auxiliary under protest. Overall, they complained that unavoidable discrimination in the industry deprived them of advancement.[9]

The Boilermakers' Jim Crow practices dated back to its 1908 convention, when a suggestion to include the ritual banning the membership of blacks in its constitution was withdrawn because it conflicted with the AFL's policy. Yet, explained Marvin C.

Harrison, special FEPC counsel at the Committee's hearing in Portland, Oregon, on November 15, 1943, the Boilermakers retained the discriminatory clause, which still had the effect of the secret ritual rules and practices. At its 1920 convention, the union's executive council, again considering its exclusionist policy, proposed unsuccessfully that African Americans be admitted "to enjoy all the rights and benefits provided for under our laws, except that of universal transfer." In 1937, the Boilermakers once more amended its constitution by extending the rights of membership to African Americans, but this time through the Jim Crow auxiliary system that it adopted.[10]

At the opening of the Los Angeles hearing on November 19, 1943, George E. C. Hayes, FEPC special counsel, said the evidence proved "to a complete certainty that this Auxiliary Lodge" was "in real fact a 'Jim-Crow' Union." In comparison with the white locals, he said, the auxiliary was "so unequal in benefits, so unjust in operation, and so violative of the principle of equal rights" that it was "impossible for any self-respecting man to join it."[11]

Northrup analyzed in detail the auxiliary system by explaining the differences it allowed in the union's treatment of both its black and white members. He noted that the only matter in which there was equality was in the dues black and white members paid. He provided the FEPC with glaring evidence of six "major discriminations" and documented the extent to which the auxiliary was subservient to the white local, to the point where the auxiliary could adopt no bylaw that conflicted with those of the supervising white local, even in minor and routine matters; the international union denied black members and locals rights to membership in the international, which meant that they were not members of the general organization at all; the international denied the black local the right to have a business agent, who was the most vital official of a local union, responsible for dealing with the employer; black locals were denied the right to have a grievance committee, and since no black sat on the grievance committee of a white local, the group was denied an essential means for investigating and remedying internal disputes or wrongs; blacks were limited to advance in status from helper to mechanic, thus denying them the rights to receive more pay and economic and job status; and there was also a limitation on the rights of blacks to transfer from one city to another, denying them membership card rights to enable them to work "throughout the length and breadth of the land."

Northrop also listed four "lesser discriminations," the first of which concerned the extent of insurance coverage, which was much less for blacks than that for whites. The auxiliary bylaws did not provide for apprentices, which meant its members would always be helpers and not be able to become mechanics, but they had a special provision to punish blacks for creating a disturbance while intoxicated; and they provided that, while white members could be admitted between the ages of sixteen and seventy, blacks could be admitted only until they were sixty.[12]

Even though Northrup's documentation was indispensable in exposing the Boilermakers' embarrassing practices during wartime, the ameliorating steps that nominally abolished the auxiliary system still left blacks in segregated locals.[13]

The International Association of Machinists

The International Association of Machinists, founded by South Carolinian Thomas W. Talbot in 1888, sought a membership that was highly skilled and of reputable social standing and character. Such emphasis on "quality" led the union from the beginning to bar acceptance of those it considered to be "social inferiors." Membership was restricted by the union constitution to "white, free born citizens." Modeled largely on the Knights of Labor, the Machinists had adopted a secret Masonic-like ritual. When the AFL refused affiliation to the IAM so long as the "whites only" clause remained in its constitution, the union's 1895 convention voted to omit it, but it transferred the clause to its secret ritual. The Machinists then applied for and obtained AFL affiliation.

In 1941 the FEPC wrote the union's executive council about discrimination complaints against some of its locals in California. Attempts by Boris Shishkin and Harvey W. Brown, IAM president, accomplished little. Although blacks were admitted to membership in some areas, FEPC complaints against the union mounted throughout World War II. Mitchell, like most FEPC staffers, strongly advocated holding FEPC hearings regarding the union, but in the end none were ever held. In 1945 the IAM's Committee on Ritual voted 10 to 3 in favor of dropping the whites-only clause, but the resolution was soundly defeated by a roll call vote at the convention that year.[14]

The Teamsters

The Teamsters Union, frequently involved in FEPC cases in Detroit and occasionally elsewhere, presented a mixed picture in its racial policies, depending on the attitudes of the locals and their leaders. Although, like many unions, the Teamsters generally tried to retain the more desirable and lucrative assignments for white members, most of its locals did admit blacks. There were a few dramatic exceptions. One was Local 299 in Detroit, led by Jimmy Hoffa. It was the only local in that city that refused to admit African Americans, but it controlled access to the lucrative long-haul truck routes, from which blacks were thus barred. Despite the intercession of Daniel Tobin, the union's international president, the FEPC had no success in getting Hoffa to end discrimination. Hoffa was openly hostile in his meetings with local FEPC officials and challenged the agency's ability to do anything about his union's antiblack policy. The FEPC held hearings on the Teamsters in Detroit in June 1945, but, although it adequately documented its cases, they were a failure. Union officials and most of the trucking companies did not attend, and the FEPC could do little more than scold the few companies there.[15]

The Seafarers International Union

During World War II, the maritime industry was dominated by two rival unions, the Seafarers International Union, AFL, and the National Maritime Union, CIO. The

NMU followed an active nondiscrimination policy, sought to secure officer and other high-level positions for black workers, operated effective educational programs in intergroup relations, permitted an active role for African Americans in union leadership positions and convention attendance, and cooperated well with the FEPC.

The SIU furnished seamen for numerous steamship lines holding war contracts. The union itself sparked numerous discrimination complaints and refused to cooperate in FEPC investigations or to negotiate with the Committee. Furthermore, the SIU complained to the Smith Committee about the War Shipping Administration's nondiscrimination policies, leading that committee to hold congressional hearings on the WSA in February 1944. Despite the attempt at intimidation, the FEPC held hearings on October 10, 1944, on the SIU's discrimination policies, which included its steadfast position that "[w]e do not mix" crews aboard ship. The Seafarers insisted on its usual practice of confining African Americans to the stewards' department and to restricting their employment there to ships on which all employees in the department were black. The FEPC, in its "Proposed Decision" resulting from its hearing, explained that its position assumed "added importance" when it was realized that the SIU's responsibilities for furnishing ship crews constituted "a very definite and integral part of the employment process." The union's policy, the FEPC said, made "the union the employment agent of management with power to a great extent to say who shall or who shall not be hired."

Skipping the issue of whether the Seafarers' segregation policy violated EO 9346 because the FEPC's mandate limited it to discrimination problems, the Committee decried the denial of "people, because of race, access to vital or essential occupations." It was "equally odious to the [Executive] Order," it said, to require that all employees in a particular occupation or department be the same race when such a work requirement inflicted distinct harm to job seekers and destroyed or impaired the efficiency "of the tried and tested system through which they" were recruited. The Committee therefore ordered the Seafarers to cease and desist from the series of discrimination policies that it had had imposed on merchant seamen. The SIU ignored the order.[16]

Other Unions

More positive were the FEPC's relationships with the United Automobile Workers (UAW), the National Maritime Union, the United Packinghouse Workers, the United Steelworkers, and the Electrical Workers. Mitchell singled out the strong antidiscrimination policies adopted by the UAW and the Packinghouse Workers as providing hope for continued advances for blacks in the automobile and meatpacking industries during the postwar era.[17]

As one of his final actions at the FEPC, Mitchell in April 1946 appraised the reports sent by key unions on their antidiscrimination efforts and presented comments for use in the *Final Report*. He praised the NMU for its vigorous antidiscrimination policies and noted the general support of the Steelworkers and the Packinghouse Workers. On the role of the International Union of Oil Workers in the protracted battles to open up the oil industry for minorities, he noted that the international leadership was often ahead of its locals in antidiscrimination efforts (in contrast to the locals of the Boilermakers and the Machinists). Referring to the problems of the Steelworkers, he noted that the achievements of that union were sometimes limited by the failure of black workers to use the available union structure to express grievances and by their frequent lack of confidence in the union.

Most historians, too, expressed mixed judgments about the accomplishments and effectiveness of the various unions in the fight against discrimination. They have noted the strong stands of some CIO unions, including those labeled as communist-led or communist-influenced, and the more ambivalent policies of most other unions that, when not actively discriminatory in policy, were often unwilling to take on locals and communities committed to segregation or to the preservation of the desirable jobs for their white members. Mitchell was thus left with plenty of work in negotiating with unions and their leaders during his postwar NAACP years.[18]

NOTES

1. For a summary of union relationships with the FEPC, see Wynn, *Afro-American and the Second World War*, 51–54. Weaver, in *Negro Labor*, provides throughout an extensive discussion of the racial practices of the unions.

2. For NAACP complaints to the FEPC regarding unions, see, for example, Walter White to Malcolm MacClean, 10/23/42; Cramer to White, 11/2/42; and White to Cramer, 11/7/42, HqR38, Central Files. Meetings. On 7/29/41, Robert Weaver provided the Tolan Committee with a partial list of unions that had bars in their constitutions against African Americans and other nonwhites from membership: Airline Pilots Association, AFL ("any moral person of the white race of lawful age and good moral character"; Brotherhood of Railway Clerks, AFL ("any white person, male or female, of good moral character"); Brotherhood of Railway Carmen, AFL ("any white person between the ages of 16–65"); Brotherhood of Dining Car Conductors (Railway Brotherhood) ("An applicant for membership must be of the Caucasian race"); Grand International Brotherhood of Locomotive Engineers (Railway Brotherhood) ("No person shall become a member of the Brotherhood of Locomotive Engineers unless he is a white man 21 years of age"); Brotherhood of Locomotive Firemen and Enginemen (Railway Brotherhood) ("any worker within the Jurisdiction who has served for at least 30 days, white, of good moral character, sober and industrious"); Railway Mail Association, AFL ("Any regular mail railway moral postal clerk or certified substitute railway postal clerk of the United States Railway Mail Service, who is of the Caucasian race, is eligible for membership"); International Organization of Master Mates and Pilots of America (AFL) ("any white person of good moral character"); Switchmen's Union of North America, AFL ("any white moral person of good moral character"); Order of Railroad Telegraphers, AFL ("any white person of good moral character"); Train Dispatchers Association of America (Railway Brotherhood) ("Any train dispatcher, white, of good moral character"); Brotherhood of Railroad Trainmen (Railroad Brotherhood) ("Any white moral person between ages of 18–65); Railroad Yardmaster of America (Railway Brotherhood) ("Any moral white person of good moral character"); Wire Weavers Protective Association of America, AFL ("Applicants for membership must be Christian, white, moral, of full age of 21"); Order of Railway Conductors (Railway Brotherhood) ("Any white man shall be eligible to membership"); Brotherhood of Sleeping Car Conductors, AFL ("Applicants for membership must be white, moral, sober, and industrious and must join of his own free will"); Commercial Telegraphers Union of North America, AFL ("Any white person of good moral character who is of 16 years of age"); International Brotherhood of

Blacksmiths, Drop Forgers, and Helpers, AFL ("Colored: Where there are sufficient number of colored helpers they may be organized as an auxiliary local and be under the jurisdiction of the white local having jurisdiction of their territory; colored helpers shall not transfer except to another auxiliary local composed of colored members and colored members shall not be promoted to blacksmiths or helping apprentices and will not be admitted to jobs where white helpers are now employed."), HqR2, Office Files of Malcolm Ross. Intergovernmental.

3. Hill, *Black Labor,* 100–6, 173–84, 375–77; Spero and Harris, *Black Worker,* 331–90; Northrup, *Organized Labor,* 14. For extensive accounts of union discrimination problems and the FEPC, see *Black Worker,* throughout.

4. FEPC, "Summary of Dr. Northrup's Testimony," n.d., HqR75, Reference File. Testimony of Herbert Northrup.

5. *Steele v. Louisville and Nashville Railroad Company et al.,* 323 U.S. 192 (1944); *Tunstall v. Brotherhood of Locomotive Firemen and Enginemen et al.,* 323 U.S. 210 (1944); and *Wallace Corporation v. National Labor Relations Board,* 323 U.S. 248 (1944); Charles Hamilton Houston, memorandum, 12/21/44, on the legal and historical importance of the Steel and Tunstall cases, NAACP II B101, DLC; George Johnson to staff, memorandum, n.d., "The Steele, Tunstall and Wallace Cases decided by the United States Supreme Court, December 18, 1944," HqR5, Office Files of George M. Johnson. Undesignated (blank) folder.

6. *Final Report,* 12–13; Houston to Association of Colored Railway Trainmen and Locomotive Firemen, International Association of Railway Employees, Arthur D. Shores, Bester William Steele, Tom Tunstall, and Thurgood Marshall, 12/20/44; Houston, memorandum, 12/21/44, both in NAACP II B101, DLC.

7. *Final Report,* 14–17.

8. For the Committee's discussions of the Boilermakers, see Transcript of Proceedings, 12/4/43, 86–112; 12/27/43, 8–22; 1/15/44, 31–33; 2/11/44, 50–58; 2/12/44, 74–88; 3/4/44, 92–108; 6/13/44, 27–89, all in HqR64, Central Files. For a general discussion of the problem, see Harris, "Federal Intervention," 325–47.

9. Harris, "Federal Intervention," 334.

10. Opening Statement of George E. C. Hayes, HqR4, Office Files of George M. Johnson. Boilermakers Union.

11. Ibid.

12. Northrup's analysis is in HqR4, Office Files of George M. Johnson. Testimony of Herbert R. Northrup.

13. Harris, "Federal Intervention," 338, 341.

14. See Weaver, *Negro Labor,* 116–18, 225–31; Mark Perlman, *Machinists,* 4, 5, 16–17, 19, 276–82, and his overall discussion in *Democracy in the International Association of Machinists;* HqR83, Correspondence Relating to Cases. (A–K), International Association of Machinists. On the Machinists cases as they appear in Mitchell's documents, see Mitchell, memoranda, 4/28, 7/7, 7/19, 9/6, 11/22/44, 1/8, 5/2, 8/17/45; reports, 11/13/44, 5/21/45. An additional memorandum of 3/7/45 has not been found. See also Mitchell, report to the FEPC at its meeting of 9/9/44, in Transcript of Proceedings, 9/9/44, 56–65, HqR65, Central Files.

15. On the Teamsters union in Detroit, see Mitchell, weekly report, 1/2/45, HqR83, Correspondence Relating to Cases. (A–K), Detroit Teamsters Union, Local 299; Transcript of Proceedings, 7/6/43, 71–74, HqR64, Central Files; *Final Report,* 22; Hill, *Black Labor,* 248–52; Kersten, *Race, Jobs, and the War,* 109–10.

16. See Mitchell, memoranda, 7/3/44, 7/19/44; Transcripts of Proceedings, 3/18/44, 38–71; 4/1/44, 94–96; 5/13/44, 38–59, all in HqR65, Central Files; *Final Report,* 22; Ross, *All Manner of Men,* 103–17. See also the records of the FEPC hearings on the Seafarers International Union, 10/10/44, and of the Smith Committee hearings regarding the SIU complaints, 2/25/44, in "Hearings Held before a Special Committee of the House of Representatives to Investigate Acts of Executive Agencies beyond the Scope of Their Authority," both in HqR18, Records Relating to Hearings. Smith Committee Hearings. For background, see Hill, *Black Labor,* 218–34; proposed decision resulting from the FEPC's hearing in Case No. 67, in the matter of respondent Seafarers International Union of North America, distributed by Mitchell on 9/17/45, to the Division of Field Operations as Field Letter no. 42-E; on the NMU, see Weaver, *Negro Labor,* 233–34.

17. See Mitchell, epilogue, for his appraisal. On the role of the UAW, see Kersten, *Race, Jobs, and the War,* 96–97, 99, 102; Weaver, *Negro Labor,* 222, 233–34; Meier and Rudwick, *Black Detroit,* 175–206, 212–22;

Hill, *Black Labor,* 260–70; Northrup, *Organized Labor,* 190–92. For the FEPC operating agreement with the UAW, negotiated 8/26/44, see *First Report,* 28; Hill, *Black Labor,* 260–62. On discrimination in the automobile industry, see also Mitchell, memorandum, 9/28/43, and notes.

18. See Mitchell's five memoranda to Ross, 4/8/46, and notes; Mitchell, epilogue. Supportive actions by unions are also discussed in Weaver, *Negro Labor,* 219–21, 223, 232–34. On the Oil Workers Union and the Shell Oil case, see also *Final Report,* 23. On the United Steelworkers of America, see Northrup, *Organized Labor,* 179–85. For the Electrical Workers, see the FEPC agreement signed 11/7/45, RG 228, Office Files of Malcolm Ross, box 70, UEW-FEPC, Agreement, DNA; King, *Separate and Unequal,* 78, 280n38; Kersten, *Race, Jobs, and the War,* 117–18, 124, 134. See also references in the headnotes to the role of various mining industry unions during FEPC investigation of Mexican Americans and mining industry cases in the Southwest.

STRIKES AND WORK STOPPAGES

One of Roosevelt's main goals for creating the FEPC was defusing social unrest that would interfere with the war effort. The FEPC was thus frequently drawn into avoiding or settling strikes, particularly those that might acerbate broader racial tensions. Labor organizations had signed no-strike pledges in support of the war effort, and various federal agencies had been established to mediate labor disputes. Nonetheless strikes did frequently occur. Although only a small percentage of work stoppages during World War II involved racial issues, those that did often created very volatile situations, particularly from mid-1943 to late 1944. "Hate" strikes, which generally were as spontaneous as wildcat strikes, were centered in the Midwest,[1] particularly in Detroit, but there were major incidents as well in Pennsylvania, Maryland, Alabama, and Louisiana. Following the 1943 Detroit riots, the Roosevelt administration strongly felt the urgency of keeping racial strife under control. Although the FEPC had no authority to settle strikes, it was sometimes called in by companies, unions, or government agencies because of its influence over black workers and its ability to negotiate the settlement of grievances.[2]

Settlements usually involved not only the FEPC and local labor and management representatives but also representatives of such other government agencies as the War Manpower Commission, the National War Labor Board, the War Production Board, the U.S. Office of Conciliation Services of the Labor Department, and military agencies such as the War Department, U.S. Maritime Commission, and labor divisions of the U. S. army and navy. Occasionally local churches and civic organizations as well as civil rights organizations like the NAACP and the Urban League also participated in settlements.[3] Of all the work stoppages in which the FEPC became involved, most were initiated by blacks and affected more workers, but those initiated by whites resulted in far more lost work days.[4]

The FEPC's greatest successes were in terminating walkouts by black workers protesting unfair work conditions or discrimination in wage rates, job classifications, promotions, layoffs, or penalties for infractions. Such strikes occurred primarily in industries that hired the most black workers, such as shipbuilding, steel manufacturing, and ordnance production. Notable racial strikes involving walkouts by blacks in which the FEPC intervened occurred at four Pennsylvania plants: Carnegie-Illinois Steel in Clairton (March 1944); Jones and Laughlin Steel in Aliquippa and Sun Shipbuilding in Chester (both in April 1944); and Dravo Shipbuilding in Pittsburgh (May 1944). Other significant walkouts occurred at American Steel Foundry's Cast Armor Plate plant in East Chicago, Indiana (July 1943); Dodge in Detroit (October 1943); Illinois Ordnance in Herrin (January 1944); Monsanto in St. Louis (March 1944); Goodyear Aircraft in Akron (April 1944); Delta Shipbuilding in New Orleans (May 1944); National Lead Company in St. Louis and American Steel Castings in Granite City, Illinois (both in July 1944).[5]

After a year of ad hoc dealings by FEPC staff members with strikes and related issues, the FEPC sought to formulate an official policy and to establish guidelines for its field representatives. Malcolm Ross, FEPC chairman, appointed a subcommittee of three—Stanley Metzger, Emanuel Bloch, and Eugene Davidson—to review the handling of racial strikes and make recommendations. The three failed to reach agreement on a common policy, and each issued his own statement in May 1944. The central point of disagreement related to how strong a stand the FEPC should take in requiring African American strikers to go back to work before it would take up their grievances. Other issues were the circumstances under which the FEPC should intervene and the hopes it could safely hold out to strikers, how much discretion regional staff members should be given in handling strikes, what role the FEPC could take in race-related strikes initiated by whites, and whether the FEPC should intervene if requested in strikes in which minorities were involved but which did not fall under FEPC jurisdiction. Of the three, Metzger held out for the greatest local flexibility and opposed blanket requirements that blacks return to work before the FEPC took action on their behalf. Bloch recommended that the FEPC insist on the immediate return to work and emphasized the political dangers the FEPC would face if it appeared to be condoning wartime strikes. John A. Davis, director of the Division of Research and Analysis, pressed for formulation of an official racial strike policy based on the cumulative experiences of key FEPC staff members who had faced such situations. After consulting Mitchell, Metzger, William T. McKnight, and Milo Manly, among others, Davis drafted a compromise policy statement for all staff members. He emphasized getting workers back on the job, but he stressed that the FEPC would be able to accomplish that only if workers felt the FEPC could succeed in redressing grievances through negotiations on their behalf.[6] By mid-1944 the FEPC began trumpeting its pacification achievements in an effort to offset attacks by its political opponents, who contended the FEPC stirred up racial trouble.[7]

More complicated were situations in which both whites and blacks walked out because of each other's actions. For example, in the Alabama Dry Dock case, white workers violently drove black workers out of the yard rather than permit their promotion to higher-level jobs where they would work on equal footing with whites. Black workers then refused to return to work until their safety could be ensured, and whites threatened further work actions unless blacks were permanently removed from their new positions. Troops had to be brought in to keep the peace. In this case,

Mitchell, along with his white colleague Ernest Trimble, visited the plant and together with other officials negotiated an agreement for a separate way on which blacks could work at higher levels. The agreement remained controversial because it seemed to sanction segregated working arrangements, which the Committee and black organizations like the NAACP and the March on Washington Movement vigorously opposed.[8] Mitchell subsequently warned FEPC examiners against sanctioning segregated work plans.[9]

The strife at Bethlehem Steel Shipbuilding at Sparrows Point, Maryland, in July and August 1943 that Mitchell helped settle also involved a walkout by blacks and whites.[10] At the Western Electric plant in Point Breeze, Maryland, Mitchell continued to monitor the situation there after the army's withdrawal. The company fell back on a compromise policy of assigning black and white workers to separate but equal locker rooms with toilet facilities attached, which each group was expected to use even though there were no separate signs or symbols designating the segregation. Since these arrangements did not directly cause job discrimination, the FEPC had no legal grounds to prevent them.[11]

Most difficult and controversial was the FEPC's involvement in walkouts and threatened strikes by white workers because of actual or anticipated new opportunities for blacks in training, hiring, and upgrading, or because of demands by whites, such as those at Western Electric, for separate toilet facilities. Severe labor shortages often encouraged concessions to blacks from employers and sometimes from unions, but the need for workers was not always enough to assuage the fears or prejudices of white workers or their communities. Consequently, mindful of the government's wish to avoid any slowdown in production, companies, unions, ad hoc groups of workers, even whole communities threatened walkouts and violence if nondiscrimination policies were implemented.[12]

In a few notable instances, the federal government stood its ground against strikes, actual or threatened, and went ahead with hearings or with issuing and enforcing directives against discriminatory policies. Most famous of these cases was the federal government's use of troops to overcome a strike in August 1944 in Philadelphia by white transit workers protesting the hiring of blacks as trolley operators. The FEPC then fought off political pressures and followed up by holding hearings and issuing directives regarding discrimination by the Los Angeles Street Railway. (See headnote on Street and Local Railways.)[13] In these cases Mitchell, like other FEPC staffers, argued that concessions to recalcitrant whites only inspired similar threats and protests elsewhere and worsened rather than reduced social tensions.[14]

Mitchell, Ross, and others repeatedly cited the case of the General Cable Company in which military officials sought to persuade the FEPC to back down in the face of opposition by white women workers to working alongside black women, but Dwight Palmer, the company's president, persuaded the workers to cooperate.[15] Nonetheless, by 1945, the government, especially under the politically vulnerable new Truman administration, became more reluctant to risk strikes and violence and blocked an

FEPC directive against the Capital Transit Company in Washington, D.C.[16] Furthermore, groups against which the FEPC stood firm, notably the Philadelphia Transit workers, the railroads, and the shipping industry, brought their cases before sympathetic congressmen. A notable result was the investigations launched by Rep. Howard Smith into the FEPC's authority and jurisdiction for such actions, ultimately helping to erode FEPC support and thus reducing, then eliminating, its appropriations. (See headnote on Jurisdictional Issues.)[17]

NOTES

1. In 6/46 the FEPC stated that employer fear of work stoppages by white workers, many of whom had migrated from the South, was a major factor in employment discrimination in the Midwest. *Final Report*, 37.

2. See Eugene Davidson, "Participation of FEPC Examiners in Settlement of Work Stoppages," [ca. 4–5/44?], and the undated summary, "Participation of Strikes, and the Statement on Work Stoppages," both in HqR4, Office Files of George M. Johnson. Strikes; Weaver, *Negro Labor*, 223; Mitchell, epilogue; Kryder, *Divided Arsenal*, 100; tables of strikes printed from FEPC records, *First Report*, 79–80, in King, *Separate and Unequal*, 243; and Kersten, *Race, Jobs, and the War*, 143–44.

3. A description of the strike settlement process appears in *First Report*, 81. Detailed examples of the process are given in Mitchell's field investigation reports, 6/8/43 (Alabama Dry Dock) and 8/6/43 (Bethlehem Steel Shipyard, Sparrows Point) in appendix 1. See also Mitchell, memoranda, 9/4, 9/9, 9/29, 11/1/43, 5/4, 6/6/44. For FBI reportage on the strikes, see Hill, *FBI's RACON*, 83–84, 274–76, 475, 715, 722, 723.

4. The charts given in the FEPC's *First Report* (79–80) record 45 percent of forty racially related strikes over eighteen months (7/43–12/44) as white-initiated, involving 30.5 percent of the strikers but 87.4 percent of the total man-days lost. Strikes by blacks constituted 52 percent of the total, while one strike was initiated by whites protesting discrimination against blacks. The FEPC also intervened in Detroit in one strike prompted by the hiring of a Japanese American citizen in 5/44 (see Mitchell, weekly report, 5/1/44). See also the threatened walkout by blacks at the General Box Company, Kansas City, Mo., discussed in the weekly report of 4/13/44, in which the FEPC was asked to intervene. Davidson's earlier report cited in note 2, above, analyzes twenty-three strikes from mid-1943 to mid-1944, while the "Statement on Work Stoppages" found in that file is based on twenty-five strikes.

5. On the strikes in Pennsylvania, see *First Report*, 80–83; Mitchell's memoranda of 9/4, 9/9, 9/29/43, 5/4/44; and his weekly reports, 1/14, 3/6, 3/27, 4/3, 4/13, 5/1/44. On the St. Louis area strikes, see Mitchell's memoranda of 7/18, 7/27, 8/08, 12/18/44; his weekly report of 12/18/44; and Metzger's testimony on the Monsanto strike in Transcript of Proceedings, 4/20/44, 33–54, in HqR65, Central Files. On the Illinois strikes, see Mitchell's weekly reports of 3/18 and 4/3/44 and his memorandum of 7/31/44. On the East Chicago strike, see the memorandum of 7/16/43. On the Goodyear case in Akron, see the weekly report of 4/14/44. On the strike at the Chrysler Tank Arsenal plant in Detroit, see Mitchell's weekly reports of 5/8 and 5/17/44. On strikes in the Midwest, see also Hill, *Black Labor*, 262–67; Kersten, *Race, Jobs, and the War*, 52–53, 55–56, 105–6, 108–9, 121–22, 123–25, 143–44.

6. See Davis, memorandum, 5/25/44, and notes, in appendix. For the recommendations of the three subcommittee members, see Metzger to Ross, 5/17; Davidson to Ross, 5/22, both in HqR4, Records of the Legal Division, Office Files of George M. Johnson. Strikes; Bloch to Ross, 5/25, HqR1, Office Files of Malcolm Ross. B. In his statement Davidson strongly recommended against any involvement in strikes not actually under FEPC jurisdiction. Metzger's arguments reiterated the stand he had taken during the Monsanto strike, when he rejected War Department demands that he insist that the workers return to work immediately. See his statements during the 4/20/44 FEPC meeting, Transcript of Proceedings, 4/20/44, 33–34, 45–51, HqR65, Central Files.

7. FEPC staffers began compiling data on strikes in 3/44, possibly for use during the House and Senate appropriations committee hearings in 5/44 and 6/44 and continued to employ such data in the

Committee's official reports. See "Statement on Work Stoppages," n.d., and related texts, HqR4, Office Files of George M. Johnson. Strikes; responses of regional directors to teletyped request for information sent 3/16/44, and other texts, grouped in HqR77, Office Files of Eugene Davidson. (Unarranged, Statements, Miscellaneous), Strikes; FEPC, "FEPC Participation in Strikes," HqR1, Office File of Malcolm Ross. Annual Reports; *First Report*, 79–83; *Final Report*, 9. The undated statement on work stoppages cited may have been the one FEPC publicist Max Berking said he prepared in mid-1944 but which was not released to congressional representatives and others at the time because of the "general delicacy of the subject." Berking to Joy P. Davis, 12/8/44, HqR1, Office Files of Malcolm Ross. D. For additional strike data, see HqR72–73, Office Files of Joy Davis. (entry 31); and work stoppage reports from regions found in HqR63.

8. On the Alabama Dry Dock case, see Mitchell, memorandum, 6/1/43; Mitchell and Trimble, field investigation report, 6/8/43, and notes, in appendix; Watson, *Lion in the Lobby*, 141–43. Copies of the field investigation report were submitted to the first meeting of the second FEPC for discussion on 7/6/43 and also can be found in various files throughout the FEPC's papers, indicating it was widely circulated among staff members.

9. For opposition to the FEPC sanction of segregated work arrangements, see Reed, *Seedtime*, 117–21; "Summary of Actions Taken by the Committee at Its Meeting in Washington, D.C.," 7/6–7/43, HqR1, Records of the Office of the Chairman, Summary Minutes of Meetings, 1/42–9/45; Transcript of Proceedings, 7/6/43, 41–44, HqR64, Central Files; John P. Davis, "Haas Compromise Bitterly Scorned," *Pittsburgh Courier*, 6/12/43, reprinted in Spero and Harris, *Black Worker*, 279–81; Field Instruction no. 21, 10/9/43, HqR78, Field Instructions, No. 20–39; NAACP, *Annual Report*, 1943, 27–28; Hill, *FBI's RACON*, 475; Mitchell memoranda [ca. 10/10/42] to Weaver; to Maslow, 8/16/43; to Ross, 2/16/44, 2/19/45; to Johnson, 11/1/43, 1/12, 5/5/44; Mitchell, weekly reports, 5/8/44, 2/20, 3/5, 3/20/45; Mitchell to Hoglund, 11/21/44; Maslow to Ellinger, 9/22/44, FR89, Region IX. Action Files.

10. On the Sparrows Point incident, see Mitchell, field investigation report, 8/6/43; digests of telephone calls, 7/31, 8/1/43, in appendix 1; Mitchell, memorandum, 11/1/43, and notes.

11. See Mitchell, memoranda, 8/26, 11/11, 12/14/43, 2/16, 3/14/44; FEPC, Transcript of Proceedings, 4/1/44, 96, HqR65, Central Files.

12. See especially the General Cable case discussed in the weekly reports of 4/3/44 and 4/13/44 and in the sources cited in note 14, below. For reports and discussion on other racially motivated strikes by white workers, see Mitchell, memorandum, 5/10/43, on Timken Roller Bearing plant, Canton, Ohio; weekly report; 4/24/44, on the Chevrolet transmission plant, Toledo; memorandum, 1/10/44, on Illinois Ordnance; memorandum, 6/28/43, on Brand and Puritz Manufacturing, Kansas City, Mo.; weekly reports, 1/22, 2/5, 5/8/44, on the Youngstown Steel plant; memorandum, 6/6/44, and memorandum of his telephone conversation of 6/9/44, on Wright Aeronautical Company, Cincinnati; memoranda, 12/8, 12/11/44, on Pullman Standard Car, Shipbuilding Division, Chicago; weekly report, 4/3/44, on the Allen Wood Steel Company, Conshohocken, Pa.; memorandum, [ca. 12/14–15/44], on Western Electric Co., Point Breeze plant, Baltimore; memorandum, 4/14/45, on Continental Can Company, Norwood, Ohio; memoranda, 7/24, 7/28/45, on Todd Johnson Dry Dock case, New Orleans.

For strike threats by whites, see also the San Diego Railway case (Mitchell, memorandum, 12/4/44), the various telephone company cases (Mitchell, memoranda, 7/5/43, 3/08/45), and the various transit company cases cited below. For an example of opposition of an entire community—East Alton, Illinois—to FEPC's antidiscrimination efforts, see Ross, *All Manner of Men*, 49–66; *Final Report*, 18–19; Kersten, *Race, Jobs, and the War*, 56–58.

13. On the Philadelphia and LARY transit cases, see headnote on Street and Local Railways; Mitchell, memoranda, 8/4, 8/7/44; Mitchell to Ross and Johnson, telegram, 8/10/44; Transcript of Proceedings, 4/20/44, 80–98; 5/13/44, 8–19, 120–21, HqR65, Central Files; files related to PRT case, FR27, Region III. Active Cases, Unarranged (includes Philadelphia Rapid Transit); Fleming's weekly report of 8/5/44, HqR51, Central Files. Reports, Region III, 4/44–; *Final Report*, 14–15; Spero and Harris, *Black Worker*, 302–31; Ross, *All Manner of Men*, 153–56; Weaver, *Negro Labor*, 160–81; Kingman, "Citizenship in a Democracy," 104–5; Philleo Nash, interview, 11/29/66, 4, 7–8, Truman Library; Winkler, "Philadelphia Transit Strike of 1944."

Mitchell later credited the successful settlement in Los Angeles to the political skills of regional director Harry Kingman (Merl Reed, interview, 8/24/78), and noted Ross's issuance of the directive before presidential aide Jonathan Daniels could reach him by phone to stop him. In his analysis, Robert Weaver stressed that both union and management requested that a directive be issued immediately, arguing that they could successfully upgrade black employees only if their actions were based on a definite government order. Like Mitchell, he believed that the strong stand in Philadelphia headed off protests in Los Angeles. Weaver, *Negro Labor,* 180–81.

14. On the counterproductivity of concessions to threats of strikes and violence, see, for example, Mitchell's memorandum of 8/4/44 on his conversation with Jonathan Daniels; Mitchell, epilogue; Ross, *All Manner of Men,* 153–62.

15. On the General Cable case, see Mitchell's reports of 4/3 and 4/13/44; his article in *NAACP Bulletin,* 7/46; *Final Report,* 18; Ross, *All Manner of Men,* 72–79; Kersten, *Race, Jobs and the War,* 124–25.

16. On Truman's thwarting of the FEPC directive against Capital Transit and the political response, see *Final Report,* 15–17; Ross, *All Manner of Men,* 160–62; Mitchell, epilogue; Ruchames, *Race, Jobs, and Politics,* 126, 132–34; Gardner, *Truman and Civil Rights,* 24–39; Eagles, *Daniels,* 145–48; Kesselman, *Social Politics,* 201–14; Reed, *Seedtime,* 332–37; Watson, *Lion in the Lobby,* 150–51.

17. For discussions of the appeal of the FEPC's Philadelphia Rapid Transit opponents to the Smith Committee and its attacks on the FEPC, see Reed, *Seedtime,* 140–43; Ross, *All Manner of Men,* 84–85, 90–93, 108–12, 134–41; Ruchames, *Race, Jobs, and Politics,* 73–86; Kersten, *Race, Jobs, and the War,* 126–29; Dierenfield, *Keeper of the Rules,* 102–55.

Clarence Mitchell Jr.

PROLOGUE

The Home Town's Race Problem

By Clarence M. Mitchell, Jr., Executive Secretary,
the St. Paul Urban League

[March 1938]

Because it is easier to sit in judgement on others than it is [to] appraise one's self, problems affecting minority groups at home do not get as much attention as those which crop up in foreign nations or in other parts of our country. Particularly is this true of the Negro problem in the Northwest and specifically in St. Paul.

The National Urban League which is interested in the integration of Negroes in American economic life, has set aside March 19 to 26 for the observance of its annual vocational opportunity campaign. The St. Paul Urban League is using this time to ask the community to be aware of the economic plight of the colored population.

Aside from the normal difficulty expected by the job-seeker in these times, the Negro of this city must hurdle an additional barrier of race. The result of this hindrance is clearly demonstrated by the fact that over 60 per cent of the 4,000 colored of this city are on direct relief or W.P.A. Entailing expenditures for their support, these people who are dependent become not merely a Negro problem, but a community problem also which should invite the interest of every person who is a citizen.

From the Urban League's point of view, there are some things which can be done about this situation by Negroes themselves and other things which must be done by the white community.

Very frequently there are those who say: "Negroes should start businesses of their own if they want to work." Few will deny that our country would soon be in economic shambles if every minority group suddenly adopted policies of employing its members only. But the challenge which opens this paragraph has been accepted by some St. Paul Negroes who are conducting successful businesses in the downtown area of our city and who also have establishments in the so-called Rondo area where the colored population is concentrated. Obviously, of course, this does not solve the problem because these enterprises could not possibly employ most of the working age people of this racial group.

In passing, it should be pointed out that even Negroes who go into business sometimes encounter difficulty in this city. Let us suppose, for example, that the business

1

operated requires the use of trucks and that such vehicles must have liability insurance coverage. In many instances insurance companies refuse to sell this type of coverage to Negroes on the grounds that the prejudices of juries prevent this racial group from getting a fair deal in accident cases.

This allegation has been found to be grossly untrue in Minnesota but the fact that it is used offers a double challenge to the white community. First, it is a terrible indictment of American justice if a man's race prevents him from being treated fairly in court. Proof that Negroes receive equitable treatment in our courts must be established by the white citizens. Secondly, it may too frequently prevent white drivers from collecting damages due them in collisions with Negroes who cannot buy insurance.

On its part, the Negro community can encourage its people to train themselves for occupations in which there is a minimum of labor turnover. The white community, on the other hand, is the only force which can see to it that the right to work is not denied them because of their racial identity.

Aside from the profit aspect, the two most important functions rendered a community by a business are supplying material for public consumption and offering available employment to any qualified person willing to work. In St. Paul Negroes benefit by the first of these functions but they do not, as a rule, benefit by the second. True, they have managed to secure opportunities in some places after persistent effort but it is unbelievably difficult for them to find employment in clerical, stenographical and practically all semi-skilled or skilled fields.

Unfortunately, the blame for this denial of work is sometimes shared by employees, as well as employers. Membership in some unions which have closed shop agreements with employers is denied Negroes. In other unions Negroes may join, but they are not permitted to work on jobs with white men. The most discouraging aspect of all, however, is summed up by the colored youth in St. Paul who charged that after his union repeatedly refused to send him out on various jobs, he finally took a job at non-union wages and was fined for doing so.

To all of this must also be added the displacement of Negroes in certain fields where they formerly found employment. What makes this acute is that opportunities in new job fields in St. Paul are not geared to provide employment for these people who are shut out of avenues in which they formerly earned a living. Notable illustrations of this desplacement are offered by Negro barbers who are being forced out by white tonsorial artists, and Negro waiters who are being displaced by white waitresses. Recently, two establishments were ready to displace all of the colored waiters in several departments. This would not have been so serious if the men could have found work in other fields, but even if other work had been available, their color and previous training would have prevented them from getting it.

No racial group has a right to special favor in the matter of obtaining a job, but all racial groups are entitled to an equal opportunity to work. St. Paul's Negroes are no different from any other group in the city. All of them must eat, must live in homes, must pay taxes and obey the laws. For the most part they do all of these things inconspicuously as do our other citizens. In the same manner they tend to influence the economic life of the city by the expansion or contraction of their purchasing power and their ability to be self supporting. They constitute a market which is an asset or a liability in accordance with the amount of money they have to spend for such things as street car service, gas, electric, fuel, clothing and the host of other things available for the St. Paul purchaser.

To crowd them on relief rolls or into the small paying and insecure types of employment is like covering a fire in a haystack with more hay. It prevents their troubles from meeting the eye immediately, but increases the damage to the rest of the community ultimately.

MS: copy, MP.

From 1938 to 1941, Mitchell was executive secretary of the St. Paul, Minnesota, Urban League. There his primary job was opening up job opportunities for African Americans, which included battling discrimination in labor unions. That work helped prepare him for the national sphere in Washington. This statement summarized his detailed 1938 annual report. That report and his 1939 annual report are in NAACP, series 13, cont. 27, DLC. For an in-depth history of his work in St. Paul, see Watson, *Lion in the Lobby,* rev. ed., 91–111.

Plate 1. An Associated Press reminder in 1944 that, although overlooked for "three centuries," African Americans played a large part in shaping the world, including the Civil War battle of Milliken's Bend. *Wide World Photos*

Plate 2. The all-black 92nd Division drew attention for their bravery in Europe during World War II. *Wide World Photos*

Plate 3. African American women in World War II doing precision work at North American Aviation in Kansas. *Walter P. Reuther Library, Wayne State University*

Plate 4. African American woman defense worker at Lockheed Aircraft Corporation, Burbank, California. *Walter P. Reuther Library, Wayne State University*

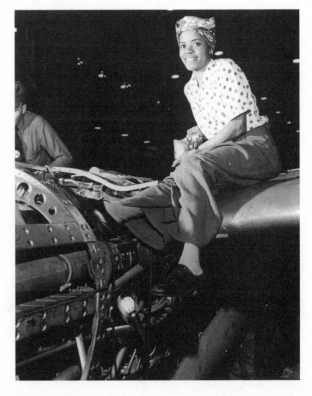

Plate 5. A. Philip Randolph, president of the Brotherhood of Sleeping Car Porters, with head of the Railroad Mediation Board, ca. 1930s. *Schomburg Center for Research and Black Culture*

Plate 6. Mark Ethridge, first chairman of the FEPC. *Getty Images*

Plate 7. Robert C. Weaver, administrative assistant at the Advisory Council of the National Defense Commission. *Wide World Photos*

Plate 8. Lawrence W. Cramer, governor of the U.S. Virgin Islands prior to his appointment as secretary of the FEPC. *Wide World Photos*

Plate 9. Frank Knox, secretary of the navy; Donald M. Nelson, chairman of the War Production Board; and Henry A. Nelson, chairman of the Board of Economic Warfare, attending first meeting of the WPB, January 20, 1942. *Wide World Photos*

Plate 10. Left to right: William Green, AFL president; Donald M. Nelson, WPB chairman, and Philip Murray, CIO president, March 7, 1942. *Wide World Photos*

Plate 11. David Sarnoff, president of Radio Corporation of America and a member of the FEPC's policy-making body. *Wide World Photos*

Plate 12. Paul V. McNutt, chairman of the WMC, with President Roosevelt. Harris & Ewing photo, n.d. *Courtesy of the* Washington Star, *Washingtoniana Division, Martin Luther King, Jr., Library, Washington, D.C.*

Plate 13. Charles Hamilton Houston. *Temple University Libraries, Urban Archives, Philadelphia, Pennsylvania*

Plate 14. Tension is evident as an armed black homeowner protects his family and property from roving crowds near the Sojourner neighborhood of Detroit in 1942. *Detroit News Photo*

Plate 15. A flaming car sets fire to a streetcar station on Woodward Street in downtown Detroit. The mob is behind the streetcars. *Detroit News Photo*

Plate 16. Whites attack a black man's car on Woodward Street near Vernor in Detroit. *Detroit News Photo*

Plate 17. The white mob sets the car afire. *Detroit News Photo*

Plate 18. Crowds of whites fill the street as smoke from a burning car rises in the background. *Courtesy of the Detroit Library*

Plate 19. Whites pummel a black man in downtown Detroit. *Courtesy of the Detroit Library*

Plate 20. Soldiers establishing peace in downtown Detroit. *Detroit News Photo*

Memorandum on COFEP Complaint against the International Telephone and Radio Manufacturing Corporation and the Federal Telegraph Company, East Newark, New Jersey

Date: January 23, 1942

To: Dr. Robert C. Weaver

From: Clarence M. Mitchell

Subject: COFEP Complaint against the International Telephone and Radio Manufacturing Corporation and the Federal Telegraph Company, East Newark, N. J.

This complaint was made through Mr. Milton P. Webster of COFEP. The persons complaining are: Messrs. Donald James, Robert Gitten, Raymond Bright and Wallace Wiggins. All of them signed a joint statement that they had seen an advertisement published for the company in the Daily Mirror asking for wiremen and assemblers.[1]

My conference was with Mr. J. A. Nelson, Personnel Manager. He represents both companies and stated that, although the men mentioned International Telephone in their complaint, they really had responded to a request for men to be assigned to Federal Telegraph. He insisted that the four men were not qualified and showed me their application cards. I made no comment. He was unable to explain why the individuals were told: "We are not hiring any colored as yet." I asked this question specifically. Mr. Nelson also said that he did not see how these men could afford to commute from New York to New Jersey. He did not adequately explain why the company advertises in New York papers for workers if it does not expect to take people from there. He said that some people are gotten from New York or persons living outside of New York "read the papers." It is interesting to note that from Mr. Nelson's own statement, the order for wiremen and assemblers has been in his hands since September 10, 1941, and he has not yet completed it. The request is for twenty-five workers and he has only been able to get fifteen.

Negroes are not employed by either concern. Each of the plants has about 1100 persons, according to Mr. Nelson. Although he professed to be interested in the hiring of colored people, he did not appear to have any plans for doing anything about his stated convictions. I would like to suggest that this case be handed back to COFEP for its New York hearings. If you do not agree, our office can continue contact with Mr. H. C. Reamer, Executive Vice-President. The firm has recently signed an agreement with Local 447 of the U.R.E.M.W. of the C.I.O.[2]

MS: copy, HqR77, Office Files of Eugene Davidson. International Telephone.

From 4/11/41 to 1/42, Robert C. Weaver was chief of the Negro Employment and Training Branch within the Labor Division of the Office of Production Management. Next, the NETB functioned in the War Production Board until 7/30/42, when Roosevelt abruptly transferred the FEPC, the NETB, and its equal, the Minority Groups Branch, to the War Manpower Commission. From then until 4/24/43, Weaver was chief of the Negro Manpower Service of the WMC (RG 179, 01.469, DNA). Weaver then served as liaison officer between the WMC and the FEPC, with the special assignment of developing a program for the fuller utilization of minority groups, until 1/16/44, when the WMC announced his resignation. He left to become director of the Mayor's Committee on Race Relations of Chicago. WMC News Release, 1/16/44, in HqR86, Press Releases. Miscellaneous Releases; Reed, *Seedtime*, 86–87.

Weaver hired Mitchell on 5/1/41 as his field assistant responsible for the New Jersey, Delaware, and Pennsylvania region. He subsequently promoted Mitchell to assistant director of the NETB. For the background of their relationship, see Watson, *Lion in the Lobby*, 122, 133–34. For more details, see "Official Steps Taken on Discrimination in Defense," in *Minorities in Defense*, which provides additional dates in its outline of the President's Committee on Fair Employment Practice, the Negro Employment and Training Branch, Labor Division, OPM, and the Minority Groups Branch, Labor Division, OPM, RG 179, Records of the War Production Board, WPB 015.737, President's Committee on Fair Employment Practice, Organization, DNA; and Current Programs of NETB, RG 179, Records of WPB, WPB 016.467, NETB Organization, DNA.

1. Initially, the FEPC was known as the Committee on Fair Employment Practice (COFEP). For background, see Reed, *Seedtime*, 10.

In their 12/13/42 letter to the COFEP, the complainants said they had been trained at the Harlem Evening Trade School and each had approximately ten years of experience in "radio installation, repairing, rebuilding and building." Each had a government operator's license, proving them "qualified to operate a station, to operate a ship to shore telephone, to operate police equipment, to operate a broadcasting station, and to construct." Indeed, they were overqualified; the job they had applied for was mass production work that did not require their range of knowledge. HqR77, Office Files of Eugene Davidson. International Telephone and Radio Manufacturing Co.

2. United Electrical, Radio, and Machine Workers of America, CIO. See Weaver, *Negro Labor*, 16–27, 201–2.

Memorandum on Westinghouse Employment Situation

January 27, 1942

Dr. Robert C. Weaver

Clarence M. Mitchell

Westinghouse Employment Situation

I have just returned from a conference with Mr. J. A. Flynn, Business Representative of Local 106, UREMW, who informed me that the union will not accept any responsibility for what happens if Mr. Robert Sharp, 112 N. Ruby Street, is restored to his position as a trainee in the Westinghouse shop. Mr. Flynn, admitting that he realized that the President's Order 8802 forbade discrimination of this kind, asserted that he thought I was just sticking my neck into a lot of trouble and that there would be violence if Mr. Sharp returned to work. I informed him that if there was any violence I would personally ask for the arrest and prosecution of anyone guilty. He then said that maybe there would not be any violence but that the men would certainly walk out. I stated that there would be ways of handling that too.[1]

Under the circumstances, I could insist that Mr. Sharp be returned to his job, but I feel that before this is done there should be some action taken from Washington to see that the union accept its responsibilities in the situation. From the stories told by Mr. J. C. Morgan, Director of Industrial Relations, and Mr. Flynn, I feel that the two have gotten together and precipitated this issue now facing us.

BRIEFLY summarized, the situation before us is as follows: Mr. Sharp was started on the job, Monday, January 26. Tuesday I received word from him that he had been laid off because the men at the plant did not consider him popular. Mr. Sharp said he was told this by a Mr. Smith and a Mr. Moore, who are plant officials. He said that he did not have any trouble. Immediately, I called Mr. J. C. Morgan and asked for his version of what happened. He stated that a number of persons had objected to Sharp and that one of them, a trainee, had said he would throw Sharp over a balcony if he continued to work. Mr. Morgan said that other persons had heard about Sharp and that they wanted to have a union meeting on the subject of his employment. According to Mr. Morgan, Mr. Flynn refused to have this meeting. (This was verified by Mr. Flynn.) I then asked Mr. Morgan for the names of the persons who led the agitation. He stated that he did not know who these persons were. (Mr. Flynn also denied knowing who the people were, but said he could have their names by Friday.) Mr. Morgan said he had taken the matter up with Mr. William W. Bardsley, Chr. of the Labor Supply Committee. I had a conference with Mr. Bardsley and informed him that I believed that the situation was arranged. Mr. Wesley Dee, Mr. Bardsley's assistant, expressed agreement with my point of view[.] I suggested that Mr. James P. Casey, Labor Representative, accompany me to Mr. Morgan's office to attempt to remedy the situation. Mr. Bardsley suggested that we also take along Mr. L. B. F. Raycroft, Management Representative on the Labor Supply Committee. He was unable to reach Mr. Raycroft, however, and I suggested that he call Commander Robinson, Naval representative on the Labor Supply Committee, to check with the plant and determine through the naval inspector stationed there whether there had been any trouble. Mr. Bardsley was unable to reach the Commander. Mr. Casey was unable to go with me because of another appointment so I confined myself to a conference with Mr. Flynn.

I shall be available for any instructions at the office. The telephone is Rittenhouse 6730.

MS: copy, HqR77, Office Files of Eugene Davidson. Birmingham.

1. In writing his study *Negro Labor,* Weaver, an economist who was a highly recognized expert on housing and labor problems, drew on the kinds of experiences with labor unions that Mitchell encountered. For a discussion of the racial policies of the United Electrical, Radio, and Machine Workers of America, CIO (UERMWA), see *Negro Labor,* 16–27, 201–2.

Memorandum on COFEP Request from Mr. Eugene Davidson

February 2, 1942

To: Dr. Robert C. Weaver

From: Clarence M. Mitchell

Subject: Regional Matters of Immediate Importance Discussed with
            Mr. [Reginald A.] Johnson

COFEP REQUEST FROM MR. EUGENE DAVIDSON

Mr. [Reginald A.] Johnson discussed with me certain cases (6) which we will supply to Mr. Davidson in response to requests from him.[1] Two of these proposed cases are illustrations of employers who have changed their hiring practices or at least hire nearly in conformity with the requirements of the President's Executive Order No. 8802. These are the Western Electric Company of Kearny, N. J., and the Federal Shipbuilding Company, also of Kearny. In both cases, Mr. Davidson's plans for making the "good" better will give these companies a chance to expand their Negro personnel and correct certain departmental difficulties we have been faced with.

Four of the firms in need of disciplinary action and which we propose to submit to Mr. Davidson are: the International Telephone Company and the Federal Telegraph Company, both of Newark, N.J.; the Walker-Turner Plant at Plainfield, N.J., and the Wright Aeronautical Company of Patterson, N.J., or the Breeze Aircraft Company in Newark, N.J. The Wright Company will possibly be used because it is likely that the training phase of the program is in need of some investigation in order to increase the admission of Negroes. The Breeze Company will be used if the most recent requests for action submitted from our office (Via Mitchell) are ignored or answered in an unsatisfactory manner. In all of these instances the final draft of material to be submitted to Mr. Davidson will be given first to you for approval. Mr. Johnson, however, will immediately notify Mr. Davidson that you have authorized the release of material[.][2]

THE WESTINGHOUSE COMPANY, ESSINGTON, PA.

In view of the alleged trouble with white employees of the Westinghouse Company over the employment of a colored machine operator,[3] Mr. Johnson and I discussed the following phases of the question:

a. Mr. Harry Block, assistant to Mr. James P. Carey, labor representative on the Regional Labor Supply Committee, is to report to Mr. Johnson the results of his (Block's) effort to secure the needed co-operation from the Union at the plant.

b. Mr. L. B. F. Raycroft, management representative on the Regional Labor Supply Committee, will report to Mr. Johnson on the results of contacts on the matter with plant representatives.

c. Mr. William W. Bardsley, chairman of the Regional Labor Supply Committee, will report to Mr. Johnson on the results of a Naval Investigation of what actually happened when the colored trainee was employed. I requested Mr. Bardsley to ask for this investigation through Commander Francis Robinson, Naval representative on the committee, since the plant has a Naval contract.

THE BENDIX AVIATION COMPANY, PHILADELPHIA, PA.

The first two trainees out of the group of nine called for interviews start to work today (Monday, February 2). I have also submitted to the management the names of twenty women who are enrolled in a light manufacturing course under the V.E.N.D. [Vocational Education for National Defense] program. In addition I have submitted the name of Mrs. Leona Highsmith, who complained that she had not been employed when she made an application previously. The management has been informed that Mr. Johnson is replacing me in the area. He will take the necessary follow-up steps.

THE FRANKFORD ARSENAL, THE NAVY YARD, THE ARMY SIGNAL CORPS, AND THE ORDNANCE DEPARTMENT-ALL OF THE PHILADELPHIA AREA.

Discussion of contacts we have had with these government agencies was held. We especially discussed plans for informing Negro women of the examination for female learners being vien [given] for these agencies. Under the examination, women without previous experience are being trained for manufacturing operations. While in training these individuals will be paid by the government.

THE BREWSTER COMPANY, HATBORO, PA.

In order to clarify our progress with the Brewster plant at Hatboro, Pa., I arranged a meeting with Mr. J. Griffith Boardman, whom I understood to be the Vice-President of the company. Mr. Boardman stated he was "only a member of the board of directors" and referred me to Mr. Philip Stevenson, executive vice president. Mr. Johnson will make the necessary follow-up in this situation since we were unable to see Mr. Stevenson before I left.

THE BALDWIN LOCOMOTIVE COMPANY, PHILADELPHIA, PA.

Being unable to contact Mr. Charles E. Acker, secretary-treasurer, on January 29 and thereafter, Mr. Johnson and I have agreed that a follow-up will be made today (Monday, Feb. 2). We are moving somewhat slowly in this, however, until such time as we have a better understanding of the situation at Westinghouse which is in the Baldwin neighborhood.

THE GENERAL ELECTRIC COMPANY, PHILADELPHIA, PA.

Further contact is to be withheld pending the outcome of the Westinghouse situation.

THE NEW YORK SHIPBUILDING COMPANY, CAMDEN, N.J(.)

We are in the process of preparing a separate memorandum on the New York Shipbuilding Company.

THE REGIONAL LAB(O)R SUPPLY COMMITTEE

We discussed the technique of action followed with the Regional Labor Supply Committee.

MS: copy, MP.

1. Eugene Davidson, FEPC senior field representative, was preparing for the Committee's hearings in New York, scheduled for 2/16, 2/17/42, which would also consider cases from northern New Jersey, a part of Mitchell's jurisdiction. Ruchames, *Race, Jobs, and Politics,* 27, 31, 36, 38, 41; Reed, *Seedtime,* 39–41. Reginald Johnson worked at the OPM with Mitchell and succeeded him in the Philadelphia office in 1942.

2. Disciplinary action available to the Committee involved submitting the case to Paul V. McNutt, chairman of the WMC, with the expectation he would use the influence of his office to obtain compliance. If that did not work, the Committee would submit the case to the president for action. See

Mitchell to Johnson, memorandum, 1/18/43; J. E. Cain, executive vice president of P. R. Mallory & Co., to Weaver, 7/8/42, indicating compliance, HqR2, Cooperative Employers; Weaver, *Negro Labor,* 202–3.

3. On the struggle to upgrade African American male and female workers throughout industry, see Weaver, *Negro Labor,* 220–23; Weaver's notes: "When management took steps to upgrade Negroes, and white workers refused to work with them, it became clear that the responsibility for initiating corrective action lay with the union" (222).

Memorandum on the Brecon Bag Loading Plant, Flora, Mississippi

April 23, 1942

To: Dr. Robert C. Weaver

From: Clarence M. Mitchell

Subject: The Brecon Bagloading Plant, Flora, Mississippi

After studying records on the case of the Brecon Bagloading Company in Flora, Mississippi, I have come to the conclusion that it is desirable to certify the Company to the President's Committee on Fair Employment Practice. This firm's complete disregard of all of the regulations governing fair employment makes it desirable that some action be taken very speedily.[1] The following is a summary of our contacts:

February 25, 1942

On this date Mr. Cy W. Record, [WPB] field representative in Region 7, stated that the town of Flora is located in the southwest corner of Madison County, 21 miles north of Jackson, Mississippi, the State's capital. Prior to the announcement that the ordnance plant would be constructed, the population was approximately 500 people. Since that time (summer of 1941) the population has more than doubled.

Canton, Mississippi, is the largest city in Madison County and also the county seat. Canton is 19 miles east of Flora and 25 miles north east of Jackson.

The workers to be employed in the Plant are expected to be drawn from the counties of Madison, Yazoo, Hinds, and Rankin. It is estimated that the total population of the commuting areas and the area from which the local labor supply could be drawn is 225, 000. The breakdown of these population figures shows that approximately 60 per cent of the inhabitants are rural; 55 per cent of the number, or more than 115,000 are Negroes.

February 27, 1942

Mr. W. O'Neill, President of the General Tire and Engineering Company, in Akron, Ohio, which is operating the ordnance plant at Flora, was advised that our office had information to the effect that Negro women would be used as maids and custodial workers only. This advice was sent in a letter signed by Mr. Sidney Hillman. Mr. C. F. Burke replied to Mr. Hillman's letter and stated that in the absence of Mr. O'Neill he was acknowledging the communication. Mr. Burke also stated that he was forwarding the information contained in Mr. Hillman's letter to Mr. A. C. Bowers, Works Manager at the Mississippi Ordnance Plant.

March 17, 1942

Mr. Burke again wrote Mr. Hillman stating that he had received a letter from Mr. Bowers in which the latter had stated that after a lengthy conference with a Miss Elsie Wolfe from the Women's Bureau of the Department of Labor:

"It appears that they agreed on the point that the local Southern Negro women are not suited for the type of operations in the bag loading plant for work requiring the skill and accuracy needed in such an operation."

Mr. Burke's letter indicated that Mr. Bowers would use Negro women in "miscellaneous places where their ability is adaptable to the requirements of the job such as in the laundry, for janitor work, etc." The Company stated that approximately 25 percent colored employees would be used when the plant reaches its maximum capacity but the men would be confined to track workers, road workers, freight handlers, yard workers, and truckers.

March 25, 1942

The Chief of the Negro Employment and Training Branch [Weaver] communicated with Miss Mary Anderson, Director of the Women's Bureau, U. S. Department of Labor. He informed Miss Anderson that Miss Wolfe was alleged to have agreed with Mr. Bowers on the exclusion of colored women from production operations at the plant on the basis of their not being qualified.

March 31, 1942

Miss Anderson replied to Dr. Weaver, stating that, "In a telegram Miss Wolfe says that she agreed with the plant manager that white and colored women could not work together on production in Mississippi. Her statement, she said, was from the production standpoint only. I fear they jockeyed her into making such a statement."

Miss Anderson indicated that she would write a letter to Mr. Burke telling him that Miss Wolfe's statement is contrary to the policy of the Women's Bureau. A copy of her letter to him on this subject was attached.

April 1, 1942

Mr. Record again talked with Mr. A. C. Bowers, and the following is an official version of the conversation:

"Mr. A. C. Bowers has stated flatly and without reservation that no Negroes will be employed in production jobs—unless it is absolutely necessary—that is, unless the total white labor supply is completely exhausted and none other than Negro workers are available for jobs. He has stated further that on the first shift he will have available enough white men and women to fill his needs, and that he expects sufficient white workers for any additional shifts that may be added as receipt of powder available for loading increases.

"Negroes will be employed—but only in such jobs as janitors, yard workers, freight loaders, truck drivers and maintenance workers. These jobs will be filled by Negro men, and Negro women will find employment only as maids and helpers in the cafeterias.

"It is quite apparent that these practices are discriminatory, especially if we take into account the fact that there is available in and around Jackson thousands of Negro men and women, many of whom on the basis of their education and experience and [a] little training could well qualify for production jobs.

"The policies now being carried out appear in bold contrast to the policies which Negro people in and around Jackson had been led to expect. It had been reported earlier that Negro women were to be employed in production jobs, and the general impression seems to have been that a majority of the workers in the plant would be Negro———Inquiring into the causes of such a change in policy, if any change has been made, indicates that there are certain local pressures being applied to the officials of the company to discourage the employment of Negroes, particularly of Negro women. Among these pressures are:

1. Middle-class white women in and around Jackson who wish to keep Negro women in their employment as maids and cooks at the rate of from $2 to $3 a week.
2. Farmers and plantation owners in the surrounding areas who wish to have available a supply of cheap day-wage farm labor, and who want to keep in effect the present $1–$1.50 a day wage scale for day laborers.
3. The local Chamber of Commerce that has been very insistent on the employment of white women living in and around Jackson."

April 8, 1942

A meeting of colored citizens in the areas from which the bag loading plant draws its personnel vigorously protested the Company's action in barring Negroes from production jobs. Mr. Record states that approximately 500 persons were present at the meeting, and all of them were anxious to have the conditions at the bag loading plant corrected.

Some of the leading colored citizens with whom Mr. Record has been in contact are:

Dr. S. D. Redmond—representing the N. A. A. C. P.
Mr. T. B. Willson—representing the Men's Civic League
Mr. William Martin—representing the "Jackson Advocate"
Rev. W. W. Blackburn—Jackson College
Mr. Joe Louis—President—Plasterers and Cement Finishers Union, Jackson
Mr. Monroe Travillian—Financial Secretary, Plasterers and Cement Finishers Union

MS: copy, HqR77, Office Files of Eugene Davidson. Flora, Mississippi.
    1. Certification was the next stage for attempting to resolve discriminatory practices of companies and unions after efforts by field assistants to do so had failed. Brecon, owned by the Coca-Cola Company, was investigated during the FEPC's Birmingham hearings held in June 1942. It subsequently modified its employment policies. See 2/5/43 and 3/29/43; the Birmingham hearings records in HqR17; and Mitchell to Johnson, memorandum, 1/18/43.

Memorandum on Portland, Oregon, Shipyards

[ca. October 10, 1942]

To: Dr. Robert C. Weaver
From: Clarence M. Mitchell
Subject: Portland, Oregon Shipyards

On Saturday, October 10, Clarence Johnson called from Portland, Ore., to say that he had just completed a meeting with Mr. Morton, chief counsel for the Kaiser Shipbuilding Company, and Mr. Murray, chief of personnel. In this conference the Kaiser representatives said that they had met with Thomas Ray of the Boilermakers Union in New York and Mrs. Anna Rosenberg, Regional director of WMC for New York. In this conference, according to the Kaiser officials, an agreement was reached that Negroes would be employed at the yards as they come in from New York, but Mrs.

Rosenberg consented to a demand from Mr. Ray that those cleared by the Boiler-makers would have to work on a segregated basis.[1]

Mr. Johnson feels that this would set a very bad precedent in Portland and particu-larly at the Company yards where between 600 and 800 Negroes are already at work on a non-segregated basis. Mr. Johnson states that to his best knowledge some of these are persons in trades covered by the Boilermaker's charter and others were cleared by unions controlling, electrical work, painting, machine operation and ship carpentry. He fears that if the segregated plan goes through it will mean that the other unions may begin asking for the same thing. I agree with him that from my knowledge of the Portland situation this would simply result in endless trouble.[2]

The company officials are to have a meeting at 10:30 a.m. Monday, October 12 with the union representatives. Mr. Johnson will not be at this meeting, but he will meet with the company officials on Tuesday, October 13. He states that 145 Negroes had come in from New York at the time of our telephone conversation and 47 others were due in on Monday. A total of 2,448 persons have come in so far.

There are two very important issues tied up with this in my opinion. The first, of course, concerns the defiant attitude of the Boilermakers. Something should be done by William Green to bring [th]em into line. I am suggesting that this might be ac-complished through Governor McNutt's labor advisory committee. The second thing affects our own operations. It appears that Mrs. Rosenberg arrived at her agreements and conclusions without the benefit of advice from Mr. Lawson of our office. It seems that in any conference so important as this Mr. Lawson should have been present or at least advised of it in advance so that he could offer suggestions. When circum-stances favor its presentation, I would like to suggest that this be ironed out through General McSherry to avoid its happening in the future.

MS: copy, HqR14, Records Relating to Hearings. Boilermakers, General Files.

1. This report was part of the response to Edward Lawson's request of 9/21/42 to Weaver, director of the Negro Manpower Service, for information on the employment practices of the Oregon Ship-building Corporation, one of the Kaiser Corporation shipyards in Portland. Lawson, a member of the WMC New York staff, reported that he had heard that the company was seeking to hire about twenty thousand men in New York City who would be transported to the West Coast to work in the shipyards there. He said that one of the administrators of the New York employment service informed him "confidentially" that Albert Bauer, assistant general manager of the Oregon corporation, had asked for the men, most of whom would be used as laborers or would be prospective trainees. Bauer, however, had stipulated "that no Negroes be referred." The employment service refused to process the discrimi-natory order. For this document and other related texts—esp. "Summary of Kaiser Recruitment Pro-gram in New York City" [ca. 10/6/42], Lawson's follow-up memoranda to Weaver of 9/22 and 9/26, and Clarence Johnson's letters to Weaver and to Lawson of 10/12/42—see HqR14, Records Relating to Hearings. Boilermakers, General Files; and, for the broader context, see the headnote on the FEPC and Federal Agencies, sections on WMC and USES (esp. for Rosenberg's role) and the section on the Boiler-makers in the headnote on the FEPC and Unions.

2. Mitchell had been in Seattle and Portland in August 1942 helping create "a great experiment—the importation of Negroes to work in the shipyards." He had helped plan "the states from which they will be drawn, the way they will come and what will happen when they get there." See Mitchell to Juanita Mitchell, n.d., quoted in Watson, *Lion in the Lobby*, 136; Mitchell, letter to Juanita Mitchell, 8/7/42, MP.

Memorandum on Suspension of War Training for Negroes in Alabama

November 28, 1942

Mr. George M. Johnson

Clarence M. Mitchell

Suspension of War Training for Negroes in Alabama

In keeping with complaints received from the Southern Negro Youth Congress of Birmingham, Alabama, the National Association for the Advancement of Colored People and the National Urban League, a conference was held with Dr. W. W. Charters, Chief of training for the War Manpower Commission.[1] The complaints charged that war training for Negroes had been stopped. The Southern Negro Youth Congress's complaint stated specifically that twelve courses for Negroes had been halted. It also alleged that although numerous white persons were being trained for aircraft work to meet the needs of the Bechtel-McCone-Parsons Company, no training was being offered for Negroes in this type of work.

After a preliminary discussion of the problem, Dr. Charters called in the following persons for a meeting on the matter: Dr. Philip Van Wyck, assistant to Dr. Charters, Mr. Edward Ludtke, southern regional director for the United States Office of Education, Dr. L. S. Hawkins, director of war training for the War Manpower Commission and Dr. H. J. McCormick, W. P. A. regional representative whose territory includes Alabama. Mr. McCormick stated that "regional representative" had been abolished as his title but that it was still most descriptive of his duties.

In brief, the conference might be summed up by saying that Dr. Charters promised a complete investigation of the matter and it is my understanding that General Frank J. McSherry's office has already begun action by sending Mr. Ernest Marbury of the operations staff into the area. Mr. Marbury, I am told, is to have Dr. Bowman F. Ashe, regional director of the War Manpower Commission, see that training in aircraft work is given to Negroes in the Birmingham area. For his own part Dr. Charters stated that he will have Mr. Ludtke and Mr. Edgar Westmorland, who is a Negro representative in the Office of Education, make a thorough investigation of the Alabama situation. This study is to be used as a basis for correcting whatever the shortcomings are. Because there is a special conference which Mr. Ludtke and Mr. Westmorland must attend. Dr. Charters stated that they could not begin work on the problem until a "Week from Monday, November 30."

During the conference the following matters came up for discussion and appear to be indicative of the peculiar circumstances which tend to hamper the training programs for Negroes in southern areas.

1. Mr. McCormick stated that he was the first to raise the question which precipitated the current difficulty. He said that during one of his visits to the

area he found forty Negro W. P. A. trainees who had been on the payroll longer than they should have been. There did not seem to be an opportunity for placing them, according to Mr. McCormick. After making some effort to find jobs for these persons, Mr. McCormick said the W. P. A. decided to drop them from its rolls. Apparently, the local council of administrators took this as a cue for deciding that the course in chipping and riveting, which was what the W. P. A. people were being given, was no longer needed and so recommended suspension of this training. At the same time there were approximately forty non-W. P. A. persons on the training rolls for the same type of instruction. There is nothing so far to show that their needs were taken into consideration.

2. I have checked with the B. E. S. [Bureau of Employment Security] and find that both Ingalls Iron in Birmingham and the Alabama Shipbuilding and Drydock Company at Mobile have been increasing their Negro personnel. Unfortunately, the B. E. S. records do not show whether these companies employed any riveters or chippers, but it is my understanding that Ingalls Iron has employed Negroes for this type of work. It is also true the North Carolina Shipbuilding Company at Wilmington, North Carolina has trained and hired a great many Negroes for riveting jobs. It is entirely possible that in an extreme emergency this last mentioned company could have been used for the placement of those trained. However, since industry generally makes use of Negroes as chippers and riveters it is entirely possible that some factor other than race caused the breakdown of the Alabama training. I venture the suggestion that such training should never have been given in the first place. The figures from the B. E. S. show the following on Ingalls Iron and Alabama Drydock:

INGALLS IRON WORKS, BIRMINGHAM, ALABAMA

Total Negro Employment Figures

July 707
August 772
September 800
October 934

Occupation Increases

	September	October
Skilled	23	23
Semi-Skilled	29	31
Unskilled	748	880

ALABAMA SHIPBUILDING AND
DRYDOCK COMPANY, MOBILE, ALABAMA

Total Negro Employment Figures

July 3,200
August 4,000
September 4,300
October 4,300

I was unable to obtain a breakdown on skills for Alabama Drydock, but its increases were substantially in laboring jobs and none above the semi-skilled level.

3. Dr. Hawkins stated that Mr. Jed B. Yingling of the United States Office of Education informed him that war training had not been stopped, but rather it had been agreed that the training would not be expanded and no new trainees would be added. I requested Dr. Hawkins to define the difference between this and ordering the training stopped. He did not seem to be able to define the difference. At this point Mr. Ludtke stated that the representatives of the Office of Education have been working on the Alabama situation and that they have made some progress. He showed a list, which is attached to this report, outlining types and location of training for Negroes in Alabama. According to Mr. Ludtke, the recommendation for halting training in Birmingham affected only the riveting and chipping courses.

4. Mr. McCormick and Dr. Hawkins seemed to make a considerable point out of the fact that the local council of administrators in Birmingham had asked that the training be halted. They also pointed out that management and labor representatives "run the council." They admitted, however, that responsibility for making such decisions rests with the U. S. E. S., local education representatives and the N. Y. A., who form the voting membership of the council.

5. In defending the efforts of the United States Office of Education in behalf of Negroes, Mr. Ludtke responded to a previous statement made by me in connection with welding equipment. I had pointed out that Alabama authorities were supposed to be trying to buy 18 new welding machines for Negroes, although the W. P. B. has issued a ruling to the effect that such equipment cannot be purchased by schools. It was my suggestion that equipment available for whites at present should be divided with Negroes. Mr. Ludtke stated that he did not believe there was enough equipment for whites which would permit such a division. He also said that he feels that if enough "pressure" is put behind the W. P. B. the new equipment can be purchased. I must admit that I do not share his views concerning the W. P. B., but if pressure can get these machines, it seems that the United States Office of Education has the responsibility for ap-

plying it since, if welding equipment had been purchased for Negroes when it was purchased for whites, we would not now be facing the problem.

In my opinion Dr. Charters will take corrective action in the Alabama matter. However, there still is considerable need for a planned approach to the whole southern problem of training for Negroes. Since Dr. Charters' office will have training responsibilities, I would like to suggest that we draw up a training program which we believe will offer substantial remedy. I recommend that we then have meetings with Dr. Charters and appropriate members of General McSherry's staff for the purpose of putting this program into effect.

Attachment

MS: copy, HqR48, Central Files. General Reports, N–Z.

1. See "Findings and Directives" in the case of "National Training Program in Alabama, Tennessee and Georgia," as mentioned in Cramer memorandum, 11/10/42, to Fenton, Brophy, and Ethridge. A copy of the findings and directives was submitted to McNutt because of his special relations with the Office of Education. HqR38, Central Files. (entry 25) Meetings. See also "Defense Training for Negroes in Birmingham, Alabama" and "The Participation of Negroes in the National Defense Training Program in Alabama," in HqR66, Central Files. U.S. Government, Aliens in Defense, Specific Groups, Mexicans (Miscellaneous).

Another manifestation of Jim Crow–type training in the South was the dismal quality of whatever programs existed. "In the South, we expect the general poor equipment and poor facilities," explained Herman Branson in *The Journal of Negro Education*. Branson's quote from John Beecher (from an article in *Science and Society* based on Beecher's observations in the spring of 1942) was revealing:

> The same thing [as the situation in Alabama] prevailed in Georgia, and Tennessee and Arkansas and South Carolina and Texas. Hardly any defense training was open to Negroes anywhere in the South, and much of what was labeled defense training was close to being outright fraudulent. I might mention one course of 150 shipfitter helpers where the sole shop equipment consisted of some shipyard pictures clipped from *Life* magazine and a bathtub navy, purchased out of the instructor's pocket at the five-and-ten. This particular course accounted for two-thirds of the Negro trainees in the state of Georgia. Somewhere else they were pretending to train Negro marine electricians in a shop where positively the only item of marine equipment was an eight-inch length of electrical cable. I recall also a class in motor mechanics where the students were forbidden to go into the motors—it was actually a class in alemiting [lubricating], tire-inflating and windshield wiping for filling station attendants. And I shouldn't forget the Negro defense shop so far out into the piney woods that it was next to impossible to get to, yet I heard such praises of and such accounts of the completeness of its equipment that I arranged to visit it. There I found a splendidly-equipped sheet metal shop with unfortunately no sheet metal to fabricate but only tin cans salvaged from the garbage pile. There I found also a gleaming row of electric welding machines but somebody had neglected to connect them with power.

Beecher, "Problems of Discrimination," 36–44, quoted in Branson, "Training of Negroes for War Industries in World War II," 378. See also Wilkerson, "Vocational Guidance and Education of Negroes," in which the author provides further critical analysis of the widespread concerns about the implications of the defense program on the American economy, particularly regarding the status of African Americans; Weaver, "Defense Program and the Negro," 324–27; and Weaver, *Negro Labor,* 41–60.

Memorandum on Wage Rate for Harvesting Sugar Cane in Florida and Louisiana

December 4, 1942

To: Mr. George M. Johnson
              Assistant Executive Secretary

From: Clarence M. Mitchell
              Field Representative

Subject: Wage Rate for Harvesting Sugar Cane in Florida and Louisiana

The U. S. Sugar Corporation published a booklet, "Sugar and the Everglades", in January of 1941. On Page 52 of that publication the following quotation is made and attributed to Mr. Otis E. Mulliken, Chief of the Labor Section of the Sugar Division, of the U.S. Dept. of Agriculture, before the Civil Liberties Committee of the U. S. Senate:

> "The standard of living of the sugarcane workers employed by the United States Sugar Corporation is higher than the standard of most other agricultural workers in the continental area. The seasonal migration of cane labor to Florida does not appear to present any problems except possibly that of controlling the supply so that the maximum amount of employment is available for the year round workers and for those who are employed only during harvesting. . . . On the whole sugarcane workers in Florida constitute a relatively privileged class of agricultural workers."

I have requested the full copy of his testimony and expect that it will be available shortly.

In view of the current charges which were brought against the U.S. Sugar Corporation by the Dept. of Justice, it seems advisable to determine whether the Dept. of Agriculture was fully aware of all of the conditions in the sugar industry when it fixed the current wage rates.[1]

I have talked with Mr. Victor Rotnem, of the Dept. of Justice, who is handling the case against the U. S. Sugar Corporation. He states that the company was indicted around November 6, along with four of its supervisors, on a charge of peonage. It is his opinion that an abundance of evidence is available to show very undesirable working conditions in the industry. During the coming week, I expect to visit his office to go over his file. I am also obtaining information from other sources on conditions in the Florida area.

Since the Dept. of Justice is not considering the wage rates as such, I presume that the Committee might well inquire of the Dept. of Agriculture on this matter.

MS: copy, HqR4, Office Files of George M. Johnson. W, Wage Increases.

1. On 11/4/42 the Department of Justice (DOJ) announced that a federal grand jury, sitting in the Southern District of Florida at Tampa, had returned a two-count indictment charging "the United

States Sugar Corporation, its personnel manager, and three of its camp superintendents with conspiracy to hold black sugar cane workers in peonage." The indictment resulted from the DOJ's investigations of complaints that the company had recruited workers to plantations near Clewiston, Florida, by offering them free transportation. Upon arrival, however, the workers were told that they owed the company the cost of the transportation and that they would not be allowed to leave unless they reimbursed the company. News release, 11/4/42, Office of War Information, Department of Justice. The DOJ's action was reinforced by the NWLB, which addressed another of Mitchell's basic concerns, namely, wage discrimination. See NWLB news release, 6/7/43, announcing that it had ruled unanimously on that day that wage classifications based solely on racial differences were "without validity." Copies of both releases are in HqR4, Office Files of George M. Johnson. W, Wage Increases.

Memorandum on U.S. Postal System

Date: December 14, 1942

To: Mr. George M. Johnson

From: Clarence Mitchell

Subject: U. S. Postal System

Following a conference with Dr. Landes on the general Post Office picture, I am suggesting that we adopt the following procedure in handling these complaints:[1]

1. I believe that we should make an immediate effort to have a hearing on Mr. Rone Sidney's case in Newport News, Virginia. I am suggesting that we have this hearing in Newport News in order to get at all of the important witnesses.

2. It is my opinion that if we recommend that Mr. Sidney be employed we can expect some reaction from the Postmaster. At that time we can suggest that we have other complaints against Philadelphia, Cleveland, New Orleans and St. Louis, Missouri. We can propose that the Committee would be satisfied if the Post Office will handle these internally in an expeditious manner. If our proposal is accepted, we can, of course, proceed to make a full presentation of all complaints. If it is not accepted, it seems we have no alternative but to continue hearings in these areas by the Staff Board of Review.

It is my understanding that Dr. Landes concurs with me in this procedure.[2]

MS: LH, DI, HqR38, Central Files. (entry 25) Memoranda, Mitchell, Clarence.

1. In 1913 President Woodrow Wilson officially implanted segregation in federal service. In reaction, the NAACP that year conducted its first study of the problem and learned that the Post Office Department had emulated practices of evicting African American employees from its dining room that had been initiated by other departments. Official segregation, which included designating separate toilets for black and white employees in several departments, long outlasted the Wilson administration. "Flagrant discrimination" in employment, as the NAACP would subsequently charge, was the

logical consequence of such practices and of those that left the selection of personnel solely to the discretion of the postmaster. King, *Separate and Unequal*, 29–30, 53.

2. The Rone Sidney case was an example of the systemic discrimination in the Post Office Department that the FEPC would battle throughout its existence. Launching an attack on this problem on 2/23/42 in a letter to Harry B. Mitchell, president of the United States Civil Service Commission, MacLean, the FEPC chairman, explained that the Committee had for some time been studying proposals for strengthening the merit principle in the commission and made a series of recommendations for doing so. In a response on 5/18/42, Harry Mitchell told MacLean that the commission was "pleased" to concur with the FEPC's recommendations and stated six steps it would take to implement them. Nevertheless, because the procedure Mitchell outlined did not work, the Committee in December 1943 held a hearing under the direction of Ernest Trimble and in February 1944 issued an order on behalf of Sidney. The department then initiated steps to correct discrimination at Newport News. See "Summary of the Evidence with Findings and Recommendation" and other materials on this case, including MacLean to Harry Mitchell, in HqR19, Records Relating to Hearings. Sidney, Rone; and the section on the Post Office Department in the headnote on Relationships with Federal Agencies. On the outcome of the case, see also the notes to Mitchell's memorandum of 5/3/44.

Memorandum on Proposed Directive to Mr. F. G. Seulberger, Chairman, Department of Industrial Relations, Northwestern University

December 17, 1942

To: George M. Johnson
          Assistant Executive Secretary

From: Clarence Mitchell

Subject: Proposed directive to Mr. F. G. Seulberger, Chairman,
          Department of Industrial Relations, Northwestern University

After reading the attached correspondence it is my opinion that Mr. Feigon did not apply for the regular Engineering Science Management War Training course which is sponsored with the help of federal subsidy. In his letter to the President's Committee on Fair Employment Practice dated August 11, 1942, Mr. Feigon states that he went to the Inland Steel Company of Indiana Harbor in an effort to get a guarantee that he would be given a job a year from the date of his application and in three month alternating periods from then on. This would mean that it could not be a regular ESMWT course because such courses are of short duration, usually from 12 to 16 weeks.[1]

I have refreshed my memory on this point by calling the office of Dean George W. Case who has charge of the program. Mr. Clark of that office stated that he was familiar with the Northwestern program and indicated that no federal funds are given for the carrying on of the type of training which was being sought by Mr. Feigon. Our best strategy of attack, therefore, would be to direct our attention fully at the employer angle which is apparently the sole reason for excluding Mr. Feigon from the other type of training offered by the University. Accordingly I am suggesting that the text of our directive be as follows:

"In your letter of October 22 which was addressed to the President's Committee on Fair Employment Practice, you stated the following: 'We have a generous sprinkling of Jewish boys—including at least one refugee. We even have a German boy, who has not yet become a citizen of the United States. We have Poles and Czechs. However, if we had a very large proportion of any one race or group we could not operate successfully since our cooperating companies demand diversity of background among the students they hire.'

The President's Executive Order 8802 forbids discrimination on the part of war industries. By honoring what you infer is a prejudice against Jews on the part of the companies, you become an accessory in the hands of those who violate the President's Order. (In his letter dated October 22, 1942, Mr. Seulberger states, 'the point I wish to make is that the boys do not hold ordinary <u>routine defense jobs</u> but are in cadet engineering training programs.' This would seem to indicate that the University regards the training as essential to the war program.)

It is the custom of the United States Employment Service to list all companies which refuse to accept individuals because of race or other factors not related to individual fitness. Such reports are then given to the Committee on Fair Employment Practice and it in turn orders these companies to comply with the clauses in their contracts requiring them to refrain from discrimination based on race, religion or national origin.

Since your letter indicates that the reason for refusing Mr. Feigon admission is based on the attitude of companies who offer employment, we should like to have a list of these companies and specific charges against them indicating that they will not accept Mr. Feigon or persons of Jewish race. When you furnish us with this information we will take the necessary steps to correct the attitudes of the companies.

Meanwhile, because of the needs for individuals who are engineers in the war program we direct you to admit Mr. Feigon to this training and inform us of your action."

I should like to point out that the Engineering Science Management Training very generally has been open to Negroes, Jews and others in northern communities.

MS: copy, MP.

1. ESMWT provided short, intensive college-level courses in engineering, chemistry, physics, and management for professional and technical workers in war industries. The program was operated by the Bureau of Training, established in the WMC to coordinate the government's several training agencies and functions. Zaid, *Inventory,* 55–58; Branson, "Training of Negroes," 378–81.

Memorandum on Tennessee Valley
Authority Employment Practices

December 23, 1942

To: Mr. George M. Johnson

From: Clarence Mitchell

Subject: Tennessee Valley Authority Employment Practices

Like many other government employers the TVA seems to be able to cite large numbers of Negroes employed as indicative of no discrimination on its part. I believe that the only way we can hope for any correction in this is to have some staff member assigned to the Authority for a period of a month or more for the purpose of making an exhaustive investigation of all complaints filed and the hiring practices of the Authority.[1]

I do not believe that we can achieve anything further via the correspondence method. Ultimately it may be necessary for us to do this in connection with some of the other large government establishments, and it is my opinion that we might well try it out on the TVA.

In order to insure the success of this undertaking, I believe that we should have some preliminary discussion of it with the members of the Authority. If it is their desire to eliminate discrimination it is very possible that they will be glad to receive this kind of assistance.

MS: copy, HqR48, Central Files. Reports, Fair Employment Practices, Reports–1.

1. The vast Tennessee River valley includes seven states: Alabama, Georgia, Kentucky, North Carolina, Mississippi, Tennessee, and Virginia. On May 18, 1933, President Roosevelt signed the Tennessee Valley Authority Act to control flooding by the Tennessee River with hydroelectric dams and to develop agriculture and industry in the region. The FEPC was seeking to prevent blacks from being confined to the customary low-level jobs on the twelve dams that the government was constructing employing twenty-eight thousand workers.

Mitchell was fully aware of the history of abysmal working conditions and discrimination on public works projects in the region as a result of investigations by civil rights groups. One done in 1933 by Roy Wilkins, assistant executive secretary of the NAACP, and George Schuyler, a writer, confirmed the deplorable conditions under which blacks were working on the Army Corps of Engineers Mississippi Flood Control project in the Delta. Wilkins, "Mississippi Slavery," *Crisis,* 4/33, 81–82.

Two later reports by Charles H. Houston and John P. Davis criticized the exclusion of blacks from training programs, model housing villages, and from all but the traditionally low-level jobs they usually held. They complained that contrary to TVA pledges, blacks were not employed in proportion to their representation in the local population, and that they were receiving much lower pay than white workers owing to the misclassifying of those doing skilled work as unskilled workers. Houston, "TVA: Lily-White Reconstruction," *Crisis,* 10/34, 290–91, 311; Davis, "The Plight of the Negro in the Tennessee Valley," *Crisis,* 10/35, 294–95, 314. Online, go to Tennessee Valley Authority Act, http://www.Chattanooga .net/uta/TVAuthorityAct.htm and http://www.tva.gov/abouttva/history.htm.

In a follow-up report on WPA flood control projects that reinforced the broad picture of discrimination Mitchell was concerned about on other large government projects, Wilkins compared the treatment of blacks he had witnessed in Cincinnati, Ohio; West Memphis, Arkansas; Louisville and

Paducah, Kentucky. Wilkins confirmed the rumor he had heard that "race prejudice had taken a vacation in Louisville during the flood disaster"; but Memphis just had "to be near the bottom in practically everything affecting the two races," in terms of grossly unequal pay for blacks, and their being "shanghaiied," peonage style, "to work on reinforcing the levees." Wilkins, "Through the 1937 Floor Area," *Crisis,* 4/37, 104–6, 124–26.

Memorandum on Railroad Complaints

December 28, 1942

To: George M. Johnson

From: Clarence Mitchell

Subject: Railroad complaints

In accordance with your assignment I am leaving to investigate complaints for the railroad hearings on January 25, 26, and 27.[1] Mr. Hubbard has given me complaints filed by witnesses who live in Chicago, Dayton, Ohio, and Cleveland, Ohio. There are one or two complaints from East St. Louis and Columbus, Ohio, but Mr. Hubbard felt that these cities need not be visited since they involve the same railroads against which a number of persons have complained in Chicago.

I understand that you will make the necessary arrangements to have Mr. Austin H. Scott work with me. Mr. Hubbard is to contact Mr. Hielman of the CIO, whose office is in Youngstown, with the request that this gentleman join me in Cleveland on December 31 or at any other time which is convenient for him for the purpose of working on the complaints we have in the Cleveland area.

While in Chicago, I expect to stop at the Southway Hotel and I can be reached there or at Mr. Scott's office. His telephone is ANdover 3600. I will advise you of other locations at which I can be reached after I confer with Mr. Scott on Tuesday. I hope to be back in the office by January 7.

MS: LH, DI, HqR37, Central Files. (entry 25) Hearings, Railroads.

1. Owing to fierce pressure from the railroads, the hearings in what would become the FEPC's legendary battle over the Southeastern Carriers Conference Agreement were not held as scheduled, creating the biggest hornet's nest in domestic politics for President Roosevelt. The roots of discrimination in the railroad industry were deep and violent, so deep that the central issues of the exclusion of blacks from closed union shops under the agreement had to be decided—in the FEPC's favor—in the *Steele v. Louisville and Nashville Railroad Company* and *Tunstall v. Brotherhood of Locomotive Firemen and Enginemen* cases. For contemporary accounts, see Jonathan Daniels, "Brotherhood Except for Negroes," *Nation,* 11/22/41, 513; "Occupational Status of Negro Railroad Employees," *Monthly Labor Review,* 3/43, 484–85; "Principal American Labor Unions: The Railroad Brotherhoods," *Congressional Digest,* 11/41, 265; "Coming Out Into the Open," *Commonweal,* 12/24/43, 244; "FEPC v. the Railroads," *Time,* 12/27/43, 18; "Railroads Demur, Notify FEPC They Won't Obey Negro-Hiring Order," *Business Week,* 12/18/43, 103; Ross, before the House Select Committee to Investigate Executive Agencies, "The

Railroad Cases," H. Res. 102, 3/14/44; Houston, in HqR6, Office Files of George M. Johnson. Railroad Cases; "Foul Employment Practice on the Rails," *Crisis*, 10/49, 269–71. See also the headnote on the FEPC and Unions; *First Report*, 62; Northrup, *Organized Labor and the Negro*, 55–64, 100–1; Watson, *Lion in the Lobby*, 139–40.

December 28, 1942, Memorandum on Complaints against the Chesapeake and Potomac Company in Baltimore, Maryland

December 28, 1942

To: George M. Johnson

From: Clarence Mitchell

Subject: Complaints against the Chesape[a]ke and Potomac Telephone Company in Baltimore, Maryland.

A great many complaints are being filed against the C&P Telephone Company in Baltimore according to the Afro-American. However, I have not seen more than two in our office, although there may be others. In any event, Mr. Julius Gardner of Region 4 has asked me to let you know that the area Manpower Director, Mr. Royden A. Blunt is at work on this problem.

In view of the fact that we will be awaiting the outcome of our Washington action before proceeding to other points, it might well be that we could call these to the attention of Mr. Blunt and suggest that he send us a statement indicating what action the Commission is planning in connection with the C&P Telephone Company.

I am attaching a suggested memorandum which you might agree to send to him through the Executive Director of the Commission.[1]

MS: copy, FR42, Region IV. Active Cases (3–624), Chesapeake and Potomac Telephone Company, Baltimore, Md.

1. Probably Johnson to Blunt, 12/26/42, filed along with numerous other related documents with this text. Complaints against the Chesapeake and Potomac Company were initiated by the *Baltimore Afro-American*, by the Baltimore Urban League, and by an umbrella organization called the Total War Employment Committee, chaired by Lillie M. Jackson, Mitchell's mother-in-law, who was president of the Baltimore NAACP branch, and Alexander J. Allen of the Urban League. The committee also included representatives of the local Communist Party, another organization backing the effort to open telephone and transit jobs to blacks. For subsequent developments, see the headnote on the Telephone Industry and the texts cited there.

Memorandum on Firms with
Fair Employment Practices

January 11, 1943

To: George M. Johnson

From: Clarence Mitchell

Subject: Firms with fair employment practices.

I have noted the contents of Mr. Fleming's memorandum dated December 21, 1942 in which he mentions the need for getting information on firms which are employing individuals without discrimination.

I shall be happy to continue working on this assignment and expect to have a report by the end of the week.[1]

MS: LH, DI, HqR38, Central Files. (entry 25) Memoranda, Mitchell, Clarence.
    1. Report not found.

Memorandum on Aircraft Training
in Atlanta, Georgia

January 11, 1943

To: George M. Johnson

From: Clarence Mitchell

Subject: Aircraft training in Atlanta, Georgia

Attached is correspondence from the Central Files concerning the aircraft training program in Atlanta, Georgia.[1] You will note that the only source of information in recent months has been Mr. William Y. Bell, Executive Secretary of the Atlanta Urban League. Mr. Record seems to have visited the school but apparently did not report.[2]

I call this to your attention because in my last telephone conversation with Mr. Record, I understood that he was not permitted to contact the Bell Aircraft personnel people. Apparently this has also prevented him from getting a first hand picture of the training program.

When you have finished with this material, I would appreciate the return of it so that I may send it back to Central Files.

MS: copy, LH, DI, HqR38, Central Files. (entry 25) Memoranda, Mitchell, Clarence.

1. See the headnote on the Aircraft Industry and the discussion of "The Runaround in Defense Training," in Reed, *Seedtime,* 175–204.

2. In his letter of 10/6/42 to Weaver, William Bell reported that aeronautical training equipment continued to "dribble in daily" to the facility. "In the meantime, [Cy] Record tells me that two personnel men, from the Bell Company, are expected in town soon and he plans to contact them immediately on the employment of Negroes at the plant." Bell said he would probably contact the man "in charge of inaugurating new defense housing in this area, in order to make certain that the company does not use the excuse of no housing facilities as the reason why it does not employ Negro workers." He thanked Weaver for the progress they had made so far and said the only thing he could further do was to wait. HqR38, Central Files. (entry 25) Memoranda, Mitchell, Clarence.

Memorandum on Request for Information from Mr. Kasper, Editor of the *Employment Security Review*

January 18, 1943

To: George M. Johnson

From: Clarence Mitchell

Subject: Request for information from Mr. [Sidney H.] Kasper,
        Editor of the Employment Security Review.

For sake of the record I am listing the points of information which I gave to Mr. Kasper at his request on Friday, January 15. It is my understanding that this material was needed for completion of the article submitted by the Committee for publication.[1]

1. Mr. Kasper wished to know the minority population of the United States. I informed him that this was approximately 25,000,000 consisting of 1,800,000 Spanish-Americans, 5,000,000 Jewish persons, 12,865,000 Negroes and 4,668,000 aliens 10 years and over. The difference between these figures and 25,000,000 is accounted for by other less important national groups.

2. Mr. Kasper requested information on the number of cases handled by the Committee. I informed him that this was in excess of 7,000 beginning June 1941.

3. The editor of the Review wished to know how many hearings the Committee has held and how many were planned. I informed him that four regional hearings have been held and five others are planned. I listed these five as Cleveland, Detroit, St. Louis, Philadelphia, and Baltimore.

4. The Review article is to contain some information concerning the 510 reports of the U. S. Employment Service. I read the section of our Operations Bulletin concerning this to Mr. Kasper.

5. Mr. Kasper wanted some information on what happened if an order of the President's Committee was defied by any corporation or union. I informed him that under the present arrangements Mr. McNutt would be expected to use the influence of his office to obtain compliance, and if this were not possible, the matter would then go to the President for action.

Mr. Kasper had asked for information on the number of persons placed in industry as a result of the Committee's activities. I informed him that we were unable to furnish this figure.

MS: LH, DI, HqR38, Central Files. (entry 25) Memoranda, Mitchell, Clarence.
    1. The *Employment Security Review,* issued by the U.S. Bureau of Employment Security (BES), Reports and Analysis Division, was superceded in 1943 by the *Manpower Review,* published by the WMC, and in 1945 by the *Employment Service Review,* published by USES, 1945–48. For background, see "The WMC and USES" in the headnote on Relationships with Federal Agencies.

Memorandum on Telephone Conversation with Mr. Cy W. Record

January 18, 1943

To: George M. Johnson

From: Clarence Mitchell

Subject: Telephone conversation, Friday, January 15 with Cy W. Record.

On the above date we talked with Mr. Record[1] by long distance telephone and he informed us of the attitude taken by Dr. B. F. Ashe, Regional Director of the War Manpower Commission concerning figures on training of Negroes in the 6 southeastern states.[2]

Mr. Record pointed out that on December 24, Dr. J. E. McDaniel, Regional Director of Training, prepared a report for Dr. Ashe in which he stated that between 1,500 and 2,000 Negroes were in training in the 6 southeastern states. In reporting this information to Dr. Charters, Acting Director of the War Manpower Commission Training Program, Dr. Ashe stated that between 15,000 and 20,000 Negroes were in training. It was my understanding that Mr. McDaniel would be in Washington on

Monday, and that he would be in need of certain information from the U. S. Office of Education.

I have obtained this information and will meet with Dr. Charters and Mr. McDaniel on Tuesday, January 19, to discuss it with them.

MS: LH, DI, HqR38, Central Files. (entry 25) Memoranda, Mitchell, Clarence.

1. Record, associate field employment assistant with the WPB, regularly kept Mitchell abreast of WMC activities involving blacks and ethnic groups in the South. The WPB had been placed within the WMC, making it easy for Record to observe closely its activities. For example, soon he would tell Mitchell that he had been assigned to the WMC's regional office around Atlanta to "work on the problem of Negro recruitment and placement in the war production industries in this area." It appeared, he said, that the office was "anxious to do an intensive job in one of the most critical labor shortage areas in this section." The situation, he said, was very bad. There were "all kinds of shortages, skilled, semi-skilled, and unskilled. Negroes, all of whom are available will be used (that is Negro males), but for the most part from present indications only in laboring jobs." Record to Mitchell, received 3/18/43, MP.

2. On training programs, see notes to 11/28/42 and 1/11/43.

Memorandum on Stabilization Agreements

January 19, 1943

To: Goerge M. Johnson

From: Clarence Mitchell

Subject: Stabilization agreements

From time to time we have questions arising involving what is commonly called "job freezing." While the entire country has not been covered as yet, a great many sections have been subjected to provisions of employment stablization formulated by Area Manpower Directors.[1]

I am familiar with the provisions of most of these and am currently studying others which have recently been agreed upon. I shall be happy to furnish information concerning any of these plans if and when a given instance warrants it.

MS: LH, DI, HqR38, Central Files. (entry 25) Memoranda, Mitchell, Clarence.

1. On the operation of stabilization plans, see especially Mitchell's memorandum of 4/13/43, and other texts of 4/5, 5/4/43, 4/28, and 9/25/44. Because such plans initially failed to include nondiscrimination provisions, agreements with discriminatory and segregated unions holding closed shop contracts raised substantial barriers for black workers in the defense industry.

Until the creation of the FEPC, the federal government did little to end the AFL's policy of racial discrimination. Those problems worsened late in 1941 when the OPM entered into a stabilization agreement with the AFL's Building and Construction Trades Department that covered eight hundred thousand workers. Intended to prevent labor disputes and obtain union cooperation, it set wage and hour standards and sought to prevent work stoppages and to stabilize labor relations in other ways to accelerate the construction of defense plants. The problem was that in return the OPM gave the AFL a virtual monopoly over the construction industry. Subsequently, similar regional agreements were made with the Metal Trades Councils of the AFL, which covered shipyards and aircraft plants. Robert Weaver explained, "Where in such instances, there was a conflict between the operation of these agreements and the announced policy of non-discrimination, OPM supported the stabilization pacts." See the headnote on the FEPC and Unions; Weaver, *Negro Labor*, 35–37, 133–34; Kersten, *Race, Jobs, and the War*, 33.

Memorandum on National Defense Research Committee

January 25, 1943

To: Lawrence W. Cramer

From: Clarence Mitchell

Subject: National Defense Research Committee

This training is carried on at the University of Chicago and the nature of it is secret and technical.[1] Mr. Hovde of the Office in Washington informed me that the University of Chicago representatives of NDRC have the right to hire an individual but such hiring must be approved by the Army or Navy. The branch of service for which the research is carried on apparently gives approval. If you wish to have me handle this matter further, I shall be glad to do so.

MS: copy, MP.

1. Lawrence Cramer handled this case, which involved Takeru Higuchi, who complained in a letter of 11/15/42 to Eleanor Roosevelt that he had asked to come to the University of Chicago for an interview for a position related to the NDRC's work. He received a response that: "We have heard that through no fault of yours and before a F.B.I. investigation was even started, your case was closed, so that we will not be able to have your services. This decision was not made by members of the project, but somewhere up along the line, and apparently is connected with current national policy (or lack of a policy). No persons of Japanese ancestry are being hired for defense projects connected with the University here at present." Upon receiving a response from the university on March 31 that a decision had been made not to use Higuchi's services, Cramer on 4/17/43 referred the case to Truman K. Gibson Jr., acting civilian aide to the secretary of war, with a request for him to investigate it. See correspondence on this case in HqR66, Central Files. U.S. Government, Aliens in Defense, Specific Groups, Japanese; headnote on Japanese Americans.

Memorandum on Telephone Call from
Mr. Cy W. Record in Atlanta, Georgia

February 5, 1943

To: Mr. George M. Johnson

From: Clarence Mitchell

Subject: Long distance telephone call from Mr. Cy Record in Atlanta, Georgia

On the above date, Mr. Record called us to give the following information:

1. He stated that the Vultee Aircraft, Gulf Shipbuilding, Brecon Bag Loading, and the McEvoy Companies, all of which were called in for hearings in Birmingham, show some numerical progress in Negro employment.[1] He stated that the Alabama Shipbuilding Company has a smaller percentage of Negroes because of overall increases in employment but the numerical figure on Negroes has increased. He states that as of January 1943 the company employed 1,056 semi-skilled Negroes and 4,181 unskilled. He notes an increase of 56 in the semi-skilled group.[2]

The Gulf Shipbuilding Company remains approximately the same except that 50 Negroes were employed several weeks ago. None of them were skilled. The Brecon Company reports 52 semi-skilled colored women employed on power sewing machines, and a total of 493 Negroes out of 3,360 persons. The Vultee Company has increased its Negro personnel from 30 to 64 out of a total of 5,527 persons. All of the Negroes are still unskilled. The McEvoy Company has increased from 550 Negroes in November to 861 in January. Some of the Negroes at McEvoy are skilled. Mr. Record also reported on the Bell Aircraft training program indicating that trainees are being turned out at the rate of 60 per month and that a total of 200 have already been trained. He feels that the company will employ a great many Negroes although it is not yet in production. Mr. Record felt that a sufficient number of persons would not be available for the Bell Aircraft Company unless there is some revision of shifts in order to accommodate persons who could not attend at the present hours.

2. We discussed the effect of his confidential material getting into the hands of the Regional Director [Burton Morley] and it was his feeling that it had a healthy effect on the situation. It was Mr. Record's belief that while no great changes for the good have taken place, the regional office would be more careful in the future when handling matters affecting Negroes.

MS: copy, HqR1, Office Memoranda. M.

1. On the Birmingham hearings, held in June 1942, see Reed, *Seedtime,* 66–74; and HqR17, Records Relating to Hearings; Weaver, *Negro Labor,* 36–37; Northrup, *Organized Labor and the Negro,* 206; headnote on Aircraft Industry.

2. Regarding a complaint against the Vultee plant in Nashville, the FEPC found that, based on the evidence, "particularly on the fact that no Negroes are employed on the production line and on evidence tending to indicate fear by the Management of racial disturbances, that the Company, contrary to Executive Order 8802, maintains a policy of discrimination in employment on account of race." FEPC, "Revised Summary and Findings," n.d. The Committee therefore directed the plant to take seven steps to comply with the executive order, including instructing its personnel officers and employees "to recruit and employ workers solely on the basis of the qualifications of applicants or workers without regard to their race, creed, color or national origin, and in the case of qualified aliens, to submit to the Secretary of War or Secretary of the Navy applications for consent to employ" such persons in accordance with War-Navy regulations. Similar directives were issued to the other firms investigated at the Birmingham hearings. See HqR77, Office Files of Eugene Davidson. Misc.; for background, see the headnotes on the Shipbuilding Industry and on the Aircraft Industries.

Memorandum on Savannah Shipyards

February 24, 1943

To: Mr. George M. Johnson

From: Clarence Mitchell

Subject: Savannah Shipyards

It is my understanding that the CIO is making an effort to organize the workers in the Southeastern shipyards in Savannah and for this reason the IUMSWA is backing the fight on discrimination.

Since we have already started an investigation through the War Manpower Commission, I am suggesting that we send the attached letter.[1]

Attachment

MS: LH, DI, FR81, Region VII. Active Cases (A–Z), Southeastern Shipbuilding Corp.

1. Probably George Johnson to Ashley Hiatt, National Representative, IUMSWA, 2/24/43, drafted by Mitchell, a copy of which is filed with this text, along with other related documents. See also Mitchell's memorandum of 3/3/43; headnote on the Shipbuilding Industry.

Memorandum on Employment of Negroes in Savannah, Georgia

March 3, 1943

To: Mr. George M. Johnson

From: Clarence Mitchell

Subject: Employment of Negroes in Savannah, Georgia.

Mr. George W. Streator of the Labor Production Division of the War Production Board left for Savannah, Georgia, during the first part of last week. Before he began the trip I discussed the recent complaints we have received from Savannah against the Southeastern Shipbuilding Company with him. He promised to look into these complaints and give me a brief statement of his version of the situation when he returned.

On his return he called me to say that it was his impression that the second mass ejection of Negroes from the Southeastern Shipbuilding Company about which we are presently concerned was a very involved situation stemming partly from the fact that the CIO is organizing in the area and partly from the fact that there is a different wage being paid common labor workers in construction jobs and at the shipyard. It is his statement that construction in the city of Savannah is paying 50¢ an hour, while common laboring jobs at the shipyard are paying 62¢ an hour. Mr. Streator stated that as far as he was able to determine by investigating the situation, some individual or individuals began a movement in the shipyard among the colored employees to ask for higher wages. He said that 3 or 4 men who are alleged to be the tools of the company or at least of contractors who need common labor in the city went among the Negroes encouraging them to quit if they did not get what they were asking for. The climax of this, according to Mr. Streator, was the formation of a committee of 18 persons who demanded a raise to $1.00 an hour. Among other things, Mr. Streator stated, workers were disgruntled because the Victory Tax was being deducted from their pay checks. The men were under the impression that this was a charge for poll taxes.

The persons who contended that they were aggrieved had a meeting on the shipyard property, Mr. Streator stated, and when they did so, approximately 200 or more workers attended. These men were forced off the grounds and hence the telegram which was sent to us from Savannah contending that a number of Negroes had been forced out by the shipyard. All of this, of course, is Mr. Streator's version of the happening and it will be interesting to keep it for further reference when we receive a report from the regional office in accordance with our previous request.[1]

By way of giving the background of the situation at [as] it is at present in Savannah, Mr. Streator stated that all of the windows of the CIO hall were shot out shortly after he arrived in town and that hammers and sickles were painted on the building with red paint.

While in Savannah, Mr. Streator stayed at the home of Mr. L. E. Carter of the Committee on Labor and Industry of the NAACP. Mr. Carter is one of those who has filed a number of complaints with this office, and we are currently handling one of his statements on training.[2]

MS: LH, DI, FR81, Region VII. Active Cases (A–Z), Southeastern Shipbuilding Corp.

1. For subsequent FEPC criticism of Streator's actions and his analysis of a dispute, see Mitchell report, 4/3/44, and notes.

2. See 2/24, 9/14/43, 1/23, 2/14 and 2/20/45, and the headnote on the Shipbuilding Industry. Filed with this text are Carter's letter to Johnson of 2/10/43, the telegrams and other complaints regarding the firm, and related correspondence of George Johnson, much of it drafted by Mitchell.

Memorandum on Susceptibility of Negroes to Industrial Diseases

March 5, 1943

To: Mr. George M. Johnson

From: Clarence Mitchell

Subject: Susceptibility of Negroes to Industrial Diseases.

On several occasions employers have taken the position that Negroes could not be employed in certain occupations because of abnormal susceptibility to diseases— such as tuberculosis (from welding fumes), lead poisoning (from the handling of various lead products), and skin diseases (from cutting oils, etc.).

I thought the staff would be interested in a reply sent by Dr. Parran in response to my inquiry on this subject. His reply is as follows:

"This will acknowledge your letter of October 21, 1942, asking whether Negroes are more susceptible to occupational diseases than are whites.

"Other things being equal, there is no current evidence of a difference between Negroes and whites in their susceptibility to this type of disease. Specifically as regards lead poisoning you will find general concurrence of this information on page 18 of the attached first section of the report of the Committee on Lead poisoning of the American Public Health Association.*

"In general our industrial sick absenteeism studies of non-occupational as well as occupational diseases have shown that as the occupation of Negro and white male become more nearly alike the magnitude of the excess in the frequency rates of disability among Negroes tends to decrease. This suggests that it is differences in the type of work performed together with the associated socio-economic status rather than race per se which have produced an unfavorable Negro health record when the type of occupation is not held specific.

"If we can be of any further assi[s]tance to you we shall be glad to hear from you again.

*Unusual and unforseen cases of lead poisoning in industry therefore should not be credited to the 'unusual susceptibility' of individuals as they might well have been before the development of adequate methods for detecting lead exposure, but should be regarded as evidence of the existence of dangerous lead exposure and should be investigated thoroughly to establish the source of such exposure."

Very truly yours,
s/ Surgeon General
U. S. Public Health Service"

MS: LH, DI, Central Files. (entry 25) Memoranda, Johnson, George M., Dec. 1941–Dec. 1943.

Memorandum on Section 35(A) of the U. S. Criminal Code

March 10, 1943

To: Mr. George M. Johnson
From: Clarence Mitchell

For a different purpose I requested a copy of Form 732-A which is used by the War Production Board, however, I happened to notice that the following quotation is printed on the form.[1]

"Section 35 (A) of the United States Criminal Code, 18 U.S.C. Sec. 80, makes it a criminal offense to make a willfully false statement or representation to any department or agency of the United States as to any matter within its jurisdiction."

It occurred to me that this particular law might contain other passages which would be helpful to us in preventing violation of Executive Order 8802. Accordingly I am passing it on to you for whatever disposition you believe it merits.[2]
Please return the form to me.
Attachment

SECTION 35(A) U. S. CRIMINAL CODE

[The law, for which the text has been removed, provided for a penalty of not more than $10,000 or a prison sentence of not more than ten years, or both.]

MS: LH, DI, HqR67, Central Files. Reports, U.S. Government-1, General A–M.

1. For the source of this form, see 3/16/43.

2. No evidence has been found that the Committee adopted these provisions into its enforcement efforts.

Memorandum on Additional Members of the President's Committee on Fair Employment Practice

March 13, 1943

To: Mr. Lawrence W. Cramer

From: Clarence Mitchell

Subject: Additional members of the President's Committee on Fair Employment Practice.

I have noted your memorandum of March 13 and wish to suggest the following things:[1]

1. For Chairman of the Committee, it is my belief that Dr. Frank Graham would make the best choice of the three mentioned. While I know him by reputation only, I have been struck with the sense of social responsibility revealed in his opinion on the Little Steel case. I fear that Professor Howard Odom would not have sufficient prestige for the Chairmanship, and I definitely would not recommend Dr. Clark Howell.

2. For members of the Committee, I believe that we need to make a sincere effort to secure some outstanding business men. Accordingly, I have previously recommended Mr. [Clarence G.] Stoll of the Western Electric Company. The company has done an outstanding job as I previously pointed out on the integration of Negroes. Prior to submitting my memorandum, I discussed Mr. Stoll's availability with Mr. Detiz [Dietz] of Western Electric. At that time Mr. Detiz figured that it might not be possible to secure Mr. Stoll. Mr. Detiz felt that if we

could not get Mr. Stoll himself, that Mr. William F. Hossford, Vice President of Western Electric, would be very desirable in that he has maintained a continuing interest in the Negro problem in the plant. Although I do not know either Mr. Stoll or Mr. Hossford personally, I feel that I know enough of the Western Electric people to believe that they are soundly approaching this problem.[2]

I do not know Bishop [Bernard J.] Shiel of Chicago personally, but I have long felt that the addition of some powerful Catholic clergyman would be of great help to our work.[3]

I have known of Mr. [Charles W.] Taussig's work with the National Youth Administration which I believe was of an advisory nature, and, of course, I am aware of Mr. Sidney Hollander's interest.

MS: copy, MP.

The FEPC was at the time soliciting recommendations for additional members of the Committee to submit a slate of nominees to President Roosevelt. The Committee's final list was submitted on 3/1/43 (see Minutes, 3/15/43, in HqR1, Summary Minutes of Meetings). The list and the suggestions submitted by others were ultimately used as a guide for members of the new committee, particularly for the choice of the new chairman, rather than for replacing members who had resigned from the old Committee. Topping the FEPC's list was Senator George Norris, who declined to serve.

Frank Porter Graham, second on the FEPC list, was Mitchell's preferred candidate. He was then a public member of the NWLB. In 1942 the WLB succeeded the National Defense Mediation Board, on which Graham also served. In 1941 the mediation board had developed a "maintenance-of-membership" compromise principle for settling the Snoqualmi Falls strike, involving a lumber company and a union in the Northwest. Rather than supporting union shops (in which all workers must eventually join the union), the formula established that unions could not compel newly hired workers to join, but those who did join were required to maintain their membership for the life of the union contract. The principle was applied in the Little Steel case by the NWLB in 1942 and in several other cases brought before the board. Graham was widely celebrated for devising the Little Steel decision, a compromise that also protected the rights of workers in closed shop situations. The decision guaranteed union membership but included clauses that protected the freedom of choice of individual workers as a means of settling a jurisdictional dispute between employer and union at the Ryan Aeronautical Company. See the text of Graham's decision, "Union Rights in Wartime," in *New Republic,* 6/29/42, 884–87; his letter on the Little Steel decision to *NYT,* 7/25/42, 12; and "Frank Graham: Effective Liberal," *New Republic,* 8/10/42, 164–66.

In addition to several other union-employer cases in which Graham used the Little Steel principle, he was celebrated for his pathbreaking opinion of 6/5/43 in the Southport Petroleum case. It abolished the separate job classifications of "colored laborer" and "white laborer" and declared that all workers must receive the same rate of pay regardless of race. Graham declined nomination to the FEPC owing to his commitments to the NWLB. See Ashby, *Frank Porter Graham,* 171–91; Ross, *All Manner of Men,* 275–76. Mitchell subsequently would cite the unanimous NWLB precedent in the Southport Petroleum case as the standard for eliminating wage discrimination based on race. For the effort to apply the wage ruling to Mexican Americans, see Daniel, *Chicano Workers,* 150–51; Mitchell, speech to National Urban League conference, 9/9/43, Chicago, HqR39, Central Files. Memoranda, Ross, Malcolm, 1944.

None of the persons Mitchell recommended ever became members of the FEPC. Only Graham and Taussig were on the list the FEPC submitted to Roosevelt. For additional information on the candidates, see the biographical directory. For discussions of the difficulty in securing members, particularly for chairman, see Ruchames, *Race, Jobs and Politics,* 54–56; and Daniel, *Chicano Workers,* 134–38.

2. No Western Electric executive ever served on the FEPC. The business leaders appointed to the new Committee were Sara E. Southall of International Harvester and Samuel Zemurray of United Fruit Company.

3. In his memorandum to President Roosevelt of 1/29/43 regarding the Committee, Attorney General Francis Biddle had included among his recommendations for membership the suggestion that "a prominent Catholic" should be included. His nominees in that category included Bishop Shiel, Monsignor Francis Haas, and Archbishop Edward Mooney of Detroit. See Official Files 4245G, Franklin D. Roosevelt Library, Hyde Park, N.Y.; Hardin, "Role of Presidential Advisers," 103–5, 110.

The prominent Catholic clergyman on the FEPC's list of nominees was Monsignor John A. Ryan, the American Catholic Church's leading expert on social and economic questions. He held several New Deal posts and headed the Social Action Department of the National Catholic Welfare Conference from 1920 to 1945. Monsignor Francis Haas, one of Biddle's candidates, ultimately became chairman of the new Committee appointed in May 1943.

Letter to Lee Seitzer on
Discriminatory Practices of Shipyards

March 16, 1943

To: Mr. Lee Seitzer
    Assistant Economic Analyst
    Bureau of Program Planning and Review

From: Clarence Mitchell
    Principal Fair Practice Examiner

Your letter of March 5 requests information on the discriminatory practices of various shipyards against non-whites. I am listing a brief statement concerning the principal yards in each of the areas included in your letter.[1]

1. In Mobile, Alabama, the Gulf Shipbuilding Company employs approximately 50 Negroes, and the Alabama Dry Dock and Shipbuilding Company employs approximately 4,881. In both of these cases there is an unnecessary restriction of the Negro labor supply in that the Gulf Company severely limits the number of Negroes it uses. The Alabama Company does make extensive use of them but it does not give them appropriate upgrading. Neither of the companies make use of Negro women in accordance with desirable hiring standards.

   During recent hearings conducted by the President's Committee on Fair Employment Practice, the Alabama Shipbuilding and Dry Dock, the Gulf Shipbuilding and the Delta Shipbuilding Companies, were directed to change their employment policies so as to conform with the requirements of Executive Order 8802. We are currently working with the Maritime Commission to insure compliance with these directives.[2]

2. In Panama City, the Wainright Shipbuilding Company employs approximately 700 Negroes according to the latest information we have received. We have

asked the Maritime Commission to investigate the failure of this company to make use of Negro women since it currently is hiring a large number of white female workers. There is no indication that Negroes are given adequate opportunities for being upgraded. The Maritime Commission has been asked to investigate this.

3. Our latest reports on the Brunswick Marine Shipbuilding Company of Brunswick, Georgia, shows a total of approximately 700 Negroes employed but they are confined to laboring occupations. The company has indicated that it will hire approximately 2,000 additional Negroes, but its failure to make use of Negroes in skilled jobs unnecessarily restricts the labor supply in the area and also violates Executive Order 8802.

4. In Baltimore, Maryland, the principal shipbuilding companies are the Bethlehem Fairfield, Maryland Dry Dock, and the Bethlehem Steel Shipbuilding Companies. The latest information we have on these companies shows that 2,800 Negroes are employed at the Bethlehem Fairfield Company, the Maryland Dry Dock Company employs 504, and the Bethlehem Steel Shipbuilding Company employs approximately 500 Negroes. We have current complaints against the Bethlehem Fairfield Company for failure to use Negro women.

5. In Pascagoula, Mississippi, the Ingalls Shipbuilding Company employs 1,048 Negroes who constitute approximately 12 per cent of its working force. However, as with the other yards, this company does not give Negroes adequate opportunities for being upgraded.

6. In Charleston, South Carolina, the principal employer of shipyard workers is the Charleston Navy Yard. There are approximately 3,757 Negroes employed. From time to time we have had problems concerning the upgrading of Negroes and having them participate in the various training programs which are set up for servicing the yard.

7. In Hampton Roads, Virginia, both the Norfolk Navy Yard and the Newport News Shipbuilding Company employ large numbers of Negroes. The Newport News Company has approximately 8,230 Negroes employed who constitute 27.4 per cent of its personnel. The Norfolk Navy Yard has 11,223 Negroes who are 26.6 per cent of its personnel. Generally speaking, these two yards seem to be making extensive use of the Negro manpower which is available.

8. In Portland, Oregon, the Kaiser, Oregon, and Willamette Companies employ a few Negroes.

9. At Vancouver, Oregon [Washington], a small number of colored persons are also employed. Recently, when the Kaiser Company was importing a number of persons into the area, restrictions against the use of Negroes were set up. The company contended that this came from the A. F. of L. Boiler Makers Union.[3]

10. In the Seattle-Tacoma area, the Seattle-Tacoma Shipbuilding Company does employ Negroes and had indicated that others will be taken.

11. At Los Angeles, California, the California Shipbuilding Company employs 648 Negroes. I should like to point out that the Moore Dry Dock Company in Oakland employs 3,200 and the Richmond Shipyard is listed as employing 8,300 non-whites. We have some complaints from Negro women at the Moore Dry Dock Company.

12. At Wilmington, Delaware, the principal shipbuilding employer will be the Dravo Company, which has made promises for the use of Negroes and indicates that it is taking them at Nevell Island in Pittsburgh. This company does employ a considerable number of Negroes in various occupations.

13. The Tampa Shipbuilding Company, Tampa, Florida, employs approximately 500 Negroes and we do not have any information on whether they are being given adequate opportunities for being upgraded.

14. In the Philadelphia-Camden area, we have another favorable picture on Negro employment in shipyards. There are approximately 4,300 Negroes working at the Sun Shipbuilding Company at Chester, Pennsylvania, 871 working at the Cramp Shipbuilding Company in Philadelphia, and they are also being used in the Philadelphia Navy Yard as well as in the New York Shipbuilding Company. We do not have current figures on the Navy Yard but the last information showed over 2,000 Negroes employed there. We have no current information on the New York Shipbuilding Company over-all figure, but the NYA has placed Negroes there in critical occupations.

15. At New Orleans, the Delta Shipbuilding Company employs 782 Negroes but has not made use of them in some of the critical occupations. The Higgins Industries also in New Orleans employs 641 Negroes.

16. At Houston, Texas, the Houston Shipbuilding Company employs approximately 1,000 nonwhites, but it does not admit Negroes to its training courses and thereby restricts the available labor supply which might be used in the war effort. The Committee has this under study with the Maritime Commission.

Thank you very much for Form 732-A which was included in your letter.[4]

MS: copy, HqR48, Central Files. Reports, General N–Z.

1. Seitzer's query of 3/5/43 is filed with this text. It indicates that data was wanted for an exhaustive WMC survey of the shipbuilding industry. Despite endemic discrimination, the shipbuilding industry played a key role in providing opportunities for black workers because here the labor market was the tightest. See Weaver, *Negro Labor*, 7, 35–37; headnotes on the Shipbuilding Industry and on the Boilermakers Union.

2. See, for example, Summary of Hearings, Birmingham, 6/20/42, with findings and directions against Delta Shipbuilding Corporation and Local 37 of the Boilermakers Union, in HqR3, Office Files of Malcolm Ross. Will Maslow; and the sources on the hearings cited at 2/5/43 n1.

3. See immediately related texts at 6/28, 8/11, 10/11, 10/18/43 ("Interview with Officials of the Oregon State Employment Service").

4. On this form, see 3/10/43.

Memorandum on Visit to New Britain
Machine Company, New Britain, Connecticut

March 23, 1943

NEW BRITAIN MACHINE COMPANY,
NEW BRITAIN, CONNECTICUT—MARCH 18, 1943

A visit was made to the New Britain Machine Works, New Britain, Connecticut, on March 18. I talked with Mr. R. S. Howe, Treasurer of the Company and Mr. Bishop, Plant Manager.

Before going to the plant I talked with Mr. Paul S. Parsons, Deputy Area Director in New Britain, Connecticut, for the War Manpower Commission. Mr. Parsons stated that the company employs 266 non-whites of whom 14 are listed as skilled, 30 semi-skilled, and 222 unskilled. He added that the company employs 54 Negro women. According to Mr. Parsons, this was one of the first companies to put Negro girls on machine tool operation. He said it is now asking for Negro NYA trainees and will accept them from other areas.[1]

The March 8 totals of the company show that there are 4,106 persons employed of whom 1,878 are skilled, 934 semi-skilled, 1,000 unskilled, and 294 in other jobs.

* * * * * * * * * * * * * *

Mr. Bishop stated that Mr. Bates had been employed at the company for approximately 1½ years and had been rejected by the Army for physical reasons. According to Mr. Bishop, Mr. Bates represents a hard worker but his foreman is supposed to have stated that he does not have the capacity to learn the type of work to which he is aspiring. At this point I read the paragraph of Mr. Bates' letter to us in which the foreman had promised him a job on the assembly line. Mr. Howe then took the position that even though Mr. Bates might be what he described as a "dumb cookie" he should be given an opportunity to qualify for the higher type of job since he had a record of being a good worker.

* * * * * * * * * * * * * *

MS: copy, FEPC FR103, Region XII. Administrative Files (A–Z), Foreign Labor Programs.
   1. This text apparently was derived from one of Mitchell's reports on his visit to New Britain. See memoranda, 5/1, 7/24/43. In letters of 3/3/43 to Iona Morris, executive secretary of the New York local division of the March on Washington Movement, and R. S. Howe, president of the New Britain Machine Company, George Johnson informed them that Mitchell was visiting the city to get a better understanding of the discrimination problems blacks were experiencing at companies there. In a letter

of 3/22/43 to Layle Lane, also of the New York City March on Washington Movement, Johnson reported that as a result of Mitchell's visit to the New Britain Machine Works, the company agreed to upgrade Lonnie F. Bates, whose complaint had sparked the FEPC's investigation. See FEPC FR 103, Region XII. Administrative Files (A–Z), Foreign Labor Programs. See Weaver, *Negro Labor,* 17–18; and the section on Segregation versus Discrimination in the introduction.

Memorandum on Declaration of Citizenship

March 24, 1943

To: Mr. Lawrence W. Cramer

From: Clarence Mitchell

Subject: Declaration of citizenship

While I was in Connecticut, the Managers of the Employment Offices in Bridgeport and Stamford said that they were having some little difficulty with the problem of persons who are unable to secure birth certificates. I raised this question with the managers because some colored persons had mentioned that difficulties were arising.

In Stamford, the Manager stated that he had received a letter from the USES, #B-39. This letter provided for the employer to handle the declaration of citizenship forms rather than the Employment Service. In Bridgeport, the Manager stated that it was not always possible to secure an Army or Navy representative to serve as a witness in the validation of such forms.[1]

MS: copy, MP.

1. Many defense jobs were open only to citizens. Noncitizens had to go through a loyalty review process. Birth certificates and naturalization papers were the customary proof of citizenship, but many African Americans and other poor or rural citizens lacked birth certificates. Their employment was therefore often delayed. Under War Department regulations promulgated 7/16/41 and revised 6/4/42, citizens could submit to employers declaration-of-citizenship forms that had to be certified by local army or navy representatives. Because those representatives were often not available, contractors still had difficulty clearing such workers for employment. See the copy of the guidelines of 6/4/42 in Field Instruction no. 19 in appendix 1. On the employment problems confronting noncitizens and the foreign born, see the headnote on National Origin, Alienage, and Loyalty.

Memorandum on Conversation with Mr. Cy W. Record

March 29, 1943

To: Mr. George M. Johnson
From: Clarence Mitchell

On March 25 Mr. Cy W. Record called me from Atlanta, Georgia, to inform me that he had received a communication from his draft board in Chicago asking him to supply the address of the local draft board in Atlanta which had had him under its jurisdiction. He stated that he had talked with the State Selective Service Director and it appeared that this was some preliminary action which will result in his being inducted into the Army. The Regional Office of the War Manpower Commission has requested a deferment for Mr. Record and he feels that some further action may be taken in his behalf. However, he wanted us to know of his status at this time.[1]

He also discussed the Brecon Bag Loading Company and mentioned that he had recently conferred with the Manager who said that the plant had been awarded an "E" for production. The Manager also expressed satisfaction with the colored employees and promised that others will be hired.

Mr. Record stated that the Bell Aircraft Company is at present only hiring persons for supervisory duties, but to all indications between 25% and 30% of the total personnel will be Negro when the plant reaches its peak employment. He stated that the International Association of Machinists of the A. F. of L. and the Aircraft Workers of the CIO are making certain overtures to Negroes which will result in the inclusion of them in the planning. I.A.M. will make some arrangement for taking care of Negroes, according to Mr. Record, and the CIO has promised them full union membership.

Mr. Record also stated that former opposition to training seems to be disappearing and a great many Negroes are taking part in the courses which are being offered. We discussed briefly the Bechtel-McCone-Parsons situation in Birmingham and he stated that training is being planned for Negroes, but it does not yet seem to be in operation.

MS: LH, DI, HqR38, Central Files. (entry 25) Memoranda, Johnson, George M., Dec. 1941–Dec. 1943.

1. In line with the government's policy regarding federal employees, the WMC had created a committee that requested deferment based on occupation. The WMC sought deferment for the following key persons: the executive secretary, assistant executive secretary, administrative assistants, and principal fair practice examiners. See Mitchell to Cramer, memorandum on staff meeting, 4/28/43, HqR38, Central Files. Meetings. Record did not receive a deferment and served in the U.S. Air Force from 1943 to 1945.

Memorandum on Material to Be Submitted for the War Manpower Commission Report

ROUGH DRAFT

[March 1943]

MEMORANDUM

To: Mr. Theodore A. Jones
From: Clarence Mitchell
Subject: Material to be submitted for War Manpower Commission report.

The following is my suggestion for material which might be submitted in response to the request of Mr. Yoder's office.[1] You, of course, may wish to revise this considerably:

The President's Committee on Fair Employment Practice was established by Executive Order 8802 of June 25, 1941. During the year from April 1942 to April 1943, it handled approximately 7,000 complaints from members of various minority groups alleging discrimination either by war industries or Government <plants> agencies. In addition, between October 1, 1942 and March 1, 1943, over 1,000 reports of discriminatory hiring practices were filed with the Committee by the USES. Such reports are filed only when employers have given an order indicating that vacancies exist but have refused to accept members of a minority group coming within the purview of Executive Order 8802. There has been some improvement in the over-all employment of minority groups in industry but there is still a {widespread} tendency to confine Negroes to unskilled jobs and to exclude altogether {Negro women and} persons who are Jewish or aliens. Generally speaking, the problem affecting another large minority group, namely the Spanish-American workers, is confined to the Southwest. In this area the conditions faced by these workers are very similar to those faced by Negroes in other areas.

A statement made by the Reports and Analysis Division of the Employment Security Office of the Social Security Board in May 1942, showed <out of> in 17,474 establishments there were 5.3% non-white, in July 1942 <out of> in 21,771 industries there were 5.8% non-white, and in November 1942, <out of> in 14,861 establishments, 6% of all employees were non-white. Numerically, the employment of non-whites in May 1942 as shown by the report was 464,095, in July it was 696,338, and in November it was 793,045.

Thus it can be seen that there has been some increase in the over-all employment, and in certain industries the percentage of non-white has been higher than the increase for all industries. <For> An example<s> of <these are> this is shipbuilding, which in July 1942 had 5.7% non-whites. In November, non-whites were 7%.

The Committee has not had called to its attention any special legislative enactments by communities or states which would prohibit the employment of Negroes in war industries. However, there are numerous agreements and constitutional provisions in various organizations which exclude members of minority groups from war employment.

<It appears that the prime problem of minorities at present is obtaining adequate opportunities for upgrading Negroes and Spanish Americans, greater use of Jewish persons and relaxation of discriminatory policies which prevent the employment of aliens {and Negro women.}>

{The prime concern of minorities at present is providing for the full utilization of the skills [illegible] of Negroes through upgrading and training, greater use of Jewish persons and relaxation of discriminatory policies which prevent the employment of aliens and Negro women. The problem regarding Negro women is particularly acute considering present employment shortages and the present emphasis on the integration of women into industry}.

MS: Draft, with emendations in the hand of Theodore A. Jones, HqR48, Central Files. Reports, General D–M.

1. This report was prepared in response to a memorandum of 3/11/43 from Dale Yoder of the War Manpower Commission to George Johnson requesting data for material for a revised version of a report on various agencies known as the Reynolds Report. The request is filed with this text, together with an enclosed "Outline Progress Report for War Manpower Commission, April 18, 1942–April 17, 1943," dated 3/12/43, and a WMC report dated 11/30/42 called "Manpower Mobilization: A Report on Progress and Problems."

Jones wrote his revisions on the text of the draft. Words he crossed out are shown in angle brackets < >. His additions and interlineations are shown in braces { }.

Memorandum on Staff Meeting of March 29, 1943

April 5, 1943

Mr. Lawrence W. Cramer
Clarence Mitchell
Staff Meeting, March 29, 1943.

At the meeting of the staff on Monday, March 29, the following matters were discussed:

1. Mr. Jones discussed the necessity for bringing all correspondence and other action up to date before the transfer of cases between staff members. He also asked that all intra-office conferences and long distance telephone calls concerning cases be made a part of the permanent records of the office by the drawing up of written reports on them. Mr. Jones stated that as of March 31, efficiency rating[s] are to be made on all employees. Special provision is being made for those who have worked less than 90 days. It was also pointed out that a certain amount of absenteeism on the part of staff members should be curtailed. Mr. Jones proposed that occasional general staff meetings be held at which time views could be exchanged between the clerical and professional personnel of the office. All complainant cards are to be checked on April 1. Mr. Jones requested that anyone having uses with such cards at the time of checking should assemble the cases on their desks to facilitate the general statistical count.

2. Mr. Trimble made a report on his visit to the Pittsburgh Plate Glass Plant at Clarksburgh, West Virginia, in behalf of seven Jehovah's Witnesses who had been ordered reinstated by the Committee. He reported that it appeared that the matter was satisfactorily settled and the individuals were to return to work on Monday, March 29. Mr. Cramer stated that apparently the union and management at this company were cooperating with the Committee and seemed willing to work out what had been a difficult problem.

3. Mr. Barron discussed the problem of Seventh Day Adventists and Jehovah's Witnesses in war plants. He pointed out that it had been difficult to establish whether in the case of Jehovah's Witnesses the refusal to purchase war bonds was a creedal tenet. He indicated that a variety of responses had been obtained on that point and also the question of whether the Witnesses were willing to bear arms in defense of the country had not been resolved. Mr. Jones was requested to make an inquiry on the matter of whether the Jehovah's Witnesses were considered conscientious objectors by the Selective Service.

On the matter of Seventh Day Adventists, Mr. Barron stated that he was considering the opinion that unless it can be established that a plant is giving other groups time off for religious purposes, failure to do so for Seventh Day Adventists would not be considered discriminatory. Mr. Cramer pointed out that the War Department gave Sabbatarians time off for worship with the right to make up such time as has been lost. He questioned whether we could ask private employers to do this same thing, however. It was his position that it must be shown that other persons similarly engaged are given time off for worship before discrimination could be shown. It was finally agreed that Mr. Barron and Mr. Cramer would draw up memoranda on this question. These memoranda will be used as a basis for securing a legal opinion from the General Counsel, War Manpower Commission.[1]

4. Mr. Davidson presented a preliminary report on the establishment of intent in complaints in employment discrimination. It was agreed that the report would be distributed among the staff members for discussion at the next meeting. Mr. Fleming made a statement concerning the Detroit area pointing out that cases of 130 companies who had been reported as discriminating through the 510 reports of the USES had not been dealt with by the Detroit staff. With the exception of 9 cases, all complaints which had been handled by the Detroit staff has been settled, Mr. Fleming stated.

Mr. Cramer, speaking of the Detroit hearings, said that such hearings would be held only after it is determined that the contracting agencies had been approached and given an opportunity to make adjustment both at the local or national levels. Mr. Cramer also stated that there should be a record that the contracting agencies have been advised of what steps should be taken to correct a complaint against a company. He agreed, that if, after a reasonable time, contracting agencies did not take action, the Committee would then be willing to hold hearings.

5. Mrs. Lawson suggested some procedures for the Staff Board of Review. She pointed out that when a case is to be submitted to the Staff Board of Review the individual handling it should summarize it so that the Board would have an opportunity to know in brief all things that had gone on in connection with the case. Decisions on whether there should be a hearing should come from the Board as a whole, she stated. When it is decided that a hearing should be held, one person should be given the responsibility for preparing the case and should have a formal plan for the hearing, Mrs. Lawson stated. A history sheet should be kept, and cases should be closed as soon as possible so that the Committee may avoid being called upon to consider collateral issues. Mr. Cramer stated that in the future Mr. Johnson will receive the recommendations of the Staff Board of Review concerning hearings and he will pass on whether they should be held.

It was decided that the discussion on War Manpower Stabilization Plans and Federal Deferment Policy would be postponed until the next meeting. Dr. Landes was also requested to have ready a report on matters involving the Social Security Board for the next meeting.[2]

MS: copy, HqR4, Office Files of George M. Johnson. S, Staff Meetings.
    1. See the headnote on Creedal Discrimination.
    2. For more on labor stabilization plans, see Mitchell to Johnson, memoranda, 1/19, 4/13/43; Weaver, *Negro Labor*, 31–37, 133–34, 140.

Memorandum on Labor Stabilization Plans

April 13, 1943

TO: Mr. George M. Johnson

FROM: Clarence Mitchell

SUBJECT: Labor Stabilization Plans

In accordance with your previous instructions and following conversations with Mr. Jones, this memorandum is prepared for circulation among staff members.

As of March 25, which was the last date on which we had an official War Manpower Commission summary, there were 52 area stabilizations plans in effect and 4 industry plans.[1] The major purposes to be accomplished by such agreements are as follows:

1. Full utilization of local labor.
2. Reduction of shifts between industries on the part of workers.
3. Provision of a system for orderly transfer of workers from less essential to more essential industries.
4. Regulations to govern the importation and hiring of workers in shortage occupations.
5. The use of the United States Employment Service as a central referring agency.

In addition to these factors, the agreements usually carry a provision that any worker who feels that he has been refused employment because of some reason not related to physical fitness to perform a job in question may appeal to the USES for remedy.

The phrasing covering such appeals ranges from a somewhat vague statement such as that in the plan covering the Needle Trades in Greater Boston which is as follows:

"Every possible effort to utilize women, older persons, handicapped persons, and other groups not ordinarily employed shall be made".

to the more comprehensive statement which is found in the Cleveland, Ohio and Louisville, Kentucky, plans which is as follows:

"Any worker applying for employment with an employer engaged in an essential activity in the Louisville Area who feels that he is being denied employment for some reason other than his lack of qualification or physical fitness for performing the job for which he is an applicant or except as required under this plan, may request the United States Employment Service to intercede in his behalf. The United States Employment Service will investigate the facts, and if it concludes that the worker is being refused employment on grounds other than lack of qualification or physical fitness for performing the job or except as required under this plan, it shall endeavor to persuade the employer to reconsider its decision and employ the worker. <u>If an adjustment satisfactory to the worker is not achieved</u>, the case shall be referred to the War Manpower Committee for appropriate action in accordance with sub-paragraph A above".

It will be noted that in the Louisville and Cleveland statement there is a reference to sub-paragraph A. This sub-paragraph relates to appeals procedures which are usually informal and may be taken by any worker who feels he is entitled to such benefit.

The Industry Plans have similar provisions for stabilization of labor, but while the area plans cover a number of industries in a specific geographic area, the industry plans cover a single industry in a number of geographic areas. Thus, the first of the industry plans cover the non-ferrous metals in several Western states.

In areas or industries where stabilization agreements are in effect workers in essential industries must obtain releases from their employers before they can be hired in other plants. If the employer denies a release, the employee may appeal to a Review unit in the USES for permission to change jobs. The following are among the valid reasons for obtaining a release:

1. Competency to perform work requiring a higher skill than that in which the employee is engaged.
2. When the person is employed for less than full time.
3. When wages or working conditions are less favorable than those prevailing in the area (or industry) for similar occupations.
4. Where there is a compelling personal reason for wanting to change.

SUMMARY OF
EMPLOYMENT STABILIZATION PLANS

(Revised March 25, 1943)

AREA PLANS IN EFFECT: 52   *INDUSTRY PLANS:*   4

REGION I

MASSACHUSETTS:

*New Bedford–Fall River
Pittsfield

REGION II

NEW YORK:

Buffalo
Syracuse

REGION III

Covered by Region-wide stabilization policy. Non-piracy agreement in effect in Northern New Jersey Area (Newark Plan.)

REGION IV

MARYLAND:

Baltimore
Cumberland
*Hagerstown

VIRGINIA:

*Hampton Roads

REGION V

OHIO:

Akron
Cleveland
Dayton
Hamilton-Warren County
*Lorain County
Marion County
Mercer County
Portage County
*Sandasky

*Sidney-Piqua-Troy
Springfield
Warren-Niles
Youngstown

KENTUCKY:

Louisville

MICHIGAN:

Battle Creek
Bay City-Saginaw-Midland County
Detroit
Grand Rapids
Muskegon
Monroe County
*Pontiac
Port Huron

REGION VI

ILLINOIS:

Springfield-Decatur

WISCONSIN:

Milwaukee

INDIANA:

Evansville
Indianapolis
*South Bend-La Porte-
  Michigan City

REGION VII

ALABAMA:

Mobile-Gulf Coast

GEORGIA:

Savannah-Brunswick

FLORIDA:

Tampa

REGION VIII

IOWA:	MINNESOTA:	NEBRASKA:
Des Moines	Twin Cities	Omaha

REGION IX

REGION X

TEXAS:

Beaumont

REGION XI

COLORADO:	WYOMING:	UTAH:
*State of Colorado	Cheyenne Area	Industrial Area I

REGION XII

CALIFORNIA:	OREGON:	NEVADA:
*Los Angeles	Portland	*State of Nevada
*San Diego		

ARIZONA:

*State of Arizona   State of Washington

* Copies not yet available

INDUSTRY PLANS IN EFFECT:

Rainwear Clothing Allied Industries—Greater Boston
Thermometer Industry—New York
Non-Ferrous Metals and Lumbering—Regions X, XI, XII
Shipbuilding—Head of the Lakes Area,
Bay Area, San Francisco

MS: LH, IN, HqR1, Office Memoranda. M.
1. For other activities related to labor stabilization programs, see 1/19 and 4/5/43.

Memorandum on Defense Training
in States with Separate Schools

April 16, 1943

TO: Mr. Lawrence W. Cramer
            Executive Secretary

FROM: Clarence Mitchell

SUBJECT: Defense training in states with separate schools.

Statistics on defense training furnished by the U. S. Office of Education for 17 separate school states and the District of Columbia indicate that as of January 31, 1942, there were 4,630 segregated training courses within the area. 4,446 or 96% were for white only, and 194, less than 4%, were for Negroes.

According to the 1940 census, Negroes constituted over 20% of the population in this area. The U. S. Office of Education does not keep statistics by courses any longer so that it would be difficult to make an exact comparison between this figure and present reports on Negroes in training. However, for these states and the District of Columbia, the U. S. Office of Education reports that as of January 31, 1942, there were 2,315 Negroes in training, and as of December 31, 1942, the number of Negro trainees was 6,625.

As of June 30, 1942, there were 29,011 training stations for whites and 2,958 training stations for Negroes. There was no figure immediately available on the number of training stations for whites as of December 31, 1942, but the number for Negroes was 6,340. The U. S. Office of Education believes that the number of training stations for whites will not vary greatly from the figure of 29,011.[1]

MS: copy, HqR1, Office Memoranda. M.

1. The U.S. Department of Education, in not keeping statistics, could have been complying with the FEPC's policy that race, creed, color, and national origin should not be included for identification purposes on application forms. For background on the WMC's "Records of the Bureau of Training," see Zaid, *Inventory,* and 11/28/42 text.

Memorandum on Civil Service Regulations on Japanese Employment

April 17, 1943

To: Mr. George M. Johnson

From: Clarence Mitchell

Subject: Civil Service Regulations on Japanese Employment

I have read the memorandum and material submitted by the United States Civil Service Commission concerning the employment of Japanese who have been in war relocation centers. I have also discussed this matter with Mr. Henderson.[1]

We both agree that Section E on Page 4 should be deleted in that it is a violation of Executive Order 8802.[2] It is also our suggestion that Article (b) under the release marked C3982-9 leaves a wide avenue for discrimination and should be changed.

MS: LH, DI, HqR66, Central Files. U.S. Government, Aliens in Defense, Specific Groups, Japanese.

1. Also in text file are Cramer to Johnson, 4/10/43, with attachment: U.S. Civil Service Commission, 3/27/43, Circular Letter No. 3982, Subject: Policy and procedure regarding utilization of American citizens of Japanese origin in War Relocation Centers. Cramer gave Johnson the circular so that he could have those staff members study it who were concerned with the problems of discrimination against Japanese Americans and in the federal civil service.

2. The Section E to which Mitchell referred said that

[i]f an appointing officer persists in objecting on grounds of their origin to any of these eligibles who have been certified to him, these eligibles should not be recertified to the same appointing officers; reports will be made, however, to the appropriate War Relocation Authority officials in the field or in Washington, D.C., as the case may be, indicating that the appointing officer or agency in question objects to the appointment of such eligibles in order that they may take appropriate steps in the matter. In such cases, however, it will not be necessary to refer them for investigation by the commission in view of the fact that they have already been investigated and cleared as to character and loyalty by the War Relocation Authority procedures.

Memorandum on Agreement on Importation of Bahamian Workers

April 26, 1943

To: Mr. George M. Johnson

From: Clarence Mitchell

Subject: Agreement on Importation of Bahamian Workers.

I have read the material on the importation of Bahamians for work in Florida.[1] I call your attention to Page 213 of the material which contains the statement, "It is expected that the terms and conditions of this agreement will apply with reference to Bahamian workers engaged in other than agricultural work in the United States pursuant to arrangements which may hereafter be made between the two Governments". This seems to indicate there may be a possibility of some of these workers going into some of the war industries. On the whole, I believe that the Department of Agriculture has done a good job in setting up safeguards with the British Government. It is my feeling that we should send them the attached memorandum as soon as I receive their own statement which is on the way.

Attachment

MS: copy, HqR67, Central Files. Reports, U.S. Government, Policies and Agreements between Government Agencies and FEPC.

1. On safeguards related to ensuring that EO 8802 was enforced for foreign workers, see Mitchell to Johnson, memorandum, 6/28/43, and other texts cited there. At a staff meeting on 3/13/43, a motion was passed that: (1) the committee did not favor importation of foreign labor; (2) workers should be imported only after efforts had been made to use local labor. On the broader question of a farm recruitment program, the committee would put pressure on the Department of Agriculture to stabilize wages. HqR38, Central Files. Staff Meetings.

Memorandum on Staff Meeting of April 12, 1943

Date: April 28, 1943

To: Mr. Lawrence W. Cramer

From: Clarence Mitchell

Subject: Staff Meeting, April 12, 1943.

At the meeting of the staff on Monday, April 12, the following matters were discussed:

1. Mr. Jones requested that material for general distribution to the staff be routed through his office in order that all persons will be sure to get such information as is available. He stated that this would avoid duplication of material which is being routed to staff members. Mr. Jones also stated that all interoffice procedures or forms should come to his office for approval. He pointed out that this would also cut down on duplication. Mr. Cramer stated that by all means this policy should prevail. Mr. Jones outlined the present policy of deferment which is followed by the Government with reference to federal employees. He stated that the War Manpower Commission has set up an Agency committee

which requests deferment on the basis of occupational activity. He also defined the various groups into which persons are classified. Mr. Cramer stated that two votes had been received from the Committee approving the use of WMC deferment plans. These called for deferment of key persons who were listed as follows: the Executive Secretary, the Assistant Executive Secretary, Administrative Assistants, and Principal Fair Practice Examiners.

2. Dr. Landes discussed matters involving jurisdiction of the Social Security Board over the State Security Commissions.[1] She outlined a case in Missouri in which an applicant seeking appointment as a Visitor in the Aid to Dependent Children Program, was turned down because of her race. It was pointed out that in Missouri the merit system appears to permit an appointing officer to consider the race of an applicant when making appointments.

It was the general opinion of the staff that such a position by the Missouri officials could be construed as a violation of Executive Order 8802, because the Missouri Commission receives federal funds for carrying on its program. It was agreed to submit the matter to the Committee for approval of further action on it. Mr. Cramer pointed out that the matter was larger than the individual case involved because it was indicative of general discriminatory practices being followed by states receiving federal grants.[2]

3. There was a discussion of labor stabilization agreements of the War Manpower Commission by Mr. Mitchell. It was agreed that a memorandum would be sent to the WMC asking that copies of action taken by area directors on complaints of discrimination be sent to the Committee.[3]

4. Mr. Davidson's discussion on motive as an element of discrimination was postponed until the next meeting.

5. Mr. Cramer reported that the Civil Service Commission has sent a circular containing instructions on methods for releasing Japanese citizens from relocation centers. He stated that so far the new action covers only those Japanese who have been in relocation centers. He stated that it was his understanding that another procedure is being prepared on handling cases of Japanese who have not been in the relocation centers. This material will be sent to the staff for reading and criticism.[4]

7. Mr. Johnson pointed out that as a matter of office procedure it would be advisable to have a limit placed on the number of persons who would sign letters concerning Committee matters. It was agreed that in the Washington office the following persons would sign official communications: Mr. Cramer, Mr. Johnson, Mr. Barron and Mr. Jones. It was also agreed that Mr. Barron and Mr. Jones would work out a statement concerning the method by which cases going to the field would be handled. It was understood that this would not go into effect until it had been discussed at the next meeting.

MS: LH, DI, FEPC RG 228, *Office Files of Malcolm Ross*, box 69, DNA.

1. Created in 1935, the SSB was at this time a subdivision of the Federal Security Agency, which later evolved into the Department of Health, Education, and Welfare. *Congress and the Nation,* 1120, 1226. On the relationship of the Federal Security Agency's functions to FEPC: "The functions of the U.S. Office of Education and the Office of Vocational Rehabilitation in training war workers come under the FEPC responsibility for eliminating discrimination in war training programs. Also the community conditions which are the concern of the Federal Security agencies are important factors in intergroup relations and in the employment of minority workers." See "Federal Security Agency," n.d., HqR5, Office Files of George M. Johnson. Misc.

2. No record of Committee action on this proposal has been found.

3. On labor stabilization agreements, see 1/19, 4/13, and 5/4/43.

4. See the headnote on Japanese Americans.

Memorandum on Compliance and Analysis Report on Six New England Companies

May 1, 1943

Mr. Lawrence W. Cramer

Mr. George M. Johnson

Clarence M. Mitchell

Compliance and Analysis Report on Six New England Companies.

I have noted the recommendations of the Compliance and Analysis Section concerning New England companies I visited in March.[1] While the person making the analysis seems to have made a thorough study of material received, unfortunately all of the material which we have in this office was not presented. My criticisms follow:

1. In the case of the New Britain Machine Company at New <Bridgeport> Britain, Connecticut, we had a complaint from a Mr. Lonnie Bates, who wished to be upgraded. The Compliance and Analysis Section recommended that some follow-up should be made to determine whether Mr. Bates was actually given the opportunity promised him as a result of my visit. There are available, in the file, letters, dated March 22 to Mr. Bates and to Miss Layle Lane of the March on Washington Movement in New York City. There is also a reply from Miss Lane which states: "On Tuesday, March 23 after an interview with his foreman and evidently after Mr. Mitchell's visit, Mr. Bates was transferred to assembling machinery . . . We are grateful to you for your help in this matter."[2]

2. In the case of the Bryant Electric Company at Bridgeport, Connecticut, the Compliance and Analysis Section recommended that correspondence should be initiated with the complainants. The file shows that on March 29, Mrs. Ira

Anderson and other complainants were advised by this office that openings were available to them if they were qualified. An excerpt from Mrs. Anderson's letter is as follows:

"A representative of this office has been in the area and has taken follow-up action in connection with your complaint. The United States Employment Service in Bridgeport has orders from the Bryant Electric Company and other companies in the area. If you are interested in war work, I am suggesting that you register at that office. They will be in a position to refer you to a job if you meet the necessary requirements. Please keep us informed of the developments in your case."

We have had no reply to these letters. In several cases the National Youth Administration has been asked to secure additional colored female workers for this area and the chief limitation is the lack of housing facilities as pointed out in my reports.

3. The Compliance and Analysis recommendation states in the case of Schick Razor Blade Company and Pitney-Bowes Meter Company of Stanford, Connecticut, that a follow-up should be made to determine whether the promise given by the company was given in good faith. I went over this entire situation with the USES and the officials of the local branch of the NAACP. On March 24, we communicated with the NAACP and on March 26 we communicated with the Employment Service. I can see no reason for additional action until such time as additional correspondence has been received by this office.[3]

4. In the case of the Firestone Rubber and Latex Company, the recommendation is that the case be "closed for the present". I am unable to understand this wording because the complainant definitely indicated that she was not interested in securing employment in this company. She also expressed satisfaction with the progress which was made in the employment of other non-whites. It is conceivable that a new case might be opened either concerning this complainant or the company but it is evident that so far as the specific complaint handled is concerned, the matter is permanently closed.

5. Concerning the Aluminum Company of America at Bridgeport and Fairfield, Connecticut, the recommendation was made that correspondence should be continued with Mr. Jacob Porter, a member of the Executive Board of Local 24 of the Aluminum Workers of America for further information regarding the distribution of Negro workers and their opportunities for training. The analysis recommends that follow-up action be initiated as of May 1. There is available in the file a memorandum dated April 2 outlining a conversation between Mr. Porter and me by long distance on March 29. It should be noted that Mr. Porter promised us a written statement concerning the matter he discussed. To date this statement has not been received. In this case Captain W. M. Ingles, who is in charge of Labor Relations of the Air Corps has a copy of my report. This report was furnished him in line with the policy suggested by you (Mr.

Cramer) in the staff meeting of March 29 which provided for use of the local and national representatives of the contracting agencies in settling complaints. At this point I have no reason to believe that the Air Corps is not following through on the matters complained of. In view of the factors involved at the plant, I believe that the date of May first would reveal little, if anything further than what we now know. The complications of the Aluminum Company of America have been clearly set forth in my report dated March 19.[4]

In this case it was desirable for the Compliance and Analysis Section to have discussed these matters with me. It also would have been happier had there been a review of the entire file. To avoid excessive intra-office paper work, I recommend that this be done in the future. I also request that the analyses made be brought into conformity with the available material before the recommendations become a part of our permanent files.[5]

MS: copy, MP.
1. See Mitchell's memorandum of 3/23/43.
2. For an excellent portrait, see Schierenbeck, "Lost and Found."
3. Letters related to discrimination problems can be found in the NAACP general files, II A-661, DLC.
4. Mitchell's report of 3/19 and memorandum of 4/2/43 have not been found.
5. See also Mitchell's report, 5/10/43.

Memorandum on Stabilization Agreements

Date: May 4, 1943

To: Mr. George M. Johnson
From: Clarence Mitchell
Subject:

Attached is a memorandum which we addressed to Mr. Bond, Deputy Executive Director, on April 22, concerning the stabilization agreements. You will note that Mr. Leo R. Werts, Assistant Executive Director, replied to this on April 27. He states that the Regional Directors will meet in Washington this weekend and the question of including the anti-discrimination clauses in stabilization plans will be discussed at that time.[1]

I should like to suggest that either you or Mr. Cramer should be present at this meeting in order that the Directors may have an appreciation of our point of view. I should also like to point out that on April 13, we addressed a memorandum to Mr.

Appley concerning appeals to Area War Manpower Directors on the part of persons who feel that they have been denied employment for some reason other than lack of physical fitness to perform a job. We have not had a reply to this memorandum as yet, but I believe it also should be discussed at the time of the meeting.

If you agree to my suggestions, I will draw up the appropriate memorandum to Mr. Werts. However, it might be better if it were handled as a telephone call from either you or Mr. Cramer.

Attachment

April 22, 1943

TO: Mr. James H. Bond
            Deputy Executive Director
            War Manpower Commission

FROM: George M. Johnson
            Assistant Executive Secretary

SUBJECT: Stabilization Agreements

Under date of April 20 we received copies of stabilization agreements in several areas. We have noted these carefully and find that in several cases there has been no statement which will offer protection to workers who are being discriminated against solely because of their race.

In his memorandum of February 2, 1943, Mr. Appley stated, "We are planning to review every employment stabilization plan to insure its conformity with War Manpower Commission policy. We shall advise the inclusion of an anti-discrimination clause in every plan where this provision is now lacking."

Accordingly, I am calling to your attention the following areas which do not have this provision in the copies which we have received: Lima; Beloit-Jamesville; Canton, Ohio; and Sandusky. We should also like to call your attention to the agreements for Oklahoma City and Hagerstown, Maryland.

In the Oklahoma agreement, there is a statement under "Objectives" which is as follows:

"Complete recruitment, registration, and orderly referral of all possible qualified workers."

Presumably this is designed to include minority groups, but it appears that a more definite and forthright statement should be made. In the Hagerstown agreement there is a statement that employers are to seek maximum utilization of local labor. This also might well be expanded to indicate more clearly that there is to be no discrimination based on race, creed, color or national origin.

A copy of the stabilization agreement for the St. Louis area apparently is incomplete, but such material as we have does not indicate that any safeguards have been included to prevent discrimination based on race, creed, color or national origin.

In view of the fact that we have had considerable difficulty with this area it is especially urged that ample provision be made to prevent needles[s] exclusion of workers for reason not related to their fitness to perform a given job.

I trust that you will take the necessary steps to bring these plans into conformity with the War Manpower Commission policy as outlined in Mr. Appley's memorandum of February 2.

MS: LH, DI, HqR67, Central Files. Reports, U.S. Government, War Manpower Commission.
   1. On stabilization agreements, see also 1/19, 4/13, 4/28/43, and 9/25/44.

Memorandum on Staff Meeting of April 26, 1943

May 6, 1943

To: Mr. Lawrence W. Cramer
From: Clarence Mitchell
Subject: Staff Meeting, April 26, 1943

1. There was a discussion by Mr. Cramer of a memorandum of agreement with the Provost Marshal General's Office. This memorandum deals with the policy of the Government concerning inquiries into race, creed, and color of applicants for civil service employment by agencies investigating loyalty. One important factor in this agreement is that the Provost Marshal General agreed to write into each contract with commercial agencies making loyalty investigations that without the written permission of the President's Committee on Fair Employment Practice, such agencies shall not divulge to any one except the Provost Marshal General's Office or his duly authorized agent, any information concerning race, creed, color or national origin of persons investigated in connection with their consideration for employment. A full text of this agreement was distributed among the staff members.[1]

2. Mr. Jones discussed itineraries of field trips and stated that a form will be drawn up to standardize information left in the office when individuals are in the field.

3. Mr. Barron discussed briefly item 7 of the compliance letter as it related to the USES form 270. He pointed out that in some cases employers have asked to be relieved of supplying statistics and monthly statements because they are already giving such material to the USES.

4. Mr. Davidson pointed out that it was his opinion that the USES could be relied upon to supply as accurate information of this type as any other agency including FEPC. Mr. Cramer also said that the volume of information which could be secured from the various USES offices would be helpful in determining employment trends. Mr. Cramer designated Mr. Jones as a person to work out, with the Employment Service, methods of obtaining accurate and complete employment information on the various war plants on form 270.[2]

4. Mr. Davidson introduced the discussion on motive as an element of discrimination. After considerable expression of opinion, it was decided that this matter would be postponed for further discussion at another meeting.

MS: copy, HqR38, Central Files. (entry 25) Meetings, FEPC.

1. See "Memorandum of Understanding between the President's Committee on Fair Employment Practice, the War Manpower Commission, and the Provost Marshal General, War Department," of March 10, 1943, included in Field Instruction no. 19, 10/4/43, in appendix 1; Cramer's memorandum to all staff members on agreement between the Committee and the Provost Marshal General, 4/27/43, HqR67, Central Files. U.S. Government, War Department A–L. For references to War Department cases investigated under the terms of this agreement, see Mitchell's reports of 1/29 and 2/17/44, and for background, see the section on the War Department in the headnote on Relationships with Federal Agencies.

2. See the sections on WMC and USES in the headnote on Relationships with Federal Agencies.

Memorandum on Employment of Negroes in Street Railways

May 8, 1943

To: Mr. George M. Johnson

From: Clarence Mitchell

Subject: Employment of Negroes in street railways

According to the information from Mr. Brotman,[1] the following is the employment picture of non-whites in the street railway industry.[2]

Mr. Brotman pointed out that the figures are based on sample reports. The same firms do not appear in a sample each month. Hence, while the March percentage is slightly lower than the January percentage, Mr. Brotman felt that this might be due to the fact that different companies were involved and not to the fact that Negroes were employed in fewer numbers.

	Total Employment	Non-white	% of Total
November, 1942	205,064	8,262	4.0
January, 1943	199,372	8,737	4.4
March, 1943	198,730	8,528	4.3

I received the following information on specific cities:

1. Detroit—The Department of Street Railways as of March 31, 1943, employed a total of 7,619 persons. Of these 385 were women and 1,090 were non-white. No figures were available on skilled breakdown for non-whites.

2. The New York City Omnibus Corporation, 605 West 132nd Street, a subsidiary of the Fifth Avenue Coach Company, employs a total of 1,957 persons, 28 of whom are women and 50 are non-white. These figures are for January 19, 1943. The report states that the company has a favorable attitude toward non-whites but does not give a breakdown on the jobs performed by these persons.

3. New York City Board of Transportation, 250 Hudson Street, as of January 23, employed 36,163 persons. There were 1,453 women and 2,260 non-white. There is no discrimination against non-whites in the operation of subways, buses and trolley lines, according to the 270 report.

4. The Triboro Coach Company, 23–29 Vernon Boulevard, Long Island City, N.Y. This is a bus line and as of March 1943 employed a total of 352 persons. 4 women and 4 non-whites. There were no non-whites driving buses.

5. Fifth Avenue Coach Company, 605 West 132nd Street, N.Y.C, as of January 21, 1943, employed a total of 1,213 persons. There are 15 women and 40 non-whites. The company was regarded as having a favorable attitude toward the employment of Negroes. There was no breakdown on jobs performed by Negroes.

6. In Minneapolis, the Twin City Rapid Transit Company as of March 17, 1943, was listed as employing a total of 2,750 persons. There were 115 women and 25 non-whites. The report stated, "The firm is broadminded about non-whites but believes car riding public and employees would resent them". I am unable to understand this information because a Minneapolis paper recently carried an article that a colored man was employed as a street car operator. I will check on this further.

7. The Municipal Railway of San Francisco employed a total of 1,375 as of March 19, 1943. There were 80 women and 16 non-whites. All non-whites are Negroes working in shop and operations. The January 20, 1943 report on this company stated that there were 33 conductors who were women and of these 3 were colored. It also stated that there were two colored motormen. Mr. Wm. H. Scott, 2600 Geary Street, San Francisco, gave this information.

8. The Market Street Railway Company, San Francisco, and the California Street Railway Company, San Francisco, showed no Negroes employed as of March 2 and 10, respectively.

9. The Cleveland City Transit System, 1404 E. 9th Street, Cleveland, Ohio, as of March 17, 1943, employed a total of 4,426 persons. Of these, 60 were women and 325 non-white. The report states that there are 124 non-white motormen and conductors including several non-white women. Mr. Morse W. Rew, Staff Engineer, gave this information.

10. There are no Negroes employed on the Cleveland Inter-Urban Railway, 1600 Terminal Tower. However, this is a small company using only 118 persons.

11. The Philadelphia Transportation Company, 1405 Locust Street, as of March 17, 1943, employed a total of 11,065 persons. There were 1,117 women employed. There are no figures on the number of non-whites.

MS: copy, HqR38, Central Files. (entry 25) Memoranda, Johnson, George M., Dec. 1941–Dec. 1943.
1. Probably Herbert B. Brotman.
2. See the headnote on Street and Local Railways.

Memorandum on Staff Meeting of May 3, 1943

Date: May 10, 1943

To: Mr. Lawrence W. Cramer, Executive Secretary
From: Clarence Mitchell, Principal Fair Practice Examiner
Subject: Staff Meeting, May 3, 1943.

1. Mr. Donovan discussed work stoppages which are caused by the inclusion of Negroes in war plants. He stated that at the Briggs Company there had been a strike which was stopped by prompt union action. In another case involving the U. S. Rubber Company, Mr. Donovan said the President of the United Rubber Workers [Sherman H. Dalrymple] came to Detroit from Akron and insisted that the union officer observe the rights of Negroes who had been upgraded by the company. Mr. Donovan mentioned several other cases in which strikes had occurred. It was his opinion that when these work stoppages take place, the President's Committee should not immediately send its representatives into the plant. He advised the strategy of first mobilizing resources of the WPB, the contracting service agency, and any other Government organization connected with the company. Mr. Cramer mentioned that Mr. J.

Lawrence Duncan of Region V had been working on a current strike which occurred at the Timken Roller Bearing Company, Canton, Ohio. This strike took place because white workers refused to train 27 Negroes who were to be upgraded. After a waiting period of several weeks, management returned the Negroes to their former duties. This resulted in the threat of a strike of the colored employees. Mr. Duncan asked the Negroes to remain on the job and they agreed to do so. It was understood that the Navy Department would insist that the company maintain its promises that these Negroes would be upgraded. Mr. Cramer reported that the Navy Department kept its part of the agreement. However, the Army had the major interest in the plant and this made it necessary to consult the Army representative. Although several calls were made in the Cleveland area, it was not possible to contact the Army representative. The latest information was telephoned into Mr. Cramer by Mr. Duncan at the time of the staff meeting.[1]

2. Mr. Jones presented a plan for referral of cases to the field. This was a joint recommendation made by Mr. Jones and Mr. Barron. After some discussion it was agreed that the proposals would remain in effect for two weeks and would be revised at the expiration of this period, if necessary.

3. Mr. Johnson discussed methods of handling reports which are made as a result of field investigations by Washington staff members. It was his recommendation that when their reports are received by the Compliance and Analysis Section every effort should be made to see that the entire file accompanies the reports. It was also suggested that drafts of communications which are to go to agencies or parties involved should be attached to the reports. Mr. Barron reported that he had drawn up a preliminary set of recommendations for material to be included in reports which would be submitted at a later date.

4. There was some discussion of whether a conference between persons making analyses and the individual making the report should be held. It was agreed that such conferences were desirable at the Washington level.[2]

5. Mr. Johnson raised a question on letters which are sent to field offices for transmittal to companies or Government agencies. In such cases, he said, the file should be returned immediately to Washington so that if companies communicate with the Washington office, the full file will be available for consultation. Mr. Cramer suggested that Mr. Jones should work out a procedure on this.

6. There was also a discussion of using 510 reports as a basis for 1–7 letters to companies. Mr. Johnson suggested that since the 510 report is something more than an ordinary complaint, a special letter should be developed for sending to companies involved.

MS: LH, DI, FEPC RG 228, *Office Files of Malcolm Ross*, box 69, DNA.
   1. See the headnote on Strikes and Work Stoppages.
   2. The issues discussed in points 3 and 4 were raised in Mitchell's memorandum of 5/10/43.

Memorandum on Conditions
at the Alabama Dry Dock and
Shipbuilding Company as of May 31, 1943

June 1, 1943

To: Mr. Lawrence W. Cramer
           Mr. George M. Johnson

From: Clarence Mitchell

Subject: Conditions at the Alabama Shipbuilding and Drydock Company
          as of May 31, 1943.

In keeping with an agreement reached on Saturday, May 29, with CIO officials and Management of the Alabama Dry Dock and Shipbuilding Company, I reported to the yard at 6:00 A M. with the first shift of workers on the above date. From an actual estimate of workers as they left the ferry entering the yard and from official counts made by the company at the request of Mr. J. M. Griser, Vice President and General Manager, 2,100 Negroes reported for duty. This meant that the repair departments of the Company had full compliments of Negroes. It meant that the shipbuilding department was close to 50% normal. I discussed this with Mr. Griser and he expressed satisfaction with the situation. He stated that he suspected some of the workers were remaining off because of a desire to have a holiday. He was optimistic about the possibility of getting all of the Negroes back.[1]

It is my urgent request that no troops be removed from the yard at this point. I talked with Captain Rice who was in charge of the Federal troops at the time I was in the yard on the above date. He stated that there were approximately 150 soldiers per shift. He also added that there were 1,000 men who were being held in reserve at Brookley Field and could be brought in.

The Alabama State Guard was still on duty on streets leading to the yard, but at the suggestion of Dr. Burton Morley, Area Director of the War Manpower Commission, the Alabama Guardsmen had been deployed so that it would not be entirely obvious that a great many of them were on hand. Dr. Morley felt that such dispersal of the troops would serve to make the situation appear less explosive to workers and thereby relieve tensions. There was also some feeling on the part of Mr. Griser and Captain Rice that it would be a good idea gradually to withdraw Federal troops from the yard. From my analysis of the situation, I do not believe that it would be safe to withdraw the troops at any time in the immediate future. It is the general opinion of the people in Mobile that the company guards are grossly inefficient. There is nothing on the record to show that they were in any sense capable of handling the disturbance on Tuesday, May 25, which resulted in the injury of some 50 workers at the yard.

When I discussed this with Mr. Griser, he admitted off-the-record, that the guard force was not an efficient organization. I trust that his confidence will be observed in this statement, but I mention his own view in order that the gravity of the situation may be appreciated. Mr. Griser stated that for some time he had been seeking to raise the wages of the Guards, but the Maritime Commission refused to permit such raises. Later, according to Mr. Griser, the Guards joined the CIO International Union of Marine and Shipbuilding Workers and the Maritime Commission permitted the company to give them a raise in pay. According to the company Vice President, the men are not the most desirable people and he is aware of their shortcomings. I regret to say that in spite of this awareness on his part he did not feel that the Federal troops should long be maintained in the Yard. He expressed the view that it would be more advisable to bring in Alabama State Police to maintain order. He also said that the company plans to organize the guard force so that the nucleus of efficient and capable men will be available for spot assignments on short notice wherever trouble develops in the yard.

After talking with dozens of colored persons and colored leaders in the community, it is my conclusion that Negroes will not feel safe in the yard if Federal troops are withdrawn in the near future. As one of them put it, "When the first soldier leaves, the Negro workers will leave". This is no criticism of the efficiency of the Alabama State Guard, nor is it a criticism of the law enforcement arm of the Alabama State Government, but it is an expression of what I believe to be a practical hazard. If new troubles are allowed it may irreparably set back the labor situation in Mobile. A full report on the investigation is being prepared.[2]

MS: copy, MP.

1. The *Mobile Press*, 5/31/43, reported on the return of African Americans to their jobs nearly a week after they had walked off their jobs owing to racial "disturbances" that had occurred in which "about a score of persons" were injured. Seven National Guard companies were stationed at the yard to assure the workers that they were being fully protected. Urging the African Americans to return to work, Mitchell said he would be present when they did so the following morning. He promised, the newspaper stated, "if you will do your best, Uncle Sam will do the rest." He said the "best cure for trouble is to forget it."

For the social background of the conflict, see Trimble's report "The Community Emergency in Mobile, Alabama," 1/12/42. He said the recent fourfold expansion of shipyard and other war employment had "sufficed to fill this far-from-modern city bank-full." Consequently, there was no place for additional workers to live in the city. "And the crest of the flood is to come." See also editorial, *Anniston Times*, 6/17/42, which urged its readers to support the war mobilization. All are in Trimble Files, IE-2-18-25-3, FEPC RG 228, DNA.

2. See appendix 1 for field investigation report by Trimble and Mitchell, 6/8/43, to which a copy of this memorandum is attached. See also the headnotes on Strikes and Work Stoppages and on the Shipbuilding Industry; transcript of the discussion of the report in Transcript of Proceedings, 7/6/43, 19–46, HqR64, Central Files; Reed, *Seedtime*, 117–22.

Memorandum on Executive Order 8802 as It Affects Bahamian Labor

June 28, 1943

To: Mr. George M. Johnson
From: Clarence M. Mitchell
Subject: Executive Order 8802 as it affects Bahamian Labor

On April 23 you instructed me to review the agreement which had been reached between the British Government and the U. S. Department of Agriculture concerning the importation of Bahamian workers to this country. Mr. William H. Tobert, Assistant to the Deputy Administrator of the Food Production and Distribution Administration in the U. S. Department of Agriculture, forwarded to me a copy of the agreement at my request.

After reviewing it, I drew up for your signature a letter to Mr. Fred Morrell, Assistant Director, Agricultural Labor Administration, U. S. Department of Agriculture, in which we asked what methods were being used to see that the provisions of Executive Order 8802 were carried out since the agreement reached with the British Government contained provision for the observance of the Order.[1] The Agreement also indicated that Bahamian workers might be used in other industries and we asked Mr. Morrell to indicate whether any specific industries or locations were being contemplated as places in which such persons would be employed.

Lt. Colonel J. L. Taylor, Deputy Administrator of the War Food Administration responded on May 14 stating that where Executive Order 8802 is violated, workers would be removed from the area of violation. He also stated that it was not contemplated that Bahamian workers would be used in any work other than agriculture. He stated, however, that if it would be necessary to consider placing any of the workers in any specific industry at a later date, the Committee would be notified.

On June 17, we addressed a letter to Lt. Colonel Taylor in which we requested that the Committee be kept informed of action taken by the War Food Administration in investigating complaints falling within the purview of Executive Order 8802. Colonel Bruton responded to our letter to Colonel Taylor. He stated that the Committee would be kept informed of such complaints and action taken. <u>This information will be furnished on all foreign nationals imported to this country for agriculture work. This will include Mexican and Jamaican nationals as well as Bahamians.</u>

I believe that the attitude of the War Food Administration is one of healthy cooperation on this matter and for this reason I am recommending that no further correspondence be forwarded at this time.

MS: copy, HqR67, Central Files. Reports, U.S. Government, Policies and Agreements between Government Agencies and FEPC.

1. Filed with this document are the letter Mitchell drafted for Johnson to send to Morrell (dated 5/4/43), related correspondence, and the "Agreement for Employment of Bahamians in the United States." For related texts, see also 4/26 and 7/24/43.

Memorandum on Long-Distance Call to Mr. Lewis W. Clymer, Region IX

Date: June 28, 1943

To: Mr. George M. Johnson
From: Clarence M. Mitchell
Subject: Long Distance call to Mr. Lewis W. Clymer, Region IX.

On the above date, I talked with Mr. Lewis W. Clymer, concerning a strike which occurred at the Brand and Puritz Manufacturing Company, Kansas City, Mo.[1] The strike occurred on May 11 when the company attempted to place some of its regular Negro employees on power sewing machine operations. When the white employees went on strike the Negroes were taken off the jobs. However, the company had asked Mr. Clymer to assist in getting priority clearance from the War Production Board so that enough sewing machines could be gotten to start a Negro production unit. I suggested to Mr. Clymer that this would not be a good procedure and indicated that the Committee would take the whole matter up with the War Department. He agreed to this.

Mr. Clymer stated that since the trouble occurred on May 11, he has been able to get the Morgan and Rice Manufacturing Company in Kansas City (Manufacturing WAAC uniforms) to employ Negroes as power sewing machine operators. At present, the company has hired 16 persons for this work, Mr. Clymer stated, and expects to take on a total of 75. The Negroes are working as a separate unit.

We also discussed the Kaiser Shipbuilding Company's recruiting program in Region IX. Mr. Clymer stated that Mr. A.W. Hill, of the Kaiser Company had informed him over the telephone that old hotels were being renovated to house workers pending the completion of Government housing in Richmond, California. Mr. Clymer felt that some of these places could be made available for immigrant Negroes. I suggested that he send a list of people who had been discriminated against by the company's recruiting agent and he promised to do this.

MS: LH, HqR38, Central Files. (entry 25) Memoranda, Johnson, George M., Dec. 1941–Dec. 1943.
1. See the headnotes on Strikes and Work Stoppages and on the Shipbuilding Industry.

Memorandum on Supplementary Training at the Alabama Dry Dock and Shipbuilding Company

[July, 1943]

To: Mr. George M. Johnson

From: Clarence Mitchell

Subject: Supplementary Training at the Alabama Dry Dock and
          Shipbuilding Company, Mobile, Alabama

At my request, Mr. Jack Wolfe who has charge of training for the Maritime Commission, secured information concerning progress of the Alabama Dry Dock and Shipbuilding Company in preparing Negroes for being upgraded.[1] Mr. Wolfe stated that between June 10 and June 24, the company referred 426 Negroes to vocational training in arc welding, acetylene welding, burning, and blue print reading. These persons are referred to the courses through the department heads.

MS: copy, HqR1, Office Memoranda. M.
    1. For overall background and cross references, see appendix 1 for report by Trimble and Mitchell, 6/8/43, and notes; headnotes on Strikes and Work Stoppages and on the Shipbuilding Industry.

Memorandum on Conference regarding Chesapeake and Potomac Telephone Company

July 5, 1943

TO: Msgr. Francis J. Haas and
           Mr. George M. Johnson

FROM: Clarence M. Mitchell

SUBJECT: Conference with Mr. August B. Haneke, Vice President and General
          Manager Chesapeake and Potomac Telephone Company,
          Baltimore, Maryland[1]

The following is my summary of what took place during the conference
we held with Mr. Haneke in the office of the Chairman on Monday, July 5, beginning at 11:00 A. M.

Mr. Haneke was present following a suggestion which he had made that he would like to come to Washington to talk over employment conditions affecting Negroes in his company. Briefly, his position was that the company had made efforts to employ Negroes in jobs different from those previously given to colored people. He indicated that Negroes were being used in the photostatic section of the company, as coin collectors, and in certain occupations involving maintenance of lines. He stated that the company has not employed any Negroes as telephone operators and felt that it could not do so for three reasons:

1. The white operators refuse to work with Negroes.
2. There had been a great deal of community resentment against using Negroes as operators.
3. The persons who would have to train operators refuse to instruct Negroes.

Mr. Haneke stated that the proximity of telephone operators on the job was different from that in any other type of work. For this reason, he said, the Telephone Company could not be compared with other firms in the Baltimore area which are employing Negroes and whites. He expressed a view that the white employees would walk off the job if Negroes were placed as operators. This, he said, would result in a major tie-up of communication facilities.

It was then suggested that since the company was advertising for telephone operators, which Mr. Haneke admitted, that some planning be done for the purpose of determining ways of making use of available and qualified Negroes. The suggestion was made that Mr. Haneke have a meeting with representatives of the President's Committee on Fair Employment Practice and also try to include Mr. Joseph P. Healey, Chairman of the Governor's Commission on Interracial Cooperation in the State of Maryland. Mr. Haneke stated that he knew Mr. Healey but did not feel a conference would accomplish anything. He finally agreed that within a week he would inform Msgr. Haas of his decision on whether a meeting would be held. It was agreed that if the meeting takes place, Messrs. Clarence M. Mitchell and Ernest G. Trimble will represent the Committee.

MS: copy, HqR1, Office Memoranda. M.

Problems with the Chesapeake and Potomac date back to 7/29/42, when the Baltimore Urban League complained about the company's refusal to hire black women as operators. See Muriel Ferris to Joseph Evans, memorandum, 5/28/45, HqR7, Office Files of Will Maslow. Relations with Other Agencies. Other parts of Ferris's background report can be found at 3/13/45 note 4. For Evelyn Cooper's later overview of the industrywide problem, see Telephone Company Cases, 3/7/45, in appendix 1; and for additional background, see the headnote on the Telephone Industry.

1. The Committee considered this case at its meeting on 7/7/43 and formally appointed a subcommittee to work on the problem. See Johnson's memorandum, 7/9/43, HqR3, Office Files of George M. Johnson, Deputy Chairman, 11/41–45, Will Maslow. See also Mitchell to Lewis W. Clymer, WMC regional fair practice examiner, 9/14/43, on subsequent, inconclusive activities, HqR38, Central Files. Memoranda, Clymer, Lewis. Despite the committee's unceasing efforts, Haneke never budged from his refusal to hire blacks as telephone operators. See 3/13/45, note 4.

Memorandum on Complaint of
Mrs. Laurence Walker, Milton, Pennsylvania,
against the Philco Radio Corporation,
Watsontown, Pennsylvania

July 5, 1943

To: Mr. George M. Johnson

From: Clarence M. Mitchell

Subject: Complaint of Mrs. Laurence Walker, Milton, Pennsylvania,
           against the Philco Radio Corporation, Watsontown, Pennsylvania

Mrs. Laurence Walker complained to the President's Committee on Fair Employment Practice concerning several firms in Pennsylvania. One of these was the above mentioned plant at Watsontown, Pa.

We referred this matter to the War Manpower Commission for an investigation and received a report on March 16. The War Manpower Commission indicated that the Superintendent of the Watsontown Ordnance Works stated that there was no discrimination. However, the Area Director of the WMC also said that it was his impression that while there was no convincing evidence that the company had discriminated it was his opinion that Negroes would not find employment at the plant until such time as there was no white help available.

Acting on the strength of this information, we communicated with the company on April 6 in Mrs. Walker's behalf. We received a reply from Mr. A. W. Whitford, Director of Public Relations on April 17. The company denied that it had discriminated against Mrs. Walker, but admitted that it had no Negroes employed at that time. On April 22, we issued a 1–7 letter to the company. The law firm, Souser and Taylor, addressed a letter to us on May 20 in the company's behalf indicating that at least three Negroes have been given employment. Since this did not comply with the requirements of our letter of April 22, a letter was addressed to Mr. Whitford on June 11 releasing the company from supplying information on item 7, but asking for the company's compliance on the other six items. The company complied with the six points, but the specific complainant was no longer available for employment.

MS: copy, FEPC, FR103, Region XII. Administrative Files (A–Z), Foreign Labor Program.

Memorandum on Conference with the
War Department Representatives, July 12, 1943

[July 12, 1943]

To: Mr. George M. Johnson

From: Will Maslow and Clarence M. Mitchell

Subject: Conference with the War Department Representatives, July 12, 1943.

A joint conference was held in the office of Mr. James Mitchell, Director of Civilian Personne[l]. Those present were Mr. Truman K. Gibson, Civilian Aide to the Secretary of War, Mr. Lewis Lautier, Assistant to Mr. Gibson, Lt. Col. John Collins, Mr. John H. Ohly, Mr. Wm. Leland, and Mr. Lemuel Foster, all of Mr. Mitchell's office.

We discussed the offices of the FEPC which will be established in the regions and some relationships which we expect will exist between these offices and representatives of the War Department. Nothing in our conversation constituted a formal agreement but was primarily exploratory, so that we would be in a position to make recommendations to the Committee at the appropriate time.[1]

The following matters were taken up:

1. On Government-owned, privately-operated plants, it was agreed that the present procedure of calling in War Department representatives after preliminary investigations have been completed appears to be working satisfactorily. It was explained tests which have been applied to this agreement have been through the representatives of the WMC who have been doing work for the Committee in the field.

2. On Government-owned, Government-operated plants, it was stated by the FEPC representatives that under the present set up complaints are channeled from the Washington Office of the Committee to the War Department and the latter makes the investigation. This procedure was discussed and the War Department representatives took the position that it should be continued even when field offices are set up. This will mean that complaints against Government-owned, Government-operated establishments would be sent to Washington from the field without contact of the party charged.

3. Privately-owned, privately-operated plants were also discussed. The War Department representatives reaffirmed their previous position that the Committee should exhaust all educative facilities at its resources before requesting assistance from the War Department in securing enforcement of Executive

Order 8802, as amended by Executive Order 9346. Some discussion centered around the R. C. Mahon Company of Detroit. This company has given evidences of refusing to comply with Executive Order 8802, and a request for War Department Cooperation on it was sent by the Committee on June 26. On July 2, Mr. Truman K. Gibson replied, stating that "Your letter of June 15 is not an exhaustion of the persuasive and educational resources at the disposal of the Committee to secure compliance with said Order (9346)."

Those present took the position that in this particular case as well as in the case of the Vultee Aircraft Corporation, Nashville, Tennessee, the Committee had not exhausted all of its educational approaches before referring the matter to the War Department.

MS: copy, HqR67, Central Files. Reports, U.S. Government, War Department A–L.

1. Inherent in this report was the nature of the formal relationship that the new FEPC was establishing with the War Department. During the previous two years, the FEPC engaged in agreements with the major contracting agencies, notably the War Department, the Navy Department, the United States Maritime Commission, as well as with the other major government bodies, such as the War Manpower Commission, dealing with the war. Documents are in HqR38, Central Files. Memoranda, Haas, Francis; with the strengthening of the Committee under EO 9346, which included establishing regional offices in concert with the WMC's regional offices, the agency proceeded to reestablish agreements with the other principal war agencies so there would be a "uniform application" of the president's nondiscrimination policy. See Transcript of Proceedings, 7/26/43, 1–13, HqR64, Central Files; and the section on the War Department in the headnote on Relationships with Federal Agencies.

Memorandum on Strike at American Steel Foundry Plant, East Chicago, Indiana

July 16, 1943

TO: Msgr. Francis J. Haas, Chairman (via Mr. Johnson)

FROM: Clarence M. Mitchell, Associate Director of Field Operations

SUBJECT: Strike at the American Steel Foundry, Cast Armor Plate Plant,
           East Chicago, Indiana

Following receipt of a copy of Mr. J. Edgar Hoover's report on the strike at the above mentioned plant, I checked with Mr. Austin H. Scott of the War Manpower Commission, Chicago, Illinois, via long distance telephone. Mr. Scott stated that he was expecting to have a meeting with the Chicago Urban League on this matter at

3:00 P. M. today. He also said that he expects to have a meeting with the company on Monday, July 19. At that time he will talk with Mr. Rishel, Works Manager.

Mr. Scott stated that the trouble at the plant is a result of an accumulation of grievances. The immediate disturbance occurred early Friday morning on the night shift when a colored man went to a white foreman to complain about the fact that another man was very close to him with an acetylene welding torch. The white foreman and the colored individual who made the complaint got into an argument, Mr. Scott said, and as a result of it the colored man struck the white man. The company guard came on the scene and took the colored man into custody. Later the Negro was turned over to the police officials of the City.

Mr. Scott stated that as Negroes found out about what had happened they protested the arrest of the colored man and suggested that if an arrest had to be made both persons should have been taken into custody. The Negroes then asked that the company intercede in getting the colored man released from jail. When this was refused by the company, the Negro employees walked out, thereby precipitating a strike. Mr. Scott said that the whole strike was of very short duration in that the men went back to work for the most part on Friday night and Saturday morning, July 9 and 10.

Mr. Scott said that Colonel Brawner, Chief of the Labor Branch, Sixth Service Command, is at work on the situation as well as Mr. Thomas Wright, Area Director of the War Manpower Commission. According to Mr. Scott, in November of 1942, Negroes were scheduled for upgrading to jobs as crane oper[a]tors. White employees threatened a strike if this happened. The matter was finally settled and Negroes were placed on crane operations. Later, the company began hiring women and refused to accept colored women. This matter was also ironed out finally.

At present, the men are complaining because they have not had an opportunity to be upgraded to jobs as foremen and in other responsible jobs for which they believe themselves capable. Mr. Scott also said that Mr. Clarence Goins, President of the Local of the United Steel Workers at the plant, has been trying to keep harmony and peace among the persons who work there. However, most of the colored employees come from Chicago, Mr. Scott pointed out, and resent the conditions of discrimination which they say exist in the plant which is located in Indiana. Mr. Scott did not know Mr. Ray Hansbrough, described by Mr. Hoover as a well-known Negro Communist leader in the south side of Chicago. It is my assumption that if Mr. Hansbrough was well known, at some time or other his activities would have come to the attention of the War Manpower Commission. Mr. Scott promised to send us a report on what happens in this matter.[1]

MS: LH, DI, HqR1, Office Memoranda. M.

1. Hoover's report has not been found. For background, see the headnotes on Strikes and Work Stoppages and on the Steel Industry.

Memorandum on Employment Conditions Affecting Negroes in West Virginia

Date: July 19, 1943

To: Mr. George M. Johnson

From: Clarence M. Mitchell

Subject: Employment Conditions Affecting Negroes in West Virginia.

Mr. George W. Streator of the War Production Board informed me on that he was going to Charleston and South Charleston, West Virginia, for the purpose of checking on employment conditions. He stated that he expected to talk with personnel representatives at the following companies:

> Electric Alloid Metallurgical Company
> Carbide and Carbon, Institute, West Virginia
> Carbide and Carbon, South Charleston, West Virginia.

Mr. Streator stated that he would also try to see the U. S. Rubber Company officials when he was in the area.

This memorandum is for informational purposes only.

MS: LH, DI, HqR38, Central Files. (entry 25) Memoranda, Johnson, George M.

Memorandum on Sample of Cases Handled Successfully by the President's Committee on Fair Employment Practice

[ca. July 24, 1943]

TO: Mr. George M. Johnson

FROM: Clarence Mitchell

SUBJECT: Sample of Cases Handled Successfully by the President's Committee on Fair Employment Practice.

In keeping with a request from Father Haas as transmitted by Mr. Malcolm Ross, with Messrs Henderson and Davis, I have prepared the following sample of important cases settled by the President's Committee on Fair Employment Practice during the months of May, June, and July, 1943.

1. HANFORD ENGINEERING WORKS, PASCO, WASHINGTON.

The Committee received complaints from the War Manpower Commission in Region VI (Chicago) and Region IX (Kansas City, Mo.) on June 12, alleging that the above mentioned company was attempting to recruit workers in the Chicago and Kansas City areas but was refusing to accept Negroes solely because of their race.[1] The reason given for refusal was lack of housing for Negroes in Pasco, Washington. The President's Committee on Fair Employment Practice wired the company and obtained a relaxation of the discriminatory hiring specifications. The company hired Negroes from Region IX on June 26. However, it did not recruit either white or Negro workers in the Chicago area, after the Committee had obtained relaxation of the discriminatory hiring practices. This was because of a change in its hiring plans.

2. AGREEMENT BETWEEN WAR FOOD ADMINISTRATION AND BRITISH GOVERNMENT ON IMPORTATION OF BAHAMIANS.

The War Food Administration voluntarily included in its agreement with the British Government for the importation of Bahamian agricultural workers on March 16, a provision that such workers would be given the benefits of Executive Order 8802 (now 9346). Lt. Colonel J.L. Taylor, Deputy Administrator of the War Food Administration, informed the President's Committee on Fair Employment Practice on May 14, that whenever Executive Order 8802 is violated, workers would be removed from the area of violation.

The War Food Administration, at the Committee's request, agreed to keep this office informed of actions taken which fall within the purview of Executive Order 8802. This information will be furnished on all foreign nationals imported to this country for agricultural work. Thus, Mexicans and Jamaicans are also covered by the arrangement.[2]

3. ALUMINUM COMPANY OF AMERICA, BRIDGEPORT, CONNECTICUT.

On March 23, a field visit was made to the above mentioned company to determine three things: 1. Whether in-plant segregation of Negroes was being stopped, 2. whether Negroes would be hired on the basis of ability, and 3, whether colored women would be hired for production work on the same terms as white women. The complaints had been submitted against the company by the Aluminum Workers of America.

The field investigator reported that the company was beginning to hire Negroes without discrimination and to end patterns of segregation. A report from the War Department submitted at the Committee's request dated June 8 stated that in-plant segregation of Negroes had been corrected in the Cylinder Head Magnesium Divisions of the Company; that Negroes were being hired on the basis of ability; and that Negro women were also being hired for production work on the same terms as white women. On June 19, the Committee requested the Bureau of Placement of the War Manpower Commission to obtain statistical data from the Manning Tables and other sources to show the extent of progress in terms of actual figures. This report is now being prepared and there is every reason to believe that the matter has been settled to the satisfaction of all parties.[3]

4. ANGELICA JACKET COMPANY, PYRAMID AND CHAMP MFG. COMPANIES, ST. LOUIS, MISSOURI.

On May 3, the President's Committee on Fair Employment Practice referred to the War Department for investigation complaints of National Youth Administration power sewing machine operators against the above mentioned companies. The companies had not cooperated with the War Manpower Commission in settling the complaints and the next step was to take the matter up with the contracting agency. On July 8, Mr. Lewis W. Clymer, War Manpower Commission representative in Region IX, reported that as a result of the War Department's intervention, the Pyramid Company employed 22 colored women. These women were first used on the night shift on a segregated basis but the owner of the plant found this impractical and integrated them on the day shift. The Angelica Jacket Company is preparing paid training for 30 colored women. The Champ Manufacturing Company agreed to employ workers regardless of race, creed, color, or national origin. Mr. Clymer stated in a telephone conversation on July 19, that the situation was progressing satisfactorily.

5. TIMKEN ROLLER BEARING COMPANY, CANTON, OHIO.

Negroes scheduled to be trained as automatic screw machine operators at Canton were transferred to other duties on April 19 because white operators refused to instruct them. With the cooperation of the War Department and the Navy Department, the President's Committee secured the restoral of the Negroes in training classifications. On July 5, Mr. J. Lawrence Duncan, War Manpower Commission representative in Region V (Cleveland), reported that some of the Negro trainees were in production and others were being trained. Also, on June 12 the Committee received a complaint from the union at the plant that a wall had been erected separating Negro and white women at the Timken Company. Mr. Duncan investigated this at the Committee's request and found that the wall had been erected by the War Department to separate work on confidential contracts from work on unclassified contracts. However, this interfered with the circulation of air and because of the complaints of white women, colored women, the union, and other persons, the wall was taken down.

6. WATSONTOWN ORDNANCE PLANT, WATSONTOWN, PENNSYLVANIA.

The Committee received a complaint against this company on June 28, that Negroes seeking employment were turned down solely because of their race. An investigation was undertaken by the War Manpower Commission in Region III (Philadelphia) at the request of the Committee. The report of the War Manpower Commission stated that it appeared that the company would not use Negroes until the available supply of white workers was exhausted in the area. The Committee instructed the company to comply with the requirements of Executive Order 8802. The company agreed to do so and the last reports as of May 20 show that it is now employing colored persons.

7. COMPLAINT OF JAMES J. KELSICK AGAINST THE SAN BERNARDINO AIR DEPOT.

Mr. Kelsick's complaint was referred to the United States Civil Service Commission and the President's Committee under date of February 12, 1943. He charged that he was discriminated against because of his race in refusal of the Depot to appoint him to the position of Junior Aircraft Engine Mechanic for which he was originally employed. An investigation was made by the Civil Service Commission representative and a report was received on May 6, 1943, in which we were informed that steps were taken to effect appointment to above named position. A letter received from Mr. Kelsick dated May 31, indicated that he had been appointed and was satisfied with the adjustment made.

8. COMPLAINT OF L. HOWARD BENNET AGAINST THE CHARLESTON NAVY YARD, SOUTH CAROLINA.

Mr. Bennet's complaint was referred to the President's Committee on January 18, 1943, on behalf of Negro women who were discriminated against by the Navy Yard solely because of their race. It was referred to the Commandant, Charleston Navy Yard, February 2, 1943. A reply was received from the Commandant on February 12, indicating that steps were being taken to facilitate employment of Negro women. A letter was received from L. Howard Bennet on July 14, stating that Negro women were being employed in occupational classifications about which the complaint was orig-inally made.

9. COMPLAINT OF MARTIN TALL AGAINST THE NATIONAL ROSTER OF SCIENTIFIC AND SPECIALIZED PERSONNEL, WAR MANPOWER COMMISSION.

The investigation of the forms of the National Roster was begun by the Committee on its own initiative, but on July 8, the Committee received through its New York Office a complaint from Mr. Martin Tall against the Roster on account of the ques-tions on race on its application blanks. Conferences were held with Dr. Carmichael, Director of the National Roster, and on July 21, he reported to this office that the ques-tions on race would be stamped off of all questionnaires. Questionnaires already filled in will also have this data stamped off before being sent on to placement officers.

11. PRESS WIRELESS INCORPORATED.

Press Wireless Incorporated, on July 6, agreed to delete all questions relating to race on its application forms.

12. COMPLAINT OF JULIA E. WHITMORE AGAINST WAR DEPARTMENT, CHICAGO, ILINOIS.

On July 4, the complainant wrote that she had been hired by the War Department against whom she had lodged her original complaint and considered her case closed.

MS: copy, FEPC RG 228, Office Files of Malcolm Ross (entry 9), box 67, DNA.

This undated, unpublished memorandum, which includes the names of companies, is a fuller ver-sion of one that Mitchell prepared 7/24/43. At the instruction of Malcolm Ross, Mitchell deleted the names from the version that was distributed for publication. Both texts are in the same file. The FEPC continued to follow a general policy of eliminating company names from its public statements.

1. Hanford Engineering Works was a massive, top secret atomic project under the jurisdiction of the Manhattan Engineer District of the Army Corps of Engineers. In 3/43 it began construction of three nuclear reactors and related facilities and a new "government city" at Richland, Washington. At its peak, it employed 51,000 workers and built housing for 17,500 workers. Plutonium produced at Hanford was used for the first atomic explosion, at Alamogordo, N.M., 7/16/45, and in the bomb dropped on Nagasaki, Japan, 8/9/45. For FEPC efforts to insure minority access to employment in the new industry, see the discussion on the atomic power industry in the introduction. On Hanford, see "Construction of Massive Plutonium Production Complex at Hanford Begins in March 1943," at http://www.historylink.org/essays/output.cfm?file_id=5363; Gannon, Joseph D. Keenan, 4.

2. See also 4/26 and 6/28/43.

3. On this case, for which Mitchell had been the field investigator, see 5/1/43.

Memorandum on Sample of Cases Handled Successfully by the President's Committee on Fair Employment Practice [Revised Version]

July 24, 1943

To: Mr. Malcolm Ross

From: Clarence M. Mitchell

Subject: Sample of Cases Handled Successfully by the President's Committee on Fair Employment Practice.

As you suggested, I have deleted identifying material from these cases which were settled by the President's Committee on Fair Employment Practice.[1]

1. A WESTERN ENGINEERING COMPANY.

The Committee received complaints from two War Manpower Commission Regions on June 12, alleging that a company was attempting to recruit workers for service in a Western area but was refusing to accept Negroes solely because of their race. The reason given for refusal was lack of housing for Negroes. The President's Committee on Fair Employment Practice wired the company and obtained a relaxation of the discriminatory hiring specifications. The company hired Negroes on June 26.

2. AGREEMENT BETWEEN A GOVERNMENT AGENCY AND A FOREIGN GOVERNMENT ON AGRICULTURAL WORKERS.

The Government agency voluntarily included in its agreement with the foreign Government for the importation of agricultural workers a provision that such workers would be given the benefits of Executive Order 8802 (now 9346). The agency informed the President's Committee on Fair Employment Practice that whenever Executive Order 8802 is violated, workers would be removed from the area of violation.

The agency, at the Committee's request, agreed to keep this office informed of actions taken which fall within the purview of Executive Order 8802. This information will be furnished on all foreign nationals imported to this country for agricultural work.

3. A NEW ENGLAND COMPANY.

In March a field visit was made to the above mentioned company to determine three things: 1. Whether in-plant segregation of Negroes was being stopped, 2. whether Negroes would be hired on the basis of ability, and, 3. whether colored women would be hired for production work on the same terms as white women. The complaints had been submitted against the company by the union representing workers in the plant.

The field investigator reported that the company was beginning to hire Negroes without discrimination and to end patterns of segregation. A report from the War Department submitted at the Committee's request dated June 8 stated that in-plant segregation of Negroes had been corrected; that Negroes were being hired on the basis of ability; and that Negro women were also being hired for production work on the same terms as white women. On June 19, the Committee requested the Bureau of Placement of the War Manpower Commission to obtain statistical data from the Manning Tables and other sources to show the extent of progress in terms of actual figures. This report is now being prepared.

4. MIDDLE WESTERN GARMENT MANUFACTURERS.

On May 3, the President's Committee on Fair Employment Practice referred to the War Department for investigation complaints of National Youth Administration power sewing machine operators against the above mentioned companies. The companies had not cooperated with the War Manpower Commission in settling the complaints, and the next step was to take the matter up with the contracting agency. The War Manpower Commission reported that as a result of the War Department's intervention, one company employed 22 colored women. These women were first used on the night shift on a segregated basis but the owner of the plant found this impractical and integrated them on the day shift. A second company is preparing paid training for 30 colored women. A third company agreed to employ workers regardless of race, creed, color, or national origin.

5. A MIDDLE WESTERN WAR PLANT.

Negroes scheduled to be trained as automatic screw machine operators were transferred to other duties because white operators refused to instruct them. With the cooperation of the War Department and the Navy Department, the President's Committee secured the restoral of the Negroes in training classifications. Some of the Negro trainees are now in production and other are being trained.

The Committee also received a complaint from the union at the same plant that a wall had been erected separating Negro and white women. Investigation showed that this wall had been erected to separate work on confidential contracts from work on unclassified contracts. However, this interfered with the circulation of air and because of the complaints of white women, colored women, the union, and other persons, the wall was taken down.

6. A PENNSYLVANIA WAR PLANT.

The Committee received a complaint against this company that Negroes seeking employment were turned down solely because of their race. An investigation showed that it appeared that the company would not use Negroes until the available supply of white workers was exhausted in the area. The Committee instructed the company to comply with the requirements of Executive Order 8802. The company agreed to do so and the last reports show that it is now employing colored persons.

7. COMPLAINT AGAINST A GOVERNMENT AIR DEPOT.

A complaint was referred to the United States Civil Service Commission and to the President's Committee on February 12, 1943. The complainant charged that he was discriminated against because of his race in refusal of the Depot to appoint him to the position of Junior Aircraft Engine Mechanic for which he was originally employed. The Civil Service Commission on May 6, informed us that steps were taken to hire the complainant. A letter received from the complainant stated that he had been appointed and was satisfied with the adjustment made.

8. COMPLAINT AGAINST A NAVY YARD.

A complaint was referred to the President's Committee on January 18, 1943, on behalf of Negro women who were discriminated against by the Navy Yard solely because of their race. It was referred to the Commandant. A reply was received from the Commandant on February 12, indicating that steps were being taken to facilitate the employment of Negro women. A letter was received from the complainant on July 14 stating that Negro women were being employed in occupational classifications about which the complaint was originally made.

MS: copy, FEPC RG 228, Office Files of Malcolm Ross (entry 8), DNA.

1. See the previous memorandum. The FEPC continued to delete identifying material from its general public relations reports.

Memorandum on Proposed Field Trip to Cincinnati during the Month of August for Ernest G. Trimble

Date: July 28, 1943

To: Mr. George M. Johnson

From: Clarence M. Mitchell

Subject: Proposed field trip to Cincinnati during the month of August
          for Mr. Ernest G. Trimble.

In response to suggestions made by Mr. Trimble when he was in Cincinnati during the month of June,[1] a number of organizations submitted what they regarded as flagrant violations of Executive Order 9346. Among the companies accused of discrimination based on race were the following:

The Crosley Corporation	American Tool Company
The Baldwin Piano Company	R. K. Le Blond Machine
The Formica Company	Sebastian Lathe Company
E. Kahn & Sons	Cincinnati Bickford Tool Co.
Cincinnati Milling Machine Co.	Eastern Machinery Co.
Proctor & Gamble Company	E. A. Kinsey Company
U. S. Playing Card Company	Jones Machine Tool Company
American Can Company	Crane & Breed Casket Company
Lodge & Shipley Machine Tool Co.	

It is suggested that Mr. Trimble return to Cincinnati to investigate employment policies of these companies. The following is a brief summary of information we have on some of them from previous contacts:

1. Crosley Radio Corporation employs no Negroes. The company stated on December 17, that it had worked out a program which would provide for the hiring of a small number of colored persons in certain operations where a minimum of "unhappiness will result". There has been no later information to show that the company has hired any Negroes.

2. The U. S. Playing Card Company was reported by the USES to be discriminating against Negroes on September 10, 1942. At the request of the Committee, the company agreed to take certain steps to bring its hiring policy into line with Executive Order 8802. However, recent complaints have been submitted against the company on the ground that it failed to employ colored persons.

3. The Baldwin Piano company was reported to the Committee by the USES on December 8, 1942. The company was charged with submitting a discriminatory hiring order. To date, the company has failed to take the steps requested by the Committee to bring its policy into line with Executive Order 9346.

4. The R. K. LeBlond Machine Company was charged with refusing to employ Negroes in other than laboring jobs. On April 2 a letter was addressed to the company asking for more information but there was no reply.

MS: LH, DI, HqR38, Central Files. (entry 25) Memoranda, Johnson, George M.

1. On Cincinnati, see Trimble's report of 6/28/43, HqR38, Central Files. (entry 25) Memoranda, Haas, Francis; and his subsequent report to George Johnson of 9/10/43, HqR48, Central Files. Company Reports to and from the Field A–J; Mitchell's report of 9/25/43; and the list of his cases of 9/14/43, in appendix 1. Regarding the proposed trip, Johnson told Trimble, "This had better be discussed in connection with the two 'fact finding hearings which are pending on Jehovah's Witnesses.'" See Johnson's memorandum of 7/29/43, filed with this text.

Memorandum on Relationship between Western Electric Company and American Telephone and Telegraph

Date: August 5, 1943

To: Mgr. Francis J. Haas

From: Clarence M. Mitchell

Subject: Relationship Between Western Electric Company and American Telephone and Telegraph

CONFIDENTIAL

This morning, I talked with Mr. Walter Diets, of Western Electric Company, concerning the relationship existing between the above-mentioned companies.[1] Mr. Diets stated that Western Electric is owned by American Telephone and Telegraph. I discussed with him the feasibility of having Mr. William F. Hossford, Vice President of Western Electric, in on the conference with Mr. Gifford. Mr. Diets said that Mr. Hossford has been interested in the whole program of Negro employment in the Western companies, as he mentioned to you previously. He also said that, since he is in the same building with Mr. Gifford, if the latter decided to call him into your conference, it would be very convenient. Mr. Diets stated that it was his impression that Mr. Gifford was aware of the progress made by the Western Electric Company in the use of the Negro employees. He, of course, cannot be quoted on any of this because of his relationship with the company.

I have checked the latest available employment figures on the Western Electric plants in New Jersey, Maryland, and Illinois. They are as follows:

Cicero, Illinois—23,657 total employment, 844 non-white;
Baltimore, Maryland—7,024 total employment, 668 non-white;
South Kearney, Bayonne, Rosselle, and Newark in New Jersey—23,508 total employment, 1,558 non-white.

These figures appear especially significant when it is borne in mind that none of these three plants had more than a hundred Negro employees in 1941. In the New Jersey and Maryland plants, Negroes are integrated throughout the plants. The Baltimore plant is especially progressive in that, in spite of prevailing Baltimore customs,[2] the company has no segregation in its employment of Negroes. All employees use the same restaurants and other facilities.

MS: copy, HqR1, Office Memoranda. M.
  1. For a history of the two companies, see Mitchell, memorandum, 8/26/43; Adams and Butler, *Manufacturing the Future.* For cross-references to other related texts, see the headnote on the Telephone Industry.
  2. For Baltimore customs, see Watson, *Lion in the Lobby,* 81–96.

Memorandum on Alabama Dry Dock and Shipbuilding Company

August 7, 1943

TO: Mr. George M. Johnson
            Assistant to the Chairman
FROM: Clarence M. Mitchell
            Associate Director of Field Operations
SUBJECT: Alabama Dry Dock and Shipbuilding Company

A letter dated August 3, from Mr. J. M. Griser, Vice President of the Alabama Dry Dock and Shipbuilding Company, stated that regulators, caulkers, testers, buffers, and painters are now being added as the work progresses.

In a previous letter dated July 10, Mr. Griser stated, "Negroes are now being employed in the following classifications:

Welders   Chippers
Burners   Erectors
Heaters   Shipwrights
Shipfitters   Groundsmen

In addition, supplementary classes in Blueprint Reading have been scheduled with the Vocational Educational Department of the State. Every encouragement is given to Negroes to avail themselves of the opportunity to take these courses in order that they may better themselves for the trades."

MS: copy, HqR1, Office Memoranda. M.
    This memorandum is a follow-up to Mitchell's field investigation report, 6/8/43, in appendix 1.

Memorandum on Conference Concerning Employment of Negroes as Telephone Operators in Baltimore, Maryland

August 9, 1943

TO: Mr. George M. Johnson
           Assistant to the Chairman

FROM: Clarence M. Mitchell
           Associate Director of Field Operations

SUBJECT: Conference Concerning the Employment of Negroes as
           Telephone Operators in Baltimore, Maryland.

At the request of the President's Committee on Fair Employment Practice the following persons met in the State Office Building of the War Manpower Commission in Baltimore on the above date. Mr. Lawrence Fenneman, State Director of the War Manpower Commission; Mr. Joseph P. Healey, Chairman of the Governor's Commission on Interracial Cooperation in the State of Maryland; Mr. August B. Haneke, Vice President and General Manager of the Chesapeake and Potomac Telephone Company; Mr. Julius M. Gardner, War Manpower Commission; Mr. Kenneth Douty, also of the War Manpower Commission.

Mr. Haneke explained the progress of the Telephone Company in the use of Negro employees.[1] He stated that at present there are about 200 Negroes employed out of a total of 5,500 persons. This represents an increase of approximately 125 colored persons in the past year. Negroes are working as clerical workers in the blue print room, coin box collectors, elevator operators, and there is one crew of Negro linemen. There is also an office located in the Northwestern section of Baltimore completely staffed by colored persons. This office employs approximately 25 persons and telephone bills may be paid there.

Mr. Healey asked for the name of the President of the union representing the operators in the Telephone Company. Mr. Haneke said that this was a Miss Crockin. He did not recall her first name.

During the course of the conference, Mr. Haneke said the Telephone Company was making plans for fuller use of Negroes in Baltimore, but he also stated that there was no plan for using colored operators in the immediate future. Mr. Healey asked what the reason was for not using Negroes as operators. Mr. Haneke replied that the opposition of his employees was the reason. Mr. Healey asked for a chance to talk with Miss Crockin and also an opportunity to go into some of the Telephone Company's buildings, as he put it, to look things over. Mr. Haneke agreed to this. Mr. Healey then stated that he would like to present his findings and suggestions to the President's Committee at its next meeting. I promised that I would lay this before Father Haas on returning to Washington. If it can be arranged, I would suggest that Mr. Healey come in and present the results of his findings to either Father Haas or the full committee.

Mr. Healey expects that a meeting of the Committee will be held in two weeks since I informed him that the Committee appeared to be meeting on that kind of a schedule. This means he will have his report ready within that time.

MS: copy, FR42, Region IV. Active Cases (3–624), Chesapeake and Potomac Telephone Company, Baltimore, Md.

Filed with this text and other related documents are Johnson's instructions to Mitchell of 8/5/43, directing him to hold a conference on the telephone company and submit a summary of the results.

1. See also texts of 12/28/42, 7/5, 9/14/43, 2/5, 12/2/44, and 2/14, 2/20, 3/8, 3/13, 3/15, 5/21/45; headnote on the Telephone Industry.

Memorandum on Complaint of Point Breeze Employees Association

August 16, 1943

TO: Will Maslow

FROM: Clarence M. Mitchell

SUBJECT: Complaint of Point Breeze Employees Association.

On the above date, an individual who identified himself as Mr. Dorsey called from Baltimore with regard to working conditions at the Western Electric Company. Mr. Dorsey stated that his union represents the employees at the Western Electric Plant. At the time of his call, Mr. Dorsey said there were approximately 23 white women in his office who were refusing to work at the company because it did not have separate rest room facilities for Negroes and whites. He wanted to know whether I would come to Baltimore to meet with the union and the plant on this grievance.[1]

He also said that he had been in communication with Mr. Charles W. Mitzell of the War Production Board. Either as a result of his contact with Mr. Mitzell or from conclusions of his own, Mr. Dorsey stated that it was his opinion that if facilities were equal they could be separate.

I told him that the Committee was familiar with the employment job at the Western Electric Company. I stated further that under no circumstances would I participate in a meeting to promote separate facilities for the racial groups employed at the plant. He then stated that the union would possibly ask the National Labor Relations Board for a strike vote on this question. I told him that the National Labor Relations Board would have to speak for itself on how it would handle such a question.

Later I talked with Mr. Stewart Meecham of the National Labor Relations Board and it was his impression that the union could ask for a strike vote on the question of separate facilities. Mr. Meecham expressed the opinion that this would also appear on the ballot,

MS: copy, FR45, Region IV. Closed Cases 108–215, Western Electric Co., Point Breeze Plant, Baltimore, Md.

1. On this case, see Mitchell, memoranda, 8/26, 11/11, 12/14/43, 2/16, 3/14, 4/5/44; headnote on Strikes and Work Stoppages. On the FEPC stand regarding segregation, see the headnote on Jurisdictional Issues and the discussion on the issue in the introduction.

Memorandum on Complaint of the Employees Association of Point Breeze, Md.

August 18, 1943

To: FATHER HAAS

From: Clarence Mitchell

Subject: Complaint of the Employees Association of Point Breeze, Md.

As a follow-up to my previous conversations with representatives of this union, I talked with Mr. Daniel Goott of the War Production Board. Mr. Goott stated that the Western Electric Company was anxious to have a meeting between union representatives and myself on the question of rest room and eating facilities at the company. This conference was originally planned for Thursday, August 19. I suggested that the Committee would not be willing to participate in the conference unless there was a request from the company. Mr. Goott agreed to have the company send such a written request. To date we have not received it.[1] Meanwhile, I talked with Mr. F. J. Bender, one of the regional directors of the CIO, whose territory includes baltimore. Mr. Bender said that the International Association of Machinists filed charges against the Point Breeze Employees Association and the case was heard before the National Labor Relations Board, on July 19. The International Association of Machinists charged that the union was company dominated. As yet, there has been no disposition of this case. Mr. Bender also stated that the United Radio, Electric and Machine Workers of the CIO is negotiating with the locals of the Western Electric Employees Association to take them into the CIO. He said that he expects to have some further word on the status of these negotiations on Thursday, August 19. I will call him at that time. <Meanwhile, the workers at the company are back on the job.>[2]

MS: copy, FR45, Region IV. Closed Cases 108–215, Western Electric Co., Point Breeze Plant, Baltimore, Md.

1. See Mitchell, memorandum, 8/26/44, and notes.

2. Additional minor cross-outs, insertions, and corrections that Mitchell marked on this text have been entered without comment in accordance with his directions.

Members of the Non-Partisan Committee, a group challenging the Point Breeze Employees Association's demands for separate facilities, alleged that the PBEA had stirred up the segregated facilities issue in an effort to prove its independence from management and offset the challenge from the Machinists' union and the CIO. See related texts in FR45, Region IV. Closed Cases 108–215, Western Electric Co., Point Breeze Plant, Baltimore, Md.

Memorandum on Complaints of Sabbatarians

Date: August 23, 1943

To: Mr. George M. Johnson

From: Clarence M. Mitchell

Subject:

Attached is correspondence concerning complaints filed by Sabbatarians who desire to have time off on their regular Sabbath.[1]

As you know, the Navy Department has ruled that its shore establishments cannot make the necessary adjustments to provide for such time off during the present emergency.[1]

On August 14 a similar statement of policy was made by the Bureau of Engraving and Printing.[2] Mrs. Marjorie Lawson prepared an extensive memorandum on this subject, which was submitted to Mr. Harry I. Barron on June 12.[3] Apparently no action was taken on it. I should like to know if it would be possible for the Committee to give consideration to this problem and make a statement of policy which will be useful as a guide to the men in the field.[4]

Attachment

MS: copy, HqR67, Central Files. Reports, U.S. Government-1, Policies and Agreements between Government Agencies and FEPC.

Copies of the correspondence from and on behalf of Sabbatarian complainants are filed with this text.

1. For statements of naval policy regarding time off on the Sabbath or on religious holidays, see especially Ralph Bard to Lawrence Cramer, 12/4/42; Secretary of the Navy to All Shore Establishments, 12/17/42; Harry B. Mitchell to Cramer, 4/20/43, all in HqR67, Central Files. Reports, U.S. Government, Navy Department; Secretary of the Navy to All Shore Establishments, 7/6/43, HqR67, Central Files. Reports, U.S. Government, Religious Discrimination.

2. Statement not found.

3. Lawson's memorandum not found.

4. Possibly a final version of Rough Draft of Operations Bulletin Re: Sabbath Observers and Absences for Religious Purposes, n.d., a copy of which is in HqR4, Office Files of George M. Johnson, 11/41–10/44, Applications: Applications for Employment.

Memorandum on Complaint of the Point Breeze Association against the Western Electric Company, Baltimore, Maryland

August 26, 1943

George Johnson

Clarence Mitchell

Complaint of the Point Breeze Association

Against the Western Electric Company, Baltimore, Maryland

On August 16, Mr. V. L. Dorsey, Director of the Point Breeze Employees' Association, which is an independent Union representing persons working at the Western Electric Company, called me from Baltimore, Maryland.

Mr. Dorsey stated that 23 white women were in his office and they refused to work at the company because separate rest room facilities were not provided for Negroes and whites. He asked whether I would come to Baltimore to meet with Union and Company representatives to discuss the problem. I informed him that in my opinion, the Western Electric Company is doing an excellent job of integrating Negroes on the basis of ability to perform vital war work and there should be no change in its policies. These policies currently provide that Negroes and whites use the same restaurant and rest room facilities. Mr. Dorsey stated that his Union was informed by the War Production Board in 1942 that under Executive Order No. 8802, separate facilities could be established for Negroes if such facilities were equal.

I declined to attend any meeting unless the company extended an invitation. Later, Mr. Daniel D. Goott of the War Production Board in Washington called and asked me to attend a conference on Thursday, August 19, at the company. I requested Mr. Goott to have the company verify this in a letter to this office. No meeting was held on the 19.[1]

The white employees returned to their jobs and are now working. This was confirmed by Mr. C.C. Chew, Superintendent of Industrial Relations at the Western Electric Company, when I talked with him on Tuesday, August 24, by telephone. Mr. Chew stated that trouble began on Thursday, August 12, when a colored woman inspector was placed with 35 whites. Some of the whites refused to work with the colored employee and the company told them they would either work or be dismissed. The employees left the job and stayed off three days, but finally they returned. Mr. Chew stated that in his opinion, the Executive Order would be violated if there were any separate facilities for colored employees. I said nothing to change this impression.

I believe that the company has taken a very desirable position on this matter. However, the Union has prepared a lengthy brief opposing the company policy. It will be appreciated if I may convey to the company and the War Production Board some affirmative statement of the position the President's Committee takes on this matter. For your information, I am attaching a copy of a letter on this matter from Mr. C. W. Mitzel, Regional Labor Representative of the War Production Board, to Mr. Carl Belschner, who wrote in behalf of the Union on June 25, 1942. Mr. Belschner addressed his letter to Philadelphia, but it was referred to Mr. Mitzel who is in Baltimore.[2]

MS: copy, HqR77, Office Files of Eugene Davidson. Follow up.

1. See Mitchell, memorandum, 8/18/43.

2. For correspondence initially referring the issues of this case to the WPB, and from there to FEPC, see C. E. Belschner to E. Browning, 6/25/42; J. M. Pohlhaus to C. E. Belschner, 7/2/42; C. W. Mitzel to J. P. Casey, 7/6/42; Robert J. Glenn to Robert Weaver, 7/15/42; Weaver to Lawrence Cramer, 7/29/42, all in HqR38, Central Files. Memoranda A–C.

In his letter to James P. Casey, WPB regional labor representative, Mitzel, the WPB field representative in Baltimore, noted that the issues were: (1) whether, under EO 8802, setting up separate washrooms, toilets, locker rooms, and cafeterias for black workers would be considered discrimination; and (2) whether the union was compelled to admit blacks as members. The union said its members did not object to working with blacks, but they felt that the company "should not impose socialization and fraternization with the colored race upon the white employees." Management did not want to bear the cost of setting up separate facilities; it also told the union that unless it admitted blacks to membership, it could be held in violation of EO 8802. In an undated letter to Belschner, Mitzel quoted Casey's response, that separate facilities would not be a violation because there was no mention of facilities in the executive order but "merely that there should be no discrimination in the employment of workers because of race, creed, color, or national origin." In his letter to Belschner, Pohlhaus, Maryland's commissioner of labor and statistics, also explicitly stated that separate facilities were not discriminatory and that unions were free to refuse admission to anyone, without regard to race, nationality, or creed. These officials were basing their views on the 1896 *Plessy v. Ferguson* case, in which the U.S. Supreme Court declared the "separate-but-equal doctrine" constitutional, and which the NAACP did not succeed in completely overturning until *Brown v. Board of Education* in 1954. The FEPC challenged successfully the right of the WPB to make rulings regarding the terms of the executive order, and the WPB staff was instructed not to make statements regarding it.

For summaries of the views of the union and management at the Point Breeze plant as expressed at a WLB hearing on the case, see Mitchell to Maslow, memorandum, 11/11/43. For additional related texts, see FR45, Region IV. Closed Cases 108–215, Point Breeze Plant, Baltimore, Md., and Western Electric Co., 4-UR-126; for background, see the headnote on Strikes and Work Stoppages. For discussions on segregation, see the headnotes on Jurisdictional Issues and on Relationships with Federal Agencies, as well as the introduction.

Memorandum on Complaint of Miss Estelle L. Lingham vs. the Civil Service Commission

DATE: 9/1/43

TO: The Files

FROM: Clarence M. Mitchell

SUBJECT: Complaint of Miss Estelle L. Lingham vs. the Civil Service Commission

Miss Lingham came into the office on Wednesday, August 18. She was formerly employed at the Adjutant General's Office but obtained leave in order to take a training course for Photogrammetrists at Bryn Mawr College. She stated that the members of her class were referred to employment, but she was told by Mr. Edwin Watson Instructor Representative of the Engineering Science Management War Training Program, that it would be necessary for her to obtain her own job through the Civil Service Commission.

Miss Lingham stated that, when she sent [went] to the Civil Service Commission, it was suggested that she visit a number of Government establishments in Washington. She did not visit many of these because, in her opinion, it was not practical.

I talked with Mrs. L. M. Bienz concerning this case. Mrs. Bienz told me that Miss Lingham's name has been certified to an agency for appointment. As yet, the agency has not indicated whether it will accept her services. I informed Miss Lingham of this and suggested that she get in touch with me again at the end of two weeks.[1]

MS; LH, FR85, Region IV, Closed Cases. Civil Service Commission, Washington, D.C., 4-GR-128, Estelle Lingham.

    1. The following handwritten notation appears at the bottom of the text: "Miss Lingham called on 9/7 to state that she had been called to an agency to be interviewed on 9/8." For the final disposition of the case, see Mitchell, memorandum, 9/23/43.

Memorandum on War Production Board Report on Jones and Laughlin Steel Plant, Aliquippa, Pennsylvania

September 4, 1943

To: Messrs. Johnson and Maslow

From: Clarence M. Mitchell

Subject: War Production Board Report on Jones and Laughlin Steel Plant, Aliquippa, Pennsylvania

On Friday, September 3, Mr. Daniel Goott, of the Labor Production Division of the War Production Board, called me concerning the Jones and Laughlin Steel Plant at Aliquippa, Pennsylvania.[1] He stated that approximately three weeks ago 450 colored persons employed in the fourteen-inch bar mill of the Jones and Laughlin Plant walked off the job and charged that the company did not promote Negroes properly. The workers also said that the company was guilty of other forms of discrimination, according to Mr. Goott.

Mr. Goott stated that this matter was handled by Mr. Joseph Koeval, Pittsburgh representative of the Labor Production Division of the WPB, and Mr. George Woomer, Commissioner of Conciliation for the U.S. Department of Labor. Both Mr. Koeval and Mr. Woomer were successful in getting men to return to work, Mr. Goott said, and promised that an effort would be made to adjust the grievances.

After negotiations with the company, Mr. Koeval and Mr. Woomer were unable to obtain adjustments of the men's grievances, according to Mr. Goott. At the time of his call, Mr. Goott said there was a threat of a second walk-out by the Negro employees. He requested me to look into this matter to determine whether the President's Committee could assist in preventing a second walk-out and, also, adjust the valid complaints of the workmen.

On Saturday, September 4, I talked with Mr. G. James Fleming, in the Philadelphia office, by long distance concerning this matter. I gave him the facts and suggested that he use his own judgment in handling the case. He stated he would discuss it with the proper War Manpower Commission officials before taking any action (in keeping with WMC Agreement). I also informed Mr. Goott of my talk with Mr. Fleming, and the former stated he would inform Mr. Koeval of my action. I then talked with Mr. Howard Colvin, Acting Director, U. S. Conciliations Service, Department of Labor. Mr. Colvin said that he would inform Mr. Woomer of the Committee's interest in the case and suggest that Mr. Woomer get in touch with Mr. Fleming.

Mr. Goott informed me that Mr. Joseph Krivan, of Local 1211 of the Steel Workers, CIO, in Aliquippa, was working on the problem. I attempted to call Mr. George Weaver, colored representative of the CIO, to inform him that Mr. Fleming is now at work on the matter. Mr. Weaver was not in his office but Mrs. LeBaron Stinnett, Secretary to Mr. James Carey of the CIO, stated that she would inform Mr. Krivan by wire that Mr. Fleming had the matter before him for further action.

Mr. Fleming called back on Saturday, September 4, and stated that he had discussed the Jones and Laughlin case with Mr. Reginald Johnson, Minorities Representative in the War Manpower Commission at Philadelphia. According to Mr. Fleming, the WMC has been working on this case for almost a year and there does not seem to be much of a change in the circumstances. The basic complaints are as follows, according to Mr. Fleming.

The colored employees charge that:

1. They are excluded from the seamless tube mill;

2. Negro employees in the fourteen-inch bar mill do not have adequate opportunities for promotions;

3. The company does not employ colored women on production work;

4. Negro employees are not permitted full participation in safety meetings, and frequently whites are asked to remain for further deliberation in such meetings after the Negroes leave;

5. The Negro workers oppose the maintenance of separate rest rooms for the two races.

Mr. Fleming said that Mr. Patrick Fagan, Area Director of the War Manpower Commission in Pittsburgh, agreed to make an immediate check on current conditions at the plant. Mr. Fagan is supposed to inform Mr. Fleming through Mr. Johnson of WMC of the status of the problem. Mr. Fleming said that he expects to be in Aliquippa on Monday to make a first-hand appraisal of the problem. He will observe the terms of our agreement with the War Manpower Commission when in Aliquippa.

MS: LH, DI, HqR63, Central Files. Tension Reports, Region III.

1. On Jones and Laughlin, see Mitchell, memoranda, 9/4/, 9/9, 9/14, 9/29/43; report, 5/1/44; for overall background, see the headnotes on Strikes and Work Stoppages and on the Steel Industry.

Memorandum on Jones and Laughlin Steel Plant, Aliquippa, Pennsylvania

September 9, 1943

TO: Messrs. Johnson and Maslow

FROM: Clarence M. Mitchell

SUBJECT: Jones and Laughlin Steel Plant, Aliquippa, Pennsylvania

As a follow-up on his investigation of the War Production Board's report of a possible strike on the part of colored employees at the Jones and Laughlin Steel Plant, Aliquippa, Pennsylvania, Mr. G. James Fleming called on Wednesday, September 8. He stated that Mr. Fagan of the War Manpower Commission in Pittsburgh did not report on conditions at the company. Mr. Reginald Johnson stated that "No news is good news," Mr. Fleming said.

However, Mr. Fleming talked with Mr. Koeval of the War Production Board in Pittsburgh, and the latter felt that, while there might not be any immediate walkout of the men, the situation is critical. Accordingly, Mr. Fleming said he would leave Philadelphia on Friday night for Aliquippa. He stated that he would have a conference with plant employees and Mr. Koeval of the WPB on Saturday.

If it is necessary to deal with the Jones and Laughlin company, Mr. Fleming stated he would not do so until he had cleared with the War Manpower Commission in accordance with the Agreement.

MS: LH, HqR38, Central Files. Memoranda, Johnson, George M., Dec. 1941–Dec. 1943.
    See the headnotes on Strikes and Work Stoppages and on the Steel Industry.

Memorandum on Conference with Admiral C. W. Fisher, Chief of Shore Establishment, Navy Department

September 13, 1943

TO: Messrs. Ross and Maslow

FROM: Clarence M. Mitchell

SUBJECT: Conference with Admiral C. W. Fisher,
                Chief of Shore Establishments, Navy Department

On the above date, a conference was held with the following persons in Admiral Fisher's office: Captain C. M. Simmers, Assistant Director, Shore Establishments (Extension 5988, Room 2032); Captain A. K. Atkins, Labor Relations Section, (Room 2026); and Commander D. G. Click, Industrial Relations Section, (Room 2414, Extension 4868). The attached statement, prepared for Regional Directors, was discussed. This statement is a condensation of previous major agreements and correspondence with the Navy Department for the guidance of the Regional Directors of FEPC.[1]

In general, it was agreed that:

1. At the Washington level, Captain Simmers would be the individual to contact concerning Government-owned and Government-operated establishments. Captain Atkins would handle Government-owned, privately-operated establishments;

2. In the field, Regional Directors of FEPC would deal with the Naval Inspectors-in-Charge in Government-owned, privately-operated plants. Admiral Fisher agreed that, if the Naval Inspector-in-Charge is not available and waiting for him would unduly delay proceedings, the FEPC Regional Director would be free to deal directly with the party charged. In privately-owned and privately-operated plants, Admiral Fisher felt that it would be desirable for the FEPC Regional Director to inform the Naval Inspectors at the plants of problems which violate Executive Order 9346. If this does not result in any success, the matter would then be sent to Washington, D. C., to be handled by the Washington office of the Committee with the Navy Department.[2]

Attachment

MS: copy, HqR67, Central Files. Reports, U.S. Government, Navy Department.

1. Statement not found. For the context, see the Navy Department, War Shipping Administration, and Maritime Commission in the headnote on Relationships with Federal Agencies.

2. Filed with this text is a follow-up memorandum from Fisher to Maslow listing government-owned, privately operated plants under the Navy Department's supervision.

Memorandum on Complaint of Miss Estelle Lingham against the U. S. Civil Service Commission

DATE: 9/23/43

TO: Files

FROM: Clarence M. Mitchell

SUBJECT: Complaint of Miss Estelle Lingham against the United States
           Civil Service Commission

It will be noted from the copy of the attached correspondence from Mr. T.L. Sharkey in the War Department, Army Map Service, that Miss Lingham was notified to report for an interview within five (5) days after September 3.

Miss Lingham informed me that she did report for the interview but felt that she was kept waiting for such a long time that it would not be desirable for her to remain at the Army Map Service office. I checked with Mrs. L. M. Bienz, of the United States Civil Service Commission, on this, and Mrs. Bienz stated that Miss Lingham had left before the person assigned to interview her could have a conversation about her case. According to Mrs. Bienz, the individual who was to interview Miss Lingham was in a conference at the time of the complainant's visit.

Miss Lingham also informed me that she was not interested in working at that particular office of the Army Map Service because it was some distance from transportation facilities. Accordingly, I suggested to the Civil Service that her name be sent to another agency for possible hiring. Mrs. Bienz informed me that this would be done.

I called Miss Lingham on September 15 and told her that her name would be certified to another Government agency.[1]

Attachment

MS: LH, DI, FR85, Region IV. Closed Cases, Civil Service Commission, Washington, D.C., 4-GR-128, Estelle Lingham.

1. According to the final disposition report on this case, 6/10/44 (filed with this text), Miss Lingham was ultimately employed as an engineering aide in the Alaska branch of the Interior Department at the appropriate salary for her position. The correspondence with T. L. Sharkey has not been found.

Memorandum on Personnel in Region V

September 25, 1943

TO: Mr. Will Maslow
Director of Field Operations
FROM: Clarence M. Mitchell
SUBJECT: Personnel in Region V.

After reviewing the problems which will be faced by the Regional Director in Cleveland, it is my impression that we should give consideration to the following matters:

1. Region V is divided into three (3) distinct areas. One of these is the State of Michigan; the other is Cleveland and the northern part of Ohio; and the third is Cincinnati and the State of Kentucky.[1] In these areas, the problems are so different that they will require careful attention at the local level on the part of some individual who understands the forces at work in the specific areas and who is able to get the confidence of the local people.

2. I was in Detroit for a brief period only. But, during that time, I heard many statements and reports concerning the Committee from local citizens. These

persons were friendly to our program but felt that considerable prestige had been lost because there had been no hearing. It is my opinion that a strong individual should be appointed in this area who will secure the cooperation of the unions and civic groups in the area.[2]

3. At present, Mrs. Lethia Clore, formerly of the New York office, and Mr. Daniel R. Donovan, of Washington, are assigned to Region V under Mr. McKnight. In neither of these cases, did the Regional Director have an opportunity to decide whether the individuals would fit the needs of his program. For this reason, I strongly recommend that, for the additional vacancy now in the Cleveland region, Mr. McKnight's judgment be the controlling factor in selection. It is also my belief that this vacancy should be filled with the understanding that the individual would be assigned to Detroit.

4. There is need for an additional person on the staff who would devote time to the Cincinnati and Kentucky area. In my opinion, if it is possible for us to obtain additional space for the Region, this should be gotten in Cincinnati and the person appointed should be stationed there to handle the Cincinnati, Dayton, Springfield, and Kentucky areas.[3]

MS: copy, HqR38, Central Files. Memoranda, Maslow, Will, 1943.

1. On recent investigations in Cincinnati by Ernest Trimble, see 7/28/43, 9/14/43, in appendix 1.

2. The first FEPC was planning for hearings in Detroit when it was replaced by the new committee. Examiners G. James Fleming and Jack Burke had been in the area preparing cases, but the FEPC did not believe that strong cases against the larger companies had yet been developed. The issue of discrimination in the area became more sensitive that summer after the Detroit riots. In 9/43, the FEPC opened a Detroit office headed by an examiner in charge, Edward M. Swan, a Michigan native. No hearings were held in Detroit until 6/45. See memoranda of 1/18, 4/5, 9/28/43 and Office of Labor Production report, 7/13/43, in appendix 1; Maceo Hubbard's analysis and the Committee's discussion, all of which was devoted to Detroit, in Transcript of Proceedings, 5/17/43, 2–69, HqR64, Central Files.

3. In late 1944, the FEPC opened a Cincinnati office under Harold James. Lethia Clore and Olcott Abbott were transferred from Cleveland as his assistants. Kersten, *Race, Jobs, and the War*, 90–91.

Memorandum on Candidates for Region X

9/27/43

Mr. Will Maslow

Clarence M. Mitchell

Candidates for Region X.

I have read Dr. Castanado's memorandum, dated September 20, in which he discusses the relative merits of Mr. L. W. [V.] Williams and Mr. Beatty, candidates for appointment in his office. I do not know either of these men personally, but, on the basis of all that I have been able to learn from persons in Texas, I would like to recommend Mr. Williams.[1]

The majority of our complaints against war industries and Government agencies in Dallas come from persons who are either in or closely connected with the Dallas Negro Chamber of Commerce. Mr. Williams, himself, has sent us a series of letters on training problems in the area and his interest is of long standing. I discussed him with Mr. Maceo Smith of Dallas, Texas, recently, and Mr. Smith felt that Mr. Williams would do a very good job.

I believe that, because Mr. Beatty has arrived in Texas only recently, there may be some local discontent in Dallas and Fort Worth if he is appointed ahead of an individual who is qualified and who has been in the area for a long time.

MS: copy, HqR38, Central Files. (entry 25) Memoranda, Maslow, Will, 1943.

1. In a 9/25/43 report, Castañeda noted that he had submitted a report on 9/20 regarding the interview of Williams and Beatty. He strongly recommended that the Committee appoint either Williams, Beatty, or John W. Rice, a third candidate, "at as early a date as possible" because it would "soon become essential to the work of this [regional] office to have a Negro Field Examiner." Williams obtained the position.

In the same report, Castañeda asked for suggestions on how to handle the employment of civilians on military stations in the area, such as Normoyle Ordnance Depot and Kelly Field. When African Americans and Latin Americans complained about discrimination based on national origin, they were "immediately charged with insubordination, lack of respect to military officers, or some other breach of discipline, and discharged." Once a civilian employee was fired for any of those reasons, he explained, it was "next to impossible to secure a reconsideration of the case." HqR55, Central Files. Reports, Weekly Reports—Chronological, Week Ending Sept. 25, 1945.

Memorandum on Ford Motor Company, Willow Run Plant

DATE: 9/28/43

TO: Mr. George M. Johnson

FROM: Clarence M. Mitchell

SUBJECT: Ford Motor Company, Willow Run Plant.

CONFIDENTIAL
= = = = = = = = = = = = =

On returning to the office, I noted that the Committee voted to give consideration to complaints filed against the Ford Motor Company and suggested that an FEPC representative confer with a designated Ford personnel representative in the future on these complaints.[1]

While in Detroit on September 23, I talked [with] Mr. Cushman, Area Director of the War Manpower Commission, concerning the Ford plant. Mr. Cushman felt that the complaints against Willow Run would have to be considered as entirely separate from over-all hiring policies of the Ford Company in its other Detroit establishments. He also said that approximately twenty per cent of the Ford personnel in other plants is made up of Negro workers.

Mr. Duncan informed me that a number of the Negro employees at the Willow Run plant were ready to quit during the week prior to my visit to Detroit. These workers felt that transportation to the plant and lack of housing made it very undesirable as a place of employment, according to Mr. Duncan. He said that union officials at the plant had succeeded in persuading the workers to remain on the job.

MS: LH, DI, HqR3, Office Files of George M. Johnson. M.

1. According to Weaver, who was active in the early negotiations with Ford, "Although many automobile plants hired colored skilled and semi-skilled production workers during the 1920's, the general pattern in the industry at the outbreak of the second World War was to restrict Negroes to foundry, general laboring and janitorial assignments. The one outstanding exception was the Ford Motor Company, where in 1941 the 11,000 Negro workers made up over 12 percent of the total number of workers, and where there was the bitterest opposition to organized labor. At the Ford plants, while there were colored production and highly skilled workers, the majority of the Negroes were concentrated in the foundry, thus, to a degree, reflecting the general pattern in the industry." Weaver, *Negro Labor*, 63.

As Mitchell indicated, Ford's new Willow Run bomber plant presented a special problem, especially after the company, by the end of 1942, reversed its comparatively progressive policy and virtually ceased hiring African American males. That year Ford exacerbated racial tensions throughout the Detroit area when it began hiring large numbers of women for Willow Run and sought to keep the workforce lily white. Ford's action triggered not only vehement protests from black trade unionists and local black organizations but mass demonstrations as well. The exclusion of black women workers was the norm among Detroit's defense industries, but Willow Run was particularly important because in the past the company had hired black labor, and the plant was enormous. Now, though, Ford made only token concessions to the FEPC, local black residents, and black union leaders. For an extended account of the confrontation, see Hill, *Black Labor*, 136–56.

This report by Mitchell does not by itself show how, or the extent to which, black Detroiters drew the FEPC into the Willow Run battle. Historically noteworthy was that before the creation of the FEPC, Robert Weaver was the most important African American in the federal bureaucracy leading the struggle against employment discrimination. At Willow Run, though, his accommodating style contrasted sharply with the militancy of local blacks, especially the Detroit NAACP branch, so much so that the FEPC eventually disregarded his counsel to "withhold action" on the NAACP's request for intervention. Perhaps a reason for Mitchell's restrained report was that he respected Weaver highly. Watson, *Lion in the Lobby*, 122–34.

The Willow Run battle was particularly important because the initiative was being taken by black leaders of UAW Local 600. It underscored the difficulty that black women encountered in getting jobs in defense industries. It again showed the extent to which the FEPC had been constrained by Paul McNutt in the WMC (in part using Weaver for that purpose at Willow Run). Not until after Roosevelt heeded black protests and removed the FEPC from within the WMC and gave it control over all discrimination cases was the FEPC able to address the Willow Run complaint.

After weeks of agitation, McNutt approved the FEPC's requests for hearings on Ford's discrimination policies. The company then began hiring black women, a few at Willow Run. Despite even more bitter racial challenges at Ford, however, the FEPC never held the hearings. Meier and Rudwick, *Black Detroit*, 150–51. For a broader picture of the FEPC's role in seeking jobs for blacks in Detroit, see Kersten, *Race, Jobs, and the War*, 94–111. The only hearings the FEPC held in Detroit were those involving, not manufacturing, but Local 229 of the Teamsters Union headed by Jimmy Hoffa and the trucking industry in 1945. See the section on the Teamsters in the headnote on the FEPC and Unions.

Memorandum on Progress Report from G. James Fleming on Jones and Laughlin Company, Aliquippa, Pennsylvania

DATE: 9/29/43

TO: Mr. Will Maslow

FROM: Clarence M. Mitchell

SUBJECT: Progress Report from G. James Fleming on Jones and Laughlin Company, Aliquippa, Pennsylvania, 3–BR–209.

On September 27, Mr. Fleming called me from Philadelphia to say that Mr. Manley of his office is in Aliquippa with representatives of the Army, Navy, and U. S. Conciliation Service on the complaints of Negro workers in the company's fourteen inch bar mill.[1]

According to Mr. Fleming, there was a work stoppage of Negro employees on Sunday, September 12. At that time, employees were protesting against failure of the company to upgrade them. Mr. Fleming said that a schedule of promotion has been drawn up by the company and currently the workers are being asked to approve it.

Mr. Fleming stated that Lt. Hewitt is representing the Navy, Captain Gallup is representing the Army, and Mr. Woomer is representing the Conciliation Service.

MS: copy, HqR48, Central Files. Reports, Fair Employment Practice Reports 1, G. James Fleming.
    1. See Mitchell, memorandum, 9/4/43.

Memorandum on Conference of the National Urban League

10/8/43

Mr. George M. Johnson
Clarence M. Mitchell
Conference of the National Urban League

In accordance with previous requests from the National Urban League, I spoke at two closed sessions of the conference on September 29 and 30.[1]

The conference members seemed anxious to cooperate with the President's Committee and were friendly in most of their expressions concerning our work. There was one statement which was made by Mr. Lester Granger, Executive Secretary of the National Urban League, which was, in my opinion, somewhat misunderstood. Mr. Ivan Willis, Manager of Industrial Relations for the Curtis Wright Corporation, was on a panel with me, as was Mr. Walter Hardin of the United Auto Workers. Mr. Willis stated that it was regrettable that in some cities the Urban League was encouraging Negroes to join unions although, in some instances, such labor organizations did not have good records on the race question. Mr. Granger arose to answer this statement by Mr. Willis. In his answer, the Urban League executive stated that the League is not pro-labor and it is not pro-management. He stated, also, it is not pro-Government as such. Mr. Granger pointed out that the first interest of the Urban League centered around the Negro and his problems. In further explaining this point, Mr. Granger said that the League is not rushing to jump on the band wagon of those who want a permanent FEPC because it was not altogether certain that the FEPC should be permanent.

On the following day, Mr. J. A. Thomas, Industrial Secretary of the National Urban League, stated that recently an official of the National Association of Manufacturers had suggested that, if the FEPC were abolished, the N.A.M. would be able to handle the integration of Negroes into industry. Mr. Thomas said that he reminded the official of N.A.M. that prior to the time the FEPC was set up, the League had approached the Association and asked that some action be taken on problems of discrimination. Mr. Thomas said at that time, the N.A.M. had insisted it did not have any responsibility for such things.

Mr. Granger's statement in its proper setting and Mr. Thomas' observation seemed to be well-balanced, and, in my opinion, did not show the League to be anti-FEPC, as it is my understanding some persons have implied.

MS: copy, HqR38, Central Files. (entry 25) Memoranda, Johnson, George M., Dec. 1941–Dec. 1943.

1. In his speech, Mitchell emphasized the importance of the unanimous order of the NWLB on 6/7/43 to the Southport Petroleum Company of Texas City, Texas, to grant wage increases to its black workers that would "place them on a basis of economic parity with white workers in the same classification." His main focus, nevertheless, was on the widespread "racial friction" that was occurring because of the "great shifts in our population" brought about by the "the demands of war." Where violence occurred, he said, "the Federal Government, citizens of local communities, the unions, representing workers in industry, and the law enforcement officers" had "the challenging responsibility of seeing that mob violence" did not interfere with war production. Mitchell's speech, "Government's Responsibility in the Present Industrial Picture," was published in the NUL's report on its conference. HqR39, Central Files. Memoranda, Ross, Malcolm, 1944.

Memorandum on Regional Office, Chicago, Illinois

DATE: 10/8/43

TO: Mr. Will Maslow

FROM: Clarence M. Mitchell

SUBJECT: Regional Office, Chicago, Illinois

I visited the regional office of the Committee in Chicago from Wednesday, September 29, through Saturday, October 2. While there, I had an opportunity to go over the general setup of the office, look at the filing system, and get some idea of how it was run. I was very favorably impressed with the manner in which everything is set up.

Mr. Henderson seems to enjoy wide community support, and the opening of the office was well publicized in English and foreign language papers. He has also established a working relationship with the Civil Service Commission, and Captain Richard E. Haugh, Assistant Chief of Labor Office, Sixth Service Command, has submitted a favorable report on conferences he has had with Mr. Henderson concerning the working relationships between the Committee and the War Department in the region. Mr. Henderson stated that the Regional Director of the Civil Service Commission is sending in to Washington a plan of working relationships between the Committee and the Civil Service Commission in the region. As soon as this is approved, we will have copies, if Mr. Henderson has not already sent them.

Apparently, a favorable relationship will exist between Mr. Henderson and the War Manpower Commission, but the latter agency is somewhat upset in that state directors are being appointed. It is not clear how much influence these directors will have, but certainly their appointment will in some way affect our operations.[1]

Mr. Davidson had requested that I discuss with Mr. Henderson some matters pertaining to the structure of reports and the sending in of docket cards. I did so while in Chicago.

Mr. Henderson informed a number of Government officials of the opening of the Committee office. Upon receiving this information, Mayor Edward J. Kelley acknowledged it and expressed a desire to give to the Committee full cooperation. Mr. Henderson will meet with Mayor Kelley for a conference during the week of October 11. He is sending us a copy of Mayor Kelley's letter for our files.[2]

MS: LH, DI, HqR38, Central Files. (entry 25) Memoranda, Maslow, Will, 1943.

1. See discussion on the War Manpower Commission and on the United States Civil Service Commission in the headnote on Relationships with Federal Agencies.

2. Henderson met with Mayor Kelly on 10/13/43. His summary of the conference, dated 10/15, is in HqR51, Central Files. Region VI, Reports, Sept. 1943–Mar. 1944. On the FEPC office in Chicago, see Kersten, *Race, Jobs, and the War*, 47–59.

Memorandum on Conference with Frank Rarig, Regional Director, WMC, Minneapolis, Minnesota

Date: 10/8/43

TO: Mr. Will Maslow

FROM: Clarence M. Mitchell

SUBJECT: Conference with Mr. Frank Rarig, Regional Director, WMC, Minneapolis, Minnesota.

In company with Mr. Henderson, I visited the office of Mr. Frank Rarig on Monday, October 4.[1] Our discussion centered around the Operating Agreement between WMC and the Committee. Mr. Henderson will submit a complete report later.

In general, it appears that the WMC of Region VIII will be very cooperative, but Mr. Rarig did not seem to be enthusiastic about the prospect of having a regional representative of the FEPC stationed in Minneapolis. It was his feeling that the affairs of Region VIII could be handled very effectively from the Chicago office of the Committee.

I have known Mr. Rarig for a number of years and feel that he will cooperate whether or not we establish an office in Minneapolis.

MS: LH, DI, HqR38, Central Files. (entry 25) Memoranda, Maslow, Will, 1943.

1. See discussion on the War Manpower Commission and on the United States Employment Service in the headnote on Relationships with Federal Agencies.

Memorandum on Field Visit to Dallas, Texas

DATE: 10/11/43

TO: Mr. Will Maslow

FROM: Clarence M. Mitchell

SUBJECT: Field Visit to Dallas, Texas

The following are items which should be taken up by me with Dr. Carlos Castaneda and his staff, in accordance with our conversation on the above date:

1. Supplementary to your memorandum of October 6, it should be suggested that the Acting Regional Director refer to state agencies only such complaints as indicate discrimination in employment outside of the jurisdiction of FEPC. Other types of discrimination should be turned over to state agencies only upon request. Care should be exercised in the wording of all official documents.

2. Field visits, as proposed in Dr. Castaneda's memorandum of September 3, may be made with the understanding that Mr. Cochran will remain in the Dallas office while Dr. Castaneda is in the field. The field visits to Louisiana should be handled by Mr. Cochran on Dr. Castaneda's return.

3. Supplementary to your memorandum of September 17, the Acting Regional Director and his staff may contact parties charged in accordance with the terms of Committee agreements with other Government agencies.

4. A review of conditions in the shipbuilding and maritime industry should be made by the Dallas office to determine whether the requirements of Executive Order 9346 are being met.[1]

5. I am carrying with me correspondence from Mr. Louis Lautier regarding the USES at New Orleans. This correspondence outlines discrimination based on race, and it is your suggestion that Mr. Cochran may be able to follow up on it when he is in Louisiana. In this connection, you desire a review of the portion of our agreement with the War Manpower Commission dealing with areas in which there are separate offices of the USES.[2]

6. It is your suggestion that there should be a special discussion of Field Instruction Number 21, dealing with satisfactory adjustment of complaints.[3] You also desire a statement on what has happened in connection with the investigation at Vanadium, New Mexico.[4]

MS: LH, DI, HqR48, Central Files. Reports 1–2, Southwest.

1. See the headnote on the Shipbuilding Industry.

2. See discussions on the War Manpower Commission and on the United States Employment Service in the headnote on Relationships with Federal Agencies.

3. For Field Instruction no. 21 on Satisfactory Adjustment of Complaints, 10/9/43, see HqR78, Field Instructions, 8/43–5/45, no. 20–39.

4. On Castañeda's investigations, see the headnotes on Mexican Americans, on the Mining Industry, and on the Oil Industry. For Mitchell's report on Vanadium, see 10/12/43.

Memorandum on Field Visit to Dallas, Texas

Date: 10/12/43

TO: Mr. Will Maslow

FROM: Clarence M. Mitchell

SUBJECT: Field Visit to Dallas, Texas

On the above date, I visited the Dallas office to confer with Dr. Carlos Castaneda, Acting Regional Director, and his staff. Messrs. Clay Cochran and Leroy V. Williams, Fair Practice Examiners in Region X, were also present. The latter had not been cleared by the Civil Service Commission at that time. I discussed in detail the ideas contained in my memorandum to you dated October 11, 1943, entitled Field Visit to Dallas, Texas. I also left cases 10-GR-60, 10-BR-61, 10-GR-62, and 10-GR-63 with Dr. Castaneda, as stated in my memorandum to him dated October 12, a copy of which is attached.[1] The following things were agreed upon during our conferences:

1. Mr. Cochran is making a field trip in Texas beginning today (October 12). He will give special attention to the complaints we have received against the Consolidated Aircraft Company of Fort Worth, and the Gulf, Texas, Sinclair, Shell and Humble Oil Companies in Houston. Mr. Cochran is also scheduled to review the problems affecting minority groups in the shipbuilding industries of Texas. It is Dr. Castaneda's belief that settlement of the complaints we have against the oil companies and Consolidated will do much to convince residents of Texas that the Committee will make an effort to adjust grievances properly presented. Both he and Mr. Cochran felt that many persons in the area are reluctant to submit complaints because they fear that nothing will be done about these complaints and, in addition, the complainants may be the victims of reprisals by the parties charged. Mr. Cochran is to visit the cities of Houston, Corpus Christi, Galveston, and San Antonio.

2. It was agreed that, following his clearance by the Civil Service Commission, Mr. Williams will make a field trip to Louisiana for the purpose of working on complaints which we have in that area. It was my suggestion that it might be well to have Mr. Cochran assist him in making contacts with the parties charged in that area after he had completed interviews with complainants.

3. We discussed the hiring policies of the North American Aviation Company and the Lockheed Aviation Company, both of which are in Dallas. Dr. Castaneda and Mr. Williams felt that North American is making some progress in the hiring and upgrading of Negroes. There was no information on the policies of Lockheed, but Dr. Castaneda stated that it did not appear that this company was using colored employees. It was agreed that a careful check would be made on both of these plants to insure full compliance with Executive Order 9346.

4. We discussed the field visit Dr. Castaneda made to Vanadium, New Mexico. He stated that his particular interest was the case of Arnulfo Holguin (10-BN-57), who is employed in the Ground Hog Unit at Vanadium. Dr. Castaneda said that his investigation of this complaint revealed general discrimination in five other mines in the area.[2]

5. Dr. Castaneda informed me that the War Manpower Commission was preparing instructions for its state offices, based on the Operating Agreement between the Committee and WMC. I read over some of these and felt that they appeared to be in keeping with the over-all agreement. However, it was my suggestion that he send copies of the revised instructions in to Washington before giving final approval to them. It appeared that WMC Form 42, providing for reports on discriminatory training practices, had not been sent to Region X by WMC at the time of my visit.[3]

6. The regional office will shortly be housed with other Government agencies in Dallas. It was my suggestion that adequate provisions be made for both of the examiners in the new office. This meant the construction of a partition in one of the larger rooms which would enable Mr. Cochran and Mr. Williams to have some privacy when interviewing complainants or conducting other official business.

Attachment

MS: LH, DI, HqR48, Central Files. Reports 1–2, Southwest.

1. Attachment not found.

2. On these investigations, see the headnotes on the Mining, Oil, Aircraft, and Shipbuilding Industries and on Mexican Americans.

3. See discussions on the War Manpower Commission and on the United States Employment Service in the headnote on Relationships with Federal Agencies.

Memorandum on Interviews with Officials of the Oregon State Employment Service

Date: 10/18/43

To: Mr. George M. Johnson

From: Clarence M. Mitchell

Subject: Interviews with Officials of the Oregon State Employment Service

On the above date I talked with Mr. Emory R. Worth, director of the Oregon State Employment Service, and Mr. Theodore Huff, placement supervisor in the Portland Office of the U.S.E.S.

Mr. Worth stated that he did not know a great deal about the hiring policies of the Kaiser Companies outside of the Portland Area and the State of Oregon because these had been handled largely out of the office of Mr. L. C. Stoll, area director of the War Manpower Commission. In some instances, Mr. Worth said, the officials of the Kaiser Company had been able to initiate clearance for hires outside of the state by going to Washington and the U.S.E.S. would find out about the recruiting of workers when new persons would arrive in area to ask for certificates of availability. These certificates, Mr. Worth explained, are supposed to be given to workers when it has been ascertained that they are coming into the area for the first time or that they are entitled to a release from an employer in the area.

The director of the U.S.E.S. also said that he did not know what special agreements exist between the Kaiser Company and the W.M.C. because these agreements were made with Mr. Stoll. In this connection I believe that I should point out that Mr. Stoll has been out of the city since my arrival, but he returned this morning and I am to have a conference with him on Thursday morning at 11:00 a.m. (October 21). Mr. Kenneth Smith, who was formerly in charge of work on minorities problems for the U.S.E.S., has resigned and is now the director of a U.S.O. in Portland. Apparently, the W.M.C. and the U.S.E.S. have not given his duties to any one person. This means that the latest information is somewhat sketchy.

The following information was obtained from the U.S.E.S. 270 reports for September, 1943, on the employment of non whites in the companies named in our complaints.

OREGON SHIPBUILDING CO.
PORTLAND, ORE.

One year ago	Current Employment
Total—33,774	33,665
Women—1,390	8,452
Non-white 95	552

KAISER (SWAN ISLAND YARD)
PORTLAND, ORE.

One year ago	Current Employment
Total—7,158	26,115
Women—276	7,958
Non-white 35	520

KAISER COMPANY (VANCOUVER YARD)
VANCOUVER, WASHINGTON

One year ago	Current Employment
Total—14,900	33,265
Women—695	8,780
Non-white 20	1,631

COMMERCIAL IRON WORKS

One year ago	Current Employment
Total—3886	8,916
Women—75	1,224
Non-white 25	(Info. Not Available)

A brief description of how persons seeking work in these yards are employed is as follows. Persons employed from the local area must have clearance from the U.S.E.S. and subsequently join the union covering their particular line of work. If they seek pre-employment training they are referred directly to such training by the United States Employment Service. If they seek training on a paid basis then they must first be cleared by a union. Thus, in the case of persons seeking paid training in trades covered by the boilermakers, it has been possible for the union to stop their employment in the Oregon Shipbuilding Company, the Commercial Iron Works and the Swan Island Yard of the Kaiser Company. These persons have been directed to the Vancouver Yard of the Kaiser Company where they were given clearance by Auxiliary A—32 of Subordinate Lodge 401. Later some of them managed to shift over to the Portland Companies, but the complainants allege that the reason so many Negroes work in Vancouver and so few in Portland is because of this practice on the part of the boilermakers. Later in this memo I will indicate how the U.S.E.S. tends to confirm these allegations on the part of the complainants. Persons coming into the area are usually transported from the point of arrival by the Kaiser Company to the U.S.E.S. where they receive certificates of availability from the employment service. They are then carried to the Union hall where they obtain clearance from the Union covering their trade. Later, they must join the union. There may be some slight variations from this procedure, but in general this apparently is the practice according to information that I have from the U.S.E.S. and the complainants. Because of the close relationship between the companies and the unions, any exceptions appear to have the consent of the union.[1]

When I talked with Mr. Huff (Earlier I learned that the statement appearing on the 510 report attributed to Mr. Knapp, who was then manager of the U.S.E.S., was really made by Mr. Huff and Mr. Knapp merely signed it) he stated that he prepared the statement included in appendix A of material given to me in Washington (See page 5 item 9 Re; Irving Johnson). Mr. Huff said that repeated efforts had been made to end the discrimination by the boilermakers and there did not seem to be any progress. Therefore, he decided to follow the path of least resistance and refer the Negroes to the Vancouver Yard of the Kaiser Company whenever they came under the jurisdiction of the boilermakers. Mr. Huff stated that he would be willing to testify at the hearing, if we obtain the permission of his superiors. He expressed the view, however, that his testifying might weaken his relationships with the unions. It is my suggestion that one of the lawyers talk with him before we decide to call him as a witness.

I obtained the U.S.E.S. file from Mr. Huff and some of the following things appear to be pertinent in it:

1. On September 7, 1943, Mrs. Amy Brown, supervisor of the Women's Industrial Division, made the following statement to Mr. Gerald Knapp, Manager of the Portland U.S.E.S., concerning the problem of minority group employment in Portland. This statement was forwarded to Mr. Worth by Mr. Knapp.

"Up until the past two months when an issue was made of the racial question, no problem of placing Negroes was encountered in this division. Heretofore, an occasional colored applicant came in and as a rule we were able to place him in some job with a minimum of difficulty. Recently, since the racial issue has been raised, an unusually large number of colored persons have been coming in asking for specific jobs in specific companies who either through their unions or via the grapevine have been labeled as discriminating against applicants because of race or color."

(Apparently, this st[a]tement does not take into consideration the fact that the needs of the companies as listed in the newspapers may have been one reason why there were large numbers of new applicants coming in and asking for specific jobs in certain companies.)

2. A local office memorandum for a report on discriminatory hiring practice dated November 30, 1942 reads as follows:

"Larry Quillopo, 10706 N. E. Liberty Street, completed a training course in burning, 42 hours and passed the burning test. Mr. Quillopo went to the Labor Temple (Boilermakers) November 30 and talked to the guard at the door of the hiring hall who wouldn't let him pass and told him that they were not hiring Filipino boys in the boilermakers union. This statement was signed by Mr. Quillopo.["]

3. A local office memorandum for a report on discriminatory hiring practice dated November 25, 1942, reads as follows:

Mildred Singleton, colored, was referred to Boilermakers Local 72 in Vancouver (Apparently Local 401 had not been established at that time) and was told definitely that Negroes were not being hired by boilermakers local. This report was signed by Mr. L. Heimel, employment service officer.

4. MEMORANDUM

File No. 55—J.W.R.

August 7, 1943

To: Mr. Ted Huff, Manager
            Placement Department

From: James W. Rintoul, Supervisor
            Men's Industrial Division

Subject: Discriminatory Practices

This refers to Mr. Knapp's memorandum of yesterday concerning discriminatory practices on the part of Portland Area employers.

At the present time we know of know cases of discrimination involving referrals from this division other than those attempted through Boilermakers Union Local #72. This local will not accept Negroes for referral through this office to any employer with whom they have contracts.

sgd James W. Rintoul
Supervisor Men's Industrial
Division.

The underscoring is mine. It should also be kept in mind that the boilermakers have contracts with all of the shipbuilders in the area.

5. Some of the complainants alleged that the Kaiser Company would not employ them in sheetmetal work. They also charged that officials of the Kaiser Company tried to persuade them to take some other kind of work. You will note from the complaint of Sidney Wolfe, already sent to you, that he was kept on the payroll as a sheetmetal worker, although actually he did no[t] perform this kind of work. The following letters are in the files of the U.S.E.S. They all read alike and were sent to the following persons on May 24, 1943.

731 S.W. STARK STREET

PORTLAND, ORE.

Mr. Odis Lee Desmuke	Sam E. Jackson, Jr.	Hiawatha P. Clemnens
Barracks 2, Section F	Barracks 2, Section F	Barracks 2, Section F
Kaiser Company	Kaiser Company	Kaiser Company
Swan Island, Portland	Swan Island, Portland	Swan Island, Portland

Dear Mr.—

Mr. C. E. Ivey of the Kaiser Company personnel office has informed us by telephone that you have chosen to remain in your original employment and that you are no longer interested in being placed as a sheetmetal worker's helper.

Inasmuch as your report to us indicates that you were not given employment in the Swan Island Shipyard as a sheetmetal worker's helper, and inasmuch as this report further indicates that such was your desire, will you confirm Mr. Ivey's statement to us in order that we might complete our records.

Very truly yours
Gerald C. Knapp
Mgr.

KFS: DLR

(The initials KFS stand for Kenneth F. Smith.)

6. A local office memorandum for a report on discriminatory hiring practice dated December 21, 1942 Re: Boilermakers Union Local 72 1313 S. W. Third Ave.

Wilbourne A. Marks, SS 568-05-9022 was referred by this office as a burner on 12-21-42 to Boilermakers Union, Local 72. While applicants was waiting in line a policeman, badge No. 73, approached him and asked what he was waiting in line for and what nationality he was. Upon receiving the answer that he was a Negro and waiting for a job, the officer told him that "Niggers had to go to Vancouver for jobs."

Sgd Wilbourne A. Marks
173 N. Halsey Street
East 5683 (Tel.)
Portland, Ore.

MS: copy, RS HqR8, Office Files of Frank D. Reeves. (Q–Z), Report on Field Investigations, Mitchell.

See the headnotes on Relationships with Federal Agencies and on the Shipbuilding Industry for cross-references to the other memoranda in this series and for background.

1. On the efforts of the Boilermakers Union (which had a ritual ban on black membership) to get around antidiscrimination directives by creating new black auxiliaries, see Reed, *Seedtime,* 277–78; and the headnote on the FEPC and Unions.

Memorandum on Report on Plan to Admit Welders to Electrical Workers Union

10/18/43

Mr. George M. Johnson

Clarence M. Mitchell

Report on Plan to Admit Welders to Electrical Workers Union

Item Number 2, of my memorandum of October 11,[1] deals with an allegation that Negro welders were being shunted to work under the jurisdiction of the Electrical Workers Union. I have the facts on this, and they are as follows:

Mr. Moses Guy, a colored member of the Grievance Committee of Local 48, I.B.E.W., informed me on October 17 that he started the plan to have colored welders taken into Local 48. He gave me this information in the presence of members of the SNOV who were vigorously opposed to the idea.

Mr. Guy said he noted that Negroes were not getting into the Boilermakers so he decided to ask his union to take them in. His union's executive board agreed to this, Mr. Guy said, and he hoped that later the number of Negroes going into the Electrical Workers Union would force the Boilermakers to admit Negroes. He abandoned the plan when it was opposed by the SNOV. I believe he was honest, but the SNOV members were annoyed with him for proposing the idea. No Negroes were ever admitted on this basis, according to Mr. Guy and Mr. Rodriquez.

Mr. Rodriquez and Mr. Carrington of SNOV stated that while Mr. Guy was probably honest, the company and union officials seized upon this plan as a way out of the boilermaker problem. The SNOV men charge that there are a few spot welders who come under the jurisdiction of the Electrical Workers in the yard. Mr. Rodriquez insisted that such welders do not have an opportunity to learn the full trade and their membership in the Electrical Workers would have no value outside the area. Since the plan was abandoned, I would suggest that it might not be helpful in the testimony. However, I shall be able to discuss it more fully in Washington.[2]

MS: copy, HqR8, Office Files of Frank D. Reeves. (Q–Z), Report on Field Investigations, Mitchell.
    1. Memorandum not found.
    2. On Mitchell's role in preparation for the West Coast Boilermakers hearings, held in Portland and Los Angeles on 11/15–20/43, see the headnote on the Shipbuilding Industry and the Boilermakers Union for cross-references to the other memoranda in this series and for background.

Memorandum on Witnesses Recommended for Hearings

10/18/43

Mr. George M. Johnson
Clarence M. Mitchell
Witnesses Recommended for Hearings[1]

As of Saturday, October 16, and Sunday, October 17, I talked with and recommend the following complainants as witnesses out of the group of attached complaints.

Category I:

    1. Robert L. Rhone, Jr. Mr. Rhone is now working on the Union Pacific Railroad as a dining car waiter. He will arrange to be off to testify. He is quiet spoken, intelligent and will made a good witness.

    2. Lee Anderson is a neat-appearing man without a great deal of imagination. He talks well and seems to follow directions. It should be noted that he goes by two different names, but, from his deposition, you will see that this is because he was at one time a boxer.

    3. Mr. A. H. Mitchell is a straightforward man, but does not express himself too well on why he feels the auxiliary is discriminatory. He knows the situation well, however, and my impression of him may be somewhat distorted by my

own shortcoming as an inquisitor. He has an excellent collection of clippings which he will make available to our attorney in Portland.[2]

4. <u>R. L. Gee</u> will make a very good witness. There are some matters concerning both Gee and Rodriguez which I will discuss with you verbally in Washington.

5. <u>John Scott Brown</u> has a very winning personality and is very intelligent. He is inclined to add a little comedy here and there, but seems to be a man of sound reasoning.

Category II:

1. <u>Paul Glover</u> is from Chicago and talks very well. I believe we should have him as a witness, but I would also like to talk with you about him in D.C.

2. <u>Henry Davis</u> is a good solid citizen from Iowa and will add considerable stability to the hearing, although he doesn't have much "spark."

Category III:

None Recommended as yet.

Category IV:

1. <u>Walter Carrington.</u> Mr. Carrington makes an excellent appearance, has a good sense of humor, but is inclined to use a few too many big words. He is somewhat talkative, but will be very helpful.

He states that his union (Local 48, I. B. E. W.) feels he should be upgraded to a leaderman, but the company has told him that it cannot promote him because he is a Negro, according to his statement. In this connection, I would like to recommend that Mr. Moses Guy, Hudson House, Vancouver, Washington, be called to state the policies of Local 48. Mr. Guy makes a very dignified appearance, talks distinctly, and is a member of the Grievance Committee of Local 48. He states he handles both Negro and white complaints. Mr. Guy's connection with the plan to take Negro welders into Local 48 was satisfactorily explained to me, and I am setting forth the full details in a separate memorandum.

2. <u>Armando Boullon</u> fits into Category IV. His statement is set forth in my memorandum on the SNOV complaint.

MS: copy, HqR8, Office Files of Frank D. Reeves. (Q–Z), Report on Field Investigations, Mitchell.

1. Mitchell conducted these interviews in preparation for the FEPC's hearings in Portland and Los Angeles. See the headnote on the Shipbuilding Industry and the Boilermakers Union and the other memoranda in this series.

2. A. H. Mitchell was connected to the Portland NAACP. See 10/20/43.

Memorandum on Testimony in Connection with Complaint of Shipyard Negro Organization for Victory, Portland, Oregon

10/18/43

Mr. George M. Johnson

Clarence M. Mitchell

Testimony in Connection with Complaint of Shipyard Negro
Organization for Victory, Portland, Oregon

In addition to the statement of Mr. Rodriquez concerning his visit to Mr. Homer Parrish, discussed in my memorandum of this date,[1] I also submit the following on this complaint:

1. On page 2, the complaint describes the structure of the SNOV. Mr. Rodriquez will testify on the structure and purpose of the organization. I am attaching a letterhead giving the officers. Briefly, the statement on the organization is that the Negroes who came to the Kaiser Company from New York in 1942 felt that they had not adequate representation from the Boilermakers' Union.

   Accordingly, they organized the SNOV. Mr. Rodriquez states that prior to November 10, 1943, the organization attempted to handle its problems in a conciliatory manner and the Kaiser Company appeared to be cooperative. On November 10, 1942, there was a government meeting with company and union officials on their (SNOV) problem, but Mr. Rodriquez charges he and his organization were denied access to this meeting even as observers. It then appeared that Mr. Thomas Ray of the Boilermakers' Union and the Kaiser Company were trying to give them the "run around," Mr. Rodriquez charges. Mr. Rodriquez charges that Mr. Murray of the personnel department of the Kaiser Company promised him that two Negroes, Bush and Wolfe (mentioned on page 4 of the complaint), would be allowed to work in the sheet metal department at the Vancouver Yard of the Kaiser Company. However, when these men went to the Vancouver Yard, Mr. Rodriquez charges, they were not put to work and were given discharge slips. Mr. Bush went back to New York, according to Mr. Rodriquez, and Mr. Wolfe went in the restaurant business.

2. On page 4, the complaint alleges that Mr. Fred Perry, a skilled Negro draftsman, was denied an opportunity to work at his highest skill. I talked with Mr.

Perry and he states this complaint was entered without his knowledge. He informed me that he has been upgraded and is satisfied.

3. Mr. Walter Carrington will testify on the Kaiser Company's policy with regard to upgrading. This is mentioned in Section D of page 4 of the complaint. Mr. Armando Boullon, who at one time was a scaler in the Swan Island Yard of the Kaiser Company, is filing the following complaint on upgrading:

He informed me that on December 1, 1942, he was employed as a scaler in the Swan Island Yard of the company. A number of white men, who were employed at the same time he was, were later upgraded to leadermen. Mr. Boullon states he noticed this and talked with his foreman about it. The foreman told him that (1) seniority and (2) qualities of leadership were the only requisites of leadermen, according to Mr. Boullon. Two weeks later, Mr. Boullon charges, white men who were employed after December 1 were upgraded to leadermen. He stated he told the foreman he would leave the job and not return until he was assured of an opportunity to be upgraded. The foreman called him later and threatened him with dismissal, Mr. Boullon states. Later, he told me, he was sent to Mr. Harry Hanson, a white supervisor for the Kaiser Company. Mr. Hanson, according to Mr. Boullon, said that "no member of <u>any</u> colored race will be a leaderman in the department." At Mr. Hanson's suggestion, Mr. Boullon says, he transferred to another shift. This was worse, Mr. Boullon charges, and he finally left the yard. He is still working for the Kaiser Company but is now a sheet metal worker.

4. Mr. Rodriquez and Mr. Gee wish to testify on the allegations on pages 6 and 8 concerning the discriminatory structure of the Boilermakers' Auxiliary. Here again I wish to discuss this with you in Washington. I recommend that Mr. Gee talk on this. Also you will recall that we sought information on what promises the Kaiser Company made to the men when they were recruited. According to Mr. Gee, the Kaiser Company representatives in New York said even if the men did not know one end of a monkey wrench from the other, they would have an opportunity to be trained and upgraded when they got to Portland. Mr. Gee, himself, came as a laborer, but Mr. E. W. Ashley, personnel manager of the Kaiser Yard at Vancouver, was responsible for his opportunity to be trained and upgraded as a welder, according to Mr. Gee.

Attachments

MS: copy, HqR8, Office Files of Frank D. Reeves. (Q–Z) Report of Field Investigation, Mitchell.

See the headnote on the Shipbuilding Industry and the Boilermakers Union for cross-references to the other memoranda in this series and for background.

1. This memorandum has not been found.

Memorandum on Information on Boilermakers Locals 72 (Portland), 401 (Vancouver), Auxiliary A-42 (Portland), and Auxiliary A-32 (Vancouver)

October 20, 1943

TO: Mr. George M. Johnson

FROM: Clarence M. Mitchell

SUBJECT: Information on Boilermakers Locals 72 (Portland), 401 (Vancouver), Auxiliary A-42 (Portland) and Auxiliary A-32 (Vancouver).

Boilermakers Local 72 is under the direction of Mr. Thomas Ray, but it will be noted from the attached newspaper clippings the International is attempting to oust him by court action. Local 401 is under the direction of Mr. Homer Parrish, but our complainants allege that although it is a separate local reporting to the International it was established by and in many respects is the creature of Mr. Ray. Auxiliary A-42 has not yet been organized, although I visited a site at 625 N.W. Couch Street which is being prepared to house this auxiliary. A more detailed statement on it will be made later in the memo. I have been unable to find any officers for Auxiliary A-32 and receipts for joining it have the stamp of Mr. Homer Parrish. The complainants allege that A-32 is strictly a paper organization, although a desperate effort is being made to give it the semblance of an organization.

In connection with the affairs of these auxiliaries and locals, I talked with the Rev. Thomas J. Tobin, chairman of the Portland Voluntary Appeals Board. He is also on friendly terms with Mr. Ray and other union leaders. The appeals board is made up of Father Tobin, Mr. Larry Rogers (Now resigned, see attached editorial) personnel manager of the Commercial Iron Works and Mr. John O'Neal of the Iron Workers Union. The board meets three times a week. It grants clearances to workers who are entitled to them but denied such by employers, it can effect payment of wages for workers improperly discharged and it can also bring about reinstatement of workers discharged unfairly. This board is an adjunct to the W.M.C., but apparently has almost complete autonomy. Father Tobin has his office at 2053 S.W. Sixth Street with the Archbishop. I talked with him there and he introduced me to His Grace, the Archbishop.

Father Tobin told me that when representatives of the F.E.P.C. were in San Francisco (referring to your visit on August 20, 1943), he went to San Francisco from Portland for a conference with Mr. Thomas Ray on the question of discrimination and at that time Mr. Ray made certain promises. At that time, Mr. Ray made the promise that he would establish a local called A-42 in Portland when he returned, according to Father Tobin. Father Tobin said Mr. Ray assured him that while this local would have some semblance of an auxiliary, it would really be a distinct local. Negroes would be cleared by it and sent on the job. Mr. Ray also promised, Father Tobin said, that he would make a fight on the convention floor of the Boilermakers to see that this local get autonomy. Father Tobin said Mr. Ray kept his word as far as possible and is using a colored man named Wyatt Williams to assist in organizing A-42. Father Tobin said it was his understanding that two months rent had been paid on a building to house the A-42 affairs and membership. Father Tobin said he gave Mr. Ray a statement to the effect that the latter was trying to set up a local giving Negroes every right possible under the ritual. This statement was published in full by one of the Portland newspapers. I will try to get a copy.

Father Tobin invited me to attend a meeting of an interracial group at the Portland Hotel on Monday, October 26 at 7:30 p.m. I told him that I expected to be in Los Angeles at the time, but would suggest that the lawyer taking my place attend.

Later in the day, I talked with Mr. Wyatt Williams at his office on the fifth floor of the Lumberman's Building. Mr. Williams informed me that he is on the Real Estate Board of the City of Portland and has been in Oregon for a number of years. He is a lawyer. He stated that when Mr. Ray first thought of starting A-42 the plan was to have Mr. James Minor, a representative of the Dining Car Workers, organize the group. Mr. Minor was unable to take the responsibility so Mr. Williams assumed it. Mr. Williams explained that A-42 would be "different from A-32." He said it would be completely independent, while "A-32 reports to the International." He estimated that A-32 has between 200 and 300 members but is really not set up as yet.

Mr. Williams showed me a form (Sample Attached) which he said he turned over to Mr. Ray to send to the International office. The money required to accompany this form was not required of the persons who signed it, he said. Mr. Williams, in response to a question from me, said he did not know whether the form had actually gone to the International office as yet, but he had given it to Mr. Ray. He tried to call Mr. Ray to check on this but could not reach him.

Mr. Williams showed me a copy of a lease for approximately 800 square feet of space at 625 N.W. Couch Street to be used for A-42. The lease was in his name and that of Local 72. Mr. Williams said he was to be an official of the union and two other persons would be hired, but he did not have a clear picture of what his title would be. He described it as, "secretary, or something like that." A-42 will pay back the Boilermakers when it is set up, Mr. Williams said. He was somewhat annoyed, however, by a letter he had gotten from the Portland Branch of the N.A.A.C.P. attacking him for starting the A-42 plan. One of the signers of this letter was a man named A. H. Mitchell and Mr. Williams at first was under the impression that I was the Mitchell. When I showed him my credentials, he appeared to be satisfied that I was another Mitchell. Mr. Williams said the A-42 arrangement would have a board of 21 persons and proportionate representation on the grievance committee of Local 72. A-42 will be able to give clearance to any yard in Portland, Mr. Williams said.

Mr. Williams took me to 625 N.W. Couch Street. A combination storage room and automobile repair shop is being converted into a union hall. Windows for paying dues have been installed, there is a large private office for Mr. Williams, restrooms for men and women are being installed, there will be a large waiting room, which, I suppose, will also serve for other purposes. In the basement, Mr. Williams said, he may later be able to have a recreation room with billiard tables and other things.

He asked me what I thought of the whole thing. I told him I assumed he had been giving a lot of thought to what he was doing and was working very hard at it. He then asked whether I thought that this type of organization would be a good thing. I told him that I preferred to make no statement since I was talking to all parties in the controversy and did not wish to say anything which might be misconstrued. We parted on what seemed to be friendly terms.

Attachment

MS: copy, HqR8, Office Files of Frank D. Reeves. (Q–Z), Report on Field Investigations, Mitchell.

See the headnote on the Shipbuilding Industry and the Boilermakers Union for cross-references to the other memoranda in this series and for background.

Memorandum on Corporate Structure and Other Information on the Kaiser Corporation and the Oregon Shipbuilding Company

October 21, 1943

TO: Mr. George M. Johnson

FROM: Clarence M. Mitchell

SUBJECT: Corporate Structure and Other Information on the Kaiser
          Corporation and the Oregon Shipbuilding Company.

These yards are building ships for the Maritime Commission. The following information was obtained from the records in the office of the Clerk of the Oregon District Federal Court in Portland:

Oregon Shipbuilding Corporation,   )
a corporation   )   Civil No. 1744
and Kaiser Company, Inc.   )
a corporation   )
                Plaintiff   )   Complaint
        v.
National Labor Relations Board;   )
Harry A. Millis individually   )

and as a member and as chairman)
of the National Labor Relations Board;)
Gerard D. Reilly individually and as a)
Member of the National Labor Relations)
Board; William Leiserson individually)
and as a member of the National Labor)
Relations Board; and R. N. Denham indi-)
vidually and as a trial examiner for the)
National Labor Relations Board.
                              Defendants

I

Plaintiff Oregon Shipbuilding Corporation (Hereinafter referred to as the "Oregon Company") is a corporation organized and existing under the laws of the State of Delaware.

Plaintiff Kaiser Company, Inc. (Hereinafter referred to as the "Kaiser Company"), is a corporation organized and existing under the laws of the State of Nevada.

The complaint sought to restrain the N.L.R.B. from holding a hearing but Judge James Alger Fee, district Judge ruled: "The motion for a restraining order is denied, the motion to dismiss is granted."

Mr. Kaiser's deposition was as follows:

Edgar F. Kaiser, being duly sworn on oath deposes and says:

"He is vice president of Oregon Shipbuilding Corporation one of the above named plaintiffs; that he has read the foregoing complaints, knows the facts set forth." This was signed by Mr. Kaiser Jan. 10, 1943 as Vice President of Oregon Ship.

An affidavit from Harry P. Morton in the case reads as follows:

"I, Harry P. Morton, being first duly sworn, do say upon oath as follows: I reside at Orinda, in Contra Costa County, State of California. I am Vice President and Industrial Relations Counsel of Oregon Shipbuilding Corporation and am also Industrial Relations Counsel for Kaiser Company, Inc.

"I act as attorney and counsel for the said corporations in matters affecting labor relations and policy thereof. I conduct negotiation with labor organizations with respect to conditions of employment of workmen employed by the said corporations, negotiating for settlement of major grievances and participate on behalf of plaintiff corporations in conferences with respect to industrial labor relations."

It is my suggestion that one of the lawyers will want to interview Mr. Morton concerning negotiations with labor unions on the subject of clearance of Negro workers.

MS: copy, HqR8, Office Files of Frank D. Reeves. (Q–Z) Report on Field Investigations, Mitchell.

See the headnote on the Shipbuilding Industry and the Boilermakers Union for cross-references to the other memoranda in this series and for background.

Memorandum on Complaints against Portland Shipbuilders

10/21/43

Mr. George M. Johnson

Clarence M. Mitchell

Complaints Against Portland Shipbuilders

I am sending the following complaints herewith:

1. Commercial Iron Works

In general, it is alleged that this company seeks to hold Negroes in low grade jobs. Beginning August, 1943, the Portland U. S. E. S. has been making a weekly report showing hires of Negroes by companies. The following is the record on Commercial:

August 4 – – – – – – – –	1 Porter, 1 Painter Helper
August 28 – – – – – – – –	3 Helpers
September 11 – – – – – –	1 Janitor, 1 Chipper
September 18 – – – – – –	1 Janitress, 1 Electrician's Helper, 1 Buffer
September 27 – – – – – –	1 Painter Helper, 1 Buffer
October 2 – – – – – – –	1 Laborer, 1 Scaler
October 9 – – – – – – –	1 Painter
October 16 – – – – – – –	1 Buffer, 3 Scalers

The following persons send complaints against this company:

Category I – – – – – – –	Booker T. Kirk
Category IV – – – – – – –	Messrs. Hayes and Jones

2. Kaiser Company, Vancouver, Washington

Category III – – – – – –	Jackie Alexander
	Gail Carey
Category IV – – – – – –	Willie Bumpurs
	A. G. Greene
	John Wesley Dews

3. Swan Island

Category IV – – – – – –	Armando Boullon

Attachments

MS: copy, HqR8, Office Files of Frank D. Reeves. (Q–Z) Report on Field Investigations, Mitchell.

See the headnote on the Shipbuilding Industry and the Boilermakers Union for cross-references to the other memoranda in this series and for background.

Memorandum on Attached Complaints Regarding Boilermakers Union

10/22/43

Mr. George M. Johnson

Clarence M. Mitchell

Attached Complaints[1]

The following documents are attached:

1. Copy of a letter from Walter R. Carrington, Chairman of Grievance Committee of the SNOV, sent to Mr. Kenneth F. Smith of the U. S. E. S. on February 17, 1943. Also, there is a covering memorandum from Mr. Smith, transmitting this letter to Mr. Stoll.

2. Complaint of Mr. Oliver D. McCray against the Commercial Iron Works.

3. Discharge slips sent to Messrs. Paul C. Richardson and Alfred E. David from the Vancouver Yard of Kaiser Company for failure to pay dues to Auxiliary A-32.

4. Statement of Raymond L. Gee, Henry Davis, Al Davis, and Jerry Westbrooks.

5. Signed Complaint of Jerry Westbrooks against the Kaiser Company at Vancouver. Also his discharge slips.

6. Complaint of Lee Russell Anderson against Kaiser Company of Vancouver with Discharge quit slip, receipt for dues stamped by Homer Parrish.

7. Complaint of Mezzellano David Metcalf who alleges he thought he was joining Local 72, but found he was really in A-32.

8. Complaint of Anthem Walker.

9. Complaint of Howard Clark.

10. Complaint of E. Davis.

11. Complaint of Elager Dubose.

Attachments

MS: copy, HqR8, Office Files of Frank D. Reeves. (Q–Z) Report on Field Investigations, Mitchell.

See the headnote on the Shipbuilding Industry and the Boilermakers Union for cross-references to the other memoranda in this series and for background.

Memorandum on Auxiliary A-32, Boilermakers Union

October 23, 1943

TO: George Johnson
FROM: Clarence M. Mitchell

Attached is a notice given to persons joining auxiliary A-32. You will note that members are requested to give information on other persons working on the job who have not joined.

As I stated in my previous memorandum on October 20, A-32 is not yet established, although it appears that a charter has been granted by the International.

I was unable to see Mr. Homer Parrish because he was not in the office when I called for an appointment; but I asked for the president of the auxiliary and was told that Mr. Parrish was the president. Thus it appears that no officers have been elected, and all of our complainants allege that they have never been notified of any meetings, nor do they know of any officers. It also appears that a number of men have not joined the auxiliary, simply because the union has not determined that they are on the job without becoming members.

In the meetings with complainants in Portland there were always persons present who said that they were working at trades covered by the Boilermakers contract, but who had not joined the auxiliary and had not been notified to join. Sooner or later the union will catch up with them, of course, but meanwhile they are remaining out of the auxiliary.[1]

MS: copy, HqR14, Records Relating to Hearings. Boilermakers, General Files.
    See the headnote on the Shipbuilding Industry and the Boilermakers Union for cross-references to the other memoranda in this series and for background.

Memorandum on Information on the Kaiser Company's Swan Island, Vancouver, and Oregon Shipbuilding Yards

October 23, 1943

TO: George Johnson
FROM: Clarence M. Mitchell
SUBJECT: Information on the Kaiser Company's Swan Island, Vancouver, and Oregon Shipbuilding Yards.

Because of his absence from the city, I was unable to see Mr. J. O. Murray, manager of Industrial Relations for the Swan Island yard of the Kaiser Company. However, I did have a talk with Mr. Clarence E. Ivey who is serving as an assistant in the personnel Department, and with a Mr. Jones who is also an assistant.

Mr. Ivey gave me some valuable information on the events which led to his appointment by the Kaiser Company. He stated that in the late summer of 1942 there was considerable unrest and unfavorable newspaper publicity in Portland because of the belief that a great many Negroes would be coming into the area and that many of these colored persons were undesirable citizens. Mr. Ivey stated that he received a long-distance call from Mr. Henry Kaiser who asked him to attend a meeting in the office of the mayor in the city of Portland to discuss the rumors and the newspaper publicity. The meeting was somewhat hastily called, Mr. Ivey stated, and the following persons were present: Mr. Ivey, a Mr. Blackburn, Dr. Denorval Unthank, Mr. Kenneth Smith, who was then with the USES, and Mr. Wyatt Williams, who, as I have previously informed you, is now attempting to organize an auxiliary for the Boilermakers Union in the city of Portland.

Mr. Ivey stated that at this meeting Mr. Kaiser informed the mayor and others that a large number of Negroes would be coming into the area to work for his company. It was explained to the city officials that these people would be used for shipyard work and the cooperation of all present was requested.

Following the meeting, Mr. Ivey stated, Mr. Murray visited him at his place of employment in the railway station and asked him to come on the staff of the Kaiser Company as a personnel worker. Mr. Ivey stated that he has been employed at the station for a number of years and if he would leave his job he would lose a number of very important pension rights. Therefore, he worked out a part-time arrangement which permits him to be at the station during the early part of the day and to work for the Kaiser yards (Swan Island and Vancouver) in the afternoon.

Mr. Ivey stated that when Negroes were recruited in other areas and brought into Portland difficulties arose which prevented the company from upgrading them. These difficulties were caused, in the main, by the Local 72 of the Boilermakers Union, Mr. Ivey charged. Following protests from the colored persons and other interested people, the Kaiser Company decided, on October 17, 1942, that it would upgrade its Negro employees in spite of any union opposition. The company made this announcement and was able to promote a number of colored workers before the Boilermakers Union insisted that the upgrading be stopped, Mr. Ivey stated.

According to his statement, the War Manpower Commission and the Maritime Commission became fearful of the possibility of labor trouble because of the Kaiser Company's stand. These two agencies then decided to call a meeting on November 10 to talk the whole problem over, Mr. Ivey said. At the meeting of November 10, the most important decision was that the President's Executive Order would be followed in the hiring and upgrading of personnel at the three yards, according to Mr. Ivey. Some of the basic issues, Mr. Ivey stated, were not settled, in that the Boilermakers Union asked for additional time in which to work out ways of handling the situation.

Mr. Ivey was unable to give the exact number of persons who had been discharged from time to time because of failure to join the Boilermakers auxiliary, A32. He stated that in his opinion these people were not discharged and the company made an effort to have all of them reinstated whenever they were able to become members of A-32.

I requested Mr. Ivey to give me some information on why most of the Negro employees were channeled to the Vancouver company. He said that this was because the company was making an effort to build up the personnel at the Vancouver yard and, therefore, was sending most of its new people to Vancouver, for a time. In this connection, I read the following statement in the recruiting manual of the Kaiser Company: "Always bear in mind that workers may go to work in any one of the three shipyards, so do not make promises that they will go to any particular yard or be housed at a particular housing unit. Also do not promise any particular shift; workers must accept shifts available at the time they arrive in Portland." (Recruiting Manual for Oregon Shipbuilding Corporation, Kaiser Incorporated, Vancouver.)

Mr. Ivey informed me that at present the company is making a sincere effort to upgrade all capable personnel, regardless of race, creed, or color. He gave me the attached lists of jobs which are held in the three yards by Negroes. This list was compiled for September, 1943, and shows a total of 2,893 persons in the three yards. Mr. Ivey admitted that in some instances the superintendents and foremen in the yards are reluctant to upgrade Negro personnel. For this reason, there are some problems connected with the move to promote workers. He stated that the company is, at present, expecting to bring in one thousand colored women to work at the Swan Island yard.

The area office of the War Manpower Commission also informed me that the Kaiser Company is now recruiting six thousand additional workers for its Vancouver yard and will use Negroes without discrimination. I noticed in the conversation with Mr. Jones and with Mr. Sheridan of the area office of the War Manpower Commission that there seems to be some tendency to think of Negro employees as possessing certain abilities which enable them to perform specific jobs; thus, there seems to be a growing tendency to think of Negroes as excellent "chippers". You will note that there are 231 employed as "chippers" in the Swan Island yard and 385 employed in the same capacity in the Vancouver yard. This is the largest occupational group of all the jobs held. It will be very regrettable if the Negro personnel is concentrated in this category, because it may result in a move to bar them from other trades. A review of the list of occupations held by Negroes will also show that some of the jobs which our complainants allege they could not enter do have Negroes in them; the number, however, is small. Mr. Jones explained that he is not authorized to give me this list, so it is for our office use only. The Kaiser Company will produce it at the hearing.

MS: copy, HqR14, Records Relating to Hearings. Boilermakers, General Files.

See the headnote on the Shipbuilding Industry and the Boilermakers Union for cross-references to the other memoranda in this series and for background.

Memorandum on Stabilization Plans in the Portland Area

October 23, 1943

TO: George Johnson

FROM: Clarence M. Mitchell

SUBJECT: Stabilization plans in the Portland area.

I had a brief conference with Mr. L. C. Stoll, Area Director, War Manpower Commission when I was in Portland. He stated that there are no agreements which supplement the master agreement on the West Coast so far as the Kaiser Shipbuilding Company and the Commercial Iron Works are concerned. As mentioned to you in my memorandum of October 18, it appears from my conversations with Mr. Stoll that some of the Kaiser orders were put on the national clearance by Washington. Also in connection with the agreements between the Kaiser Company and the union, the suit filed against the National Labor Relations Board mentions that the Kaiser Company, Incorporated, and the Oregon Shipbuilding Company are signators to the master agreement.[1]

Mr. Thomas Sheridan, Utilization Consultant, W.M.C discussed the stabilization plans and the Appeals Board of Portland with me. The voluntary plan for labor stabilization went into effect on April 7, 1943 in Portland. This plan is attached, and I will discuss it fully with you when I arrive in Washington. It is marked "Exhibit 1". You will note that it provides for an Appeals Board to hear cases of workers who have been denied clearance by an employer. Mr. Sheridan explained that the Appeals Board felt that it did not have jurisdiction over cases of individuals discharged by companies because they would not join the auxiliary A-32 of the Boilermakers Union. It will also be noted that this board is made up of an impartial chairman (Father Thomas J. Tobin), a representative of management and a representative of labor. The impartial chairman is paid, but the other two members serve without pay, and the expenses of the board are borne by labor and management.[2] On November 1, or thereabouts, this plan is to be replaced by a new employment stabilization program which is marked "Exhibit 2" and attached. I have noted some of the important passages in the new plan.

MS: copy, HqR14, Records Relating to Hearings. Boilermakers, General Files

1. See the headnote on the Shipbuilding Industry and the Boilermakers Union, and on FEPC Relationships with Federal Agencies for cross-references to the other memoranda in this series and for background.

2. On the appeals board, see also 10/20/43.

Memorandum on Conference with Officials of Auxiliary A-35

October 26, 1943

TO: George M. Johnson

FROM: Clarence M. Mitchell

SUBJECT: Conference with officials of auxiliary A-35

In company with Mr. Brown of the Los Angeles office and Mr. Floyd Covington, executive secretary of the Los Angeles Urban League, I talked with Mr. Garner Grayson, acting secretary of A-35 and Mr. H. S. Griggs, assistant secretary, on the above date in their office at 4150 South Main Street. The offices are new and arrangements appear to be made for the accommodation of a large number of individuals who may be paying dues. There are a number of girls on the office force, all of whom are Negroes.

Mr. Grayson informed me that the auxiliary was set up July 7, 1943. He admitted that there had been no meetings of the membership and stated that he was appointed by officials of subordinate Lodge #92. The first meeting of stewards who will serve in the yards was held on September 1, according to Mr. Grayson. I asked him about the length of time an individual is given before he is suspended from work for failure to pay union dues. Mr. Grayson said that the auxiliary is giving sixty days to all delinquent members, and adds an extra thirty days before requesting termination of such employees. It was his estimate that since July, 1943, approximately five hundred persons have been recommended for termination at the three yards in question. (Western Pipe and Steel; Consolidated Steel, Shipbuilding Division; and California Shipbuilding Company). In order for an individual to be terminated, A-35 compiles a list which is sent to Local 92 for checking. Local 92 sends this list with a covering letter to the shipbuilding company requesting that the accordance with the provisions of the master agreement the employees named on the list be terminated.

When an employee receives notice of termination for failure to pay union dues, he comes to the auxiliary and is given a slip which he takes to Local 92. At Local 92 he is given a green slip which he takes to the employer. The employer is supposed to keep this green slip and permit reinstatement of the individual. The notices sent to the employer are from Local 92, but signed by Mr. Grayson.

In response to the question of how an individual referred by USES receives employment, Mr. Grayson gave the following outline: Persons referred from USES come to A-35 for an interview. A-35 refers them to Local 92. Local 92 then sends them to the company hiring hall. From the company hiring hall they are sent to the job. Thus, persons referred by the auxiliary make an extra trip in order to obtain employment. Mr. Grayson stated that the parent Local 92 calls the employer each day to determine what hires will be made. A-35 calls 92 at 9 a.m. and determines how many persons it will be permitted to refer. Thus it appears that the actual hiring of individuals depends on the pleasure of Local 92.

Mr. Grayson stated that he has approximately four thousand members in the auxiliary and hopes to hold a meeting in the near future.

The acting secretary of A-35 appears to be a very intelligent man and is a graduate of one of the California schools of pharmacy. He was at one time the proprietor of a drugstore in Los Angeles. The assistant secretary is a prominent church worker and at one time was connected with the Golden State Mutual Insurance Company. Thus it appears that two former business men are now acting as the union representatives. Both of these men appear to serve at the pleasure of Local 92. They seemed straightforward and capable, but did not anticipate that Local 92 would make an effort to have them made the stewards of a subordinate lodge.

MS: *copy, HqR8, Office Files of Frank D. Reeves. (Q–Z) Report on Field Investigations, Mitchell.*
    See the headnote on the Shipbuilding Industry and the Boilermakers Union for cross-references to the other memoranda in this series and for background.

Memorandum on Meeting with White Members of Boilermakers Local 92

October 27, 1943

TO: George M. Johnson

FROM: Clarence M. Mitchell

SUBJECT: Meeting with white members of Boilermakers Local 92

On the above date eight white members of the Boilermakers Union met at the office of the President's Committee in Los Angeles at 8 p.m. to discuss their views on A-35. The following persons were present: Mrs. C. Benowitz, c/o Koski, 1324 Lincoln St., Long Beach, Calif.; R.E. Brooks, 1021 B.E. Court, Wilmington, Calif.; Mrs. Ruth Teeter, c/o Koski, 1324 Lincoln St.; Long Beach, Calif.; Louis Rapellin, 2826 Cincinnati, Los Angeles, 33, Calif.; Norman Doran, 1024 Dundas St., Los Angeles, Calif.; John Garrish, 351 Paseo de Gracia, Redondo Beach, Calif.; Frank Kadish, 933 South Kingsley Drive, Los Angeles, Calif.; Jack Diamond, 1324 Crenshaw Blvd., Los Angeles, Calif.;

Mr. Rapellin stated he had been a member of the Boilermakers for thirteen years, but believed that the auxiliary set-up was inimical to the welfare of the trade union movement. Those present expressed that in the beginning Negroes were admitted to the Local 92 as members at large, with the understanding that they were affiliated with an auxiliary in Kansas City. Dues were collected from Negroes at the local source, according to these persons, but such money as was taken in went to Kansas City. Here it should be noted that these are the views of the persons present and may not necessarily represent what actually happened.

According to all those present, there is nothing in the ritual of the Boilermakers Union which bars colored persons from holding membership. They stated that the question of admitting colored persons first arose in 1941 and was discussed on the floor at one of the meetings. Mr. Blackwell, the business agent of the union, made the statement that Negroes could not be admitted to the union except as auxiliary members and there was nothing that could be done about it. White union stewards have not been told to handle Negro grievances, nor have they been told to refrain from handling them, according to those present. Thus it is left largely to the discretion of the steward, according to those who attended the meeting. The persons present stated that although the Boilermakers Local 92 has approximately 40,000 members, usually only a small number of persons attend the meetings which are held twice each month. Sometime this number is as small as 35 persons and sometimes it might be as high as 400, according to these individuals.

The jurisdiction of Local 92 includes in California the counties of Santa Barbara, Kern, Inyoo, San Bernadino, Los Angeles, Ventura, Orange, Riverside, San Diego, and Imperial; and in Nevada the 2 counties of Emeralda, Nye, Lincoln and Clark.

The persons present stated that they were opposed to the auxiliary set-up because it divides the workers into separate groups and will permit the quick disbanding of the union. They also said that the Axis propagandists, especially the Japanese are making use of the discrimination and separation of trade unions in America to show that the United States does not believe in democracy. Those present pointed out that all other racial groups are taken into the Boilermakers and said that before the declaration of war Japanese were in Local 92 as full members. Mr. Blackwell was quoted as saying that if Negroes are in the union they will have to stay in after the war. In response to the question of what would happen to auxiliaries after the war, Mr. Blackwell is said to have stated that they would be dissolved. The persons present charged that the auxiliaries have no power to refer people to jobs and that Local 92 gets all the orders but is supposed to have some scheme of prorating them so that the auxiliary can refer persons to the job.

Negroes are excluded from field construction jobs and job shops, according to Mr. Kadish, one of those present. The Boilermakers have a shipyard office at Wilmington, California which refers persons to shipbuilding, according to Mr. Kadish, and an office at 108th and Broadway, which makes referrals to field construction jobs and job shops. Negroes are not sent out from the 108th and Broadway office, according to Mr. Kadish. Those present stated that Negroes are not permitted to get jobs as welding instructors in the yard although some of them are qualified for it. However they stated that such promotions depend on the foremen or superintendents and that the union generally takes the position that setting up of a man is a company prerogative. This applies to whites as well as to Negroes.

About a year and a half ago, according to Mr. Kadish, a Negro was qualified for lay-out work but was not given it. There was some discussion and his fellow-workers were in favor of his having the job, according to Mr. Kadish. However, the individual was not promoted. This was at the California Shipbuilding Company and Mr. Kadish did not recall the man's name. Those present contended that if the International of the Boilermakers Union desired to change the policy of refusing Negroes full membership, it could be done without a meeting of the membership.

According to these persons, some months ago the International sent a circular letter to all Locals informing them that it was powerless to do anything about the question of admitting Negroes to union membership. However, according to those present there was a referendum on whether women should be admitted to the Boilermakers and this referendum was defeated; but by Executive Order the Board of the International ruled that women should be admitted and they are now members. Those present stated that for the time being they did not wish to have their names used in any publicity, but at the time of the hearing they expected to have a large number of white persons who would protest against the auxiliary set-up. They also said that if necessary they could provide a white witness who would testify against the auxiliary, but would prefer to do so only if Mr. Blackwell is called on the stand first.

It is my recommendation that Mr. Rapellin be called to testify since he has been in the Boilermakers Union for a number of years and seemed to have a definite conviction that having separate auxiliaries are very undesirable.

MS: copy, HqR8, *Office Files of Frank D. Reeves.* (Q–Z) Report on Field Investigations, Mitchell.

　　See the headnote on the Shipbuilding Industry and the Boilermakers Union for cross-references to the other memoranda in this series and for background.

Memorandum on Conference with Mr. George Toll, Local Manager, USES, Long Beach, California

October 27, 1943

TO:　　　　George M. Johnson

FROM:　　　Clarence M. Mitchell

SUBJECT:　Conference with Mr. George Toll, Local Manager, USES, Long Beach, California

Mr. Toll opened the office of the Employment Service at Wilmington, California on August 1, 1941. This office has been receiving orders from the California Shipbuilding

Company, Western Pipe and Steel, and Consolidated Steel from that period up until present. Mr. Toll left Wilmington only recently.

It was the function of his office to place the California clearance orders from the three companies. This included approximately 18 offices in Southern California, with the exception of San Diego.

Mr. Toll stated it had been his experience that Consolidated and Western Pipe and Steel were reluctant to hire Negroes as machinists helpers and shipfitters helpers. Recently they have begun taking Negroes in these occupations, but only because of the manpower shortage, according to Mr. Toll.

He is willing to testify at the hearing on the effect on these matters. It is my suggestion that Mr. Dreyfus may wish to talk with him at an early date.

Mr. Toll also suggested the name of Mr. John Marshall, Personnel Manager of the Standard Shipbuilding Company as a witness who would give favorable testimony on the utilization of minority groups. He also suggested the name of Mr. Frank Schirer of I.B.E.W., Local B-11, as a union witness who would give favorable testimony. Mr. Schirer's address is 1669 East Anaheim Street, Wilmington.

MS: copy, HqR38, Office Files of Frank D. Reeves. (Q–Z) Report on Field Investigations, Mitchell.

See the headnote on the Shipbuilding Industry and the Boilermakers Union for cross-references to the other memoranda in this series and for background.

Memorandum on Case of Mr. Thomas Madison Doram

October 27, 1943

To: George M. Johnson

From: Clarence M. Mitchell

Subject: Case of Thomas Madison Doram
              717 1/2 E. Vernon Ave.
              Los Angeles, Calif.
              Tel.: Adams 13649

One of the most unusual cases connected with the current shipyard controversy is that of the above-mentioned complainant. Mr. Doram is 29 years old and was initiated by Local 92 as a full member March 25, 1942. At that time he was a helper. Apparently the union was under the impression that he was white, or at least not a Negro, because he was given an insurance policy and a union book, neither of which make any mention of auxiliary. Mr. Doram mentioned that he was initiated with a great many white persons and there was no reference to race in the initiation ceremonies.

His work began at the California Shipbuilding Company on December 29, 1941. At that time he was a janitor. Within 20 days he went into production as a burner. From January to June, 1943, he served in the yard as an instructor of burners, but states that he was not paid for doing this. All the trainees under him at that time were white, according to his statement. He made an effort to have his status raised from a helper to a mechanic, but was unable to do so. He then wrote a letter to Mr. Blackwell of Local 92, asking that his status be changed, but did not receive a reply, according to his testimony. Mr. Doram also states that he wrote to a man named Jerry Doolan in the Personnel Department of the California Shipbuilding Company requesting that he be given an opportunity to become a mechanic but did not receive a reply.

While he was on the job, a man by the name of Youlen Dixon, a white leadman, would frequently make adverse reports on him, Mr. Doran stated. On June 29 an argument arose between Dixon and Doram, according to the latter's statement, which resulted in a fight. According to the complainant, Mr. Doram, Mr. Dixon tried to hit him but missed, and when he did so Doram tried to hit Dixon and did not miss. Dixon fell, according to Doram, but while prostrate sought to pull a knife. Doram states that he jumped on Dixon to prevent him from pulling out the knife, when Paul Morris, shipfitter's foreman who had been talking with both of them, leaped on his (Doram's) back. Doram stated that he was able to fight Morris off, but Dixon ran to another section of the ship where the argument occurred to get a hammer. He was unable to get this hammer, but returned with the knife. Finally the fight was stopped and later it was discovered that Dixon's jaw was broken. Dixon was permitted to return to work after talking with plant protection authorities. Shortly after that, Doram states, a number of persons began to petition his superiors to have him moved from each job he held at the California Shipbuilding Company. At one time he reported this to the Federal Bureau of Investigation, Mr. Doram said, but this did not stop those who sought to have him moved by petition. Finally he obtained a release from the WMC and went to work at the Bethlehem Steel Company. On July 6, 1943, he went to the paymaster to pick up his check, Mr. Doram said, and while there was arrested by police from San Pedro, who jailed him on the charge of assaulting Dixon.

Doram states that he placed his case with Thomas Griffith, an attorney for the National Association for the Advancement of Colored People. However, Griffith took the case as a part of private practice and charged him $50 for it. Mr. Doram said that he paid $25 of this $50. His trial was set for July 27, and according to his statement he did not see his lawyer until the day of the trial. On July 28 Mr. Doram said he was referred to the Probation Department and appeared before Judge LeRoy Dawson on August 11. Judge Dawson sentenced him to 30 days, according to Mr. Doram, and the case was appealed. He stayed in jail for four hours and was released on bond of $500.

He stated it was impossible for him to get in touch with his lawyer immediately and later the lawyer's brother filed his appeal in Mr. Doram's behalf, but did so in the wrong court. This resulted in renewal of the jail sentence, according to Mr. Doram.

Mr. Doram now has his case in the hands of Walter Gordon, another lawyer in Los Angeles. This lawyer has requested that the jail sentence for Mr. Doram be stayed until November 4. Mr. Doram feels that part of his troubles are due to persecution on the part of the Boilermakers Union because he is a full member and refuses to join the auxiliary. He is now employed at the Consolidated Steel Company. It should be noted that this is not the Consolidated Steel Shipbuilding Company. He is working as a burner.

MS: LH, DI, HqR14, Records Relating to Hearings. Oregon Shipbuilding Corporation, Vancouver and Swan Island Shipyards, and International Brotherhood of Boilermakers, Iron Shipbuilders, Welders and Helpers of America Hearings, Los Angeles Complaints.
   See preceding texts on the shipbuilding industry.

Memorandum on Bethlehem Steel Shipbuilding Corporation, Sparrows Point, Maryland

November 1, 1943

TO: Mr. George M. Johnson
           Mr. Will Maslow

FROM: Clarence M. Mitchell

SUBJECT: Bethlehem Steel Shipbuilding Corporation, Sparrows Point, Maryland

On Thursday, July 29, 1943, I was assigned to work on a problem which had arisen at the Bethlehem Steel Shipbuilding Company at Sparrows Point, Maryland. At that time, Negro employees of the company had walked off the job because the company had stopped training Negroes for jobs in the riveting department.[1] This action was taken by the company following a walkout by whites who were said to be opposed to having Negroes receive this type of instruction.[2] The matter was finally settled, and the Negroes who had been in training were restored to the class.

On the above date, Mr. J. B. Knotts, management's representative in charge of industrial relations at the yard, visited our office on another matter. He informed me that the training of Negroes was continued, and there are now five (5) gangs of colored riveters. This means a total of fifteen (15) persons, a riveting gang being made up of one riveter, one holder-on, and a heater. A passer is also a member of the gang, but he is not a trained person.

MS: copy, HqR38, Central Files. Memoranda, Johnson, George M., Dec. 1941–Dec. 1943.
   1. On the epidemic of "hate strikes" that occurred in 1943, see the headnote on Strikes and Work Stoppages.
   2. According to Philip H. Van Gelder, national secretary-treasurer, Industrial Union of Marine and Shipbuilding Workers of America, the "disturbances" were initiated "by irresponsible individuals and

agitators, who were not officers or members of the Union." The union's position, he said, was "firmly against any form of racial discrimination" and the executive board of Local 33 had reaffirmed that policy two days before the disturbances. Van Gelder, statement, 7/30/43, HqR1, Office Memoranda, R.

The Bethlehem Shipbuilding Corporation had 8,500 workers, 1,400 of whom were African Americans. In a memorandum of 8/2/43 to Monsignor Haas, Ross reported on a meeting that he, George Johnson, and Mitchell had attended with representatives of the Baltimore NAACP and other local civil rights groups, of Local 2610 of the U.S. Steelworkers of America, and of the IUMSWA and its Local 33. About 600 African Americans and 5,000 white workers were members of Local 33. Despite Van Gelder's statement, Ross said Gene Crossetti, president of Local 33, led a delegation in 1942 protesting against African American workers becoming welders, and he was elected to head the union local on that ground. The 2,000 welders in the union controlled the local. Ross asserted that Crossetti allegedly knew of the school for white and African American riveters six weeks earlier and "did nothing to make it open successfully." Ross, "Meeting with Baltimore Group on Sparrows Point Situation," 8/2/43, HqR1, Office Memoranda. R. See also appendix 1 for George Johnson to Haas, 7/31/43 on Mitchell's "Telephonic report on Bethlehem Shipyard at Sparrows Point on July 31 from 9:35 to 9:45"; Haas's 8/1/43 digest of other telephone calls to him on the case; and Mitchell's Progress Report, 8/6/43, on Bethlehem Steel Company.

Memorandum on Western Pipe and Steel Company Complainants

11/1/43

Mr. George M. Johnson

Clarence M. Mitchell

Western Pipe and Steel Company Complainants

1. <u>WARREN G. BURRIS</u>, 1517 1/2 West Thirty-Fifth Place, Los Angeles, California. Mr. Burris states that he has been employed for approximately a year at the Western Pipe and Steel Company. He charges that his complaint is against Local 92 of the Boiler Makers' Union and the company. He states that, when A-35 was set up, he believed it to be unconstitutional and objected to the payment of dues into it. His work card was pulled on July 14, 1943. He was called back to the job after being off for one day. A week later, his card was again pulled, Mr. Burris charges, and this time by paying five ($5.00) into Auxiliary A-35 he was reemployed, but he sent in a protest card to the President's Committee. Since that time, he has not paid any money to the Auxiliary, according to his statement, and has received three notices telling him that his card will be pulled again. He states that he does not object to paying dues into a union which is not segregated. About five weeks before October 27, Mr. Burris states, his foreman came to him with two Negro women helpers. After introducing him to the helpers, the foreman told him that eventually there would be enough helpers on the

outfitting dock for an all-Negro shipfitting crew. The foreman informed him that he was entitled to the position as leadman of the crew, according to Mr. Burris. Mr. Burris' statement is that, "I explained to him how I thought this was a discriminatory set up, and didn't want it. . . Finally my helpers increased in number until I had five, and one Improver. I was then given a time book and checked their time with my foreman, with no increase in pay. I now have two helpers but I don't keep their time. I believe any action to set up a separate crew is entirely wrong and will greatly hinder the war effort. I work with whites and get along fine and see no reason why democratic believing people can't work together. . . I also told this to an A-35 steward and told him to discuss this in his next meeting."

2. ANTONUIA WILLIAMS, 739 1/2 East Forty-Eighth Street, Los Angeles, California. Mr. Williams is employed as a riveter's helper at the Western Pipe and Steel Company. He charges that the company has discriminated against him because he is qualified as a crane operator but has been denied the job solely because of his race. Mr. Williams did not seem to be able to give a good picture of his problem. He has loaned the Committee some exhibits, one of which is an insurance policy, and also a dues book. This material will be valuable. I am not certain that it would be a good idea to call Mr. Williams to testify on his complaint against the Western Pipe and Steel Company.

3. MR. MARYLAND STAMPS, 4150 South Main Street, Los Angeles, Telephone AD 0507. Mr. Stamps is employed as a burner for the Western Pipe and Steel Company. He charges that he applied for membership in Local 92 on March 11, 1943. At that time, he was under the impression that he was joining the union but found later that he was a member of the Auxiliary, A-35. Mr. Stamps states that he continues to pay his dues to the union but does so under protest because he knows that if he does not pay them he cannot work at the company.

4. MISS OLA C. ROSBOROUGH, 125 East Thirty-Sixth Place, Telephone AD 15343. Miss Rosborough is employed as a shipfitter helper at the Western Pipe and Steel Company. She charges that she sought to join Local 92 of the Boiler Makers' Union but was unable to do so solely because of her race. She states that, at the time she first paid her dues, she was under the impression that she was getting into Local 92. This occurred on August 20, 1943.

In addition, we have the names of nine (9) persons who signed individual statements to the effect that they are paying dues into this Auxiliary in order to continue their employment at the Western Pipe and Steel Company, but such payments made are under protest.

MS: copy, HqR38, Central Files. (entry 25) Memoranda, Johnson, George M., Dec. 1941–Dec. 1943.

See the headnote on the Shipbuilding Industry and the Boilermakers Union for cross-references to the other memoranda in this series and for background.

Memorandum on California Shipbuilding Company Complainants

11/1/43

Mr. George M. Johnson

Clarence M. Mitchell

California Shipbuilding Company Complainants

1. <u>MR. WALTER WILLIAMS</u>. Mr. Williams informed me that he finished a war training course in September, 1942, in welding.[1] He went to the USES and was given a referral card to the California Shipbuilding Company hiring hall. From there he was sent to Local 92 of the Boilermakers union for clearance. He stated that he talked with a clerk who told him he would have to pay a deposit of $7.50 and a balance of $7.50 within thirty days as a joining fee. Mr. Williams said that there was no indication at the time that he would not be a member of Local 92. He was then sent back to the hiring hall of the company and assigned to the night shift on the same date. Mr. Williams stated that he paid $2.45 each month from September until May, 1943. At that time he was instructed to pay dues into the auxiliary by a clerk in the union office. The auxiliary was not opened until June 6, Mr. Williams said, but Local 92 would not accept his money in May. At first he refused to pay dues, but in August he began paying monthly sums to the auxiliary after receiving a notice from his employer that his services would be terminated if he did not pay his dues to the union.

He states there have been no meetings of the auxiliary to his knowledge, and there are no elected officers. Mr. Williams talked of the manner in which the Shipyard Committee for equal participation had its origin. The organization began in January, 1943, Mr. Williams said, when Negro workers at the yards began noticing that the word "auxiliary" was printed on their receipts for dues. In February, 1943, or thereabouts, Mr. Williams received an insurance policy also bearing the word "auxiliary," according to his statement. The first meeting of the Shipyard Committee for Equal Participation was held in February at the Y. M. C. A. but Mr. Williams was not present at the time. Mr. Grayson, the current secretary for the Boilermakers auxiliary A-35 was acting as chairman at the time, Mr. Williams stated. About the middle of March, Mr. Williams stated, Mr. Grayson began to change his tactics and tried to sell Negroes on the idea of using the auxiliary. This did not get the approval of the majority of the members and Mr. Williams took the presidency in the latter part of March, according to his statement. At the present time the organization has about 75 paid members according to Mr. Williams and about 1,000 unpaid persons who are sympathetic and affiliated with it. Although the auxiliary has been in existence since June, Mr. Williams stated that he did not hear of a stewards committee until a month ago when certain individuals were designated as stewards by the auxiliary but apparently have not functioned. The white stewards of the Boilermakers tell the men that they do not represent colored workers, according to Mr. Williams.

Mr. Williams is a young man of 25; he is married and has two children. His draft status is 3-A. Apparently he has considerable ability, and while he did not finish college, did enroll for six months in the Los Angeles Junior College. I recommend him as an intelligent and capable witness.

2. HERMAN JAMES HENDERSON, 1458 East Forty-Eighth Place, Los Angeles. I did not interview Mr. Henderson, but he has registered a signed complaint with the Los Angeles office charging that he has been discriminated against by the California Shipbuilding Company and the Boilermakers Union because he was terminated by the company on October 11 for failure to pay dues into the auxiliary. Mr. Henderson is recommended by Mr. Burke as a desirable witness.

3. ANDREW BLAKENEY, 812 1/2 East Forty-Second Street, Los Angeles, Telephone: Adams 15523. I interviewed Mr. Blakeney concerning his complaint that he was terminated by the California Shipbuilding Company in July, 1943, when he refused to pay dues into the auxiliary, A-35. Mr. Blakeney stated that he went to work for the company in October, 1942, as a welder. He paid his initiation fee into Local 92 and assumed that he was a member, according to his statement. In July he stated he received a notice to pay his dues at the office of A-35. He refused to do this and was terminated by the company. Mr. Blakeney informed me that he is a musician by profession and is now earning more money than he would at the shipyard. However, he is ready to return to work at the yard whenever he can obtain admission to the Boilermakers Union. He stated that his main reason for becoming a welder was to do his bit for defense, since he earned more money as a musician.

Mr. Blakeney was a very forthright man and I believe that he will make a good witness for the hearing.

4. MISS HELEN C. GRIGGS, 1542 Seventh Street, Santa Monica, California. Miss Griggs was employed by the California Shipbuilding Company as an arc welder. However, according to her statement, this did not agree with her health and she requested a transfer to burning. When she went to the union hall to discuss this matter with Mr. Grayson of A-35, he told her that the only jobs available were for shipfitters helpers, according to her statement.

She feels she was discriminated against because according to her statement, there were jobs available for burners but she was refused solely because of her race. Miss Griggs is a member of auxiliary A-35 but has not been referred to any employment by the organization since September 10, 1943. I do not recommend Miss Griggs as a witness because it is difficult to understand why she would feel that burning would be less injurious to her than arc welding. It is my suggestion that Mr. Dreyfus may wish to talk with her a second time and if in his opinion she should be called as a witness, this can be done.

5. MR. JEFFERY NEAL, 699 East Fifty-Fourth Street, Los Angeles. Mr. Neal is a chipper at the California Shipbuilding Company. He stated that he was dissatisfied with membership in the Boilermakers auxiliary and while he has paid his dues previously, he has not paid them recently. He gave me a letter dated October 15, signed by Mr. Grayson of the auxiliary. This letter informs Mr. Neal that if he has not paid his dues by October 31 he will be terminated in accordance with the provisions of Section 2 of the master agreement. Mr. Neal stated that he also had a grievance against the company because Negroes were barred from water-stop chipping as long as this job paid $1.55 an hour. When it was reduced to $1.38 an hour Negroes were then placed on it, Mr. Neal stated. He did not give a clear picture of whether he had sought employment on this type of job. At one time he stated that when it came his turn to be employed on water-stop chipping he did not object because he was not assigned since he was too large to get into the place where it was necessary to do the work.

If Mr. Neal is called as a witness, I suggest that his statements be confined to the auxiliary since he does not seem to have a particularly good case against the company personally, although there may be something to his argument so far as other persons are concerned.

6. MR. OSCAR P. TYLER, 962 East Twenty-Second Street, Los Angeles. Mr. Tyler is employed at the California Shipbuilding Company and charges that he is being discriminated against because he is made to belong to Local A-35 in order to hold his job as a chipper. Mr. Tyler charges that the Local A-35 never holds any meetings and does not have officers. He states that it is also impossible to have grievances handled. I recommend Mr. Tyler as a witness.

7. MR. CARL C. DAVIDSON, 1156 East Forty-Ninth Street, Los Angeles. Mr. Davidson is employed at the California Shipbuilding Company as a welder. Mr. Davidson charges that he was transferred from a type of employment which was relatively easy to a type that was harder and he was unable to get his union to adjust the grievance. He also said that on July 5, 1943, he sought upgrading to a job of welder-leadman and was refused by the superintendent of the department. The superintendent said that it would be necessary to have an all-colored crew in order to give Mr. Davidson the job of leadman, according to the complainant. Mr. Davidson charges that the company refused to upgrade him, transferred him, and, therefore, discriminated against him and forced him to belong to A-35 in order to hold his job. Mr. Davidson has a tendency to try to explain the complaints of other persons rather than his own, but I believe that he will make a good witness with proper handling.

8. HENRY MELVYN MILLER, 1251 East Adams Boulevard, Los Angeles. Mr. Miller was employed by the California Shipbuilding Company as a shipfitter's helper. He charges that the company discriminated against him because it refused to

upgrade him to a journeyman shipfitter. Mr. Miller states that he studied architecture for several years and has had a number of years in sheetmetal training. He worked six months as an apprentice fitter for the California Shipbuilding Company. He charges that when he asked Mr. A. C. Cummings, foreman of the midship crew, area 8, for a job as a journeyman shipfitter Mr. Cummings said there were no openings. The following day a white journeyman shipfitter was hired, according to Mr. Miller's charge. When he was unable to get promoted, he became discouraged because of the company's policy, Mr. Miller said. He also feels that he has been discriminated against because he has not been admitted to Local 92 of the Boilermakers Union but is requested to pay dues into auxiliary A-35. He left the company on October 20 with the intention of staying away, Mr. Miller said, and on October 21 his card was "pulled" at the request of the Boiler Makers, according to his statement. This witness has lost his thumb and three fingers on his left hand. Apparently, this injury did not interfere with his duties at the company because he was employed there and could have remained on the job if he had been satisfied with conditions. He talked very well and I recommend that he be called to testify.

9. JAMES A. JACKSON, 4006 Wadsworth Avenue, Los Angeles, California. Mr. Jackson is employed as a welder at the California Shipbuilding Company. His three-page complaint against the company and the union may be summarized by stating that he has had several grievances at the company and he was unable to talk with Mr. Grayson of Local A-35 to have these grievances adjusted. At one time, he was dismissed from the yard for failure to pay dues and sought to get a release but was unable to obtain it. He is now working at the yard after having paid $12.10 to A-35. Mr. Jackson charges the acting secretary, Mr. Grayson, has no control whatever over the yard workmen. Mr. Jackson said, "This is just a means of collecting dues for services not rendered." I recommend Mr. Jackson as a witness.

10. MR. MILTON BERRYMAN, 1841 West Thirty-Sixth Street, Telephone RO 3031. Mr. Berryman is a member of the Boiler Makers' Union and was admitted because he was registered in the State of Louisiana as a Portuguese. He gives the following statement of his complaint:

"I, Milton Berryman, an employee of Calship, and who have been employed by Calship for the past 28 mos., entered the yard as a production welder and since March 1942, I took the Bureau of Marine Inspection and Navigation certification test and successfully passed it on Plate and Pipe for some unknown reason have not been upgraded.

"About July 1943, Mr. Tom Rice, on the recommendation of several foremen in the yard, promised to use me as a welding instructor. But when the requisition for Change of Status came to Mr. Sides' office, Mr. Sides refused to sign it. He, Mr. Sides, told me over the phone that he did not doubt my qualifications, but he did not approve of discrimination, and if I taught any one it would have to be Negroes and since that was the company's policy, too, he was in no position to override their policy. He referred me to Mr. Cecil Jackson's office, the chief labor coordinator. When I approached him with my problem, he said he thought that, in view of the facts that I had stated to him, and the length of my employ I certainly was entitled to at least an instructor's position, but he was only union's representative and he had no right and no authority to change a man's rate status.

"He in turn referred me to Mr. Bergerman [Bergemann], who is mgr. personnel. After about 3 attempts to make an appointment with Mr. Bergerman I was given a pass to see him. I stated my case to him, giving him full details, including length of time in the company's employ and my qualifications and length of experience as journeyman welder. After a prolonged conversation discussing my case and similar other ones, he promised me he would take it up at the next Labor-Management meeting, and if I would come to his office after the meeting, he would have a definite answer for me. I came in as I was asked to.

"He told me Mr. Berryman, in our opinion that would not be to the best interest of the company and that I could take any steps that I so desired. At that point, I asked him, in his opinion didn't he think Calship was practicing or using discriminating methods. At this question, his reply was "No." No. 1—that Calship was the first to employ Negroes. Second—that Calship employed the greatest number of Negroes. I then asked him if in his personal staff there were the Negroes represented. His reply, no, not at the present. When I said good day to him as I was leaving, his curt reply was you can do anything you want to in reference to your case Mr. Berryman."

11. <u>FRED JONES</u>, 647 East Fifty-Third Street. Mr. Jones is employed as a production welder at the Calship Company and has been working there for a period of eighteen months. He charges that he joined Local 92 on September 8, 1942, and paid dues for three months. A man at the union hall told him that he should pay dues just as any of the "white fellows," Mr. Jones stated. At that time, the people in the Boiler Makers' Union were under the impression that he was not a Negro, according to Mr. Jones. Later, Mr. Jones says, he was informed that he would have to pay his dues at the Auxiliary. When he asked why, he was informed that he would have to join whether he liked it or not, according to his statement. One union official tried to get the dues receipts back from him, Mr. Jones stated, but he refused to surrender them. An argument resulted and Mr. Jones stated that he told the union official that if he would step outside for a few minutes the entire matter would be settled permanently. The union official did not step outside, Mr. Jones said. Later, Mr. Jones charges, he received a letter telling him to send in the receipts or be fired. I asked for a copy of this letter but Mr. Jones did not have it and promised to send it. He is paying his dues into the Auxiliary but under protest. I recommend that he be called as a witness.

12. <u>PERCY YOUNG</u>, 772 East Forty-Eighth Street, Los Angeles, California. Mr. Young is employed at the California Shipbuilding Company and charges that the Boiler Makers' Auxiliary is a discriminatory union set-up. However, he

does not express himself well, and I would not suggest that he be called as a witness.

Complaints from the following persons are also attached:

1. Taylor Gilbert (Complains of Separation)
2. Michael Fisher (Separation)
3. R. Watkins (Separation)
4. W. R. Henry (Separation)
5. Lonnie T. Pickens (Separation)
6. Hannah Washington (Charges she was forced off job)
7. Clinton Rayford (Separation)
8. J. W. Mills (Separation)
9. Joyce Ray Washington
10. Theodore J. Hutchison (Complains against Auxiliary)
11. Arthur Hall (Separated but back on the job)
12. Reginald J. Morris (Complains because he was not admitted to 92)
13. John F. Brown (Complains against Auxiliary).

I am submitting the names and addresses of sixty-five (65) employees of the Cal-ship Company, who charge that they are paying dues into the Boiler Makers' Auxiliary under protest.[2]
Attachments

MS: copy, HqR8, Office Files of Frank D. Reeves. (Q–Z) Report on Field Investigations, Mitchell.
　　1. See the headnote on the Shipbuilding Industry and the Boilermakers Union for cross-references to the other memoranda in this series and for background.
　　2. A copy of the list of names is filed with this text in HqR8, Office Files of Frank D. Reeves. (Q–Z) Report on Field Investigations—Mitchell. See also the voluminous materials related to the hearings on the shipbuilding industry in HqR14, 15.

Memorandum on War Contractors Failing to List Number of Non-whites on ES 270 Reports, Region IX

DATE:　　　　　　　　　　　　　　　　　　　　　　　　November 5, 1943
TO:　　　Mr. Will Maslow
FROM:　　Clarence M. Mitchell
SUBJECT:　War Contractors Failing to List Number of Non-Whites on ES 270
　　　　　　Reports, Region IX

The following companies and Government establishments were cited by the War Manpower Commission in Region IX as refusing to supply information on the number of non-whites employed.[1] This information was to be used for USES 270 Reports:

Kansas City, Missouri

Aluminum Company of America
Ford Motor Company
Kansas City Power & Light Company
Kansas City Quartermaster Depot
Oldsmobile (Kansas City Div.) General Motors Corp.
Pratt & Whitney Corporation of Missouri
Standard Oil Company (Indiana)

St. Louis, Missouri

Chevrolet Motor Company
Emerson Electric Manufacturing Company

Oklahoma City, Oklahoma

Douglas Aircraft Company, Incorporated

Independence, Kansas

Independence Army Air Field

Coffeyville, Kansas

Coffeyville Army Air Field

Pauline, Kansas

Army Air Forces Supply Depot

Pine Bluff, Arkansas

Pine Bluff Arsenal

Bauxite, Arkansas

Alumina Plant Incorporated—
Aluminum Ore Company—of
Aluminum Company of America

Letters setting forth the policy of the Committee with reference to this matter were sent to all of them except the War Department establishments, and the Oldsmobile and Chevrolet Motor Companies. In the case of the latter two, it was thought that the matter might be handled better through the central office of the General Motors Corporation.

The following companies have indicated that they will comply with the requirements and send in information on non-white employment:

Pratt & Whitney Corporation, Kansas City
Douglas Aircraft Company, Oklahoma City
Emerson Electric Company, St. Louis
Standard Oil Company, Kansas City

On September 7, the Aluminum Company of America sent in a letter stating that it did cooperate with the War Manpower Commission in giving information but added that its application did not carry any information on race, color, or creed. There is nothing in the file to show that this letter was answered.

I do not have any information on the current status of these cases because, as you will recall, these are among the cases turned over to Region IX for further handling.

MS: copy, HqR38, Central Files. (entry 25) Memoranda, Maslow, Will, 1943.

1. This was a broad problem that would eventually crystallize in the FEPC's fight with General Motors Corporation over the issue. See 3/27/44, note 5, later texts involving GM, and the headnotes on Race, Creed, Color, or National Origin on Employment Application Forms and on Creedal Discrimination.

Field Investigation Report on California Shipbuilding Corporation, Western Pipe & Steel Company's Shipbuilding Division, and Consolidated Steel Corporation's Shipbuilding Division

November 6, 1943

To: Mr. George M. Johnson
           Deputy Chairman

From: Clarence M. Mitchell
           Associate Director of Field Operations

Re: California Shipbuilding Corporation, Western Pipe & Steel Company's
           Shipbuilding Division, and Consolidated Steel Corporation's
           Shipbuilding Division
           Investigation by: Clarence M. Mitchell

I. Brief Summary of Complaint

The President's Committee on Fair Employment Practice, during the summer of 1943, received over four hundred complaints from persons employed in the shipbuilding industry of Los Angeles and vicinity. These complaints came, for the most part, from the Shipyard Committee for Equal Participation. It was charged that Negroes employed in shipbuilding trades coming under the jurisdiction of Boiler Makers' Local 92 were being forced to join an auxiliary, A-35. Those refusing to join the auxiliary were dismissed from employment by the shipbuilding companies, according to the complaints.

The yards involved were the California Shipbuilding Company at Wilmington, the Consolidated Steel Corporation's Shipbuilding Division at Wilmington, and the Western Pipe & Steel Corporation's Shipbuilding Division at San Pedro.

II. Description of Parties Charged

The California Shipbuilding Company employed 40,421 persons as of October 8, 1943, according to Mr. Russell A. Bergemann, Manager of Industrial Relations. It builds cargo vessels and tankers.

The Western Pipe & Steel Company employed a total of 12,285 persons as of October 9, 1943, according to Mr. W. H. Lewis, Administrative Manager. This yard is building coast guard and naval vessels.

The Consolidated Steel Corporation's Shipbuilding Division employs a total of 18,000 persons, according to the latest information from Mr. Clarence R. Johnson, Minorities Consultant of the War Manpower Commission in Region XII. Mr. Johnson stated that the Consolidated Company was not very cooperative and had not supplied information similar to that given by Western Pipe & Steel and the California Shipbuilding Companies.

The employment figures in these yards as of October, 1943, were as follows:

CALIFORNIA SHIPBUILDING CORPORATION
WILMINGTON, CALIFORNIA

September, 1942			*Current Employment*
Total	—	37,000	40,421
Non-White	—	469	3,802

WESTERN PIPE & STEEL COMPANY
SHIPBUILDING DIVISION
SAN PEDRO, CALIFORNIA

November, 1942			*Current Employment*
Total	—	13,500	12,285
Non-White	—	207	783

CONSOLIDATED STEEL CORPORATION
SHIPBUILDING DIVISION..
WILMINGTON, CALIFORNIA

August, 1942			*Current Employment*
Total	—	3,500	18,000
Non-White	—	17	1,800

*Figures supplied by Clarence R. Johnson,
War Manpower Commission, Region XII.

Local 92 of the International Brotherhood of Boiler Makers, Iron Ship Builders and Helpers of America has jurisdiction over the following counties in the area: In California—the counties of Santa Barbara, Kern, Inyo, San Bernardino, Los Angeles, Ventura, Orange, Riverside, San Diego, and Imperial. In Nevada—the counties of Esmeralda, Nye, Lincoln, and Clark. It is estimated that this local has approximately 40,000 members. Mr. H. G. Coryell is President of the Union and Mr. E. V. Blackwell is the Secretary and Business Agent. This union has set up an auxiliary known as A-35, which has an office in the City of Los Angeles at 4150 South Main Street. At the time I was in the City, Mr. Garner Grayson was serving as acting secretary of the union and Mr. U. S. Griggs was acting assistant secretary. Messrs. Grayson and Griggs estimated that they have approximately 4,000 persons in the auxiliary.

The California Shipbuilding Corporation, the Western Pipe & Steel Company's Shipbuilding Division, and the Consolidated Steel Corporation's Shipbuilding Division have closed shop contracts with the Metal Trades Council of the A. F. of L., in accordance with the provisions of the Master Agreement affecting the shipbuilding industries on the West Coast. The principal union in the Metal Trades Council, from the standpoint of membership and prestige, is the International Brotherhood of Boiler Makers, Iron Ship Builders and Helpers of America. The provisions of the contract require that the unions of the Metal Trades Council supply workers to the companies from their membership and, when they are unable to do so, the companies are free to recruit non-union workers. However, all persons recruited must become members of the union and pay dues or their employment must be terminated by the companies.

III. Prior or Related Cases Involving Parties Charged

From time to time, the Committee has received complaints from various individuals who charged that they were not given employment at one of these three yards. There are others who charged that they have not been upgraded in accordance with their skills and abilities. These individuals allege that they were being discriminated against solely because of race.

Mr. George Toll, Local Manager of the U.S.E.S. in Long Beach, California, informed me that he opened the office of the Employment Service at Wilmington, California, on August 1, 1941. This office has been receiving orders from the California Shipbuilding Company, Western Pipe & Steel, and Consolidated Steel from that period up until present. Mr. Toll left Wilmington only recently. It was the function of his office to place the California clearance orders from the three companies. This included approximately eighteen (18) offices in Southern California, with the exception of San Diego. Mr. Toll stated it had been his experience that Consolidated and Western Pipe & Steel were reluctant to hire Negroes as machinists helpers and shipfitters helpers. Recently, they have begun taking Negroes in these occupations, but only because of the manpower shortage, according to Mr. Toll.

IV. Efforts of the War Manpower Commission to Obtain Compliance

Beginning in 1941, Mr. Clarence R. Johnson, Minorities Consultant for the War Manpower Commission in Region XII, has been at work on the problems of these three yards. Mr. Johnson began his efforts when he was with the Minorities Division of the Office of Production Management and the Negro Employment and Training Branch of the War Production Board. Later, the Negro Employment and Training Branch of WPB was transferred to the War Manpower Commission, and Mr. Johnson continued his work under WMC. On February 24, 1942, Mr. Blackwell wrote the following letter to Mr. Johnson:

> "In confirmation of our telephone conversation of February 23, I have instructed our Wilmington office to clear colored applicants when properly referred to that office."

Local 92 cleared some Negroes for employment and a few actually became members of the union because their racial identity was not known. On July 7, 1943, the union established Auxiliary A-35 and insisted that all Negroes become members of it or have their employment terminated.

159

V. Efforts to Obtain Compliance

When the auxiliary was established in July of 1943, many Negroes employed at the three yards refused to pay their dues. According to Mr. Grayson of the Auxiliary, approximately 500 Negroes were terminated by the companies for this reason.

In addition to your visit to the West Coast for the purpose of holding conferences with the Boiler Makers' and the shipbuilding interests on this problem, Judge James Wolfe, Chief Justice of the Supreme Court of the State of Utah, and Mr. Daniel R. Donovan, of the Committee's staff, went to Los Angeles in an attempt to adjust these problems in a manner which would be in harmony with the requirements of Executive Order 9346. On those occasions, the union representatives did not offer any solution which would adjust the complaints before the Committee.

In its meeting of August 28, 1943, the Committee voted to have a hearing in the City of Los Angeles on these complaints. I arrived in Los Angeles on Friday, October 22, 1943, and remained until the morning of Thursday, October 28. During that time, I interviewed complainants and the following persons:

1. Mr. Burt Harnish, Area Director of the War Manpower Commission, and members of his staff.
2. White members of the Boiler Makers' Local 92.
3. Officials of Auxiliary A-35.

I did not talk with management or Local 92 representatives because you had already discussed the problem with them in your meeting at San Francisco on August 20, 1943.

The results of these interviews are set forth in the following memoranda:

1. Employment Reports re California Shipbuilding Corporation, Western Pipe & Steel Company's Shipbuilding Division, and Consolidated Steel Corporation's Shipbuilding Division, dated 10-8-43, 10-9-43, and 11-3-43, respectively.[1]
2. Conference with Officials of Auxiliary A-35, 10-26-43.[2]
3. Meeting with white members of Boiler Makers' Local 92, 10-27-43.[3]
4. Case of Thomas Madison Doram, 717 1/2 E. Vernon Avenue, Los Angeles, California, Telephone: Adams 13649, 10-27-43.
5. Conference with Mr. George Toll, Local Manager, USES, Long Beach, California, 10-27-43.
6. California Shipbuilding Company Complainants, 11-1-43.
7. Western Pipe & Steel Company Complainants, 11-1-43.[4]
8. Consolidated Steel Corporation Complainants, Shipbuilding Division, 11-1-43.[5]
9. Statement Signed by Persons Protesting Against A-35.

In summarizing, I believe I should say that there were some persons who charged the companies with discrimination, but the bulk of the charges was against Local 92 for setting up A-35. A number of Negroes who signed pledges that they would not pay dues were dismissed. It appears that some of these found employment in other places. Many of the complainants began paying dues into the auxiliary, but signed statements indicating that they did so under protest.

VI. Recommendations

In view of the evidence submitted by complainants and other information set forth in my memoranda, it is my recommendation that the Committee proceed with the hearing.

MS: copy, HqR48, Central Files. Reports 1–2.
    See the headnote on the Shipbuilding Industry and the Boilermakers Union for cross-references to the other memoranda in this series and for background.
    1. The reports of 10/8, 10/9, and 11/3/43 were not found.
    2. The report of 10/26/43 is published herein.
    3. This report is published under the date of 11/27/43.
    4. The two reports of 10/27 and the two of 11/1/43 are published herein.
    5. This report was not found.

Memorandum on OPA Policy Statement Regarding Executive Order 8802

Date: November 8, 1943

To: Mr. Will Maslow
From: Clarence M. Mitchell
Subject: OPA Policy Statement Regarding Executive Order 8802

In keeping with our conversation on November 6, I talked with Mr. T. Arnold Hill, of the Office of Price Administration, concerning Mr. Jack Burke's memorandum of October 30, regarding the Office of Price Administration.

Mr. Hill stated that the press release which was attached to Mr. Burke's memorandum was based on an administrative order which was sent out by Mr. Brown. This order, Mr. Hill said, will remain in effect unless rescinded by Mr. Bowles. Mr. Hill will send me a copy of the order, and we can forward it to all of the regional offices.

Mr. Hill also suggested that it would be desirable for FEPC to request that Mr. Bowles reaffirm this order. It was Mr. Hill's belief that the letter of request might well include a brief statement about the contents of Mr. Burke's memorandum and two cases from the California area, which I mentioned to him.

If we send such a letter to Mr. Bowles, I would prefer to have the administrative order before me before preparing it. Accordingly, I shall wait until the order arrives before doing so.

October 30, 1943

To: Harry L. Kingman
   Regional Director

From: Jack B. Burke
   Fair Practice Examiner

Subject: OPA policy statement regarding Executive Order 8802

The attached copy of an undated press release, which sets forth a statement by Prentiss M. Brown, former Price Administrator, regarding OPA policy in connection with racial discrimination in Government agencies and defense industries, recently came into this office.

It occurs to me it might be a good idea to suggest to the Washington office that Clarence Boldes [Chester Bowles], the new Price Administrator, be urged to publicly reaffirm this policy.

Reports have been received here that the local OPA set-up is lax in its employment policy, where certain members of minority groups are concerned.

July 15, 1943

MEMORANDUM

To: All OPA Employees

From: Prentiss M. Brown
   Administrator

Subject: Office of Special Assistant to the Administrator

I am today signing Administrative Order No. 84, which sets forth the functions and responsibilities of the Special Assistant to the Administrator who will deal with racial matters. I am hereby appointing Mr. T. Arnold Hill to this position.

I am anxious to avoid any criticism of OPA's relationship to our Negro citizens; to insure a reasonable and fair participation for them in our program; and to take all possible steps to enlist their support and cooperation for our program.

I am directing that in the National Office all communications and all questions pertaining to Negro participation, support and cooperation, and all questions dealing with matters of policy, racial discrimination, and arrangements for conferences with delegations that want to be heard on Negro matters, and the like, be cleared with this Office of the Special Assistant to the Administrator.

Communications addressed to the Administrator or simply to the Office of Price Administration when referring to the above mentioned matters should be transmitted to Mr. Hill's office for appropriate disposition.

I am likewise anxious that the regional administrators and district directors take full advantage of the services rendered by Mr. Hill's office, and make use of it whenever his advice or assistance will be helpful to them.

November 12, 1943

MEMORANDUM

To: Mr. Jack B. Burke
           Fair Practice Examiner
From: Clarence M. Mitchell
           Associate Director of Field Operations
Subject: Your Memorandum of October 30, Regarding OPA Policy Statement

In keeping with your request, I have checked with OPA, and the press release attached to your memorandum refers to Administrative Order No. 13, Supplement No. 6, of the Office of Price Administration. This was issued by Mr. Prentiss M. Brown on February 16, 1943.

The Office of Price Administration states that this order is still in effect and will remain so unless rescinded by the present Administrator. There is no reason for assuming that the present Administrator will revoke this order, but, for practical purposes in the field, we are requesting Mr. Chester Bowles to reaffirm this statement. As soon as he does so, this information will be sent to the field.

Meanwhile, it is advisable to make full use of the provisions of Administrative Order No. 13 in dealing with the Office of Price Administration.

MS: LH, DI, HqR67, Central Files. Reports, U.S. Government-1, General N–W.

Copies of related documents, including Administrative Order no. 13, the press release, and Hill's 11/8/43 memorandum to Mitchell in which the administrative order by Brown was enclosed, are filed with this text.

Memorandum on War Department Forms 6 and 6a

DATE: 11/9/43
TO: Mr. Will Maslow
FROM: Clarence M. Mitchell
SUBJECT: War Department Forms 6 and 6a

On two occasions, we have had requests for information concerning these forms. During my absence, Mr. Truman K. Gibson wrote a letter concerning them, but which, I observe, you have noted.[1]

I had a talk with a War Department representative concerning these documents, and he stated that they are supposed to be confidential. This means that we could not give them to anyone other than our own staff members.

I have requested copies of the forms and, as soon as they are available, I believe we should discuss them further.

MS: copy, HqR67, Central Files. Reports, U.S. Government, War Department A–L.

1. Jewish organizations in New York had objected to questions regarding race or religion included on these employment application forms used by the War Department. The query to Truman Gibson, civilian aide to the secretary of War, drafted by Mitchell and sent under the signature of George Johnson on 9/15, and Gibson's reply of 10/28/43, are filed with this text. According to a letter of 11/12/43, drafted by Mitchell and signed by Malcolm Ross, to Eli E. Cohen of the Coordinating Committee of Jewish Organizations, the forms were used in connection with loyalty investigations of persons in war industries and were permissible under the FEPC's agreement with the Provost Marshal General's office of 3/10/43. For these and related texts, see HqR67, Central Files. Reports, U.S. Government, War Department A–L. For background, see the headnote on Race, Creed, Color, or National Origin on Employment Application Forms and the section on the War Department in the headnote on Relationships with Federal Agencies.

Memorandum on War Labor Board Panel Hearing on Case of Point Breeze Employees Association Versus Western Electric Company, Baltimore, Maryland

November 11, 1943

TO: Mr. Will Maslow

FROM: Clarence M. Mitchell

SUBJECT: War Labor Board Panel Hearing on Case of Point Breeze
Employees Association versus Western Electric Company,
Baltimore, Maryland.—4-UR-126

In the absence of Mr. Joseph H. B. Evans, Associate Director of Region IV, who was on other official business, I attended the hearing before a War Labor Board Panel on the case of the Point Breeze Employees Association v. the Western Electric Company of Baltimore. The hearing was at 10:00 A. M. on Tuesday, November 9, 1943, in the assembly room of the Brown Memorial Presbyterian Church, Lafayette and Park Avenues, in Baltimore. Members of the panel were: the Rev. Guthrie Speers, chairman; Joseph Conway, labor representative; and E. St. John Huberman, industry representative. Mr. Eli Rock, regional representative of W. L. B., was also present.[1]

The Point Breeze Employees Association won a strike vote held on October 4 and 5, 1943. Out of 6,300 eligible employees, 2,960 voted. The results were 1,802 for a strike, 1,144 against, 12 void ballets, and 2 blank ballots. The union states the strike is for separate facilities for colored and white employees. The W.L.B. granted the company and the union a hearing and the strike, which was scheduled for Friday, November 5, was called off by the union.

Because this matter is still being handled in the regional office, I am making no recommendations at this time. However, I attempted to make a full report on what happened at the hearing. The Regional Director will, no doubt, wish to make certain suggestions for further action after he reads this memorandum. A copy of it is being transmitted to him.

The following is my record of what occurred at the hearing. [Emphasis added]

STATEMENT BY CHARLES H. DORN
ATTORNEY FOR THE POINT BREEZE
EMPLOYEES ASSOCIATION

Mr. Dorn charged that, since the summer of 1942, the company decided to remove racial designations from toilet doors. When this action took place, there was considerable trouble, Mr. Dorn charged. He said there have been numerous "incidents" involving Negroes and whites on this issue. The last incident which occurred was in August, 1943, Mr. Dorn said. At that time, a colored girl was brought into a department where no Negroes had worked before, he stated. There were no other lavatory facilities in the area and it was necessary for this girl to use those used by the white employees. The white girls in the area walked off the job in protest, he stated.

Mr. Lucien F. Rye, a conciliator from the United States Department of Labor, came down to try to settle the matter, Mr. Dorn said. According to Mr. Dorn, Mr. Rye said it would not be discriminatory if equal facilities were set up for Negroes. As a result of Mr. Rye's efforts, the white girls who had gone on a strike because the colored girl had been brought into the department returned to work, Mr. Dorn stated. The understanding was that a settlement would be made later, Mr. Dorn indicated.

A petition was submitted to the company with the names of 1,500 employees on it, asking that separate facilities be instituted, Mr. Dorn told the panel. When the petition was submitted, it did not have 1,500 names on it, he admitted, but at present it does contain 1,500, according to his testimony. There were no dates on the copies submitted to the panel. Some of them were written in longhand and others had a typewritten statement on them with signatures attached. As a result of this petition, Mr. Dorn said, the union felt that something should be done about the matter. Up until the time the petition was received, the union had tried to stay away from the issue, according to his statement. Mr. Dorn admitted that he did not know whether only salaried employees, union members, or members of the supervisory force signed the petition. He stated that he had not even checked to determine whether the persons who signed it were union members. He charged that the company had always stated that Executive Order 8802 made it necessary that there be no separation of the lavatory facilities. Mr. Dorn said that he proposed that such facilities could be established without violating the Executive Order, and he also said that the union would take action in behalf of Negroes if the company failed to set up facilities for them which would be equal to those established for whites.

One Government representative, who came to the plant, stated that if separate facilities were discriminatory, the Western Electric plant was the only one south of the Mason and Dixon Line which was not discriminating, Mr. Dorn said. He also charged that, when the strike vote was taken on October 4 and 5, the voting places were not conveniently located, but, in spite of the difficulty that confronted workers who wished to vote, they still came out and cast their ballots. Mr. Dorn also charged that the A. F. of L., the C. I. O., and the Baltimore Afro-American newspaper were all campaigning to persuade the workers to vote against having a strike. In spite of these efforts, he said, 63.3 per cent voted "yes," 39.2 per cent voted "no," and .4 per cent of the ballots were void. According to Mr. Dorn, an NLRB representative named Seff said he had never seen an election where the vote came out so heavily and where the issue involved was so thoroughly settled. According to this NLRB man, as quoted by Mr. Dorn, the majority was so overwhelmingly for an interruption of war production that it was astounding.

Mr. Speer raised the question of whether both Negroes and whites had voted. Mr. Dorn's reply to this was in the affirmative.

Mr. Conway asked whether those eligible to vote had done so. Mr. Dorn said that he would not be in a position to say because he did not know whether it would be permissible to give out that type of information on a war plant. He suggested that, since representatives of management were present, they might wish to answer the question. Mr. Chew responded by saying that there were 6,300 hourly rated employees who were eligible to vote and of those 1,700 were colored. Mr. Chew said the vote was 1,802 for a strike, 1144 against the strike, 12 void ballots, and 2 blank ballots. Mr. Dorn then said that a number of persons had waited an hour in order to be able to vote. The election was not held on company time, he said, but was held on the employees' own time. Mr. Dorn pointed out that the number of votes against having separate facilities was less than the number of Negroes employed. He stated that the union did not want to have a strike because the Army had said that the work of the plant was very important. Mr. Dorn stated that, immediately after the balloting, the union could have called the strike and pulled its members off the job. He said, however, that the contract between the union and the company provides for a thirty-day notice before the calling of a strike, and it was decided that the work stoppage would be on Friday, November 5, at 6:00 A. M., unless the company changed its policy. On Thursday, November 4, Mr. Dorn said, representatives of the War Labor Board came in seeking to have the strike called off. He alleged that this was the first time that anything had been done to settle the matter between the date of the strike vote and November 4.

Mr. Dorn completed his statement by saying that he had legal opinions proving that the establishment of separate facilities is not discriminatory, if such facilities are equal.[2]

STATEMENT BY C. C. CHEW
SUPERINTENDENT OF INDUSTRIAL RELATIONS,
WESTERN ELECTRIC COMPANY

Mr. Chew, speaking for the company, mentioned that Mr. Dorn had said the dispute resulted from a demand for separate facilities. On June 25, 1941, the President issued his Executive Order that there should be no discrimination, Mr. Chew s[ai]d, and this was followed by Executive Order 9346. The Western Electric Company has entered into a number of contracts which contained provisions that the company would not discriminate, Mr. Chew said. Without reference to the merits of the President's Order, Mr. Chew said, the company felt that it should comply with it. At the time the Order was issued, Mr. Chew said, there were no colored employees at the Baltimore plant of the Western Electric Company. Therefore, there were no separate facilities for employees. He stated that, prior to the time colored persons were hired, on some occasions, colored truck drivers came into the plant and a facility had been installed for their convenience and in order to comply with the Baltimore City Plumbing Code. The first colored employee was hired October 6, 1941, Mr. Chew said, and, in accordance with the requirements of the Baltimore Plumbing Code, the following facilities were set up: one in the Cable Shop, one in the Wire Shop, and one in the Canton Warehouse. There was also a drinking fountain on the trucking platform, Mr. Chew said. On February 13, 1942, the Plumbing Code was amended and it was no longer necessary to provide separate facilities, Mr. Chew said. The company then decided that it needed to develop a policy on the matter. This policy was based on two things, Mr. Chew said—(1) the management knew that it had to comply with the requirements of the Executive Order, and (2) since a large number of Negroes would be employed, it would be very impractical to have separate facilities for them. The company had to consider that it was made up of a number of separate buildings and departments, Mr. Chew stated. Frequently, it is necessary to transfer employees and equipment between departments and buildings, Mr. Chew pointed out. In order to have a flexible working force and to make certain that it did not discriminate in doing this, the company felt that it was necessary to have facilities which would be available for the use of all of its employees regardless of race. Mr. Chew said that the percentage of movement and transfer of employees cannot be foreseen to the extent that separate facilities could be provided by the company. Western Electric also feels that it cannot discriminate in the movement of its employees between departments and buildings, Mr. Chew stated. He said there was no serious argument against this arrangement until October of 1942. It had been discussed with both the salaried employees and the hourly rated employees, Mr. Chew said, and both of these groups had agreed to it. The October grievance in 1942 was built around incidents in the main, which were supposed to have occurred in the washrooms. It was finally agreed that these incidents would be handled on an individual case basis, Mr. Chew stated, and there was no further difficulty until August 12, 1943, when twenty-two white women refused to work because a new colored employee had been assigned to their group. The company suspended the twenty-two employees for thirty days, or until such time as they were willing to return to work under conditions in keeping with the company policy, Mr. Chew said.

The union met with management and the controversy crystallized into a demand for separate facilities, Mr. Chew told the panel. The employees involved returned to work on August 16, 1943. Mr. Chew stated that the question of the lavatory facilities was not raised at first when the August 12 trouble occurred but was subsequently raised in meetings with management.

Mr. Chew reminded the panel that Mr. Dorn had charged that the location of the balloting places on October 4 and 5 was inconvenient. This location was decided upon by the Labor Board, Mr. Chew said, and the company had nothing to do with it. The dispute is one on which the company and the union cannot agree, Mr. Chew said, because the union has said it cannot accept less than its full demands, and the company feels that it will be violating Executive Orders 8802 and 9346 if it makes a change. Mr. Chew stated that the company would not change unless ordered to do so by the proper Government agency.

In replying to Mr. Chew's statement, Mr. Dorn made the assertion that: "It goes without saying that among the colored race venereal disease is greater than among whites." Mr. Dorn then picked up a large volume which, he said, was a medical publication, and was about to quote certain passages based on an analysis of 1,895,778 cases. The panel called for a recess at this point and, when it returned to the hearing room, asked that Mr. Dorn give the page references of the material he was reading instead of quoting it at the hearing. Mr. Dorn agreed to do this and then read Executive Order 8802.

Mr. Dorn insisted that, when the colored employees first started to work at the plant, the company did have separate facilities and then read the Plumbing Code as revised by the City of Baltimore. He stated that, while the Plumbing Code has been revised, the city itself still maintains separate facilities for Negroes and has five public bathhouses for whites and one for colored. He also cited several court cases which he said substantiated his point providing that separate facilities were not discriminatory if equal. He told the panel that the City of Baltimore does not permit Negroes to play golf on all of its golf courses but restricts them to one course known as the Carroll Park Course. This course is for Negroes only, Mr. Dorn said, and whites may not play there.

Mr. Dorn then charged that the company still has separate facilities for Negroes in its Haven Street plant and that "the higher ups in personnel" have separate washrooms for themselves, which are kept locked. He stated that, at the Haven Street plant, there are no signs designating facilities for racial groups, but one set of washrooms is kept locked and whites only may have the key. Mr. Dorn then said that the American Telephone and Telegraph Company controls Western Electric Company and the Chesapeake and Potomac Telephone Company in Baltimore. The latter has separate facilities for Negroes, he stated, and the policy for Western Electric should be the same. He also cited a list of war industries in Baltimore which, he said, have separate facilities for Negroes. Among these, he listed the following companies: Rustless Iron and Steel, Crown Cork and Seal, Bendix, Westinghouse, and the Bethlehem Steel Shipyard. Mr. Dorn stated that he had a number of other companies on the list and submitted this to the panel. He then made the charge that there have been work stoppages at the plant and older employees were leaving because of the mixed facilities. He said that a number of new white employees would begin working at the company and upon discovering that Negroes and whites used the same facilities would leave. This, he charged, slowed down production.

Mr. Chew, replying to Mr. Dorn's statement, said that the twenty-two girls who went on strike in August did so because they refused to work with a colored woman employee. Later in the discussion concerning the work stoppage, Mr. Chew said the girls agreed that they would work with the colored employee if separate facilities were set up. One of the panel members asked Mr. Chew whether he knew of any other Baltimore plants in which the facilities were mixed instead of separate. Mr. Chew stated that he knew of certain establishments but did not care to mention the names because he, of course, was primarily concerned with the affairs of the Western Electric Company. He said that there was one large plant very close to the Western Electric Company which had arrangements similar to those in his plant.

Replying to Mr. Dorn's charge that "the higher ups in personnel" had facilities for themselves, Mr. Chew said that the door to the facility which he has occasion to use had never been locked in ten years. He stated that the present policy of the Western Electric Company has been in effect for one and one-half years and, if changed, in his opinion, would lead to further trouble. He reiterated his statement, however, that the company would abide by any decision of a proper governmental body.

STATEMENT BY EUGENE BARNES

Mr. Eugene Barnes, a colored member of the Point Breeze Employees Association, was granted an opportunity to speak as an individual. Mr. Barnes made his request from the floor and the panel members conferred among themselves before giving him the opportunity to speak. The chairman pointed out that, because of the nature of the case, it seemed desirable to have some statement from a colored employee. Mr. Barnes said that he is a floor hand in a Punch Press area at the company. He charged that many colored and white employees are opposed to the Point Breeze Employees Association's attempt to have a strike for separate facilities. He stated that there are 800 colored persons who are in the PBEA and they, with the majority of white persons in the plant, oppose the strike. He stated that the union does not reflect the views of the employees because it has membership meetings once a year only and is governed by thirty-three selected representatives. These representatives started the petition for the strike, Mr. Barnes charged, and he added that no vote of the membership was taken on this question. Mr. Barnes stated that Mr. Dorn, the union's attorney, was in error when he said production in the plant was being slowed down because of mixed facilities. The plant has won three "E" awards for production. This, Mr. Barnes said, shows that the worker morale is high. He also said that the President's Committee on Fair Employment Practice has already held that any change from the present conditions would be a step backward which could not but lead to discrimination based on race and would, therefore, violate Executive Order 9346. Mr. Barnes said that, in addition, this is the first case of its kind which has come to his attention, and he believed that, if any change was made in response to the pressure brought by the PBEA, a dangerous precedent would be set. This precedent would lead small but articulate groups in other plants in many parts of the country to use the strike threat to accomplish similar objectives, Mr. Barnes said. He repeated his charge that the Point Breeze Employees Association had stimulated the petition among the workers and had told many persons that they were voting for separate facilities and not for a strike. He challenged Mr. Dorn's statement about the policy of Baltimore city with reference to golf courses and stated that the Carroll Park Course is not open at all since it has been "plowed up." He said that colored persons are playing on all courses in the city. The speaker then stated that he regretted that the question of venereal diseases had been raised by Mr. Dorn, but, since it had been raised, he was prepared to give an answer. The panel members requested that he submit his views in writing for their information as Mr. Dorn had been asked to do. He agreed to do this.

Mr. Barnes gave the Eastern Aircraft Company of Baltimore as an illustration of a war plant which has a policy similar to that of Western Electric. He charged that the persons who went on strike in August had previously been stationed in an area where he was working and, from his observation, he believed that the real purpose for the strike was to keep the colored employee out of their department altogether. He charged that Mr. Dorn was incorrect in his statement on the Haven Street plant. Mr. Barnes said that he had worked in this location for seven months. The building, he said, was formerly used by the Heffberger Ice Company. This company had two sets of sanitary facilities, he stated, but he was not certain of whether these facilities had racial designations on them when they were being used by the Heffberger Company. In any event, Mr. Barnes stated, the Western Electric Company has never had any regulations requiring a separation of the races in the Haven Street plant, and, during his seven months there, he used both sides himself. Mr. Barnes stated that he was present at a meeting of officials of the PBEA prior to the time the strike was supposed to take place. After attending this meeting, he said, he concluded that the union officials are not really interested in separate facilities or winning the war, but only in perpetuating themselves in their offices. He stated that the action of the PBEA was one of the worst things that could have been done to injure morale of workers and said that it was a terrible slap at the colored employees. These employees are paying dues to the extent of over $400 a month, Mr. Barnes charged.

At the end of Mr. Barnes' statement, Mr. Dorn arose to say that he suggested that the panel members visit the Haven Street plant and find out for themselves what the conditions were. He admitted, however, that he had received his information on the separation of facilities from another person and did not know it from his own investigation.

Mr. Chew said that he would like to point out that, when discussing incidents which occur in the plant, it should be kept in mind that his company did not have many incidents but such as did occur were between Negroes and Negroes, whites and whites, and sometimes between Negroes and whites.

Both sides were given four days in which to present briefs setting forth their positions.

Also present at the hearing, as observers, were Major J. P. Rhudey and Captain H. J. Lidoff, labor officers of the Signal Corps, who came down from Philadelphia. Major Rhudey was given an opportunity to make a statement, and he said he did not wish to express an opinion on the merits of the case but he would like to say that, while the Army needs all of the things that the company manufactures, there is a particular need for the field wire, which the company is making. This need is so urgent, the Major said, that plans are being made to establish other plants where there is an available labor supply. He said that the Army appeals to both sides that there be no stopping of the production of field wire because it is urgently needed and especially since there are expanding operations in military areas.

At the close of the hearing, Mr. Speers, the chairman, told me that he would communicate with the President's Committee if the panel needed any further information which the Committee might have. He seemed very cooperative, and I felt that, in the hearing, both sides were given an opportunity to present their points of view. I also thought that the panel was very fair in giving the colored employee an opportunity to state his views.

MS: copy, HqR68, Office Files of John A. Davis. Mitchell.

This text marks the continuance of a long struggle in which a central issue was demands by white women for separate bathrooms. Underlying this issue was whether the FEPC would sanction segregation. Neither EO 8802 nor EO 9346 gave the FEPC specific jurisdiction over the issue; but the Committee consistently opposed introduction of segregated facilities of any kind in places where they did not already exist. See 8/5, 8/26, 11/13 note 2, 12/14/43, and 1/7, 3/14/44. For additional background, see the headnotes on Jurisdictional Issues and on Strikes and Work Stoppages, as well as the introduction.

1. See the section on the NWLB in the headnote on Relationships with Federal Agencies.

2. Those opinions were based on the U.S. Supreme Court's decision in *Plessy v. Ferguson* (1896).

Memorandum on Western Electric Company, Baltimore, Maryland

November 13, 1943

Mr. George M. Johnson

Clarence M. Mitchell

Western Electric Company, Baltimore, Maryland

I thought that you might be interested in receiving these copies on the Western Electric case. You will note that Father Haas' letter of September 7, which he dictated himself in my presence, states that the establishment of separate facilities would be a violation of the Executive Order in this case.[1] Also, you will note that the Company takes a very strong position and indicates that it arrived at the policy of mixed facilities in order to meet the production requirements of the plant, and also to conform to what it believed to be the requirements of the Executive Order.

Since the Committee is meeting, I assume this matter will come up for discussion.[2]

MS: copy, HqR38, Memoranda, Johnson, George M.—3, Dec. 1941–Dec. 1943.

1. This case led the FEPC to adopt the position that it could oppose segregation, despite lack of specific authorization to do so, when its practice contributed to employment discrimination. See Mitchell, memorandum, 11/11/43 and the headnote on Jurisdictional Issues.

2. At its 12/4/43 meeting, the Committee approved the following statement (originally adopted 11/16/43): "the Committee takes the position that in the circumstances of this case where there are frequent and temporary transfers of workers from department to department such installing of segregated duplicate facilities cannot but lead to discriminatory employment practices and would be in violation of Executive Order 9346." At that meeting, the associate director of Region IV (Joseph Evans) also reported on the hearing on separate facilities at Western Electric before the NWLB. See Minutes, 12/4/43, HqR1, Summary Minutes of Meetings; Mitchell, memorandum, 11/11/43.

Memorandum on Complaint of Robert Nelson Craig

November 13, 1943

TO: Mr. George M. Johnson
        Deputy Chairman

FROM: Clarence M. Mitchell
        Associate Director of Field Operations

SUBJECT: Complaint of Robert Nelson Craig, 12-UR-1103

Attached is a memorandum sent to me by Mr. Robert E. Brown of the Los Angeles office. It is self-explanatory.

Attachment

[ATTACHMENT]

TO: Mr. Clarence L. Mitchell
            Associate Director of Field Operations and/or
            Attorney Marvin Harrison

FROM: Robert E. Brown, Jr.
            Examiner in Charge

SUBJECT: Boilermakers A-35 and Robert Nelson Craig

The enclosed statement was taken this morning. Mr. Craig was working in the California Shipyard Company. Unfortunately, he is reporting to Fort McArthur on November 9, 1943, for induction into the Army; yet it may be possible that he will be stationed nearby so that he can be present to testify at the Hearing if it is deemed advisable. Mr. Dreyfus was present during the interview.

You will note that two members of A-35 are mentioned. It is suggested that their statements may be important. Follow-up work will be conducted along this line. I do not recall other statements that were made by stewards or acting stewards of Local A-35. We await your suggestions on the importance of such statements.

Mr. Walter Williams has been unsuccessful in collecting further statements from workers at the Consolidated Shipyard Company and Western Pipe and Steel Shipyard Company. Every effort is being made to get additional statements from workers who have been victims of discrimination in these companies.

[ENCLOSURE]

November 8, 1943

Mr. Robert Nelson Craig
1265 East 27th Street
Los Angeles 11, California

I do not think that A-35 has any advantages at all to warrant the advancement of the colored people. A-35 has not had a general meeting since its organization in June, 1943. The reason they have not had a meeting is, according to Mr. Grayson, because they could not have a meeting without Blackwell's consent. Blackwell said he did not think the time was right to have a meeting for the reason that he thought the "hoodlums" might come in and break it up.

I was approached for the job as a steward and I accepted this job, but I was in no official capacity. We had no authority—that is, none other than what Mr. Grayson would give us. We could not leave the area to settle any disputes without the consent of our superior.

At one of the stewards' meetings, I brought up the question of what official capacity the stewards were in. At that particular time, Mr. Grayson said he did not know, but would let us know later. Then the stewards' instruction cards were printed and issued to the stewards. I showed my card to several white stewards and I understand that none of them had seen cards like it before. Therefore I feel that the cards were printed for the benefit of Local A-35, although they carry the designation of Local 92. It was stipulated that the Negro steward job was to deal only with Negroes.

Mr. Elmo Jacobs would testify to the truth of these statements, as would Mr. William Hayman.

Robert Nelson Craig
November 8, 1943

MS: LH, DI, HqR14, Records Relating to Hearings. Oregon Shipbuilding Corporation, Vancouver and Swan Island Shipyards, and International Brotherhood of Boilermakers, Iron Shipbuilders, Welders and Helpers of America Hearings, Los Angeles Complaints.

See the headnote on the Shipbuilding Industry and the Boilermakers Union and manuscript documentation 10/28/43.

Memorandum on Final Disposition Reports

11/15/43

Mr. Will Maslow
Clarence M. Mitchell
Final Disposition Reports

10-BR-41-45-

I have noted that in this Report, we addressed a communication to the parties charged, although it should have been evident that they were not within the Committee's jurisdiction.

It is my suggestion that regional directors should guard against addressing any communications to or having contact with parties charged similar to those in this complaint.

10-BA-29—

It strikes me that this report does not show why the complainant's service record was broken in 1942 as a result of his being discharged by the company and re-employed several days later. It seems that there should be some explanation of this because, according to the report, "his break in service made him ineligible under the terms of the Vacation Agreement for a paid vacation during 1943."

This observation on my part is merely for the purpose of recording a criticism which may be helpful in the suggestions we will compile and send to regional directors on FDR's.

10-BR-2—

In this case, the complainant submitted a complaint which he said involved forty or fifty colored employees working in the Casting Shop. The reason given for final disposition is, "The request of the complainant made on Oct. 13, 1943, that the case be closed in view of the circumstances."

Since our field instruction on satisfactory adjustment provides that persons with complaints similar to that of the individual presenting the charge are entitled to a remedy, it seems undesirable to have one person close a case involving so many others. There is nothing in the report to show that the names of the other complainants were obtained. This may be a fallacy in the original investigation.[1]

As I have mentioned to you previously, I believe we should have a special field instruction on the handling of cases involving wage discrimination.

10-GR-56—

It appears that there was nothing further to be done in view of the statement that the complainant failed to submit further proof of racial discrimination in her case. However, in view of the fact that the complainant lives in Dallas, it would have been a good idea to show that she was called into the office for a conference on this matter before it was disposed of.

MS: copy, HqR38, Central Files. (entry 25) Memoranda, Maslow, Will, 1943.

1. See Field Instruction no. 10 in HqR78, Field Letters, Aug. 1943–June 1945, and the transcript of the discussion of it during the FEPC meeting in Transcript of Proceedings, 9/14/43, 97–101, HqR64, Central Files.

Memorandum on Conference at General Accounting Office in re 6-GR-248, Employment of Japanese Americans

11-17-43

TO: Mr. Will Maslow

FROM: Clarence M. Mitchell

SUBJECT: Conference at General Accounting Office in re 6-GR-248

Mr. Elmer W. Henderson, Director of Region VI, referred a complaint to this office stating that the War Relocation Authority had been unable to place American citizens of Japanese origin in the Chicago office of the General Accounting Office at 366 West Adams Street. He requested an investigation at the Washington level to determine whether the General Accounting Office did hire workers in keeping with the provisions of Executive Order 9346.

I arranged an appointment with Mr. E. Ray Ballinger, Director of Personnel for the General Accounting Office, on the above date. Also present at the conference was Mr. Herschel Parham, Chief of Recruitment and Placement.

Mr. Ballinger admitted that the General Accounting Office does not employ citizens of Japanese origin. He stated that he had recently discussed this problem with Mr. Lindsay C. Warren, Comptroller General, and Mr. Warren felt that Japanese could not be used in the GAO. Mr. Ballinger also said, in his opinion, it is difficult to tell whether the Japanese who are born in this country ever give up their citizenship and allegiance to the Japanese government. He stated that the problem had been emphasized to some extent by the recent disturbance in the Tulelake area in California.[1] Although it was pointed out to Mr. Ballinger that the Tulelake Center is for persons who are loyal to Japan, he stated that, in his opinion, the Japanese in the Center must have received cooperation from other Japanese who had not been designated as loyal to the Japanese government.

Mr. Ballinger said he doubted that the President had intended to include citizens of Japanese ancestry under the provisions of Executive Orders 8802 and 9346. I read to him the section of FEPC Field Instruction No. 20, which deals with the President's message to the United States Senate, concerning citizens of Japanese origin, on February 14, 1943, Senate Document Number 96. Mr. Ballinger then said he assumed that the President must have meant to include citizens of Japanese origin under the terms of the Executive Order.[2]

I also described the War Department's attitude on the question, as I understood it. I mentioned that, in February of 1942, the War Department had issued a memorandum asking that all Japanese employees be suspended indefinitely. I pointed out that Hawaii was the first place to request an exception to this order on the ground that it employed so many Japanese in War Department establishments that it would cripple operations if they were taken out. An exception was made in War Department installations, according to the information I have received.

I also told him that the GAO in Chicago was said to have made the statement that Japanese were not employed in Army arsenals, but, when I talked with the War Department on this, I was informed that citizens of Japanese ancestry are employed in these arsenals. An investigation of their loyalty is made before they are permitted to work. I stated that the War Department has established a Japanese-American Joint Board in the Provost Marshal's Office, and several other Government agencies are using citizens of Japanese ancestry.

Mr. Ballinger wanted to know whether there was a large supply of citizens of Japanese ancestry available in the Chicago area, and I told him that we have no information that there are a great many. However, I informed him that the report sent to us did state that citizens of Japanese origin had been turned down from time to time by the GAO. Mr. Ballinger said that, in his opinion, there would possibly be sections of various Government agencies to which citizens of Japanese ancestry could be sent, and, at the same time, there would be no possibility of such employees coming into contact with vital war information. He finally conceded that there might be some departments in the General Accounting Office where Japanese-Americans could be employed. He also admitted that GAO does employ citizens of German descent as well as citizens of other enemy alien descent.

Mr. Ballinger stated that a letter should be sent to Mr. Warren if the Committee desired a change in the policy of the GAO. I told Mr. Ballinger that I would discuss with him the contents of any letter sent to the Comptroller General in order that such portions of it as touched on our conversation would have his agreement. I also stated that I would ask that a copy of the letter to the Comptroller General be sent to him for his information.[3]

It is my recommendation that this letter be sent following the next Committee meeting in Washington. I am attaching copies of pertinent War Department memoranda dealing with the employment of Japanese.[4]

Attachments

MS: copy, FEPC FR89, Region IX. Japanese Employment.

1. Tulelake is a rural town in Siskiyou County in northeastern California. Unlike the town, the name of the camp is usually spelled Tule Lake. Considered one of the most infamous of the internment camps, it held those who refused to take the loyalty oath to the United States. Prisoners there held frequent demonstrations and strikes that resulted in violence, army occupation, and the imposing of martial law. At its peak it held 18,789 internees. "Tule Lake Committee": http://www.gaylonn .com/tulelake/history.html; http://www.tulelakecalifornia.com/history.html.

2. Field Instruction no. 20 and its revisions are on HqR78, Field Instructions, Aug. 1943–June 1945, 20–29 folder. See also the headnotes on Relationships with Federal Agencies and on Japanese Americans and the sources cited there.

3. On Ross's letter to Warren, 12/27/43, and the subsequent negotiations, see 1/5, 2/4, and 2/5/44.

4. This text of Mitchell's memorandum to Maslow was enclosed in Maslow to Regional Director Roy A. Hoglund, memorandum, 12/9/43, along with a War Department memorandum of 10/13/43 on Employment of Persons of Japanese Ancestry in Plants and Facilities Important to the War Effort and

the attached Instructions Concerning Employment of Persons of Japanese Ancestry in Plants and Facilities Important to the War Effort (FR89, Region IX, Japanese Employment). Those attachments are probably the same as those Mitchell sent Maslow with this memorandum.

Weekly Report, Week of November 13, 1943

November 20, 1943

TO: Will Maslow
Director of Field Operations

FROM: Clarence M. Mitchell
Associate Director of Field Operations

SUBJECT: Weekly Report, November 13, 1943

During the past week, I have worked on the following cases:

1. Bechtel, Price and Callahan	—12-BR-138 (Pending)
2. Point Breeze Employees Association	—4-UR-126 (Pending)[1]
3. Teamsters Local 299	—3-UR- (Pending)
4. War Shipping Administration	—10-GR-11 (Pending)

Other Special Assignments:

1. Reviewing personnel applications
2. Working with DFO on Western Cartridge Company
3. West Coast shipbuilding hearings
4. Reviewing Final Disposition Reports
5. Reviewing Weekly Reports of Regional Directors
6. War Department Form 6a

cc: Johnson
Davis
Davidson
Jones

MS: RG 228, FEPC (entry 40 PI-147), Office Files of Clarence Mitchell, Bi-Weekly Reports, Clarence Mitchell.

1. See 11/11/43 for Mitchell's report on the WLB's hearing on the case. For other background, see discussion on Western Electric Company in the introduction and the corporate directory.

Weekly Report, Week of November 20, 1943

November 20, 1943

MEMORANDUM

TO: Will Maslow
        Director of Field Operations

FROM: Clarence M. Mitchell
        Associate Director of Field Operations

Subject: Weekly Report, November 20, 1943

During the past week, I have worked on the following cases:

1. General Accounting Office	—6-GR-246 (Pending)
2. Point Breeze Employees Association	—4-UR-126 (Pending)[1]
3. Pendleton Shipyard	—10-BR (Pending)

Other Special Assignments:

1. Reviewing personnel applications
2. Working with DFO on Western Cartridge Company
3. Reviewing, commenting and acting upon Weekly and Final Disposition
   Reports of Regional Directors
4. Hiring Policy of O.P.A
5. Investigation of complaints by Civil Service Commission
6. Complaints against Treasury Department

cc: Johnson
      Davis
      Davidson
      Jones

MS: copy, FEPC RG 228 (entry 40 PI-147), Office Files of Clarence M. Mitchell, Bi-Weekly Reports, Clarence Mitchell, DNA.

1. On this case, see 11/11/43 memorandum and notes.

Memorandum on Conversation with
Dr. Castañeda Concerning His New Appointment

December 4, 1943

TO: Malcolm Ross, Chairman
          FEPC

FROM: Clarence Mitchell
           Assistant Director of Field Operations

SUBJECT: Conversation with Dr. Castaneda Concerning His New Appointment

In keeping with your instructions, and our conversations, I discussed with Dr. Castaneda the proposed new position of Special Assistant to the Chairman on Latin-Americans.[1] I explained to him that there were many important factors connected with this new responsibility which you had not entrusted to your written memorandum, and which you relied upon me to convey to him in the course of our conversation. He is agreeable to the acceptance of new responsibilities, and understands that this work will require, in addition to the handling of Latin-American problems in Region X, trips to and work in Regions 12 and 11.

At the start of our conversation I had thought that it would be advisable to suggest that Dr. Castaneda accompany me to Washington for further discussions with you. However, I learned that Mr. Clay L. Cochran of his staff will shortly go to the Army, and we have agreed that a trip to Washington by Dr. Castaneda at this time would be inadvisable. We discussed the filling of the vacancy created by Mr. Cochran's resignation, and I explained that as soon as you have decided on a suitable person for Regional Director, the addition of that person to the Dallas office will serve to meet the staff needs. I made it clear that in view of our staff needs at Kansas City, that any person of an Examiner status added to the staff would no doubt have to spend the initial portion of his time in Region 9 because of the small staff which that office has. Dr. Castaneda understands that he will serve as Acting Regional Director until we have been able to obtain and decide upon a suitable person for Regional Director. He also understands that Dallas will continue to be his official station, although he did make the suggestion that a possible base in Austin for him would be more geographically convenient for handling the other problems in Texas.

We discussed the salary of the new position, and I explained that your conversations did not indicate that there would be an increase from his present status. However, I told him that in view of the new responsibilities, that it might be possible to make some re-adjustment in salary if we can obtain the necessary green light from the Bureau of the Budget. It is clear to Dr. Castaneda that any statements on my part were not a commitment insuring a raise in salary, but merely an expression of our wish to see that he is entirely satisfied with our efforts to make his remuneration consistent with his new and heavier responsibilities.

As soon as we are able to obtain a person suitable for Regional Director, Dr. Castaneda will be able to come to Washington for further conversations, but in any event we agree that his advice to the new Director will be very helpful in seeing that there is no break in the fine work he has been doing here for all minorities.

I am leaving a copy of this memorandum with Dr. Castaneda for his confidential file.

MS: copy, HqR1, Office Memoranda, M.

1. Castañeda, who had been serving as acting director for Region X, was now assigned to handle all cases involving discrimination against Mexicans, an authority that extended beyond the boundaries of any one region. A draft report, "FEPC and Discrimination against Mexicans," [n.d.], apparently prepared in late 1943, said the committee had "been most active in processing individual complaints of discrimination because of Mexican origin." It then had 172 such cases. "From Region X alone (New Mexico, Texas and Louisiana) the Committee has docketed 123 cases, many of them involving from 2–10 complaints. From Region XII which includes in the territory California, Nevada and Arizona 59 docketable complaints have been received and from Region IX (Kansas, Oklahoma, Missouri and Arkansas) have come 2 such complaints." Those complaints involved wage differentials, refusal to hire, refusal to upgrade, work conditions, and discharge. See HqR6, Office Files of Will Maslow. Malcolm Ross. For background, see Almaráz, *Knight without Armor;* and the headnote on Mexican Americans.

Memorandum on Transcripts of Fact Finding Conferences in Corpus Christi, Texas

December 6, 1943

TO: Will Maslow
           Director of Field Operations

FROM: Clarence Mitchell
           Associate Director of Field Operations

SUBJECT: Transcripts of Fact Finding Conferences in Corpus Christi, Texas

Herewith are copies of the transcript taken by a court stenographer for Dr. Castaneda in his investigation of complaints against the Southern Alkali Corporation, the American Smelting and Refining Company, the United Gas, Coke, and Chemical Workers, and the Zinc Workers Federal Labor Union.

Mr. Cochran is working on an analysis of these cases and I have requested that any recommendations be sent to you in Washington for study before they are sent to the parties charged. No other records of this kind are planned.

MS: LH, DI, HqR38, Central Files. (entry 25) Memoranda, Maslow, Will, 1943.

Among other things, the transcripts list the complaints and the companies that were charged with discrimination. Transcripts of Castañeda's Corpus Christi investigation can be found in HqR19, Records Relating to Hearings. Southwest (Mexicans).

Memorandum on Consolidated Aircraft

December 8, 1943

TO: Will Maslow
          Director of Field Operations
FROM: Clarence Mitchell
          Associate Director of Field Operations
SUBJECT: Consolidated Aircraft

As stated in Dr. Castaneda's Weekly Report, Col. Roy E. Ludick, Air Corps Representative at the Consolidated Plant, agreed to furnish information on this date concerning conferences with the company on upgrading of Negroes. I called Col. Ludick and he informed me that the company stated 100 Negroes had been upgraded and that it needed 75 additional colored workers. Twenty-five are to be upgraded, and fifty are to go into the so-called janitorial pool.[1]

In order that we may evaluate his conference with the company, I requested that he send us a written statement. He agreed to do this and if after scrutinizing this statement we are not satisfied it represents sufficient progress, we can take the matter up with the Air Corps in Washington, or the company's national management.[2]

MS: LH, DI, HqR38, Central Files. (entry 25) Memoranda, Maslow, Will, 1943.

1. Copies of Castañeda's reports are on HqR38, Central Files. (entry 25) Memoranda, Castañeda, Carlos.

2. For background, see the sections on the Aircraft Industry and the War Department in the headnote on Relationships with Federal Agencies.

Memorandum on Conference with WMC Regarding New Orleans, Louisiana, and Other Problems

December 9, 1943

TO: Will Maslow
          Director of Field Operations
FROM: Clarence Mitchell
          Associate Director of Field Operations
SUBJECT: Conference with WMC re New Orleans, Louisiana, and other problems

On the above date I requested Mr. Glenn O. Mc Guire, Liaison Representative of the War Manpower Commission, to come to the office for a conference concerning the report that 10,000 trainees are to be imported for work in Louisiana.

Mr. Mc Guire stated that the Deputy Director of WMC [J. H. Bond] had been in the Louisiana territory and felt that there should be a downward revision of figures on the estimated labor needs for the area. Mr. Mc Guire said that he had been unable to find any indication that there would be 10,000 persons imported to work as paid trainees. He stated that the Higgins Aircraft Corporation is operating a paid training program, but the plant does not have a contract at this time, and it may have to revise its estimates on the number of trainees needed.

It was agreed that Mr. L. Virgil Williams of this office will go to New Orleans on December 10 for the purpose of obtaining information on the number of Negroes registered in the active files of the USES, the number of Negroes trained and placed in the VTW program, and the number of courses now open for Negroes in that area. I have prepared a memorandum to Dr. Castaneda concerning Mr. Williams' visit. A copy of this memorandum is attached.[1]

We also discussed with Mr. Mc Guire 510 reports from the New Orleans area. He stated that he was making an effort to get such reports and local offices were reluctant to submit them. I pointed out that under our terms of agreement with WMC we would ultimately have to insist upon receiving these if we did not get them voluntarily.

I also pointed out that the North American Aviation, Inc., is recruiting workers through the USES, and there has been some indications that Negroes are not being accepted, but at the same time we did not have any 510 report on this company. Mr. Mc Guire agreed to check this also and report to us.[2]

MS: HqR38, Central Files. (entry 25) Memoranda, Maslow, Will, 1943.

1. Mitchell to Castañeda, memorandum, 12/9/44, filed with this text.

2. See the headnote on the Aircraft Industry and discussions on the WMC and USES in the headnote on Relationships with Federal Agencies.

Memorandum on Expression of Appreciation for Dr. Castañeda's Work

December 9, 1943

TO: Malcolm Ross
        Chairman

FROM: Clarence Mitchell
        Associate Director of Field Operations

RE: Expression of Appreciation for Dr. Castaneda's Work

In looking over the correspondence in the office, I came across the attached communications addressed to Dr. Castaneda. They are complimentary and you will be

pleased to note the high regard in which he is held. Copies of these letters, or excerpts from them, are attached.[1]
CC Will Maslow

MS: copy, HqR39, Central Files. (entry 25) Memoranda, Ross, 1943.
    1. The attachments are filed with this text.

Report on Visit to Western Electric Plant
by Clarence Mitchell

12-14-43

Mr. Will Maslow
Clarence M. Mitchell
Visit to Western Electric Plant, Baltimore, Maryland

On the above date, I went to the Western Electric Plant in Baltimore to determine conditions resulting from a strike called by the Point Breeze Employees Association.[1]

I arrived at the plant at approximately 2:45 P.M. At that time, a group of white pickets was walking in front of the Wire Building and greeted the colored persons who got off the streetcar by yelling, "Here come the niggers," "Haven't seen many of them today," and "I guess they must be scared." I talked with a policeman and learned that a lieutenant of the Baltimore Police Force was in charge. I talked to this Lieutenant and informed him of what I had heard. He stated that he had been on duty since 8:00 A.M. and had not observed anything which would lead to disorder. He did agree that he would try to prevent any disturbance from taking place.

I then went into the plant and talked with Major Long, Labor Officer of the Third Service Command, and Mr. C. W. Stoll. Mr. Stoll stated that the plant had been reduced to about fifty per cent of its normal personnel.

I went outside to the entrances to the Cable Building and the Wire Building. At the time of my arrival, shifts were being changed, and a great many colored workers were coming on the job. A scattering of whites also was coming in. In front of the Cable Building, the white pickets formed a solid group, which made it impossible for some of the colored workers to get through. Finally, some of the Negroes pushed their way through and went into the building. Some of the white incoming workers were accosted by the white pickets and upbraided for going to work.

In front of the Wire Building, the pickets continually yelled various insulting remarks at the Negroes and also seized several whites coming out of the plant. Apparently, the white persons who were seized by the pickets were on friendly terms with them because this did not result in any violence. However, the police who were present made no effort to interfere with what was going on.

Later in the day, I called Commissioner Hamilton Atkinson, of the Police Department of the City of Baltimore, and informed him of the incidents which I had observed, stating that, if these continued, they might cause some trouble. He promised to instruct his men to see that these things were stopped.

At 8:00 A.M. on Wednesday, December 15, I went to the plant again and noticed that the picket line was much thinner and more orderly. This may have been due to the extreme cold weather.

I talked with the Police Commissioner, who happened to be at the plant at the time, and he stated that his men were instructed to see that the matters I called to his attention were corrected. An Inspector of the Police was with Mr. Atkinson and denied that any of the incidents had taken place.

I called Major Long and asked whether he had any new developments. He stated that he had met with the Union but had been unable to persuade its leaders to call off the strike. He also said that it appeared that an effort was being made to close down the company's power plant, which would result in complete suspension of operations.

So far as I could determine, most of the Negro workers were on the job.

MS: copy, FR45, Region IV. Closed Cases 108–215), Western Electric Co., Point Breeze Plant, Baltimore, Md.; undated copy, without addressee, and with other minor variations, HqR63, Central Files. Reports, Tension Area Reports, Region IV.

1. A subsequent undated draft of a strike report summarizes the information in this memorandum and reports activities following Mitchell's visit. It adds the following information:

White workers alleged that they were striking against the company's policy of allowing Negroes to use the same lavatory facilities used by whites. The Company contended that the nature of its operations required common facilities to provide the greatest flexibility in use of its working force.

Incipient disorders, such as whites seeking to prevent Negroes from going to work, were directed to the attention of local police by the FEPC representative [Mitchell]. Negroes were also cautioned against any actions which would lead to disorders and urged to remain on the job. There were no disorders from the Negroes, although one white person was arrested when evidence was produced alleging that he was letting air out of the tires of parked cars belonging to workers in the plant.

Because of the failure of whites to return to work and increasing tensions the Army took the plant over on December 19, 1943. The Army is still operating the plant and production is now normal.

See HqR77, Office Files of Eugene Davidson. (Unarranged, Statements, Miscellaneous) Strikes; Mitchell's report of 2/16/44. For background and cross-references, see the headnote on Strikes and Work Stoppages; Adams and Butler, Manufacturing the Future, 142–47.

Memorandum on Pittsburgh Telephone Cases

DATE: 12-21-43

TO: Mr. Will Maslow

FROM: Clarence M. Mitchell

SUBJECT: Pittsburgh Telephone Cases

I talked with Mr. Fleming via long distance after receiving his report on the Pittsburgh Telephone cases. I suggested that he should indicate whether it would be possible to get additional material which would enable the Committee to have a hearing. Mr. Fleming stated he did not believe it would be possible to do this and stated that all of his efforts to obtain information from citizens in Pittsburgh had not borne very much fruit in the way of specific complaints.[1]

I suggested that he make one last effort to determine the full status of the case and make a specific recommendation to us on whether there should or should not be a hearing. He agreed to do this.

MS: LH, DI, HqR38, Central Files. (entry 25) Memoranda, Maslow, Will, 1943.

1. Complaints alleging discrimination against the Pittsburgh office of the Bell Telephone Company of Pennsylvania date back to 10/41. In a 7/9/43 memorandum George Johnson explained that complaints against the Pittsburgh office represented one of four cases in which black applicants were refused consideration for jobs as switchboard operators despite the companies having advertised those job openings. The other companies were the Chesapeake and Potomac Company in Baltimore, Southern Bell and Telegraph Company in Louisville, and Bell Telephone Company of Pennsylvania in Philadelphia. At its meeting of 2/11–12/43, the FEPC accepted Johnson's recommendation not to hold a hearing on the complaints against the company because the evidence was insufficient. However, the committee continued to monitor the Pittsburgh telephone office's activities.

See Johnson to Francis Haas, 7/9, 7/17/43, HqR3, Office Files of George M. Johnson. Maslow, Will; Minutes, HqR1, Summary Minutes of Meetings; headnote on the Telephone Industry.